MW00574289

Brandeis and the Progressive Constitution

Brandeis and the Progressive Constitution:

Erie, the Judicial Power, and the Politics of the Federal Courts in Twentieth-Century America

EDWARD A. PURCELL, JR.

Yale University Press New Haven and London

Copyright © 2000 by Yale University.
All rights reserved.
This book may not be reproduced, in whole or in part, including
illustrations, in any form (beyond that copying permitted by
Sections 107 and 108 of the U.S. Copyright Law and except by
reviewers for the public press), without written permission from
the publishers.

Designed by Gregg Chase.
Set in Monotype Fournier type by Tseng Information Systems.
Durham, North Carolina.
Printed in the United States of America.

Library of Congress Cataloging-in-Publication Data
Purcell, Edward A.
Brandeis and the progressive constitution : Erie, the judicial
power, and the politics of the federal courts in twentieth-century
America / Edward A. Purcell, Jr.
          p.   cm.
Includes bibliographical references and index.
ISBN 0-300-07804-8 (cloth : alk. paper)
1. Brandeis, Louis Dembitz, 1856–1941.   2. Judges—United
States—Biography.   3. Law and politics.   4. Progressivism
(United States politics)   I. Title.
KF8745.B67P84   2000
347.73'2634—DC21   99-31555
                                                      CIP

A catalogue record for this book is available from the British
Library.

The paper in this book meets the guidelines for permanence and
durability of the Committee on Production Guidelines for Book
Longevity of the Council on Library Resources.

10 9 8 7 6 5 4 3 2

For Rachel

Contents

Acknowledgments

Work on this book was carried out sporadically over a long period of time, and I was able to complete it only with the generous help and encouragement of friends and colleagues and the support of a number of schools and institutions. Finishing the book gives me the gratifying opportunity to express my deep appreciation to them all.

For their illuminating scholarly assistance I thank my colleagues at New York Law School and the members of the legal history colloquium at New York University Law School who read and commented on early drafts. In addition, I owe a special debt of gratitude to a number of individuals who gave their time with special generosity and provided particularly helpful comments: Richard B. Bernstein, Robert Blecker, Mary Ann Case, Erwin Chemerinsky, Barry Cushman, Lawrence Fleisher, Helen Garfield, Dan Hamilton, Morton J. Horwitz, Alfred S. Konefsky, William P. LaPiana, David W. Levy, Scott L. Matthews, Eben Moglen, William E. Nelson, Steven Newman, Rudolph J. R. Peritz, John Henry Schlegel, Peter H. Schuck, Richard Sherwin, James F. Simon, Henry Steiner, William M. Wiecek, Harry H. Wellington, and Donald H. Zeigler. Finally, I acknowledge the late Clifford S. Griffin for his encouragement and inspiration.

For their financial and administrative support I express my appreciation to the American Philosophical Society, the Social Science Research Council, the National Endowment for the Humanities, the American Council of Learned Societies, Harvard Law School, the University of Missouri—Columbia, New York University School of Law, and the law firm of Paul, Weiss, Rifkind, Wharton & Garrison.

More recently, New York Law School has been generous in providing research assistance and in arranging my schedule to maximize the time available for writing. Dean Harry H. Wellington and Associate Dean Ellen Ryerson have been particularly supportive and encouraging. Professor Joyce Saltalamacchia, the director of the school's library, and her entire staff, especially Joseph Molinari and Michael McCarthy, have faithfully and happily supplied me with an unending flow of research materials. My research assistants, Elenor Reid, Anthony G. Di Maria, and Jennifer C. Argabright helped immensely in reviewing the manuscript and preparing it for publication, and my secretaries, Nicole Fischer, Billy Coleman, and Rosetta Reid, provided assistance in every way possible.

I also thank the following libraries for permission to cite and quote from material in their manuscript collections: Bancroft Library, University of California—Berkeley (Papers of Hiram W. Johnson and J. F. T. O'Connor); Library of Congress, manuscript division (Papers of Newton D. Baker, Hugo L. Black, Felix Frankfurter, Charles Evans Hughes, La Follette Family, James M. Landis, George W. Norris, Richard Olney, Donald Richberg, Harlan F. Stone, Willis Van Devanter, Thomas J. Walsh); Harvard Law School Library (Papers of Louis D. Brandeis, Felix Frankfurter, Learned Hand, Henry M. Hart, Jr., Oliver Wendell Holmes, Jr., and Roscoe Pound); Herbert Hoover Presidential Library (Papers of Herbert Hoover); Herbert Hoover Institution Archives, Stanford University (Papers of James Henry MacLafferty); Law Library, William Mitchell College of Law (Papers of William D. Mitchell and family); Franklin D. Roosevelt Presidential Library (Papers of Franklin D. Roosevelt); University of Virginia Law Library Special Collections (Papers of James C. McReynolds); Southern Historical Collection, Wilson Library, University of North Carolina—Chapel Hill (Papers of John J. Parker).

Similarly, Yale University Press provided a particularly supportive and helpful editorial process. I thank Clyde Spillenger for a particularly thorough and helpful review, and John Covell and Nancy Moore Brochin for their insightful comments and their careful reading and thorough editing of the manuscript.

My greatest thanks goes to my family. My wife, Rachel Vorspan, my son Dan, and my daughter Jess have filled my life with joy, and their companionship and support have encouraged my work and eased its burdens. My in-laws, Max and Sandy Vorspan, were unfailingly hospitable and supportive during my working visits to California. Finally, Professor Rachel Vorspan contributed her insights as both lawyer and historian, helping immeasurably to focus and strengthen the book.

Brandeis and the Progressive Constitution

Introduction

From the moment that Justice Louis D. Brandeis announced the Supreme Court's decision in the spring of 1938, *Erie Railroad Co. v. Tompkins* has fascinated members of the legal profession.[1] Reaching far beyond Harry Tompkins's personal injury claim, Brandeis's decision addressed fundamental constitutional issues involving the locus and scope of lawmaking authority in the American legal system. Overruling *Swift v. Tyson,* a ninety-six-year-old decision that had expanded the power of the national courts to create a "general" federal common law independent of the common law of the states, it sought to limit that judicial power and rebalance the lawmaking structure of American government.

As massive historical changes altered the social and political significance of *Swift,* however, they did the same to Brandeis's creation. To view *Erie* through the historian's eyes — to consider its complex social origins, its purposeful human crafting, and its shifting but nevertheless patterned reinterpretation over the years — is to explore both the sweep of American experience in the twentieth century and the practices of its legal and political elites in molding the nation's rules, concepts, principles, and ideologies of law. The changing national experience and the evolving ideas and legal practices are examined here, as much as or more than Brandeis and his decision. This book is a work of history, not of law.[2]

In Part 1, Chapters 1 through 3 provide an overview of the period from 1877 to 1937, highlighting a range of developments that helped create the distinct politico-constitutional age that shaped Brandeis's views and ultimately gave birth to *Erie.* This period was marked by a fundamental premise concerning the role of the federal courts and the relationship between the legislative and judicial branches. Legal commentators of all stripes came to see the judiciary — especially the federal judiciary — as the branch of government that would most consistently protect private property and interstate corporate enterprise. They viewed state and federal legislatures — and sometimes even state courts — as the branches most likely to threaten those interests. In the decades surrounding the turn of the century the Supreme Court expanded the reach of federal judicial power to increase the ability of the federal courts to review government regulatory efforts, while Progressives* came to believe that significant social and economic reform could take place only if that power were limited and state and national legislative powers were expanded. These developments, this book argues, underlay Brandeis's constitutional theory.

Part 2 focuses on Brandeis — his judicial practice, his evolving constitutional philosophy, and his opinion in *Erie* for a bare five-justice majority. Chapters 4 through 7 argue that Brandeis played the preeminent role both in forging a majority and in shaping the Court's final opinion, and they provide insight into the meaning of Brandeis's decision by relating it to his values, politics, personal motivations, and overall constitutional jurisprudence. These chapters conclude that Brandeis was animated by broad personal and social purposes and that he sought to use his opinion to institutionalize the goals and values of early-twentieth-century Progressivism.

Part 3 considers the fate of Brandeis's decision and his Progressive ideals in a new and different postwar world. Chapters 8 through 10 argue that tumultuous historical changes ripped his opinion from its cultural moorings and propelled it into a drastically different world where judges and legal scholars viewed it with new eyes. These chapters explore the subsequent interpretations that fundamentally reshaped Brandeis's opinion as later generations struggled to control the scope and function of the federal judicial power in a new politico-constitutional age.

Chapter 11, the final chapter, sketches developments of the past quarter century. Writing "recent" history (where the conscious and unconscious promptings of contemporary concerns are powerful) is difficult, especially when the subject is law. *Erie* remains deeply embedded in continuing professional disputes, and its history bears an immediate normative significance that other historical subjects often lack. The scholarly commentary, moreover, has reached staggering proportions. To treat that literature with justice would require a separate book, and to identify its most significant and enduring contributions would require a perspective that is as yet unavailable. Thus, the final chapter brings the story of Brandeis and *Erie* to century's end by noting its highlights.

*The word *Progressive* is capitalized to refer to the ideas, values, and assumptions that characterized many of the reform movements of the early twentieth century, particularly their widely shared if somewhat varied commitments to science, expertise, efficiency, popular education, democratic government, the rights of labor, the limitation of corporate power, and the use of government to ameliorate the harsh consequences of industrialization. The term does not refer to the formal Progressive party that was organized around Theodore Roosevelt.

Through its three parts, the book explores the complex relationship between changing American politics and evolving ideas concerning the practice of constitutional government and the role of the federal judiciary. On one level, it examines the origins and intended significance of the Court's landmark decision in *Erie*. Recognizing the complexities and ambiguities of the issues involved, it nevertheless concludes that the case has been widely misunderstood, in large part because judges and legal scholars have too often divorced it from its full and vital historical context. It was neither a simple articulation of the positivism of Justice Oliver Wendell Holmes, Jr., nor the inevitable result of a "philosophical revolution" in the Court's understanding of "law." The book suggests that commentators have persistently overemphasized *Erie*'s "philosophical" content while minimizing or ignoring other more important elements. Similarly, the decision was not designed primarily to protect "federalism" or special enclaves of state law. Rather, its more vital concern lay in broader ideas about judicial lawmaking and separation of powers. Nor, again, was *Erie* simply a product of the "constitutional revolution" that the Supreme Court carried out after spring 1937. It was closely related to that pivotal period, but it bore an oblique and problematic relationship to the jurisprudence of the "Roosevelt Court."

On a second level, the book is a study of Brandeis and his work as a constitutional judge. It explores the tensions that arose from his political Progressivism, his role as a justice, his strategic position on a historically specific Court, and his developing and purposeful constitutional jurisprudence. The book posits that *Erie* reflected Brandeis's deepest concerns and illuminated central elements of his judicial practice and philosophy. More particularly, it argues that his purpose in *Erie* was not only to destroy the doctrine of *Swift v. Tyson*, reject its ostensibly outmoded jurisprudence, and terminate its generally pro-corporate consequences. Instead, his broader goal was twofold. First, Brandeis sought to restructure the American judicial system to increase both its operational efficiency and its capacity to provide practical justice. *Erie* was an integral part of his long-term effort to adapt the court system of the states and the nation to the demands of a new interstate society. Second, Brandeis sought to constrain a pervasive if amorphous judicial practice by which the Supreme Court had, for more than half a century, used common law techniques to expand its lawmaking powers and, all too often, to serve anti-Progressive purposes. Brandeis wrote *Erie* not only to terminate the "federal general common law" but also to cabin more generally the lawmaking powers of the national courts in a variety of cognate areas.

On a third level, the book uses *Erie* as a case study to explore the ways in which historical processes shape and reshape fundamental ideas about legal doctrines, the role of the judiciary, and the nature of constitutional government. The world of early twentieth-century Progressivism inspired both Brandeis and his decision in *Erie*, but that world was expiring as Brandeis drafted and delivered his opinion. His reasoning and purposes could hardly have maintained their full intended meaning in a radically new age. The book shows how succeeding generations of judges and scholars worked, sometimes consciously and sometimes not, to remake both Brandeis's image as a constitutional judge and his opinion in *Erie*. The decision was not the "founding document of modern American judicial federalism," as one distinguished scholar has termed it, nor was it the case that "shaped the agenda and analysis of the legal process school" that grew to prominence in the postwar decades, as another equally distinguished commentator has declared.[3] True, it was subsequently tailored to those purposes, but Brandeis's intent was quite different. Indeed, *Erie* was quite different from the polestar version that Professor Henry M. Hart, Jr. — the decision's most brilliant and influential scholarly advocate — imagined and confidently proclaimed to the world.

Brandeis's decision, the book argues further, was also quite different from the famous precedent that the United States Supreme Court repeatedly applied during the succeeding half century. It was not the case Justice Felix Frankfurter explained so carefully in *Guaranty Trust Co. v. York*, nor the decision Chief Justice Earl Warren implemented in *Hanna v. Plumer*, nor the opinion Justice Lewis F. Powell, Jr., invoked so forcefully in *Cannon v. University of Chicago*.[4] Because of the Court's immense power and prestige — and because its pronouncements constitute "authoritative" statements of "the law" — its interpretations over the years tend to blur, obscure, and then replace broad and complex historical understandings with formalized doctrines. That elaborate formal practice of redefining and remaking legal rules is an essential part of the legal process. As a matter of historical understanding, however, it is dysfunctional. Equally important, as a matter of legal doctrine, the practice is also a powerful force for covert change. In both its origins and subsequent interpretation, the history of *Erie v. Tompkins* illuminates the way individual perspectives and social pressures have driven the law's contingent evolution. In this critical sense, the book explores *Erie*, an unusual case in so many respects, as representative.

As the book explores the complex dynamics of legal change, it suggests a number of conclusions. It points, for example, to the historicity of that most exalted, rigorous, and frustrating law school course (labeled differently from school to school), "Federal Courts." Inspired by the confrontation between progressivism, professionalism, and the conservative politics of the 1920s, this now standard course and respected field of study was largely inspired by Brandeis and molded by Frankfurter in the process of grappling with the legal parameters of pressing social and political conflicts. Born of political commitment and ideological conviction, the idea of "Federal Courts" as a special field of scholarly study spread in the 1930s and 1940s and then grew to maturity following

World War II. Historical changes between the Great Depression and the cold war, however, altered the field of study, fragmented its assumptions, and confused its purposes. Thus, the field changed substantially in the decades following World War II, with few students recognizing the exact nature of those changes. Indeed, only recently have "Federal Courts" scholars even begun to consider the extent to which their subject is the confected product of distinctive historical developments.

The book shows, too, that aspects of the grand historical synthesis that Frankfurter designed over the course of his life as scholar and judge were highly misleading. In particular, it highlights significant issues that divided Brandeis and Frankfurter after the mid-1930s and emphasizes Frankfurter's changing views, his role in remolding *Erie*'s significance for his own purposes, and his subsequent efforts to recast Brandeis's judicial image to provide support in his constitutional battles with Justice Hugo L. Black and the early Warren Court. It also explores the differences that developed between Frankfurter and Hart, his brilliant student and colleague, over the nature of the federal judicial system and the constitutional role of the national courts. During the period of Hart's greatest intellectual achievements, from World War II into the 1960s, he was far more a judicial activist and nationalist (and had a far more ambiguous relationship to both Frankfurter and the Warren Court) than has been commonly acknowledged.

More generally, the book points to the critical role "branch affinities" played in the ideological commitments of diverse political partisans to the different branches of government. It suggests that such foundational ideas as federalism, separation of powers, and the respective constitutional roles of the various branches of government are rooted largely in expectations concerning the practical consequences that varying allocations of institutional authority would likely cause. The legal meaning and political significance of those foundational ideas shift, fragment, and realign over time as controlling social and political expectations are transformed.

Finally, in the process of probing for a "historical *Erie*," the book raises deep, if familiar, doubts about the concept of a knowable and authoritative "original intent."[5] To provide insight into Brandeis's purposes and strategies, the book addresses a single decision, on a clearly defined issue, well known and widely discussed both prior to and contemporaneously with the decision, and made by a group composed of a mere five individuals who acted only sixty years ago and who bequeathed to us a relatively extensive and informative documentary record. Indeed, arguing that Brandeis was *Erie*'s dominant author, the book focuses largely on a single individual who left behind an extraordinarily rich and voluminous collection of relevant materials, including especially valuable and revealing private letters and working judicial papers. Despite these quite exceptional advantages, however, the inquiry relies unavoidably on the historian's inference and speculation. Thus, answers to even relatively simple, recent, and specific questions—even when based on unusually abundant and illuminating sources—remain tentative and incomplete.

The analysis, moreover, highlights problems and ambiguities that plague efforts to use "original intent" as an authoritative legal norm. It argues, for example, that Brandeis's reasoning in *Erie* was flawed because he had to navigate around the views of the four justices who joined him to create his bare majority. At least two, and possibly all four, of them apparently misunderstood, doubted, or disagreed with the constitutional language Brandeis chose. The opinion was also flawed because Brandeis made conscious tactical decisions to obscure and avoid as well as to illuminate and effectuate.[6] Thus, the Court's opinion was, in places, opaque and misleading by design. The analysis, in short, supports those who argue that the idea of a normative "original intent" makes historical inquiry the oracle of answers that it often cannot provide. Equally important, the analysis also suggests that a fully "authentic" original intent—even if discoverable and applicable to the questions that later generations pose—may not be persuasive, serviceable, or even recognizable to those later generations who ask new questions on the basis of their new and different perceptions and assumptions.

Seriously qualifying and limiting (although hardly rejecting) ideas of original intent, the book suggests that historical evolution creates limitations and imperatives that infuse with new meaning the words of authoritative documents. The test of the wisdom and validity of those new meanings is only partially a historical question. We can learn far more by recognizing and understanding that continuous process of change and reinterpretation than by pretending that we can discover and apply an objective and legally directive "original intent" free from the limitations, pressures, and needs of our time.

Although the book questions both the utility and validity of most purportedly normative and directive ideas of original intent, it shows that historical analysis carries distinctive virtues. Historical analysis can clarify the ways in which changing values, problems, and circumstances drove the evolution of constitutional assumptions and practices; it can aid us in understanding how past generations strove to make complex socio-legal processes work; and it can illuminate the ways in which the various institutions and rules of law affected the diverse elements of American society. Historical analysis need not boast complete truth or promise authoritative answers to specific legal questions in order to help us—and future generations—learn how we might continue to shape those processes to sustain and enhance a decent, ordered, and relatively democratic life.[7]

Accordingly, the book hazards a broader historical, constitutional, and normative conclusion. It suggests that Brandeis and his opinion in *Erie,* although flawed, were admirable. This conclusion is based on a complex judgment that in his opinion, as in his judicial career, Brandeis successfully combined four paramount virtues: he articulated sound and fundamental constitutional principles; he served the cause of popular, representative government; he adapted legal rules effectively to serve desirable institutional goals; and he improved the ability of the legal system to provide practical justice to the weak and disadvantaged.

The Federal Judicial Power
and Progressive Reform

PART I

The Premise of an Age

I

LAW, POLITICS, AND THE FEDERAL

COURTS, 1877–1937

Legalized race-based slavery, the issue that dominated American politics in the middle third of the nineteenth century, ended with the Civil War and the Thirteenth Amendment; the resulting question of the status of free blacks faded in national importance after the end of Reconstruction in the 1870s. The dominant constitutional issues of the earlier period—the nature of American federalism and the scope of national sovereignty—similarly appeared settled by the war and the two other constitutional amendments that followed. By the end of the 1880s the North and South had reunited in sentiment as well as law, in large part by consigning the "race question" to the states.

During the last third of the nineteenth century, rapid and tumultuous changes transformed the United States from a rural, agricultural, and decentralized society into an urbanized and industrialized nation in the process of centralizing. The changes equally transformed American politics. In place of slavery and the issue of race, problems of industrialism emerged as the paramount concerns of a new politico-constitutional age. Beginning in the 1870s a variety of groups—southern and midwestern farmers, incipient labor organizations, middle-class "reformers," and small businesses adversely affected by the growth of national corporations—began calling for government "regulation." In the 1890s populism, a movement and then a political party based on agrarian interests in the South and Midwest and silver mining interests in the western mountain states, carried the fight against "big business." By the turn of the century farm groups had joined industrial workers, social reformers, urban consumers, middle-class professionals, and disadvantaged and opportunistic business groups to raise the banner of "Progressivism." This was a broader and more diverse movement aimed at controlling corporations, rationalizing social and economic institutions, ameliorating the harsh consequences of industrialism, utilizing science and expert knowledge for democratic ends, and, in the name of "the people," taking control of government from political "bosses" and "special interests."

The agencies of government responded to the changing politics and the challenges of industrialism in divergent and conflicting ways. All branches of state and national governments tried to foster economic expansion, and all saw the need to deal with the worst excesses of industrialism. Erratically and unevenly, state legislatures took the lead. By 1900 most had enacted anti-trust laws, asserted some control over local railroads and transportation facilities, and adopted programs to supervise banking and insurance. Most had also adopted measures to control elements of the employer-employee relationship, improve the conditions of factory labor, and expand the liability of employers for workplace injuries. With passage of the Interstate Commerce Act in 1887 and the Sherman Anti-Trust Act in 1890 Congress tentatively joined the effort. The reactions of the courts varied, although generally they appeared more solicitous of established property rights than did the legislatures. For a century after the nation's founding, American courts had exercised the power of judicial review over legislative enactments only sparingly, but in the late nineteenth century they grew increasingly willing to invalidate legislation that restricted the rights of private property and economic liberty. In place of questions about the relations between states and nation, conflicts between the legislative and judicial branches of government dominated debate.

After the turn of the century, legislative efforts intensified. On the state level Progressives pushed through measures to improve working conditions, restrict the use of child labor, and limit work hours for female and, in some occupations, male employees. They enacted minimum wage laws for women and established workmen's compensation programs in forty states. Led by two reform-oriented presidents, Theodore Roosevelt and Woodrow Wilson, the national government moved toward stronger enforcement of the anti-trust laws and broader efforts to regulate the new national economy. Congress strengthened federal legislation designed to control corporate activities, initiated the national regulation of food and drug products, and for interstate railroads established significant safety requirements, a strong employers' liability law, and the eight-hour day for employees. Facing a close reelection fight in 1916 and needing to win the support of independent and Republican Progressives, President Wilson supported and Congress passed a key Progressive proposal, the first federal child labor bill, which was designed to end one of the worst abuses of the new industrialism.

Although reform groups enjoyed numerous victories in the legislatures, they were less successful in the courts.[1] The doctrines of the common law, often interpreted narrowly by a cautious judiciary, seemed biased in favor of organized wealth and against disorganized and weaker parties. Contract law, emphasizing formalities and defining inequitable agreements as "voluntary," supported the position of those able to impose harsh terms on others. Tort law, upholding narrow rules of liability, helped relieve corporations of some of the costs of industrialism and transferred those costs to vulnerable segments of the population. Although the courts began to moderate some common law doctrines in response to the rigors of industrialism, they remained generally less responsive to reform than the legislatures. Corporate interests increasingly relied on the courts as their ultimate bulwark against regulatory action, and Progressives increasingly identified them with social conservatism, corporate power, and the protection of private property.[2]

Inspired by the political ideals of democracy and the social possibilities of science, Progressives sought to bring social justice and efficiency to industrial society by rationalizing its structures and practices. Although skeptical of the partisanship and corruption of legislatures, they committed themselves to broad programs of legislative reform. The legislative branch was popularly elected and hence closer to the people, and it had the authority to investigate social problems methodically and ameliorate them broadly. The legislature also had the power to establish expert commissions and regulatory agencies capable of supervising business and ensuring that the law was wisely applied and properly followed. "[T]here is coming to be a science of modern legislation," Roscoe Pound, a Progressive law professor declared in 1908, and "modern" statutes were the result of detailed legislative investigations and "long and patient study by experts."[3] Felix Frankfurter, a young Progressive lawyer and activist, packed those assumptions of legal Progressivism together tightly in 1912. "Growing democratic sympathies, justified by the social message of modern scientists," he announced, "demand to be translated into legislation for economic betterment."[4]

Conversely, Progressives doubted the intellectual capacities of the courts and believed them unsuited to deal with the complex problems created by modern industrial society. Progressivism, declared Learned Hand, a young attorney in New York, "reflects a suspicion of courts."[5] Judges were deemed incapable of investigating the facts, freeing themselves from old and hardened conceptions, and designing intelligent and systemic reforms. "Incidentally, it is beyond belief what courts don't know," Frankfurter exclaimed. "I do not mean their views but their ignorance of facts and events."[6] Their reasoning, therefore, was often abstract and ill-informed. Herbert Croly, founder of the Progressive magazine *The New Republic*, emphasized that courts "cannot be sure of being confronted by the real facts or all the facts." The "common-law judge" was consequently disabled by his position and training, Croly concluded, and "cannot become a satisfactory or a sufficient servant of a genuinely social policy."[7] Pound made the point bluntly. "Judicial law-making for sheer lack of means to get at the real situation, operates unjustly and inequitably in a complex social organization."[8]

Not only were the courts intellectually backward, many Progressives believed, but often they were simply biased in favor of property. Charles F. Amidon, a Progressive federal judge in North Dakota, charged that judicial opposition to reform legislation made "the courts odious,"[9] and a steelworker accused the judiciary of always defending employers. "It is useless to strike or fight the big corporations," he complained bitterly, because "the courts"—like the government and the police—were "on their side."[10] A young lawyer had little opportunity for success unless he "absorbs the theory of the vested rights of wealth," Samuel Gompers, the president of the American Federation of Labor (AFL), complained in 1900. "What hope has he to become a judge in the city or in the State or in the United States unless he is in line with the prevailing thoughts of the protection to vested wealth?"[11] Hand blamed public dissatisfaction on "the very ill-advised and lawless attitude" of the courts in construing the Constitution.[12] Judges were, he believed, "almost inevitably drawn from the propertied class and share its assumptions."[13] The historian Charles Beard sought to demonstrate that the Constitution had been designed by wealthy investors for the very purpose of protecting their interests and that judicial review had been one of their chosen instruments of social control.[14]

Although state courts were often hostile to reform efforts, the federal courts gradually became the principal target of Progressive criticism.[15] By virtue of membership in the "national" judiciary, federal judges seemed to feel a greater responsibility to protect national corporations and to guard against local pressures that might impinge on interstate commerce and the national market. Because federal judges were appointed for life (by the 1890s state judges in all but eight states were subject to popular election), they also appeared more aloof from popular demands and hence less "democratic."[16] Because they were typically selected from the ranks of prominent lawyers whose class status and professional practice linked them with national corporations, their ideological biases seemed to run in favor of national business.[17] Moreover, as a single and readily identifiable national judiciary, the federal courts were more visible than state courts, and their constitutional rulings voiding state legislation provided explosive national symbols of both an alleged class bias in favor of corporate business and a centralizing assault against the rights of the states. As Progressivism moved from the state to the national level after the turn of the century, so its criticisms of the judiciary came to focus on the federal courts.

The United States Supreme Court, dominated by prominent upper-middle-class Anglo-Saxons who commonly had practiced corporate law before taking their seats, largely determined the federal judiciary's political image.[18]

In the decades following Reconstruction, the Court seemed to grow increasingly sympathetic toward business and began to reshape the law in ways that strengthened the position of national corporations. Most broadly, it protected the integrating national market that industrialism and the railroads were creating. Increasingly, the Court used the Commerce Clause to limit state efforts to impose taxes and other restrictions on interstate business,[19] and in the 1880s it began reshaping the federal common law of torts and contracts, strengthening the legal position of railroads, manufacturers, and insurance companies.[20] It construed the Sherman Anti-Trust Act broadly to prohibit local organizing efforts of labor unions, but narrowly to prevent the federal government from regulating companies that manufactured goods for interstate commerce.[21] In an unusually controversial decision in 1894 the Court invalidated a minimal and slightly Progressive federal income tax.[22]

Perhaps most controversial, the Court embraced the doctrine of "substantive due process."[23] In 1886 it held that the term *person* in the due process clause included corporations,[24] and four years later it announced that due process extended beyond procedural matters and created substantive and judicially enforceable limits on the powers of government.[25] By the end of the century it was enforcing the doctrine of "liberty of contract," holding that the due process clauses of the Fifth and Fourteenth Amendments prohibited state and federal legislation from unduly restricting the freedom of workers and employers to agree "voluntarily" on terms of employment.[26] "The supremacy of the legislature" has been "challenged by the courts," Donald Richberg, a Progressive labor lawyer, declared in 1923. Since the late nineteenth century "the courts have gradually increased their authority until they have reached their present position of supremacy."[27]

The Court's major constitutional decisions fastened a pro-business and anti-Progressive label on the federal courts. Most Populists and Progressives identified them as pillars of the new corporate economy and repeatedly criticized their decisions and political bias. Corporate lawyers and business groups, though characterizing the role of the federal courts quite differently, essentially agreed with the critics' premise. They praised the national courts as guarantors of individual liberty and social stability, and with near unanimity they preached the need to preserve the courts' prestige and influence. William D. Guthrie, a conservative leader of the New York bar, advised that it was "often of vital importance to proceed in the first instance, if at all possible, in a federal court."[28] Over the last quarter of the nineteenth century, the critics and defenders of the federal courts labored in tandem to construct one of the fundamental ideological premises of the new age: the courts, especially the federal courts, were pro-business; and the hope — or threat — of significant Progressive reform lay with legislative innovations and, as perhaps the only way to ensure the success of those reforms, serious restrictions on federal judicial power.

The adversaries chose their formalisms accordingly. Conservatives portrayed the courts—especially the federal courts—as the institutional embodiment of the ideals of law, reason, and justice. They examined the legislative branch, in contrast, with cold and unforgiving eyes, focusing on every corruption, failing, and flaw. Progressives, conversely, pictured legislatures and their expert administrative agencies relatively abstractly and as they wished them to be, as authentically popular, problem-solving, and even "scientific" branches of government. They scrutinized the courts, in contrast, with a searing realism that revealed judicial work as ill-informed and socially biased.[29] In the long period of industrialization from 1877 to 1937, the politico-constitutional debate across a wide range of disparate legal and social issues revolved around that underlying premise and found voice through those contrasting ideological approaches.

The Evolution of Professional Legal Culture

Much of the debate and most of its detailed argument occurred within the legal profession, and personal values as well as the interests of clients helped determine how lawyers responded. Advocates of states' rights persistently criticized the federal courts, while nationalists defended their vital role. Small-town plaintiffs' lawyers protested the advantages large corporations enjoyed, and corporate counselors bemoaned the local prejudices that victimized their clients. In spite of the variety, however, the weight of the legal profession—and certainly the orientation of its organized and elite elements—shifted during the late nineteenth century toward a staid social conservatism, a commitment to the interests of national corporations, and an intense identification with the judiciary—especially the federal judiciary. By the 1890s the upper echelons of the bar had grown acutely apprehensive about "radical" political proposals and fervently devoted to the defense of established property interests.[30]

The shift in professional attitudes was part of a general rigidification of American legal culture in the late nineteenth century. Structurally, socially, and intellectually the profession's leadership became narrower, more insulated, and increasingly unwilling to address the social inequities that came with industrialism. The rigidification was in part a reaction to massive and bewildering social change, the result of a desperate adherence to the common law as a symbol of principle, precedent, and continuity. Partly, too, it was the reaction of an Anglo-Saxon Protestant social elite to the turmoil associated with the demands of a new and largely immigrant working class. By the late nineteenth century, in fact, immigrants and their children—including rapidly growing numbers of Catholics and Jews from Southern and Eastern Europe—constituted a majority of the American industrial work force. Given "the great army of discontents, and their apparent power, with the growth and development of universal suffrage," declared Christopher G. Tiedeman, a leading treatise writer, the "conservative classes stand in constant fear of the advent of an absolutism more tyrannical and more unreasoning than any before experienced by man, the absolutism of a democratic majority."[31]

Beyond the broader social conflicts, the rigidification was rooted in three internal changes that altered both the structure and culture of the American legal profession. First, lawyers were becoming more organized and "professionalized." In the decades following the Civil War legal education underwent rapid changes as the old apprenticeship system broke down and training at university-based law schools took its place, especially for members of the middle class able to afford some or all of a college education. With rising admissions standards, lengthened programs of instruction, and full-time faculties increasingly separated from practice, professional law schools made legal education more formal, technical, rule-centered, and homogeneous.[32] At the same time, practicing lawyers began to organize state and local bar associations across the country, and in 1878 members of the northeastern legal elite founded the American Bar Association to provide national leadership. Indicative of both its membership and its orientation, the ABA for almost a quarter century continued to hold its annual meetings in Saratoga Springs, New York, the traditional and elegant summer resort of the East's upper middle class. Sixty bar associations existed in the United States in 1880, and by 1916 there were 48 state and 623 local ones.[33]

The second change occurred at the end of the nineteenth century, as urban law firms and elite corporate lawyers became the dominant molders of professional attitudes and the preeminent symbols of professional success. This change helped to infuse specific, if often implicit, social content into the professional ideal. The "dominant type," the ABA's official history proudly proclaimed, was "the railroad lawyer and the businessman-lawyer."[34] Although the vast majority of attorneys were solo practitioners who earned minimal or average livelihoods, by the turn of the century the most successful corporate practitioners were commanding six-figure incomes. They organized rapidly growing and departmentalized firms to serve the specialized needs of thriving corporate clients. Attracting the ablest graduates from the top law schools and restricting their hiring to those from "proper" social and ethnic backgrounds, the new firms monopolized the most lucrative areas of practice and exerted a controlling influence in most bar associations.[35] Drawn from the same social, ethnic, and religious backgrounds as the leaders of American business, the members of the new corporate legal elite defended their clients with the greatest professional skill and the resolute confidence born of representing one's highly successful social peers.[36]

Third, lawyers, especially the elite, were coming to hold the common law in the highest reverence. "There is no necessity in these days of American idolatry of the common law," one scholar remarked wryly, "to dwell upon the development and perfection to which the local common law of England has been brought."[37] The common law represented continuity in an age of tumultuous change, stability in an era of sharpening conflict, and authority in an age of scientific questioning. Finally, and perhaps most important, the common law represented the ideal of narrow and reliable law made by judges, in contrast to the more sweeping, unpredictable and potentially radical statutory law of the legislature. Most lawyers preferred the common law because it was the basis of their professional expertise, social influence, and economic livelihood. Many, especially the elite, favored it because it placed authority in the hands of judges. They trusted the courts and feared that legislatures were likely to pander to the demands of an uninformed and inflamed populace. "Much is to be dreaded and guarded against," Guthrie warned, "in the despotism of the majority wielding and abusing the power of legislation."[38]

The developments that helped rigidify professional legal culture also contributed to another change. During the late nineteenth century elite practitioners and law teachers embraced the centrality of federal constitutional rights and began cultivating a special reverence for the national judiciary. The authority of the federal courts under the Fourteenth Amendment, Guthrie declared, was "the bulwark on which we place our reliance." Lawyers, "the great conservative force in American politics," had a professional "duty to preach constitutional morality to the rich and to the poor, to all trades and to all vocations, to all ranks and to all classes." That duty, like the Constitution, was sacred. "We," Guthrie proclaimed grandly, "are the guardians of the Federal Constitution."[39]

The national courts were fewer in number than the state courts, and the quality of their judges was almost universally regarded as higher.[40] After Congress granted "federal question" jurisdiction in 1875,* the national courts gradually became the principal forum for litigating major national issues. They handled a much smaller number of cases than did the state courts; their criminal dockets excluded ordinary common law crimes and were limited to special federal statutory offenses; and they heard relatively few civil actions that involved small, and therefore presumably unimportant, monetary claims. For elite lawyers representing national corporations, the federal courts were generally attractive because of their presumed solicitude for the interests of national business

---

*From 1789 to 1875 the lower federal courts did not have general jurisdiction to hear cases "arising under" federal law, that is, cases where the claim was based on federal law. As part of its effort to reconstruct the South and enforce federal law, Congress granted the lower courts general jurisdiction to hear all actions based on federal law — so-called federal question jurisdiction.

and because appearance in federal court was synonymous with a more elevated type of practice in a more prestigious forum. For law teachers, a distinct and newly influential professional subgroup, the federal courts were equally attractive, though for somewhat different reasons. The law teachers saw the national courts as instruments of a broader national viewpoint and appropriate forums for a unifying national law. The case method they used in their classes disdained consideration of "local" law and its many variations, focusing instead on identifying the true, enduring, and universal principles of the common law. There was a natural professional affinity between the practicing and teaching elites on the one hand and the federal judiciary on the other. Neither group wished to see the authority or prestige of the national courts impaired.

Simeon E. Baldwin, a quintessential pillar of the bar, exemplified the attitudes that characterized the professional elite in the decades surrounding the turn of the century. A congregationalist and a Yankee, Baldwin was the scion of an old and prominent Connecticut family. He enjoyed a long and successful corporate practice, helped found the American Bar Association, served on the Connecticut Supreme Court, won election as governor, and taught intermittently at the Yale Law School. Emphasizing that law represented the rule of reason and principle, his survey of *The American Judiciary* reflected the ideological biases of the profession's elder corporate elite.[41] "The courts stand for conservatism," he announced firmly, and their recognized virtues "put Americans in a friendly attitude toward the judiciary."[42] Of course, "federal judges stand higher in public estimation than the State judges."[43] Conversely, "Americans have become distrustful of their legislatures," he announced with pride. "They believe that much of their work is ill considered, and that some of it has its source in corruption."[44] The only noteworthy threat to the nation's stability arose from "those representing certain labor unions" and from "the development of collectivism."[45] Dissatisfaction with the courts, in fact, was limited to "foreign immigrants" and was rooted in ignorance. "The membership of a Labor Union, in many parts of the country, is apt to be largely of foreign birth," Baldwin warned. "The leaders not infrequently know little of the English language and less of American institutions."[46] Fortunately, however, a deep respect for the judiciary and the existing social order characterized the attitudes of truly American unions and was also "the prevailing feeling of non-union men."[47]

Progressivism and the Federal Judiciary

By the 1890s the obverse but compatible images of the federal courts — as the biased guardians of corporate wealth and the courageous champions of individual liberty — were widely if imprecisely fixed, and the political role of the national judiciary emerged as a persistent issue in national politics. In the presidential campaign of 1896 Populists and Democrats made the Supreme Court's political orientation a major issue, the first time since 1860 that the Court had figured prominently in a national election.[48] Addressing the Georgia Bar Association in 1898, a Populist lawyer exemplified the change in Southern politics. Passing over the race issue, he condemned the "arbitrary powers" of the national courts and their unholy alliance with business.[49]

In the years following 1900, Progressives turned the Populist attack on the judiciary into a staple of political debate. "The most momentous question before the people of this country today," wrote one Progressive attorney, "is undoubtedly the question of the limits of the power of the judiciary to annul legislation for alleged unconstitutionality." [50] In 1905 the Supreme Court applied its liberty of contract doctrine in *Lochner v. New York* to invalidate a New York statute that prohibited the employment of bakers for more than ten hours a day or sixty hours a week.[51] Progressives attacked it ferociously, and Learned Hand voiced their underlying refrain: the decision was not only unsound, but the result of social and political bias. "There is an inevitable bias upon such vital questions in all men," he charged, "and the courts are certainly recruited from a class which has its proper bias, like the rest." [52]

Progressives advanced a wide variety of proposals to limit the powers of the courts.[53] Many suggested restricting or abolishing judicial review, while others sought to restrain the use of injunctions, limit the courts' jurisdiction, make federal judgeships elective, and expand the role of the jury. Some argued for the recall of judicial decisions, urging that the people be authorized to overturn constitutional decisions by popular vote.[54] Although it ignored more radical proposals, Congress did respond. On four occasions between 1903 and 1920 it restricted the power of individual federal judges to issue injunctions against regulatory activities,[55] and on three other occasions it limited federal removal jurisdiction* to assist injured employees who wanted to avoid the burdens of federal litigation.[56]

Although World War I and the subsequent Red Scare fragmented Progressives, two events in the early 1920s combined to reenergize their criticisms of the federal judiciary. One was Prohibition, and the other was a seemingly even more anti-Progressive Supreme Court. The first created a crushing docket crisis that generated powerful demands for substantial changes in the federal judicial

---

*Federal law allowed defendants in state court actions to transfer their cases to the federal courts—to "remove" them—when the case was within the original jurisdiction of the national courts. Removal was a defendant's tool to counter a plaintiff's right to choose the court where his or her claim would be heard. In its legislation restricting removal, Congress assisted railroad employees and merchant seamen who sued their employers for personal injuries by making their choice of forum absolute. Commonly, such plaintiffs strongly preferred to litigate in the state courts, whereas their employers preferred the national courts and used removal regularly.

system, and the latter guaranteed that the political battle lines of the preceding decades would help determine what changes, if any, would be made.

Legal and social changes had brought growing caseloads to the federal courts since the 1870s, but nothing matched the staggering and immediate impact of the Eighteenth Amendment, which became effective in January 1920.[57] Because the states made only feeble efforts to enforce Prohibition the burden fell almost entirely on the national government, and prosecutions inundated the federal courts. In 1916, the year before America entered the war, 20,243 criminal cases were filed in the federal courts and 20,432 terminated. By 1926 the numbers had more than tripled to 68,582 filings and 76,536 terminations. During the four years from 1926 to 1929, 196,000 Prohibition-related suits swamped the national courts, accounting for more than 40 percent of their caseload. The press of crowded dockets became a lightning rod for clashing passions over Prohibition, and together they transformed the abstruse issue of judicial reorganization into a hotly contested political issue.[58]

Initially, Congress responded to the flood of cases by creating new judgeships, but opposition quickly developed to such wholesale expansions of the judiciary. While judges, lawyers, litigants, and the press protested "congestion in the courts," Congress examined a wide range of possible solutions including "streamlined" procedures and more efficient administrative techniques. "The courts have as great need as the factories of the efficiency engineer," the *American Bar Association Journal* argued.[59] "[I]f there are more cases than the Federal courts can dispose of under the present judicial structure," a congressman declared to the rousing applause of his colleagues, "it is high time that the Congress enact legislation to relieve the situation."[60] The applause, however, was hollow, for there was little agreement on what legislation to enact. Forced to confront the problem of congestion, politicians realized that alterations in the structure or jurisdiction of the federal courts necessitated far-ranging and fundamental policy choices.

Those policy choices seemed particularly apparent in the early 1920s because the Supreme Court, with a new majority, was becoming more actively anti-Progressive. The conservative and anti-labor William Howard Taft was appointed chief justice in 1921, and the following year two more highly property-conscious new justices, George Sutherland and Pierce Butler, joined the Court. Together with Justices James C. McReynolds and Willis Van Devanter, they formed a solid five-justice bloc that pushed the Court into a renewed anti-Progressive activism. Symbolizing the decade's pro-business orientation, the Taft Court invalidated state and federal regulatory laws in greater numbers and more frequently than any previous Court.[61] Consistently, it favored the interests of private business, appeared sharply hostile to the cause of organized labor, and reasserted the doctrine of liberty of contract to void regulatory statutes.[62] The Court had invalidated the first federal child labor law in 1918, and four years later the Taft Court invalidated the second one. The rulings used such broad language that it seemed only a constitutional amendment could allow Congress to address the problem.[63] "Much higher judicial barricades to political progress had been constructed since the World War began," Richberg complained. The Court's decisions were sometimes "so bad" that they were "laughable." [64]

Progressives rallied in opposition to the Taft Court.[65] Throughout the decade they joined states' rights advocates in urging measures to restrict the federal courts, ranging from radical efforts to terminate the power of judicial review to technical proposals to reduce the judge's control over the jury.[66] "For years I have seen the day coming when the Federal judiciary must be made, to some extent at least, subject to the will of the people," Senator Robert M. La Follette of Wisconsin declared. "We have created, or at least have suffered, to grow up within our land a Frankenstein which must be destroyed or else it will destroy us." The child labor cases, he charged, were "typical of the conduct of the Federal judiciary and particularly the Supreme Court whenever Congress has sought to enact progressive and humane legislation which was offensive to great financial interests." [67]

Calling on Progressives to unite, La Follette organized a new Progressive Party and campaigned for the presidency in 1924. Drawing the support of many leading insurgent politicians, social reformers, and farm and labor groups, the new party adopted a platform that advocated constitutional amendments to require the popular election of federal judges and to confer on Congress authority to override the Court's decisions.[68] Republicans bitterly attacked the Progressive planks, while Democrats were divided and equivocal.[69] Party loyalty, prosperity, and the aura of doom that typically surrounds third parties kept many Progressive sympathizers out of La Follette's camp. Although he received almost five million votes, the landslide for Republican incumbent Calvin Coolidge buried him and his party. La Follette's campaign, however, continued the prewar Progressive attack on the federal judiciary, and for the next thirteen years reformers continually hammered at the political bias they saw in the national courts.

Among conservatives, the fear of Bolshevism and the threat of La Follette cemented their allegiance to the federal judiciary, and supporters of the status quo rallied to the Court's defense. The judiciary, the *American Bar Association Journal* declared in 1926, was "the main support of a government of laws and not of men" and "the conservator of the interests of the years against the passions of the moment." [70] Justice McReynolds, perhaps the most reactionary member of the Taft Court, voiced the basic conviction of many conservatives. "The Supreme Court of the United States is the keystone of the arch that sup-

THE PREMISE OF AN AGE   23

ports our whole system of government," he declared. "Take it away and the entire structure would fall." [71] Worship of the Constitution and the judiciary had become fundamental articles of faith among conservatives, and throughout the 1920s and 1930s the ideological and emotional gulf between conservatives and Progressives yawned ever wider.

Typical of their long struggle was the battle over federal injunctions against rate-making orders of state regulatory commissions. [72] Beginning in the late nineteenth century, the states had increasingly utilized special commissions to regulate rates and conditions of service of common carriers and public utilities. Central to their efforts was the massively complex task of rate-making—evaluating a company's total assets and costs and establishing rates that would prevent "monopoly exploitation" while providing a "fair return" on investment. The rate-making process required extensive factual investigation and difficult judgments of economic value, and it inevitably brought railroads and public utilities to the doors of the federal courts seeking relief. The Supreme Court held that "unreasonable" rates were "confiscatory," and that the federal courts could enjoin state officials from enforcing them. [73] It also held that affected parties had a right to select a federal over a state court in which to press their constitutional claims [74] and, further, that they enjoyed a constitutional right to an immediate stay pending judicial review of any rate order alleged to be confiscatory. [75]

The federal rate injunction drew its notoriety from cases relatively few in number but highly visible and politically explosive. [76] Usually they were brought by major utility companies, often a corporation chartered out of state. The suits involved tens and sometimes hundreds of millions of dollars in capital stock, affected the utility rates paid by entire cities or states, and impinged directly on the administrations and careers of incumbent state officials. In 1907 the governor of North Carolina openly defied a federal court in a rate case, and the attorney general of Minnesota deliberately violated a federal injunction in an effort to enforce his state's rate schedule. [77] In 1928 a federal district court enjoined New York City and its Transit Commission from blocking a subway fare increase, and it did so in spite of a series of contracts in which the company promised to retain the five-cent fare in exchange for franchise rights and financial incentives. [78] In response, two leading New York Progressives, Senator Robert F. Wagner and Congressman Fiorello LaGuardia, introduced bills in Congress to deprive the lower federal courts of jurisdiction over such rate suits. [79]

Critics of the rate injunction charged that it was a gross interference with the authority of the states and an unfair tool of powerful private interests. Assailing the district court's injunction in the subway case, Wagner insisted that "the appropriate forum for the litigation of a strictly local issue is the State court." The suit, like most actions involving utility rates, turned initially, if not

wholly, on local issues such as the construction of private contracts, state statutes, and municipal ordinances. "The Federal Courts have been most aggressive
in the steady encroachment of Federal power upon the sovereignty of the States,"
Wagner declared. More than the executive or the legislature, they were "the
greatest offender against the principle of local self-rule."[80] LaGuardia charged
that "such flagrant misuse of the Federal courts" was a "national scandal." The
availability of federal jurisdiction enabled companies to delay and often defeat
administrative orders regardless of the merits involved. The federal courts, La-
Guardia insisted, were "used for the purpose of legalizing the exploitation of
these greedy corporations."[81]

Defenders of the federal courts maintained that constitutional rights were
at stake and that utilities had a right to seek protection from the national courts
in order to avoid local prejudice and inadequate state procedures and remedies. David E. Lilienthal, a Progressive Chicago attorney who also represented
utilities, acknowledged that federal procedure gave greater protection to regulated companies than the procedure in most states, particularly the "facility and
speed with which temporary relief may be obtained." He denied, however, that
recourse to the federal courts was either unfair or "an acute public problem."
In fact, Lilienthal argued, it was most appropriate for such suits to be heard in
the federal courts because of the greater "ability of the [federal] judges to com-
prehend the complexities of a rate case" and because most rate cases presented
federal, not local, issues.[82]

By the end of the 1920s the efforts of Progressives and states' rights
advocates to curb the federal rate injunction were rapidly gaining strength.
Gassification, electrification, and the growth of urban rail transportation systems increased the importance of public utilities and brought them into daily
contact with millions of consumers. The onset of the Depression undermined
the credibility of business leaders and led to the collapse of elaborate public
utilities holding companies. Those economic disasters, in turn, led to revelations
of systematic financial chicanery, and public utilities quickly became objects
of widespread anger and suspicion. When the elections of 1930 and 1932 gave
Democrats and Progressives large majorities in both houses of Congress, legislative action became politically feasible.

State and local governments petitioned Congress, and by 1932 the railroad and utilities commissions of thirty-two states had gone on record favoring
legislation that would deprive the national courts of jurisdiction to enjoin rate
orders.[83] The president of the California Railroad Commission charged that
federal review was disruptive, inefficient, and unnecessarily costly and time-
consuming. "We face," he warned, "the elimination not only of state control of
state rates, but of effective state control of service and safety." The only solu-

tion lay with congressional action that would free the commissions from "the present intolerable interference by lower federal courts." [84]

At the request of the California commission, Senator Hiram Johnson introduced a bill aimed at ending that "intolerable interference." [85] The undisputed leader of California Progressivism, Johnson had for three decades been a dedicated opponent of private utilities and a forceful advocate of public ownership. Elected governor in 1910, he strengthened the California Railroad Commission by giving it authority to set rates and subsequently extended its jurisdiction to all public utilities. [86] Serving in the Senate after 1916, he was a jealous defender of state authority who nevertheless supported Progressive national legislation and repeatedly denounced the evils of the "power trust." Only by defeating the power of the utility companies, he maintained, could there be "a semblance of either economic or political freedom in our commonwealth." [87]

The bill Johnson introduced was hardly radical. It deprived the lower federal courts of jurisdiction, on the basis of both federal question and diversity of citizenship, to enjoin the enforcement of any order of a state commission involving rates. The limit on jurisdiction, however, was subject to three significant conditions: the order could not affect interstate commerce; it had to be made after reasonable notice and hearing; and it had to be reviewable in a state court with authority to provide a "plain, speedy and efficient remedy." [88] The second condition seemed minimal and unobjectionable. The first condition, however, limited the bill's reach substantially, while the third lacked established legal meaning but clearly imposed a federal standard for state judicial remedies. Those two conditions offered the national courts considerable leeway to expand or contract the bill's scope.

Regardless of its vague language, the purpose of the Johnson bill was clear. Private utilities flooded Congress with letters and telegrams in opposition, while their law firms submitted briefs condemning the bill as discriminatory, unnecessary, and unconstitutional. [89] The Association of Railway Executives relied on the American Bar Association to lead the opposition, and the ABA responded with stinging denunciations and a massive effort to organize opposition from local bar groups across the country. [90] "There was a tremendous opposition to this bill from the public utilities of course, and the power trust very insidiously did everything possible to hamstring the law," Johnson complained to his son. "In addition, the lousy American Bar Association butted into the situation and opposed it." [91]

States' rights and Progressive hostility to the perceived alliance between business and the federal courts dominated the debate. Johnson urged his allies "not to make legal arguments, but to draw the line sharply between the power companies on the one hand, and the people on the other." [92] One congressman charged "that 99 percent of the cases brought in our Federal courts are brought through deceit or trickery," and another accused the utilities of "undue activity" in securing the appointment of federal judges.[93] "If the Federal judiciary is in any disrepute," he declared, "it is largely because the people believe that the utilities have unduly used the local Federal courts as a means to an end which they did not deserve."[94] Congressman James M. Beck, the leading Republican constitutionalist in the House, conceded that the bill was constitutional but insisted that Congress had a "moral" mandate to preserve the federal question jurisdiction of the national courts in rate matters.[95] The Johnson bill, Beck charged, was "a destructive proposal, which seeks to tear up by the roots the sturdy oak of the Federal judiciary."[96] If the Johnson bill were enacted, a past president of the ABA wrote, "there will be disastrous results."[97]

President Franklin D. Roosevelt tipped the scale.[98] As governor of New York, he had protested a federal injunction that allowed the New York Telephone Company to raise its rates. "This power of the Federal court," he had proclaimed, "must be abrogated."[99] Urged to support the Johnson bill by numerous Progressives, Roosevelt signaled his approval,[100] and the bill became law in May 1934. Johnson was delighted. "I can't imagine any other president during my time would have done a thing like this, and have done it of his own volition."[101]

The Johnson Act was noteworthy for two reasons. First, it confirmed once again the breadth of the conviction among Progressives and states' rights advocates that the federal courts served the interests of powerful corporations. Second, it suggested the extent to which most of them were reluctant to undermine too severely the general supervisory role of the federal courts. Indeed, as much as the act showed that political hostility existed, it also showed that the characteristic twentieth-century idea of the federal courts as the primary protectors of federal constitutional rights had taken root across the political spectrum. The Johnson Act limited federal judicial supervision, but only narrowly and conditionally. It preserved federal jurisdiction over rates that affected interstate commerce, created a federal standard of judicial relief by requiring the states to provide "a plain, speedy, and efficient remedy," and, of course, preserved the Supreme Court's jurisdiction to review resulting state court decisions. In spite of its narrow scope, however, the Johnson Act was a classic victory for legal Progressivism as well as for the advocates of states' rights. "I feel very proud of this," Johnson wrote to a friend, "and I am tickled to death."[102]

Countermovement: Professional Law Reform and Conservative Politics

Professional law reform was a product of growing specialization within the legal profession, formal institutionalization in multiyear law schools and

local and national bar associations, and particularly the emergence of elite corporate law firms and the establishment of a national profession of law school
teachers. Like Progressives, professional law reformers were inspired by ideas
of science and efficiency. They sought to alleviate the pressures of continuously
mounting caseloads and an increasingly complex legal environment by making
court procedures and institutions simpler, less costly, and more easily understood. Unlike Progressives, however, they proclaimed themselves politically and
socially neutral. Eschewing problems of substantive law, professional law reformers concentrated on technical improvements that were ostensibly unrelated
to partisan politics.[103] Emphasizing the complex nature of "efficient" reform,
they assumed that technical expertise alone made rational improvement possible.
Further, they assumed that lawyers' associations were the natural repositories
of such knowledge and that those associations should be entrusted with the responsibility for improving the legal system.

Although neutrality and expertise were its proclaimed hallmarks, professional law reform had unavoidable political resonance. Initially, both political
conservatives and the bar associations reacted with hostility to Progressive calls
for judicial reform.[104] Proposals to strengthen the courts and preserve the common law appeared increasingly safe and expedient after the turn of the century,
however, when an ever more aggressive plaintiffs' personal injury bar began
exerting increasing pressures on corporate defendants and some Progressives
began pushing for the adoption of the radically majoritarian judicial recall. Indeed, leaders of the bar began to realize that attributing "popular dissatisfaction"
with the law to inadequate and archaic judicial procedures was an ideal strategy
to counter Progressive attacks, check the plaintiffs' personal injury bar, deny
the need for major changes in substantive law, and portray legitimate reform as
an abstruse matter best left to the profession itself.

Taft, with impeccable credentials and enormous prestige at the bar,
emerged as the pivotal figure. While still president of the United States, he began
a sedulous campaign to defeat Progressive judicial reform by galvanizing the
profession behind a calculated and narrow reform program of its own. Subsequently, as law professor, president of the ABA, and chief justice of the United
States, Taft continued to preach the twin gospels of preemptive procedural reform and protection of the federal judiciary. Progressivism threatened a wild
and lawless assault on basic social institutions, he believed, and only the federal
courts — guarded by the constitutional guarantee of life tenure and providing
tight judicial control over juries — could guarantee the security of private property. Repeatedly, he insisted that the only "real objections" to the courts were
their "lack of dispatch of business and the cost of litigation."[105] Those objections
could be remedied and the federal courts protected, he exhorted bar associations

across the nation, by efficient administrative centralization and the simplification of judicial procedure.

Professional law reform appealed to many Progressives as well as conservatives. Both groups agreed that the courts should be made more efficient and their dockets controlled, and both believed that litigation should be less expensive and time consuming. During the 1920s and 1930s the movement helped achieve significant changes in the federal judicial system. It contributed to the passage of several procedural reform acts, including the Judges Bill of 1925, which gave the Supreme Court almost complete control over its appellate docket. Additionally, aided by the spur of Prohibition-induced congestion, professional law reformers helped persuade Congress to pass a series of measures that created a centralized administrative structure for the federal courts in order to increase their efficiency.[106]

For many professional law reformers, conservatives as well as some Progressives, the idea of court-made rules of procedure became the centerpiece of their efforts.[107] The movement for court-made rules was, in part, a response to the legislative codification of civil procedure that characterized the latter half of the nineteenth century. Following New York's adoption of the Field Code in 1848, numerous states had enacted similar procedural codes, and over the years many lawyers and judges, especially conservatives, criticized the codes for being unnecessarily rigid and elaborate. Law reformers began to argue that the legislative process made systematic amendment too difficult and that, if rules were made by the courts, they would be more flexible and efficient. The federal courts were necessarily caught in the middle of the debate because the Conformity Act of 1872 denied them authority to make rules of procedure in actions at law. The act mandated, instead, that they follow the "modes of proceeding" that were used in the states in which they sat.[108]

Taft quickly embraced the idea that the federal courts should make their own procedural rules for actions at law. In 1910, while still president, he recommended the approach to Congress and heralded it as "the best method of securing expedition in the disposition of cases."[109] The American Bar Association, under the leadership of Thomas W. Shelton, a Virginia practitioner, quickly took up the cause. The ABA drafted a bill and had it introduced in Congress in 1912 and reintroduced thereafter in each succeeding Congress for the next two decades.[110] Rejecting the requirement of conformity to state practice, the ABA bill transferred authority to prescribe procedural rules in actions at law from Congress to the Supreme Court, freed the federal courts from their dependence on state practice, and promised a nationally uniform system of procedure for the federal courts. The cause of court-made rules, Shelton believed, was a "sacred matter."[111]

Advocates of the ABA bill made a strong case. They maintained that procedural reform was essential to eliminate unnecessary technicalities and insisted that federal practice under the Conformity Act was hopelessly complicated.[112] Their argument focused on the inherent flexibility of court-made rules and the rigidity of legislative prescriptions.[113] Further, it emphasized that the Supreme Court had successfully drafted rules governing procedure in equity and the federal specialties of admiralty, bankruptcy, and copyright. Such wide experience proved the wisdom and utility of court-made rules, they argued, and promised equal success in reforming common law procedure. Finally, the bill's advocates maintained that in drafting the rules the Court would receive the assistance of the nation's most respected procedural specialists at the bar and in the law schools. The creation of a simplified and modernized set of rules, especially rules that merged law and equity, would serve as a national model and inspire similar improvements throughout the nation.

Although the ABA proposal was reasonable in many ways, it involved far more than mere technical simplification. Regardless of the bill's merits, many of its supporters were animated by concerns that were, at their root, highly political. Elite lawyers began to complain seriously about the "complications" of judicial procedure only after a newly specializing plaintiffs' personal injury bar began using those procedures vigorously in suits against their corporate clients.[114] Facing that new challenge, the legal elite soon came to regard the courts — which they had hailed as near perfect in the late nineteenth century — as victims of flawed procedures and antiquated administration. Further, the ABA exploited its commitment to procedural reform to serve a variety of unacknowledged, and perhaps even partly unconscious, political goals: to deflect attention from substantive legal issues and egregious inequalities in the distribution of legal services, to identify proper legal reform with politically arcane issues beyond the competence of the public, and to demonstrate the civic virtue of the legal elite.[115] There was, too, a practical motive. Nationally uniform procedure would serve the interests of elite law firms representing national corporations by simplifying their task of monitoring and conducting their clients' legal business across the nation.[116]

Ideologically most compelling, the ABA bill resonated profoundly with the legal elite because it served their most fundamental goal, the denigration of the legislature and the elevation of the judiciary. Praising the courts for their expertise and integrity, John H. Wigmore, the increasingly conservative dean of Northwestern Law School, rejected one of the fundamental assumptions of legal Progressivism. Legislatures, he charged, possessed "an inferior grade of knowledge." They inevitably became "the catspaw of a few intriguing lawyers" who sought only "to serve selfish ends or to vent petty spite or to embody [in legislation] some personal narrow view."[117] The *American Bar Association Jour-*

nal hammered at those galvanizing themes. The "whole trend of modern professional thought," it proclaimed in 1921, "is towards the increased autonomy of the judicial institution." [118] Disappointed with Congress's failure to act, the journal announced five years later that "the remedy is for the courts themselves to resume the inherent powers of which the legislature had no authority to deprive them." [119] Taft confided to Shelton that "the danger to this country is in the enlargement of the power of Congress," and Shelton agreed wholeheartedly.[120] "The Judicial Department," he declared privately, "must depend for its protection upon some sort of an alliance with the Executive." [121]

The fact that the ABA sponsored the bill automatically provoked suspicion, if not opposition, from many Progressives. As governor of New York, Franklin Roosevelt had gotten "fed up" with bar association suggestions for judicial appointments. "They never, under any circumstances, suggested a 'man of the people,' " he complained. "Always someone from a big law firm, all of which did and do the same type of legal business." [122] Many Progressives, especially those from the South and West, agreed.[123] The ABA, Hiram Johnson instructed his son, "may be relied upon always to favor exploitations of our people." [124]

The ABA was surely vulnerable. It consistently opposed Progressive proposals, from child labor legislation to minimum wage laws. Although its advocates frequently appealed to the virtues of decentralized federalism, when the power of the federal judiciary was involved they suddenly became ardent centralizers. The ABA claimed, for example, that one of its principal goals was to simplify procedure and bring uniformity to federal and state practice. If so, an amendment to the Conformity Act, requiring actual conformity and specifying unavoidable exceptions, might well have been a more desirable approach.[125] Similarly, the association claimed that another of its major goals was to improve the general administration of justice. If that were true, a campaign directed at the state courts would certainly have had a broader impact. Not only did the state courts handle the overwhelming amount of litigation in the United States, but improvements in their procedures would have accrued to the federal courts automatically under the Conformity Act.[126] The ABA, however, scorned that path and largely ignored the states. Its paramount goal was to strengthen the authority and independence of the national judiciary. Amending the Conformity Act or improving state practice would have maintained congressional control over procedure and continued to subordinate the federal courts to state rules. Ultimately, the association's campaign for uniform court-made rules was driven by its twin ideological commitments: politically, to the more conservative federal courts as the foundation of stability and property; professionally, to the more prestigious federal courts as the forums they and their corporate clients preferred.

Support for the ABA bill was not, however, limited to corporate lawyers and political conservatives. Learned Hand, who had become a federal judge in New York in 1909, and Dean Charles E. Clark of Yale Law School were among the Progressives who supported some version of the proposal.[127] Within the profession as a whole, in fact, division on the ABA bill followed status and practice lines as much as political ones. Many law teachers and law reviews favored the bill almost as strongly as the ABA did, and prominent academic specialists were virtually unanimous in urging the bill's passage. Conversely, large numbers of nonelite lawyers opposed it. Although law school teachers who specialized in "procedure in general" inevitably saw "confusion and uncertainty" in federal practice across the nation, state practitioners were typically satisfied with their local rules. The leaders of the bar repeatedly proclaimed the profession's support for the bill, but they well knew that opposition was widespread. Clark acknowledged that "the general professional reaction is, quite naturally, against change," and Charles Evans Hughes, another supporter, admitted privately to his awareness of the sharp division of opinion.[128] "I have had occasion to learn," he wrote, "that there is strong opposition throughout the country to the project of uniform rules in common law causes." [129]

Senator Thomas J. Walsh, a Progressive Democrat from Montana and one of the ablest lawyers on the Judiciary Committee, became the most outspoken antagonist of the ABA bill. Uniform federal procedure "would be convenient, no doubt, for Mr. Shelton and his associates among the members of the American Bar Association who try cases in many States," he exclaimed, "but the humble lawyer whose practice is confined to the State in which he resides may be pardoned for looking at the matter in quite a different light." [130] Walsh defended practice under the Conformity Act, protested the confusion that new rules would cause, and objected to the burden their preparation would impose on the Supreme Court.[131] Further, he questioned the bill's constitutionality, arguing that it would be an unauthorized delegation of legislative power to the judiciary.[132] Finally, Walsh argued that uniform national rules would intrude on the states, which embraced "radical differences in social, financial, and political organization," and impose on all a single set of inevitably rigid rules.[133]

In the early 1920s success seemed within the ABA's grasp. Landslide Republican victories in 1920 and 1924, the growing pressure of Prohibition-induced congestion, the appointment of Taft as chief justice, and the endorsement of President Calvin Coolidge generated powerful support for passage of its bill. By the mid-1920s every state bar association in the nation had endorsed it, as had innumerable local bar groups, civic and business organizations, and law reviews and law school deans.[134] In early 1924 Shelton told Roscoe Pound that "we have a large majority in favor of the bill if it ever reaches the floor." [135]

Unfortunately for the ABA, the floor proved beyond reach. Although support was strong in the House, the Senate refused to act. In the Judiciary Committee Walsh, backed by other Progressives, battled the bill to a stand-still.[136] Regular Republicans, Taft fulminated, were being "buffaloed" by "these yahoos of the West and crafty damage lawyers like Walsh." [137] When the congressional elections in 1926 increased Democratic and Progressive strength in both houses, the opportunity was lost. Confidently bringing the bill to a vote before the new Judiciary Committee, Walsh carried a ten to six majority for an adverse report.[138] The federal courts, Taft complained bitterly, were "at the mercy of their enemies." [139]

The onset of the Depression focused congressional attention on more immediately critical issues, and the further infusion of Democratic and Progressive strength in Congress after the election of 1930 dashed the ABA's hopes. Then Shelton died, and the twenty-year effort flagged. In 1932 the ABA concluded that prospects for the bill's passage appeared nonexistent, and the next year it formally terminated its campaign.[140] Apparently guaranteeing the bill's demise, after the election of 1932 the newly elected president, Franklin D. Roosevelt, named Walsh as his attorney general.

Fate, however, intervened. Shortly before Roosevelt's inauguration, Walsh was struck with a fatal heart attack. His last-minute replacement, Homer S. Cummings, a moderate Democrat from Connecticut, shared neither Walsh's deep suspicion of the ABA and large Eastern law firms nor his solicitude for the small-town practitioner and the variegated rules of state practice. Cummings was, in fact, an enthusiastic law reformer who believed strongly in the desir-ability of court-made rules of procedure.[141] Equally important, his energy and loyalty soon won Roosevelt's complete confidence, and by 1934 he had become one of the president's most trusted advisors.[142] Adopting the language of the ABA bill, Cummings revived the cause of court-made rules and threw his support behind the proposal.

Suddenly, the time was right. With his basic New Deal recovery program in place, Roosevelt was marking time while awaiting signs of an economic upturn. Congress, freed from the intense demands of the previous year, had the opportunity to consider other less pressing measures. The president, fully supporting the policy of the National Industrial Recovery Act to encourage co-operation between economic groups, was determined to maintain his contacts with business and, when possible, to heed its advice. Backing the procedural reform bill seemed an easy way to show his solicitude.[143] Additionally, the administration was happy to signal the courts that it was concerned with their needs and prestige.

Quickly and easily the Cummings bill passed both houses and became law in June 1934. The Rules Enabling Act authorized the Supreme Court, subject to the approval of Congress, to establish general rules governing the "practice and procedure" of the district courts in actions at law. Further, it authorized the Court to merge the rules with those for suits in equity, thereby creating "one form of civil action" in the federal system. The act imposed one limitation, that the rules "shall neither abridge, enlarge, nor modify the substantive rights of any litigant."[144]

In a few months Cummings accomplished what the ABA had failed to do in twenty years. Although Walsh's death and the appointment of Cummings as attorney general were prerequisites, the ease of the bill's final passage revealed the critical importance of the political context that surrounded it. The bill finally passed because the ABA had essentially withdrawn, and the Roosevelt administration adopted its abandoned cause. Neither Republican nor Democratic Progressives were willing to fight the New Deal, especially on a bill that enjoyed so much professional support. Most Southern and Western Democrats readily fell into line, and conservative Republicans voted for a bill they had long supported. Two decades of controversy over a professionally important but politically arcane issue faded when endorsement by the New Deal lifted the deep suspicions of Progressives in both parties.

Culmination and Disintegration: The Court-Packing Fight

From the beginning, both Progressives and their adversaries anticipated a confrontation between the New Deal and the federal courts.[145] Whatever actions Roosevelt planned would surely require the exercise of expansive national powers and would, with equal certainty, be subject to elaborate and well-financed constitutional challenges. Roosevelt himself expressed the basic Progressive conviction in the final days of his campaign in 1932. "After March 4, 1929, the Republican Party was in complete control of all branches of the Federal government," he charged, "the Executive, and the Senate and House of Representatives — and, I might add, for good measure, the Supreme Court as well." William Nelson Cromwell, the chairman of the New York Committee of the Bar for Hoover, reacted immediately. Berating Roosevelt for "his unfair aspersion," Cromwell loftily proclaimed that the Court "has kept itself immaculate from the stain of political partisanship." Revealing both the power of the professional ideal and the ideology of the legal elite, Cromwell was able to insist — in a document that appeared a week before the election, accusing Roosevelt of "desperation," and carrying the label of an overtly partisan political group — that his committee was acting for no reason but to defend "the administration of justice uninfluenced by any partisan considerations." In private, Roosevelt acknowledged that his remark might have been unwise, but he refused to retract it. "What I said last night about the judiciary," he told a friend, "is true."[146]

For two years New Dealers and their opponents anxiously waited for a wave of constitutional challenges against Roosevelt's program to reach the Supreme Court. In spring 1935 the results came in, and the Court handed down a series of decisions invalidating several New Deal measures, including the pivotal National Industrial Recovery Act. Deeply anxious over the fate of the Agricultural Adjustment Act (AAA) and several new measures that Congress had adopted in 1935 (including the Social Security Act and the National Labor Relations Act), Roosevelt began thinking seriously about ways to counter the Court's hostility and intransigence.[147]

Meanwhile, friction between the New Deal and the federal courts intensified. The lower courts were seriously disrupting the administration, issuing nearly two thousand injunctions against various government programs, the majority involving taxes under the AAA. Although a federal statute prohibited such injunctions, Cummings told Roosevelt in exasperation that "the Courts seem to have found a way of declaring it inapplicable" and have enjoined federal agencies "rather freely."[148] Then in early 1936 the Supreme Court's conservative majority began another string of anti–New Deal decisions over the consistent opposition of the Court's Progressive wing—Justices Louis D. Brandeis, Harlan F. Stone, and Benjamin N. Cardozo. Most strikingly, the Court revived the doctrine of liberty of contract to hold a New York minimum wage law unconstitutional and invoked the Tenth Amendment in invalidating the AAA on the ground that agriculture was a "local" concern reserved to the control of the states.[149] Writing for Brandeis and Cardozo, Stone exploded in dissent. Scorning the majority's claim that federal power should be curtailed "because it may be abused by unwise use," he sounded the Populist and Progressive battle cry of the preceding half century. "So may judicial power be abused."[150]

New Dealers were furious, never doubting that the majority was driven by social and economic bias. The Court had "established its ascendency over the entire government," charged Robert H. Jackson, one of the New Deal's top lawyers, and it used its supremacy "to disable the nation from adopting social or economic policies which were deemed inconsistent with the Justices' philosophy of property rights."[151] Proposals to counteract the Court were widely discussed, and congressmen introduced more than a hundred bills aimed at expanding congressional authority and limiting judicial review.[152]

Emboldened by staggering majorities in Congress after the 1936 elections, Roosevelt decided to carry the fight directly to the Court. On February 5, 1937, he recommended that Congress "reorganize" the federal judiciary.[153] Focusing on the need to dispose of "our overcrowded dockets," he maintained that "lowered mental or physical vigor" meant that judges over the age of seventy were often unable to deal with their caseloads or adapt to "complicated and changed conditions." For the Supreme Court he proposed that the president be empowered to make an additional appointment for each judge who was over seventy and refused to retire, limiting the expansion to a maximum of six.[154] Unable to resist criticizing the judiciary for its "[g]overnment by injunction," however, Roosevelt ended with a threat. "If these measures achieve their aim," he declared, "we may be relieved of the necessity of considering any fundamental changes in the powers of the courts or the Constitution."[155]

The proposal, particularly its transparent rationale based on age and efficiency, quickly boomeranged. Not only did it fail to deceive, but it outraged the president's opponents and embarrassed his supporters. Pouncing immediately, Herbert Hoover stripped away the facade. "The real issue," he insisted, "is whether the President by the appointment of additional judges upon the Supreme Court shall revise the Constitution."[156] A week after his message a swelling chorus of criticism forced Roosevelt to acknowledge that his proposal was an attempt to protect the New Deal.[157] In a nationwide radio broadcast he confronted the issue squarely. "[W]e must take action," he proclaimed, "to save the Constitution from the Court."[158]

Attacked furiously as an attempt to destroy the Constitution and establish a presidential dictatorship, Roosevelt's Court bill provoked the most intense and bitter struggle of his presidency. The White House staff directed a nationwide campaign to win popular support and wielded the patronage power ruthlessly to marshall local Democratic organizations behind the bill.[159] Raising money and providing direction behind the scenes, the Republicans carefully avoided making the bill a "party" matter and encouraged "pro-Court" independents, Progressives, and Democrats to spearhead the opposition. To their delight, Senator Burton K. Wheeler — a Democrat, a Westerner, and a well-known Progressive who had been La Follette's running mate in 1924 — agreed to lead the anti-administration forces. Opponents organized nationwide, exhorting citizens to "save the Supreme Court from domination by President Roosevelt."[160]

The Supreme Court contributed to its defense. First, responding to Wheeler's inquiry, Chief Justice Hughes secured the assent of Brandeis and Van Devanter, de facto representatives of the Court's divergent wings, to a letter stating that the Court was "fully abreast of its work" and insisting that an increase in membership "would not promote the efficiency of the Court." To the administration's surprise and chagrin, Wheeler introduced the letter while testifying before the Senate Judiciary Committee in late March, not only discrediting the president's contentions about age and delay but also signaling publicly to Progressives that the revered Brandeis disapproved the bill.[161] Second, the Court seemed to reverse its course abruptly. On March 29, with Hughes and Justice Owen J. Roberts joining the three Progressives, it upheld a Washington state minimum wage law that was indistinguishable from the New York statute it had voided only the previous year.[162] Two weeks later, by the same five to four vote, it approved the crucial National Labor Relations Act.[163] In late May, in another pair of identical five to four votes, it upheld pivotal provisions of the Social Security Act.[164] Each succeeding decision sapped the support for the bill.[165] Third, Van Devanter announced in mid-May that he would retire at the end of the Court's term, only weeks away. Roosevelt would thus be able to make his first Court appointment and, of critical importance, to make it from the ranks of the Court's anti-Progressive wing. Together with the Court's apparent acceptance of the New Deal, Van Devanter's retirement meant that Roosevelt had won the war if not the immediate battle.[166]

Although the president continued to push his bill, by summer it was dead. Furious at the rebuff, Roosevelt finally agreed to withdraw it and accept a face-saving compromise, passage of a pair of mildly Progressive judicial reform bills. One, the Judiciary Act of 1937, allowed the attorney general to intervene in any suit in which a federal statute was challenged on constitutional grounds and provided for accelerated appeal to the Supreme Court of any decision invalidating such legislation. It also precluded single judges from enjoining enforcement of federal statutes and required that suits for such injunctions be heard by special three-judge courts.[167] The second bill, the Tax Injunction Act, was modeled on the Johnson Act.[168] It denied the federal courts jurisdiction to "enjoin, suspend, or restrain" the collection of state taxes if there was "a plain, speedy, and efficient" remedy available under state law.

The statutes were not insignificant. Their provisions embodied reforms that Progressives had supported for three decades. In the wake of Roosevelt's climactic six-month pitched battle, however, they seemed inconsequential and humiliating.

On one level, Roosevelt had obviously succeeded. Once Van Devanter retired and the conservative majority was lost, the constitutional battle was over. Other resignations followed quickly, Sutherland's within months and Butler's within two years. By 1941 Roosevelt had made seven appointments, and one of the two holdovers was the Progressive Stone, whom Roosevelt elevated to chief justice in 1940. The new Court did not invalidate a single New Deal measure, and over its first several years it expanded broadly the power of the national government.

The results of the Court fight were far reaching and pervasive. Institutionally, the battle seemed to guarantee the independence of the Court and to place it in an almost sacred position in the structure and ideology of American government. Popular faith in the Court's special role defeated the dominant president of the twentieth century at the summit of his power. It seemed unlikely in the extreme that any president or party in the near future would again challenge the Court so directly and boldly. Indeed, the Court fight would prove fraught with ironies, and the extent to which the anti–New Deal forces succeeded in using Roosevelt's proposal to elevate the Court to a seemingly untouchable position would have a continuing impact in the radically altered world of the coming decades.

Jurisprudentially, the Court fight offered Progressive constitutionalists two conflicting lessons. One was that the justices of the old Court had incurred the wrath of the American people by repeatedly overstepping their authority and reading their personal values into the Constitution. In the absence of clear and compelling constitutional language, many of them reasoned, the Court should defer broadly to the legislature and exercise judicial self-restraint when exercising the awesome power of judicial review.[169] The other lesson was that the old Court had chosen to enforce the wrong substantive values. Some concluded that future Progressive Courts should allow extensive economic regulation but enforce vigorously the personal liberties that were enshrined in the Bill of Rights. The Court's future would turn in large part on which lesson its members accepted.

Politically, the consequences were profound. The Court fight marked the beginning of the end of the New Deal. It severely tarnished Roosevelt's aura of political mastery and signified to many that he was devious, untrustworthy, and power hungry. The fight fragmented the president's congressional support and drove a deep wedge between loyal New Dealers and the party's sizable, critically situated, and primarily Southern conservative wing. Moreover, it taught conservative Democrats the utility of cooperating with the Republicans. As their mutual distrust of Roosevelt and their antagonism toward executive centralization grew, the two groups coalesced into a cohesive bloc that brought the New Deal to a halt. An economic downturn in late 1937 helped discredit the New Deal, while the growing menace of Nazism and the threat of a new war in Europe placed ominous new issues at the center of American politics. In November a special session of Congress marked the change. Presented with a batch of Roosevelt's "must" bills, Congress refused to take action and adjourned within weeks.[170] The following year the huge Democratic majority passed only one significant piece of reform legislation, and the elections of 1938 substantially increased Republican strength in both houses. Roosevelt remained popular, but the New Deal was dead.[171]

The Court fight marked the beginning of a fundamental realignment in the basic contours of American politics.[172] Initially, the confrontation had pitted Roosevelt and the Democratic Congress against the conservative and "Republican" Supreme Court, but by the summer of 1937 it had been transformed into a struggle between an aggressive and overreaching executive and a suspicious legislature jealous of its prerogatives. The anti–New Deal coalition in Congress, forged to protect the Court, emerged as the primary institutional antagonist to an expanding executive branch which came to represent centralization, bureaucratization, and a new kind of urban liberalism sharply distinct from the older Progressivism. Increasingly, Roosevelt's strength rested on the support of the large cities, nationally oriented social reformers, the newly muscular labor movement, and the ethnic and religious minorities that together could carry the large industrial states. Congress, conversely, fell under the control of a bi-party majority rooted in the merging interests of those opposed to Roosevelt and his new coalition: the business sector, farmers, states' rights advocates, small-town America, and Protestant and nativist groups hostile to the ethnic and cultural changes that New Deal urban liberalism symbolized. Progressives and states' rights advocates, who had frequently found common ground in the early twentieth century, especially in their attacks on the federal courts, divided sharply and reoriented their politics. Progressives who embraced New Deal liberalism soon became bitter adversaries of those who continued to uphold the doctrine of states' rights. Concurrently, the federal courts, the common enemy that had so often united the two groups, faded from the political arena. The Supreme Court dismantled the anti-Progressive Constitution, and Roosevelt's appointees reshaped the social and political orientation of the national judiciary. In the name of judicial restraint the "New Deal Court" announced resolutely that it would seldom challenge either state or national legislatures, especially on issues of economic regulation.

As the judiciary receded from the center of national politics, Roosevelt was left to confront Congress. As he won reelection for two more terms, the conservative coalition grew in cohesiveness, determination, and frustration. By the 1940s the fundamental politico-constitutional world that Populists and Progressives had inhabited for the preceding half century—the "popular" and therefore sometimes reformist legislative branch that opposed the activist and property-conscious federal judiciary—had, like the world of pre–Civil War America, "gone with the wind." In its place a new world was taking shape that pitted the powerful executive reformer—the "representative of all the people" who could identify the common good and protect the "Free World"—against the conservative legislature—the home of lobbyists, special interests, powerful and reactionary committee chairmen, and all that was local and narrow. This alignment lasted for another decade and a half, until the Republicans finally broke the Democrats' twenty-year hold on the executive and almost simultaneously the federal judiciary reemerged—this time on the "progressive" side—as the dynamic and divisive force in American politics.

Expanding the Federal Judicial Power

2

JUSTICE DAVID J. BREWER AND

THE "GENERAL" COMMON LAW

Neither the Progressives nor their adversaries were entirely accurate in their complementary portraits of the federal judiciary. The national courts allowed far more economic regulation than Progressives acknowledged, and they protected far fewer individual "liberties" than their conservative defenders proclaimed.[1] Not surprisingly, historical reality was more complicated than political rhetoric.

Still, however, both sides had reasons for their views of the judiciary. The federal courts did foster the growth of the national market, protect private property, and encourage corporate enterprise. "Corporations are a necessary feature of modern business activity," the Supreme Court explained in 1906, "and their aggregated capital has become the source of nearly all great enterprises."[2] Further, in cases of far-reaching importance the federal courts did rule against workers and labor unions, construe the ideal of legal equality to exacerbate social inequality, and invoke the principle of private contract to allow powerful parties to take advantage of weaker ones. Although the Supreme Court accepted the vast majority of regulatory efforts, it restricted or invalidated reform measures that Progressives considered of particular importance, and its constitutional rulings created doctrinal obstacles to many other reforms they proposed.

Although the often repeated saga of the turn-of-the-century Court has focused on a relatively small number of politically controversial decisions that involved bitterly contested social issues, the most pervasive and enduring achievement of that Court was not political, social, or economic. It was institutional. The Court strengthened the power of the federal courts and moved—albeit somewhat erratically and incompletely—to establish the primacy of the national judiciary in American government. Its unifying thrust lay not in preventing the exercise of government power but in expanding the ability of the national judiciary to review exercises of that power, especially by the states. The more industrialization changed the United States, the more the institutions of government responded and the more the Court approved. The more it approved, the more concerned many people, including the justices, became with the question of limits. By expanding the supervisory role of the national judiciary, the Court created the ultimate security blanket to buffer the unnerving challenges raised by an age of rapid, disruptive, threatening, and inescapable social change.[3]

The turn-of-the-century Court altered the institutional balance of American government. On one front it helped shift power from the states to the nation, and on another front it expanded the power of the federal judiciary over all other branches of government—over state courts and over the legislative and executive branches of both states and nation. Many of the ideas associated with substantive due process were rooted in the jurisprudence of state courts, for example, but the turn-of-the-century Court shaped those ideas to meet new social problems, gave them a wider national effect, and channeled their enforcement to the lower federal judiciary. Despite its continuing commitment to the values of federalism, after 1890 the Supreme Court became a powerful centralizing force in American government.

Expansion and Reorientation

The doctrine of substantive due process represented more than the creation of new constitutional law that limited government regulation and fostered corporate enterprise. It exemplified the Court's active expansion of federal judicial power. As the justices made clear when they announced the doctrine in the famous Minnesota Rate Case in 1890, the constitutional point was not the assertion of limits on government but the assertion of the judiciary's power to pronounce what those limits were. The "reasonableness" of transportation rates, the Court explained, "is eminently a question for judicial investigation."[4] Dissenting with two others, Justice Joseph P. Bradley noted the significance of that ruling. "The governing principle" of the Court's prior decisions, he declared, "was that the regulation and settlement of the fares of railroads and other public accommodations is a legislative prerogative and not a judicial one."[5]

Substantive due process meant that the ultimate power to judge the "reasonableness" of rate regulation and other legislative actions lay with the federal judiciary. In its subsequent decision in *Lochner v. New York* (decided in 1905), which invalidated a state statute that limited the number of hours that bakers could work, the Court defined the relatively heavy burden that such legislation bore. "The law must have a more direct relation [to a valid public purpose], as a means to an end, and the end itself must be appropriate and legitimate."[6] The burden of proving a statute's reasonableness was substantial, and it rested on the legislature. The Court would decide in each case whether that burden had been met.

Regardless of its high political visibility, substantive due process was merely one part of the Supreme Court's expansive efforts. The Court also employed the long-used Contract Clause to check government actions and in 1905 enlarged the range of rights that the clause protected.[7] It incorporated the Fifth Amendment Takings Clause into the Fourteenth Amendment, thereby making the clause applicable to the states, and extended to corporations Fourth Amendment protections against unlawful searches and seizures.[8] Throughout the period, too, the Court applied the Commerce Clause to police both state and federal governments. With respect to state governments, it used the "dormant" Commerce Clause—the provision's inherent force in the absence of congressional legislation—to limit state regulatory efforts that impinged improperly on interstate commerce.[9] With respect to the federal government, it approved substantial expansions of national legislative power, showing greater deference to Congress than to the states while continuing to enforce significant limits on that power.[10]

Similarly, the Court used its authority to construe federal statutes to help shape national economic policy and protect the expanding market. The practical significance of that power grew dramatically in importance after 1887, when Congress began to enact regulatory programs. By the early twentieth century, actions based on congressional enactments accounted for a substantial and growing part of the federal caseload. The Court checked the new Interstate Commerce Commission closely in its early years, especially when it attempted to set rates, for example, but it readily approved congressional efforts to impose rigorous national safety requirements on railroads.[11] After struggling with the Sherman Anti-Trust Act for two decades, it held in 1911 that the statute's provisions should be construed according to a "rule of reason," which, in effect, authorized the federal courts themselves to draw the line between lawful and unlawful economic concentration.[12] Most broadly, the Court used "preemption"— the doctrine that congressional legislation could "occupy a field" and thereby exclude state law—to strike down numerous state provisions and thereby create a more uniform national law of interstate commerce. It often employed the doctrine, moreover, in the absence of any clear congressional intent to preempt.[13]

To help enforce national law in its rapidly expanding reaches, the Court also increased the supervisory capabilities of the lower judiciary. In essence, it reoriented the federal trial courts toward cases involving issues of federal law while expanding access to them for parties who asserted federal rights. This reorientation stemmed from the Court's realization that, by itself, it could no longer adequately monitor the burgeoning work product of state courts and administrative agencies. Moreover, because regulatory and rate-making cases involved complex factual issues, fact-finding efforts at the trial level played an ever more critical role in the adjudicatory process and highlighted the potentially decisive role of the trial courts.[14] Finally, the fact that federal consideration was reserved solely to appellate review by the Supreme Court placed ever greater burdens on the justices, while imposing on parties the disadvantage of a long-delayed and less certain federal remedy and the risk that decisions would be based on closed records and frozen findings of fact made by state courts and agencies. The Court's solution was to expand the role of the federal trial courts and transform them into the front-line defenders of federal rights. Unlike their state counterparts, federal judges held guaranteed lifetime appointments that protected them from popular pressure. As a group, they tended to share a broader national viewpoint. They were, moreover, appointees of the national government, directly responsible to the federal appellate courts and the United States Supreme Court. The lower federal courts promised to enforce federal law more consistently, more reliably, and more readily than the state courts, and the Supreme Court trusted them to shoulder much of its increasingly heavy burden.

Accordingly, beginning in the 1890s and culminating in the years between 1900 and 1917, the Court restructured federal procedural and jurisdictional law to expand the ability of the lower courts to deal with economically important disputes, claims based on federal law, and challenges to state regulatory actions. It effectively negated the Eleventh Amendment as a bar to federal jurisdiction over suits against state officers,[15] and it expanded the lower courts' ability to handle challenges to state regulation in cases where issues of local law were raised along with federal law claims.[16] Concurrently, it expanded the reach of federal equity. The Court endorsed a sweeping increase of judicial power in appointing receivers and exercising continuing supervision over corporate reorganizations,[17] sought to ensure federal jurisdiction over shareholder derivative suits,[18] and approved more readily the issuance of injunctions against state court actions when they threatened to interfere with proceedings or prior judgments of federal courts.[19] Additionally, it authorized exceptions to the doctrine that equity would not enjoin threatened criminal proceedings and allowed the lower federal courts to block such prosecutions when they were used to enforce regulatory schemes.[20]

The Court's 1908 decision in *Ex parte Young* was a crowning achievement.[21] There, the justices upheld the jurisdiction of a lower federal court to enjoin the attorney general of Minnesota from enforcing the state's rate regulations against a railroad. The decision not only expanded the ability of the federal courts to review state regulatory actions, but also synthesized many of the Court's decisions since 1890 and reshaped federal law in four distinct areas. It was a major breakthrough in authorizing federal injunctions against threatened state criminal prosecutions, and it established what became the broad and standard constitutional rationale for avoiding the limitation of the Eleventh Amendment.[22] State agents who tried to enforce unconstitutional laws were "stripped" of their official status, the Court ruled, and therefore injunctions against them did not operate against the state itself.[23] Even more innovative, *Young* further extended federal judicial authority by creating, in effect, a judge-made cause of action for injunctive relief directly under the Constitution. It established that a claim under the Fourteenth Amendment was cognizable in the federal courts without an allegation that state agents had committed any type of common law tort or other act that constituted an independent legal wrong.[24] Finally, by creating a new constitutional cause of action, the Court circumvented the strictures of the "well-pleaded complaint" rule. That rule limited the lower courts' federal question jurisdiction to cases in which plaintiffs, and plaintiffs alone, presented properly pleaded federal claims.[25] As long as the allegation that a state was acting in an unconstitutional manner served only as a defense in state enforcement proceedings, parties seeking to challenge regulatory efforts had to wait for a state to take action and then raise their defense in the forum of the state's choosing—invariably, one of its own courts.[26] By creating a new constitutional cause of action, *Young* transformed the challengers' defense into an affirmative claim for relief that they could initiate as plaintiffs. By avoiding the "well-pleaded complaint" rule, the decision allowed challengers to control the choice of forum and force states to defend their actions in the national courts.

Justice John Marshall Harlan dissented, advancing two closely related principles fundamental to nineteenth-century American jurisprudence.[27] One was that the state courts were "under an obligation equally strong with that resting upon the Courts of the Union to respect and enforce the provisions of the Federal constitution." The other was that the proper remedy for a state court's denial of a federal right was by a writ of error from its highest court to the United States Supreme Court.[28] In *Young,* Harlan believed, those two principles meant that the railroad should not be able to initiate its action in a lower federal court. Not a single justice, joined him, however. Without rejecting the general principles, the other justices ignored the first and qualified the second. A federal trial court, they decided, was precisely the forum that should be available for such a suit.

The Court did not disguise *Young*'s activist consequences. The very next year it went out of its way to defend and encourage the lower courts in using their supervisory powers. In *Willcox v. Consolidated Gas Co.* it reprimanded attorneys for a state agency who criticized a lower court because it took jurisdiction over a challenge to the agency's action. Counsel "assume[d] to criticize that court for taking jurisdiction of this case, as precipitate, as if it were a question of discretion or comity," the Court noted. But, it thundered in response, "there was no discretion or comity about it." When a party "properly appealed" to a federal court, that court had a "duty" to exercise its jurisdiction. "The right of a party plaintiff to choose a Federal court where there is a choice," the justices proclaimed, "cannot be properly denied." [29]

By 1913 the Court was prepared to announce that "the Federal courts are charged under the Constitution" with the duty of protecting federal constitutional rights and, further, to suggest that they were "the primary source for applying and enforcing the Constitution of the United States." [30] Given that both the existence and jurisdiction of the lower federal courts were matters within the discretion of Congress, and that they had not been given general federal question jurisdiction until 1875, the Court's statement seemed dubious as both history and law.[31] It did, however, articulate the essence of its reorientation of the federal judiciary.

With *Young* and its related doctrines as a centerpiece, the Court reshaped federal law in three other areas to serve the same purposes. First, it blocked a series of state efforts to restrict the jurisdiction of the national courts. In 1908 it established the principle that states could not create administrative appeal procedures to preclude claimants asserting federal rights from challenging state regulatory decisions in a federal court.[32] Then, beginning in 1910, it developed the doctrine of "unconstitutional conditions" to prohibit a variety of devices that states were using to force foreign corporations—those chartered in other states—to abandon their federal right to use the national courts.[33] Similarly, it extended federal equity jurisdiction by limiting the effect of new state-created "legal" remedies. Because federal equity courts could hear suits only when there was no "adequate remedy at law," new state remedies "at law" threatened to defeat their jurisdiction and, if the state restricted the remedies to its courts, prevent parties from seeking their legal relief in a federal court. In a long series of decisions the Court gradually established the rule that an "adequate remedy at law" capable of defeating federal equity jurisdiction required a legal remedy that was available in a federal court.[34] Thus, if states created new legal remedies that were available only in their own courts, the remedies could not defeat federal equity jurisdiction.

Second, to accommodate what *Young* referred to as "a great flood of litigation of this [regulatory] character" that might enter the federal system,[35] the Court decided to trim the national dockets of less important diversity cases. Conferred originally in the Judiciary Act of 1789, diversity jurisdiction—which allowed the federal trial courts to hear suits between citizens of different states—had been the principal source of the lower courts' business. Although their numbers were large, diversity cases typically involved routine and socially inconsequential private-law disputes. Therefore, large numbers of them could be cut from the federal dockets with relatively little impact on national concerns; in any event, such cases commonly were less important than the kinds of cases the justices were funneling into the federal system. Accordingly, in the first decade of the twentieth century the Court issued a series of decisions that promised to eliminate from the dockets large numbers of run-of-the-mill diversity actions.[36] Confirming its supervisory purpose, moreover, the Court tailored its restrictions carefully. It maintained diversity jurisdiction over shareholder derivative suits and petitions for railroad receiverships—two types of proceedings with great economic importance.[37] Indeed, it expanded diversity jurisdiction to enable the lower courts to hear a third type of case with special economic significance: actions challenging compensation awards made in state property condemnation proceedings.[38]

Third, the Court imposed greater control over the state courts themselves to ensure that they properly enforced federal law. In 1903 it held that federal law, not state law, controlled the *res judicata* effect of federal court decisions on federal law issues. "[A] right claimed under the Federal Constitution, finally adjudicated in the Federal courts," the Court insisted, "can never be taken away or impaired by state decisions."[39] Five years later it declared that if the Eleventh Amendment barred a federal court from hearing a challenge to state action based on federal law, the Constitution required state courts to provide a judicial forum for its adjudication. Equally important, it made clear that resulting state decisions would be reviewable in the United States Supreme Court.[40] Upholding the second Federal Employers' Liability Act (FELA) in 1912, the Court declared that the state courts had a duty to hear suits under the act, and two years later it held that federal law controlled all issues, including related common law matters, that arose in connection with FELA claims.[41] Finally, the Court expanded its ability to review state court judgments that involved issues of federal law. In early 1912 it handed down three decisions qualifying the long-established rule that it was bound by state court findings of fact.[42] Then, only months later, it declared that "settled" principles allowed it to review state court findings of fact when federal rights were denied on dubious or inadequate factual grounds.[43] The Court made the point of its new rule abundantly clear. It was "necessary to examine the evidence," it explained, in order "to prevent an evasion of real issues."[44] The "real issues," of course, were federal rights, and the feared evaders were state courts that might minimize, avoid, or deny them.

In the quarter century preceding World War I, then, the Supreme Court reshaped federal law across the board, from sweeping constitutional mandates to arcane rules of jurisdiction and procedure. Its purpose was manifest. "[I]n no other way can the obligation of the Federal courts under the Constitution be discharged," it asserted in cumbersome but passionate language, "than by rigidly adhering to the right and duty to maintain the ultimate right of the Federal courts to protect the citizens of the United States, and of every State, in the enjoyment of rights and privileges guaranteed by the Federal Constitution." [45]

Justice David J. Brewer and the Ideal of Judicial Primacy

Justice David Josiah Brewer was an ardent proponent and creative architect of the Court's complex restructuring of federal law. During his tenure, from early 1890 until his death in 1910, Brewer's ideas and drive played a key role in the Court's expansive thrust. [46] Unlike his colleagues, moreover, he proclaimed the primacy of the judiciary publicly and vigorously.

A product of New England and its religious heritage, Brewer was born in 1837 in the city of Smyrna, Asia Minor. [47] His father, Josiah, a devout Congregationalist missionary trained at Yale, was stationed there serving his second tour of duty bringing Christian education to the Near East. His mother, Emilia, a devoted woman who married Josiah between his missionary assignments abroad, was the sister of the remarkable Field brothers, David Dudley, Stephen, Cyrus, and Henry. [48] The family returned to Connecticut before David's second birthday. After his early schooling, the young man attended Yale College, where he was deeply influenced by its president, Theodore Dwight Woolsey. Woolsey was a Congregationalist minister who taught a moralistic blend of politics and religion that the young Brewer found compelling. [49] His intense religious upbringing, as well as his connection to the Field family, shaped his life and values.

After graduating from college with honors in 1856, Brewer focused his attention on law and politics. For a year he read in the Albany office of his uncle David Dudley Field, a major figure at the New York bar and the preeminent legal reformer of his day, and then spent another year studying at Albany Law School. In the turmoil of the 1850s both family commitments and religious conviction turned him into a fierce anti-slavery Republican. Naturally energetic and outspoken, he used the party's press to attack the pro-southern Pierce administration and to excoriate the *Dred Scott* decision. After receiving his law degree in 1858, he decided to head west, fascinated by the struggle for "Bleeding Kansas" and inspired by his uncle Stephen J. Field, who had just been elected to the California Supreme Court. Just as he had turned down the opportunity to stay in New York and practice law with one uncle, he refused to join another in California. Determined to succeed on his own, he decided to make his fortune in the Midwest and, after scouting the area, settled in late 1859 in Leavenworth, Kansas.

As a young attorney, Brewer struggled to establish a practice, joining a variety of community activities and participating avidly in local Republican politics. He served in the local militia, organized the Leavenworth Mercantile Library Association, and helped establish the First Congregational Church, where he taught Bible classes and supervised the Sunday school. Combined with his intellectual abilities and engaging personality, his community service quickly won him a series of public offices. In 1861 he was appointed commissioner for the federal circuit court in Kansas; and the following year, after failing to obtain the Republican nomination for the state legislature, he won election to the county probate court. From that point he ascended steadily through the judicial hierarchy. From 1865 to 1869 he served as a state district judge, and in 1870 at the age of thirty-three he was elected to the Kansas Supreme Court. Twice reelected, he was appointed in 1884 to the federal circuit court for the Eighth Circuit. Five years later, with a Republican president back in office, he was nominated to the United States Supreme Court.

On January 6, 1890, Brewer took his seat. Awaiting him there was his uncle Stephen, the primary exponent of substantive due process, then in his twenty-seventh year on the Court. In protecting individual economic rights, advancing the doctrine of liberty of contract, and advocating an active role for the federal courts, Brewer shared and would carry on many of his uncle's ideas and values.[50]

Rather than quieting his public voice, appointment to the Court encouraged the new justice to speak freely and forcefully on public issues. Across the country, especially during the strife-torn 1890s, Brewer preached the same fundamental message: the nation confronted grave dangers, and only the courts could save it. Government centralization, political demagoguery, labor unions, greedy legislatures, and non–Anglo-Saxon races threatened to disrupt American society and destroy its institutions. A rising "spirit of paternalism"[51] threatened to centralize government and destroy liberty, while a "movement of 'coercion' " driven "by the mere force of numbers" sought "to diminish protection to private property."[52] Unions were "a step toward despotism," and a "tempestuous democratic flood" threatened the nation.[53] "Unrestrained, unchecked, it will sweep onward, bearing all things to certain destruction," he warned; "but subjected to restraining law, its tremendous and irresistible force will be transmitted into beneficent light and power to illumine the upward ways of humanity."[54]

The United States Constitution was the supreme statement of that "restraining law." It provided "the measure of all rights and the limitations of all powers."[55] Regardless of social and economic developments, moreover, its meaning remained unchanged. "That which it meant when adopted," Brewer declared, "it means now."[56] It was "the inviolable rule of action."[57]

The Constitution's true authority, Brewer believed, came from the fact that it incorporated the principles of the Declaration of Independence and the divine truths of Christianity.[58] It affirmed the "sacredness of life, of liberty, and of property," and it proclaimed that government was based on and limited by "inalienable rights" that were "given not by man to man, but granted by the Almighty." [59] Consequently, the Constitution's command was one of "absolute and eternal justice." [60] Suggesting the extent to which he identified the mandate of the Constitution with his religious beliefs, he charged that the popular movement against property not only transgressed the Constitution but "in spirit, if not in letter, violates both the eighth and tenth commandments." [61]

The nature of the Constitution determined the role of the courts. The most "distinctive feature of the Constitution," Brewer declared, "is its judicial system, with the Supreme Court at its head." The founders conferred "vast powers" on the Court and made it "a most potent factor in shaping the course of national events." That Court "stands today," he declared reverently, "a quiet but confessedly mighty power, whose action all wait for, and whose decisions all abide." [62] When it acted, it simply "lifts its staying hand and says 'Thus reads the Constitution.' " [63]

The judiciary was society's providential guardian, and the judge was "a priest ministering at the most sacred altars." [64] Alone, the courts ensured "that popular action does not trespass upon right and justice as it exists in written constitutions and natural law." [65] Consequently, Brewer maintained, the judiciary must be protected and strengthened. "If you want to have justice administered in the most expeditious and best way, untie the hands of the judges," he urged; "give them a greater freedom, and you may be sure that the outcome will be for the best interests of this state and every individual within it." [66] To social turmoil and economic conflict he had one answer: "My reply is, strengthen the judiciary." [67] Because politicians and legislators catered to popular will and were ultimately unreliable, there "arises the urgent need of giving to the judiciary the utmost vigor and efficiency." Long after the turmoil of the 1890s had passed, he continued his campaign. "It is just at this time that it is of the supremest importance," he insisted in 1903, "that the judiciary of the State and nation should be upheld in the utmost stretch and reach of their power." [68]

The federal judiciary's paramount power lay in its equity jurisdiction, and Brewer sought to defend and expand that jurisdiction wherever possible. Repeatedly, he appealed to the doctrine that federal equity was a system of "independent" remedies authorized by the Constitution itself. "It is a mistake to suppose that for the determination of equities and equitable rights we must look only to the statutes of Congress," he declared for the Court in 1906. "The principles of equity exist independently of and anterior to all Congressional legislation." [69] Similarly, he insisted that federal equity was also insulated from state action, maintaining that the creation of new state remedies at law should not deprive a federal equity court of jurisdiction. [70] The independence of federal equity conferred broad discretion on the national courts, and it offered Brewer a wide field where he could apply his "convictions of right and wrong."[71] Equally important, he considered equity's classic remedy, the injunction, as the ideal instrument for protecting private property and enforcing public order. Declaring that he was "as much opposed to government by judges as any man," Brewer maintained that equitable relief had nothing to do with discretion or policy. "[T]he writ of injunction is not an act of legislation," he explained. "It creates no new law." Rather, it was simply the law's most useful remedy. "It only enforces rights which the Constitution and the law have theretofore declared sacred."[72]

Repeatedly, Brewer sounded the tocsin against a radical "movement to displace the courts." "It is part and parcel of the scheme to array the many against the few, the masses against the classes." There was, he warned, a "constant tendency in the legislation of this country to tie up the hands of the court and the judge."[73] Such a course was folly. "In no country in the world, under no form of government, is a firm, strong, stable judiciary more needed than in a 'government of, by, and for the people'."[74] Predatory majorities would be held at bay only "so long as constitutional guarantees lift on American soil their buttresses and bulwarks against wrong," he maintained. Those guarantees, in turn, would operate only "so long as the American judiciary breathes the free air of courage."[75] Above all, the Supreme Court must never be "shorn" of its powers. "No specious plea against government by injunction should ever be permitted to take from it that wholesome restraining influence which has been so powerful for good."[76]

Brewer's frequently emphatic off-the-bench pronouncements, together with his judicial opinions attacking government regulation, earned him a reputation as a "rugged individualist," an anti-government "activist," and a staunch proponent of "laissez faire constitutionalism." To a considerable extent, his reputation was deserved. He embraced the doctrine of substantive due process and its corollary, liberty of contract, and he was prepared to scrutinize state and federal regulatory actions closely.[77] In controversial cases, he often sided against workers, labor unions, and tort claimants.[78]

Vigorously, if sometimes unsuccessfully, he sought to establish greater protections for private property and broader restrictions on government regulation.[79] Shortly after he took his seat, warning of threats to liberty and property, he announced forthrightly that "we must re-cast some of our judicial decisions."[80] He launched a long-term assault on the doctrine of *Munn v. Illinois,* a major Court decision in 1877 that allowed the states wide latitude in regulating the uses of private property.[81] Enthusiastically, he joined the majority in the Minnesota Rate Case and praised the decision publicly for putting judicial limits on *Munn*'s doctrine of legislative discretion.[82] On a parallel front, he pushed to expand the right to compensation when government regulation affected private property, arguing that owners were entitled to "a full and perfect equivalent for the property taken." On this issue, too, he trumpeted his signature theme. The "measure of compensation," he insisted, "is a judicial and not a legislative question." [83]

Although Brewer's reputation as a defender of property was well founded, it was also, like much of his rhetoric, somewhat overinflated. Most obviously, his judicial opinions were usually more sophisticated and varied than his most fervid public pronouncements.[84] As a judge, too, he accepted many regulatory efforts of both state and national governments.[85] His interests, moreover, ranged far beyond issues of economic regulation. Maintaining his membership in the Congregationalist church throughout his life, he never faltered in his religious commitment. Largely from that inspiration, he was a sincere, if somewhat abstract and limited, social reformer. He showed considerable sympathy for African Americans and Chinese immigrants, and he became an early supporter of women's rights. Perhaps his strongest reform commitment was to world peace. He criticized the United States for its colonialism after the Spanish-American War and worked earnestly to advance the cause of international law and arbitration. During the last decade of his life, his strident rhetoric seemed to moderate, and he criticized the materialism of the age and the excesses of its wealthy.[86]

Brewer's fundamental goal was not, in fact, simply to protect private property. Rather, it was to ensure more broadly that the judiciary — in his view the most reliable, effective, and just institution of government — would be able to maintain the rule of the Founders' law and God's justice.[87] To an unusual degree, he believed that his personal values were embodied in the Constitution, and he was determined to see them enforced. Dissenting in 1892, for example, he felt no compunction about asserting the relevance of his personal views to a question of constitutional law. "The paternal theory of government," he wrote, "is to me odious." [88]

The equation Brewer made between his personal views and the requirements of the Constitution was evident in 1891 when he denounced the "police power" — the doctrine that state governments could regulate property and behavior to serve important public goals. The power was "undefined and perhaps indefinable," he explained, and accordingly it suggested little limitation on government action. Consequently, it became "the refuge of timid judges" who sought "to escape the obligations of denouncing a wrong." Brewer scorned such judges. "The absence of prescribed limits to this [police] power," he maintained, "gives ample field for refuge to any one who dares not assert his convictions of right and wrong." [89] In his view, the "undefined" police power was limited not only by the express terms of the Constitution but by a judge's proper "convictions of right and wrong." [90] In placing limits on that dangerous and otherwise "undefined" power, Brewer was fully ready to assert his convictions.

Those who regard Brewer as merely "property-conscious" or "anti-government," then, miss the essence of his judicial career. First and foremost, he was a religiously inspired advocate of judicial power, especially federal judicial power. At the center of his jurisprudence lay a fervent belief in the authority of the courts to enforce the nation's fundamental moral and economic proprieties in a time when social conflict, disruptive change, and a largely immigrant and dangerous industrial work force threatened to exploit the frailties of popular government.[91] It was that belief, and his consequent and methodical efforts to expand the federal judicial power, that made him a major force in the Court's history.

The Supple Power of the General Federal Common Law

Nowhere was the nature of Brewer's jurisprudence more apparent than in his uses of what was called "general law" or "federal common law." Since 1842, following its decision in *Swift v. Tyson*, the Supreme Court had held that the federal courts were not required to follow the decisions of state courts in matters of "commercial" or "general" jurisprudence, but only on issues of "local" law.[92] Written by Justice Joseph Story, a widely respected legal scholar and broad-visioned nationalist, *Swift* was designed to expand the role of the federal judiciary and help generate a uniform national commercial law.[93]

Technically, the opinion interpreted Section 34 of the Judiciary Act of 1789, a provision called "the Rules of Decision Act," which required the federal courts to follow "the laws of the several states" in actions at common law where the federal Constitution and statutes did not govern.[94] *Swift* held that the word *laws* in the provision meant only laws that were "strictly local," that is, state constitutions, statutes, and rules established by long usage that related to immovable property within the state. The term did not include judicial decisions that dealt with the "general principles" of judge-made or "common" law. Such judicial decisions involving "general" issues were not actually "law" but merely "evidence" of the law. Story's construction meant that Section 34 did not require the federal courts to follow state judicial decisions on issues of "general" common law. Instead, it allowed them, in the absence of properly controlling "local" authorities, to exercise their "independent" judgment in determining the applicable "general" common law rule.[95] Thus, *Swift* seemed to rely on what was called the "declaratory" theory of law, the idea that the common law consisted of principles existing independently of judicial decisions. In that view, the role of judges was to find, declare, and apply those preexisting principles to new fact situations.[96]

During the second half of the nineteenth century the federal courts ignored state court decisions with increasing frequency. Steadily expanding the scope of the *Swift* doctrine, they developed their own extensive body of independent decisional rules that came to be called "general law" or "federal common law." By century's end they had inflated the domain of general jurisprudence to encompass most common law subjects, and in 1910 the Supreme Court extended it further to issues of real property law—an area that in the nineteenth century had seemed clearly "local." [97] To many, especially elite lawyers and national corporations, the federal courts under *Swift* were establishing a nationally uniform common law that would facilitate interstate commerce in the burgeoning national market.[98]

Brewer, of course, reveled in the idea of general law. Like the independent system of federal equity, it was a charter of federal judicial freedom that enabled him to serve his ideas of right and justice. Moreover, it was a highly useful complement to the Court's powers to construe the Constitution and federal statutes. The idea of a federal common law fostered an amorphous concept of law that allowed the Court to make rules without identifying their source or legitimating their creation. It was also particularly useful because it allowed the Court to cover whatever gaps might result from narrowing or invalidating state and federal statutes. Once legislation had been avoided or overturned, the *Swift* doctrine allowed the federal courts to make their own law in the area newly freed from statutory control. Indeed, the Constitution's limitations on legislative power stood sentinel over the realm of the federal common law. If legislatures abolished general law rules that the Court deemed essential, it could revive the rules by striking the statutes down on constitutional grounds.[99] Indeed, the generative power of "general" jurisprudence could itself shape the nation's fundamental law. When "interpreting the Constitution," Brewer pointed out, "we must have recourse to the common law." [100]

Exploiting the potential of the general common law, Brewer employed it in a variety of contexts and for a variety of purposes. All, of course, served to expand federal judicial power. His general common law decisions reflected that purpose and highlighted the nature of his jurisprudence.

Brewer used the *Swift* doctrine, for example, to assert federal judicial control over the field of tort law, especially over personal injury claims by employees against their employers. His decision for the Court in *Baltimore & Ohio Railroad Co. v. Baugh* in 1893 was a landmark twice over.[101] Broadly, it established that industrial tort law was an area of "general" jurisprudence over which the federal courts properly exercised their independent judgment under *Swift*.[102] More narrowly, it announced a sweeping version of the "fellow-servant" rule that made it exceptionally difficult for workers to prevail in tort suits against their employers.[103] *Baugh* and its resulting federal common law of industrial injuries exemplified both Brewer's commitment to national judicial power and his willingness to subordinate the claims of workers to the welfare of national corporations. The property of interstate railroad corporations, he had boasted shortly before his decision came down, "stands as secure in the eye and in the custody of the law, as the purposes of justice in the thought of God."[104]

Only two justices dissented in *Baugh*. Chief Justice Melville W. Fuller rejected the decision as "unreasonably" harsh to the victims of industrial injuries, while Field scorned his nephew's opinion as an affront to "justice and humanity." More to the point, Field brought into the open the practical truth that animated the *Swift* doctrine. It "has been often advanced in judicial opinions of this court," he confessed, "to control a conflicting law of a state." Escalating his attack, Field maintained that he and the other justices who had refused to follow those "conflicting" state law decisions had erred profoundly. The general federal common law intruded into areas reserved to the states by the Tenth Amendment, he charged, and it was, therefore, unconstitutional.[105]

Although Brewer usually agreed with Field and frequently denounced the evils of centralization, in *Baugh* he turned a deaf ear to his uncle's fervent appeal on behalf of state authority. Instead, he urged the Court to assert control over the law of industrial torts, and in subsequent cases he applied the anti-plaintiff federal fellow-servant rule repeatedly and ruthlessly.[106] *Baugh*'s twofold thrust served Brewer's purposes well. Its narrow holding assisted corporations by discouraging employee tort claims and relieving the companies of potentially serious liabilities.[107] Its broad holding promised uniform federal law for the national market and enhanced the power of the federal judiciary by bringing a fiercely contested and economically important area of the common law under its control. The constitutional rights of the states carried little weight, in his mind, when centralization brought power not to Congress or the executive but to the federal judiciary.

In a second area, the law of common carriers, Brewer's use of the federal common law revealed that his goal was not simply to protect property and commerce but to ensure a broader rule of federal judge-made law and justice. In 1901 he wrote for the Court in *Western Union Telegraph Co. v. Call Publishing Co.* and placed judicially mandated regulatory norms above the self-aggrandizing claims of an interstate corporation.[108] There, the publishing company sued Western Union for allegedly charging unjust and discriminatory interstate rates, and the question was whether the Nebraska courts had authority to grant relief. Seeking to have an unfavorable jury verdict overturned, Western Union advanced a bold three-pronged argument to establish what Brewer termed the "startling" proposition that interstate telegraph rates were entirely free from legal restrictions.[109] First, the company maintained that it could not be held liable under Nebraska law because "Congress has sole jurisdiction over such [interstate] matters." Second, it pointed out that Congress had failed to enact any controlling legislation. Finally, it maintained that "there is no national common law." Thus, the company concluded, "in the absence of a statute by Congress" regulating interstate telegraph rates "there was no law upon the subject" and presumably "no limit" on the rates it could charge.[110]

Understandably, the Court refused to accept the claim that anyone could act in a context that was wholly "lawless." To dispose of its arguments, moreover, an easy and effective rejoinder lay ready at hand: absent relevant congressional legislation, the state's common law controlled. The Nebraska Supreme Court had upheld the verdict on precisely that ground.[111]

For Brewer, such a resolution was unattractive. It meant deferring to both Congress and the states, and it meant squandering a golden opportunity. He saw no reason to accede to the proposition that Congress had "sole jurisdiction" over interstate commerce nor to the proposition that mere legislative inaction could prevent the federal courts from enforcing desirable social norms. Similarly, he saw no need to rely on state law or to accept the proposition that there was no "national" common law. He was, indeed, prepared to jettison that last proposition despite the fact that the Supreme Court had repeatedly affirmed it as fundamental. "There is no common law of the United States in the sense of a national customary law," the Court had declared in 1888.[112] Indeed, the *Swift* doctrine was premised on the theory that common law rules were matters of "state" law and that the federal courts merely exercised an "independent judgment" when the issue was "general."

Brewer, however, was not deterred. He seized the opportunity to expand the elastic *Swift* doctrine by force of assertion. There was, he proclaimed baldly, "a general common law existing throughout the United States." That national common law existed "not, it is true, as a body of law distinct from the common law enforced in the states, but as containing the general rules and principles by which all transactions are controlled except so far as those rules and principles are set aside by express statute." [113] Brewer did not bother to explain exactly what his words meant in terms of the Court's prior doctrine or how the "general rules and principles" that he invoked differed from the kind of "national" common law that did not exist. Instead, he ruled. In *Western Union* he asserted explicitly national authority and created truly national judge-made law, not local law that state legislatures could control or overturn. "[T]he principles of the common law," he declared, "are operative upon all interstate transactions except so far as they are modified by Congressional enactment." [114] On the ground that the Nebraska courts could enforce that interstate national common law, he held that the state judgment against the telegraph company was valid.

Western Union was classic Brewer. Asserting the existence of a national common law, he held that it governed interstate commerce and that it was independent of both Congress and the states. By recognizing a distinctly national common law, moreover, he implied that it reached to the limits of national power and established that the Supreme Court of the United States was its authoritative voice. Finally, he imposed on interstate business only a minimal and flexible limit that was controlled by the federal courts, the general principle that common carriers could not charge "unreasonable" and "discriminatory" rates. As important as private property and corporate enterprise were to Brewer, neither was as important as the primacy of federal judicial power in ensuring that the law recognized the proper "convictions of right and wrong." [115]

In a third area, the law of insurance, Brewer used the general law even more aggressively. As *Western Union* created a national judge-made law that stretched at least to the limits of congressional power, the federal common law of insurance stretched the judicial power beyond the lawmaking authority of Congress. Story himself, on the heels of *Swift*, had brought insurance within the general common law. "[T]he construction of a contract of insurance," he had ruled, presented "questions of general commercial law" that were "by no means local." [116] Subsequently, in a series of cases following the Civil War the Court had held that insurance contracts did not constitute "commerce" within the meaning of the Commerce Clause. [117] The decisions prevented Congress from regulating insurance under the commerce power, while at the same time they freed the states to act without regard to restraint by the dormant Commerce Clause. Thus, by the late nineteenth century three issues were settled: Congress could not regulate insurance matters under the Commerce Clause; the states exercised general supervisory authority in that area; and, by imposing constitutional limits on state regulation and shaping their own general common law, the federal courts could exert substantial lawmaking authority in the area. The federal judiciary stood as the only branch of the national government empowered to make law covering insurance contracts.

Brewer embraced that disjunction of power. Repeatedly, he voted to reaffirm the constitutional limitation on congressional power, [118] and just as regularly he used the authority of the federal courts to make general common law rules for insurance contracts. Indeed, he joined the Court in a series of decisions that shaped the general common law to protect the interests of insurers and made the federal courts highly favorable forums for them. The justices made it easier for the companies to claim forfeitures against their policyholders and to avoid liability for the dubious or improper acts of their agents. [119] Brewer was prepared, moreover, to construe state legislation narrowly to guarantee ample room for the operation of general law. [120]

More important, Brewer sought to maintain the disjunction between federal legislative and judicial power. The critical point occurred after 1905 when state investigations produced sensational evidence that the insurance industry was marked by waste, fraud, and mismanagement. Many Progressives began calling for national legislation, and Congress considered enacting a regulatory program. In the name of decentralization, Brewer publicly and forcefully denied the authority of Congress to act.[121] Insurance, he insisted in 1906, "has been repeatedly held by the Supreme Court to be not a part of interstate commerce, and only a matter of local law." Congressional intervention threatened "danger," he warned, and the principle of decentralization demanded that the states continue to control insurance legislation.[122] For purposes of national legislative power, Brewer insisted that insurance was "local" and therefore beyond federal authority. For purposes of national judicial power, however, he denied that premise and insisted that insurance was "general" and, therefore, within the scope of the *Swift* doctrine. As he had dismissed Field's appeal to state authority in *Baugh*, so he turned away from decentralization in insurance law when it was the federal judiciary that was making the national law.

Although Brewer helped make the federal common law more favorable to insurance companies and opposed Progressive national legislation, his goal was not narrowly political. In fact, since 1890 some insurance companies had been urging congressional action to overcome basic industry problems and to preempt the stringent regulatory programs that a number of states had established.[123] Indeed, many Progressives were committed to state regulation and suspicious of the motives behind proposals for national action. Brewer, then, acted primarily not to assist the companies but to protect the independent national lawmaking power of the federal judiciary. He believed in limiting government regulation, fostering corporate enterprise, and protecting the national market; even more, however, he believed in the judicial rule of right and justice. The best way to achieve that goal was to maintain the primacy of the federal judiciary by limiting the reach of Congress and allowing the national courts to make the only national law in that area.

The general common law, Brewer realized, was a remarkably potent and supple tool. Exemplifying the turn-of-the-century Court's underlying instrumentalism, his decisions repeatedly exploited its potential and revealed in the process his hierarchy of values.[124] As his decisions in all three areas established, the virtues of decentralization disappeared when it was the national courts that made national law. The expansion of federal judicial power was primary, for with it he could serve his fundamental substantive values. On that list of substantive values, *Western Union* demonstrated that a general regime of judicially determined law and justice came first. As his insurance decisions showed, protecting corporate enterprise and the national market held a high rank. As *Baugh* and his other employee tort decisions revealed, providing compensation for injured workers did not appear.

Establishing Judicial Primacy: Twin Triumphs
of the General Common Law

The boldness of Brewer's institutional enterprise emerges in sharpest relief when two of his masterpieces are juxtaposed: *Kansas v. Colorado* and *In re Debs*. The cases arose from entirely different types of disputes, addressed wholly dissimilar legal issues, and arrived at the Court a dozen years apart in radically contrasting political climates. They were, nonetheless, jurisprudential twins.

Decided finally in 1907, *Kansas v. Colorado* initially raised technical and relatively narrow legal issues involving the Court's Article III jurisdiction over suits between states and the law of nonnavigable interstate streams.[125] In 1901 Kansas filed suit in the United States Supreme Court to enjoin Colorado from diverting the waters of the Arkansas River before they flowed into Kansas. Both states relied on the common law doctrine of riparian rights, but Colorado contended for the particular version that a number of arid Western states had adopted.[126] Thus, the principal legal question between the states was which substantive common law rule applied to their dispute.

The significance of the suit was transformed, however, when the United States government intervened in order to protect the Roosevelt administration's program to "reclaim" lands in the Western states through the construction of dams and irrigation systems. The attorney general urged the Court to reject the laws of both Kansas and Colorado and to decide the case on the basis of "a new law of waters on interstate streams," a law which would be national in scope and founded on the Constitution.[127] The attorney general asserted three broad claims. First, he argued that the United States was a single nation and that the federal government alone was capable of properly settling disputes between states.[128] Second, acknowledging that the Court had jurisdiction over suits between states, he suggested that the mere fact of jurisdiction did not give the Court authority, or at least exclusive authority, to establish a substantive federal law of interstate streams. For, he emphasized, "the court is not a legislature."[129] Third, he argued that the dispute between the states involved the "function and power of the Government, on the legislative and executive side."[130] Stressing the national importance of the administration's reclamation program, he told the Court that it was "indispensable to the future growth and prosperity of the Nation that the public lands be reclaimed and cultivated."[131] For that overriding national purpose, Congress had constitutional authority to legislate under the Commerce Clause and on the basis of "the doctrine of sovereign and inherent power."[132] Concluding, the attorney general asked the Court for a decree that would provide "a recognition of the national law and of the Government's right to direct the matter of water distribution on this non-navigable interstate stream." [133] The administration's intervention thus forced on the Court a second issue: which branch or branches of the federal government had authority to create a national law for interstate streams?

Carrying a bare five votes, Brewer once more seized the opportunity. [134] He was consumed, of course, not by the question the states presented but by the claims the attorney general made. He readily accepted the premise that the United States was a single nation and that disputes between states necessitated a national law. Between the powers of Congress and those of the federal judiciary, however, he insisted that there was a "significant difference." [135] The Constitution gave Congress "no general grant of legislative power" but only a delegation of certain limited and specified powers. Conversely, Article III "granted the entire judicial power of the Nation" to the federal courts, and its charter was "not a limitation nor an enumeration." Rather, Article III granted "all the judicial power which the new Nation was capable of exercising." [136] Brewer continued, "[t]hese considerations lead to the propositions that when a legislative power is claimed for the National Government the question is whether that power is one of those granted by the Constitution, either in terms or by necessary implication, whereas in respect to judicial functions the question is whether there be any limitations expressed in the Constitution on the general grant of national power." [137] Brewer had already noted that, with the exception of the Eleventh Amendment, the "general grant" of judicial power in Article III was "unrestricted.' [138] Thus, he established a more flexible and expansive test for judicial power than for legislative power, necessarily broadening the reach of the former beyond that of the latter.

Brewer developed that fundamental premise with a complex and partly implicit argument. Reviewing the enumerated powers of Congress, he found them inadequate to justify general congressional control over interstate streams. The attorney general's "inherent" power argument he dismissed bluntly. It was, Brewer declared, "in direct conflict with the doctrine that this is a government of enumerated powers." [139] Then, sowing the seeds of a pivotal distinction, he pointed out that the Tenth Amendment reserved undelegated powers to the states "or to the people." The amendment reserved to the states all "powers affecting the internal affairs of the States," while "all powers of a national character which are not delegated to the National Government by the Constitution are reserved to the people of the United States." [140] One obvious conclusion was that "Congress cannot enforce either rule [of riparian rights] upon any State." [141] Then, having laid his groundwork, Brewer reshaped the Constitution and the federal judicial power: "It does not follow, however, that because Congress cannot determine the rule which shall control between the two States or because neither State can enforce its own policy upon the other, that the controversy ceases to be one of a justiciable nature, or that there is no power which can take cognizance of the controversy and determine the relative rights of the two States." [142] Reaping the harvest of his distinction between the Tenth Amendment powers reserved to the states and those reserved to the people, he then summoned forth the image of the general common law enshrined in *Swift* and stretched broadly in *Western Union*. The common law "does not rest on any statute or other written declaration of the sovereign," he explained, but its "principles" were "in force generally throughout the United States." [143] Assuming, then, that "the people" were the source of authority for common law principles, he concluded his tour de force. In matters national in scope but not delegated to Congress, where power was reserved not to the states but to "the people," the national courts were necessarily the authorized voice of a truly "national" common law. Because the Supreme Court had jurisdiction over disputes between states, the "clear language of the Constitution vests in this court the power to settle those disputes." [144] Consequently, while Congress did not have power to make the governing law, the Supreme Court did. Brewer thus brought to the law of interstate disputes the same disjunction in lawmaking power that marked insurance law. The only difference was that in the former area, unlike the latter, he was able to negate the lawmaking authority not only of Congress but of the states as well.

As in *Western Union*, the specific decision in the case was mere detail and the resulting rule merely one of general reasonableness to be determined in individual cases by the Court. Declaring that "[e]ach State stands on the same level with all the rest," Brewer concluded that the law should "recognize the equal rights of both and at the same time establish justice between them." In such disputes "this court is practically building up what may not improperly be called interstate common law." [145] That law required only "the equitable apportionment of benefits between the two States." [146] Quickly skimming the facts, he ruled that Kansas had not shown sufficient injury to offset the benefits Colorado received from its use of the Arkansas River.

Kansas v. Colorado was a breathtaking performance, the work of a constitutional virtuoso—indeed, of a constitutional framer. In a single opinion Brewer denied the power of the national legislative and executive branches, elevated the federal judiciary to a position of constitutional primacy over both Congress and the states, and carved out an important area of conflict where the Court's interstate common law would reign free and unchecked. His opinion had much to commend it. The subject matter unquestionably required that final authority rest with the national government, and the doctrine of delegated powers made his analysis plausible. It was the Court's regnant theory of general common law, however, that underwrote his opinion. It justified his audacious use of the Tenth Amendment and anchored his conclusions in established doctrine.

Neither his arguments nor his conclusions, however, were necessary. Just as he could have easily relied on state common law in *Western Union,* he could readily have found congressional power in the Commerce Clause or the Necessary and Proper Clause.[147] Moreover, his distinction between powers reserved to the states and those reserved to the people, though clever, was at bottom merely a result-oriented stratagem. He cited no authority to support it. His analysis of the judicial power was logical only because it begged the question of the scope of that power: it assumed that a grant of jurisdiction carried with it power to make substantive rules unfettered by parallel congressional power. In any event, his arguments and conclusions were determined neither by the language of the Constitution nor by the nature of interstate disputes. In *Kansas v. Colorado* Brewer produced the ultimate statement of his political and judicial philosophy.

The full import of his judicial coup d'etat in *Kansas v. Colorado* stands out with particular clarity when his opinion is compared to his more famous decision a dozen years earlier in the Court's first great labor injunction case, *In re Debs.*[148] In May 1894 the employees of the Pullman Company, a manufacturer of railroad cars, went on strike, and the American Railway Union, led by Eugene V. Debs, agreed to support them. The strike spread south and west from Chicago, shutting down much of the nation's rail traffic and heightening the already acute social tensions that the fierce depression of the 1890s had generated. The national government sent troops to protect the mails, and federal courts enjoined the strike as an obstruction of interstate commerce. When protests and sporadic violence erupted, Debs and several other union leaders were jailed for contempt, and the strike soon collapsed. Affirming Debs's conviction, Brewer wrote for a unanimous Court in holding that it was proper for the national government to guarantee the free movement of interstate commerce and "to appeal to the civil courts" for injunctive relief.[149]

A variety of factors defeated the strike, but the injunctions appeared decisive to many, including both Debs and the United States attorney who prosecuted him.[150] Brewer, a firm believer in the labor injunction, agreed wholeheartedly.[151] Two years before *Debs,* defending the ability of the courts to resolve social problems, he had argued that judges were fully capable of settling such economic and social conflicts. Indeed, he had done so himself a decade earlier as a federal circuit judge.[152] "[W]hile as for speed," he had asked dramatically, "is there anything quicker than a writ of injunction?"[153] As a result of the Court's approval and the injunction's effectiveness, *Debs* quickly became a landmark case and helped spur a widespread use of the injunction against labor in the early twentieth century.[154]

Again making the most of his opportunity, Brewer used *Debs* for purposes far broader than merely stopping the Pullman strike. Refusing to rely on the Sherman Act, which the lower courts had invoked to support their decrees, Brewer declared boldly that "we prefer to rest our judgment on the broader ground."[155] To furnish that "broader ground," he pulled together a varied set of precedents, analogies, and assertions that accomplished the same result he wrought in *Kansas v. Colorado,* the expansion of federal judicial power.[156]

Brewer framed the case in terms of two questions: whether the "general government" had authority to prevent interference with interstate commerce; and whether, if it did, a federal equity court could issue an injunction to aid its efforts. He answered the first by invoking the power of Congress under Article I to regulate interstate commerce and to establish a postal system.[157] Next, he called on the dormant Commerce Clause for the principle that states could not "legislate in such a manner as to obstruct interstate commerce." Then, he drew an inference. "If a state, with its recognized powers of sovereignty, is impotent to obstruct interstate commerce, can it be that any mere voluntary association of individuals within the limits of that state has a power which the state itself does not possess?" Acknowledging that Congress could pass legislation dealing with such obstructions, he asked incredulously: "But is [legislation] the only remedy?"[158] He reached his answer — not surprisingly, a negative one — by offering a non sequitur and then begging the question.

Brewer's non sequitur was his leap to the clause in Article III that provides for a jury trial of federal crimes in the state where the crime was committed. That provision, Brewer explained, meant that "a great body" of people in a state — by using local juries to protect obstructionist neighbors — could combine to subject "the whole interests of the nation" to the "absolute mercy of a portion" of the state's inhabitants. "But," Brewer added quickly, "there is no such impotency in the national government."[159] His argument, then, was that a constitutional right to a local jury trial existed and that the right could hypothetically serve to prevent the local enforcement of federal laws.[160] Thus, he used an entirely hypothetical speculation together with a constitutional right unrelated to the powers of the national government — indeed, a constitutional right intended to limit the powers of that national government — to justify a powerful intervention by the "general government" into local affairs.

The question-begging immediately followed. Because the national government could not be defeated by "such impotency," the "entire strength of the nation," including its army and militia, was necessarily "at the service of the nation, to compel obedience to its laws."[161] That conclusion, however, assumed away the very question Brewer purported to answer: *whether* the national government was legally authorized to intervene. Brewer answered the question, in effect, by saying that the government had a right to intervene because it had an inherent right to enforce its laws. At no point, however, did he either identify any federal law that authorized such action or specify any federal law that the strikers had violated.

Although Congress could surely have legislated on the subject, as Brewer noted,[162] neither the Commerce Clause nor the Postal Clause imposed any duty directly on the strikers. To the contrary, the Court's jurisprudence dealing with commerce, contract, and competition emphasized the freedom of individual actors except where limited by common law or reasonable statutes. Brewer's citation to the numerous congressional statutes regulating interstate commerce and the mails made painfully clear that not a single one of them authorized the injunctions at issue.[163] Brewer subsequently admitted as much. "We held in *In re Debs*," he declared in 1903, "that the United States had a right, even in the absence of a statute specially authorizing such action, to come into the Federal courts by an original bill to restrain parties from obstructing and interfering with interstate commerce."[164]

Having answered his first question by asserting that "the nation" could act against the strikers, Brewer turned to his second question, whether the general government had any "alternative" to the use of force. Here, he invoked the common law of public nuisance, in particular the doctrine that obstruction of a highway was "subject to abatement at the instance of the government."[165] The jurisdiction of the courts, Brewer asserted, "exists in all cases of nuisance."[166] The federal government had a right to seek injunctions against the strikers because it had a property interest in the mails and because it had a duty to protect the general welfare in areas committed to its authority. Equitable relief was appropriate, furthermore, because the nation's "vast interests" in interstate commerce were threatened with "irreparable damage" and "great public injury."[167]

Brewer's approach in *Debs* was noteworthy for several reasons. First, it reflected the same amorphous idea of general law that underlay the *Swift* doctrine. The Court could beg the question of what law authorized the federal courts to act because the justices conceived of law not as specific and positively authorized rules but as an amorphous collection of judge-made rights, duties, and principles that courts properly enforced. Second, it revealed the extent to which an instrumentalist orientation suffused the Court's non-positivistic approach to judicial lawmaking. "If ever there was a special exigency, one which demanded that the courts should do all that courts can do," Brewer declared bluntly, "it was disclosed by this bill."[168] *Debs'* underlying rationale was quite clearly one of expedience, and the justices unanimously embraced both Brewer's obvious purpose and his promised results. Third, Brewer's approach manifested his determination to expand the power of the federal courts and make them as independent of Congress as possible. To that end, he refused to rely on the Sherman Act, upheld the lower court's equitable jurisdiction on common law nuisance grounds, and created — as the Court would subsequently do in *Ex parte Young* — a cause of action and the remedial power of the federal courts directly from the Constitution itself. He made Congress irrelevant. Finally, in the service of federal judicial power and injunctive remedies against labor, Brewer accepted precisely the kind of claim about "inherent" governmental power that he scorned so harshly when the attorney general raised it in *Kansas v. Colorado*. In the latter case, of course, the claim was raised on behalf of "the legislative and executive side" of the national government, not on behalf of the judiciary.

The nature of Brewer's constitutional enterprise was manifest. In *Debs*, two relevant constitutional provisions granted powers to Congress. Brewer defined them as grants to "the nation" and reasoned that the federal courts necessarily shared in those grants and were thereby authorized to make law within their scope. The fact that Congress had not passed any relevant statute was of no significance, for the federal courts could make law in advance of national legislative action. In contrast, in *Kansas v. Colorado* a constitutional amendment "reserved" nondelegated powers to the states. Brewer defined the amendment as limiting only Congress and not the judiciary. Further, he proclaimed that the amendment not only exempted the federal courts from its restriction but also, in fact, conferred on them profound and far-reaching powers, the very "reserved powers" of the people themselves — indeed, "all powers of a national character which are not delegated to the National Government." [169] Finding a deep well of federal judicial power in the Tenth Amendment was a supreme act of creation — as boldly inventive as finding it, as he had in *Debs*, in the constitutional limitation on federal judicial power that guaranteed a trial by local jury.

Brewer, the impassioned advocate of judicial power, outdid himself. In *Debs*, Congress had power, even if it were merely presumed and admittedly unexercised. The federal courts, therefore, had equal power and could exercise it forcefully irrespective of congressional inaction. In *Kansas v. Colorado*, Congress had no power. The Supreme Court, therefore, had it all.

A son of missionaries forged in the fires of mid-nineteenth-century New England congregationalism, Brewer equated God's justice with the law, the law with the courts, and the federal courts with the salvation of the nation. He saw one solution to the threats, dangers, and disruptions that menaced his country. He was determined, as he repeatedly exhorted his audiences, to "strengthen the judiciary" and "untie the hands of the judges." For those purposes, he found the general common law an ideal tool.

Progressive Judicial Reform
After World War I

3

DIVERSITY JURISDICTION AND

THE LABOR INJUNCTION

Progressives bristled at Brewer's exhortations. They were convinced that he and too many other federal judges imposed their values on the law in the service of wealth and property. Brewer, Theodore Roosevelt remarked derisively, simply "translate[d] his private surmises into public decisions."[1] Consequently, Progressives sought repeatedly to restrict the national judiciary and limit the powers of its judges.

One of their targets was the jurisdiction that the federal courts exercised over suits between citizens of different states, the core area where *Swift* and the general common law reigned. Diversity jurisdiction symbolized for both Progressives and their adversaries the de facto alliance between corporations and the national judiciary. In two important but quite different types of social conflicts the jurisdiction gave national corporations substantial advantages that Progressives believed were both unfair in operation and biased in intent. When individual plaintiffs filed claims against corporations, the jurisdiction gave the defendants a variety of litigation advantages that helped them discourage and defeat their weaker adversaries. When workers attempted to strike or unionize, the jurisdiction gave employers powerful legal weapons to counter their efforts. Corporations continuously exploited their advantages in both situations, and their practices quickly pulled the abstruse subject of diversity jurisdiction into the overarching politico-constitutional conflict that dominated American politics.

Individual Plaintiffs and the Corporate Use of Diversity

Congress conferred diversity jurisdiction on the federal courts in the Judiciary Act of 1789, apparently seeking to protect nonresidents from various forms of "local prejudice" by providing them with a neutral alternative to the state courts. The jurisdiction was "concurrent" with that of the state courts; that is, it did not displace state jurisdiction but simply offered parties an additional forum option. Thus, plaintiffs suing citizens of other states could bring their suits in either a federal or a state court. In addition, to protect nonresident parties when they were defendants in state court actions, the statute conferred a similar choice of forums on them. It allowed nonresident defendants to trump plaintiffs' forum choices by "removing" actions brought in state courts into the corresponding federal courts.

Following the Civil War, as the nation expanded and corporations began to operate across the country, legal and social changes gave diversity jurisdiction a new and growing significance. First, for purposes of diversity jurisdiction the law came to consider corporations as citizens of the states where they were chartered. Because most corporations held charters from only one state, they were considered "nonresident citizens"—and "foreign" corporations—in all other states. Thus, by the late nineteenth century it was settled that, as plaintiffs, corporations could invoke federal diversity jurisdiction and, as defendants, they could use it to remove suits brought against them in every state but their state of incorporation. Second, sweeping social changes—industrialism, westward expansion, and the growth of a national market—generated massive numbers of disputes between aggrieved individuals and nonresident corporations operating in the growing national market. Third, the forum preferences of individual plaintiffs and corporate defendants were usually adverse. For a variety of practical reasons—including fewer locations, longer delays, higher litigation costs, and more burdensome procedures—the federal courts were generally more expensive, inconvenient, and time-consuming than were the state courts. Accordingly, individual plaintiffs chose to file the overwhelming majority of their claims in the state courts. Conversely, corporate defendants usually removed those suits whenever they could.[2]

Corporations defended their preference for the federal courts on two grounds. First, they argued that the federal courts offered them protection from "local prejudice." They claimed that state courts, especially in the South and West, were unpredictable and sometimes biased, and removal allowed them access to "fairer" forums. The federal courts, unlike many state courts, required unanimous jury verdicts, and they drew their juries from larger geographical areas, thereby diffusing the danger of local prejudice. Federal judges exerted more control over their juries and, unlike most state judges, held life tenure, which insulated them from political pressures. Second, corporations heralded the uniformity of the federal common law that the *Swift* doctrine made possible. State laws varied widely and made it difficult for them to plan efficiently, they maintained, while the existence of a uniform federal common law simplified their operations and thereby facilitated interstate commerce.

Beyond the convenience of uniform law and protection against local prejudice, corporations found advantages in the national courts that their representatives minimized, ignored, or denied. One was informal but highly effective: The ability to remove suits allowed corporations to exert significant out-of-court leverage against their weaker individual adversaries. Because federal suits were more inconvenient and expensive, and because those burdens weighed much more heavily on parties with few resources, removal often placed heavy and disproportionate pressures on relatively poor individual plaintiffs. Consequently, corporations were often able to use removal to exploit those practical burdens and thereby induce individual plaintiffs to abandon their claims or settle them for minimal amounts.[3]

The other advantage corporations enjoyed, a formal and "legal" one, was the fact that *Swift* allowed the federal courts to ignore state decisions and apply their own general common law. The advantage, however, was hardly limited to legal uniformity. Rather, the existence of an independent federal common law conferred two more specific, and quite practical, benefits on corporate defendants. First, by continually expanding the scope of the general law and creating areas of uncertainty as to which common law rule would apply, the *Swift* doctrine made litigation less predictable and therefore riskier and more expensive.[4] In litigations between unequal parties, such increased costs and risks exerted far greater pressure on the weaker. When the stronger party was a national corporation, those pressures became further inducements for individual plaintiffs with few resources to abandon or discount their claims. Second, and of broader and more obvious significance, the substantive rules of the federal common law tended to favor national corporations. In two common types of cases—for example, tort suits brought by injured employees and insurance actions brought by individual claimants—the federal common law grew distinctly more favorable toward business in the late nineteenth century and was far more favorable than the common law of many states.[5] Brewer's 1893 decision in *Baugh,* which expanded the fellow-servant defense, was a landmark in that process.

The expansion and pro-corporate consequences of *Swift* and diversity jurisdiction increasingly spurred opposition. By the late nineteenth century both were coming under sharp attack from three distinct but partially overlapping sources. The first was social and political. Populists, Progressives, labor representatives, and plaintiffs' lawyers protested both the pro-business and anti-worker bias of the general common law as well as the unfair practical burdens that federal litigation imposed on parties with few resources. The *Swift* doctrine, complained one writer, created "the anomaly of a plaintiff fully entitled to recover in a State Court" who could be "divested of his rights" by the mere tactic of removal to federal court.[6] Corporations consistently "sought shelter in the federal courts," William Jennings Bryan charged in 1907. They did so to move suits "so far away from the plaintiffs as to make litigation expensive" and to bring their cases before judges who typically owed their appointments to "the recommendation of corporate representatives."[7]

The federal general common law resonated broadly as a political issue because it implicated one of the fundamental divisions that separated Populists and Progressives from their conservative opponents. The former placed their reform hopes in legislative action and eyed the judiciary with suspicion. The latter feared the dangers of legislative radicalism and revered the judiciary as the foundation of stability and liberty. Populists and Progressives saw *Swift* as a license for judicial subjectivism and biased decision making; conservatives saw it as a guarantor of security and the reign of common law principles.

The second source of hostility to *Swift* grew from the states' rights tradition that rejected both diversity jurisdiction and the federal common law as intrusions on state sovereignty. States' rights critics maintained that the state courts alone had authority to determine state common law, and they deplored the fact that the outcome of a case could depend on which party could maneuver into the more favorable forum. They emphasized that inconsistent laws operating within the same state caused confusion and impaired economic development.[8] Many of the states'-rights advocates, however, were political and social conservatives who had little sympathy for Progressivism and harbored a deep distrust of legislation. Private law issues, they agreed, "can be better developed by the courts of [the] State than by its legislature."[9] Unlike Progressive critics who denounced the federal common law as an illicit tool of judicial aggrandizement, defenders of states' rights protested it as an illegitimate doctrine of national power.

The third source of criticism was intellectual. While *Swift* seemed to assume that the common law involved preexisting principles, the nineteenth century witnessed the emergence of powerful ideas that challenged that premise. The positivist jurisprudence that stemmed from the work of Jeremy Bentham and John Austin defined law as the "command of a sovereign," thus locating the origin and authority of law in a specific and identifiable source. Darwinian science suggested that legal rules and institutions responded to social changes, an emphasis that undermined faith in unchanging principles and directed analysis away from formal rules and toward their de facto social context. By the beginning of the twentieth century the jurisprudential assumptions underlying the declaratory theory of law and attributed to *Swift* were subject to intense theoretical criticism.[10]

The most telling attack came from the emerging figure of Oliver Wendell Holmes, Jr., who would become the preeminent legal historian and theorist of the age. Sitting on the Massachusetts Supreme Judicial Court from 1882 until he was appointed to the United States Supreme Court in 1902, Holmes rejected ideas of preexisting law and emphasized the social origins and functions of legal rules. Law was positive and practical, drawing its authority from a sovereign power and operating to satisfy the society's dominant needs. It was, he wrote in 1897, "the prediction of the incidence of the public force through the instrumentality of the courts."[11] When judges decided cases, Holmes argued, they drew on constitutions, statutes, and precedents, but those formal sources frequently failed to provide specific conclusions. "The felt necessities of the time, the prevalent moral and political theories, intuitions of public policy, avowed or unconscious, even the prejudices which judges share with their fellow men," he announced, "have a good deal more to do than the syllogism in determining the rules by which men should be governed."[12]

Holmes was hostile to *Swift* — "a very fishy principle started by Story" — because it violated the constitutional authority of the states and, more important for him, rested on what he saw as a false and outmoded jurisprudence.[13] In his view *Swift* gave voice to the theory of preexistent law, implied that judges reached their decisions through a deductive process, rejected the idea that judicial decisions "made law," and denied that law was based on the authority of a sovereign. The idea of an "independent judgment" on common law questions was theoretically absurd, he declared, and, even if "preexisting principles" did exist, they would have no claim to authority within a sovereign state that rejected them.[14]

In 1910 Holmes had his first chance to confront *Swift* from the supreme federal bench. In *Kuhn v. Fairmont Coal Co.*, the Court extended the doctrine to allow the federal courts an independent judgment on the construction of a contract for the sale of subsurface mineral rights, an issue of real property law that seemed clearly "local."[15] Writing for three dissenters, Holmes maintained that *Swift*'s "fiction" about preexistent law "had to be abandoned." The only relevant law was the law of the states, and state judges, equally with state legislatures, had the authority to make that law. "The law of a State does not become something outside of the state court and independent of it by being called the common law," he declared. "Whatever it is called it is the law as declared by the state judges and nothing else." *Swift*, Holmes suggested, was disruptive and "arbitrary" in creating exceptions to otherwise established state laws.[16]

The new jurisprudence to which Holmes gave voice quickly took on political coloring. Its challenge to ideas of preexisting law suggested that the application of legal rules involved not deduction but discretion and, by extension, that the personal values of judges influenced their decisions. That inference supported Populist and Progressive claims that the "pro-corporate" decisions of the federal courts were not logical dictates of "the law" but the results of social bias. Indeed, Holmes himself seemed to say as much in 1905 in his resounding dissent from the Court's archetypal anti-Progressive decision, *Lochner v. New York*. "This case is decided," he charged, "upon an economic theory which a large part of the country does not entertain." [17]

Given his positivism, his attack on *Swift*, and his rejection of substantive due process, Holmes had little sympathy with Brewer's activist and religiously inspired jurisprudence. As *Lochner* illustrated, many of their most basic views were sharply at odds. Brewer was "a man of great power," Holmes wrote privately, but he "made me shudder many times." [18]

As the Holmesian critique merged with Progressive and states' rights attacks, defenders of the federal common law increasingly stressed *Swift*'s status as an established precedent and its practical role in unifying the national economy. Largely dismissing the importance of the philosophical critique, they defended the federal common law on the pragmatic grounds of interstate business stability and the sanctity of contract. [19] "General relaxation of the obligation of *stare decisis* would foster commercial anarchy," one defender argued, especially since disregard of *stare decisis* was "on the increase in most of the state courts." [20] Another writer insisted that the common law was based on the foundation of *stare decisis* and could easily dispense with theories of preexistent law. "The fundamental problem in each jurisdiction," he explained, "is the systematic, consistent, and, so far as possible, certain development of the law by means of the cases decided by the courts." [21]

Regardless of the attacks, business and the organized bar, especially its elite corporate wing, remained firmly committed to both diversity jurisdiction and the federal common law. In the early twentieth century the leadership of the bar, moving away from the states' rights traditionalism that characterized many of the elite's elder statesmen, increasingly became ardent judicial nationalists ready to accept doctrines or proposals that increased the prestige of the federal judiciary and its power to protect corporate enterprise. The social and political commitments of the elite bar were clear. [22] In 1920, for example, the ABA considered possible amendments to the removal statute. Its Committee on Jurisprudence and Law Reform enthusiastically recommended one reform to clarify and strengthen the rights of removing defendants. It readily quashed a second proposal designed to bar corporations from removing in those states where they regularly conducted business. [23]

The Labor Injunction and the Hitchman Structure

Brewer's opinion in *Debs* had encouraged employers to resort to the labor injunction with increasing frequency, and the judiciary responded with ever more sweeping prohibitions on the activities of organizers and strikers.[24] In 1908 the Supreme Court held that labor activities fell within the prohibitions of the Sherman Anti-Trust Act, and three years later it held that circulation by a union of an "Unfair" list that urged people not to patronize certain employers could be illegal and therefore enjoinable.[25] Between 1880 and 1920 courts issued almost a thousand injunctions against labor, and the federal courts proved especially attractive to employers.[26]

The labor injunction quickly became a major political issue. In 1896 the Democrats denounced it in their platform, and Populists and Progressives urged Congress and state legislatures to limit its use. Although state courts were often as hostile toward unions as the federal courts, critics frequently focused on the more prominent and powerful national judiciary. "The federal courts have long needed" to be curtailed, Samuel Gompers declared. "They have been encroaching, meddling, adding to their powers, acting in arrogant, high-handed ways and assuming to be the whole government."[27] A writer in the *Nation* recorded the obvious. "We cannot ignore the fact," he explained, "that a large number of our citizens think that the Federal judges are inclined to sympathize with employers when they quarrel with laborers."[28]

Organized labor hated the injunction, and Progressives increasingly joined the effort to restrict its use. Several states adopted anti-injunction statutes, and Congress considered such measures for two decades beginning in the 1890s.[29] Three times between 1897 and 1912 anti-injunction bills passed one house of Congress but failed in the other, and President Theodore Roosevelt urged action in five separate messages to Congress. In 1908 and 1912 the AFL supported the Democratic presidential nominees, primarily because they endorsed anti-injunction legislation.[30] Following his election in 1912, President Wilson refused to support labor's demand for complete exemption from the anti-trust laws. He did agree, however, to accept legislation limiting the injunction and providing jury trials in contempt proceedings.[31]

In 1914 Congress passed the Clayton Act, which included two sections that seemed to restrict the labor injunction. One provided that the Sherman Act should not be interpreted to prevent labor unions from "lawfully carrying out" their "legitimate objects," and the other limited the use of injunctions in labor disputes.[32] In 1921, however, in *Duplex Printing Press Co. v. Deering*, the Supreme Court construed the vague provisions to be essentially meaningless.[33] With Holmes, Brandeis, and Clarke dissenting, the Court authorized an injunction that prevented unionists from interfering with plaintiff's business in any way, including "even persuasion" directed toward third parties.[34] Most Progressives saw the Court's treatment of the statute as the result of the majority's personal opposition to organized labor, and they denounced both the decision and the majority's partisanship. Learned Hand voiced the common refrain. Declaring himself "absolutely convinced that the case was wrongly decided," he confessed privately that "the worst part of it is that I fear it is decided from bias." [35]

Later in the same term, the Court dealt even more harshly with a state anti-injunction statute. *Truax v. Corrigan* invalidated an Arizona law that denied an injunction to a restaurant owner confronted with a strike and boycott by his employees.[36] Emphasizing that the continued operation of the restaurant was "a property right," the Court held that the strikers had harmed the business, created an unlawful conspiracy, and engaged in "moral coercion by illegal annoyance and obstruction." The statute was unconstitutional, *Truax* declared, because it violated the owner's "fundamental rights." Holmes, Brandeis, and Clarke again dissented, this time joined by Justice Mahlon Pitney.

While the Court was preserving the labor injunction, employers were developing a complementary tool to expand the injunction's utility. In the late nineteenth century some businesses began to require their workers to sign contracts promising that they would either refrain from joining a labor union or quit their jobs if they did. Such agreements gave employers numerous advantages. They helped eliminate union sympathizers, who often refused to sign such agreements, from the employer's work force. They allowed employers to threaten workers who did sign with breach of contract actions and loss of employment if they joined unions. They allowed employers to threaten labor organizers with tort actions for inducing breach of contract if the organizers attempted to unionize their workers. Finally, by creating a "legally protectable interest," the agreements served as a basis on which employers could request injunctive relief against strikes and organizing campaigns. Such contracts, labor complained bitterly, treated workers like "yellow dogs."

Unlike injunction suits under the anti-trust laws which could be heard in the national courts under federal question jurisdiction, actions based on "yellow dog" contracts presented common law issues that could enter the federal courts only under diversity jurisdiction. As the yellow dog contract came into wider use, then, diversity began to play a more prominent role in labor cases. By the end of the 1920s critics of the labor injunction estimated that two-thirds of federal injunction cases came to the national courts on the basis of diversity.[37]

The economic coercion behind the yellow dog contract and its effectiveness in discouraging unionization angered organized labor as well as Progressives and many moderates. In 1898 Congress responded with the Erdman Act,[38] which made use of the agreement a misdemeanor, and by 1914 the legislatures of fourteen states had adopted similar statutes.[39] The Supreme Court, however, invalidated the legislation. In 1908 it ruled in *Adair v. United States* that the yellow dog provision of the Erdman Act violated the Due Process Clause. It was not an authentic regulation of interstate commerce but rather "an arbitrary interference with the Liberty of contract which no government can legally justify in a free land."[40] Seven years later in *Coppage v. Kansas* the Court held a similar state statute unconstitutional on the same grounds. In signing the agreement, the majority stated, the employee was acting voluntarily as "a free agent."[41]

With *Adair* and *Coppage* the Court created constitutional barriers to both federal and state legislation outlawing the yellow dog contract. Their significance for injunction suits resting on diversity jurisdiction became apparent two years after *Coppage* when the Court decided *Hitchman Coal & Coke Co. v. Mitchell*.[42] With both Congress and state legislatures apparently barred by the Constitution from making yellow dog contracts unlawful, the Court had a free hand to create and enforce its own controlling law. The substantive due process doctrines of *Adair* and *Coppage* created the statutory void that was a prerequisite for the unhampered operation of the general jurisprudence of the federal courts. *Hitchman* showed how diversity, substantive due process, the federal labor injunction, and the lawmaking independence of the national judiciary leveraged the power of employers to defeat the labor movement.

In 1903 the United Mine Workers succeeded in unionizing the Hitchman Coal & Coke Company, a West Virginia corporation operating in that state. Three years later the miners went on strike, and the company decided to bring in new workers and required them to sign yellow dog contracts. In late 1907 the UMW tried to unionize the replacement miners, and many of them agreed to join the union if and when it received the support of a majority of workers. The company sought to enjoin the organizing effort, and a federal judge granted a temporary and then a "perpetual" injunction.[43] For nine years the union fought the order through a series of hearings and appeals, all the while barred from further efforts to unionize the Hitchman workers. The injunction and other obstacles would have defeated or broken most other unions, but the UMW persisted. It was one of the few strong national unions in the country, and the Northern companies it had unionized were insisting that it either organize the competitive Southern coal fields or risk losing its recognition in the North. In 1917 the case reached the United States Supreme Court.

The issues were squarely presented, and diversity was the sole basis of federal jurisdiction. The company, a "citizen" of West Virginia, had named as defendants a group of union officials who were nonresidents, and it advanced only state law claims, one for common law conspiracy and one for tortious interference with contract. Relying on *Adair* and *Coppage*, the Court reaffirmed the constitutional right to liberty of contract and the employer's right to require yellow dog contracts.[44] "In the present case, needless to say," a six-justice majority declared, "there is no act of legislation to which defendants may resort for justification." [45] Free from legislative constraint, the Court held the yellow dog contracts lawful and recognized them as creating legally protectable property interests in the "good will" of the company's employees. The "pecuniary value" of the employee contracts was "reasonably great," and it lay in the "reasonable probability" that the employer would enjoy a stable work force. "The right of action for persuading an employee to leave his employer is universally recognized — no where more clearly than in West Virginia, — and it rests upon fundamental principles of general application." [46] Because the company would sustain irreparable injury if the union succeeded, an injunction was proper. Making minor modifications, the justices affirmed the lower court's decree. Holmes, Brandeis, and Clarke dissented.

Hitchman expanded the power of the federal labor injunction substantially. First, it broadened the concept of legally protectable property to include the "good will" of employees bound by yellow dog contracts, and it allowed the mere fact that the employees had signed such contracts to serve as legal proof of that "good will." [47] Second, it made the special requirement for equitable jurisdiction, lack of an "adequate remedy at law," a condition that would be fulfilled almost automatically in labor cases. "That the damage resulting from a strike would be irremediable at law," the majority stated, "is too plain for discussion." [48]

Hitchman also revealed the Court's anti-union bias. The UMW organizer had not induced any workers to join the union while remaining at work, an action that would have constituted a violation of Hitchman's yellow dog contracts. Instead, he had urged them to agree to join if and when a majority of workers were ready to take action. "But, in a court of equity, which looks to the substance and essence of things and disregards matters of form and technical nicety," the Court declared, "it is sufficient to say that to induce men to *agree* to join is but a mode of inducing them to join." It concluded that, "for practical purposes," the organizer had induced the workers to become union members.[49] As far as it went, such an analysis was both reasonable and consistent with the practical orientation of traditional equity. The problem was, however, that the Court paid heed to such "practical purposes" only to defeat the union's defense. When it considered comparable arguments that would defeat the company's position, its approach shifted radically. Under an equally "practical" analysis, numerous traditional equitable maxims — duress, overreaching, unclean hands, lack of mutuality — were available to deny enforcement to the employment contracts. The Court, however, dismissed those doctrines and ignored the company's "practical purposes." When upholding the yellow dog contracts it rested, instead, squarely on "matters of form and technical nicety": The company's contracts were valid because the workers had given their "free assent" [50] and signed them "voluntarily." [51]

The Court's disparate treatment of the parties was even clearer when it addressed the agreements that the union organizer had made with the workers. To support its conclusion that he had used "deception and abuse" in obtaining the agreements, the Court seized on a previously unmentioned fact. The organizer had induced the workers by telling them that Hitchman would reduce their wages if the mine were not unionized. He had "prophesied," the Court declared, "in such a way that *ignorant, foreign-born miners, such as he was addressing,* naturally might believe him to be speaking with knowledge." [52] When discrediting the organizer's contracts, in other words, the Court saw the "ignorant, foreign-born" nature of the work force as a significant factor impairing their ability to give free and knowing "assent." When addressing the "assent" given to the company's contracts, however, it failed to see those characteristics as relevant. [53]

Hitchman confirmed and authorized a powerful anti-union instrument by linking three separate legal doctrines—diversity jurisdiction, substantive due process, and the "independence" of federal equity. In doing so, it crystallized a structure of law for labor disputes that could stop union organizers cold, and it made the federal courts the dominant source of the controlling substantive law.

The first element of the *Hitchman* structure was diversity itself. The widely perceived anti-union bias of the federal courts made them attractive forums for employers, and diversity allowed them easy access. The companies could choose among the possible defendants—local workers or out-of-state organizers, resident union members or nonresident national officials—and align parties to ensure the existence of diversity. Hitchman, for example, was a local corporation, so it elected to sue nonresident union officials. The tactic worked equally and more commonly for foreign corporations which, of course, sued only resident workers, organizers, or union members. [54]

The second element of the *Hitchman* structure was the leverage provided by substantive due process. Relying on *Adair* and *Coppage,* the Court in *Hitchman* noted specifically that legislatures could not make yellow dog contracts unenforceable. "This court repeatedly has held that the employer is as free to make non-membership in a union a condition of employment, as the working man is free to join the union," it declared, "and that this is a part of the constitutional rights of personal liberty and private property." [55] The opinion proceeded immediately to add a broadly worded dictum. "In the present case, needless to say, there is no act of legislation to which defendants may resort for justification." [56] The latter statement seemed to mean that no such statute would have been constitutional: it immediately followed a citation to *Adair* and *Coppage,* and it used the permissive "may" instead of the factual "can." The Court was fully aware that *Adair* and *Coppage* freed it to create its own substantive law covering labor contracts.

The third element of the *Hitchman* structure was the explicit holding that yellow dog contracts were enforceable and that federal equity would protect them. The Court made it clear that it was relying not on local law but on "fundamental principles of general application."[57] It cited cases from a variety of jurisdictions—federal, state, and British. "In our opinion, any violation of plaintiff's legal rights contrived by defendants for the purpose of inflicting damage, or having that as its necessary effect, is plainly inhibited by the law as if it involved a breach of the peace," the majority declared. "A combination to procure concerted breaches of contract by plaintiff's employees constitutes such a violation." For that central proposition the Court cited a Pennsylvania case, a New Jersey case, and a British case.[58] Even though it claimed that West Virginia decisional law favored the company, the Court carefully refrained from relying on local authority. Instead, it indicated specifically that issues relating to yellow dog contracts were matters of general federal law, thus explicitly nationalizing its decision and making its anti-union law available in federal courts across the country.

Although the Court asserted that the principles it relied on were "universal," its contention was demonstrably incorrect. The common law action for tortious interference with contract developed in the United States only in the 1890s, and in many states there were few decisions defining the action and widespread variation as to its elements and defenses. Moreover, by 1930 the common law of seven states had explicitly refused to recognize the action.[59] The "independent" law of *Hitchman* thus gave a tort action under yellow dog contracts to employers in at least seven states where the action was otherwise unavailable, and it provided in many others a broader and more certain remedy than existed under local law.[60]

Analogous to the "independent judgment" of state law that the federal courts rendered under *Swift*, the rule laid down in *Hitchman* rested on a different doctrinal basis. *Swift* construed the Rules of Decision Act, which applied only to "trials at common law." In equity, then, *Swift* and the statute were technically irrelevant. Federal equity, rooted in the constitutional grant of the "judicial power" in Article III, was considered a "special system" of federal jurisprudence "independent" of state systems. In matters of procedure and allowable remedies, it was wholly independent of state law. The generally accepted theory was that the federal courts followed independent substantive principles of equity but that they would usually enforce specific rights that had been created by state statutes.[61] In practice, the relationship between federal equity and state law was similar to that which existed at common law under *Swift:* Federal judges would enforce state statutory rights but frequently, perhaps usually, ignore state judicial decisions. In 1923 the Supreme Court explicitly suggested that the relationship between federal equity and state law was the same as that which obtained for actions at law under *Swift*. The Rules of Decision Act, it stated, was "merely declarative of the rule which would exist in the absence of the statute." [62] Thus, although the formal basis of *Hitchman*'s doctrine was different from *Swift*'s, they shared similar theories of federal judicial independence and the same idea of general federal law. The similarity of their pro-corporate results, moreover, was apparent.

Although the *Swift* doctrine was confined to common law actions, it was relevant to federal equity in two ways. First, by establishing the "independent judgment" of the federal courts on common law issues, it strengthened the view that federal equity was properly a system independent of the state courts. *Swift* was the legal analogue of the "independent system" of federal equity, and the two doctrines supported one another by fostering the idea that divergence between the substantive laws applied in state and federal courts was normal rather than anomalous. Second, by enabling the federal courts to develop their own common law rules, *Swift* created rights cognizable in the national courts that could provide substantive predicates to justify the intervention of federal equity. The general jurisprudence of the national courts created substantive rights that differed from those existing under state decisional law, and it thereby widened the differences between the rights that federal equity would protect and those that the state courts would recognize. [63]

After *Hitchman* the labor injunction swelled to flood tide. The fear of Bolshevism and the Red Scare that followed World War I made unionism widely suspect, while strikes confirmed the belief that labor was dangerously radical. [64] The power that a union asserted left "no limit upon its domination over the employer's affairs," charged one federal judge in 1920. "Such an organization as a 'shop committee' becomes, in substance, if not in name, a 'soviet.' " [65] Accelerating prosperity and Republican control of the national government deprived unions of political influence, and the Taft Court kept labor tightly in check. *Duplex* and *Truax* were both decided in 1921, and the following year a series of all-encompassing injunctions crushed the massive railway "shopmen's strike" centered in Chicago. [66] "The only class which is distinctly arrayed against the Court is a class that does not like the courts at any rate, and that is organized labor," the chief justice wrote his brother in 1922. "That faction we have to hit every little while." [67]

By leveraging diversity jurisdiction, substantive due process, and the independence of federal equity, *Hitchman* expanded the power of the national courts and provided employers with a lethal anti-union weapon. [68] Prior to 1917 yellow dog contracts had not been used extensively, but by the end of the

1920s they bound approximately 1,250,000 workers.[69] To enforce them the courts issued hundreds of injunctions.[70] In the repressive atmosphere, union membership dropped by 1,500,000, while unionized workers fell from 19.4 percent of the nonagricultural work force in 1920 to half that number a decade later.[71]

Progressive Failure: The Campaign to Abolish Diversity Jurisdiction

Since the late nineteenth century, reformers had sought to restrict the *Swift* doctrine and the reach of federal diversity jurisdiction. Although broad attacks consistently failed, on several occasions Progressives succeeded in trimming removal jurisdiction and the federal common law, most notably in the Federal Employers' Liability Act in 1908, amendments to that act in 1910, and the Jones Act in 1920.[72] Those statutes, together with other legal and social changes, had substantially reduced the inequitable social impact of diversity, especially in employee injury claims. Ironically, as the practical grounds for their hostility declined, Progressives in the late 1920s faced their most promising opportunity to strike fatally at the corporate use of diversity jurisdiction.

The conservative wing of the Republican party dominated the federal government throughout the decade, but its control of Congress weakened after 1926, especially in the Senate. The Republican majority was slim, and several of the party's most prominent members were Progressives. Indeed, in December 1926 seniority made Republican George W. Norris of Nebraska chairman of the Senate Judiciary Committee. A former state court judge and congressman who had served in the Senate since 1912, Norris was one of the most dedicated Progressives in Congress and possibly the most successful legislator in the Senate's history.[73]

Angered by the conservative bias of the judiciary and the administration's pro-business appointments, Norris sought to limit the power of the federal courts and make them more responsive to popular sentiment and less to the opinions of business.[74] "Continued association with the overrich," he chided Chief Justice Taft, "will cause men to forget those who toil and suffer." [75] In 1922 Norris cemented his reputation as a judicial radical and earned the permanent hostility of conservatives when he called for the abolition of the entire lower federal judiciary. Coming from a rural state and exhibiting a deep sympathy for the poor, Norris was sensitive to the practical leverage that diversity jurisdiction gave corporations. "I lived for a number of years in a town which was 250 miles distant from the nearest Federal court," he explained. "I knew from my experience that a man of ordinary means could not afford to hire a lawyer, pay his expenses, perhaps to be in court five minutes, have his case adjourned and then to pay the expenses of witnesses coming perhaps from places great distances away." [76]

On the other side of the aisle, Democratic Senator Thomas J. Walsh, a Progressive from Montana and the great adversary of the ABA's procedural reform bill, seconded Norris's attacks. Walsh consistently opposed efforts to strengthen the legal position of large corporations, and in the early 1920s he, too, turned his attention to diversity jurisdiction. Charging that "innumerable corporations" had obtained out-of-state charters "for no reason except to enjoy" the advantages of federal jurisdiction, Walsh tarred the practice as "a reproach to our judicial system." Congress, he insisted, should end "the scandal of the 'tramp' corporation."[77]

The Supreme Court spurred opposition to diversity in 1928 when it reaffirmed *Swift* in *Black and White Taxicab Co. v. Brown and Yellow Taxicab Co.*,[78] a case that presented a flagrant, if unusual, example of corporate jurisdictional manipulation.[79] Facing unfavorable Kentucky law in a conflict with a local competitor, a Kentucky taxicab company assigned its assets to a new corporation chartered in Tennessee. The new corporation, able to allege diversity with its Kentucky-chartered rival, then sued for an injunction in the Kentucky federal court. Holding under *Swift* that it was not bound by Kentucky common law, the federal court applied divergent federal common law and granted the new corporation an injunction against its competitor. The Supreme Court affirmed.

Holmes, joined by Brandeis and Stone, dissented. Expanding on his 1910 dissent in *Kuhn*, Holmes charged that *Swift* was based on a "subtle fallacy" about the nature of law and the role of the federal courts. The idea that the national courts could render an "independent judgment" on state law assumed that the common law was "a transcendental body of law outside of any particular State but obligatory within it unless and until changed by statute." But "there is no such body of law," Holmes insisted. "The common law so far as it is enforced in a State" was "not the common law generally but the law of that State existing by the authority of that State." When states declared their law through their courts, those decisions were "laws" which the federal courts were bound to follow equally with state statutes. "If I am right the fallacy has resulted in an unconstitutional assumption of powers by the Courts of the United States."[80]

Outraging opponents of diversity and embarrassing its supporters, the *Taxicab* case quickly became a symbol of corporate exploitation of federal jurisdiction.[81] The prestige of Holmes, Brandeis, and Stone—popularly linked as the Court's dissenting "progressive" wing—further tarnished *Swift* and encouraged political opposition and academic criticism. When the justices delivered their opinions, Walsh sat listening intently in the front row of the Court's chamber. Later the same year he introduced a bill to overrule *Swift*.[82]

While the *Taxicab* case spotlighted one abuse of diversity, intellectual changes within the legal profession were inducing legal scholars to view *Swift* and diversity with ever sharpening hostility. As part of prewar Progressivism, a number of writers had begun to develop a "sociological jurisprudence," an approach that emphasized the social functions of law. By the mid-1920s some began pushing those insights into an even more critical approach that became known as "legal realism." Downplaying the general significance of abstract rules and formal doctrines, the realists argued that the study of law should be broadened to include all the social considerations that shaped its development.[83]

On the level of theory, the new jurisprudence embraced Holmes's ideas. It rejected concepts of "preexisting" law, highlighted the positive basis of legal rules in the authority of the state, and equated the judicial function with "making"—not "finding"—law. After the *Taxicab* case, assaults on *Swift* filled the law reviews. Critics maintained that its doctrine was philosophically untenable and that it violated state sovereignty, created an incoherent distinction between "local" and "general," and led to growing confusion in the common law. Scholarly defense grew faint.[84] Assuming that the decision was too well established for the courts to reverse, writers repeatedly called upon Congress to take action.[85]

On the level of research, scholars interested in realist and sociological approaches investigated the practical operation of diversity jurisdiction, and during the 1920s and early 1930s they helped focus attention on its de facto social significance.[86] Yale University law school, an institutional center of realism, organized a massive empirical study of thirteen selected federal judicial districts that was published by the American Law Institute in 1934.[87] Charles E. Clark, the school's Progressive dean, directed the study and then highlighted its finding that corporate defendants dominated the diversity docket. They were involved in 75 percent of all diversity cases and 87 percent of all removed diversity actions. "The realities," Clark concluded, were that diversity placed "the ordinary citizen" at a disadvantage when dealing with corporations and created a "sense of unfairness." Given the way the system worked in practice, he declared, "inherent arguments of equity and fairness" required serious restrictions on corporate use of the jurisdiction.[88]

While *Swift* and diversity came under intensifying scrutiny, the most sustained academic assault came from Felix Frankfurter. A Progressive lawyer and political activist who began teaching at Harvard Law School in 1914, Frankfurter had gained prominence and notoriety by the 1920s for his involvement in a series of unpopular causes associated with the political Left. Repeatedly he attacked the social biases of the Taft Court, and in 1924 he supported La Follette's presidential campaign. In both his scholarly and popular writings he insisted that law, especially constitutional law, was a product of relatively unrestricted policy choices. "The simple fact is that in these matters the Court, under the guise of legal form, exercises political and economic control," he declared in 1930. "Let us face then the fact that five Justices of the Supreme Court are moulders of policy, rather than impersonal vehicles of revealed truth." [89] The fact that he was a Jew deepened the enmity that many conservatives felt for him and helped convince them that he was both radical and dangerous. [90]

Frankfurter tried to use his academic position to offset his political reputation, draping his legal Progressivism in neutral scientific and professional language. In *The Business of the Supreme Court*, [91] published in 1928, he proposed that the goals of jurisdictional reform were administrative efficiency and the preservation of the Supreme Court's ability to oversee the nation's legal system. He praised the legal establishment, from Chief Justice Taft to the ABA, for supporting efforts to improve federal judicial administration. Judicial efficiency and craft values demanded an end to congestion in the federal courts, he argued, and they demanded equally that the national judiciary confine itself to issues that it was professionally most competent to handle — issues of federal, not state, law. The obvious conclusion was that federal jurisdiction had to be seriously restricted and that restriction was most appropriate in those cases that involved only issues of state law. Restrictions were necessary, in other words, in diversity actions.

Behind Frankfurter's scientific language and neutral phrasing lay the familiar critique and agenda of legal Progressivism. *Swift* was "untenable in theory" as well as "mischievous in its consequences, baffling in its application." [92] The federal common law created widespread divergences between state and federal law and provided a constant "temptation" for federal judges "to make law according to their own view when untrammeled by authority." [93] Diversity jurisdiction was "consciously abused" [94] by designing parties who used it to "escape from state tribunals." [95] It created "unmitigated" hardships for individual plaintiffs who sued national corporations [96] and stamped the national courts "as the resort of powerful litigants." [97] Because corporations were parties in approximately 80 percent of recent diversity cases, Frankfurter argued, meaningful reform required a substantial reduction in corporate litigation — "the key to diversity problems." [98]

While docket problems, the *Taxicab* case, sharpening scholarly criticism, and a growing body of empirical evidence steadily fueled the attack on diversity, political and economic pressures gave the effort new immediacy. Prohibition prosecutions continued to overwhelm the federal courts, and political conflict over the Eighteenth Amendment intensified. In his inaugural address in 1929 President Herbert Hoover put federal judicial reform on the front page by recommending the creation of "a national commission" to study Prohibition enforcement in the context "of the whole structure of our Federal system of jurisprudence." [99] By the middle of 1930, moreover, the Depression dominated American politics, inflaming a growing hostility toward corporations and reviving the appeal of Progressive ideas. "As a natural result of the general depression we probably shall have some curious political times," Justice Van Devanter confided anxiously prior to the congressional election of 1930. "Both parties will have an increased number of Senators and Representatives who are inexperienced and disposed to turn to wild theories and to invoke untenable remedies." [100] Van Devanter's anxiety proved well-founded. In 1930 the Republicans lost eight seats in the Senate and fifty-three in the House.

Encouraged by the influx of Democratic and Progressive strength, Norris believed he could at last strike successfully at diversity. Soliciting information from federal district judges, he produced a useful, if spotty, report in support of a bill to abolish the jurisdiction. Frankfurter encouraged him, sending copies of his work on the federal courts together with draft bills and supporting memoranda.[101] Recognizing the powerful political support for diversity and counseling a narrow approach, Frankfurter urged a series of specific proposals designed to carve away the most offensive parts of the jurisdiction without wholly abolishing it.[102] Norris utilized Frankfurter's materials and some of his arguments, but he would not abandon his wholesale approach.[103] In 1931, he reintroduced and vigorously pushed his bill to abolish diversity.

The strong case presented, the growing anger against corporations, and the added Progressive strength in Congress made passage a possibility, but the mere fact that Norris and Frankfurter were in the forefront guaranteed passionate opposition. The elite bar reacted with instinctive hostility. Some were prepared to acknowledge in the abstract that there might be imperfections in diversity jurisdiction, but they were loath to accept any significant change. Gurney E. Newlin, who had served as president of the ABA in 1929, conceded that *Swift* sometimes created "unfair" results, but he fervently praised diversity for encouraging nationwide investment of capital.[104] Judge John J. Parker of the Fourth Circuit defended both *Swift* and diversity as sources of legal "uniformity" that strengthened the nation and encouraged business. Although he was willing to consider minor changes,[105] he feared that efforts to restrict "the power of the federal courts" were the product of "socialists and near socialists." [106]

More extreme conservatives refused to admit any flaw with the jurisdiction. Edward W. Everett, a Chicago attorney and past president of the ABA, simply denied that there was "any real objection to the present jurisdiction of the Federal Courts." Everett supported his claim that no "real objection" existed by citing evidence that demonstrated the social insularity of many legal conservatives. He had, Everett explained, "received many letters from lawyers of prominence" who were "unanimous in expressing their preference to a Federal Forum in which to try their cases." [107] The agreement of such "lawyers of prominence," he believed, was entirely sufficient to settle the matter. Similarly, Paul Howland, a Cleveland attorney who chaired the ABA's Committee on Jurisprudence and Law Reform, claimed that opposing Norris was equivalent to defending "the supremacy of law." [108]

Howland defended even the *Taxicab* case, and his argument revealed starkly the mentality of the bar's conservative elite in the early 1930s. He repeatedly stated that the reincorporating party had sought to avoid a "Kentucky statute," and he suggested ominously that the "statute" could have been "enacted by the Kentucky Legislature for the express purpose of putting the Taxi Cab Co. out of business." [109] It was, of course, a stunning suggestion, stunning because it misstated the essential fact in the case. The state "law" at issue was a common law rule, not a statute. Indeed, had the "law" at issue been a statute, *Swift* would not have been applicable. [110] The misstatement was both obvious and central to the entire controversy over *Swift*, yet Howland, his colleagues, and the editors of the *American Bar Association Journal* all somehow missed it. Their error illuminated brilliantly the conservatives' world view. In the heat of national debate, Howland justified the Supreme Court's notorious *Taxicab* decision, mistakenly or by design, as a corporation's necessary effort to avoid an intentionally evil statute. His misstatement summoned up, and perhaps unconsciously arose from, the profound terror that haunted the conservatives—the fear of radical legislative attacks on business and property. Equally, it suppressed the very possibility that the federal courts and their general law could somehow be at fault.

Both President Hoover and his attorney general, William D. Mitchell, opposed the Norris bill [111] and maintained that diversity was necessary to protect interstate business. When support for the Norris bill grew, however, Mitchell offered a narrower counterproposal that limited the ability of corporations to utilize diversity in states where they did business. [112] The administration gave the proposal no support and did little more than acknowledge formal sponsorship. By presenting an alternative to the complete abolition of diversity, Mitchell's bill complicated the legislative situation and provided an additional basis on which to oppose Norris. Hoover, who had fervently hoped for Norris's defeat in 1930, continually tried to undercut his influence. [113] "The strategy," his secretary wrote, "is to keep the fire centered on Norris and to cut him out from the rest of the herd." [114] Shortly after the attorney general had his bill introduced in the House and almost ten months before he requested Norris to introduce it in the Senate, Mitchell sent a copy to the ABA so that it "may give the proposal attention." [115] His action, of course, was a clarion to the elite bar, warning that vigorous opposition was essential to protect diversity.

National business organizations and bar associations responded forcefully, recognizing that the administration's counterproposal was a tactical diversion. "I do not think the insistence is very strong upon the part of the Attorney

General," Howland informed the House Judiciary Committee bluntly and without contradiction.[116] The American Bankers Association and the Chamber of Commerce urged their members to contact Congress, while insurance companies and railroads protested the bills' dangerous consequences.[117] The bars of numerous cities and states unanimously registered their disapproval.[118] The ABA submitted a long brief devoted almost exclusively to arguing the unconstitutionality of the bills, and its *Journal* poured out a stream of criticism.[119] Members of the ABA's executive committee even sought and secured a private meeting with Hoover to urge him to veto the Norris bill if it passed, and the president indicated that he would do so.[120]

Unfortunately for Norris, Progressives split over his bill. Although most of them favored restrictions and believed that corporations abused diversity, many also agreed that the jurisdiction was a protection against prejudice and a proper instrument of national authority. The jurisdiction, declared the realist Herman Oliphant of the Johns Hopkins Institute of Law, "is probably a very useful and desirable thing in some classes of cases."[121] Newton Baker, who had been a member of Wilson's cabinet, suggested excluding foreign corporations from diversity in those states where they were licensed to do business, while Clark supported the attorney general's bill.[122] None of the three, however, backed abolition. Progressives who opposed the Norris bill were guided by social and professional commitments to the national role and technical superiority of the federal courts, and most regretted that Norris had not opted to push narrower restrictions aimed specifically at corporate abuses of the jurisdiction.[123]

Focusing on the more pliable House, the defenders of diversity pressed for public hearings.[124] "Mysterious pressure was brought to bear" on the House Judiciary Committee after it voted favorably on the Norris bill, Congressman Fiorello LaGuardia reported, and consequently "the committee reconsidered its action to give the bar associat[ion] a hearing." The reversal, LaGuardia confessed, made him "just a little bit discouraged."[125] At the subsequent House hearing, business groups and the ABA appeared in massed ranks. For the association, Howland orchestrated the testimony of numerous banking, insurance, and manufacturing associations. Rejecting arguments made against the jurisdiction, the business groups stressed the desirability of uniform national laws and the threat of local prejudice. Several argued that diversity was a constitutional right, and one declared it "a mandate of the Constitution."[126]

The House hearings on the bill were important, not for the empirical evidence or legal analysis they produced, but for the social realities they documented. Business groups put on a massive display of their commitment to diversity. There was no doubt as to the powerful interests that opposed change. The ABA and the elite corporate bar, moreover, showed the extent to which a partisan ideology controlled their thinking.[127] Seriously misstating the law, ignoring evidence and arguments their adversaries presented, and allying with clearly defined corporate interests, they insisted that they spoke for no client but the public. "All we want, all we hope for in the world," Howland told the association's annual meeting, "is to be of assistance to our lawmakers and, without any ulterior motive, to cooperate with them in a joint effort to secure the best possible legislation for our common country."[128]

Norris attempted to meet the opposition. His committee report indicated many of the reasons behind the attack on diversity, and it pointed to support from small-town lawyers and a few legal scholars. It accused "large corporations, mainly through their attorneys" of conducting "nationwide propaganda in opposition to this legislation."[129] The real motive behind their "misleading" campaign was the fact that diversity was "of great value" to corporations and that it imposed "extreme hardship and detriment to the other party to the litigation."[130] Rejecting the argument that the bill was unconstitutional, the report maintained that congressional power to limit diversity was beyond question.[131]

Norris's effort was not enough. Although the Senate Judiciary Committee reported his bill favorably and voted down the attorney general's, the Senate leadership refused to bring the measure to the floor. The House Judiciary Committee voted both bills down. Coming as close to abolishing diversity as a Progressive ever would, Norris succeeded only in dividing his sympathizers while uniting national business and the elite bar in a fervent campaign to preserve the jurisdiction.

The Norris bill and the attorney general's bill failed for a variety of reasons. Many people, including some Progressives, believed that diversity was an important jurisdiction for the federal courts. The fact that it had existed since 1789 together with the claims of local bias made them reluctant to support abolition. The political opposition, too, was powerful, entrenched, and well organized, while support for restriction was scattered, largely voiceless, and without organization. Moreover, the Depression, while strengthening hostility to corporations and enlarging the Progressive bloc in Congress, also created countervailing pressures. It spurred the business community to throw its full weight behind diversity, and it made congressmen keenly sensitive to problems of economic stability and less willing to make arcane changes that business opposed so fiercely. In addition, the state of constitutional law in the early 1930s, together with the prestige and certitude of the elite lawyers who argued that the bill was unconstitutional, seemed to persuade a number of congressmen that restricting diversity was simply beyond their power.

Finally, much of the blame fell on Norris himself. His legal knowledge was limited; his committee report did not do justice to his case; and his reputation for hostility toward the federal courts undermined his credibility. He failed, moreover, to rally any significant and visible political support at the House hearing. Perhaps most important, his unwillingness to compromise and either present a narrower bill or throw his support behind the attorney general's proposal allowed the moment of opportunity to pass.

Progressive Triumph: Restricting the Federal Labor Injunction

Throughout the 1920s, on both state and national levels, labor and its supporters fought the injunction as their highest legislative priority.[132] Its use, *The New Republic* warned, led "only to more war." [133] In 1924 the AFL endorsed La Follette's Progressive campaign, which stood on a pro-union platform and castigated the federal courts for their anti-labor bias.[134] Four years later the federation tried to make the injunction a major issue in the presidential campaign. It received a platform pledge from the Democrats and a personal promise from their presidential candidate, Governor Alfred E. Smith of New York, to sponsor legislation to curb the injunction. The Republicans' platform confined itself to general criticism, while Hoover, the Republican candidate, mentioned the injunction unfavorably but made no promises.[135]

After the early 1920s, support for anti-injunction legislation began to grow. The Red Scare had dissipated, and cries of "Bolshevism" no longer struck a broadly responsive chord. As the number of strikes declined, the public's sense of danger eased. Many of the decade's injunctions were coercive and unjustifiable in scope, repelling a growing number of legal traditionalists and moderates. Following an injunction in a Virginia strike, for example, a local barber, neither a member of the union nor a participant in the strike, placed a large sign in the window of his privately owned business that read "No Scabs Wanted in Here." The local federal court convicted him of contempt, and in 1923 the Fourth Circuit upheld his conviction.[136] The following year Senator George Wharton Pepper, a conservative Republican from Pennsylvania, criticized the sweep of recent labor injunctions and warned against the festering hostility they engendered toward the federal courts.[137]

The Supreme Court's dissenting wing, led by Holmes and Brandeis, nourished criticism of the labor injunction, and Progressive legal scholars documented its abuses. Donald Richberg criticized the injunction in terms of the newer legal theory associated with sociological jurisprudence and legal realism. "[I]t is most important for the lay public to get an understanding of the fact that the judges make law," he insisted. Otherwise, "public opinion is not properly directed toward the responsibility of the judiciary for the persistence of old bad law and the promulgation of new bad law." [138] By the beginning of the 1930s scholars had produced a substantial body of literature that subjected the injunction to sharp, and in many cases devastating, criticism.[139]

As he pushed the campaign against diversity jurisdiction, Frankfurter helped carry the assault on the labor injunction. *Duplex* had shocked and exasperated him. "[F]or the court to say that all those [statutory] words mean nothing," he wrote privately, was "a strong dose."[140] He resented not only the political bias that the federal labor injunction revealed but also what he regarded as the professional debasement that it caused the national courts. The "serious abuses in the exercise of this power by the federal courts" harmed labor, he warned Walsh in 1926, and with their abuses "the federal courts are seriously hampering the prestige they ought to have."[141]

In 1930, with his colleague Nathan Greene, Frankfurter published *The Labor Injunction*, an examination of equity's growth and power as an anti-union weapon. Merging the attack on the injunction with Frankfurter's earlier criticism of diversity, the book emphasized that the corporate manipulation of the jurisdiction proved the "eagerness of employers to be heard by a federal court."[142] He pointed to *Swift* as a source of trouble because its doctrine allowed the national courts to make law "untrammelled by state decisions."[143] The book indicted the federal judiciary forthrightly. "The most ambitious decrees have always issued from the United States courts."[144] In private, Frankfurter was even more blunt, stating that the federal courts were "partisans in class conflicts."[145] Determined that his work should have as wide an influence as possible, he sent dozens of copies to scholars, lawyers, judges, and members of Congress.[146]

Norris, who regarded the labor injunction as another example of the political bias of the federal courts,[147] turned his attention to the issue in 1927. In April the Supreme Court, over a devastating Brandeis dissent in which Holmes joined, expanded the reach of the Commerce Clause and the anti-trust laws to uphold an injunction against a small local strike.[148] A week later, in the *Red Jacket Coal* case, the Fourth Circuit alienated the labor movement when it approved a massive injunction that protected virtually the entire coal industry of West Virginia from union pressures.[149] Three months later Senator Henrik Shipstead of Minnesota, the only Farmer-Laborite in the upper house, introduced an anti-injunction measure endorsed by the AFL, and Norris decided to take up the cause. As chairman of the Judiciary Committee, he stacked a special subcommittee to hold hearings, naming himself as chairman with Walsh and Senator John Blaine, a Wisconsin Progressive, as its only other members.

The subcommittee's hearings, held in early 1928, proved only that the anti-injunction forces were badly split. One group, led by the intense and magnetic Andrew Furuseth, the president of the Seamen's Union, hoped to abolish the injunction entirely and to do so on the basis of a restrictive definition of "property" and the authority of the Thirteenth Amendment. The Shipstead bill, introduced at Furuseth's urging and backed by the AFL, adopted that approach.[150] The second group, which included some labor leaders and almost all the union lawyers,[151] disagreed with both the scope and theory of the Shipstead bill. They argued that it was undesirable to deny certain types of intangible property, such as patents or copyrights, equitable protection, and they insisted that Congress would never pass a bill that absolutely prevented injunctions in labor disputes.[152] Moreover, given its vague and imprecise language, they maintained, the Shipstead bill would be easy for hostile courts to negate by construction.[153]

When the hearings ended inconclusively, Norris took a bold step. Distressed at the division among union leaders and unsure in his own mind as to the proper approach, he decided to scrap the Shipstead bill and sponsor an alternate that would have the best possible chance to survive the courts and accomplish its purpose. In April he invited Richberg, Frankfurter, Oliphant, and two other academic labor law specialists, Edwin E. Witte of the University of Wisconsin and Francis B. Sayre of Harvard, to come to Washington to draft a completely new bill.[154] Locked in the offices of the Senate Judiciary Committee, the five specialists carefully reviewed the relevant judicial decisions and produced a bill radically different from the one Shipstead had introduced.

The draftsmen assumed that congressional control over the jurisdiction of the lower federal courts presented the strongest constitutional theory on which to base the statute and the one that would be most difficult for the courts to reject or avoid. They cast the bill, therefore, in jurisdictional terms. Their proposal deprived the federal courts of jurisdiction in "labor disputes" to enjoin a number of specifically named activities, including striking, organizing, and publicizing. Further, it deprived the federal courts of jurisdiction to issue any labor injunction except in accord with a rigorous procedure designed to eliminate abuses, guarantee workers a hearing before any order issued, and impose heavy evidentiary requirements on the complainant and the court. It also granted a right to trial by jury in most contempt cases, severely restricted the use of "conspiracy" charges, and freed unions from liability for unlawful acts performed without their approval. Finally, the proposal denied the federal courts jurisdiction to hear suits based on yellow dog contracts and, further, provided that such agreements were unenforceable at law or in equity. A series of comprehensive definitions made clear the breadth of the bill's intended coverage, and the drafters implemented language to prevent the courts from doing to their bill what *Duplex* had done to the Clayton Act.[155] The drafters had apparently taken the advice of Judge Amidon, the old North Dakota Progressive. The federal courts, he warned Frankfurter, "will have to be hog-tied or they'll squirm out." [156]

After extensive internal debate the AFL decided to support the new bill, and Norris's effort gained momentum.[157] Hoover unintentionally aided the cause with a series of judicial nominations that spurred an extended debate on the abuses of the injunction. One was his nomination to the Supreme Court of Judge Parker, who only three years earlier had written the opinion in the hated *Red Jacket Coal* injunction case.[158] Another was the nomination to the Seventh Circuit of an infamous "injunction judge" who had issued, among others, the sweeping orders that broke the railway shopmen's strike of 1922.[159] Both nominations failed.[160] In addition, the Supreme Court—after the moderate Charles Evans Hughes succeeded Taft as chief justice in 1930—also lent encouragement. It unanimously upheld a provision of the Railway Labor Act of 1926 that protected unions against company pressure. Distinguishing *Coppage* and *Adair,* it assumed that Congress could regulate the employment relationship under the commerce power and recognized that employer pressure could "override the will" of employees.[161] The opinion undercut the constitutional certainty of the bill's opponents and signaled to its supporters that the Court's position might be shifting.

Beyond the confines of government, the deepening Depression generated a popular demand for government intervention in the economy and spurred a widespread sympathy for the cause of labor. In 1930–31 New York and Wisconsin adopted stringent anti-injunction statutes, and reform groups such as the American Civil Liberties Union and the National Civic Federation joined the campaign for the Norris bill.[162] In the congressional elections of 1930 the AFL obtained pledges in favor of the bill from many congressmen who represented industrial areas, and the Democrats, committed to its support, made major gains in both houses.[163]

Working again with LaGuardia, who sponsored the bill in the House, Norris steered his anti-injunction measure through the Senate Judiciary Committee. Bar associations and business groups denounced it, but they exercised a declining influence in the new Congress.[164] More ominously, the possibility of a veto by a noncommittal president hung over the measure. Hoover's secretary of labor, meeting with counsel for the National Association of Manufacturers, went so far as to offer Richberg a federal judgeship if he would announce his opposition.[165] In spite of the difficulties, public support and labor backing was strong. Norris, Walsh, Blaine, and other Progressives presented a carefully organized and well-prepared defense,[166] and in March 1932 the bill passed both houses by landslide votes.[167]

Attention shifted to the White House. Hoover was particularly concerned that the bill could prevent injunctions against boycotts, and he seriously considered a veto.[168] Letters and telegrams from business groups inundated his office urging him to do so. Henry W. Taft, the brother of the late chief justice, told Hoover that the bill was "the most glaring instance of class legislation that has been passed by Congress in many years." It would seriously harm the federal courts, Taft maintained, and its section outlawing the yellow dog contract was "unconstitutional."[169] Hoover's personal secretary feared that the bill could "set the stage for the purposes of the Communists."[170] The President, however, was preoccupied with the Depression, Prohibition, and his reelection. The overwhelming majorities in both houses, moreover, made a veto pointless.[171] At the last moment Hoover reluctantly signed.

Beyond the political leadership that Norris and other Progressives provided, passage of the bill rested on three principal factors. First, the Depression drastically altered the nation's social attitudes toward corporations and labor, and the election of 1930 strengthened Progressive forces in Congress and induced many representatives to give greater attention to union demands. Second, legal scholars and the bill's sponsors made a powerful case against the injunction. They documented its excessive sweep, the unfair procedures under which it was issued, and the unjustifiable power it gave to employers. In the lengthy debates only one congressman claimed that its abuses were less than serious.[172] Third, organized labor presented a fervent and united front. Furuseth was the only nationally known leader to oppose the bill, and by 1931 his influence had waned.[173] Labor harbored its doubts, but publicly it supported the Norris-LaGuardia bill unequivocally.

The success of the anti-injunction bill stood in sharp contrast to the failure of the parallel effort to abolish diversity jurisdiction. Norris viewed both as parts of his general effort to restrict the federal courts and, on that point at least, the ABA agreed with him completely. Both bills were directed against well-established jurisdictional doctrines that could serve legitimate social purposes. Both struck at legal advantages that corporations enjoyed, and both provoked extreme and nearly unanimous opposition from business associations and leaders of the corporate bar.

The contradictory results were even more striking given the different legal considerations that marked the two bills. Although the diversity proposal was attacked on constitutional grounds, it was clearly within the power of Congress.[174] Moreover, although it eliminated a major category of federal jurisdiction, the proposal did not restrict the authority of the national courts over any suit that raised a federal law claim. The anti-injunction measure, in contrast, raised unsettled and far-reaching questions of constitutional law by using congressional control over jurisdiction to strike at specific social interests and specific substantive rights. Yet, it was the diversity bill that failed to reach the Senate floor or even pass the House committee, while the doctrinally more radical anti-injunction measure passed by crushing majorities.

A number of factors explained the diverse fates of the two bills. The labor injunction had a dramatic simplicity and an obvious social significance that was lacking in the case of general diversity jurisdiction. The injunction starkly pitted employers against workers, "capital" against "labor," in a direct and dramatic confrontation that had obvious national repercussions. Injunctions affected thousands and sometimes tens or even hundreds of thousands of workers. The injunctions in *Debs* and the railway shopmen's strike reached workers across the nation, while Judge Parker's order in *Red Jacket Coal* protected 316 separate mining companies against the unionizing efforts of the United Mine Workers, an organization with 475,000 members.[175] By contrast, claims potentially subject to diversity jurisdiction, though numbering tens and perhaps hundreds of thousands each year, involved unknown and individual plaintiffs, relatively small amounts of money, and ordinary issues of everyday life. They sparked no headlines, involved no major organizations, and rallied no national constituencies.

Additionally, it was far easier to recognize and document the social operation of the labor injunction than of diversity jurisdiction. Although the labor injunction rested on a complex set of legal doctrines, including diversity, those technicalities did not obscure its obvious and clearly pro-employer consequences. The operation of diversity jurisdiction, in contrast, lacked any such single and unequivocal result. Its consequences varied in different states, and its general significance emerged only statistically. Moreover, the corporate use of diversity jurisdiction involved nothing as identifiable and dramatic as an injunction. In the vast majority of cases, in fact, it led only to routine and unreported out-of-court settlements—private agreements that were diverse, difficult to evaluate, and for the most part simply unknown. The operation of general diversity jurisdiction, in short, could hardly command general and sustained national attention.

Further, while the labor injunction grew in importance after World War I, the inequitable social impact of diversity jurisdiction had been declining for twenty years. The *Hitchman* structure was a relatively recent and dynamic innovation, and the yellow dog contract was widely used and resented. In contrast, a variety of legal reforms and social changes had curtailed the ability of corporations to exploit diversity jurisdiction against individual plaintiffs, and by the early 1930s its inequitable social impact affected a much smaller number of persons than it had in earlier decades.[176]

Finally, the anti-injunction bill was conceived more effectively and defended more persuasively than was the diversity bill. It dealt clearly and carefully with the legal problems the injunction raised, and it focused narrowly on the particular abuses that most required remedy. Its supporters were well prepared for the extended debate, and they defended the bill with powerful evidence and arguments. Conversely, the diversity bill was drawn too broadly and defended too weakly. Norris failed to make the case for abolition, and he made a major blunder when he refused to narrow his efforts to particular elements of the jurisdiction that led to the greatest abuses.

Although Norris failed to exploit his opportunity to limit diversity, he did succeed in restricting the labor injunction and eliminating the yellow dog contract. His achievement destroyed the *Hitchman* structure and deprived corporations of two of their most effective anti-labor tools. Norris, moreover, learned a legislative lesson that served Progressives well two years later. In 1934 he agreed to shelve his bill to abolish diversity in order to concentrate his efforts and unite Progressives in support of Johnson's narrow and more promising bill to limit federal jurisdiction over state rate-making orders.[177] Both his successes and his failures echoed in the minds of legal Progressives throughout the 1930s.

Brandeis, *Erie*, and the Complexities of Constitutional Judging

PART **2**

Litigant Strategies and Judicial Dynamics

4

In early 1934, as Senator Norris joined the Progressive drive to pass the Johnson Act and the New Deal's recovery program sputtered along, Harry J. Tompkins, a twenty-seven-year-old factory worker, was laid off from his job. The mild mannered and slightly built Tompkins lived with his wife and young daughter in the small mining town of Hughestown, Pennsylvania, far from the political turmoil of the nation's capital. A half block from their white frame house lay a one-track rail line belonging to the Erie Railroad, whose freight trains often awakened the young man in the middle of the night as they rumbled through town.[1] In the fifth year of the nation's long and grinding Depression, Tompkins was one more unnoted casualty of hard times.

On July 27 of that year Tompkins ate dinner and spent the evening at his mother-in-law's house. Shortly after midnight he began the six-mile trip home, riding with some friends for much of the way. At approximately 2:00 a.m. the friends dropped him off near a well-trod footpath that ran along the freight tracks toward his home. He had only a short distance to go, and as he walked along the path a train approached. Suddenly, and too late, Tompkins looked up. Protruding from the train and coming right at him was "a black object that looked like a door."[2] It slammed into him and threw him under the passing wheels. Neighbors found him unconscious, lying against a rail, his severed right arm lying between the tracks. At a nearby hospital the remainder of the arm was amputated.[3]

Tompkins recovered rapidly and, when released from the hospital, sought counsel. Asking around town for advice, he was given the name of a New York attorney named Bernard Nemeroff, whose father happened to be a local businessman. Tompkins retained Nemeroff, who quickly secured the assistance of a young Columbia Law School graduate named Aaron L. Danzig to do his legal research. Subsequently, to try the case, he brought in G. Everett "Stub" Hunt, an experienced trial lawyer who specialized in personal injury actions. Fortunately, or so it seemed, Tompkins's attorneys proved able, clever, and successful.[4]

Doctrine and Strategy: The Art of Forum Shopping

The seriousness of Tompkins's injury and the consequent value of his claim made it worthwhile for his attorneys to explore their available forum options with the greatest care. Because the railroad was incorporated in New York and operated in both New York and Pennsylvania, they knew they could obtain personal jurisdiction over it in either state.* Because the railroad's New York incorporation made it a citizen of that state for federal jurisdictional purposes, and because Tompkins was a resident of Pennsylvania, they also knew that a federal court in either state would have subject matter jurisdiction over Tompkins's claim on the basis of diversity of citizenship. Thus, they knew that they could bring the suit in either New York or Pennsylvania and that they could file it in either a state or a federal court.[5] For carefully calculated reasons, they chose the United States District Court for the Southern District of New York.

The federal forum was essential if their client were to avoid what appeared to be a settled and highly unfavorable rule of Pennsylvania common law. Under the decisions of the state's supreme court, Tompkins had no legal right to use the footpath and was a "trespasser." Consequently, the railroad owed him no "duty of care." It would be liable to him only for a "willful" injury.[6] Because the railroad had obviously not injured Tompkins "willfully" he seemed destined to lose his case if Pennsylvania law were applied. His chances appeared much better, however, in a federal court. The general common law rule applicable under the *Swift* doctrine imposed a broader duty of care on the railroad that would allow Tompkins to recover for a merely "negligent" injury. Understandably, then, his attorneys chose to file in a federal, rather than a state, court.

The attorneys chose a federal court in New York, rather than one in Pennsylvania, for equally well-calculated reasons.[7] They concluded that the federal courts in the two states tended to apply the federal common law in significantly different ways. The United States Circuit Court of Appeals for the Third Circuit, whose jurisdiction covered Pennsylvania but not New York, tended to push the district courts in its circuit to defer to local common law and apply divergent federal rules only sparingly. Conversely, the United States Circuit Court of Appeals for the Second Circuit, whose jurisdiction included New York, tended to

---

*A court must have two different kinds of jurisdiction in order to hear a case. "Personal jurisdiction" refers to the court's authority over the specific defendant. It exists when the defendant has a sufficient connection with the state in which the court is located, such as physical presence, incorporation, or the conduct of regular business in the state. "Subject matter jurisdiction" refers to the court's authority to adjudicate specific types of cases. Federal courts, for example, have subject matter jurisdiction over cases that raise federal questions and over those between citizens of different states.

sanction wider uses of the federal common law.[8] Thus, it seemed that a federal court in New York would be more likely to apply the divergent federal rule to Tompkins's claim than would a federal court in Pennsylvania. Hence, Tompkins would have the best chance of prevailing in a federal court located in New York.

The choice proved shrewd. The district court for the Southern District of New York applied the federal rule, and on November 16, 1936, Tompkins won a jury verdict for the handsome sum of $30,000. When the Erie Railroad appealed,[9] the Second Circuit affirmed the judgment.[10] As Nemeroff and Danzig had expected, the appellate court ruled that under the *Swift* doctrine the district court had properly applied the federal rule rather than the conflicting state law. At that point, the matter should have been settled. "There wasn't a chance in the world," Tompkins's attorneys believed, "that the Supreme Court would grant *certiorari*."[11]

Then lightning struck. Incredibly, Harry Tompkins's action captured the attention of the United States Supreme Court. On October 11, 1937, it granted the railroad's petition to hear the case.[12]

Doctrine and Strategy: The Art of Appellate Lawyering

While Tompkins's attorneys relied on *Swift,* the railroad's attorneys, led by Theodore Kiendl, a partner in John W. Davis's prestigious New York law firm, cleverly sought to narrow its doctrine and turn it to the railroad's advantage.[13] Kiendl — "iron gray hair, striped gray suit," Danzig recalled, "pure Westchester" — was an experienced trial lawyer and able appellate advocate who planned his strategy with care.[14] "We do not," his brief announced, "question the finality of the holding of this Court in *Swift v. Tyson.*"[15] Instead, Kiendl advanced a shrewd interpretation of *Swift* that not only avoided the compulsion of the general common law but also required the federal court to apply Pennsylvania law. *Swift* called for the application of federal common law, Kiendl argued, "only when the pertinent principle or rule of law has not been definitely settled, foreclosed or established" in a particular state.[16] But "where the evidence in the form of state decisions is sufficiently conclusive," he continued, *Swift* held that the "federal courts are bound to recognize an asserted rule of state law."[17] In Tompkins's case the applicable Pennsylvania law was clear and authoritatively settled by the state's supreme court.[18] In that case, Kiendl concluded, *Swift* itself directed the federal court to apply the law of Pennsylvania.[19]

Although no advocate could doubt Kiendl's skill or judgment in trying to narrow *Swift* so adroitly, it seemed curious that he did not also argue that the case should be overturned. *Swift* had been widely and vigorously criticized for decades, and there was surely reason to believe that the Court might be ready to abandon it. Such a fundamental challenge, moreover, could be advanced quite safely in the alternative without compromising the narrow argument that he had constructed so artfully. Several years later Kiendl gave two reasons for his decision not to challenge *Swift*. The precedent was too widely accepted and long established to challenge, he maintained, and "a head-on attack" might prove "fatal" to his client's cause.[20]

Although Kiendl wisely advanced the narrow ground that turned an obstacle into an advantage, the reasons he gave for not raising the more fundamental challenge in the alternative were unconvincing. If he had been worried that a frontal attack might somehow offend or distract the Court, he could have presented the alternative argument relatively briefly and placed it inoffensively at the end of his brief. There, the challenge to *Swift* would have appeared as a conventional final fallback position offered by a thorough and dedicated advocate. Kiendl, however, portrayed himself as unaware of that tactical option. He claimed, instead, that he confronted a "dilemma" and was forced to choose between two mutually exclusive approaches: "attacking the doctrine of Swift v. Tyson directly or endeavoring to suggest that this doctrine was inapplicable."[21] Kiendl was not, however, confronted with an either/or dilemma. Arguing in the alternative is one of the most common—and safest—tactics in the advocate's arsenal.

Further, contrary to Kiendl's statements, neither *Swift*'s pedigree nor the risk of attacking its doctrine appeared particularly weighty at the beginning of 1938. Although an argument urging a court to overrule a ninety-six-year-old precedent would ordinarily seem unpromising, when Kiendl was drafting his brief he confronted a situation that should have suggested, and even invited, such a "head-on attack."[22] For decades *Swift* had been subjected to increasingly severe criticism. Justice Oliver Wendell Holmes, whose ideas enjoyed enormous respect and inspired numerous followers, had attacked it harshly—most recently in the *Taxicab* case, where he had charged that its doctrine was "unconstitutional."[23] By the mid-1930s he and other critics had convinced a large majority of legal commentators that *Swift* was fundamentally misguided and unsound.[24] Even more significant, by the fall of 1937 only three members of the *Taxicab* majority remained on the bench, while the other six justices had either joined Holmes's *Taxicab* dissent or shown themselves willing to limit *Swift*.[25] Further, in early January of 1938, more than three weeks before the oral argument in *Erie*, the *Swift* doctrine became even more vulnerable. One of the three remaining members of the *Taxicab* majority resigned, and Roosevelt replaced him with a second New Dealer who seemed likely to join the Court's anti-*Swift* wing. Finally, the fact that the Court granted certiorari in a diversity action involving a routine common law tort claim was by itself sufficient to fire the imagination of an attorney as experienced and sagacious as Kiendl.

Had there been any doubts about the Court's purpose in granting certiorari, the oral argument on January 31, 1938, quickly dispelled them. "I had
not proceeded very far," Kiendl recalled, "before Mr. Justice Brandeis pointedly inquired about our views with regard to the Swift v. Tyson case." [26] Indeed,
Brandeis was quite pointed. "Mr. Kiendl," he asked, "do you think *Swift v. Tyson*
was rightly decided?" [27] Most of the other justices joined the ensuing discussion, and Kiendl was forced to devote the greater part of his oral argument to
the issue. Despite prodding from Brandeis, whose hostility to *Swift* was widely
known, Kiendl still failed to attack the case "head on." The description he gave
of his response to Brandeis evidenced his deep reluctance to do so. "I could not
refrain from expressing my view," he recalled, "that the doctrine of that case
was unfortunate in its consequences but that nevertheless its acceptance by so
many courts for so many years precluded me from suggesting that the doctrine
be overruled." [28]

Kiendl's response raises a number of questions. Why would an advocate
characterize his behavior in such circumstances so passively, and almost apolo-
getically, as a seemingly forced inability to "refrain from expressing my view"?
Why would he do so when his sought-after view addressed the critical issue that
seemed to captivate the Court and ultimately proved to be the dispositive issue
that won a famous victory for both himself and his client? Why, even more puz-
zlingly, would he emphasize the fact that *Swift* had been accepted "by so many
courts for so many years"? Why would he do so when it was also true that *Swift*
had been subjected to fundamental criticisms and that the Court itself had for
the past several years seemed to view it with doubt, if not dislike? Why, especially, would an advocate in Kiendl's circumstances dare make the suggestion
that *Swift*'s precedential status was of such longevity that it might reasonably
be thought to "preclude" a fundamental reconsideration of the case?

Why, finally, would he suggest such a self-denying possibility when it
was Brandeis who spearheaded the attack? Only six years earlier, in a striking
dissent that had drawn widespread attention, Brandeis had declared that the
doctrine of *stare decisis* was neither "inflexible" nor "a universal, inexorable command." Rather, it was "a question entirely within the discretion of the court." [29]
He had then demonstrated that the Court had overruled some three dozen of its
own opinions and substantially "qualified" many more.[30] His point was plain.
"The Court," Brandeis had announced sweepingly, "bows to the lessons of experience and the force of better reasoning." [31] Kiendl surely knew that the justice
who pressed the question did not, in the least, feel "precluded" from reconsidering *Swift*.[32]

The explanation for Kiendl's tactic is straightforward: he did not want
Swift overruled. He shaped his response in the oral argument so blandly for the

same reason that he crafted his brief to avoid questioning *Swift*'s continued authority. His paramount goal in litigating *Erie* was, ironically, not to defeat Harry Tompkins but to preserve *Swift v. Tyson*.

Kiendl's appellate strategy is significant because it reveals the high economic value that his client placed on preserving the federal common law. The railroad wanted to protect *Swift* because, from its long-term perspective, the federal common law was more valuable in litigating and settling claims brought against it than was a victory in Tompkins's individual suit.[33] Understandably, then, Kiendl's brief showed a special solicitude for *Swift:* He did not merely avoid the case but expressly defended it. "[T]he persistent criticisms of *Swift v. Tyson* and succeeding cases," he argued, "have been largely misdirected."[34] He went further and declared that his narrow interpretation "furnishes the fundamental answer to the many criticisms of the doctrine of *Swift v. Tyson*."[35] Because Pennsylvania law was clearly established and highly favorable, he hoped to exploit it for his client's benefit without affecting *Swift*'s precedential status. If his strategy succeeded, he would save his client the substantial sum of $30,000 while at the same time preserving the general federal common law. If *Swift*'s abolition were the price of victory, however, he knew that his client preferred defeat. Hence, Kiendl had, at all costs, to deflect the Court from overturning *Swift* and focus only on distinguishing it.

Professor Irving Younger, who examined Kiendl's appellate brief in *Erie*, termed it "an exercise in virtuosity" and "a *tour de force*."[36] Indeed, it was. Kiendl's argument was masterful, however, not merely because—as Younger correctly noted—it cleverly transformed the ostensibly unfavorable law under *Swift* into a positive force that supported his client's position. It was a truly virtuoso performance because it was designed to accomplish even more: to protect his client's broad, long-term interest in maintaining a doctrine that usually served the client's interests while, at the same time, mounting a sharp but narrow attack on its applicability in an individual case where it happened to cut against the client's specific, short-term interest.

Contrary to his later claim, then, Kiendl was not worried that a "head-on attack" on *Swift* might prove fatal to his case. Rather, he was worried that such an attack might prove fatal to *Swift*. In shaping his litigation strategy, Kiendl showed himself an exceptionally able advocate who quite methodically sought to advance his client's interests in both the short and long term. His only problem was that the Court had its own agenda. In retrospect, it is probable that Kiendl's subsequent description of his strategy in *Erie* was a rationalization offered because he preferred to be seen as a somewhat surprised and fortunate winner rather than as a somewhat devious and overreaching loser.[37]

This insight into Kiendl's strategy also throws light on one of the charges commonly leveled against *Erie:* that the Court acted improperly in overruling *Swift* because the parties had neither asked for such a ruling nor briefed the relevant legal issues.[38] The charge is valid primarily because the Court's allegedly hasty action supposedly deprived Tompkins's attorneys of the opportunity to present a fully developed defense of *Swift*. An understanding of Kiendl's strategy, however, makes it clear that the inability of Tompkins's attorneys to defend *Swift* was counterbalanced by Kiendl's studied refusal to offer any serious critique of the case and his failure to raise any argument that his adversaries had been precluded from answering.[39] This understanding also suggests the possibility that the Court acted as it did in some part, at least, because the majority justices clearly understood his strategy. They may have discounted the utility of ordering a reargument on the issue because they doubted Kiendl's freedom and willingness to mount an all-out attack on *Swift*. The justices may have regarded his strategy as too clever by half and believed, accordingly, that it should not be allowed to cabin their judgment and prevent them from deciding the case as they thought best.

Inside the Court: Forming a Majority

It should have been no surprise that it was Justice Louis D. Brandeis who interrupted Kiendl and propelled *Swift* to the forefront of the oral argument. Brandeis had long considered its doctrine legally unsound and socially divisive. He believed that it intruded on the law-making authority of the states, encouraged manipulative litigation tactics, and unfairly enhanced the litigation position of national corporations. In 1917, in his first term on the Court, he had joined Holmes's dissent in *Southern Pacific Co. v. Jensen,* which protested the expansion of federal general law in admiralty,[40] and a decade later he joined Holmes's dissent in the *Taxicab* case.[41] In 1930, writing for the Court, he openly expressed his doubts about *Swift*'s fundamental legitimacy. It was, he declared, "for the state courts to interpret and declare the law of the State." [42]

Sometime in late 1937 or early 1938 Brandeis decided to make the Erie Railroad's appeal the instrument of *Swift*'s demise. The Court's decision to overrule *Swift,* and especially its decision to do so on constitutional grounds, was largely due to him. Since Holmes's resignation in 1932, Brandeis had become the Court's recognized leader in opposing the federal common law, and in early 1938 he was ready to seize his opportunity.

Brandeis was confident that he had allies in his opposition to *Swift*. He counted primarily on the support of Justice Harlan F. Stone. A successful practitioner and later dean of Columbia Law School, Stone served as attorney general under President Calvin Coolidge before joining the Court in 1925. At first occasionally, and by the end of the 1920s often, Stone joined Holmes and Brandeis in their dissents from the Court's constitutional decisions. In 1928, his initial acceptance of *Swift* turned to flat opposition when he concurred with Brandeis in Holmes's *Taxicab* dissent.[43] Three years later Stone termed the dissent Holmes's "greatest exposition of the nature of the common law." [44] A careful legal craftsman and frequent advocate of judicial restraint, Stone increasingly came to view the law as a social product. The proper function of the judiciary, he believed, was the responsible adaptation of established doctrine to meet changing social needs. When he gave the address on American law at Harvard's tercentenary celebration in 1936, he pointedly chose Holmes's dissent in *Jensen* — which also attacked the idea of a general law that existed independent of any identifiable sovereign — to illustrate the principle that "bad precedent must on occasion yield to the better reason." [45] Stone and Brandeis worked together with increasing closeness during the 1930s, going so far as to meet privately, along with Justice Benjamin N. Cardozo, to prepare a common strategy for the Court's Saturday conferences. Although they had their differences, they shared a deep personal respect for one another as well as similar views on most of the major issues that confronted the Court. In pushing to overrule *Swift*, Brandeis was confident that he could count on Stone's support.

Only six other justices were sitting with Brandeis and Stone when *Erie* was argued. Cardozo had been absent for several weeks, stricken with the illness that within months would take his life.[46] Justices James C. McReynolds and Pierce Butler, the two remaining members of the *Taxicab* majority, were staunch supporters of *Swift* and made it clear that their views had not changed. Of the four new members who had come onto the Court since 1928 — Chief Justice Charles Evans Hughes and Justices Owen J. Roberts, Hugo L. Black, and Stanley Reed — Brandeis and Stone needed at least three to forge a majority for overruling.

When the Court met in conference after the oral argument, the majority quickly coalesced. The chief justice, siding with Brandeis and Stone from the beginning, introduced the matter bluntly. "If we wish to overrule *Swift v. Tyson*," he announced, "here is our opportunity." [47] As expected, McReynolds and Butler supported *Swift*, while Brandeis and Stone urged its abolition. Then, in succession, the Court's three newest members each cast his vote in favor of overruling, creating a six-justice majority for abolishing *Swift*. The chief justice, recognizing Brandeis's leadership in the matter, assigned him the opinion.[48]

While Brandeis and Stone led the attack on *Swift*, Hughes's concurrence was crucial. A man of immense prestige, the chief justice had been governor of New York, an associate justice of the Supreme Court from 1910 to 1916, the Republican presidential candidate in 1916, and then secretary of state in the 1920s. He combined leadership of both the Republican Party and the corporate bar with a moderate Progressivism, and in his years of private practice he had been one of the nation's most successful and sought after advocates. Appointed chief justice in 1930, Hughes guided the Court through the turbulent New Deal years, frequently siding with the conservative wing but in a number of major decisions voting with the Progressives. He was a highly effective chief justice, an excellent administrator, and a tactful moderator. With no special commitment to *Swift*, Hughes acknowledged many of the criticisms made against it. During his tenure as chief justice, in fact, the Court restricted *Swift*'s scope even while it continued to honor and sometimes apply its doctrine. Hughes was keenly aware, too, of the incentives the doctrine created for forum shopping and the added burdens it placed on the federal dockets.[49] Sensitive to the need to preserve local law in the midst of the New Deal's centralizing drive, Hughes may also have seen termination of the federal common law as a useful balance to the Court's decisions of the previous year that had substantially expanded federal power.[50]

Roberts was the fourth vote in favor of overturning *Swift*. A law professor, private practitioner, and district attorney in Philadelphia, he was a lifelong Republican. Roberts had come to national attention as a special investigator probing the government's oil lease transactions that had erupted into the Teapot Dome scandal. Appointed to the Court by President Herbert Hoover in 1930, he tended to join the anti–New Deal justices on constitutional issues though in some cases, unpredictably, he sided with the Progressives. His apparently inconsistent behavior, especially his widely criticized "switch" to the Progressive wing in the spring of 1937, earned him a reputation for vacillation and mediocrity. His opinions, in fact, revealed neither a sophisticated nor a coherent constitutional theory.[51] Following his retirement in 1945 he acknowledged the undistinguished nature of his tenure on the Court. "I have no illusions about my judicial career," he wrote poignantly. "Who am I to revile the good God that he did not make me a Marshall, a Taney, a Bradley, a Holmes, a Brandeis, or a Cardozo."[52]

Roberts tended to look to Hughes for guidance and assurance, and he was likely drawn to the *Erie* majority because the chief justice supported Brandeis's position.[53] Over the years Roberts had developed a warm and sympathetic relationship with Hughes. "My companionship with Justice Roberts," Hughes later wrote, "was most agreeable throughout the entire period of my service as Chief Justice."[54] For his part, Roberts declared simply that Hughes had been like a "father" to him.[55] Like Hughes, Roberts sought to preserve areas of local law, and abolishing *Swift*—especially after the Court's landmark decisions of the previous year—probably appealed to him for that reason.[56] After the demise of the "old" Court in 1937, Roberts demonstrated his readiness to follow the emerging new majority in a number of areas.[57] He had joined the Court's decisions in the mid-1930s that limited *Swift*'s scope, and, when Hughes, Brandeis, and Stone came out in favor of overruling *Swift*, he was unwilling to stand with Butler and McReynolds in opposition.

The fifth vote to overrule came from Justice Black, Roosevelt's first appointee to the Court. A hardened Southern Democrat who was deeply distrustful of corporate business, Black had specialized in personal injury actions and represented a number of local labor unions as a young lawyer in Birmingham, Alabama. Early on he had learned the shrewd tactical uses that corporations made of federal diversity jurisdiction, and he shared the animosity of both Progressives and states'-rights advocates toward *Swift*.[58] "I am not now, and have never been, a railroad, power company, or corporation lawyer," he repeatedly proclaimed when he ran successfully for the United States Senate in 1926.[59] Once in Washington, Black quickly allied himself with the Progressives. He became a close friend and ally of Norris and consistently supported the Nebraskan's efforts to limit the federal courts. Backing his bill to abolish diversity jurisdiction,[60] Black praised Norris as "the greatest Senator of all."[61] With the coming of the New Deal, Black emerged as a controversial national figure, one of Roosevelt's fiercest defenders, and a persistent antagonist of the anti–New Deal Supreme Court. When Justice Willis Van Devanter, a member of the Court's anti–New Deal wing, retired in the middle of 1937, Roosevelt selected Black as his replacement. The president was not particularly impressed with Black's legal skills, but he was confident that his first nominee would provide an energetic and reliable voice for Progressivism on the high bench.[62]

Black's appointment was widely perceived, in fact, as a "political" event, and few seemed to doubt either Roosevelt's result-oriented expectations or Black's willingness to fulfill them.[63] Norris, understandably, reacted with enthusiasm. "The scales of justice in his hands," the old Progressive announced, "will bring renewed hope to millions of our common people throughout the country."[64] Once on the Court, Black proved eager to press for changes in the legal doctrines that he believed favored corporate interests. As the sole dissenter in *McKart v. Indianapolis Water Co.*,[65] for example, he became the first justice since 1890 to attack the basic concept of judicial participation in administrative rate-making decisions.[66] In *Connecticut General Life Insurance Co. v. California*,[67] again dissenting alone, he challenged the fundamental constitutional doctrine that corporations were to be considered "persons" within the meaning of the Due Process Clause.[68] In his first term, Black dissented in sixteen cases, twelve of them in the face of an otherwise unanimous Court. He was primed to overrule *Swift*, and he joined Brandeis readily and enthusiastically.

The last member of the majority was Justice Reed, Roosevelt's second and most recent appointee.[69] A politically moderate Democrat from Kentucky, Reed had worked on the state level for such Progressive causes as workmen's compensation and limitations on child labor. Although he was skeptical about the New Deal's bureaucratization and centralization, the unprecedented scope of the Depression and his faith in Roosevelt's leadership moved him to accept the New Deal and most of its programs. Reed was staunchly loyal to the president, serving the administration as a special assistant to the attorney general and then as solicitor general. Arguing many of the New Deal's major constitutional cases, he had experienced firsthand the harsh questions and hostile attitudes of the Court's anti–New Deal majority.

Reed was nominated to the Court in mid-January to succeed the retiring Justice George Sutherland, the second of the anti–New Deal justices to retire. Confirmed by the Senate on the twenty-fifth, Reed heard oral argument in *Erie* his first day on the bench. As a loyal New Dealer he was predisposed to vote with Brandeis and Stone, especially in cases where McReynolds and Butler appeared together on the opposing side. Also, as a southerner and self-styled Jeffersonian, Reed was sensitive to *Swift*'s derogation of the authority of the states.[70] During oral argument in *Erie* and in the Court's subsequent Saturday conferences, he came to believe that the trial court had applied a rule inconsistent with Pennsylvania common law, and that belief convinced him that the appeal presented a proper case in which to overrule *Swift*.[71] Although he lacked Black's ardor for change, Reed had no qualms about dispatching the ninety-six-year-old case.

The Art of Appellate Judging: Writing an Opinion and Holding a Majority

With a six-justice majority, Brandeis set to work on his opinion in early February. He read widely in the law reviews, distilling the criticisms made against *Swift* and gathering examples of conflict between general common law rules and those of the various states.[72] He first set out a statement of facts and then, in early March, reviewing a printed draft of his factual summary, he formalized the threshold decision that the six justices had made. With his pen he scratched in what would become the opinion's well-known and blunt opening sentence, forcing the issue that Kiendl had struggled so assiduously to avoid. "The question for decision is whether the oft-challenged doctrine of *Swift v. Tyson* shall now be disapproved."[73]

Brandeis's first draft that reached the legal issues, dated March 7, rested on the proposition that Holmes had laid down ten years earlier in his *Taxicab* dissent. *Swift* was unconstitutional. "Except where a rule of decision is one to be determined by the federal authority," Brandeis wrote, "the law to be applied is necessarily a state rule, whether it be enunciated by the legislature or by the courts of the State."[74] Such "recognition of the substantive law of a state is required by the Constitution." Thus, from the beginning, Brandeis rested his opinion on the Constitution. The March 7 draft contained both the statement that *Swift* represented an "unconstitutional assumption of powers" and an adumbration of the opinion's supporting constitutional theory. "Congress," Brandeis wrote in the early draft, "has no power to declare the law general." [75]

In his next draft, dated March 9, he began a second line of argument, one that Holmes had ignored but which was central to Brandeis. "Experience in applying the doctrine of *Swift v. Tyson*," he explained, "taught the difficulty of drawing the line between the province of general jurisprudence and that of local law." Pointing to the "resulting uncertainty," he sketched an argument that *Swift* rendered "impossible equal protection of the law." Because rights varied depending on the forum in which a case was heard, and because noncitizens had an advantage over citizens in determining which forum would hear a case, he maintained that *Swift* and diversity jurisdiction "instead of preventing discrimination against the non-citizen operate[s] to discriminate against the citizen." [76] On the following day he added to that argument a discussion of the evils of jurisdictional manipulation that *Swift* engendered, particularly on the part of corporations. "The injustice became glaring when this [discrimination] was accomplished without change of residence by the facile device of incorporation under the laws of another State." [77] Succeeding drafts elaborated the manipulation point and added examples of the erratic spread of the federal common law into a variety of substantive fields.

By March 21, Brandeis had completed a draft that he considered ready for circulation. It began with a discussion of the facts, introduced *Swift* through a long quotation, commented on the doctrine's growth, referred to the historical research of Charles Warren dealing with the origin of the Judiciary Act of 1789, and then discussed the *Taxicab* case at length. [78] The second section analyzed the "defects, social and political" which "experience in applying the doctrine of *Swift* v. *Tyson*" had revealed. The third section argued that *Swift* was, in Holmes's words, "an unconstitutional assumption of powers by courts of the United States." Except where federal constitutional or statutory law controlled, Brandeis explained, the law to be applied was the law of the state, whether statutory or judicial. "There is no federal common law," he wrote. "Congress has no power to declare rules of common law applicable in a State whether they be local in their nature or 'general,' be they commercial law or a part of the law of torts." The fourth and final section disposed of the case itself. It reversed the decision of the court of appeals because it had applied general law instead of state law. Because the parties disputed the nature of the applicable Pennsylvania rule, Brandeis's draft ordered the case remanded for a determination of that issue. [79]

Black responded quickly. "Your requiem over *Swift v. Tyson* is one of your best—and that is saying much." He was concerned only that there might be a possible "misunderstanding as to the application [of the new doctrine] to this particular case." Black pointed out that the plaintiff's brief had argued that the leading Pennsylvania case, unfavorable to his cause, was not applicable. He asked Brandeis to insert a comment to the effect that "this Court realized there was a further controversy as to the applicability" of the ostensibly controlling Pennsylvania precedent.[80] Brandeis agreed, adding a footnote to the opinion's final section.[81]

The episode, minor in itself, was characteristic of both justices. While Black was delighted with the fall of *Swift*, he hoped to avoid an unfavorable result for the injured Tompkins. His concern with the practical result in "this particular case" foreshadowed the sympathy that he would so frequently manifest for relatively poor litigants, especially those involved in personal injury suits. For his part, Brandeis was already aware that his decision would likely deprive Tompkins of his large award. He had, in fact, previously directed his law clerk to determine what the relevant Pennsylvania rule was, and the clerk had concluded that under state law "a verdict should have been directed" in favor of the railroad.[82] The episode illustrated the methodical way in which Brandeis explored the relevant issues, and it suggested that he avoided declaring Pennsylvania law—an omission for which he was subsequently criticized—not only out of deference to the state courts but also because he would otherwise have had to rule against the plaintiff.[83] With his case remanded, Tompkins had the option to salvage something by settling his claim before the railroad took further legal action. Regardless of his thoughts about Tompkins, however, Brandeis focused on general social and institutional concerns, not on the individual result.

Reed also responded quickly. He regarded the opinion as "splendid" but thought that "an expression or two" should be "modified." He cut to the heart of the opinion's constitutional theory. It would be wise, Reed suggested, "to make clear there is no denial of Congressional power to fix rules of the law for Federal courts." His objection was threefold. First, Reed believed that Brandeis's statement about congressional power was simply wrong. "When Federal courts were given jurisdiction over citizens of different states," he explained, "I think Congress could prescribe the applicable law in the trials." Second, although he agreed that *Swift* was wrongly decided, he questioned "the advisability of calling such action 'unconstitutional.' " Third, he suggested that the issue could be resolved, and *Swift* interred, by simply changing the "statutory interpretation" of the word "laws" in Section 34, the Rules of Decision Act.[84]

Brandeis attempted to persuade Reed of the necessity to rest on the Constitution. Reed proved adamant, but so did Brandeis. Two days later, Reed sent him a proposed concurrence, arguing that the word *laws* in Section 34 should merely be reinterpreted to include judicial decisions. The effect of Brandeis's opinion, Reed contended, was to hold Section 34 "invalid, *in toto,* as a exercise of a non-delegated [congressional] power."[85]

Stone, who apparently expressed approval when he first read the draft, began to hesitate.[86] On the twenty-third, before he had seen Reed's draft concurrence, Stone wrote Brandeis stating that "[u]pon reflection there is one part of your opinion in *Erie Railroad v. Tompkins* which gives me some concern." The disturbing section was "that in which you say in effect that there is no constitutional power in Congress to require federal courts to apply rules of law inconsistent with those in force in the state, unless Congress is acting under one of the substantive powers granted to the national government." Stone asked Brandeis to "eliminate" or "rephrase" the language, claiming that "the matter is not, in my mind, entirely free from doubt — the power may be implicit in the judicial sections [of the Constitution]." Moreover, Stone argued, the statement about congressional power was "unnecessary" to the decision. Finally, he called Brandeis's attention to the problem his language would create with respect to the new Federal Rules of Civil Procedure. "I am apprehensive of a doctrine which would require this Court constantly, without any aid from Congress, to draw the line between the rules of law applied by the federal courts which are substantive and those which are procedural."[87]

Worse for Brandeis and his wavering majority, Stone and Reed were not alone in their doubts. The chief justice was also suspicious of the constitutional argument, and, given the doubts of those three, it is likely that Roberts was also uncertain.[88] Black alone expressed the "hope that not a word will be changed relating to the last repose of *Swift v. Tyson.*"[89] As of the twenty-third, it looked as though Brandeis might have lost a majority for his constitutional rationale if not for the overthrow of *Swift.*

Brandeis, however, set to work and persuaded Stone to stay with him. On the twenty-fourth they conferred, and Brandeis convinced his colleague to accept his constitutional rationale. Stone "was in 3:30 — 24th," Brandeis noted on Stone's letter of the previous day. "Says after our talk will abide by the opinion — unless he lets me know to the contrary."[90] On the following day, after reading Reed's concurrence, Stone wrote Brandeis. He had decided to accept the constitutional language, but he was now bothered by Reed's comments. On the one hand, Stone was attracted by Reed's proposal to base the decision on a reinterpretation of the statutory language. On the other hand, he was reluctant to jettison the construction of a statute that had been settled by the Court, and accepted by Congress, for ninety-six years. Given the long-standing nature of the construction, Stone explained, it should be altered only if there were a compelling reason for doing so. "In view of the long history of our support of *Swift v. Tyson,*" he wrote to Brandeis, "I realize the force of the constitutional aspects of the case as an impelling reason for overruling *Swift v. Tyson* and the long line of cases which have followed it." Thus, Stone not only accepted the constitutional language but now urged that the opinion make clear that only constitutional considerations justified the Court in changing the long-established statutory construction of Section 34. "I think it is important that we should not discuss the constitutional question unless we definitely conclude that without it we would not overrule the precedents of one hundred years." [91]

Both to avoid the force of Reed's proposal and to explain the necessity for the constitutional language, Stone suggested a change to indicate that the Court did "definitely conclude" that the constitutional basis was essential. Brandeis's draft had read: "*We need not determine whether the objections disclosed by experience are alone sufficient reason for* abandon*ing* a doctrine so widely applied throughout nearly a century. *For* the unconstitutionality of the course pursued has now been made clear and compels us to do so." [92] Stone asked that the passage be, in his word, "reframed" to read: "*If only a question of statutory construction were involved we would not be prepared to* abandon . . . a doctrine so widely applied throughout nearly a century. *But* the unconstitutionality of the course pursued has now been made clear and compels us to do so." [93] If the change were not acceptable, Stone stated, he would concur separately, "making plain my position that I come to the constitutional question only because otherwise I should, as Mr. Justice Holmes said, leave *Swift v. Tyson* undisturbed." [94] Brandeis readily agreed to Stone's new language.

With Stone aboard, Brandeis was able to solidify his majority at the Saturday conference on the twenty-sixth. [95] Brandeis outlined the minor changes he was making in his previously circulated draft, and, with Stone's support, he overcame whatever hesitations Hughes and Roberts may have felt. Black reaffirmed his enthusiastic acceptance of the opinion, while Reed stood by his concurrence but failed to persuade anyone to join him. McReynolds and Butler registered their dissents, but neither could influence the other six. On the twenty-eighth Brandeis circulated a new draft that incorporated the changes discussed. Hughes, Stone, Roberts, and Black all signed on, the chief justice adding that the opinion was "admirable." [96] Brandeis's draft, by a bare majority, had become an opinion of the Court.

False Leads: The Alleged Contributions of Stone and Black

A number of writers have emphasized the importance of Stone and Black to the Court's decision in *Erie*. Their claims, however, are inaccurate. Brandeis was the primary architect of *Erie*. He was the dominant force in leading the Court to overturn *Swift,* in pressing to base the decision on the Constitution, and in drafting the specific constitutional language that the Court adopted.

Two of the most important, and ostensibly authoritative, accounts of the Court's deliberations attributed the constitutional basis of *Erie* largely or wholly to Stone. Merlo J. Pusey, Hughes's biographer, based his account in significant part on a series of interviews with the chief justice after his retirement.[97] According to Pusey, Hughes reported that after reading the first draft of Brandeis's opinion he "consulted Brandeis and learned that he [Brandeis] had originally written his opinion without reference to any constitutional issue." Brandeis told Hughes, Pusey wrote, that Stone "had induced him [Brandeis] to change [his draft opinion] by arguing that *Swift v. Tyson* had stood so long that Congress must be regarded as having accepted its doctrine."[98] Similarly, Alpheus T. Mason, Stone's biographer, relied primarily on Stone's papers to provide a somewhat more complex but ultimately confused account. He also portrayed Stone as a major force in ensuring that *Erie* was decided on constitutional grounds. It was Stone who pressed Brandeis to invoke the Constitution, Mason wrote, and it was Stone who first advanced "the astonishing premise that the prior decision in *Swift v. Tyson* was unconstitutional." Moreover, Mason continued, Stone regarded the constitutional foundation as so essential that he threatened to withdraw his support for Brandeis's opinion if the latter did not rest his opinion on constitutional grounds. "So vital did Stone regard this suggestion," Mason declared, "that he threatened to write a separate opinion if Brandeis did not acquiesce." As a result, the biographer concluded, "Brandeis adopted Stone's suggestion verbatim."[99]

When the successive drafts of Brandeis's opinion in *Erie* are reviewed along with other documentary evidence, it is clear that the accounts by Pusey and Mason are both inaccurate.[100] Pusey's is simply mistaken. The earliest draft of Brandeis's opinion that reached the legal issues sketched the constitutional argument, and all the succeeding drafts retained and developed it. Stone's response to the first draft that Brandeis circulated among the justices establishes that Stone was initially concerned not with the lack of a constitutional rationale but with the presence of one: the language pertaining to the power of Congress.[101] Further, Pusey's discussion of *Erie* contains, within two pages, several inaccurate or misleading statements.[102] Finally, Pusey's account is based on Hughes's recollections, and there is strong reason to believe that Hughes gave Pusey a mistaken account. Pusey does not indicate *when* Hughes spoke with Brandeis. The record suggests that Hughes recalled a conversation that almost certainly took place after Brandeis had received Stone's letter of the twenty-fifth requesting the "reframed" language. If the two had spoken then, Brandeis would have told Hughes that (as of that time) Stone was insisting that the decision rest on a constitutional basis. Such a conversation probably was what Hughes recalled and recounted, in vague terms, to Pusey. Given the documentary evidence, the early drafts of Brandeis's opinion, the inaccuracies in Pusey's account, and the fact that Hughes's recollections came in old age and some ten years after the event, no reason remains to credit Hughes's reported recollection of Stone's role in the case.

Mason's account is distorted not by reliance on faulty recollection but by the author's inability to review all the relevant documents.[103] The misleading nature of Mason's account can be more clearly understood by recognizing that there were two related though distinct constitutional points involved: first, the conclusion that the doctrine of *Swift* led to an unconstitutional assumption of powers by the federal courts and, second, the supporting ground that "Congress has no power to declare substantive rules of common law applicable in a State."[104] Mason argued that Stone was responsible for the former and hoped to restrict or eliminate the latter.

On the first issue—that the course of judicial action following *Swift* was unconstitutional—the documents establish that Stone was responsible only for a minor stylistic change, not for an "astonishing premise." The declaration that *Swift* was an unconstitutional assumption of power by the federal courts appeared in Brandeis's original draft, and Stone's "reframed" language did not constitute a substantive change. The alteration Stone suggested had the advantage of addressing Reed's concurrence, and it did reorient the logic of the decision away from problems of "experience" to the proprieties of "statutory construction." The change was not significant, however, in terms of either the decision to rest *Erie* on a constitutional basis or the theory that underlay that constitutional basis.

On the second issue—the opinion's basis concerning congressional power—the critical language was in Brandeis's original draft, and it survived intact into the final opinion.[105] Brandeis's note on Stone's letter of the twenty-third indicates that Brandeis persuaded Stone to accept the congressional power language. Stone's second letter, on the twenty-fifth, abandoned his earlier objection to that part of the opinion. On this second constitutional issue, then, it was Brandeis who initiated and prevailed, and Stone who acquiesced.[106]

While Stone had but a minor impact on the opinion's language, Black had almost none. Several scholars have attributed significance to Black's dissent in *New York Life Insurance Co. v. Gamer,* which the Court handed down two months before *Erie.*[107] *Gamer* dealt with a question involving burden of proof under state law, and it ruled in favor of an insurance company. Black wrote one of his solo first-term dissents, arguing that under state law the majority's decision was incorrect. He pointed out that the Court's rule was based neither on a federal statute nor on state law, and he criticized the approach which allowed different common law rules to be applied in state and federal court. "Neither the company nor the policyholder should obtain an advantage by the application of a different law governing the contract," he maintained, "merely because the case can be removed to a federal court."[108] Given Black's lone attack on the divergent federal common law rule and the Court's subsequent decision in *Erie*, some observers concluded that his dissent in *Gamer* triggered *Swift*'s overthrow.[109]

Although his dissent did implicitly criticize *Swift*, Black was neither the catalyst in the *Erie* decision nor an influence within the Court. First, and most conclusively, the Court had already reached its conference decision on *Erie* before Black's *Gamer* dissent was circulated among the justices.[110] Second, it appears likely that Black did not discuss *Swift* or his *Gamer* dissent with Brandeis before Brandeis had circulated his first draft of *Erie*. On his "return" of Brandeis's *Erie* draft, at least, Black considered it necessary to inform Brandeis that "[m]y dissent in *New York Life Insurance v. Gamer* was based on a challenge of the rule announced in *Swift v. Tyson* although I did not specifically refer to it in my opinion."[111] Third, Black's dissent in *Gamer* seemed designed neither to analyze and undercut the rule of *Swift* nor to persuade the Court to reject it. His dissent did not even mention *Swift* by name. It focused on the specific context of insurance law and dealt hastily and dubiously with several complicated issues. Perhaps most significant, it failed even to allude to the possibility that a constitutional issue might be involved. The dissent, instead, emphasized what would become one of Black's most characteristic concerns. The federal rule, he maintained in the dissent, "in my judgment transfers jury functions to judges."[112]

More broadly, it was unlikely that Black's attack on *Swift* influenced the Court because, at the time, he did not command the intellectual and professional respect of the other justices. Stone was deeply distressed by Black's radical dissents and poor craftsmanship;[113] Brandeis[114] and Hughes[115] shared his concerns. Black struck them as too anxious to assert his own beliefs, much too radical in attempting to change the law, and deficient in learning and in his understanding of the judicial role. Given the apparent views of those three dominant figures, it seems likely that Roberts and Reed also regarded Black as suspect or worse.[116] Indeed, all the justices who voted to overturn *Swift* were unsympathetic to the aggressive political views that infused Black's first-term dissents.

Thus, in spite of the power that he would eventually wield over many of his colleagues, and in spite of the reputation he would ultimately earn as one of the giants in the Court's history, Black did not move the Court or any individual justice in *Erie*. His dissent in *Gamer* was irrelevant, and he did not command the respect of the majority justices. Although his vote was essential, his influence was nonexistent.

The Majority Justices: Doubt and Dissatisfaction

The reasons for Brandeis's success in carrying a majority for his opinion in *Erie* are not entirely clear. Apparently, Black alone was untroubled by the constitutional issue. Beyond elaborating the general theory contained in his opinion, Brandeis's March 24 note to Reed and an undated draft footnote, not included in the final opinion, suggest that Brandeis may have stressed two considerations to his doubting colleagues. First, he emphasized that his opinion did not, under any interpretation, hold Section 34 unconstitutional. Hence, it did not repudiate the legislation passed by the first Congress, and it did not limit any otherwise valid power of Congress. Second, Brandeis pointed out that prior Court decisions had stated that *Swift*'s interpretation of Section 34 was merely "declarative" of what the law would be in the absence of the statute. Those statements implied that the *Swift* doctrine was based on constitutional grounds. Hence, it would be appropriate, indeed necessary, to overturn *Swift* by setting aright the underlying constitutional principles. Brandeis's final opinion emphasized both those points more explicitly than had his March 21 draft.[117]

Doubts about *Erie*'s constitutional foundation may have lingered among the justices until the last minute. As late as the conference on April 9, Hughes was still trying to bolster the opinion by reading a long quotation from Field's dissent in *Baugh*, which had also maintained that *Swift* was unconstitutional. In his early drafts Brandeis had not quoted from Field's opinion, and in later drafts he had excerpted only two sentences from it. In response to Hughes's eleventh-hour effort, however, he decided to include in his final opinion the much longer quotation that the chief justice had read.[118]

On April 25, 1938, Brandeis finally delivered the Court's decision and opinion. His efforts, however, apparently failed to convince fully either Hughes or Stone. Nine years after *Erie* was announced, the chief justice told Pusey that he had sided with Brandeis for the sake of harmony and because a majority opinion was necessary in so important a case.[119] Hughes also recalled that he had regarded the opinion's constitutional language as unnecessary and that he had actually preferred Reed's approach.[120] For Stone's part, four days after the opinion came down, he confided to Frankfurter that he agreed with the assertion that "the Court itself has been acting unconstitutionally" in applying *Swift* but that he nevertheless thought "it was unnecessary to say how far or to what extent Congress might legislate." Like Hughes, he went along with Brandeis's language largely because he felt that the drastic change resulting from the decision would require a majority to make it authoritative. "I thought that enough were writing," he explained, "without my risking the final result by putting in my own oar."[121]

The available records show, then, that Brandeis was the primary force behind the decision to use *Erie* as the vehicle for overthrowing *Swift* and that he was almost solely responsible for the opinion's constitutional rationale. The carefully constructed draft that he originally circulated on March 21 became, with relatively minor changes, the Court's final opinion. In his effort to overturn *Swift v. Tyson*, Brandeis had three ready and generally enthusiastic supporters and, in Hughes and Roberts, two others with no apparent qualms. For the declaration that the federal courts had pursued an "unconstitutional" course under *Swift*, however, he probably had only two supporters who joined him without reservations, Stone and Black. Finally, for his statements concerning congressional power—which embodied the opinion's underlying constitutional theory—he may well have had no supporters who accepted them fully and without reservation. Reed, in his concurrence, explicitly disavowed the statements; Stone, in private correspondence, expressed serious reservations; and Hughes subsequently told his biographer that they were simply unnecessary. Given those pervasive doubts and Black's enthusiastic support, Roberts may also have harbored reservations. The opinion's apparent evocation of the Tenth Amendment, however, may have quelled any doubts he might have had. Finally, Black, Brandeis's one unflinching if perhaps slightly embarrassing ally in the matter, may not have thought seriously about, or even considered, the possibility that *Swift* was unconstitutional until Brandeis circulated his March 21 draft.

Erie v. Tompkins was the result of a confluence of factors at a particular moment in history. It reflected sweeping political, social, and legal developments that extended back for more than half a century, along with a range of highly individualized human and institutional factors.[122] Most immediately, however, it was due to Brandeis. The Court's decision was largely due to his drive to overrule *Swift*, and its opinion was almost wholly due to his insistence that it rest on constitutional grounds and, more important, on specific constitutional grounds of his own choosing. *Erie* was, perhaps to an unusual degree, a decision of the Supreme Court that embodied the well-considered and fundamental constitutional theory of only a single justice.

Brandeis

THE JUDGE AS HUMAN

5

Born on November 13, 1856, Louis Dembitz Brandeis grew up in a family of German Jewish immigrants that had settled in Louisville, Kentucky.[1] His father was a successful grain merchant, providing his family with a comfortable home that emphasized education, culture, and a respectable middle-class liberalism. At sixteen Brandeis began two years of study in Dresden, where he received a German pre-university education, and then he attended Harvard Law School. After graduating in 1877, he practiced briefly in St. Louis and then returned to Boston to open a partnership with a friend and law school classmate. Brandeis possessed unflagging energy, a brilliant analytical mind, and an ability to master complicated factual details. By the 1890s he was head of a large firm with a successful corporate practice and enjoyed both a growing professional reputation and considerable personal wealth.[2]

His background and experience drew him into the emerging coalition of reform movements that constituted early twentieth-century progressivism. His Kentucky origins and the family business engendered a strong sense of localism, a faith in the small economic unit, and a deep suspicion of corporations and their concentrated power. His family's middle-class liberalism and faith in orderly social progress inspired in him an intense concern with the public responsibilities of lawyers and businessmen. A strong sense of personal integrity induced him to look critically at the ways in which the legal profession enhanced the power of organized wealth.

As a successful corporate lawyer, Brandeis knew and dealt with members of the New England social and economic elite; as a Jew, he increasingly felt the social distance that separated him from that elite, especially as social tensions sharpened and anti-Semitism intruded in the 1880s. Most commonly, he represented businesses owned by Germans and Jews, and the adversaries he fought on their behalf were frequently the established New England banking and railroad interests that the Protestant elite controlled. His clients, almost exclusively manufacturing and retailing firms, required ready access to capital and inexpensive transportation, while the railroads and their New England banking allies sought to "rationalize" the transportation system and guarantee high dividends on their investments. Increasingly, Brandeis's personal values and professional activities overlapped, focusing his attention on the growing conflicts between large corporate interests on the one side and various groups of economic outsiders, including small business, on the other. He regarded concentrated power as overbearing and began to criticize "bigness" in all its forms.

Brandeis saw political strife as the result of the inevitable confrontation between individuals and an increasingly organized industrial society. Believing that such conflicts were rationally resolvable, he devoted himself after the turn of the century to public issues. He served without compensation as a "people's lawyer" in cases that pitted concentrated financial interests against the diverse claims of individuals, localities, small groups, and what Brandeis deemed the common good. Testifying before Congress on a piece of proposed regulatory legislation, he was asked what "the effect of this measure will be on investments." He replied politely that "I was thinking of its effect upon the much larger number of our people, who have no investments and no money to invest." [3]

Believing fervently in the importance of educating the people on public issues and in the power of the press, Brandeis wrote and spoke widely on a variety of reform subjects. He popularized the idea of "scientific management" as part of his effort on behalf of Boston shippers to prevent a railroad rate increase, and he argued that the roads were inefficient because they were too large and cumbersome for effective administration. [4] Repeatedly he insisted that careful study of the relevant facts could suggest new ways to increase the efficiency of economic organizations and allow a fairer distribution of the nation's growing wealth.

As Progressivism flourished, Brandeis established himself as one of its major spokesmen and the legal profession's most controversial reformer. He fought the efforts of New York and Boston investment bankers to consolidate their control over transportation and public utility services in Massachusetts, and in 1908 he won a landmark Progressive victory before the Supreme Court in *Muller v. Oregon,* defending an Oregon statute that limited the employment of women factory workers to ten hours a day. [5] Two years later, in the notorious "Ballinger-Pinchot affair," he helped expose the dubious if not fraudulent transfer of valuable mining claims from the Interior Department to private financial interests. His dogged probing eventually forced President William Howard Taft and his attorney general to acknowledge predating an official report in an effort to exonerate the secretary of the interior. Congress canceled the transfers, and

Taft and his allies never forgave Brandeis for the public humiliation he inflicted on them.

As his influence grew, Brandeis moved into presidential politics.[6] A friend and admirer of Senator Robert M. La Follette, he stumped a number of states supporting the latter's campaign for the Republican presidential nomination in 1912. When La Follette's effort failed, Brandeis, formally a Democrat, shifted to Woodrow Wilson, who had emerged as a strong Progressive force in the Democratic Party. By the end of the year he had become one of Wilson's key advisors. After the election he worked with the new administration on several major bills and became the president's most trusted consultant on economic issues. Repeatedly urging that the anti-trust laws be strengthened, he helped draft the Federal Trade Commission Act of 1914, which created a new federal agency to supervise business behavior and restrict efforts to consolidate corporate power.

In January 1916, bidding for Progressive support in what promised to be a closely contested reelection campaign, Wilson nominated Brandeis to the Supreme Court. Business groups and conservative Republicans reacted fiercely. With a largely covert anti-Semitism fueling their deep hostility, they charged Brandeis with lack of a "judicial temperament" and unethical conduct in his law practice. "Where others were radical," insisted the *Wall Street Journal,* Brandeis "was rabid." Taft sought his revenge. Privately, he denounced Brandeis sweepingly as "a muckraker, an emotionalist for his own purposes, a socialist, prompted by jealousy, a hypocrite," as well as a man of "unscrupulous" methods and "infinite cunning" who had "much power for evil."[7] Publicly, he joined several past presidents of the American Bar Association in a formal statement that proclaimed Brandeis "unfit" to hold judicial office.

Progressives rallied to Brandeis's side, and Wilson informed the Senate that he was firmly committed to his nominee. Brandeis, the president announced, was a man "singularly enlightening, singularly clear-sighted and judicial, and, above all, full of moral stimulation."[8] The Senate Judiciary Committee held extensive hearings to investigate the charges against him, but the voluminous evidence proved little more than the existence of a political and professional chasm between the two sides. In a near perfect party vote on June 1, 1916, the Senate approved the nomination 47 to 22. Only three Republicans—including La Follette and George W. Norris—voted for confirmation, while only a single conservative Democrat opposed the nominee. Many Republican Progressives compromised by abstaining.

Evolution of a Judicial Philosophy: Values and Choices

Once on the Court, Brandeis refused to write or speak publicly and devoted himself to the judicial task. He often wrote for the majority and was personally on good terms with all the justices except James C. McReynolds, an irascible anti-Semite who got along well with no one on the Court and few off it. Brandeis operated quietly and effectively, adapting to the constraints imposed by the Court's institutional structure and sometimes modifying its decisions even when he could not command a majority for his preferred position.[9] In spite of his quiet influence, he was usually in the minority on pivotal and divisive constitutional issues. It was in the context of his twenty-year experience as a dissenter that he developed the two outstanding themes of his judicial career, Progressivism and restraint.[10]

Although Brandeis no longer engaged in public politics, his judicial opinions frequently articulated the values of Progressivism and nourished the activism of others. He repeatedly criticized the assumptions of the Court's conservative majority, calling for a greater flexibility in interpreting the Constitution and a greater attention to the harsh human consequences of industrialism. He appealed to both legal doctrines and empirical evidence to support the "reasonableness" of Progressive legislation and seldom tired in his efforts to persuade the Court to accept reform legislation.[11]

During Brandeis's first year on the bench, the Court voided an award made under the New York Workman's Compensation Act. In *New York Central Railroad Co. v. Winfield* it ruled that the Federal Employers' Liability Act (FELA) preempted the field of compensation for workers injured in interstate commerce.[12] In the circumstances of the case the New York act provided the injured plaintiff with a remedy, but the federal statute did not. Deeply committed to industrial compensation programs, Brandeis dissented. Examining the history of workmen's compensation laws and the FELA, he argued that Congress did not intend to preempt the field and that the award under state law should be upheld.

Winfield presented a clear example of conflicting judicial values. The language of the FELA was inconclusive on the preemption issue. The majority found the argument for preemption compelling because it valued "uniformity" in the rules of liability affecting interstate commerce.[13] Such uniformity might have simplified the legal obligations of interstate carriers, and it tended to restrict their liability.[14] Brandeis, however, found the argument against preemption compelling for a more specific social reason: "our individualistic conception of rights and liability no longer furnished an adequate basis for dealing with accidents in industry."[15] The lesson of the workmen's compensation movement, he maintained, was that "[a]ttention should be directed not to the employer's fault, but to the employee's misfortune."[16] States had the right to protect their citizens and a duty "to avert misery and promote happiness so far as possible."[17] Brandeis's view expanded the authority of state legislatures, broadened the possibilities for comprehensive state compensation programs, and upheld the more rigorous safety standards that many states had adopted. Essentially, he argued that the majority gave no substantial practical reason for interpreting an inconclusive statute as preemptive, and he attempted to show why it should be construed otherwise. Only one other justice joined him: the Progressive John J. Clarke, another Wilson appointee. The majority's decision, Brandeis confided privately, "laid me low."[18]

Although relations with his colleagues were cordial, Brandeis felt keenly the differences in substantive social values that separated him from the majority. The "lines of cleavage on the court" did not derive from party affiliations, he explained in the mid-1920s. The "[r]eal line of difference is on progressiveness." The justices, Brandeis believed, held profoundly contrasting "views as to property."[19] In 1920, for example, the Court ruled in *Eisner v. Macomber* that Congress could not tax certain kinds of stock dividends, and Brandeis dissented, emphasizing the decision's inequitable social results.[20] "If stock dividends representing profits are held exempt from taxation under the Sixteenth Amendment," he protested, "the owners of the most successful businesses in America will, as the facts in this case illustrate, be able to escape taxation on a large part of what is actually their income."[21]

His early years on the Court confirmed for Brandeis the widely shared Progressive conviction that the conservative majority was sometimes driven by class bias. Until he joined the Court, he declared, he "never realized" the extent to which the justices were "diverted by passion and prejudice and how closed the mind can be."[22] His colleagues were influenced in "large part" by "personal considerations," and they were frequently directed by a pervasive social prejudice that "unconsciously operates."[23] Most striking was the Court's bias against labor unions. "There," Brandeis declared, "its prejudices become active."[24]

From the nation's high bench Brandeis gave voice to that fundamental Progressive complaint. Many citizens believed that "the social and economic ideas of judges" were readily "translated into law," he declared, and they believed further that those ideas "were prejudicial to a position of equality between workman and employer."[25] Dissenting in the early 1930s, he turned the complaint into a warning. In exercising the "high power" of judicial review, he admonished the Court, "we must be ever on our guard, lest we erect our prejudices into legal principles."[26]

Burns Baking Co. v. Bryan illustrated his minority plight.[27] There, the Court held unconstitutional a Nebraska statute designed to protect consumers from short-weighted bread by prohibiting bakers from selling loaves which exceeded various maximum weight limits. Brandeis defended the statute, and three other justices initially voted with him to uphold it. Then the anti-Progressives "got busy," Brandeis complained, and they induced two of the justices—George

Sutherland and Edward T. Sanford—"to suppress their dissents." When the decision was announced, a solid seven-member majority confronted the dissenting Brandeis, who was joined only by Holmes. "Results are thus achieved," he complained, "not by legal reasoning, but by finesse and subtlety." [28] The decision, he moaned, was "worse even than *Lochner*." [29]

Brandeis's dissent in *Burns Baking* echoed the assumptions of Progressivism and characterized his approach in dealing with due process challenges to the "reasonableness" of regulatory legislation. Starting with the statute's rational purpose, he examined the realities of bread-making and the difficulties of protecting consumers from short-weighting. Then, in considerable detail, he reviewed empirical evidence that demonstrated the practical utility of the regulatory scheme the Nebraska legislature had adopted. "Knowledge is essential to understanding," he chided the majority in characteristic Progressive tones; "and understanding should precede judging." [30] Repeatedly appealing to "experience," he cited government investigations, congressional hearings, and the "experiments of competent scientists" to show how and why the statute would operate effectively. Completing the survey, he ended abruptly.[31] "To decide, as a fact," that the statute was unreasonable "is, in my opinion, an exercise of the powers of a super-legislature—not the performance of the constitutional functions of judicial review." [32]

Evolution of a Judicial Philosophy: Counterstrategy and Counterpoint

Brandeis's dissent in *Burns Baking* illustrated not only his Progressive method and values but also his insistence that the Court allow legislatures broad leeway and confine its own work narrowly. In the context of his seemingly permanent minority status, Brandeis's Progressivism helped inspire the second major theme of his judicial career, the desirability of judicial restraint. "[T]he most important thing we do," he told Frankfurter, "is not doing." [33]

Judicial restraint for Brandeis took three forms. First, on the level of judicial review, he believed with Holmes that legislatures possessed broad power and that the courts should sustain statutes unless unquestionably contrary to the Constitution. "Statute-Killers when confronted with an objectionable law say: How can I manage to hold it void?" he explained. "Constitutionalists say— How can I manage to sustain it?" [34] Second, quite different from Holmes, he emphasized the importance of keeping the courts strictly within the confines of their jurisdiction, not merely the clear limits imposed by statutes but also the vaguer limits implied by the "case" or "controversy" clause of Article III. Courts should not hear suits unless they constituted "actual" disputes between concretely adverse parties, where the claim was "ripe" for adjudication and the court could render an effective judgment.[35] Finally, Brandeis urged the necessity of restraint in the application and elaboration of constitutional doctrine. Opinions should be written narrowly to deal with the specific case presented, and the Court should avoid ruling on constitutional issues if any valid alternative ground was available.[36]

Brandeis adumbrated his philosophy of judicial restraint in numerous cases, but he articulated it most fully in his 1936 concurrence in *Ashwander v. Tennessee Valley Authority*.[37] There, Brandeis drew together a wide range of cases and used them to formulate what he described as the rules under which the Court "has avoided passing upon a large part of all the constitutional questions pressed upon it for decision." He identified them as follows. First, "[t]he Court will not pass upon the constitutionality of legislation in a friendly, nonadversary, proceeding." Second, "[t]he Court will not 'anticipate a question of constitutional law in advance of the necessity of deciding it.' "[38] Third, "[t]he Court will not 'formulate a rule of constitutional law broader than is required by the precise facts to which it is to be applied.' " Fourth, "[t]he Court will not pass upon a constitutional question although properly presented by the record, if there is also present some other ground upon which the case may be disposed of." Fifth, "[t]he Court will not pass upon the validity of a statute upon complaint of one who fails to show that he is injured by its operation."[39] Sixth, "[t]he Court will not pass upon the constitutionality of a statute at the instance of one who has availed himself of its benefits." Finally, the Court would not pass upon the constitutionality of a statute without first ascertaining "whether a construction of the statute is fairly possible by which the question may be avoided."[40]

Those rules of judicial restraint appealed to Brandeis for a variety of reasons. First, they conformed to his belief in the power and limitations of human reason as well as his sense of personal and institutional integrity. While he understood that legal issues which directly implicated divisive social conflicts would often fragment the Court, he believed that issues relating to technical jurisdictional and procedural matters commonly were resolvable by settled norms and careful reasoning. One function of law (committed for the most part to the legislature) was to adapt established rules to changing human conditions, while another function (entrusted to the courts) was to maintain systematic rules for the fair and rational processing of disputes. Brandeis's intense concern with jurisdictional matters was in part the outgrowth of his belief in the possibilities of human reason and his belief that reason could enjoy its widest scope in dealing with such issues.

Second, Brandeis believed in judicial restraint as an instrument for limiting the jurisdiction of the federal courts, preventing the continued expansion of their caseload, and preserving their quality and prestige. The heavy dockets that came with Prohibition meant that the courts were pressed to dispose of cases quickly and that they could not give them proper judicial scrutiny. The rising caseload also created pressures for the appointment of additional judges, a result that Brandeis believed would lower the general quality of the federal bench, especially given the appointments that the Republican presidents were making in the 1920s. The Coolidge administration, he complained, "is debauching the judiciary with inexcusable political appointments." [41] As the caseload mounted, he spoke increasingly of the need to "generally reduce federal jurisdiction." [42]

Third, Brandeis embraced the idea of judicial restraint because it embodied the authentic ideals of early twentieth-century Progressivism. It reflected commitment to popular government and democratic processes. It reflected faith in the scientific power of factual investigation and the benevolent potential of legislative experimentation. It reflected suspicion of the courts, bodies that were limited by an abstract doctrinal method and, all too often, by the conservative social biases of their judges.[43] Judicial restraint, the plea of the elaborately fact-based "Brandeis brief" that he had originated in *Muller v. Oregon*, provided a constitutional theory that accorded with his deepest political and social values.

Fourth, Brandeis's commitment to judicial restraint was rooted firmly and purposely in his acute awareness of its tactical uses. For Brandeis, unlike Holmes, judicial restraint was a method to defend Progressive values threatened by a hostile judiciary. It was intended to narrow the number and breadth of their anti-Progressive decisions, to broaden the range of allowable legislative authority, and to block some of the avenues down which corporate litigants marched when seeking the haven of a federal forum.[44]

Finally, the idea of judicial restraint appealed to Brandeis on an intensely personal level. As a socially marginal figure, a spectacularly successful Jew from Brahmin Boston in a profession dominated by Anglo-Saxon Protestants, he sought to identify with and create symbols of judicial propriety.[45] As a justice who had been the target of an organized anti-Progressive and tacitly anti-Semitic campaign to block his appointment, Brandeis strove to exhibit a rigorous judicial demeanor. His philosophy of restraint provided an effective repudiation to the charges his adversaries had brought against him in his confirmation battle. It undoubtedly gave the austere Brandeis deep satisfaction to raise before the elite bar the most meticulous of jurisdictional and procedural standards and to do so in the general, if usually implicit, service of Progressive ends.

It was in the early 1920s, with Progressivism in eclipse and the conservative wing of the Republican Party in control of all three branches of the national government, when Brandeis began methodically to formulate and preach his "philosophy" of judicial restraint. Responding to the anti-Progressive decisions of the Taft Court in 1922, he outlined to his friend and confidante Felix Frank-furter the basic ideas that he would later announce in *Ashwander.* "The remedy for the prevailing discontent" with the Court, he explained, "must be sought" in technical jurisdictional rules that would prevent or delay it from reaching the merits of cases.[46] Such jurisdictional rules, he declared a month later, were "the only effective remedy" for the Court's excessive actions "in holding statutes un-constitutional."[47]

Brandeis's advocacy of restraint was seldom far removed from his Pro-gressive goals. Sometimes he carried a majority with him. His tact, craftsman-ship, and insistence that the Court had no right to judge the "wisdom" of legislation helped forge a bare five-justice majority that sustained an Arizona workmen's compensation statute in 1919 and smoothed the way for the Court's acceptance of similar laws in other states.[48] Three years later his forceful insis-tence upon the careful application of doctrine again allowed him to persuade a majority to limit the reach of the federal courts in imposing burdens on labor unions under the anti-trust laws.[49]

More frequently, however, his pleas came in dissent.[50] In *Pennsylvania v. West Virginia,* for example, he urged that a suit challenging the constitutionality of a statute intended to regulate companies operating natural gas pipelines be dismissed because it did not present a justiciable controversy within the scope of Article III.[51] Privately, he identified his social goal. The Court's decision, which his jurisdictional argument would have prevented, "means rich states can with-draw power from poor states."[52]

Indeed, in *Ashwander* itself, Brandeis was moved by social concerns. Agreeing with the Court's constitutional ruling upholding certain powers of the New Deal's Tennessee Valley Authority, he concurred separately to protest the majority's threshold ruling that stockholders had standing to seek an injunction against corporate officials who complied with allegedly unconstitutional stat-utes. Such a broad rule of standing, he believed, would open the federal courts to a wide range of corporate challenges to legislative action. Only months after *Ash-wander* it was just such a stockholders' suit that provided the procedural vehicle that allowed the Court to hear *Carter v. Carter Coal Co.,* where, with Brandeis dis-senting on the merits, it held the New Deal's Guffey Coal Act unconstitutional.[53]

The persistent congruence between Brandeis's advocacy of restraint and his Progressive values was illustrated clearly in *Dahnke-Walker v. Bondurant,* a case that presented an abstruse jurisdictional question apparently far removed from social issues.[54] The Court, invalidating the particular application of a Ken-tucky statute that regulated local activities of foreign corporations, reversed a decision of the state's highest court by taking jurisdiction on the basis of a writ of error as opposed to a writ of *certiorari.* The former represented an appeal as of right for the losing party, an appeal that the Court was required to hear; the latter was a discretionary writ, one granted only when the Court chose for its own reasons to hear a case. Brandeis dissented, maintaining that under the appropriate jurisdictional statute the suit was reviewable only on *certiorari*.[55] He sought to draw a relatively clean line between the kinds of suits that were reviewable by each writ, to limit those that gave rise to an appeal as of right, and to effectuate the purpose of the jurisdictional statute "to relieve an overburdened court."[56]

Brandeis's argument was highly technical, but it was driven by his Progressive social concerns. The result of the majority's decision, Brandeis pointed out, was that an appeal as of right would depend "not upon the nature of the constitutional question involved but upon the skill of counsel" in framing issues for appeal.[57] As a result, "large classes of cases" would become reviewable as of right. He identified three: "proceedings under State Workmen's Compensation Acts or State Employers' Liability Acts," suits challenging the validity of state taxation, and "suits in state courts against foreign corporations."[58] His point was clear, if not fully elaborated. The majority's decision rewarded parties who could retain the most skilled counsel and who could afford additional appeals. Workers asserting claims for industrial injuries and plaintiffs seeking relief against foreign corporations would be faced with the knowledge that their adversaries could impose substantial additional costs and delays on them by taking appeals, as of right, all the way to the Supreme Court of the United States. The broader the scope given to the writ of error, Brandeis understood, the greater the practical litigation leverage that wealthier parties would enjoy.[59]

Thus, in this most arcane and technical area, Brandeis remained attuned to the likely social consequences of legal rules in the context of actual litigation. As someone who had been an artful and tenacious litigator, he understood well that to litigants and their attorneys jurisdictional and procedural rules were only tools to be used as partisan weapons in any advantageous way possible. "[E]xperience affords ample basis," he insisted in 1936, that expanded procedural options enabled "wealthy and litigious" corporations to "practically nullify" regulatory legislation.[60] As a Progressive judge, he sought to limit the practical harms and inequitable results that such weapons could cause. In the 1920s and 1930s the prescription of "judicial restraint" served that purpose well.

Crucible: The Declaratory Judgment

Although Progressivism and restraint were generally compatible, there were exceptions.[61] The most striking occurred when Brandeis confronted the declaratory judgment, a "remedy" that he regarded as dangerous and disruptive. The declaratory judgment, Brandeis insisted to Frankfurter, was "so obviously bad in American affairs."[62] It would magnify judicial power by turning "specific questions of fact" into abstract matters of "law."[63] It would encourage anti-Progressive judicial activism and discourage reform legislation by simplifying and expediting due process challenges to government action. It would defeat Progressive legislation at birth and thereby deny society the opportunity to implement, learn from, and improve its regulatory methods. Finally, it would deny Progressives the practical successes that would demonstrate the "reasonableness" of their reform proposals.[64]

The declaratory judgment was a remedy recognized in Scottish jurisprudence and added by statute to British equity practice in the middle of the nineteenth century.[65] It was a final and binding adjudication of rights that issued without an accompanying order of execution, and its supporters hailed it as a preventive or facilitative device that could determine rights prior to actual injury and prevent wasted time and needless effort. Considered an equitable remedy, it issued at the court's discretion. Unlike the injunction, however, declaratory relief did not require a showing of immediate and irreparable harm nor was it necessarily barred by the existence of an adequate remedy at law. The declaratory judgment was used primarily to resolve questions of status, such as matrimony and ownership, and to construe written documents whose meaning was disputed. Compared with other remedies, it offered three distinct advantages. First, it allowed parties to seek adjudication relatively early, for it did not require actual injury. Second, it could provide relief against threatened injury, not solely actual harm. Third, it allowed parties to seek declarations not just that they had a certain right but that their adversaries did not have an inconsistent right. Hence, it allowed "party reversal." Those who would otherwise have had to await action by their adversaries and enter court as defendants, in other words, could take the initiative as declaratory judgment plaintiffs and seek preemptive adjudications denying whatever rights their adversaries could claim.

Because the declaratory judgment was not part of traditional equity, American courts regarded its use as beyond their inherent powers. Before World War I, in fact, the declaration of rights was scarcely known in the United States, and not until the New Jersey legislature authorized it in 1915 did any state adopt an effective declaratory procedure.[66] During the next few years a number of law school teachers began urging its wider use, and Edwin M. Borchard, a professor at Yale Law School, emerged as its most fervent advocate. In a stream of law review articles and letters to judges, he extolled the device as a method of increasing judicial efficiency by making suits simpler, less expensive, and less time-consuming.[67] Soon, the American Bar Association and numerous state and local bar groups endorsed it.[68] By 1921 five states had passed legislation authorizing their courts to issue declaratory relief, a number that jumped to twenty-three by 1928 and then to thirty-four six years later.[69]

Use of the declaratory judgment by American courts raised a special problem. The United States Constitution and the constitutions of many states limited the exercise of judicial power to "cases" and "controversies," actual and immediate disputes between concretely adverse parties in which courts could render final and binding judgments. The federal courts and most state courts were thereby precluded from rendering "advisory opinions," generalized rulings on pending legislation or on legal disputes that were hypothetical, premature, or somehow collusive. Frequently, courts assumed that a constitutional case or controversy required a showing of actual injury that could be remedied by a mandatory order of execution. The appearance of the declaratory judgment, then, raised two related constitutional questions: whether judgments that were merely "declaratory" constituted unauthorized "advisory opinions"; and whether Congress and state legislatures could, under their respective constitutions, authorize their courts to grant such declaratory relief.

The proponents of the declaratory judgment argued persuasively that enabling legislation was constitutionally permissible. Denying vehemently that the declaratory judgment was an advisory opinion, they insisted that it would issue only in actual and concrete controversies. The remedy was entrusted to the court's discretion, and any dispute that was inchoate, hypothetical, or contrived would be dismissed pursuant to established practice. Further, they argued that an enforcement order was often unnecessary in a society that recognized the rule of law.[70] Neither equitable doctrines nor constitutional limitations, they pointed out, precluded courts from granting preventive relief as such.[71]

In 1920 the Supreme Court of Michigan became the first state supreme court to pass on the issue. In *Anway v. Grand Rapids Railway Co.* it held that the state's enabling statute violated the Michigan constitution because it attempted to authorize the exercise of judicial power "in advance of any existing controversy."[72] State legislatures continued to authorize the device, however, and by 1925 the supreme courts of five other states had upheld their enabling acts.[73]

Despite the growing support for the declaratory judgment, to some Progressives *Anway* was a warning shot. The Michigan legislature had passed a statute prohibiting street railway companies from employing motormen and conductors "more than six days in any consecutive seven days."[74] In 1918 the Grand Rapids Railway Company signed a contract with the local railway workers union which required that disputes be submitted to binding arbitration. When disagreement over the six-day law arose, an arbitrator enforced the statute's limiting provision. Bound by its agreement with the union, the company had no further legal remedy. Suddenly, and quite soon thereafter, Charles Anway, a nonunion conductor, came forward and sued the company for a judgment, declaring that the statute did not prohibit the company from allowing him to work a seven-day week. The company answered, "admitting the allegations of the bill." [75] The union hastened to intervene as a party defendant in support of the arbitration decision and the six-day statute. In a jumbled opinion the court's majority dismissed the suit on the ground that the declaratory judgment statute violated the state's constitution.

The suit, almost certainly collusive, failed to invalidate the six-day law, but it did reveal the advantages that the declaratory judgment offered to companies fighting unions or challenging regulatory laws. By inducing third parties to sue, they could avoid any limitations imposed in their union contracts while having the issue presented to the courts and the public as a matter of "individual" freedom. By appearing as defendants, moreover, they could concede critical facts, avoid elaborate trials, and scuttle any serious defense. Further, they could challenge regulatory statutes more quickly and without proof of actual injury or irreparable harm, and they could obtain a declaration of unconstitutionality without bringing the government in as a party defendant. Revealingly, Borchard saw the plaintiff in *Anway* simply as an individual nonunion member who "wished to work more than six days a week." [76] The secretary-treasurer of the International Seamen's Union described the case differently. *Anway,* he informed William Green, the president of the AFL, was a "frame-up" against the local union. [77]

Although Brandeis could not join the public debate, Frankfurter made the case against the declaratory judgment for him. Ostensibly replying to a law review article that defended advisory opinions, Frankfurter argued that all procedural devices that accelerated judgment served primarily to strengthen the power of the judiciary over the legislature and to restrict the possibilities of intelligent social legislation. Accelerated adjudication of constitutional issues meant that legal questions would be determined "abstractly" and would necessarily "result in sterile conclusions unrelated to actualities." [78] The "controversy between legislature and courts, in issues which matter most," he maintained, "is not at all a controversy about legal principles, but concerns the application of admitted principles to complicated and often elusive facts." [79] Hoping to preserve as much sway as possible for the "Brandeis brief," which had saved so many Progressive statutes, Frankfurter argued that accelerated adjudication deprived legislatures of their "creative function," prevented the growth of social knowledge through legislative experiments, and weakened "legislative and popular responsibility." [80] Moreover, judicial review was ultimately a "political function," he warned, and "grave dangers" loomed if the courts did not rigorously restrict its use. [81] "To meet the intricate, stubborn, and subtle problems of modern industrialism," Frankfurter pleaded, "the legislature must be given ample scope for putting its prophecies to the test of proof."[82] Premature adjudications were "ghosts that slay."[83]

Corporate lawyers and anti-Progressives, of course, were well aware of the uses of accelerated adjudication. Everett P. Wheeler, the chairman of the ABA Committee on Jurisprudence and Law Reform, argued that the declaratory judgment would "decrease the volume of litigation" because actions for such relief "would necessarily be in most cases [based] upon conceded facts."[84] His reasoning suggested precisely what some legal Progressives feared — collusive suits upon "conceded facts." Similarly, in 1933 and 1934 Republican Senator Arthur H. Vandenburg of Michigan, a vigorous opponent of the New Deal, explored the possibility of a constitutional amendment that would authorize the Supreme Court to render advisory opinions on constitutional issues. Congress repeatedly confronted constitutional questions, he wrote privately to a number of anti–New Deal attorneys, and uncertainty about their constitutionality blocked some measures and left many of those enacted in limbo for years. There was, he wrote, "grave danger *today* from the lack of a 'short cut' to conclusive constitutional determinations." Admitting that he was not a lawyer, Vandenburg stressed that "I do know the precise objective which I want to reach."[85]

Congress had considered declaratory judgment legislation since 1921 when proponents, spearheaded by the ABA, introduced an enabling bill. Although Senator Thomas J. Walsh and a number of Progressives opposed it, the bill gradually gained support.[86] The House Judiciary Committee reported it favorably in 1925 and again in 1926, and in January 1928 the full House passed it. Pressure mounted for action in the Senate, and in April and May the Senate Judiciary Committee held hearings on the bill.

In an eleventh-hour move, Brandeis seized what came to hand.[87] Three days after the Senate Judiciary Committee ended its hearings, he announced the Court's opinion in *Willing v. Chicago Auditorium Association*.[88] Holding that a suit to establish title to land was not cognizable in federal equity, Brandeis sought to deal a lethal blow to the pending bill. "What the plaintiff seeks is simply a declaratory judgment," he declared. "To grant that relief is beyond the power conferred upon the Federal judiciary."[89] That jurisdictional bar, he emphasized, was constitutional. "The proceeding does not present a case or controversy within the range of judicial decision as defined in Article 3 of the Federal Constitution."[90] To support the conclusion that the nature of the relief sought created the constitutional bar, Brandeis emphasized that the suit was not moot, that the parties were clearly adverse, that the plaintiff had a "substantial interest" to protect, and that the suit presented "no attempt to secure an abstract determination."[91] Jurisdiction failed, then, only because the suit sought what was, in effect, a declaratory judgment. Such relief, Brandeis insisted, did not fall "within the meaning of Article 3 of the Constitution."[92] His point was fundamental. The Constitution itself precluded the federal courts from granting declaratory judgments, and Congress therefore could not grant them the power to issue such relief.

As a practical matter, the decision seemed unwise. Plaintiffs were seeking to build a $15 million commercial facility in Chicago, but uncertainties over provisions in their leaseholds on the property had brought the project to a halt. An authoritative ruling settling the respective rights of the various parties would have allowed plaintiffs to proceed fairly and confidently. *Willing* seemed, in fact, to present exactly the kind of controversy that the declaratory judgment was designed to remedy. The fair and reasonable plea, however, failed to move Brandeis. On a critical issue of social and political policy, it conflicted with his broader agenda.[93]

As a legal matter, moreover, the decision's constitutional language was clearly unnecessary. It was adequate to say, as Justice Stone pointed out in his concurrence, that such relief was simply "unauthorized under any statute."[94] Indeed, Stone gently but deftly skewered Brandeis on his own principles. "And the determination now made seems to be very similar itself to a declaratory judgment to the effect that we could not constitutionally be authorized to give such judgments."[95]

Brandeis's opinion, however, was directed not to courts or lawyers or constitutional theorists but to the Senate, where the declaratory judgment bill was literally on the verge of passage. His stratagem came in the nick of time. Andrew Furuseth, the president of the International Seamen's Union and the tireless opponent of the labor injunction, was one of the Progressives who picked up his signal. Upon reading *Willing,* Furuseth immediately called Senator Norris's attention to Brandeis's warning and urged him to block the pending bill.[96] Support in the Senate Judiciary Committee dissipated, and the bill died without a vote.

For five years the matter hung in the balance. The House Judiciary Committee twice more reported the declaratory judgment bill favorably, and in 1932 the full body passed it a second time.[97] Not only did the House contain fewer Progressives who occupied less strategic positions than those in the Senate, but many Progressives and states'-rights advocates were convinced of the bill's desirability. The fact that so many states had already adopted the device reassured states'-righters, and many Progressives were attracted by its promises to simplify procedure and increase judicial efficiency. "I believe it is a piece of Progressive legislation," LaGuardia told the House. "We have a similar statute in New York."[98]

The bill's academic supporters, in the meantime, were assiduously and effectively undermining the authority of the Court's language in *Willing.* A

dozen law review articles demonstrated that the Court's constitutional assertions were dicta and that none of its prior decisions actually held that Congress
could not authorize the federal courts to grant declaratory relief."[99] Criticizing
Brandeis's supererogatory language in *Willing*, Borchard insisted that the claim
of a constitutional impediment "can hardly be supported."[100]

Challenged by the powerful counterattack, the rapidly dwindling Progressive opposition gave ground, reluctant to acknowledge that their true
objection was political, not doctrinal or logical. Frankfurter claimed that the
declaratory judgment faced "barriers in the Constitution not revealed to the unsophisticated eye of the layman," and he suggested vaguely but portentously that
it raised "distinctively American problems of political science."[101] His position
inspired an anonymous note, published in the 1932 *Harvard Law Review*, pushing Brandeis's argument as far as decorum allowed. Admitting that *Willing* was
flawed, the note suggested that Brandeis's opinion was nevertheless based on
"the existence of some strong reason which urged the undesirability of declaratory judgments in federal practice."[102] The Court was the final arbiter "of our
political and economic systems," and declaratory rulings were especially "likely
to be a mere speculation as to policy on the part of the Court."[103] The political message, though costumed in the garb of institutional efficiency, was clear
enough. "Thus, if the declaratory judgment works perfectly," the note warned,
"there will be nothing to prevent the presentation of all legislation to the Court
immediately upon its passage."[104]

Defenders of the declaratory judgment replied quickly. Responding in
the *Harvard Law Review*, Dean Charles E. Clark criticized the note and deni-
grated *Willing* as a "conceptualistic declaration."[105] Borchard identified the ille-
gitimacy of the note's defense. He upbraided its author and, if its analysis were
correct, Brandeis himself for the "unfortunate" practice of relying on "inarticulate major premises" to support "occult" decisions. The author's "imaginative
fears" about constitutional litigation, Borchard declared, were without empirical support and belied by "vast experience."[106]

Responding privately to Clark, Frankfurter exploded in sarcastic and
condescending rage. Brandeis, he declared, was "seeking to enforce a social
policy that is to him very important," and the case or controversy clause was
simply "the only intellectual device open to him." He made both of the salient
points. The declaratory judgment would magnify "the ways of the Supreme
Court of the United States toward social legislation" and increase the "ease" with
which "astute counsel" could manipulate procedures "on sterilized statements of
fact." Brandeis, Frankfurter concluded sharply, might "know more about these
matters than even the most brooding student of [the] declaratory judgment."[107]

Clark represented the views of many Progressives, particularly academics interested in rationalizing the legal system.[108] The declaratory judgment was a "convenient" device for adjudicating certain kinds of issues, he replied, and Brandeis's constitutional language represented an unwise judicial technique. "[W]henever a judge uses the Constitution to solidify procedure," Clark explained, "I must confess I see red for it seems to me it vitiates the whole process of law administration." Moreover, he continued, Brandeis's "great fears" about judicial intervention were "well-nigh fantastically remote." The Supreme Court, Clark concluded "does not and should not delay necessary and important decisions in the hope that light will break upon it through such delay." [109]

Increasingly trapped doctrinally and isolated politically, Brandeis and Frankfurter at last fell silent as events overtook them. First, the Court changed. Stone overcame whatever remaining doubts he had after exchanging a series of letters with Borchard, and Holmes, who had been unwilling to oppose Brandeis on the issue, left the Court in 1932.[110] Holmes's successor, Benjamin N. Cardozo, was already on record as favoring the declaratory judgment.[111] Second, the states continued to adopt the declaratory procedure, and by 1932 eighteen state supreme courts had upheld the legislation under their constitutions.[112] Finally, widespread acceptance in the states resulted in a dilemma for the Supreme Court. If state practice utilized the declaratory judgment but the United States Constitution placed it beyond federal judicial power, then the Supreme Court would be forced either to surrender its right to review state declaratory judgments involving federal questions or to create some special, implicit, and possibly awkward constitutional exception.

Resolution came quickly. In 1933 a unanimous bench ruled in *Nashville, Chattanooga & St. Louis Railway Co. v. Wallace* that the Court could hear and decide appeals from state decisions rendered under local declaratory judgment acts. Writing for the Court, Stone held that Article III allowed the Court to rule on declaratory judgment actions "so long as the case retains the essentials of an adversary proceeding, involving a real, not a hypothetical, controversy, which is finally determined by the judgment below." [113]

In effect, *Nashville* established the constitutionality of the declaratory judgment.[114] "The bogey which for so long confused the declaratory judgment with an advisory opinion on a moot case," Borchard crowed, "has thus finally been laid to rest." [115] Virtually alone, Frankfurter tried to emphasize *Nashville*'s limited nature. It was "not an enunciation of new criteria," he maintained, and the difficult questions were still "postponed to the future." [116]

The dam, however, had burst, and supporters of the federal bill turned expectantly to Congress. In early 1934, the House again passed it. With Walsh dead and Homer S. Cummings, Roosevelt's law-reforming attorney general, supporting the measure, the Senate Judiciary Committee reported it favorably.[117]

Citing *Nashville,* the committee announced that doubt concerning the constitutionality of the bill "has now been dissipated." [118] Shortly thereafter, Congress passed a bill authorizing the federal courts to grant declaratory relief.

Brandeis's effort had failed. He had, as Frankfurter told Clark, sought to enforce a "social policy" that was "very important to him." He fought to protect Progressive regulatory actions, limit corporate tools to challenge them, and minimize judicial opportunities to invalidate them. He was willing to violate his *Ashwander* principles to do so. Indeed, he not only reached an unnecessary constitutional question, but he did so for the precise purpose of imposing a substantive constitutional limitation on the power of Congress.

When Brandeis embraced a constitutional bar as his ultimate objection to the declaratory judgment, advocates of the device pushed him into a corner where he had no compelling argument save the political one. And that argument he could not make publicly, for it demonstrated that his constitutional position was merely pretextual. Moreover, admitting his true motive would have required him to defend the proposition that constitutional rights should be subservient to procedural limitations that were not only discretionary and manipulable but also designed to serve covert political purposes. As Borchard charged, such an "inarticulate major premise" was improper judicial technique. It was also a tool of dishonesty or unconscious prejudice. The latter vice, of course, was one of the principal judicial abuses that Progressives had condemned for half a century.

Brandeis's fight against the declaratory judgment revealed his willingness to use jurisdictional doctrines to serve his broader social and political goals. It showed the depth of his concern about the dangers of judicial power, the fate of Progressive legislation, and the threat of sophisticated and abusive litigation tactics. The fact was that few Progressives, at least by the early 1930s, shared his acute fear of the declaratory judgment or accepted his dire warnings about its consequences. Brandeis, however, had not been dissuaded from his views. He had merely lost a fight.

Approaching Erie: *Means, Motives, and Opportunity*

When *Erie* appeared on the Court's docket in late 1937, the *Ashwander* decision was less than two years old. Although three of its rules were not relevant, four were. The Court should not "anticipate" questions of constitutional law, Brandeis had written in *Ashwander,* and it should not "formulate a rule" broader than required by the "precise facts" of the case. In *Erie,* Brandeis declared that Congress lacked constitutional authority to legislate rules of "general federal common law." The "precise facts" of the case included no such congressional statute, and his statement seemed to "anticipate" the constitutional question that such a hypothetical statute would present. Further, he argued in *Ashwander* that the Court should avoid even a properly presented constitutional question if the case could be disposed of on "some other ground" and, finally, that it should construe statutes where possible so that "the [constitutional] question may be avoided." [119] Justice Reed's concurrence offered some "other ground," and that ground was the alternate construction of a statute. Indeed, Reed's approach fulfilled all four of *Ashwander*'s relevant injunctions.

Those injunctions, however, did not stop Brandeis. Was *Erie*, then, like *Willing*, animated by political and social considerations? Was it also, like *Willing*, a product of Brandeis's personal values and motives? The answer to both of those questions is yes.[120]

Was *Erie*, like *Willing*, a strained and unsound opinion? Was it also, like *Willing*, an improper or pretextual interpretation of the Constitution? The answer to both of those questions is no.

Judging, especially on the United States Supreme Court, is a special kind of human act, and in *Erie* Brandeis acted as both an understandable and reasonable human being and a wise and broad-visioned constitutional judge. His unflinching determination to use *Erie* to overrule *Swift* sprang from a combination of three quite different types of considerations. First, in terms of his tactical decision to act, the time was simply ripe. The opportunity and the instrument came to his hand, and Brandeis—like Justice Brewer in so many of his major decisions—would not see them wasted. Second, by the beginning of 1938 powerful personal motives—private and intimate as well as social and political—impelled him to act. *Erie* represented not merely another case, albeit a major one, but a special occasion that stirred him deeply. Third, *Erie* allowed Brandeis to achieve two Progressive goals that he considered fundamental: improving the social efficiency and practical fairness of the legal system, and bringing the lawmaking structure of American government into proper constitutional balance. The third consideration was crucial, for it justified him as a constitutional judge in seizing his opportunity and indulging his personal inclinations.

THE IMPETUS OF TIME: CARPE DIEM

Tactically, the overriding fact was that at the beginning of 1938, with the changes in the Court's personnel, there were at long last enough votes to overrule *Swift*. Cardozo's absence, too, may have strengthened Brandeis's ability to muster a majority for a flat overruling.[121] A genius at making the law appear changeless as he changed it, Cardozo had written opinions in the early 1930s narrowing *Swift* significantly.[122] Had he been present in 1938 to argue for a continued case-by-case whittling, his views might have influenced the Court.[123] Moreover, the ease with which he avoided *Swift* most likely reinforced Brandeis's belief that the general federal common law was so malleable that it would be futile merely to try to cabin it. The power that *Swift* conferred on the federal judiciary undeniably appealed to many of its judges, and a constrained *Swift* could always be set free. A flat overruling on constitutional grounds was necessary to lay the doctrine to final rest.[124]

Action by the Court also seemed essential because the altered political situation dispelled whatever hopes Brandeis had entertained that Congress would deal with *Swift* and diversity jurisdiction. The kinds of judicial reforms that Norris and Walsh had sponsored no longer commanded its attention. The Court-packing plan had shattered Roosevelt's congressional coalition, and the rapid emergence of foreign policy issues increasingly occupied national attention.[125] By late 1937 it was apparent that if the federal common law were to be interred, the Court itself would have to do it.

Finally, at the beginning of 1938 the Court was in the mood to make changes. After a long and bitter struggle, the justices of the emerging new majority were psychologically ready to jettison doctrine identified with the "old Court." They had begun the process the preceding term, and Brandeis shared the sense of excitement and vindication.[126] The pent-up political anger against the old Court encouraged the new majority to institutionalize what they regarded as the proper limits of the federal judiciary's lawmaking function.[127] In a period of turmoil and change strong measures seemed possible and necessary. As one of his former law clerks suggested, during 1937 and 1938 "the day-by-day pragmatic aspect" of the cases became paramount for Brandeis.[128]

THE IMPETUS OF THE PERSONAL: POLITICAL AND SOCIAL VALUES

If the mood and personnel of the Court in early 1938 made the overthrow of *Swift* possible, Brandeis was especially eager to bring it about. He believed deeply in the virtues of a decentralized federalism and in the advantages of small units of social organization.[129] The local unit, whenever it could function with reasonable efficiency, was the ideal unit, whether in government or industry.[130] Although he believed that small-unit organizations tended to be more efficient than large ones, he viewed the primary value of decentralization as moral. Only in small and local organizations could most individuals be responsible for themselves and develop their abilities to the fullest extent.[131] "The great developer," he claimed, "is responsibility." [132]

Brandeis's faith in the virtues of decentralization informed much of his jurisprudence, and on the Court he exhibited an acute concern for the preservation of the authority of the states. Defending the necessity and propriety of national power, he insisted "that recognition of Federal powers does not mean denial of State powers." [133] Decentralization worked to the advantage of both the nation and the cause of Progressivism. "It is one of the happy incidents of the federal system," he declared, "that a single courageous State may, if its citizens choose, serve as a laboratory and try novel social and economic experiments without risk to the rest of the country."[134]

His special devotion to the small unit extended to an appreciation for the integrity of local law, which, he believed, should be protected from unnecessary federal intrusions.[135] The proper scope of national law should be determined by practical social analysis; and, when uniformity was required, national standards should be enforced. Such a judgment, however, required careful study of specific issues, and the bias should be in favor of local organization. *Swift*, of course, represented precisely the kind of unnecessary centralization that offended Brandeis. It allowed federal judges to disregard state common law rules and frustrated the states' attempts to implement their local policies. Abolishing it would prevent unnecessary federal interference with those policies and give state judges their proper share of responsibility.[136]

Brandeis's faith in decentralization compounded his resentment against *Swift*, and it imbued him with special fervor in the late 1930s. Although he happily agreed with the emerging new majority in giving constitutional sanction to most New Deal measures, he was apprehensive about the increasing centralization that resulted. He was delighted with such measures as the Public Utilities Holding Company Act, which promised to break up utility combines, but other measures made him wary.[137] Above all, the National Industrial Recovery Act, which suspended the anti-trust laws, outraged him; and he readily joined the Court's unanimous decision invalidating it as an unconstitutional delegation of legislative power.[138] "This is the end of this business of centralization," he angrily told Tommy Corcoran, one of Frankfurter's students who had served as his law clerk and was currently a top Roosevelt advisor, "and I want you to go back and tell the President that we're not going to let this government centralize everything."[139] Like many of the older Progressives, and unlike most younger New Dealers, Brandeis saw dangers as well as benefits in the course Roosevelt was charting.[140] *Erie* could help counterbalance the New Deal's centralizing impact.

Brandeis also detected unwanted centralization in another area, far less significant politically but more immediately relevant to the judicial system. In 1934, the Rules Enabling Act, which he and Walsh had so long opposed, had authorized the Supreme Court to promulgate rules of procedure for both legal and equitable actions, and in December 1937 the newly drafted Federal Rules of Civil Procedure came before the Court for review. Brandeis alone dissented from the Court's approval, and he cherished the hope that Congress might veto the new rules.[141] He feared their potential rigidity; he felt that the Court should not take responsibility for a set of rules to which it could not give adequate consideration; and, likely most important, he believed that they represented yet another example of needless centralization.[142] By overruling *Swift*, the Court would establish a new area of decentralized authority and counterbalance the new centralizing Federal Rules.

The immediate political situation may also have prompted Brandeis to act. Roosevelt's court-packing plan offended him deeply — personally as well as constitutionally. Roosevelt had dispatched Corcoran to warn Brandeis about the plan, and the justice bluntly informed the messenger that he was "unalterably opposed to the President's action."[143] The Court's independence and integrity were at stake, he believed, and in the long run the plan would do far more damage than good. After the battle had raged for two and a half months, Brandeis announced his opposition when he approved the letter Chief Justice Hughes submitted to the Senate Judiciary Committee stating that the Court was fully abreast of its work.[144] The Court fight revealed the depth of popular anger at the Court and encouraged Brandeis in his efforts to constrain the national courts. *Erie*, a self-denying internal reform, would serve that goal.

THE IMPETUS OF THE PRIVATE: HOLMES AND RETIREMENT

The Court fight focused Brandeis's attention on another factor that pressed him to seize the opportunity *Erie* presented. Although he was one of the Court's staunchest Progressives, he was also its oldest member. Two months before Roosevelt announced his plan, Brandeis had marked his eightieth birthday.[145] The president's plan spawned in Brandeis an angry resentment against its emphasis on the advanced age of the Court and, in particular, its insinuation about the declining abilities of judges over seventy. Brandeis, Hughes observed, was "deeply wounded" by Roosevelt's remarks.[146] Nonetheless, as the oldest sitting justice he could hardly have failed to reflect on his inevitably hastening retirement. By 1937, in fact, Brandeis was showing unmistakable signs of physical frailty and declining energy. He had severely restricted his social activities, and during 1937 and 1938, his last two full years on the Court, he wrote fewer than half as many opinions as he had in earlier years.[147] In 1937, too, he was deeply shaken by more immediate and haunting events. Three of his oldest and closest friends died, two of them relatively suddenly.[148]

The fight over the Court bill forced Brandeis to confront his inevitable retirement in a particularly personal and distressing way. The bill implicitly identified him, the oldest justice, as the one who should most appropriately and promptly retire. Recognizing the growing impatience of Roosevelt and his supporters to remake the Court, Brandeis resented the mounting pressure he felt to resign, especially because it came from many whom he regarded as his longtime friends and supporters.[149]

Although Brandeis had no intention of leaving, especially in the face of pressure, the political battles and personal wounds of 1937 forced him to recognize that only a short time remained to him and that the end of his tenure could come quickly and unexpectedly. It was most unlikely that he would have another chance at *Swift*. Consciously or unconsciously, the promptings of age surely contributed to his determination to act with dispatch.[150]

Finally, Brandeis was inspired by a related motive, private and compelling. Perhaps because of his advancing age, he viewed *Erie* as an opportunity to pay his last respects to the departed Holmes. When Brandeis was nominated to the Court in 1916, he informed President Wilson's attorney general that "[m]y views in regard to the Constitution are as you know very much those of Mr. Justice Holmes."[151] The two had frequently been in agreement, especially on broad and bitterly divisive constitutional issues. "There seems a pre-established harmony between Brandeis and me," Holmes wrote a friend in 1928. "He agrees with all my dissents and I agree with the only one that he will propound [this term]."[152] By the 1920s, the phrase "Holmes and Brandeis dissenting" had become nationally known as a symbol for the opposition to the Court's conservative majority.

An element of opportunism existed in Brandeis's relationship with Holmes. By cultivating his widely respected senior colleague, Brandeis was able to draw Holmes and his prestige to the Progressive side on many of the most controversial issues that divided the Court. Pressing Holmes to study the "facts" of modern industry and encouraging him to dissent in cases where he might otherwise have remained silent, Brandeis helped cast Holmes as a great "Progressive" dissenter.[153] As Holmes grew weaker with age during the 1920s, in fact, Brandeis exerted a noticeable influence over him. Holmes had fallen "so completely under the control of Brother Brandeis," Chief Justice Taft complained, that the latter had "two votes instead of one."[154]

The personal bond between the two, however, was deep and genuine. Strikingly different in background and attitudes, they had developed during their years on the Court a special and profound mutual respect. Professional admiration, intellectual appreciation, judicial companionship, and personal affection bound them together. They not only consulted with one another and usually voted the same way, but also lived only a block apart and daily traveled to and from the Court together.[155] "Brandeis is in good shape—we generally go home together," Holmes wrote Frankfurter in 1924, when he was eighty-three and Brandeis only sixty-eight. "He insists on coming to my door and I express fears to trust him to get back across the street."[156]

Yet, at the same time, their friendship remained somewhat formal, the result of their styles of restraint in personal affairs as well as their mutual recognition of their differences. It was a friendship in which a deep, but largely unspoken, mutual bond had developed.[157] "I had a delightful note from Brandeis who told me that your companionship was the crown of his life," Harold Laski wrote Holmes in 1924. "As you know, he does not waste words."[158] "I am glad at what you say he wrote," Holmes responded on another occasion, "because he is a great comfort and help to me."[159] Holmes told Frankfurter that "I have known Brandeis for forty years and I have never left his presence without feeling that I have left a good man." Frankfurter remembered the remark clearly. "To me that observation was always most interesting," he explained, "because of no other man have I ever heard Holmes express himself in ethical terms."[160] Brandeis repaid the tribute in the appropriate coin. Holmes, he confided admiringly to Frankfurter, was "as wonderful in character as in brain."[161] The two justices conveyed their feelings toward one another largely through their conduct. They conveyed them through their words, perhaps, almost wholly through third parties. Brandeis, one of his finest biographers concluded, "loved Holmes."[162]

After Holmes's wife died in 1929, his health deteriorated dramatically; by the end of 1931 it was clear that he could no longer continue on the bench. After consulting with several members of the Court, Hughes approached Brandeis and asked him to speak with Holmes. Many years earlier Brandeis had promised Holmes that he would tell him when the time had come, but the promise proved one that Brandeis could not bear to keep. Agreeing that Holmes had to resign, he told Hughes that as chief justice, he would have to carry the burden. In January 1932 Hughes visited Holmes's townhouse and secured his agreement to retire. The chief justice left with tears in his eyes, and shortly thereafter Brandeis appeared at the door. He went into Holmes's office, and the two spoke for some time.[163]

Holmes's retirement, Frankfurter observed, left a "great personal void" in Brandeis's life.[164] Two or three times each week Brandeis faithfully visited Holmes, and the old man's face would light up when his maid announced Brandeis's presence. Rising feebly from his chair, Holmes would welcome his visitor and embrace him, repeating "My dear friend, my dear friend."[165] When Holmes died in 1935, Brandeis was so distressed that he could not attend the funeral.[166]

Two years after Holmes's death, during the Court term that preceded *Erie*, Willard Hurst served as Brandeis's law clerk. When he first read *Erie*, he was struck by the profound feelings of affection, respect, and loss for Holmes that he detected. "I was interested in the considerable stress on Mr. Justice Holmes in the Justice's opinion," Hurst wrote less than a month after *Erie* came down. "Several small indications seemed to me last year to warn one off the subject of Mr. Justice Holmes in speaking to the Justice." There was, Hurst came to believe, "feeling there so very deep as to be avoided."[167]

The challenge to *Swift* had become particularly identified with Holmes, whose opening broadside in *Kuhn* appeared twenty-eight years before *Erie*.[168]

In Brandeis's first term on the Court he had joined Holmes's dissent in *Southern Pacific Co. v. Jensen*, protesting an analogous development of federal common law in admiralty.[169] Then, in 1928, Holmes had broken his own rule never to dissent twice on the same issue. Writing for Brandeis and Stone, he had proclaimed the *Taxicab* case "exceptional" and charged *Swift* with authorizing unconstitutional federal judicial lawmaking.[170]

Brandeis was acutely aware of Holmes's special passion in striking at *Swift*. The *Taxicab* case was one "I care about," Holmes had written privately,[171] and he had confided to Frankfurter that it "is the only one that has stirred me much lately." [172] To Laski, he had declared that "I will have my whack if I live, if it is my last word." [173] The ideas that united his dissents in *Kuhn, Jensen,* and *Taxicab*—that the common law was no "brooding omnipresence," that there was no "law" that was not the law of some particular sovereign, and that *Swift*'s fallacious theory allowed the federal courts to act unconstitutionally—represented core elements of Holmes's jurisprudence.[174] "Holmes' dissent in the *Black & White Taxicab* case will stand among his notable opinions," Brandeis wrote after the decision came down. "It was," he noted, "delivered with fervor." [175]

Brandeis may even have sensed a parallel between Holmes's "fervor" concerning the *Swift* doctrine and his own implacable opposition to the declaratory judgment. A decade earlier, when Brandeis used *Willing* to block efforts to pass the declaratory judgment bill, Holmes had wished for a different decision. Nonetheless, he had refused to abandon Brandeis on an issue that was so important to him. "I do not care to join in the criticism of his opinion," Holmes informed Stone, refusing to sign on to the latter's narrow concurrence that invited the very congressional action Brandeis sought so desperately to forestall. "I also regret the conclusion that we cannot [issue] declaratory judgments." [176] Brandeis undoubtedly knew Holmes's views on the issue, and he surely appreciated what his friend had done for him.

Brandeis's opinion in *Erie* directly quoted and approved Holmes's earlier dissents, and it emphasized that the decision was turning on Holmes's analysis. "The fallacy underlying the rule declared in *Swift v. Tyson* is made clear by Mr. Justice Holmes," Brandeis wrote. And, again, "the doctrine of *Swift v. Tyson* is, as Mr. Justice Holmes said, 'an unconstitutional assumption of powers'." [177] Brandeis placed unusual weight on the words of one justice, especially in view of the fact that the words appeared only in dissent. Moreover, in his initial drafts Brandeis ignored Justice Field's earlier constitutional attack on *Swift* in his *Baugh* dissent, relying solely on Holmes. Although he subsequently incorporated a brief excerpt from Field, it was only after Hughes read from Field's dissent at the conference on April 9 that Brandeis decided to include in the final published opinion the longer quote from *Baugh*. Had Brandeis not been motivated by a desire to pay special homage to Holmes, it seems probable that he would have drafted his opinion differently: he would not have relied so heavily on the dissents of one justice, and he would have used the full relevant quote from Field in his earlier drafts as an authority equal in weight to Holmes. Perhaps, too, he might even have attempted to articulate the constitutional theory of *Erie* more fully than he did.

A year and a half after Holmes's retirement, Brandeis had sent him on his ninety-second birthday a copy of four lines from Goethe's *Iphigenie:* [178]

> *Blessed is he who cherishes the memory of his fathers*
> *Who, proud of their deeds, their greatness*
> *Entertains the listener, and quietly delights*
> *In seeing himself included at the end of this illustrious line.*

Brandeis meant the lines as praise for the retired justice, but the evocation of respect and loyalty expressed equally his own deep sense of personal connection and continuity with his predecessor, his colleague, and his friend.

At the beginning of 1938, the opportunity appeared, and Brandeis felt deeply the need to seize it. He had special, intense, and quite personal reasons for acting immediately and decisively. At the same time, however, he was guided by deeply cherished and fundamental convictions about public policy and constitutional structure. In shaping his opinion, he implemented the Progressive values that he had absorbed, nourished, and articulated for a lifetime.

"Defects, Social" 6

THE PROGRESSIVE AS LEGAL CRAFTSMAN

Although Brandeis used *Erie* to honor Holmes, he cast his opinion along his own chosen lines. "[E]xperience in applying the doctrine of *Swift v. Tyson*," he stated, "had revealed its defects, political and social."[1] Holmes's animosity toward *Swift* rested largely on intellectual grounds, his contempt for the idea of a "transcendental body of law."[2] Not surprisingly, in his *Taxicab* dissent he had not even alluded to *Swift*'s social impact or its tactical significance. For Brandeis, however, those factors were profoundly important shortcomings that constituted one of the two paramount reasons *Swift* had to be overturned.

Brandeis's view of *Swift*'s "social defects" flowed from his intertwined commitments to the Progressive ideals of social justice and efficiency. The former nourished a deep resentment of large national corporations and the unfair advantages they reaped from *Swift* and diversity jurisdiction. The latter generated an acute concern with the proliferation of elaborate litigation tactics that complicated the law and wasted social resources, tactics that *Swift* and diversity encouraged. Together, the doctrine and the jurisdiction enhanced the importance of extraneous social factors and tactical procedural maneuvering, frustrated the purposes of substantive legal rules, and compromised the ability of the legal system to provide practical justice. Those interrelated considerations inspired Brandeis when he indicted *Swift*'s "social defects."

Corporate Litigation and the Politics of Diversity Jurisdiction

Brandeis was wary of the growing size and power of modern corporations.[3] Repeatedly, he urged the Court to sustain statutes that placed special restrictions on their activities. In *Quaker City Cab Co. v. Pennsylvania* the Court held that a statute imposing a gross receipts tax on corporations, but not on individuals or partnerships in the same business, violated the Equal Protection Clause.[4] Dissenting, Brandeis termed the statute not only "reasonable" but also desirable. Its classifications, he asserted, were based on distinctions "real and important."[5] There were "intelligent, informed, just-minded and civilized persons," he insisted, "who believe that the rapidly growing aggregation of capital through corporations constitutes an insidious menace to the liberty of the citizen; that it tends to increase the subjection of labor to capital; that, because of the guidance and control necessarily exercised by great corporations upon those engaged in business, individual initiative is being impaired and creative power will be lessened."[6] He urged rigorous enforcement of the anti-trust laws and reform of state incorporation laws to undo economic concentration,[7] and he hoped privately for a "supercorporation tax, progressive in nature" based on "all values over $1,000,000."[8] During the 1920s, angered and frustrated over the corporate concentration that the Republican administrations fostered, he came to favor the public ownership of utilities and power companies.[9]

Antagonism toward corporate concentration was a cornerstone of Brandeis's philosophy. "Bigness" was the central evil, and national corporations represented the most aggressive and dominant form of bigness in twentieth-century America. They made state lines irrelevant and overwhelmed the capacity of local governments to restrain their activities. They destroyed the ideals of industrial democracy and oppressed the cause of labor. Most crucially, they defeated the hopes and aspirations of small and mortal individuals. "It's clear, I think," Brandeis declared in 1925, "that the gentle enslavement of our people is proceeding apace—politically, economically, socially." His faith in the individual, however, remained strong. "[T]he only remedy is via the individual," he insisted. "To make him care to be a free man and willing to pay the price."[10]

Believing that economic concentration was largely responsible for the Great Depression, Brandeis dissented alone in *Liggett v. Lee* in 1933 and issued his most extreme judicial condemnation of large corporations. Two hundred non-banking corporations controlled one-fourth of the national wealth, he pointed out; regardless of the formalities of corporate governance, they were in fact controlled by only a few hundred persons. The result was an extreme disparity in individual incomes, "a major cause of the existing depression," and "the negation of industrial democracy." Such concentrations of power were "sometimes able to dominate the State," he warned, and they threatened "the rule of a plutocracy." By failing to enforce reasonable controls on corporate size and power, the states had created a "Frankenstein monster."[11]

Brandeis's dissent in *Liggett*, like his dissent in *Quaker City*, gave voice to his deepest social and moral beliefs. The reactions of his frequent allies, Justices Stone and Cardozo, marked the depth and intensity of his personal feelings.

In *Liggett* Cardozo was the only other justice to dissent, but he refused to join Brandeis's opinion. In *Quaker City* Holmes and Stone both dissented. While the former joined Brandeis's dissent, the latter drew the line. The discussion of corporations "weakens the whole opinion," Stone warned Brandeis. It "will suggest to many minds that this is the real germ of your opposition."[12]

Of course, it was. Brandeis shared the Progressive hostility toward large corporations on the grounds that they exploited the availability of diversity jurisdiction and the advantages of the federal common law.[13] In 1922, commenting on Senator Walsh's criticism of the federal judiciary, he concluded flatly that "it was a great mistake to hold that corporations were citizens entitled to sue in Federal Courts on the grounds of citizenship."[14] Ten years later, dissenting alone, he defended the right of the states to revoke the license of foreign corporations to do local business if they removed suits to federal court.[15] He favored many of the proposals offered to limit jurisdiction, including raising the jurisdictional amount and prohibiting devices to "manufacture" diversity jurisdiction. Legislative restrictions would mean at least some contraction of the advantages that corporate litigants enjoyed, and throughout the 1920s and 1930s he encouraged Senators Norris and Walsh — old Progressive allies of his — in their efforts to remedy the problem.[16]

Brandeis had first worked with Norris in 1910 during the sensational Ballinger-Pinchot affair. The Nebraskan, then in the House, played a critical role in blocking the attempt of Republican stalwarts to pack the congressional committee that was to investigate the matter. His effort gave Brandeis the opportunity to make his case publicly and with full effect.[17] Two years later when Norris first ran for the Senate, Brandeis stumped Nebraska on his behalf.[18] Subsequently, the two cooperated in pressing the investigation of one of Brandeis's principal targets, the New York, New Haven and Hartford Railroad, and in 1916 Norris was one of only three Republicans who broke ranks and voted to confirm Brandeis to the Supreme Court.[19] Norris, Brandeis believed, was one of the nation's great Progressive leaders.[20]

Brandeis first met Walsh during his confirmation battle. As a member of the subcommittee conducting the hearings, Walsh quickly emerged as the nominee's most tenacious defender. "The real crime of which this man is guilty," the Montana Progressive declared, "is that he has exposed the iniquities of men in high places in our financial system." Brandeis "has not stood in awe of the majesty of wealth."[21] The two men quickly became friends, and over the years Walsh visited the justice's home frequently. Among their many shared views was their mutual opposition to the proposed Rules Enabling Act, and Brandeis encouraged Walsh's efforts to block the bill.[22] Although Brandeis regarded Norris as the leading Progressive in Congress, he considered Walsh one of its finest legal minds.

Although Brandeis did not publicly engage in political activity while on the Court, he remained in close and purposeful contact with those who did. Through his regular Monday afternoon teas, as well as frequent dinner parties, he kept in touch with a wide range of Progressive politicians, labor leaders, social reformers, law professors, and intellectuals.[23] These gatherings were typically small, and the conversation tended to be serious. Aside from providing a welcome social outlet, they served a more important function as opportunities for political consultation. Walsh, for example, contacted Frankfurter in 1926 to indicate his interest in bills that restricted the jurisdiction of the federal courts. "Recently," he wrote, "I had a talk with Justice Brandeis who is impressed with the wisdom of that course."[24] At every opportunity Brandeis urged congressmen to limit diversity.[25] "Senator Blaine was in the other day," he informed Frankfurter in 1928. "I took occasion to talk to him and Sen. La Follette jointly on restricting federal jurisdiction whenever they saw a chance."[26]

In addition to his private efforts, Brandeis exerted a public influence through Frankfurter.[27] His letters to Frankfurter were organized into brief numbered items and often read like directives from a commanding general. He repeatedly urged Frankfurter to have his students publish work on controversial jurisdictional topics,[28] and he encouraged and guided Frankfurter in producing his own immediately useful scholarship.[29] *The Business of the Supreme Court* and his articles attacking *Swift* and urging the restriction of diversity jurisdiction bore Brandeis's stamp of approval. When they appeared, Brandeis directed Frankfurter to send copies to influential politicians and judges.[30] Finally, he supported Frankfurter's efforts financially. From 1924 to 1939 he contributed funds for the support of research assistants, and from 1917 to 1938 he provided his friend and de facto agent with a substantial yearly stipend.[31] With good reason did Brandeis consider Frankfurter "clearly the most useful lawyer in the United States."[32]

Brandeis's activities in 1928 illustrated his method of operation. In March, while dining with Congressman R. Walton Moore of Virginia, he proposed the desirability of restricting diversity jurisdiction and suggested that Moore cooperate with Frankfurter in drafting an appropriate measure.[33] Calling the congressman's attention to the importance of *The Business of the Supreme Court*, he offered to write Frankfurter to obtain a copy for him. Brandeis then told Frankfurter of the discussion and noted that his law clerk, Henry J. Friendly, had grown "keenly interested" in jurisdictional matters. The same year, Friendly published a study in the *Harvard Law Review*, originally written for Frankfurter's seminar on federal jurisdiction, entitled "The Historical Basis of Federal Diversity Jurisdiction."[34] "When the time comes for work on your part," Brandeis informed Frankfurter, "Friendly can, I think, be drafted by you."[35] The result was a series of bills that restricted the scope of diversity jurisdiction. Frankfurter and Friendly drafted them, and Moore introduced them in the House of Representatives.[36]

Brandeis took special interest in a bill designed specifically to overrule the *Taxicab* case. Such a bill "would be an excellent idea," he responded to Frankfurter's inquiry. "The draft bill should go to Sen. Tom Walsh."[37] Two days later Frankfurter wrote Walsh, pointing out the need to change the rule and enclosing a draft bill intended to end the "mischievous" doctrine.[38] Walsh, who had sat in the Court chamber while Justices Butler and Holmes delivered their opinions, responded immediately, agreeing with Frankfurter's comments and promising to introduce the bill.[39] Less than a month later he did so. "I suppose," Brandeis wrote Frankfurter subsequently, "you saw that your *Black & White* taxi bill was introduced in the Senate by T. J. Walsh."[40]

Walsh's death in early 1933 crimped but did not terminate Brandeis's efforts to restrict diversity jurisdiction. The following year he used a case involving a special diversity removal provision to pull together a collection of statutes and shape them into what he termed an "established trend of legislation limiting the jurisdiction of the federal trial courts." Restriction of federal jurisdiction, he proclaimed, represented a "long-existing policy" of Congress.[41] Off the bench he continued to urge congressional action, and in early 1936 he again tried to instigate specific legislation. Diversity, he told Frankfurter, should be "abolished."[42] Two days later Frankfurter pushed forward. "Is this not a very propitious time," he wrote Norris, to push "for restricting the present unwarranted jurisdiction of the United States District Courts?" Passing along Brandeis's suggestions as his own, he urged that diversity be "abolished."[43] The following month Frankfurter contacted two of his ex-students who had clerked for Brandeis, and they subsequently met with Norris and drafted two bills that severely narrowed federal jurisdiction.[44] Once again, however, the effort proved abortive.

The Spectre of the Labor Injunction

Brandeis's campaign to abolish *Swift* and diversity was further motivated by his recognition of their role in fostering the federal labor injunction. He had been sympathetic to the cause of organized labor at least since the Homestead strike in 1892, and he repeatedly supported labor's efforts to improve wages and working conditions. He was suspicious, especially in his early years, of the potential for oppression that powerful trade unions presented, and his instinct for individualism and the small unit made the existence of large national organizations seem regrettable. Nevertheless, he recognized that they were necessary and, in the context of industrial concentration, highly desirable. By 1908, moreover, Brandeis had become convinced that the injunction was an unfair and nearly insurmountable obstacle to unionism. It was, he concluded, "most unsound in practice." [45] By World War I he had established himself as a consistent, albeit sometimes critical, supporter of unions and a convinced opponent of the labor injunction. [46]

As a justice, Brandeis repeatedly faced the labor injunction, and four of the leading cases the Court heard during his tenure involved diversity jurisdiction. [47] One was *Hitchman*. There, Brandeis rejected the employer's appeal to liberty of contract, disdained the company's use of "yellow dog" contracts, and stressed that both the union and its organizing efforts were lawful under applicable state law. Responding to the company's claim that the union intended to use economic pressure to "coerce" it, he pointed out that its "whole case is rested upon agreements secured under similar pressure of economic necessity or disadvantage." The courts should treat all the parties equally and apply the same law to the union and the workers that it applied to the company. "If it is coercion to threaten to strike unless plaintiff consents to a closed union shop," he insisted, "it is coercion also to threaten not to give one employment unless the applicant will consent to a closed nonunion shop." [48]

Brandeis's angriest dissent came in 1927 in *Bedford Cut Stone Co. v. Journeymen Stone Cutters' Association,* a decision upholding an injunction on the ground that a strike created a "restraint of trade" in violation of the Sherman Anti-Trust Act. [49] The union was small and weak, and the employers were powerful and nationally organized. Only "a national union," Brandeis declared, could begin to offset the employers' advantages and allow "the individual stonecutter" to "protect his job." [50] The issue was the "reasonableness" of the restraint that the strike created. "And the restraint imposed was, in my opinion, a reasonable one." His references to the legal principles that should control the decision were followed by a blunt acknowledgment of his own values and, by implication, those of the majority. "Tested by these principles, the propriety of the unions' conduct can hardly be doubted by one who believes in the organization of labor." [51]

In *Bedford* Brandeis again suggested the existence of class bias. The Court interpreted the Sherman Act "to permit capitalists to combine" even when the result was the creation of a huge corporation that could dominate an entire industry. It interpreted the same act "to deny to members of a small craft of workingmen the right to cooperate in simply refraining from work, when that course was the only means of self-protection against a combination of militant and powerful employers." He concluded with passion. "If, on the undisputed facts of this case, refusal to work can be enjoined, Congress created by the Sherman Law and the Clayton Act an instrument for imposing restraints upon labor which reminds of involuntary servitude." [52]

The split on the Court was deep. The barely veiled accusation was not lost on Chief Justice Taft. "Brandeis," he wrote his son, "has written one of his meanest opinions."[53] For his part, Brandeis forwarded a copy to Frankfurter as new ammunition. "If anything can awaken Trade Unionists from their lethargy," he declared angrily, "this should."[54]

As he had directed Frankfurter to press for the abolition of diversity jurisdiction, so he urged him to work for abolition of the labor injunction. The Supreme Court's labor cases "make a terrible story," he confided.[55] "[T]he employers['] resort to the injunction must be discontinued."[56] Brandeis encouraged Frankfurter to produce scholarly and popular work criticizing the injunction, and he congratulated him when his anonymous editorial condemning *Bedford* — using as its title a quotation from Brandeis's dissent — appeared in *The New Republic*. "Your 'Reminds of Involuntary Servitude' is a stirring document," the justice cheered.[57] Learning of Senator Henrik Shipstead's inartfully drafted anti-injunction bill, he directed Frankfurter to review it and "get it changed, as you deem wise."[58] The major scholarly result of his encouragement was Frankfurter's powerful 1930 indictment, *The Labor Injunction*, formally dedicated "To Mr. Justice Brandeis." The book was, in essence, a brief for the Norris-LaGuardia Act. Brandeis not only encouraged the work but also advised Frankfurter on how and to whom he should distribute copies.[59] As the book demonstrated, diversity jurisdiction and the general law of the federal courts were integral parts of the history of the labor injunction.

When *Erie* was argued in January 1938, the bitter battles that surrounded the labor injunction were still being fought before the Court. Although the justices had held the New Deal's pro-union Wagner Act constitutional the previous year, some lower federal courts continued to enjoin actions of the National Labor Relations Board.[60] On January 31, the day *Erie* was argued, Brandeis announced the Court's decision in *Myers v. Bethlehem Shipbuilding Corp.*,[61] reversing a lower court decision that enjoined the labor board from investigating a complaint charging an "unfair labor practice" under the act.[62] More directly, Brandeis was concerned with the labor injunction in early 1938 because the Court had finally agreed to hear its first appeals under the Norris-LaGuardia Act. Since the act's passage in 1932, the justices had avoided passing on either its constitutionality or its construction. In contradictory leading cases, the Second Circuit had construed the act broadly and denied an employer relief,[63] while the Seventh Circuit had held the act inapplicable and approved an injunction in a strike situation.[64] In each case the Supreme Court had refused to grant *certiorari*. Given the volatile political context of the mid-1930s and a badly divided and uncertain Court, neither the Progressive nor conservative wing was anxious for a showdown.

For six years the fate of the Norris-LaGuardia Act hung in doubt. Its careful draftsmanship and its form as a restriction on jurisdiction, over which

Congress admittedly had almost complete control, seemed to place it on solid constitutional ground. Nevertheless, the fact that it denied equitable relief to persons allegedly suffering legal wrong shrouded the status of the act in uncertainty. This uncertainty was magnified by the anti-Progressive political orientation of the old Court, the authority of such cases as *Truax v. Corrigan*,[65] and the style of statutory construction exemplified in *Duplex v. Deering*.[66] Moreover, the pivotal statutory definition of a "labor dispute" required a clear and authoritative interpretation. While the Second Circuit construed it broadly,[67] the Eighth Circuit and the District of Columbia Circuit held it inapplicable to different types of labor turmoil.[68] Most blatantly, the Seventh Circuit held the act inapplicable in a series of four suits, decisions that the *Harvard Law Review* termed "flatly opposed to the terms of the statute." [69]

Some of the opinions emanating from the lower courts, moreover, were stunning in their recalcitrance. Despite the meticulous and all-encompassing definitions of a "labor dispute" and persons "interested" in labor disputes, two members of a special three-judge federal court in *Donnelly Garment Co. v. International Ladies' Garment Workers' Union* found that the act was silent as to its intended scope.[70] "The failure of Congress to define what constitutes a bona fide labor dispute," they declared, adding the term "bona fide" where Congress had excluded it, "has left the question open for judicial determination." Abandoning the explicit and comprehensive terms of the statute, the judges relied on the definition of a "dispute" in *Bouvier's Law Dictionary* and upheld a temporary injunction against a union-organizing effort.[71] By 1937, the *Yale Law Journal* warned that "restrictive and unsympathetic judicial interpretation" threatened to "nullify" the Norris-LaGuardia Act.[72]

Then, in the spring of 1937, the logjam began to break. With Chief Justice Hughes and Justice Roberts joining the three Progressives, the Court clearly distinguished *Truax* and upheld against constitutional challenge Wisconsin's "little Norris-LaGuardia Act." [73] The subsequent appointments of Justice Black in October and Justice Reed the following January meant that the Norris-LaGuardia Act had at least become constitutional and that its scope had broadened.

Promptly, the new Court granted *certiorari* in two cases in which lower courts had held the act inapplicable and issued injunctions. In each one, with Justices Butler and McReynolds dissenting alone as they would in *Erie*, the Court construed the term *labor dispute* broadly and denied the lower court's jurisdiction to enjoin labor activity.[74] Neither case directly raised a constitutional issue, but the Court seemed to foreclose any challenge by applying the statute and commenting in passing that "the power of the court to grant the relief prayed depends upon the jurisdiction conferred upon it by the statutes of the United

States."[75] The first of the cases was argued three weeks before *Erie;* the second, a month after.

To compound the impact of the two cases, the union's appeal from the ruling of the three-judge court in *Donnelly,* filed at the end of January, was also before the Court at the same time. There, the willful recalcitrance of the majority judges seemed undeniable, and the highly unusual and blunt opinion of the single dissenting district judge forced the issue of good faith.[76] Arguing that the statute's meaning was crystal clear and that it properly barred the injunction the majority had issued, the dissent concluded with a harsh reprimand. "And the judges must apply the law, whether it is good or bad," it declared. "They have taken a solemn oath that they will do that very thing."[77] Three weeks after *Erie* the Court issued a unanimous *per curiam* opinion vacating the order in *Donnelly.*[78]

While Brandeis was drafting *Erie,* then, the issue of the labor injunction was immediately before him and raised pressing issues of law and judicial administration. Its lessons were clear. The federal courts had been especially sympathetic to employers; they had allowed corporations to exploit easily manipulable and unfair procedural advantages; they had used substantive due process, diversity jurisdiction, and the independent lawmaking authority of the federal courts to undercut Progressive state and national policies. As the three appeals in early 1938 demonstrated, many lower court judges were still blatantly fighting unionism and straining the language of the statute in order to do so. While diversity jurisdiction lay in the hands of Congress, the independent judgment of the federal judiciary, like the scope of the Norris-LaGuardia Act, lay in the hands of the Court.

Tactical Escalation and the Demands of Social Efficiency

Swift's third social defect was also rooted in Brandeis's fear of corporate power and manipulation, but it transcended that fear. Since the late nineteenth century, litigation had grown increasingly expensive and elaborate as more and more parties adopted sophisticated litigation tactics and methodically used an expanding variety of procedural moves and countermoves. By increasing the differences between state and federal courts, *Swift* magnified the importance of forum control and helped stimulate a variety of rival techniques to secure and deny access to the national courts. Thus, *Swift* and diversity jurisdiction helped spur an escalating process of tactical innovation that generated massive amounts of litigation that addressed not the claims of the parties but the tactics of their lawyers. Brandeis resented the accelerating trend and bridled at the inequitable results and social waste that accompanied it.

The trend was particularly noticeable in suits involving interstate forum shopping, cases where out-of-state plaintiffs filed in courts that had little or no connection to their underlying claims because the forums offered special tactical benefits. Plaintiffs' attorneys, some of whom methodically solicited cases in apparent violation of professional ethics, largely drove the development, funneling cases to states where the courts promised more favorable procedures, higher jury verdicts, or other comparable advantages. Since the 1870s the Supreme Court had used the Due Process Clause to limit the ability of states to assert personal jurisdiction over nonresident defendants, but that limitation seemed increasingly inadequate to control the new plaintiffs' tactics.[79] By the early 1920s the Court began experimenting with new statutory and constitutional doctrines to provide additional limits, and Brandeis took the lead.[80]

Interstate forum shopping had become most notorious in actions under the Federal Employers' Liability Act (FELA). The statute not only provided injured workers a promising cause of action, but also allowed them to sue in any state or district where a defendant railroad did business and denied defendants the right to remove. By the 1920s thousands of claims were being brought from halfway across the country to a handful of favored plaintiffs' forums, including Minnesota, Missouri, and New York. Employers, especially railroads and their insurance companies, protested strenuously. They argued that suits brought in forums distant from the place of injury were expensive, disruptive, and unnecessary and that they constituted a form of extortion instigated by unethical "ambulance chasers." To fight the tactic, the companies generated counterstrategies, which included preemptive suits at the place of injury or the worker's residence and requests for equitable relief against "vexatious" litigation in the plaintiffs' chosen forum. The result was a proliferation of complex legal and equitable issues and a substantial increase in the time and effort necessary to resolve mushrooming issues of practice and procedure.[81]

Sympathetic to injured workers, Brandeis nevertheless objected to the tactics of their attorneys. Interstate forum shopping symbolized for him the ethical failings of the legal profession. It was often the result of unethical claims solicitation, and its success represented the triumph of the lawyer's cleverness over the law's integrity. Further, at a time when the courts were under intense docket pressures, the practice overloaded the legal system by multiplying disputes and wasting limited judicial resources in resolving complex issues that arose only because parties purposely created them for tactical advantage. Finally, the practice offended Brandeis's Progressive commitment to social efficiency and systemic rationalization. Interstate forum shopping put unnecessary burdens on the courts and distributed cases among the states in socially disruptive and undesirable ways. The practice imposed excessive costs on parties, particularly defendants, and burdened business by forcing employees and other witnesses to spend weeks traveling and living in locations distant from their jobs.

Believing that the Court should restrict such abusive practices, Brandeis was willing to deprive injured workers of important tactical advantages and to invent new doctrine to do so. In 1923, writing for the Court in *Davis v. Farmers Co-Operative Equity Co.*, he used the Commerce Clause to impose limits on plaintiffs' choice of forum, holding that the added costs and inconveniences of suits brought in forums distant from the place of injury could unduly burden interstate commerce.[82] *Davis* gave voice to Brandeis's deep concern with promoting the rational and efficient allocation of judicial business across the nation. The "requirements of orderly, effective administration of justice," he declared, "are paramount."[83] Six years later, again writing for the Court, Brandeis reversed another plaintiff's judgment and held that the *Davis* doctrine applied to suits under the FELA.[84]

Similarly, Brandeis sought to restrict interstate forum shopping by limiting the incentives that divergent state laws offered to sophisticated litigants. Since the turn of the century the Court had used the Due Process Clause to limit the authority of states to apply their own law to activities occurring largely or wholly outside their borders.[85] Although Brandeis had serious qualms about the clause, he agreed that judicially imposed constitutional limits were necessary. By imposing some constraints on state choice-of-law rules, at least, due process served both to make federalism coherent and to choke off a potentially powerful incentive for interstate forum shopping.[86]

Even more striking was Brandeis's effort in the early 1930s to expand the reach of the Full Faith and Credit Clause, an area where his desire to restrict interstate forum shopping trumped his commitment to federalism and local law.[87] The "constitutional limitation imposed by the full faith and credit clause," Brandeis declared in 1935, "abolished, in large measure, the general principle of international law by which local policy is permitted to dominate rules of comity."[88] The next year he wrote for the Court reversing a judgment for a widow who had moved to Georgia to avoid unfavorable law in New York, the state where she had lived with her husband until his death.[89] "[T]he room left for the play of conflicting [state] policies," he declared, "is a narrow one."[90] To the extent that the Constitution positively mandated the choice of another state's law (as opposed to merely limiting the ability of forum states to apply their own law), it would limit more narrowly the incentives for interstate forum shopping. Moreover, to the extent that such a limit could be imposed under the Full Faith and Credit Clause, it could be accomplished without invoking and thereby broadening the sway of the politically dangerous Due Process Clause, the foundation of many of the anti-Progressive decisions that Brandeis had fought.

One incentive for interstate forum shopping that particularly attracted Brandeis's attention was the divergence that existed among state workmen's compensation statutes. Between 1917 and 1923 forty-two states enacted such statutes, and their substantive terms varied widely, especially in the amounts of compensation they provided. In addition to covering injuries that occurred within the enacting state, most statutes also reached injuries that occurred outside the state if the injured person was a resident of the enacting state or if the employment contract had been signed there. Increasingly, injured workers whose residence, employment contracts, or work assignments involved two or more states had the option to choose between different compensation plans. The widow of a Tennessee worker, for example, moved to Georgia and then sued for workmen's compensation in Ohio, where her husband had been killed. The Ohio statute provided $4,910.64, more than double the amount the Tennessee statute offered.[91]

In 1932 Brandeis took aim at such tactics. In *Bradford Electric Light Co. v. Clapper* an employee who resided and worked in Vermont was killed while on special assignment in New Hampshire.[92] His widow brought suit in the latter state, where a more promising statutory cause of action was available. Writing for a seven-justice majority, Brandeis held that the Constitution compelled New Hampshire to apply Vermont law. The Full Faith and Credit Clause, he wrote, "prevents the employee or his representative from asserting in New Hampshire rights which would be denied him in the state of his residence and employment." [93] The most striking fact about the decision — and the basis for its potential breadth — lay in the fact that New Hampshire, as the place of injury, had a substantial connection to the case and that traditional choice-of-law rules recognized the law of the place of injury as the properly applicable substantive law. Brandeis, however, easily dismissed that fact. Workmen's compensation statutes, he explained, were commonly regarded "as substituting a statutory tort for a common law tort." [94] The traditional rule, therefore, did not apply, and the Full Faith and Credit Clause mandated a special and highly restrictive new one in its place.

Two decades earlier, in one of Brandeis's first opinions for the Court, he had heard a case involving a property dispute that turned on a choice between the conflicting statutes of two states. In *Kryger v. Wilson* he restated nineteenth-century doctrine, declaring that a state court's decision to apply its own law instead of the law of another state was at most "a mistaken application of doctrines of the conflict of law." Such an issue was "purely a question of local common law" and, therefore, "a matter with which this court is not concerned." [95] *Kryger* revealed none of his later concerns with the burgeoning problems of methodical interstate forum shopping. To the contrary, at the beginning of his judicial career Brandeis was concerned primarily with protecting the scope of local law, limiting the Court's due process doctrine, deflating conflicts to the status of ordinary choice-of-law questions, and preserving the rule that claims under the "federal common law" did not raise federal questions for review in cases coming from state courts.[96] Although *Kryger* and *Clapper* were distinguishable, the casual sweep of Brandeis's comments in the earlier case contrasted sharply with the purposefulness of his contrary reasoning in the later one. Together, they revealed the extent to which the growth of interstate forum shopping forced him to rethink fundamental questions of constitutional policy.

Brandeis's determination to limit interstate forum shopping was highlighted by his disagreement with Stone, usually one of his consistent allies on the Court. In *Clapper*, Stone merely concurred separately, objecting to the Court's extension of the Full Faith and Credit Clause to compel application of one state's law to an event that occurred in another state.[97] He advanced two arguments that ordinarily would have appealed to Brandeis. First, Stone argued that a decision on the constitutional issue was unnecessary. A federal court made the ruling under review, and the state courts had not yet established a relevant choice-of-law rule. A New Hampshire court might, therefore, decide on its own to apply Vermont law in such cases. "Hence, it seems unnecessary to decide whether that result could be compelled" by the Constitution.[98] Second, appealing to the principle of local autonomy that Brandeis so often upheld, Stone stressed the basic right of states to regulate the behavior of persons acting within their territory.[99] New Hampshire's legitimate interest in regulating the matter "derived from the presence of the employer and employe [*sic*] within its borders" and from "the commission of the tortious act there."[100] In *Clapper*, however, neither of those Brandeisian arguments persuaded Brandeis.[101]

While Brandeis battled forum shopping on the interstate level, *Swift* and diversity jurisdiction continued to spur the practice on the intrastate level. Studying cases from the previous thirty years, two researchers concluded in 1929 that the "application of the doctrine of *Swift v. Tyson* has resulted in many states in two different conceptions of what the general commercial law is."[102] A review of reported appellate decisions in 1930 discovered from a random sample of fifty-eight diversity cases that federal courts relied on state precedents in only twenty, or approximately 35 percent.[103] In 1934 a two-volume study of federal contract law concluded that areas of divergence had "rapidly grown in number in the more recent years."[104]

The split between federal and state common law was particularly sharp in the area of insurance law.[105] Federal common law was distinctly favorable to insurers, and during the 1920s and 1930s it helped generate a rapid influx of cases into the national courts and a desperate struggle for forum control in suits between insurers and policyholders. Insurers developed tactics to expand their ability to remove and found new ways to gain access to federal equity, while policyholders countered with a range of procedural innovations designed to anchor their claims in state courts. Their battles forced a steady stream of insurance cases to the Supreme Court. Only months before *Erie* was argued, in fact, the Court confronted some of the problems raised by the expanding access to federal equity that insurers had won. Its opinion in *American Life Insurance Company v. Stewart* was notable for two reasons.[106] First, it attempted only a tentative resolution, acknowledging that the issues raised were complex and the practice context volatile and fiercely contested. Second, it recognized the practical importance of the lawyers' tactics. In *Stewart* the company's attorneys had snookered their adversaries into giving up their opportunity to proceed in a state court.[107]

Only months before the oral argument in *Erie* Brandeis was further reminded — this time with special force — of the incentive *Swift* created for federal-state forum shopping. The Declaratory Judgment Act, which he had fought so resolutely in *Willing*, came before the Court for the first time. By 1937 the constitutional question seemed settled, and in *Aetna Life Insurance Co. v. Haworth* the Court readily upheld the statute.[108] Beyond the constitutional issue, however, Brandeis was concerned with the impact that the declaratory judgment would have on the dynamics of litigation practice.[109] In that regard, the Court's decision was particularly distressing.

Haworth upheld two important tactical innovations that the companies had developed. First, it approved an insurer's use of the declaratory remedy to obtain a judgment of nonliability, a type of action that the company could not otherwise have brought. In so doing, *Haworth* confirmed Brandeis's fear that the declaratory remedy would, in effect, expand the jurisdiction and caseload of the federal courts, encourage potential defendants (especially foreign corporations) to initiate preemptive federal suits to avoid unfavorable state law, and magnify the importance of diversity jurisdiction and the general common law. Second, *Haworth* also sanctioned the tactic the company used to overcome the jurisdictional barrier posed by the required amount in controversy. If it were left to the policyholder to bring suit, he could have claimed only the benefits that had accrued under his disability policies, an amount that would have been less than the $3,000 jurisdictional minimum. Indeed, in *Haworth* the policyholder argued that "there was no present right of recovery of an amount sufficient to give a federal court jurisdiction."[110] Able to initiate suit for a judgment of nonliability, however, the company could claim that the true amount in controversy was the total value of reserves that it would have to set aside to fund its full potential liability. A total reserves theory easily placed its claim above the jurisdictional minimum. Accepting the company's theory, *Haworth* found the jurisdictional amount satisfied.[111] In so doing, it promised to expand the federal caseload, deprive policyholders of an important forum-control tactic, and make the federal common law more readily available in preemptive strikes by insurance companies.

Haworth suggested that most of the justices failed to understand the dynamic potential of the declaratory judgment. The opinion proclaimed that the device was "procedural only" and that its party reversal potential was legally irrelevant.[112] Whatever those statements might mean as matters of doctrinal logic, in terms of litigation practice they were quite off the point. Because the declaratory judgment allowed parties to sue prior to actual or imminent injury, it brought the judiciary into disputes earlier than was otherwise possible. Because it allowed parties to sue for judgments declaring that their adversaries did not have a certain right, it enabled sophisticated litigants who might otherwise have been defendants to take preemptive action and initiate lawsuits themselves. That option allowed them to appear as aggrieved parties and to control the timing of suits, the party structure, and the scope of the pleadings. Most important, the declaratory judgment enabled them to determine which forum would hear the suit, allowing them to exploit any possible advantages in a particular court. As long as *Swift* reigned, litigants could determine whether federal or state common law would govern their claim. Considered realistically and dynamically, the declaratory judgment was a device that promised to magnify the importance of tactical maneuvering, encourage the creativity and audacity of litigators, and provide disproportionate advantages to wealthy and knowledgeable litigants with multistate contacts and "astute counsel."

More than most of his contemporaries, Brandeis recognized that the declaratory judgment — simplistic and one-dimensional in the abstract way many of its proponents framed it — would prove in practice volatile, expansive, and disruptive. He sensed, too, the dramatic synergism inherent in the explosive combination of *Haworth* and *Swift*. Given diversity jurisdiction and the new availability of the declaratory judgment, *Swift* could only swell in importance as an incentive for more frequent, aggressive, and sophisticated federal-state forum-shopping efforts.

Crafting an Opinion: Remedying Social Defects in a Constitutional Revolution

Brandeis devoted almost half of his opinion in *Erie* to outlining the "mischievous results" of *Swift*. It was, he began *Erie*'s second section, "[e]xperience in applying the doctrine of *Swift v. Tyson*" that revealed its social defects. First, he noted, "the benefits expected" from *Swift* had not appeared. State courts, persisting with their own rules, prevented "uniformity" in the common law. Moreover, the "impossibility of discovering a satisfactory line of demarcation" between questions of local and general law made the doctrine erratic and "developed a new well of uncertainties" as to whether federal courts would follow state decisions.[113]

Second, in spite of diversity's accepted rationale of protecting out-of-staters from local prejudice, Brandeis emphasized that "in practice" *Swift* altered that function.[114] "*Swift v. Tyson* introduced grave discrimination by non-citizens against citizens."[115] The existence of the general federal common law meant that rights varied between state and federal courts, and "the privilege of selecting the court in which the right should be determined was conferred upon the non-citizen." *Swift* and diversity, therefore, gave a significant advantage to the non-citizen and "rendered impossible equal protection of the law." Two further developments made the resulting discrimination "far reaching." One was the "broad province accorded to the so-called 'general law'," which expanded the areas in which conflicting federal and state rules existed.[116] The other was "the wide range of persons held entitled to avail themselves" of diversity.[117] Individuals could move from one state to another to create diversity, he explained, and "without even change of residence, a corporate citizen of the State could avail itself of the federal rule by re-incorporating under the law of another State, as was done in the *Taxicab* case."[118]

Although the claim that *Swift* caused unfair "discrimination" was central to his analysis, Brandeis's opinion was paradoxical. It did not analyze the specific social operation of the doctrine, nor did it detail the evidence that supported its factual contentions. Brandeis referred to the *Taxicab* case,[119] but he mentioned only once the particular advantages that the "corporate citizen" enjoyed.[120] Moreover, his reference to the "wide range of persons" who could exploit diversity was somewhat puzzling and vague. The opinion, in sum, was brief—perhaps even gnomic—and devoid of detailed legal and social analysis. Its purposes were Brandeisian, but its argument was not.

Indeed, Brandeis's pivotal argument concerning *Swift*'s social operation was general and abstract. The citizen was denied equal protection by a discrimination in favor of the noncitizen. It seemed surprising that Brandeis, of all judges, would reverse a long-established doctrine that had allegedly caused "far-reaching" social discrimination "in practice" without more fully explaining and documenting its operation. In his "citizen/noncitizen" dichotomy, however, Brandeis purposely used formally neutral language to minimize and obscure the anticipated social consequences of his decision.

This abstract description of *Swift*'s operation implied the existence of a world of undifferentiated legal units roaming the nation in search of advantage in particular courts. "Through this [diversity] jurisdiction individual citizens willing to remove from their own State and become citizens of another might avail themselves of the federal rule," Brandeis explained. "And, without even change of residence, a corporate citizen of the State could avail itself of the federal rule by re-incorporating under the laws of another State."[121] Individuals and corporations thus appeared equal in their ability to manipulate diversity and exploit *Swift*. His abstract analysis projected the image of rational and free litigant atoms—individuals and corporations alike—following their self-interest in an interstate judicial marketplace.

There was, of course, some truth in the image he sketched. Individual litigants had played an important role in the tactical escalation that marked American litigation, and during the previous twenty-five years they had begun to engage in interstate forum shopping as well. They used, for example, the appointment of both out-of-state administrators and assignees—presumably two examples of the "wide range of persons" who used diversity—to create or defeat jurisdiction.[122] They filed suits in states other than their own and even changed their citizenship in order to obtain tactical advantages.[123] The Tennessee widow who moved to Georgia in order to collect an Ohio workmen's compensation award had used the latter strategy, for example, and Harry Tompkins himself had adopted the former.

The image that Brandeis projected contained two fundamental flaws. First, it was inconsistent with the dominant social patterns of individual interstate forum shopping. Second, it was inconsistent with both Brandeis's social beliefs and his expectations concerning *Erie*'s practical significance.

The first problem, the fact that the image was empirically inaccurate, was apparent in several ways. One was that individuals who used interstate forum-shopping tactics rarely did so to "avail themselves of the federal rule." Tompkins's motivation was, in fact, quite uncharacteristic. Instead, when plaintiffs adopted interstate tactics, they were usually lured by advantages other than differences in applicable substantive law. Commonly, they sought to impose on their adversaries the burdens and costs of litigating in distant forums, or they expected to win larger judgments in locations known for having particularly generous juries. Often, too, they sought to exploit particular procedural advantages that some state forums offered, including helpful discovery rules, non-unanimous jury verdicts, favorable allocation of the burden of proof, minimal trial court control over juries, or appellate courts that deferred broadly to jury verdicts and damage awards. In most cases, too, plaintiffs brought their suits in distant forums simply because they had succumbed to solicitations from distant, big-city tort specialists who promised them higher recoveries. Moreover, in those cases where plaintiffs adopted interstate tactics because of the federal common law, their purpose was generally to avoid the federal rule, not to obtain its benefits. Both out-of-state administrators and out-of-state assignees, for example, were used primarily to destroy diversity and defeat anticipated removals in order to avoid unfavorable federal law, not to create diversity to gain access to an advantageous federal rule.[124]

Further, even in those relatively rare cases where plaintiffs specifically sought to exploit a favorable general common law rule, they seldom had to "create" diversity to obtain its benefits. If they wished to avail themselves of the rule in a suit against a nonresident, all they had to do was file in their local federal court. Tompkins, for example, who had that option available, had done nothing to "create" diversity with the Erie Railroad. If the local court could not assert personal jurisdiction over the nonresident, plaintiffs could still obtain the advantage of the federal rule by suing in a federal court in the defendant's state of residence. In either case, no questionable "forum shopping" would be involved and no unusual or special tactic would be necessary to create diversity.[125] The only situation in which individuals would be tempted to create diversity involved suits against their co-citizens. Such cases were quite common, of course, but they were almost invariably brought in local state courts. Individuals seldom changed their residence in order to bring claims in a federal court against individual co-citizens. The most notorious example of changing citizenship for diversity purposes was the *Taxicab* case, which was an instance of corporate rechartering, not an individual's change of residence.

Finally, Brandeis's image was inconsistent with dominant social patterns for another reason. The interstate forum shopping that had become common practice among individuals had little to do with *Swift* and diversity jurisdiction. Brandeis had been particularly concerned with two significant categories of individuals who brought suits in distant forums and changed residence for litigation purposes, but neither of those classes did so to obtain the benefits of federal common law. One category, probably the largest and surely the most notorious, was FELA claimants. They relied, however, not on diversity jurisdiction or the common law but on a federal statute that established nationwide substantive law and gave plaintiffs a wide selection of venues and the absolute right to choose between federal and state forums. When FELA plaintiffs used interstate tactics, then, they did so for reasons unrelated to either *Swift* or diversity jurisdiction.[126] The other category of interstate forum shoppers was made up of claimants under state workmen's compensation statutes. Unlike FELA plaintiffs, they did shop among the states for more advantageous substantive law, but their focus was on the differences among state statutory provisions — binding on the federal courts under *Swift* — and not on any divergent general common law rule. Although some did use diversity, most preferred the state courts and sought to keep their claims out of the federal courts. Thus, while individuals did "remove from their own State and become citizens of another," as Brandeis recounted, it was seldom either diversity or the federal common law that inspired their efforts.

The second problem with Brandeis's abstract image of interstate forum shopping was that it reflected neither his true views nor his expectations about *Erie*'s social significance. Indeed, his image was arresting, coming as it did from the justice who argued passionately that it was not only reasonable but highly desirable to allow legislatures to classify corporations differently from natural persons and impose heavier burdens on the larger entities. "The difference in power between corporations and natural persons," he wrote in his classic dissent in *Liggett v. Lee*, "is ample basis for placing them in different classes."[127] Privately, he spoke even more directly. "[S]uper corporation taxes" on "larger corporations" were essential, he maintained, "in recognition of bigness as a curse." Higher corporate taxes were necessary to protect individuals from "the menace, social and economic, which inheres in size by reason of its dominant position and its power of endurance."[128]

Erie's easy equation of individual and corporate litigants was foreign to Brandeis's fundamental view of the world. He believed in neither a universe of free and mobile litigant atoms nor a practical equality between individuals and corporations. Against the large and powerful chain stores, he had written in *Liggett v. Lee*, "the individual retailers of Florida are engaged in a struggle to preserve their independence — perhaps a struggle for existence."[129] "[W]hat approximately equal individual traders may do in honorable rivalry," he had written in another context, "may result in grave injustice and public injury, if done by a great corporation." The reality of massively differential social power was critical, and Brandeis's point was basic. "In other words, a method of competition fair among equals may be very unfair if applied where there is inequality of resources."[130] Brandeis's abstract language in *Erie* contradicted his fervently held views concerning the relationship between individuals and corporations.

Equally, *Erie*'s abstract analysis was foreign to Brandeis's habit of mind. "He sought continuously," wrote Dean Acheson, one of his law clerks, "to make the case before him as concrete as possible, to develop fully all the facts involved in the dispute and, beyond them, the great body of factual knowledge which surrounded the particular episode."[131] Holmes described his friend's approach in similar terms. Brandeis "always desires to know all that can be known about a case," he observed. He "loves facts" and in drafting opinions was "the most thorough of men."[132] Yet in *Erie* Brandeis treated the social facts sketchily and quite inaccurately, and he relied on a picture of the world that he fundamentally rejected.

That abstract image and general language did, however, frame Brandeis's opinion in socially neutral terms. It emphasized a kind of discrimination that even many defenders of *Swift* acknowledged as an unfortunate result of the doctrine. More important, it obscured the corporate exploitation of diversity by transforming the problem of a specific and socially based legal inequality into one of generalized and abstract "discrimination" between generic categories of citizen and noncitizen.

Brandeis stated, however, that *Swift*'s defects were revealed by "experience" and occurred "in practice." *Erie*'s abstract citizen/noncitizen dichotomy became socially meaningful only from that quite different perspective—by reading into it the social reality that Progressives had decried for half a century. Few ordinary individuals sought to bring suits in federal court, and fewer still sought to do so in out-of-state federal courts. Of the relative handful who did, few tried to take advantage of a favorable federal common law rule. In contrast, large corporations had the resources regularly to seek and find the most favorable forums available. More important, because they conducted business as "noncitizens" across the nation they were continuously in a position to remove diversity suits against them and secure the advantages of *Swift* and a federal forum. Indeed, as Brandeis well knew, foreign corporations dominated the diversity docket and were the removing parties in the overwhelming majority of all removed diversity actions.[133] That social exploitation of diversity and the enhanced extralegal litigation leverage that it gave corporate defendants—not an abstract discrimination between conceptual categories—was the de facto "experience" that constituted, in Brandeis's view, an unjust discrimination that was "in practice" systemic and "far reaching."[134]

Although conceptualism was foreign to his thought, Brandeis could use its techniques when they served his purpose.[135] "He never ceased," Alexander Bickel wrote, "to exercise, and perhaps delight in, a ruthless technical ingenuity in the contrivance of distinctions."[136] His generalized citizen/noncitizen analysis was such a contrivance, for it drained his opinion of identifiable, partisan, and concrete social consequences while effectively altering the balance of sociolegal power in litigation practice. Indeed, Brandeis invoked the tactics of those individual litigants who "remove[d] from their own State and became citizens of another" for that exact purpose. He trumpeted the misleading proposition that *Swift* stimulated forum shopping not only by corporations but also by individuals—indeed, by an unspecified and seemingly innumerable "wide range of persons." The assertion made *Erie* seem socially neutral and obscured its practical significance.

Brandeis reinforced that neutral effect with an otherwise curious omission. As usual, he relied on a wide variety of sources in his opinion, ranging from standard judicial decisions to less conventional materials such as law review articles and reports of congressional hearings. He even included more questionable citations to jurisdictional reform bills that had been introduced in Congress during the preceding decade but had failed to become law. He did not, however,

cite the single most rigorous, comprehensive, and authoritative source of information about the federal diversity docket that was then available, the massive
quantitative survey that had been conducted by Yale Law School and published
by the American Law Institute only four years earlier.[137] Not only was the study
relevant to "experience" under *Swift,* but its elaborate statistical results clearly
demonstrated one salient fact concerning diversity "in practice": Progressives
were right when they charged that corporations dominated the diversity docket
and used removal methodically and extensively. The fact that Brandeis did not
draw on that finding or cite the study suggests again that he designed his opinion to obscure the significance of corporate litigation practices and minimize the
importance of *Erie*'s expected social consequences.

That Brandeis's view of the world differed from the abstract analysis he
presented in *Erie* was confirmed by three other facts. First, the change Stone
made in the opinion, though minor, did reorient its logical thrust. Stone wrote:
"If only a question of statutory construction were involved we would not be
prepared to abandon a doctrine so widely applied."[138] Brandeis had originally
written that "[w]e need not determine whether the objections disclosed by experience are alone sufficient reason for abandoning a doctrine."[139] The final version emphasized, and then avoided, an issue of statutory construction, whereas
Brandeis had originally structured his opinion to consider, but then avoid, a
social analysis.

Second, an early fragment of his draft, neither completed nor included in
the final opinion, further suggested that Brandeis was thinking of the Progressive critique of *Swift.* "To a large extent the diverse citizenship jurisdiction was
invoked by non-citizens not for protection against apprehended local bias but
to get the advantage of some federal ruling, made or expected, more favorable
than that embodied in the decisions of the highest court of the State," he wrote.
"Thus the Court held that whether an employer was liable for injuries suffered
by an employee through the negligence of a fellow servant was a question of
gt. . . ."[140] There the fragment broke off. It revealed, however, that Brandeis
began an argument that stressed more strongly the purposive social use of *Swift*
and, further, that he initially thought of emphasizing not only the *Taxicab* case
but also the socially more important and divisive *Baugh,* Brewer's harsh 1893
fellow-servant decision. The fragment, of course, is ambiguous. Since Brandeis
did not include it in his final draft, he may have been unpersuaded by the line of
argument it suggested. That, however, seems implausible. He had nothing but
the keenest antipathy for *Baugh* and the values it represented, and he certainly
believed that corporations had exploited the availability of a pro-defendant federal common law. The more convincing explanation for his decision to eliminate
the discussion of *Baugh,* then, was that Brandeis made a conscious choice to

depoliticize *Erie*. *Baugh* was inconsistent with that neutralist purpose, while the *Taxicab* case served it perfectly.

Third, and by far most convincing, Brandeis stated the pivotal jurisdictional law on which he relied in a mistaken, but unusually revealing, manner. "[T]he privilege of selecting the court in which the right should be determined was conferred upon the non-citizen."[141] That statement was obviously inaccurate; the correct statement of law was embodied in clear and long-established statutory provisions.[142] As plaintiff, a citizen might sue a noncitizen in either federal or state court in the citizen's home state, and a noncitizen had the same choice.[143] It was only in the removal context where the noncitizen enjoyed the advantage. Sued in the state courts of her home state, the citizen could not remove; sued in the state courts of an adversary's home state, the noncitizen could remove. The widely recognized and dominant social pattern of diversity litigation showed that individual plaintiffs brought suit in their home states and that foreign corporations removed. The law that Brandeis stated in *Erie*, in other words, was the law that related only to the difference between citizens and noncitizens with respect to their right of removal. Brandeis, then, ostensibly speaking in general terms, stated the relevant law that applied only in a specific subcategory of cases. That lapse confirmed that he was focused not on the law considered most generally—not on abstract citizens and noncitizens—but on the law that controlled in the specific and paradigmatic social situation in which diversity jurisdiction operated, to the Progressive mind, most notoriously and unfairly.

Brandeis's misstatement of the law was particularly revealing, too, because its effect was consistent with the effect of two other apparent lapses in his opinion. One of those was Brandeis's misleading analysis of interstate forum shopping, with its puzzling image of equal litigant atoms in the judicial marketplace. Both the analysis and the image had the virtue of focusing his opinion steadily on the proliferating and abusive tactics that plaintiffs employed.[144] The other apparent lapse was Brandeis's surprising failure to utilize, or even cite, the Yale Law School survey demonstrating that corporations were the removing party in 87 percent of all removed diversity actions. By ignoring that study, Brandeis could ignore its powerful confirmation of the Progressive charge that corporations systematically exploited diversity removal jurisdiction. Thus, all three of the apparent lapses in his opinion—the inaccurate analysis and puzzling image of interstate forum shopping, the inexplicable failure to cite the best available body of empirical data, and the obvious misstatement of the relevant jurisdictional law—served the same rhetorical function: they deflected attention from removal, the key element in the corporate use of diversity jurisdiction and the area where Swift had operated most notoriously.

Erie's artful design provokes an obvious question. Why would Brandeis write such a flawed, abstract, oblique, and misleading opinion? Reflection suggests that, in the context of early 1938, he had quite a number of reasons for doing so.

First, the Progressive critique of *Swift* and diversity was difficult to demonstrate conclusively. Although it was widely recognized that diversity operated to favor corporate interests and much evidence supported the claim, this fact was exceptionally difficult to "prove" empirically. Statistical evidence was incomplete, legal analyses were subject to dispute, and personal testimony was partisan and divisive. In addition, corporations defended their use of diversity as a necessary recourse against local prejudice, a danger that was difficult to disprove and unwise to disparage wholly. Moreover counterexamples showed that individual plaintiffs could also exploit diversity. Indeed, *Erie* itself was such a counterexample—one that fit nicely with, and may even have helped inspire, Brandeis's neutral conceptual analysis. It was easier and safer to rest on a theory of general discrimination than attempt to establish a theory of specific social bias.[145]

Second, Brandeis's characteristic method of examining and documenting the social operation of legal rules was unnecessary. His "fact-based" opinions grew not only from his pragmatic orientation but also from his persistent efforts to demonstrate the "reasonableness" of regulatory measures.[146] In *Erie*, there was no contested statute and no need to show its reasonable operation. The case was to turn, he had decided, upon a rule of law, and a rule of constitutional law at that. Social facts, therefore, could appropriately play a peripheral role.

Third, and far more important, to argue the existence of a particular social discrimination would have been politically divisive and partisan. The spring of 1938 was a critical and volatile period: The Depression dragged on, the New Deal was fragmenting, and war loomed in Europe. The Court had just survived the tumultuous Court-packing battle and was in the process of effecting a constitutional "revolution." *Erie* itself, even dressed in the most neutral language, was a startling reversal of established law that would almost certainly be viewed as radical and disruptive. There was simply no reason to make the opinion appear any more socially inspired than was minimally necessary.

Fourth, a neutral analysis would not only prevent *Erie* from engendering bitter or extended controversy, but it also guaranteed Brandeis his bare majority. He had reason to doubt the complete support of Hughes and Roberts. More important, he undoubtedly recalled that Stone had refused to join his dissent in both *Quaker City*, which condemned the "menace" of corporations, and *Bedford*, which suggested the majority's class bias. At most, Brandeis could afford to lose only one vote—his constitutional language threatened to, and did, accomplish that. An opinion that emphasized *Erie*'s social purpose and consequences would have endangered and quite likely scuttled his majority opinion. He dared not run that risk.

Finally, Brandeis realized that he was in a new position on a new Court. After twenty years as a "great dissenter," he was suddenly in an emerging and profoundly different constitutional majority. Having criticized and castigated the old Court for its social bias, he had no desire to call attention to his own values when he was at last establishing new and Progressive doctrine. The Court needed, perhaps above all, to establish its social neutrality and to decide cases upon the basis of generalized and evenhanded principles. The fact that Black alone—the author of a dozen solo and sometimes radical dissents—championed his opinion may have cautioned him further. While Brandeis was helping the Court set a new constitutional course with a new social orientation, he also recognized the importance of setting for the nation an example of a judiciary that was disinterested, reasoning, and fair.

Erie's "social" component was thus paradoxical. It constituted both a triumph for Brandeis's Progressive social values and an exemplar of the rule of general and neutral legal principles. Had the opinion been the work of Holmes, it would surely have been different. Had it come from Cardozo or Stone, Hughes or Roberts, Black or Reed, different still. But *Erie* was Brandeis's opinion, to an exceptional degree. In it he tried to reconcile through a "form of words" his Progressive commitments to social justice and efficiency, with a broader commitment to the ideal of law as principled and evenhanded. Unfortunately, he drafted his opinion so artfully and cautiously that he allowed the latter ideal to obscure not only the decision's immediate social results but also an integral part of his Progressive ideal, the vital principle that law should be equitable and just "in practice," not merely in form. That Brandeis served his values and ideals with a heavy dose of the expedient and disingenuous illustrates the fact that Supreme Court judges are, after all, intelligent but imperfect—as well as purposive and crafty—human beings who must operate in an unusually complex, demanding, and pragmatic majoritarian institution.

"Defects, Political" 7

THE PROGRESSIVE AS

CONSTITUTIONAL ARCHITECT

S*wift*'s "defects" were "political" as well as "social," Brandeis wrote, and its paramount political flaw was its elevation of the judiciary over the legislature. Brandeis believed in the constitutional primacy of the legislature, and *Erie*—rooted in the political ideals of Progressivism—implemented that principle. "Primacy," of course, did not mean "supremacy." Like most Progressives, Brandeis did not wish to abolish judicial review or give unlimited power to the legislature. Instead, he sought to limit the judiciary, constrain its anti-Progressive activism, and force it to defer more broadly to legislative policy.[1] Although his decision fostered decentralization, ultimately it rested not on the distinction between local and national authority but, rather, on the relationship between federal judicial and legislative power.

Progressivism and the Legislature

Proclaiming that "we are committed primarily to democracy,"[2] Brandeis devoted his career to what he regarded as the compatible causes of social justice, organizational efficiency, and popular government. All required, and were based on, "rule by the people."[3] The nation was founded on faith in popular government and the authority of elected legislatures. "In America, as in England," he declared, "the conviction prevailed then [at the founding] that the people must look to representative assemblies for the protection of their liberties."[4]

As did most Progressives, Brandeis viewed the courts as obstacles to reform and the legislatures, however imperfect, as the means of achieving it. The latter half of the nineteenth century had been a period of revolutionary change, and "[p]olitical as well as economic science" tried to study that change carefully. "But legal science—the unwritten or judge-made laws as distinguished from legislation—was largely deaf and blind."[5] He identified the judiciary with social ignorance and doctrinal rigidity and the legislature with factual investigation, expert planning, and scientific reform. "In the course of relatively few years," he declared, voicing the common Progressive complaint, "hundreds of statutes which embodied attempts (often very crude) to adjust legal rights to the demands of social justice were nullified by the courts." [6]

Sharing the Progressive commitments to popular government and expert administration, Brandeis understood the legislature as the essential and proper instrument of social reform. With its members popularly elected from relatively small districts, the legislature constituted the voice of the people and comprised the voices of the localities. The courts were further removed, and in many cases essentially insulated, from the educative pressures of electoral politics. Further, the legislature was properly the "lawmaking" body of government, the repository of the people's legitimate power to remake the law, create new governmental institutions, and finance the programs that social amelioration required. Although the courts could also "make law," they did so properly only within a narrow range, and they lacked power to authorize new institutions and fund their operations. Finally, the legislature had the capacity to investigate social problems and utilize the knowledge of society's experts. Conversely, the courts were too often mired in outworn doctrine and unable to gather, let alone master, the relevant social facts.

Faith in the power of facts and the methods of reason and science was central to Brandeis's social philosophy. What "the welfare of the community demands," he emphasized, "is intelligent and wholehearted cooperation in attaining the greatest efficiency of production and the avoidance of waste." [7] Although he recognized the pervasive power of entrenched interests, he believed that careful study of social problems, meticulous attention to detail, and elaborate presentation of evidence could guide the people and compel legislative majorities to act. Social research, "if published in proper form," he commented in 1909, "must prove of paramount importance." It would "profoundly affect public opinion" and furnish "a broad foundation for legislative action." [8]

His argument in *Muller v. Oregon*, in which he successfully defended an Oregon statute that regulated the hours of women factory workers, characterized his approach. [9] His brief—widely known as the "Brandeis brief"—contained two pages of legal analysis and over a hundred devoted to empirical evidence demonstrating the social harm that resulted from excessive hours of factory labor. Subsequently, he heralded the statute as an example of intelligent social experimentation and pictured the Oregon legislature—with perhaps some artistic license—as an organized, intelligent, and highly methodical social scientist using careful research to solve modern problems. [10] It was essential, he maintained, that legal analysis proceed through an understanding of social facts and not merely through the "logical" analysis of legal principles. "Whether or not [an experiment] is arbitrary, whether it is reasonable," he insisted, "must be determined largely by results where it has been tried out."[11] Judicial deference to legislative innovations was essential if society was to benefit from the "logic of facts." It was small wonder that he feared so intensely the anti-legislative potential of the declaratory judgment.

Ten years later, dissenting in *International News Service v. The Associated Press*, Brandeis spoke in the same voice of Progressivism from the bench of the Supreme Court.[12] There, he opposed the majority's decision to allow one news service to enjoin another from "appropriating" its "property" in the news reports it distributed to clients. "[W]ith the increasing complexity of society, the public interest tends to become omnipresent," he explained, "and the problems presented by the new demands for justice cease to be simple." Growing social complexity meant that "the creation or recognition by courts of a new private right may work serious injury to the general public."[13] The reason, to Progressives at least, was obvious. "Courts are ill-equipped to make the investigations which should precede a determination of the limitations which should be set upon any property right in the news." Moreover, if courts tried to create such new rights, they "would be powerless to prescribe the detailed regulations essential to full enjoyment of the rights conferred or to introduce the machinery required for enforcement of such regulations."[14] Conversely, legislatures could "consider such facts and possibilities" that "appropriate inquiry" disclosed, establish rational and ordered structures of limited rights and tailored remedies, and "provide administrative machinery for enforcing the rules." It was precisely because of those institutional capacities, Brandeis maintained, that "the effort to meet the many new demands for justice incident to a rapidly changing civilization" compelled the "resort to legislation."[15]

Brandeis's faith in the power of facts and the potential of legislation dovetailed with the values he identified in both expert administration and decentralized federalism.[16] "There is great advantage in the opportunity we have of working out our social problems in the detached laboratories of the different states," he argued in 1912. Decentralization was ideally suited to encourage legislative experiments inspired by social research and directed by specialized administrative agencies. "[W]e ought to get the full benefit of experiments in individual states before attempting anything in the way of Federal action."[17] Twenty years later, dissenting from the Supreme Court's invalidation of an Oklahoma statute that regulated private business, he reaffirmed his faith. "It is one of the happy incidents of the federal system that a single courageous state may, if its citizens choose, serve as a laboratory," he declared, "and try novel social and economic experiments without risk to the rest of the country."[18]

Although Brandeis's faith in popular government and the legislative process was profound, it was not unrealistic. "[W]e are living in a Democracy, & some way or other the people will get back at power unduly concentrated," he commented in 1906, "and there will be plenty of injustice in the process."[19] He was well aware, too, of legislative corruption and compromise, and he knew that even able and dedicated Progressives would be unable to remake the world. "[D]o not pin too much faith in legislation," he cautioned.[20] The process of social improvement was difficult, uncertain, and slow. Still, Brandeis believed, it was essential for society to remedy the disruption caused by industrialization, and participation in the common effort was, for the individual, a moral duty. The primary instrument in practice, and the proper one in principle, was the popularly elected and potentially "scientific" legislature.

Given Brandeis's belief in the primacy of the legislature, he was especially sensitive to the fact that the federal courts under *Swift* made national rules of law in areas where Congress did not legislate and, far more egregious, in areas where it could not legislate. In *Erie* he identified property conveyances, contracts entered into and performed wholly within one state, and "torts committed within the State upon persons resident or property located there."[21] Those categories seemed purely "local," and Congress had not tried to legislate for any of them and, to some extent at least, almost certainly could not do so. But if they were beyond the power of Congress, that fact made no difference to the federal courts under *Swift*. The federal common law was illegitimate, Brandeis believed, because it was based on the fallacy that the scope of congressional power had no relevance to the reach of the federal judicial power. The fatal flaw in *Swift*, he wrote in his unsuccessful effort to placate the dubious Justice Reed, was that it created an area of judge-made law "untouched by [congressional] legislation."[22]

"Untouched by Legislation": The Anomaly of Insurance Law

The existence of federal judicial law-making power "untouched" by congressional authority manifested itself starkly in the area of insurance law, a realm where *Swift* was widely applied and in which Brandeis had a special interest. In 1905 a struggle had erupted for control of the Equitable Life Assurance Society of New York, and a group of Massachusetts policyholders retained Brandeis as counsel to study the situation and advise them.[23] Angered over the company's high-handed methods and outraged by the results of a contemporaneous insurance investigation in New York, he launched a campaign to reform the industry and create an alternate source of protection for workers. He was largely responsible for the development of the Massachusetts plan for savings bank life insurance and a primary force in urging it on the state legislature. In 1907, despite powerful and organized opposition, the Massachusetts Assembly enacted his program.[24] The success, Brandeis believed, was his "greatest achievement," and it was the beginning of what became a lifelong commitment.[25]

Savings bank life insurance was typically Brandeisian. Its purpose was to create a more efficient system of providing socially necessary protection; it was designed to allow individuals to become responsible for their own needs; it used a decentralized and cooperative instrument; and it was based on an antipathy toward concentrated wealth and uncontrolled power. The major insurance companies fired Brandeis's hostility. Foremost, they represented an unbridled concentration of economic power that had to be tamed. Detailing the financial operations of the companies, Brandeis highlighted their amassed wealth and abuse of public trust.[26] "The greatest economic menace of today," he charged, was the "great insurance companies which are controlling so large a part of our quick capital" and which "exercise a predominating influence over the business of the country."[27] Moreover, he argued, the companies' methods were abusive, inefficient, and fraudulent.[28] The three largest companies spent excessive amounts of their premiums on unjustifiable administrative expenses, and policyholders consequently shouldered the burden of unreasonably high rates.[29] Finally, "oppressive provisions in the policies" frequently provided inadequate compensation or even prevented recovery when insured persons filed claims.[30]

Brandeis supported savings bank life insurance throughout his life, and the commitment of his early Progressive years remained intense in 1938. Less than two months after *Erie* came down he criticized the "recent attempt of the [insurance] companies to secure in Massachusetts restrictive legislation" regarding savings bank life insurance, and he pointed to "the urgent need of intensive widespread education."[31] On March 5, while drafting *Erie,* he wrote to a friend expressing his hope that Governor Herbert H. Lehman would succeed in his effort to institute a savings bank life insurance plan in New York "[d]espite insurance company wiles."[32]

The revelations of the insurance investigations in 1905 flowed from and strengthened the tide of Progressivism. Across the nation pressure for insurance reform grew, and by 1908 twenty-nine states had passed new legislation, a good many substantially altering their regulatory laws. Recognizing the role that *Swift* and diversity jurisdiction played in augmenting the social power of the insurance companies, moreover, some states adopted statutes designed to prevent insurance companies from removing suits against them to the federal courts.[33] Simultaneously, a drive began in Congress to pass legislation that would establish a national licensing requirement for all interstate insurance companies. While championing strict state regulation, Brandeis was initially wary of the proposed congressional action. Suspicious of unnecessary centralization, he believed that the particular bill under consideration would serve primarily to preempt the increasingly rigorous and nearly universal state regulation of insurance and thereby protect the companies rather than their policyholders.[34]

By 1913, however, Brandeis's opposition to national legislation waned when Congress at last considered legislation that he regarded as truly Progressive. Then, he was forced to confront the awkward constitutional problem that had repeatedly stymied congressional action.[35] For fifty years the Supreme Court had held that insurance was not "commerce" and, hence, that Congress could not reach it under the commerce power.[36] To avoid the judicial roadblock, Brandeis proposed that "Congress has ample power" to regulate insurance "indirectly by virtue of its control of the mail privilege or through the taxing power."[37] His recognition that Congress could only legislate for the insurance industry "indirectly" underscored the pivotal institutional anomaly that marked American insurance law. Congress was barred from regulating insurance matters, while the federal courts were free under *Swift* to develop a federal common law to govern the area.

By the 1920s insurance law not only presented a lawmaking anomaly but had become one of the most obvious areas where federal common law diverged from state law and favored insurance companies over their policyholders.[38] Claimants' attorneys avidly sought to avoid the national courts, while insurance companies worked assiduously to force their adversaries to litigate there. By the early 1930s their tactical battles were escalating, and a stream of difficult procedural questions poured into the appellate courts. Repeatedly, Brandeis and the other justices were forced to confront the complex doctrinal problems that insurance litigation generated in the battle for forum control. *Haworth* and the declaratory judgment, in his view, highlighted the constitutional anomaly and promised to exacerbate the practical problems it generated.

The federal common law of insurance contracts provoked Brandeis's hostility for yet another reason. Consistently defending exercises of legislative authority and upholding the right of the states to supervise insurance, he rejected the substantive due process rationale used to invalidate state regulatory efforts.[39] In 1918 his confrontation with the Court's anti-Progressive majority in *New York Life Insurance Co. v. Dodge* taught him a lesson.[40] As *Hitchman* had revealed how substantive due process coupled with federal judicial lawmaking could create powerful legal obstacles to unionism, *Dodge* demonstrated how the two could combine to further restrict the ability of the states to regulate insurance.

The New York Life Insurance Company challenged a Missouri statute designed to minimize the opportunities for insurance companies to declare policies forfeit. The statute provided that, upon failure to meet a premium payment, a policy's paid-up reserve—minus up to three-fourths of the reserve value if needed to cover any other indebtedness—would be applied to premium pay-

ments until it was exhausted. Dodge had taken out a policy in Missouri and subsequently pledged it as security for a loan from the company. When he failed to
pay the premium due on his policy, the company appropriated the reserve value
to cover the loan obligation and held the policy forfeited. Upon his death, his
widow sued the company in a Missouri state court, claiming under the statute
that premium payments due from the reserve value had kept the policy in effect.
The company answered that the subsequent loan agreement had been consummated in New York, that its actions were valid under New York law, and that the
Missouri statute could not constitutionally be applied to a loan agreement made
in New York. A Missouri appellate court rejected the company's arguments and
affirmed a judgment for the widow. The statute, it held, was constitutional and
applied "notwithstanding any contrary agreement" between the parties.[41] Accordingly, the court found that the policy was still in force and that, after the
proper deductions, the company owed Dodge's widow $2,233.45.

The United States Supreme Court reversed. Its prior decisions upheld the
power of a state "to control insurance contracts made within its borders," the majority explained, but those cases "do not rule the question presently presented."
The subsequent loan agreement was a separate contract, and "competent parties
consummated the loan contract now relied upon in New York where it was to
be performed." As Missouri "lacked power" to control a New York contract, the
statute as applied exceeded the state's authority. A contrary ruling, the majority
concluded, would "permit destruction" of the policyholder's right to borrow
and would "sanction the impairment of that liberty of contract guaranteed to all
by the Fourteenth Amendment."[42]

Brandeis disagreed with the majority at every point. "There is no constitutional limitation by virtue of which a statute enacted by a State in the exercise
of the police power," he charged, "is necessarily void, if, in its operation, contracts made in another State may be affected." Maintaining that the proper test
was whether the regulation was "reasonable," he explored the social and legal
reasons the statute was constitutionally valid as applied.[43] The policyholder was
at all times resident in Missouri, the company was licensed to do business in the
state, and the statute sought a legitimate goal without depriving the company
of its rights to collect on the policyholder's debts.

Most important, Brandeis called special attention to the fact that *Dodge*
turned necessarily on an unexamined choice of law and an indirect but crucial
application of the assumptions behind *Swift*. The Missouri courts selected and
applied local law, construing the statute as controlling the policy regardless of
the second agreement. The Supreme Court ruled that the state's choice was unconstitutional on the basis of a threshold determination—unspecified as to its
legal source—that the second contract was "made" in New York. The Court's

source was the law of neither Missouri nor New York, Brandeis pointed out, but rather "general law." [44] Only after deciding that the second agreement was "made" in New York could the Court rule that the statute as applied violated the Fourteenth Amendment. Realizing the extent to which insurance company attorneys could manipulate the "place of making," Brandeis stressed the authority of the state to protect its citizens "against acts of insuring corporations." [45]

Dodge was an ominous warning to Brandeis, signaling *Swift*'s pervasive anti-Progressive and anti-legislative influence. The majority used general law to limit the reach of a state statute beyond the direct command of due process doctrine. In deciding that the "place of making" was determinative and that the contract was made in New York, the Court exploited the assumptions behind *Swift* to read the Missouri statute as transgressing the Fourteenth Amendment. It held in effect that state rejection of a general law choice-of-law rule could constitute a violation of the Constitution. Common law concepts suffused the law of contracts, and, as long as the *Swift* doctrine existed, federal general law could indirectly determine and then constitutionally limit the scope of state statutes. *Dodge* suggested to Brandeis that *Swift* was a threat, not just to the authority of Congress and the state courts, but to state legislative authority as well.

Constitutional Erie: The Principle of Legislative Primacy

When the opportunity arrived to overrule *Swift*, Brandeis did so to curb the power of the federal courts. He believed that *Swift* violated the Constitution's structural balance, which mandated that the legislative branch hold lawmaking primacy over the judiciary.[46] Brandeis's constitutional theory was not based on any particular limitation on congressional power, nor was it based on a commitment to decentralization as such. Rather, it was grounded on two related principles. The first, which Brandeis regarded as inherent in the constitutional structure, was that legislative and judicial powers were coextensive. The second, which he regarded as a prudential but nevertheless essential corollary, was that federal judicial power was also limited to those areas—not involving constitutional rights—where Congress had chosen to act. Absent compelling reason, the federal courts should not make law even in areas within the national legislative power unless and until Congress made the initial decision to assert national authority in that area.[47] In its theory of legislative primacy, *Erie* was a constitutional statement of the political ideals of early twentieth-century Progressivism.[48]

Swift's essential constitutional error was that it denied the existence of legislative power as a prerequisite to judicial lawmaking. "The federal courts assumed, in the broad field of 'general law,' the power to declare rules of decision which Congress was confessedly without power to enact as statutes." [49] The key word was *confessedly:* the Court itself admitted that it had acted beyond the power of Congress. The quotation Brandeis selected from *Swift* made the point. There, the Court had not considered the scope of congressional authority even relevant to its lawmaking powers, and it had accepted its obligation to follow state statutes when they extended into a "general law" area. Thus, the Court acknowledged that it was making law in an area properly governed by state legislative authority. The quotation made it apparent that the Court viewed itself as a court of general common law jurisdiction irrespective of any limitations that restricted Congress.[50] Brandeis enumerated a variety of instances in which the federal courts had made common law rules in areas that were unrelated to any accepted theory of national legislative power.[51] There was "no federal general common law" because "Congress has no power" to make such law. That absence of power did not turn, as *Swift* in theory had turned, on whether the issue was "local" or "general." Rather, it turned on the absence of congressional authority as determined by reference to the constitutional grant of powers to the national government.

Brandeis made his premise clear in his effort to persuade Reed to join the majority. The point of his analysis, he explained, was not that Congress lacked certain powers but that the federal courts ignored the relevance of whatever those powers were. "Since [the *Swift* doctrine] admits that the state rule must be followed if declared in a [state] statute," he explained, "it admits that [the state rule] is not a matter within the authority of Congress."[52] The axiom of coextensive powers served as his implicit premise. Indeed, because state legislatures could in effect modify or abolish federal common law rules within their jurisdiction, Brandeis's statement that *Swift* created an area of judicial lawmaking "untouched by legislation" made no sense without the axiom of coextensive powers and the premise that national legislative power was the touchstone for the scope of the federal judicial power.

To that constitutional axiom, Brandeis added a critical and prudential corollary that further restricted the judiciary: even in areas within congressional power, the federal courts should not, absent compelling reasons, make nonconstitutional law in advance of applicable legislation. "Except in matters governed by the Federal Constitution or by Acts of Congress," he asserted, "the law to be applied in any case is the law of the State."[53] *Erie* involved an alleged tort committed by an interstate carrier moving in interstate commerce, and it seemed relatively clear that Congress could enact rules of law that would cover its particular facts. Brandeis, however, wanted to establish the principle that the mere possibility of valid congressional legislation was by itself insufficient to authorize the national courts to make law in an area. Congress, not the courts, should determine when and where national lawmaking authority was exercised.

Brandeis had four reasons for ignoring *Erie*'s "interstate" context, each based on his assumption of legislative primacy. First, congressional abstention in any area within its authority represented a political judgment by the representative branch that states should exercise control in that area, and the courts should defer to that judgment. In fact, the regulation of interstate commerce was an area where Brandeis believed such deference was particularly desirable. Although Congress could assert exclusive control over interstate commerce, in many areas it had not done so. In the absence of national legislation the states were free, within the imprecise boundaries of the "dormant" Commerce Clause, to regulate some aspects of it. The recurring question was whether various state statutes impinged improperly on national commerce, and Brandeis believed that Congress, not the judiciary, should make that decision. "My own opinion," he explained, "had been that it was wise (1) to treat the constitutional power of interstate commerce as very broad and (2) to treat acts of Congress as not invading State power unless it clearly appeared that the federal power was intended to be exercised exclusively."[54] To counter the aggrandizing tendencies of the federal judiciary in needlessly preempting state law, the states could persuade Congress to define explicitly the scope it intended for its legislation. "[I]f [the states] wish to preserve their police power," he urged, "they should, through the 'state block' [*sic*] in Congress, see to it in every class of Congressional legislation that the state rights which they desire to preserve be expressly provided for in the acts."[55] Regardless of the "facts" in *Erie*, then, because Congress had not asserted national authority in the area, the judiciary should follow suit and apply state law.

Second, Brandeis considered the judiciary, in contrast to the legislature, unsuited to the task of establishing the kind of laws that were necessary to deal with complex social and economic issues. Given the sporadic, limited, and reactive nature of judicial intervention, he reasoned, the courts were "ill-equipped" to initiate significant changes in the law.[56] Without legislative guidance and support, their ad hoc efforts could easily cause more harm than good.

Third, Brandeis understood that if the federal courts could make rules in advance of congressional legislation, they would frequently be forced to frame decisions in hypothetical and "advisory" terms. Could Congress pass legislation that would apply to the facts in *Erie?* What kind of legislation could it be? What would be its limits? How far would or should it be extended? Any test of the scope of judicial lawmaking power based on unexercised congressional authority would force the courts to evaluate the limits of that authority abstractly, and Brandeis was adamantly opposed to such "advisory" opinions, especially in matters of constitutional adjudication.[57] The strength of the judiciary lay in its capacity to scrutinize past events; the strength of the legislature lay in its ability to adapt the law broadly to present and future needs.

Fourth, Brandeis knew that a limit based on possible but hypothetical congressional legislation would, as a practical matter, be wholly insufficient to restrain the national courts. And he also knew, as his long experience with congressional efforts to overthrow *Swift* had shown, that in most cases judge-made rules would stand without subsequent correction by Congress. Even the formidable Progressive assault on diversity jurisdiction and the reformist congressional majorities of the early 1930s had not been sufficient to overrule *Swift* or even remedy the specific abuse that had occurred in the *Taxicab* case. Jurisdictional issues were abstract and technical, and specific common law rules seldom commanded congressional attention. By itself, the axiom of coextensive powers would prove only slightly more constraining in practice than the general law doctrine of *Swift*. It was essential, Brandeis believed, that the lawmaking power of the federal courts be restricted, beyond constitutional mandates, to areas already controlled "by Acts of Congress."

During his early years on the Court, Brandeis had faced an analogous problem in a series of admiralty cases.* There, the Court took peremptory action in setting aside state and federal workmen's compensation acts—reforms which Brandeis considered of the greatest social importance. This action heightened Brandeis's sensitivity to the danger of allowing judicial lawmaking in areas within congressional authority but where Congress had chosen not to act. Beginning in 1917 in a series of decisions written by the anti-Progressive Justice McReynolds, the Court declared that the constitutional grant of admiralty jurisdiction gave the federal courts exclusive judicial authority to make relevant substantive rules in maritime cases. It held further that the "general maritime law" could not be altered by state law, that it required uniform rules throughout the United States, and that Congress—though enjoying exclusive legislative authority in maritime matters—was constitutionally barred from adopting as national law the differing legislation of the states. State workmen's compensation laws, therefore, could not govern maritime employment. Subsequently, the Court ruled unconstitutional two successive congressional enactments that attempted to incorporate state workmen's compensation statutes into the federal maritime law.[58]

The battle lines were familiar. In the leading case, *Southern Pacific Co. v. Jensen*,[59] Brandeis and Clarke joined Holmes's dissent, charging that the Court conceived the maritime law as the familiar and delusive "omnipresence," this

---

*Article III, Section 2, of the Constitution extended the federal judicial power to "all Cases of admiralty and maritime Jurisdiction," and from 1789 Congress conferred this jurisdiction on the federal district courts. Its jurisdictional statute embodied an inherent tension, making "admiralty" jurisdiction exclusive to the federal courts but "saving" to suitors the right to seek a common law remedy in state court "when the common law is competent to give it." It was thus up to the Supreme Court to draw the line between "admiralty" matters, which were exclusive to the federal courts, and related "common law" issues, where federal jurisdiction was concurrent with that of the state courts.

time found brooding over the seas.[60] Brandeis and Clarke also joined Justice Pitney's separate and more elaborate dissent, which argued that, at least in the absence of a congressional mandate, the admiralty jurisdiction provided a forum only and not the basis for an exclusive and substantive federal judge-made maritime law.[61] Subsequently, Brandeis dissented when the Court declared that state courts must apply the federal admiralty law,[62] and he dissented in both cases which held that Congress could not simply incorporate the various state statutes into federal maritime law.[63]

Brandeis had two objections to the Court's doctrine. One was that it enforced by judicial fiat an absolute uniformity without examining the social context to ascertain whether or not uniformity was desirable.[64] The other was that the *Jensen* line of cases consistently limited the reach of otherwise applicable workmen's compensation laws. Brandeis invariably voted to sustain and expand the coverage of those laws, whether state or federal.[65]

In 1924 Brandeis wrote his major dissent from *Jensen* in *Washington v. Dawson,* and his views were strikingly consistent with his later opinion in *Erie.*[66] Protesting the Court's second invalidation of a congressional statute authorizing application of state workmen's compensation laws in admiralty, he noted the frailty of a mere jurisdictional grant as a basis for judicial lawmaking and argued that the nature of the issue presented was "wholly of state concern."[67] Most important, he stressed the significance of the fact that "Congress has, in express terms, given its sanction" to the state legislation.[68] "Congress may, at least in large measure," he insisted, "determine whether uniformity of regulation is required or diversity is permissible."[69] That was true under the Commerce Clause, and it was true to some extent even in the area of bankruptcy where the Constitution itself called for "uniform laws."[70] Moreover, Brandeis declared, "[e]xperience and discussion have also made apparent how unfortunate are the results, economically and socially," that stemmed from the Court's decisions in *Jensen* and its progeny. "It has, in part, frustrated a promising attempt to alleviate some of the misery, and remove some of the injustice, incident to the conduct of industry and commerce."[71]

Jensen and its progeny represented a quest for national uniformity in which the federal courts used a jurisdictional grant as the basis for asserting substantive lawmaking authority not only independent of state courts but mandatory upon them. The Court neither waited for Congress to address the issue nor deferred to its decentralizing statutes once it had acted. It recognized congressional authority as supreme, but it required that the legislature impose uniform national rules. The central flaw in all the cases, Brandeis believed, was that they denied the lawmaking primacy of the legislature. The federal courts occupied the field before Congress had chosen to act and rejected the subsequent judgments of Congress that uniformity was unnecessary. Thus, *Jensen* and its progeny demonstrated that a mere theoretical primacy of the legislature was not by itself sufficient to curb the national courts. The judiciary must have its law-making power limited not merely to areas of national legislative authority but also to areas where Congress had specifically chosen to act.

That restriction on judicial lawmaking, Brandeis believed, was especially necessary in diversity cases. If *Jensen* was bad, *Swift* was far worse. Admiralty represented a smaller amount of judicial business, a circumscribed class of cases, and a relatively limited intrusion on the interests of the states. Indeed, dealing with the law of the high seas, admiralty had from the nation's beginning been recognized as a core area for the proper exercise of federal authority. In contrast, diversity cases constituted a substantial amount of business and allowed parties to bring any and every issue of state law to the federal courts. Unlike *Jensen*, *Swift* provided the opportunity for extensive and persistent displacement of state laws on the most ordinary and fundamental issues. Additionally, Congress had from the nation's beginning passed legislation dealing with the maritime law and responded repeatedly to *Jensen* and its progeny with statutes providing workmen's compensation coverage to maritime workers.[72] In contrast, it had never been able to respond legislatively to *Swift* or the substantive rules that had been declared in its name. Finally, and constitutionally most significant, in admiralty the Court at least recognized the direct legislative authority of Congress, whereas *Swift* allowed the federal courts to operate where Congress was "confessedly" without power.[73]

Erie's declaration that *Swift* was unconstitutional, then, was a conclusion drawn from two premises: first, that the Constitution inscribed the principles of coextensive powers and legislative primacy; and, second, that *Swift* stood for the proposition that the federal courts could make law in areas where "Congress was confessedly without power" to act.[74] Brandeis was not deciding or implying anything in *Erie* concerning the ultimate scope of congressional power, nor was he necessarily suggesting that Congress could not legislate for the specific fact situation that *Erie* presented under some constitutional grant of power. He was only affirming two points. One was that *Swift* permitted the federal courts to act beyond the constitutional reach of the federal judicial power because it allowed them to make rules presumptively beyond the scope of congressional authority. The other point was that the federal courts should not, without compelling reason, displace state rules with those of their own making because Congress had not passed legislation to cover the facts of *Erie*.

The Derivative Role of the Tenth Amendment

Although Brandeis based his opinion in *Erie* on the principle of legislative primacy, he seemed to refer—albeit obliquely and reluctantly—to the Tenth Amendment. His analysis implicated that provision, but it did so only derivatively, only as a result of the controlling constitutional principle of coextensive powers. According to Brandeis, the Tenth Amendment, by itself, did not create any particular substantive limitation on the powers of Congress. He held, instead, that the authority of the national judiciary was limited to the same areas over which the national legislature could make laws, and that because Congress did not have authority over every area that the federal courts ruled under *Swift,* its doctrine allowed federal judicial lawmaking beyond the constitutional power of the national government. Consequently, this allowed an unlawful incursion into state authority which, as a corollary, violated the Tenth Amendment.

Brandeis had powerful political and social reasons for avoiding reliance on the Tenth Amendment. In the late 1930s the Court was expanding federal power under the Commerce Clause, but its outer boundary remained uncertain.[75] A substantive interpretation of the amendment would impose an independent limit on federal legislative power, precisely the type of constitutional constraint that opponents of the New Deal favored as a method of restricting Progressive legislation. Throughout his tenure on the Court, Brandeis supported far-reaching assertions of national legislative power, and he joined in one of the Court's most powerful repudiations of a substantive Tenth Amendment.[76] Justice Stone, too, was flatly opposed to a substantive Tenth Amendment, and any direct reliance on its independent mandate would surely have lost his vote.[77] Brandeis believed in decentralization, but he did not believe that decentralization should restrict Congress to anything less than the full range of its Article I powers.[78]

Brandeis's opinion contained only two apparent references to the Tenth Amendment. He quoted from Justice Field's dissent in *Baugh,* which cited the provision;[79] and he concluded with the declaration that the federal courts under *Swift* "have invaded rights which in our opinion are reserved by the Constitution to the several States."[80] The successive drafts of his opinion reveal the reluctance and the caution with which he made both references.

With respect to the first apparent reference, Field's *Baugh* dissent, Brandeis was meticulous in his usage. Most obviously, he did not quote any part of the dissent that mentioned the Tenth Amendment by name. Further, in the draft that he circulated to the Court on March 21 he used only two sentences from *Baugh,* not the entire quote that appeared in the final opinion. In that earlier draft he excluded the subsequently incorporated sentence that suggested most strongly a substantive Tenth Amendment: "There stands, as a perpetual protest against

[*Swift*], the Constitution of the United States, which recognizes and preserves the autonomy and independence of the states—independence in their legislative and independence in their judicial departments." [81] Instead, Brandeis originally quoted only two sentences which highlighted his axiom of coextensive powers: "Supervision over *either the legislative or the judicial action* of the States is in no case permissible except as to matters by the Constitution specifically authorized or delegated to the United States. *Any interference with either, except as thus permitted*, is an invasion of the authority of the State and, to that extent, a denial of its independence." [82] The reference to the parallel nature of legislative and judicial power implied that they properly had equal scope. Moreover, although the sentences did suggest a narrow construction of national power, they clearly implied that the sections of the Constitution that "specifically authorized and delegated" power to the national government, not the direct force of the Tenth Amendment, constituted the proper criteria by which to measure that power.

Brandeis added the rest of the Field quotation only as a bow to Chief Justice Hughes, who read the passage at the conference on April 9. [83] Hughes, like Justice Roberts, [84] had suggested that the Tenth Amendment created substantive restrictions on national power, and both may have considered the provision as *Erie*'s constitutional basis. [85] With only one easily distinguishable exception, however, the Court's invalidation of the NIRA in *Schechter*, Brandeis had pointedly refused to join the Court's anti–New Deal opinions that suggested a substantive Tenth Amendment. [86] Moreover, even if Hughes and Roberts did consider the Tenth Amendment *Erie*'s constitutional foundation, there was no reason to think that Brandeis accepted their view. Similarly, there was no reason to think that Brandeis accepted Field's views. Although his *Baugh* dissent expressed a strong concern for the constitutional rights of the states, Field and Brandeis differed so fundamentally in their views on constitutional law and their personal political values that Field's views cannot be attributed to Brandeis. Indeed, the longer quote Brandeis used in his final opinion ended two sentences before Field mentioned the Tenth Amendment. [87] Thus, rather than relying on the Tenth Amendment, Brandeis purposely avoided it, minimized its shadow, and rendered it superfluous.

Erie's second apparent reference to the amendment, the statement about "reserved" rights, was also omitted from Brandeis's March 21 draft. That draft ended its constitutional discussion with the quote from Holmes that declared *Swift* "an unconstitutional assumption of powers by courts of the United States." [88] In the middle of April, after the conference on the ninth, Brandeis considered the necessity of responding to the dissenters. Butler, writing for himself and McReynolds, charged the majority with deciding a needless constitutional issue and insisted that the Court had a duty to "indicate precisely the principle or provision of the Constitution held to have been transgressed."[89] It was only at that point that Brandeis decided to add the reference to "reserved" powers. "It does not seem to me that Justice Butler's opinion requires any change in the statements in my opinion," he wrote. "But I think it would be helpful to add the following: In disapproving [*Swift*] we do not hold unconstitutional Section 34 of the Federal Judiciary Act of 1789 or any other Act of Congress. We merely declare that in applying the doctrine this Court and the lower courts have invaded rights which in our opinion are reserved by the Constitution to the several States."[90] Thus, with a bare majority that contained two and probably three doubters and against a strong dissent that highlighted the opinion's constitutional vagueness, Brandeis finally decided to add a reference not to the Tenth Amendment itself but to less specific "reserved" rights. Purposely, he kept the statement vague. He refused to cite the amendment by name or to put any part of his statement in quotation marks.

Brandeis walked a narrow line. He apparently felt compelled to hint at the Tenth Amendment, but he was unwilling to give it independent force as a substantive limitation on national legislative power. His goal, after all, was to limit the power of the national judiciary and to assert the lawmaking primacy — not some limitation — on the legislative branch. The principles of coextensive powers and legislative primacy, however, were not found in the explicit language of the Constitution, and he reluctantly accepted the need to suggest some specific constitutional anchor. Rejecting a substantive Tenth Amendment, he made the provision applicable only derivatively, only as a corollary of the principle of coextensive power and the conclusion that the federal courts had made law in areas where Congress was "confessedly" without power.

Stone, in fact, understood Brandeis's opinion in exactly that manner. Commenting on the March 21 draft, he stated its theory clearly. There was "no constitutional power in Congress to require federal courts to apply rules of law inconsistent with those in force in the state," Stone paraphrased, "unless Congress is acting under one of the substantive powers granted to the national government."[91]

Although his assertion that "Congress has no power to declare substantive rules of common law" seemed to some to impose a limitation on national legislative power, it did not.[92] Lack of congressional power was the reason *Swift* was unconstitutional, but *Erie*'s reasoning involved no determination concerning the scope of national legislative power. It reasoned only that the federal courts could not make substantive common law in an area *if* Congress were without authority in that area as, in *Swift*'s case, it "confessedly" was.[93]

Legislative Primacy and Legal Positivism

Swift declared that the common law consisted of "principles" and that judicial decisions were merely "evidence" of the law. Quoting Holmes, *Erie* rejected that view, scorning the idea of "transcendental" principles, declaring that decisions made law, and identifying law with the power of a sovereign. To many, those ideas symbolized a transformation in legal philosophy from the nineteenth to the twentieth century: the decline of customary, historical, and natural rights jurisprudence and the rise of positivism and legal realism. Thus, many viewed *Erie* as the triumph of a positivist and skeptical Holmesian realism.[94] The jurisprudence that informed *Erie*, however, was neither a skeptical realism nor a full-fledged Holmesian positivism. Rather, it was gnostic and pragmatic, focused on the social function and consequences of procedural rules. It was, in fact, characteristically Brandeisian: epistemologically confident, theoretically principled, institutionally rooted, and morally committed.

Holmes rejected *Swift* primarily on philosophical grounds.[95] He identified the decision with what he regarded as the absurd idea that the common law was a "transcendental" body of principles.[96] That conviction, in turn, rested on his philosophical empiricism and deep personal skepticism. "I hate (intellectually)," he wrote in 1924, "every appeal to intuitions that are supposed to *transcend* reason."[97] Law was only what the courts would enforce, and the common law of any state was only what that state's government would back with force. "The question of what is the law of Massachusetts or of Louisiana is a matter that Mass. or La. has a right to determine for itself," he wrote, whether "the voice of the state" was its courts or its legislature.[98] "The Common Law in a State is the Common Law of that state deriving all its authority from the State,"[99] and judges were "directors of a force that comes from the source that gives them their authority."[100] If that source could not give them authority, they could not properly direct its force. Hence, when the federal courts declared the common law in an area beyond the sovereign authority of the national government, as they did under *Swift*, they were acting without authority and impinging on the rightful powers of another sovereign.[101]

In *Erie* Brandeis incorporated the narrowly positivist elements of Holmes's jurisprudence that equated judicial decisions with "law" and law with the power of an identified sovereign. In his opinion he included five separate quotes from Holmes's *Taxicab* dissent, including the derogatory reference to *Swift*'s assumption of a "transcendental body of law."[102] The quotes served to indicate that *Swift* violated state sovereignty[103] and that it disregarded the principle of coextensive powers.[104] What appealed to Brandeis was only the narrow positivist argument, consistent with but a part of Holmes's legal philosophy, that courts made "law," that "law" was derived from the authority of a sovereign, and that *Swift*, therefore, allowed illegitimate incursions into state sovereignty.

Brandeis did not, however, adopt any broader skeptical, positivist, or "realist" legal philosophy. He did not accept the proposition that law meant only what the courts would enforce or that any rule the courts enforced was immune from meaningful philosophical and moral critique.[105] He did not stress the importance of separating the "is" and the "ought" in order to study the operations of the law objectively, nor did he embrace any cynical prediction theory of law. Nor did he question the idea that legal and moral "principles" existed, that they could be known and developed by human reason, and that they could and should guide judicial reasoning.[106]

Quite the contrary. Brandeis opposed *Swift* for the morally and legally principled reasons of social justice and efficiency and constitutional balance. Terminating *Swift* and grounding *Erie* on the Constitution, he proclaimed that legal principles existed and provided guidance for judicial decisions. *Swift* was unconstitutional because it violated fundamental principles Brandeis believed were valid despite the fact that the Supreme Court had previously made "law" that rejected them. Indeed, his opinion held that what the federal courts had been enforcing was not properly "law," but instead a usurpation. In its recognition that courts made "law" and derived their institutional legitimacy from a sovereign authority, *Erie* reflected positivist ideas. In its emphasis on the power of reason, the authority of constitutional principles, and the legal and moral imperative of seeking fairness and justice, it rejected more extreme skeptical and realist contentions and affirmed a relatively traditionalist, principled, and Progressive jurisprudence.[107]

More important, *Erie*'s narrow positivism was grounded ultimately not in any distinctively Holmesian or realist jurisprudence, or any other general legal philosophy, but in Brandeis's practical understanding of the structural and operational requirements of American constitutional federalism in an age of burgeoning multistate activities. The constitutional basis for his brand of positivism, moreover, was not the Tenth Amendment but the Due Process Clause and the Full Faith and Credit Clause.[108] It was based not on the "reserved powers" of the states but, ironically, on the tightening constitutional limits that the Court itself was placing on the lawmaking power of the states.

Developments in communications and transportation during the nineteenth century and the establishment of a national market following the Civil War multiplied the number and variety of interstate activities. Combined with a proliferation of new state regulatory and remedial legislation, the changes forced courts ever more frequently to confront difficult questions involving the extraterritorial reach of state law.[109] Beginning in the 1870s the Court adapted the Due

Process Clause to prohibit state courts from asserting personal jurisdiction over parties not present within their borders,[110] and shortly thereafter it began to use the clause to prevent states from taxing property or transactions in other states[111] and from making their debt instruments nontaxable to residents of other states.[112]

The Court was reluctant to use the Constitution to control state choice-of-law questions and initially relied on common law principles to resolve or avoid alleged conflicts.[113] In the early twentieth century, however, it began cautiously and only half-consciously to utilize a constitutionally based concept of "legislative" or "regulatory jurisdiction" to guide its decisions. In 1912, for example, it ruled that a Wisconsin court had to enforce a Minnesota statute in an action brought by the receiver of an insolvent Minnesota corporation. The subject of the Minnesota statute — enforcement of a special statutory liability against the company's shareholders — was "peculiarly within the regulatory power of the State of Minnesota," Justice Van Devanter wrote for a unanimous Court; "so much so that no other State properly can be said to have any public policy thereon."[114]

Van Devanter's statement suggested both halves of the Court's embryonic doctrine: some issues were so specially related to a particular state that the Full Faith and Credit Clause would require other states to apply that state's law in their courts; other issues were so remotely related to a state that the Due Process Clause would prohibit that state from applying its own law in its own courts. First, and more sparingly, the Court deployed the Full Faith and Credit Clause to give state law extraterritorial effect when that law had created a special relationship between two or more parties.[115] In 1914 in *Supreme Council of the Royal Arcanum v. Green*, for example, it held that the clause required the laws of the chartering state to be applied to a shareholder's suit against a fraternal benefit corporation. "[T]hose laws were integrally and necessarily the criterion [*sic*] to be resorted to" in construing the corporation's constitution and bylaws and in determining "the intrinsic relation between each and all the members."[116] Second, and more broadly, the Court used due process ideas, without always citing the constitutional clause, to prevent forum states from applying their laws to claims with which the forum states had insufficient connection. "[A] State may not consistently with the due process clause of the Fourteenth Amendment," it declared in 1914, "extend its authority beyond its legitimate jurisdiction."[117] Ten years later, in *Aetna Life Insurance Co. v. Dunken*, it ruled that a Texas court could not apply Texas law to "a Tennessee contract," an agreement completed in Tennessee and subsequently delivered in Texas. "The Texas statute was incapable of being constitutionally applied to it," the Court stated, "since the effect of such application would be to regulate business outside the State of Texas."[118]

Brandeis arrived on the Court just as it was beginning to shape its double constitutional limit on state "legislative jurisdiction," and he was deeply involved in developing both. Reflecting the Court's highly tentative and uncertain approach when he arrived on the Court in 1916, he joined an opinion during his first term that avoided an alleged conflict between state laws while noticing — and expressly holding open — the question whether one state could refuse to enforce a contract validly made in another "consistently with the very nature of the relations between the several States resulting from the constitutional obligations resting upon them."[119] Indeed, in one of Brandeis's first opinions, he readily dismissed a due process challenge to North Dakota's refusal to apply a Minnesota statute on the ground that the issue was an ordinary conflicts question that did not rise to constitutional stature.[120]

During the 1920s, however, Brandeis began to recognize the need for constitutional limits on state choice of law. In *Clapper* he sought to expand the Full Faith and Credit Clause to restrict interstate forum shopping, emphasizing the importance of identifying and enforcing a state's proper "legislative jurisdiction."[121] In 1935 he again insisted that "a State can legislate only with reference to its own jurisdiction."[122] Similarly, writing for the Court in *Home Insurance Co. v. Dick* in 1930, Brandeis held that the application of a forum state's statute violated the Due Process Clause when "nothing in any way relating to the policy sued on, or to the contracts of reinsurance, was ever done or required to be done" in the forum state.[123] Although he continued to try to restrain the Court's use of the Due Process Clause in this area, as elsewhere, he fully agreed "that a State is without power to impose either public or private obligations on contracts made outside of the State and not to be performed there."[124]

By the early 1930s, courts and law reviews were commonly invoking the concept of legislative jurisdiction. The American Law Institute adopted the phrase in its *Restatement of the Law of Conflict of Laws* in 1934, and Justice Stone employed the cognate term "constitutional jurisdiction" in developing his approach to choice-of-law questions in the mid-1930s.[125] It was "unavoidable," Stone wrote for the Court in 1935, "that this Court determine for itself the extent to which the statute of one state may qualify or deny rights asserted under the statute of another."[126]

When Brandeis considered the authority of state decisional law in *Erie*, when he pondered the proper scope of state lawmaking power, his thinking was informed by more than two decades of experience with the judicial effort to articulate constitutional rules of interstate order for a dynamic society with a federalized lawmaking structure.[127] The concept of legislative jurisdiction — the constitutional right of governments to make law in certain areas and for certain classes of transactions — focused his attention on the sovereign authority that backed constitutionally allowable lawmaking. The concept also implied that the scope of that allowable lawmaking should be no broader for one branch of a government than for its other branches.[128] The American Law Institute's *Restatement* expressly made the connection between the concept of state legislative jurisdiction and the theory of coextensive powers. "A state exercises its legislative jurisdiction," it declared in 1934, "by adopting certain principles of law as part of the common law of the state, or by an act of a legislative body."[129]

Erie's positivism, then, was ultimately not philosophical, or realist, or even Holmesian. It was Brandeisian, the result of Brandeis's practical recognition that divided sovereignty required limits on all branches of state lawmaking authority as well as the restriction of each state's lawmaking to its proper sphere. Similar to the Court's developing law of legislative jurisdiction, *Erie*'s positivism was based on a practical recognition of the changing demands of constitutional federalism. It was part of a broader working approach that sought to adapt the architecture of American government to the challenges of a new, expanding, and dynamic interstate society.[130]

Legislative Jurisdiction and Supreme Court Review: From Anomaly to Defect

In addition to underscoring the anomaly of federal judicial lawmaking in areas where Congress was "confessedly without power," the concept of legislative jurisdiction highlighted a second anomaly. "Persistence of state courts in their own opinions on questions of common law," *Erie* declared, allowed two different and often conflicting sets of common law rules to exist in the same state.[131] The result "rendered impossible equal protection of the law."[132] The Supreme Court had not remedied that perplexing problem of dual and conflicting laws because, quite simply, it could not.

The Court had long held that there was no "national" common law of the United States. According to long-established doctrine, *Swift* authorized the federal courts only to make an "independent judgment" on common law principles as to what was properly "state" law. As the Court acknowledged in 1903, the federal common law was not "the creation of the Federal [lawmaking] power."[133] As a result, the rules of the federal common law did not come within the mandate of the Supremacy Clause and did not give rise to "federal questions" for purposes of either original jurisdiction or Supreme Court review.[134] Because the Court lacked jurisdiction to hear appeals from state courts on such common law questions, then, it could not impose its federal common law on the states. When dealing with questions of general law, the Court explained in 1871, "the Federal courts and the State courts, each within their own spheres, deciding on their own judgment, are not amenable to each other."[135] Regardless of otherwise relevant common law decisions by the federal courts, including those by the United

States Supreme Court, a state court remained free to "administer the common law according to its [own] understanding and interpretation."[136]

Few lawyers or judges maintained that the Supreme Court should be able to review the common law decisions of state courts. The limited nature of the Court's appellate jurisdiction had long been established, and as a practical matter the multiplying number of federal statutory and constitutional issues on its docket prevented it from effectively supervising the federal common law that existed under *Swift*.[137] Most important, allowing the Court to review and determine state common law issues would nationalize the legal system and destroy much of what remained of the states' lawmaking autonomy and authority.[138]

From his earliest years on the Court, Brandeis was determined to preserve the independence of state common law and to maintain the rule that, in actions coming from the state courts, common law issues did not present federal questions for review.[139] Although the Court could review independent judgments on state law issues that the lower federal courts rendered under *Swift*, it could not review those same issues in actions that were decided in the state courts. In 1930 in *Brinkerhoff-Faris Co. v. Hill* Brandeis went out of his way to stress that limitation.[140] The *Swift* doctrine, he emphasized, "is, if applied at all, confined strictly to cases arising in the Federal courts."[141]

As the idea of legislative jurisdiction gained prominence, it made that bifurcated appellate practice seem increasingly troublesome. If the federal and state governments had their distinctive legislative jurisdictions, and if the lawmaking authority of both their courts and their legislatures were equally limited to that jurisdiction, at least two consequences would follow. One, implicit in Brandeis's constitutional theory but not addressed in *Erie*, was that the established rule limiting the Court's appellate jurisdiction over state courts to truly "federal" issues was constitutionally required. The other was *Erie*'s constitutional holding that state courts were the authoritative voices of state law and, consequently, that the federal courts were obliged to follow their decisions in state law matters. To Brandeis, the idea of legislative jurisdiction and the challenges of twentieth-century federalism transformed the significance of a "federal" law that lacked "supremacy." The arrangement could no longer be considered a mere procedural or theoretical anomaly. Rather, it had become an irrational and substantive institutional defect that demanded remedy.

The Brandeisian Enterprise: Countering Brewer and the Supple Tool of Judicial Primacy

On the same day that *Erie* came down, Brandeis announced a second decision that illuminated *Erie* and paralleled its constitutional theory. On February 10 and 11, as he was beginning to draft his opinion in *Erie*, the Court heard oral argument in *Hinderlider v. La Plata River & Cherry Creek Ditch Co.*[142] Assigned to write for the Court, Brandeis researched and drafted the two opinions concurrently. Although *Hinderlider*'s significance has often been missed and some commentators have even seen it as inconsistent with *Erie*, it was an apt companion that Brandeis used to amplify *Erie* and his vision of the proper structure of balanced constitutional government.

In 1923 Colorado and New Mexico approved an interstate compact that apportioned between them the waters of the La Plata River. Two years later Congress approved the compact, and the states established agencies to implement their agreement. Under the distribution plan, Hinderlider, the Colorado administrator, denied to the La Plata River & Cherry Creek Ditch Company a part of the flow which it had been granted by an 1898 Colorado state court judgment. Incorporated in Colorado, the company filed suit in state court seeking to enjoin Hinderlider from depriving the company of the full amount of water to which it was entitled under its prior judgment. Hinderlider raised the interstate compact as his defense, and the trial court dismissed the company's bill. On appeal, however, the Colorado Supreme Court ruled that the compact did not constitute a valid defense. "It is a mere compromise of presumably conflicting claims, a trading therein, in which the property of citizens is bartered, without notice or hearing and with no regard to vested rights."[143] It held that Hinderlider's action deprived the company of a "vested right" to a specified amount of water and reinstated its bill. Subsequently, a trial court issued the injunction sought, and the Colorado Supreme Court affirmed.

Avoiding the question of whether the compact itself presented a federal question, the United States Supreme Court ruled that the decision "denied an important claim under the Constitution" and was therefore reviewable.[144] "For whether the water of an interstate stream must be apportioned between the two States," Brandeis wrote for a unanimous bench, "is a question of 'federal common law' upon which neither the statutes nor the decisions of either state can be conclusive."[145] On the basis of the Court's 1907 decision in *Kansas v. Colorado* he ruled that federal law mandated the equitable apportionment of such water between the states.[146] Reversing the Colorado Supreme Court, he held that the company could have no vested right to anything more than the state's equitable share of the water and that the valid interstate compact properly governed the apportionment.

On the surface, *Erie* and *Hinderlider* were wholly different. The substantive legal issues and relevant facts were entirely dissimilar. Jurisdictionally, *Erie* reviewed the decision of a lower federal court in a diversity action, while *Hinderlider* reviewed the judgment of a state court on the ground that it had denied a federal constitutional claim. *Erie* upheld the independence and authority of the state courts; in contrast, *Hinderlider* imposed on them the command of a federal rule. Finally, and superficially most arresting, *Erie* declared that there was no "federal general common law," while *Hinderlider* ruled that the Colorado Supreme Court had transgressed the "federal common law." Despite the differences, however, the two opinions constituted parallel statements, and their political and constitutional unity became apparent against the backdrop of the case that Brandeis cited in *Hinderlider* and pondered deeply during the early months of 1938 — Justice Brewer's stunning tour de force in *Kansas v. Colorado*.

Brewer's opinion in *Kansas v. Colorado,* written three decades earlier, was perhaps his greatest jurisprudential triumph. He had linked the idea of general law to the Tenth Amendment and on that basis established the exclusive authority of the Supreme Court to make law in disputes between states. His opinion denied the power of both Congress and the states, and it held that the Court alone — unchecked by any other branch of government — had constitutional authority to make the controlling national law.

In *Hinderlider,* Brandeis responded.[147] He accepted without comment Brewer's assertion (technically, dictum) that Congress could not legislate over interstate streams, but he reduced the decision's substantive holding to the vague mandate that apportionment between states must be "equitable."[148] More important, he made explicit the source of the Court's authority: not vague principles of "general law" but the Constitution itself. He thus brought *Hinderlider*'s "federal common law" (a phrase that he placed in quotation marks) within the limits announced in *Erie:* State law applied "[e]xcept in matters governed by the Federal Constitution or by Acts of Congress."[149] Most fundamentally, however, Brandeis used *Hinderlider* to reinterpret the constitutional structure of authority over interstate streams and disputes between states and to balance the Court's purportedly exclusive power with the power of the legislature.

Brandeis exploited an obvious constitutional loophole in Brewer's opinion. "As Congress cannot make compacts between the States, as it cannot, in respect to certain matters, by legislation compel their separate action," Brewer had written, "disputes between them must be settled either by force or else by appeal to tribunals empowered to determine the right and wrong thereof."[150] Brandeis avoided that unacceptable choice by invoking a second constitutional alternative, one which Brewer, determined to deny legislative power, had ignored. "The Supreme Court of Colorado," Brandeis wrote, "held the Compact [between Colorado and New Mexico] unconstitutional because, for aught that appears, it embodies not a judicial, or quasi-judicial, decision of controverted rights, but a trading compromise of conflicting claims. The assumption that judicial or quasi-judicial decision of the controverted claims is essential to the validity of a compact adjusting them, rests upon a misconception. It ignores the history and order of development of *the two means provided by the Constitution* for adjusting inter-state controversies. *The compact—the legislative means—*adapts to our Union of sovereign States the age-old treaty making power of independent sovereign nations."[151] *Hinderlider* thus countered *Kansas v. Colorado* by highlighting and honoring the alternative "legislative means" available to settle interstate disputes. The power that the Court aggregated to itself in *Kansas v. Colorado*, Brandeis emphasized, was not exclusive. The constitutional provision authorizing interstate compacts—requiring agreement by the relevant state legislatures and approval by Congress—created a source of legislative authority over interstate disputes equal, and historically prior, to the Court's interstate common law.[152] "But resort to the judicial remedy," Brandeis proclaimed defiantly to Brewer's ghost, "is never essential to the adjustment of interstate controversies."[153]

Thus, in spite of their differences, *Hinderlider* and *Erie* were parallel statements of Brandeis's constitutional philosophy. First and foremost, each attempted to make the reach of legislative and judicial powers coextensive. *Hinderlider* was not *Erie's* contradiction but its complement. *Erie* restricted the power of the federal courts to the limits of the congressional power to legislate, while *Hinderlider* extended the legislative powers of the states and nation together to the limits of federal judicial power established in *Kansas v. Colorado*.

Beyond that fundamental parallel, the two cases had other common elements. Both tacitly accepted the proposition that the Tenth Amendment limited national power only derivatively, only in the absence of a constitutional grant of legislative authority. *Hinderlider* acquiesced in the rule that Congress, by itself and absent some other constitutional rationale, could not legislate over interstate streams, and *Erie* assumed that there were some areas which Congress could not reach. Neither, however, suggested an independent and substantive Tenth Amendment, and neither held that the amendment precluded Congress from legislating in any particular area. Both, moreover, implicitly rejected Brewer's adroit bifurcation of the reserved powers. Indeed, properly understood, *Hinderlider* confirms the conclusion that Brandeis did not base *Erie* on the Tenth Amendment. *Kansas v. Colorado* showed that the amendment's category of reserved powers could serve as an independent basis of federal judicial power free from legislative check, and that was precisely what Brandeis sought to extinguish. Both, too, nourished the powers of the states, *Erie* by empowering their courts and *Hinderlider* by prodding their legislatures. Finally, each restricted the advantages of established wealth. *Erie* curbed a glaring de facto abuse of diversity jurisdiction, and *Hinderlider* narrowed the "vested rights" that were beyond the power of "legislative means" to modify. Although neither opinion had the majestic sweep—or sheer audacity—of *Kansas v. Colorado*, together they countered Brewer's constitutional philosophy with a profoundly different one, equally comprehensive and equally rooted in its author's deepest political and social values.

In overthrowing *Swift*, then, Brandeis was extinguishing not only the federal general common law but, more significantly, a fertile, amorphous, and dangerous assumption about the reach of federal judicial power.[154] The *Swift* doctrine, as it had developed for almost a century, stood not simply for a general federal common law, or for *Western Union*'s assertion of a broader and more powerful "national" common law, or even for *Kuhn*'s extension of national judicial power into narrowly "local" issues. It stood not merely for the major social oppressions of *Baugh* or the minor corporate manipulation of the *Taxicab* case. *Swift* symbolized more broadly and ominously the political and institutional primacy of the anti-Progressive federal judiciary: it stood for the idea that the federal courts had authority to impose substantive rules of law free from legislative alteration, and it exemplified the Supreme Court's willingness to use its power to ordain its own institutional primacy. The imperative of judicial primacy led Brewer to insist that insurance law was "local" with respect to legislation — hence, beyond the power of Congress — but "general" with respect to the common law — hence, within the lawmaking power of the federal judiciary. It drove him in *Debs* to ignore statutory grounds and invoke independent common law authority for exercising judicial power. It inspired him in *Kansas v. Colorado* to exploit the Court's jurisdiction over interstate controversies in order to fashion an area of law where the Court stood constitutionally supreme over both Congress and the states. The quest for judicial primacy enabled the Court, after erecting constitutional bars against federal and state legislation in *Adair* and *Coppage*, to enforce in *Hitchman* the coercive yellow dog contract and assert control over the pivotal law of employment relations. In *Jensen*, it spurred the Court's aggressive decision to transform the admiralty jurisdiction into a judicial mandate that defeated state workmen's compensation laws and required both Congress and the states to honor uniformity in the national maritime law. Finally, it allowed the Court in *Dodge* to create and apply *sub silentio* general common law rules controlling choice of law and thereby empowering the Court to narrow state legislative power even further than its express due process doctrine required.

For Brandeis, the *Swift* doctrine ultimately posed an issue not of philosophy or even of federalism but of political accountability and constitutional balance. "Checks and balances were established in order that this should be 'a government of laws and not of men,'" he declared in 1926. "The doctrine of separation of powers was adopted by the Convention in 1787, not to promote efficiency but to preclude the exercise of arbitrary power."[155] Brandeis repudiated the general common law because he was both a Progressive who believed passionately in the principle of legislative primacy and a legal craftsman who discerned the pervasive role that *Swift*'s ductile doctrine played in justifying and inspiring expansive judicial lawmaking free from legislative checks. *Swift* was the private law counterpart of the public law doctrine of substantive due process—twin pillars of the activist federal judiciary that had crimped and barred Progressive reforms for half a century. Its overthrow allowed the substitution of an alternate and Progressive premise, one that in Brandeis's view was rooted in the Constitution itself. In *Erie* and *Hinderlider* he established the basics of that premise, balanced the unchecked power of the federal judiciary, and affirmed the fundamental constitutional principle of legislative primacy.

History and the Dynamics
of Legal Change

PART 3

Erosion and Creation of Meaning in an Age of Transition

8

E*rie* was a response to a half century of American history whose most characteristic legal, social, and political concerns were passing away as Brandeis delivered his opinion. The crises of the 1930s and 1940s, followed by a sustained postwar economic boom, the explosive pressures of the cold war, and the long and divisive struggle for black civil rights restructured American society, reshaped its culture, and reoriented its politics. They also transformed the social role and political significance of the federal courts. Embodying a set of assumptions forged in one politico-constitutional age, *Erie* could hardly maintain its intended social and political significance unchanged in a dramatically new one.

The opinion's abstract, abbreviated, and to some extent purposely misleading reasoning invited multiple interpretations. Further, its numerous doctrinal implications guaranteed that it would generate a large technical literature and countless disputes. The shifting meanings that judges and law writers found in Brandeis's opinion, however, also stemmed from broad historical changes. Consciously and unconsciously, later generations elided the social and political values of Progressivism and replaced them with the goals, ideals, anxieties, and branch affinities of a new age.

Erie *in the Twilight of Progressivism*

Although the general public took little notice of *Erie*, the legal profession was stunned. "Whhew [*sic*]!!! What will your Court do next?" Frankfurter exclaimed to Stone two days after the decision came down.[1] "I haven't yet caught my breath over the Tompkins case."[2] It was a "remarkable performance," Stone admitted. "I haven't gotten over my own surprise at it."[3]

Many writers expressed shock and even anger that the decision came

without warning, disrupted settled doctrine, and contained broad but vague constitutional language. Few were willing to defend either Brandeis's constitutional
statements or his precipitate and uncalled-for dispatch of *Swift*. The *Harvard Law
Review* concluded that the opinion "lacks much of the precision" that the profession had a right to expect.[4] Another commentator chastised the Court for "not
hearing argument specifically on the *Swift* question."[5] Even many of Brandeis's
friends and admirers were disturbed. "I really do not like the way it was handled
by L.D.B. and much preferred Stanley Reed," Judge Augustus N. Hand confessed, and Professor Thomas Reed Powell of Harvard Law School upbraided
Brandeis for "violating many of the canons of constitutional adjudication upon
which he has often strongly insisted."[6] However desirable the result, many concluded, the Court had not treated the case properly. "In view of the Justices
who comprised the majority," commented Harry Shulman, one of Brandeis's be-
mused ex-clerks, the resort to constitutional language "was extraordinary."[7]

Aside from their shared surprise, commentators agreed that the decision
would have important social consequences. Most seemed to acknowledge that
Swift had led to serious abuses, and many noted its social and economic significance.[8] "[I]n nine cases out of ten," commented two writers, *Swift* had worked
"to the advantage of a corporate litigant."[9] Judge John J. Parker, a longtime
proponent of *Swift*, bemoaned the dangers that would result for those "trading,
travelling or lending money throughout the country."[10] The fall of the general
common law, other articles noted, would likely cause problems for municipal
bondholders and insurance companies.[11]

The familiar battle lines of the preceding half century largely remained in
place. The *American Bar Association Journal* published an attack that denounced
Erie's constitutional language as "untenable" and its likely consequences as "ap-
palling."[12] Predictably, it warned that the decision might threaten federal judicial
power. *Erie*, the article cautioned, could hinder the ability of the national courts
to make their own procedural rules and to administer the independent system of
federal equity.

On the Progressive side, the most striking response came from Robert H.
Jackson, Roosevelt's solicitor general. Only the previous year, he had attacked
the Court's long train of "judicial abuses" when he testified before the Senate
Judiciary Committee in support of the Court-packing bill.[13] As luck would have
it, Jackson was scheduled to address the ABA's impending annual convention in
1938. Known for his stylistic flair and barbed wit,[14] Jackson decided to address
the federal judiciary's most devoted apostles on "The Rise and Fall of *Swift v.
Tyson*."[15] Ostensibly an account of *Swift*'s history, Jackson's speech was a mocking jab at ABA pieties and a political defense of both Brandeis and his decision.

Blandly introducing *Erie* as a technical decision unrelated to economic concerns, Jackson explained how *Swift* had served the interests of organized wealth, provided special benefits to corporations, and inflated by dubious means the power of the politically conservative federal judiciary. He lingered in lurid detail over one of the more unseemly episodes in the Court's history, emphasizing the determination of the justices to protect municipal bondholders at all costs. He pointed to the way the federal courts had voided reform legislation and then created common law rules of narrow corporate liability. "The most serious objection [to *Swift*]," he commented, drawing out Brandeis's premise, "is that the national legislature was powerless to alter rules of law after they were declared by the Federal courts." Indeed, Jackson gleefully spotlighted the irony of the argument that *Swift* had been justified because it allowed the creation of a uniform national commercial law. "The need for uniformity has never been allowed to operate as a basis of power in Congress, which was not granted in the Constitution," he noted dryly, "and it is hard to see why it should supply power, otherwise not granted, to the Federal judiciary."[16] Jackson concluded with a vigorous twist of the knife, skewering the federal judiciary with the ABA's anti–New Deal rhetoric. *Erie* "in effect has declared that hundreds of judges have done daily what, in the case of administrative officers, is called exercising an unlawful discretion."[17]

Those who heard or read Jackson's remarks in 1938 understood his barbs full well. What neither he nor they could have known, however, was that his speech would quickly become a dusty and almost unrecognizable monument to the branch affinities of a bygone age.

Transitions

Within a relatively few years, the landscape of American life changed dramatically. The New Deal established a centralized administrative state far more comprehensive than anything that the old Progressives had ever attempted, while the Supreme Court shaped the Constitution to expand federal power and validate the institutional changes. State and federal legislation established a partial welfare state and replaced ever larger parts of the common law with statutory schemes. Congress and the Court, the Depression-born sympathy for labor, a new union militance, and an era of booming prosperity created a powerful and institutionalized labor movement unlike anything that had previously existed.[18]

The frightening challenge of world war and cold war spurred a vast military and industrial effort. The nation seemed more united, and government and business more structurally intertwined, than ever before. Suddenly, national corporations no longer appeared as monstrous intruders in a decentralized society. Instead, they were institutions essential to national survival. Charges of "monopoly" and "exploitation" grew faint, and the political rhetoric of Progressivism suddenly appeared quaint and even archaic. Corporations were the instruments of mass productivity, objects of national pride, and rich sources of new jobs, the paramount social commodity of the new age. In the Employment Act of 1946 Congress announced the government's responsibility to work toward "maximum employment," but it indicated that the goal was to be achieved primarily through the efforts of "free competitive enterprise." [19] The act was a tepid version of the original Full Employment Bill of 1945, and its provisions evidenced both the increasingly conservative orientation of Congress and the return of business to a dominant national position. [20]

Through world war and cold war, the frightening challenges of Nazism and Communism — and the image of "Totalitarianism" — inspired a profound reaffirmation of American institutions and values. Compared to Nazi Germany and Stalinist Russia, the United States appeared admirable and even ideal, and it became increasingly easy to ignore Roosevelt's "one-third of the nation" that was ill-housed, ill-fed, and ill-clothed. When the postwar economy boomed, Americans embraced the new prosperity with surprise, enthusiasm, and gratitude. Liberal social scientists proclaimed that the nation had solved the basic social problems of modern industrial society. The remaining challenges were to maintain a stable international order and to foster the triumphant domestic economy. [21]

The political terrain was equally transformed. Robber barons and the social gospel disappeared, and many of the issues that had inspired Progressives — child labor, unionism, anti-monopoly, workmen's compensation, the yellow dog contract, municipal ownership, employers' liability laws, public utilities regulation — faded from the scene. In their place stood the challenge of communism and the threat of internal subversion. The term "Progressive" fell from the political vocabulary, replaced more or less by the label "liberal," a designation that encompassed attitudes associated with Progressivism but implied a stronger national orientation, rooted in the New Deal, and a greater concern with civil rights and civil liberties, rooted in the reaction against Nazi racism and totalitariarism. In 1948, left-wing Democrats organized a new Progressive Party and ran as its presidential candidate an old New Dealer, former Vice President Henry A. Wallace. They received support from the American Communist Party, drew charges of being "un-American" and even treasonous, and suffered a disastrous defeat that buried the label of "Progressive." Although Democratic president Harry S Truman won a surprising victory on a platform that promised to continue the New Deal, Congress refused to act on his legislative requests and repeatedly passed conservative-backed measures over his vetoes. Accusations that prominent New Dealers were Communists or "fellow travelers," shocking revelations of espionage, the discovery in 1949 that the Soviet Union possessed the atomic bomb, and the start of the Korean War in 1950 generated an intense fear of Communist subversion and Soviet aggression. By the early 1950s anti-communism was the nation's touchstone political issue, and the New Deal forces were scattered and in retreat.[22]

The institutions of government reflected the changes. A pervasive desire for stability and security came to dominate American politics, and Congress and the state legislatures moved away from the values of the New Deal. Elected majorities no longer seriously considered innovative and far-ranging social reforms, and talk of "legislative experimentation" carried connotations wholly different from those during Brandeis's lifetime. Both Congress and the states responded to the perceived threat of subversion with probing political investigations and ominously restrictive legislation, forcing new issues of civil liberties and individual freedoms to the forefront of legal and political debate.

Conversely, the image of the federal courts was shifting in a more liberal direction. In the late 1930s and 1940s the national judiciary became highly deferential to legislative action, especially in matters of economic regulation. Twenty years of Democratic rule had reshaped the political values of the federal courts, and its new judges tended to accept broad exercises of national powers. No longer were they closely identified with private property and corporate wealth. The federal courts began to demonstrate increased sensitivity toward issues of civil rights and civil liberties and developed an image as protectors of individual noneconomic rights.[23] After a period of timidity in the late 1940s and early 1950s, the Supreme Court began to restrict the domestic campaign against subversion and to expand protections for a variety of individual rights. Most dramatically, in 1954 it declared legalized racial segregation in the public schools unconstitutional.[24] Quickly, a new image — "the Warren Court" — crystallized and captured the nation's imagination. Its positive side proclaimed the federal courts the bulwark of individual freedoms, the vindicators of federal rights, and the protectors of the poor and downtrodden. Its negative side painted the federal courts as centralizing liberal activists, destroyers of states' rights, and (on occasion) the designing allies of Communist subversion.

Cumulatively, the changes scrambled and largely reversed the politico-constitutional premises and branch affinities of the half century that preceded 1937. Political liberals began to seek ways to limit the newly conservative legislative branch and expand the powers of the transformed federal courts. Economic conservatives and business groups found Congress ever more sympathetic to their views, while anti-Communists received strong support from both national and state legislatures. Together with the defenders of segregation, economic conservatives and anti-Communists increasingly came to view the federal courts as dangerous captives of liberal centralizers.

The transformation induced lawyers to perceive *Erie* anew. First, as problems of economic inequality faded from view in the new and sustained postwar boom, lawyers were increasingly unable to see any connection between Brandeis's decision and more general problems involving the relationship between economic inequality and the judicial system. As society accepted national corporations, their dominance of the diversity docket no longer seemed suspicious or inappropriate. Second, because Congress and the federal courts were in the tentative, yet apparent, process of reversing their respective political orientations, *Erie*'s constitutional implications concerning congressional power and its limits on the federal courts no longer carried the political relevance they had possessed for Brandeis. The postwar context rendered *Erie*'s social significance and constitutional principles newly problematic and ambiguous.

Equally important, social and legal changes altered the practical operation of diversity jurisdiction itself. The abolition of *Swift* together with improvements in transportation and judicial administration eliminated many of the burdens that had made the federal courts disadvantageous venues for individual plaintiffs, while new procedural and jurisdictional rules often assisted those same plaintiffs substantially in suing corporate defendants. Further, Democratic appointments to the lower federal bench made the national courts increasingly attractive to individual claimants. By the late 1940s, one of the basic premises that had animated Progressives — that diversity jurisdiction seriously burdened individuals who sued national corporations — had been essentially eliminated.[25]

Further, the constitutional context changed, giving *Erie* a strikingly different doctrinal significance. Most important, the Court expanded congressional power dramatically, abandoning earlier limits on the Commerce Clause[26] and construing the spending power to allow a potentially vast range of new federal social and regulatory programs.[27] The new breadth of congressional power weakened the constitutional limits that *Erie* could impose on the federal judicial power. In 1943 the Court further minimized *Erie*'s constitutional significance by reversing the long line of cases that had excluded insurance from the category of "commerce."[28] By allowing national regulation of insurance under the Commerce Clause, the Court extended the power of Congress to encompass what had been the most salient area where the federal common law under *Swift* had reigned "untouched by legislation." The Court thus removed another limit that *Erie* had set on the judicial power.

Finally, the Court further diminished *Erie*'s potential significance when it announced a new type of truly "federal" common law: judicial decisions based not on "independent" judgments of state law but on interpretations of the federal Constitution, statutes, and "interests." Recognizing the overwhelming challenge the national government faced in financing the new world war, the Court construed federal statutory provisions broadly in two decisions in the

early 1940s in order to identify what it deemed national policies designed to protect federal financial institutions and federal commercial paper. The decisions
held that the federal courts could displace state law and apply judicially created
rules of federal law to effectuate those policies even when the rules went far
beyond the scope and terms of the relevant congressional statutes.[29] Although
both decisions involved national interests and at least implicated issues of federal statutory construction, the Court failed to explain when the national courts
could properly displace state law and when an issue not clearly controlled by
federal constitutional or statutory provisions was properly considered "federal."
The cases suggested that if the courts ignored or minimized the significance of
Brandeis's prudential corollary, vast and uncharted leeway existed under *Erie*
for federal judicial lawmaking.[30]

The Court's decisions expanding the commerce power and establishing
a new federal common law exemplified the virtually immediate change in the
social and legal context that surrounded *Erie*. The new federal common law decisions, for example, were the products of a distinctly new Court and a shattering
new world war. They seemed necessary to strengthen the federal government
and help it deal with the staggering financial burdens that confronted it in a time
of the gravest national peril. Had there been no war, federal power would not
have expanded exponentially, and *Erie*'s meaning and significance would not
have changed so quickly and so substantially.

The Roosevelt Court: A New Deal *Erie*

During the late 1930s and early 1940s a new "Roosevelt Court" took
shape. In addition to Hugo Black and Stanley Reed, the president appointed
Felix Frankfurter and William O. Douglas in 1939 and Frank Murphy in 1940.
The following year he placed Robert H. Jackson and James F. Byrnes on the
Court. In 1943, Wiley B. Rutledge succeeded Byrnes, who had resigned to serve
as director of the Office of Economic Stabilization. Thus, four years after the
Court fight, only Stone and Roberts remained. It had taken almost a decade, but
Roosevelt had finally remade the Court.

The new Court's primary goals were to reorient the Constitution, validate the New Deal, and constrain the power of the federal courts. The Court
buried the doctrine of liberty of contract, interpreted federal law more favorably
toward organized labor, and expanded the reach of federal legislative power
while allowing wide latitude for state economic regulation. It also moved halt-
ingly to strengthen the individual protections offered by the Bill of Rights and,
on occasion, showed a new sensitivity toward the values protected by the First
Amendment.[31]

The Roosevelt justices rejected what they regarded as the "activism" of the old Court and proclaimed the constitutional theory of Progressivism, the wisdom and necessity of "judicial restraint." The courts, they maintained, should defer broadly to legislative efforts and construe statutes sympathetically to achieve their underlying purposes. Similarly, the justices developed doctrines designed to restrict the opportunities of the lower courts to "intrude" into areas of state and congressional authority.[32] Beginning in the early 1940s personal and ideological disagreements began to wrack the Court, especially in cases involving the Bill of Rights. Throughout its existence, however, the Roosevelt Court never questioned the "plenary powers" of Congress in matters of social and economic legislation.

Similarly, the Roosevelt Court readily effectuated what its members considered *Erie*'s social goal. They sought to prevent parties from using diversity jurisdiction to avoid state laws and policies, and they were sensitive to the need to control corporate litigation tactics. Consequently, the justices implemented *Erie* vigorously to minimize incentives for forum shopping between federal and state courts.

Although they readily adopted a policy against forum shopping, the Roosevelt justices shared a common concern about the opinion's constitutional language. They feared that it might lead to substantive limitations on the powers of Congress. *Erie* referred specifically to subjects that were beyond the authority of Congress, and it contained an apparent invocation of the New Deal's constitutional bête noire, the Tenth Amendment. Reed had voiced his concern in *Erie* itself, and Rutledge repeatedly emphasized the danger of limiting Congress in developing the *Erie* doctrine. Even Stone, who had joined Brandeis's opinion, continued to harbor doubts. *Erie*, he explained to Roberts in 1941, had not settled the issue of whether Congress could enact substantive rules of law for the federal courts in diversity suits "notwithstanding some unfortunate dicta in the opinion."[33] Unsure of the nature of Brandeis's constitutional theory, but anxious about its implications, the Roosevelt Court vigorously enforced its anti-forum-shopping interpretation of *Erie* while ignoring Brandeis's constitutional language.[34] Indirectly, the Court negated any inference that the decision could be based properly on the Tenth Amendment by repudiating the idea that the amendment constituted a limitation on national power.[35]

In turning the Court away from *Erie*'s constitutional foundation, Frankfurter's role was pivotal.[36] Although he was "delighted with the result of the Tompkins case because *Swift v. Tyson* always seemed to me bad policy," he refused to accept what he saw as Brandeis's dubious and dangerous constitutional reasoning.[37] From the day that *Erie* came down, Frankfurter rejected it.[38] "I disagree *in toto* with Brandeis' constitutional view as to *Swift v. Tyson*," he told

Reed in 1942.[39] A constitutional ruling, as Reed's concurrence had shown, was unnecessary. More important, it threatened the powers of Congress.

Brandeis's opinion, Frankfurter insisted privately, was based not on Holmes's theory but on the profoundly different theory that Field had sketched in his *Baugh* dissent. There, Field had charged that the creation of an independent federal common law was an unconstitutional intrusion into state sovereignty that violated the Tenth Amendment.[40] "It is significant," Frankfurter explained privately, "that while Holmes in the *Black & White Taxicab* case spoke of *Swift v. Tyson* as 'an unconstitutional assumption of powers by courts of the United States,' Brandeis put unconstitutionality on a much broader ground, that is Field's ground, namely, that by the *Swift v. Tyson* doctrine 'this Court and the lower courts have invaded rights which in our opinion are reserved by the Constitution to the several states.' "[41] Frankfurter identified the difference he saw between the two theories: "It is noteworthy that Field in this [*Baugh*] dissent first expressed the view that *Swift v. Tyson* offended against the Constitution and it did so, not [as Holmes reasoned] because the judiciary assumed authority that belonged to the Congress, but because the formulation of the law relevant to diversity cases was one of the reserved powers of the states, since it did not concern the making of law in a domain which the Constitution gave to the Congress."[42] The difference, Frankfurter believed, was fundamental. Field and Brandeis based their views on principles of federalism and accepted the Tenth Amendment as a substantive limitation on the powers of Congress; Holmes advanced a theory based on separation of powers and rejected a substantive Tenth Amendment.[43]

Frankfurter claimed to be the authoritative expositor of Brandeis's constitutional philosophy.[44] His close and long-term association with Brandeis, his repeated invocations of the latter's authority, and the seemingly broad similarities in their political and constitutional views justified that privileged status. His confident assertions concerning *Erie,* made to an uncertain Court newly filled with Roosevelt appointees who were acutely solicitous of congressional power, must have been compelling.

Frankfurter, however, misconstrued Brandeis's constitutional theory. In defending his interpretation he relied primarily on the two obvious textual grounds. *Erie* quoted at length from Field's *Baugh* dissent, and it referred—as Field had done—to the "reserved" powers of the states.[45] In contrast, Holmes's *Taxicab* dissent neither cited Field's dissent nor referred to "reserved" powers. Those textual grounds, however, provided weak support for Frankfurter's interpretation.

First, *Erie* itself did not distinguish between the theories of Field and Holmes. Brandeis had precious little authority to cite for his constitutional position, and he used both dissents to lend it support. Despite differences between the two, in fact, both emphasized the importance of state authority, and both maintained that *Swift* was unconstitutional because it allowed the federal courts to intrude on that authority. For that basic proposition, *Erie* simply equated the two dissents.

Second, Brandeis's opinion clearly relied on Holmes more strongly and more centrally than on Field. It used five quotes from the *Taxicab* dissent, as opposed to one from *Baugh;* it twice invoked Holmes by name, as opposed to once for Field; and it stated its constitutional holding by both quoting and expressly naming Holmes, not Field, as its oracle. "Thus, the doctrine of *Swift v. Tyson* is, as Mr. Justice Holmes said, 'an unconstitutional assumption of powers by courts of the United States which no lapse of time or respectable array of opinion should make us hesitate to correct.'" Indeed, Brandeis placed that quotation from Holmes immediately before his statement of the Court's holding that contained the reference to "reserved" powers.[46]

Third, Brandeis's successive drafts of *Erie* show that he relied on Holmes, not on Field. When he initially framed his argument, he quoted only Holmes. Later, when he added a quotation from *Baugh,* it consisted of only two sentences and did not include any of Field's references to the Tenth Amendment. When his opinion was essentially complete and *Erie*'s constitutional theory in place, Brandeis acquiesced to pressure from Hughes and included the full quotation from Field that appeared in the final opinion. The drafts suggest strongly that Field's dissent had no significant influence on Brandeis while he was conceiving and drafting his opinion.

Beyond the weakness of those textual grounds, however, the contents of the three opinions themselves show that Frankfurter's interpretation was badly distorted. In the first instance, he simply misread Holmes's dissent. He maintained that Holmes had deemed *Swift* unconstitutional on the ground that "the judiciary assumed authority that belonged to Congress."[47] Neither in his *Taxicab* dissent nor in his earlier *Kuhn* dissent, however, did Holmes articulate that rationale. Rather, in both dissents he argued that *Swift* improperly allowed the federal courts to intrude into state lawmaking authority.[48]

Further, Frankfurter failed to acknowledge the similarities that united all three opinions and misread the critical differences that divided Field from both Holmes and Brandeis. On one hand, Frankfurter ignored the fact that *Erie* voiced a variety of jurisprudential propositions that Field and Holmes fully shared. Both dissenters rejected the existence of an authoritative "general law"—and did so with surprisingly similar metaphors.[49] Both equated judicial decisions with "law," insisted that states made their laws equally by legislation and by judicial decision, and based "law" on the positive authority of the state.[50] Finally, both assumed a theory of coextensive powers, maintaining that the authority of a state's judicial decisions was equal in scope to the authority of its legislative enactments.[51] Thus, to a large extent Brandeis adopted a set of propositions that Field and Holmes had equally articulated. On the other hand, and more important, Frankfurter ignored the critical differences between Field, on one side, and Brandeis and Holmes, on the other. One was their use of the Tenth Amendment: Field cited it twice; Holmes and Brandeis never did so.[52] The other critical difference was that Holmes and Brandeis emphasized the lawmaking authority of the states, while Field emphasized and repeatedly referred to the states' "independence," "autonomy," and "separate" spheres.[53] Field, in other words, expressly relied on the Tenth Amendment and on a relatively rigid theory of the states as constitutionally separate and independent sovereigns. In contrast, Holmes and Brandeis refused to cite the Tenth Amendment and relied on a narrower theory that affirmed only the states' authority to make laws in areas where Congress lacked power.

Those similarities and differences make it clear that Brandeis followed Holmes, not Field. Although Brandeis accepted the ideas about judicial lawmaking and the legislative authority of the states that both dissents shared, he sided unambiguously with Holmes on the two critical points on which Holmes differed from Field. Brandeis refused to cite the Tenth Amendment, and he based his reasoning on a theory of the constitutional distribution of lawmaking authority, not on any theory of state autonomy. Indeed, aside from the language he quoted from Field, Brandeis did not refer to the states' "independence," "autonomy," or "separate" spheres.

Finally, Frankfurter misconstrued *Erie* because he failed to give weight to a crucial difference between the constitutional ideas of Field and Brandeis. Frankfurter argued that Field — and, allegedly following him, Brandeis — considered *Swift* unconstitutional because "the law relevant to diversity cases was one of the reserved powers of the States, since it did not concern the making of law in a domain which the Constitution gave to the Congress." [54] That proposition implied agreement between Field and Brandeis that the Tenth Amendment recognized or created independent enclaves of state authority. Field accepted that interpretation of the Tenth Amendment, but Brandeis did not. More important, Frankfurter's statement elided a fundamental difference between Field and Brandeis that gave radically divergent meanings to the proposition they allegedly shared: it ignored their quite different views concerning the constitutional scope of congressional power. Field believed that the national government was strictly limited to "delegated" powers that should be construed narrowly.[55] Brandeis, in contrast, believed that the national government possessed expansive powers that should be construed flexibly. Thus, even if Frankfurter had been correct in his assumption that Brandeis shared Field's view of the structural significance of the Tenth Amendment, he was wrong in implying that they agreed on what was the truly dispositive question: the constitutional scope of national lawmaking power.

If Frankfurter misconstrued *Erie*, however, a second and more puzzling question arises. Of all people, how could Felix Frankfurter — Brandeis's close friend, loyal confidant, fellow Progressive, and long-time collaborator — have made such a mistake? What of his special relationship with Brandeis? Did that relationship not give him a true insight into *Erie?* The answer is that, ironically, Frankfurter's relationship with Brandeis contributed to his misinterpretation of *Erie*.

Brandeis seldom talked with Frankfurter about pending cases, and *Erie* took Frankfurter completely by surprise when it came down.[56] More important, at the time when Brandeis was writing *Erie*, the confidential relationship that had existed between the two in the 1920s and early 1930s had been disrupted. By late 1937 Brandeis was not likely to have confided in Frankfurter about the case, and personal motives may have predisposed Frankfurter to view *Erie* in an unfavorable and distorted light.

The central fact is that their relationship changed significantly during the mid-1930s. As Frankfurter became more deeply involved with Roosevelt and the New Deal, he developed an increasingly close relationship and an intense personal loyalty to the president. At the same time, Brandeis and Roosevelt were moving apart. The justice was growing ever more disturbed by the New Deal's growing tendency toward centralization, while the president began to feel that Brandeis "was losing sight of the fundamentals."[57] A series of policy disagreements, which Frankfurter initially attempted to minimize, created a growing tension, and by the summer of 1935 Frankfurter's deepening loyalty to Roosevelt had begun to chill his relationship with Brandeis.[58]

The Court-packing episode almost caused a complete rupture. Brandeis was virulently opposed to Roosevelt's plan.[59] As soon as it was announced, he wrote Frankfurter asking bluntly whether Roosevelt had consulted him about it. The president, Brandeis warned, was "inviting some pretty radical splits in the Democratic Party & allies."[60] Roosevelt had not, in fact, sought Frankfurter's advice about the plan, but immediately after announcing it he had phoned and exacted a promise that Frankfurter would remain publicly silent on the issue.[61] Roosevelt told Frankfurter that he hoped to put him on the Court at some point and that he did not want him compromised by involvement in what could become a nasty partisan fight.[62] Frankfurter could hardly have refused the request, nor could he have failed to feel the most profound sense of gratitude and exhilaration. In public, he obediently remained silent. In private, he encouraged Roosevelt enthusiastically and arranged for Professor Henry M. Hart, Jr., of Harvard, one of his most highly prized former students and a former law clerk to Brandeis, to make a public defense of the president's bill. Sending Roosevelt a copy of Hart's article, Frankfurter proudly identified the author as "one of my pet products." [63] Outraged by many of the Court's anti–New Deal decisions and bristling from the criticism of friends who urged him to speak out against the president's plan, Frankfurter became deeply and emotionally ensnared in what proved to be the paramount political battle of Roosevelt's presidency.[64] In a letter to Roosevelt dated two days after Brandeis's note warning about "radical splits," Frankfurter turned his back on the justice and pledged his fealty to the president. "[T]he momentum of a long series of decisions not defensible in the realm of reason nor justified by settled principles of Constitutional interpretation," he affirmed, "had convinced me, as they had convinced you, that means had to be found to save the Constitution from the Court, and the Court from itself." Although Frankfurter had reservations about the plan, he had no reservations about committing himself to Roosevelt. "I have, as you know," he wrote the president, "deep faith in your instinct to make the wise choice." [65]

Subsequently, when Brandeis signed Hughes's adroitly timed letter that embarrassed the president and helped defeat the Court bill, Frankfurter—like many New Dealers—was stunned. Brandeis, he felt, had betrayed the president.[66] To Roosevelt, he confessed that Brandeis's action was "a source of sadness to me." [67] To mutual friends, he charged that the Hughes letter was "indefensible" and "disingenuous." Most important, he vented his outrage at Brandeis by accusing him of betraying not only the president but also his own oft-proclaimed constitutional principles. Because the Hughes letter made statements concerning Article III of the Constitution, Frankfurter charged, it "grossly violated the settled practice of the Court against giving advisory opinions." [68]

Frankfurter's bitterness boiled over in the spring of 1937 when the Court suddenly reversed direction. While New Dealers rejoiced at their dramatic constitutional victories, Frankfurter expressed anguish and disgust at the Court's dishonesty. "To me it is all painful beyond words—the poignant grief of one whose life has been dedicated to faith in the disinterestedness of a tribunal and its freedom from responsiveness to the most obvious immediacies of politics." [69] The Court's decision in *West Coast Hotel v. Parrish*,[70] the first of the series, was based on "the indefensible misrepresentation of the record" and showed that "the real nature of the problem" with the Court was "purely personal." The decision was due to Roberts's "shocking" change of heart. "I say shocking because no conceivably relevant, intellectual, legal reason can account for his flop." [71] When

Brandeis wrote him happily after the decision, Frankfurter replied politely but inconsolably. There was satisfaction in the result, he declared, "but, unhappily, it is one of life's bitter-sweets and the bitter far outweighs the sweet." [72]

The feelings Frankfurter expressed—suffering, bitterness, betrayal—were undoubtedly genuine and deeply felt, but his explanation for those feelings—the Court's doctrinal reversal—was wholly insufficient. Frankfurter approved without qualification the substance of the Court's doctrinal change and knew, moreover, that it was essential to safeguard the New Deal. Only the year before, in fact, he had given a series of lectures on the Commerce Clause and urged precisely the kind of broad national powers that the Court seemed finally to accept.[73] The reversal constituted a great New Deal victory, and Frankfurter had every reason to celebrate its long-desired and, in his view, constitutionally proper results.

More important, Frankfurter did not believe that the Court merely expounded timeless law or stood immune from politics. Indeed, while castigating the Court for its duplicities, he could not resist an assessment similar to those he had made on many prior occasions. The Court's behavior, he charged in April 1937, would provide "a very healthy education of the public mind to an understanding of what the Supreme Court really does when it decides constitutional controversies." [74] What the Court "really" did, Frankfurter believed, was make policy judgments that were informed by the political and social values of the justices. "[T]he words of the Constitution" were "so unrestrained by their intrinsic meaning, or by their history, or by tradition, or by prior decisions," he had explained a decade earlier, "that they leave the individual Justice free, if indeed they do not compel him, to gather meaning not from reading the Constitution but from reading life." [75] The justices inescapably read "life" through the lens of their values and preconceptions. "But the process of constitutional interpretation compels the translation of policy into judgment," he had explained, "and the controlling conceptions of the Justices are their 'idealized political picture' of the existing social order." [76] More bluntly, he had told Holmes that judges who pretended to legal certainty were "but translating their own unconscious economic prejudices or assumptions." [77]

Even more significantly, Frankfurter did not believe that the Court was "really" oblivious to changing political pressures. Thirteen years earlier he had maintained that Theodore Roosevelt's campaign for the judicial recall had moderated the anti-Progressive attitudes of the judiciary. "The public opinion which the Progressive campaign aroused," he had boasted, "subtly penetrated the judicial atmosphere." Political pressure had worked. "No student of American constitutional law can have the slightest doubt that Mr. [Theodore] Roosevelt's vigorous challenge of judicial abuses was mainly responsible for a temporary period of liberalism which followed in the interpretation of the due process clauses." Indeed, supporting La Follette's Progressive Party campaign in 1924 and its effort to restrict judicial review, Frankfurter had written approvingly of such political threats: "[Theodore] Roosevelt shrewdly observed: 'I may not know much about law, but I do know one can put the fear of God into judges.' The 'fear of God' was needed to make itself felt on the bench in 1912. The 'fear of God' very much needs to make itself felt in 1924." [78]

Frankfurter's anger and grief in the spring of 1937, then, were not caused by a sudden discovery that the Court did not pronounce timeless law, that it lacked "disinterestedness," or that it bent to political pressures. It was rooted in other, quite different, factors: distress at Brandeis's betrayal of the president; personal embarrassment over his own seemingly cowardly and dishonest public silence on the Court bill; and, perhaps most keenly felt, anguished exasperation over the political humiliation that the Court, Congress, the Republican Party, political conservatives, and the American Bar Association were inflicting on his beloved Roosevelt. The president had invested a great deal in his effort to confront and overcome the anti-Progressive Supreme Court. Suddenly the Court, by abandoning its doctrine under political pressure and seemingly at the last moment, appeared to be defeating the president's effort, tarnishing Roosevelt's reputation, fragmenting the New Deal, perhaps endangering Frankfurter's future appointment to the Court, and—bitterest irony—emerging in the process as itself newly sanctified and triumphant. To Frankfurter, that turn of events was an outrageous and unendurable injustice, and it was the true source of his bitterness.

Frankfurter responded fiercely. The Court's craven reversal, he insisted repeatedly, was Roosevelt's vindication. "[T]he man who won these cases," he declared passionately, was "a somewhat inactive lawyer who did not argue them named Franklin D. Roosevelt." Whatever the outcome of the Court bill, "the President will win because he has already won." [79] To the government lawyer who argued one of the New Deal's critical victories, Frankfurter was as unyielding as he was ungracious. "[I]n the inner recess of your mind you know as well as I know," he preached fervently, "the lawyer who won these cases is the lawyer who never argued them—Franklin D. Roosevelt." [80] The result, Frankfurter insisted, desperate to make his wish the fact, was that "F.D.R. will have got what he wanted—the people will know and his prestige will not have been lowered." [81]

His response suggests two conclusions. First, it further undermines his claim that the Court's lack of "disinterestedness" caused his personal "grief." For, if the president was truly the lawyer who won the New Deal's victories, he had succeeded only by mounting intense political pressures against the Court— by doing exactly what Frankfurter had praised Theodore Roosevelt for doing a quarter of a century earlier. If the second Roosevelt were to be praised, then the pressure he generated had been necessary and desirable; if that were true, then, the Court's "shocking" reversal had been equally necessary and desirable. Although Frankfurter regretted many things about the Court's past behavior, in the spring of 1937 he could hardly have been distressed about the very decisions that he hailed as the president's political triumph and personal vindication. Second, and more obviously, the response suggests the depth of Frankfurter's personal commitment to Roosevelt, which was all-consuming. In the turmoil and conflict of 1937, that commitment pushed Brandeis beyond his sympathies and into the shadows.

Most revealingly, when *Erie* came down the next year, the same theme of betrayal dominated Frankfurter's reaction. The opinion "runs counter to those fundamental canons for constitutional adjudication which Brandeis has been most uncompromising in espousing." [82] Brandeis, he insisted, had acted in "really violent disregard of the professed constitutional canons of adjudication." Indeed, Frankfurter — the longtime critic of *Swift*, diversity jurisdiction, exploitative corporate litigation tactics, and the political biases of the anti-Progressive federal courts — identified "the vital aspect" of *Erie* as nothing that was social, or economic, or political. Rather, he announced, its "vital aspect" was its violation of judicial propriety, its "disregard of constitutional postulates when a desirable result is to be reached." [83] In his mind *Erie* was exactly like the Hughes letter — demonstrably illegitimate and wrong because it transgressed the canons of judicial propriety. Still harboring his rancor toward Brandeis for betraying Roosevelt, Frankfurter seized on *Erie* as both symbol and proof of Brandeis's faithlessness to principle.

A comparison of Frankfurter's reaction to *Erie* to his diametrically opposed response a decade earlier to Brandeis's opinion in *Willing* demonstrates the nature and extent of his altered loyalties. Knowing that Brandeis used Article III to block passage of the declaratory judgment bill for essentially illegitimate personal and political reasons, Frankfurter nevertheless supported him faithfully. Indeed, he acknowledged Brandeis's covert motives and defended his purposeful judicial opportunism. By any conceivable standard, *Erie* was less dubious and more soundly based than *Willing*. Moreover, *Erie* lacked both *Willing*'s pretextual reasoning and politically preemptive thrust. Frankfurter nevertheless defended *Willing* vigorously and loyally. *Erie* he peremptorily condemned.

Following *Erie*, the relationship between Brandeis and Frankfurter suffered further strain when the two were informally forced into competition. Frankfurter yearned for a place on the Court, and in 1938 he began through innumerable surrogates to lobby Roosevelt ceaselessly for the next available nomination. "Felix Frankfurter," Roosevelt told Jim Farley, "wants to get on [the Court] in the worst way."[84] Rumors spread about Frankfurter's possible appointment, the likelihood and desirability of Brandeis's retirement, and the uncertain future of the Court's "Jewish" seat. Harold Laski, Tommy Corcoran, and Harold L. Ickes were among the New Dealers who hoped to see Frankfurter succeed Brandeis as soon as possible. If Brandeis refused to resign before the end of Roosevelt's term, Ickes wrote in July 1938, he "will have something to answer for to the liberals of the country."[85] The rumors quickly reached the justice, particularly reports that Corcoran was upset that Brandeis's continued presence on the Court was blocking Frankfurter's appointment.[86] Brandeis refused to consider retirement and responded to the rumors coldly. Frankfurter, he declared stonily, could probably "do more" by staying at Harvard.[87]

The two maintained a friendship, but its nature had changed profoundly. Frankfurter's response to Brandeis's critical comments about Black in early 1938 illustrated the change. "Frankly," he informed the justice blithely, "I don't share your concern."[88] When Frankfurter received his appointment to the Court and took his seat in early 1939, he most likely considered himself, at long last, the true equal of Brandeis and probably experienced an intense desire to be his own man. Shaping and limiting *Erie* according to his views may have seemed a particularly appealing course toward self-definition. No longer was he a protégé, assistant, or even "half brother/half son."

Two years after *Erie,* with Brandeis retired from the Court, Frankfurter still nursed his bitterness at Brandeis's betrayal of Roosevelt. When Hart, his "pet product" who had defended the Court bill, sent him some confidential files from his clerkship with Brandeis in the early 1930s, Frankfurter pounced vindictively. Reviewing the documents, he announced that he liked the clerks' "minds so much better than that of Brandeis." The documents showed Brandeis "at his worst devious." They revealed that Brandeis purposely twisted precedents "to use them or evade them to support a conclusion that he prefers." They demonstrated, too, that Brandeis's reasoning was "plain stupid or crooked." Indeed, Frankfurter exploded, "Brandeis should have been ashamed." He concluded smugly that "it makes me feel all the more keenly that righteousness is not a satisfactory substitute for rectitude." Savoring the moment, Frankfurter could not suppress a vengeful regret. "It is a pity that the documents are confidential and so can't be the subject of an article."[89]

The drastic change in their relationship suggests three conclusions. First, it seems highly unlikely that the two men discussed *Erie* in confidence or that Frankfurter had any special or inside information concerning Brandeis's constitutional thinking in the case. Indeed, Frankfurter seemed wholly unaware of the key facts about the textual bases for his claim that *Erie*'s constitutional theory was the same as Field's: that Brandeis had agreed to include the long quote from *Baugh* only belatedly and reluctantly; that he had added his reference to "reserved" powers only at the last minute and only in response to the pointed challenge in Butler's dissent; and that in his early drafts he had relied solely on Holmes and omitted both those items.

Second, it is likely that Frankfurter's view of *Erie* was deeply colored by his resentment of Brandeis and his intense loyalty to Roosevelt. He surely knew from Corcoran — almost certainly in vivid detail — about Brandeis's direction to "go back and tell the President that we're not going to let this government centralize everything." [90] *Erie* was a decentralizing opinion, easily interpreted as an indirect reaction against the New Deal. Far more important, Frankfurter believed that Brandeis had betrayed Roosevelt in the Court fight, and it was his intensely felt sense of betrayal — not constitutional principles — that informed his reaction to *Erie*.

Third, if Frankfurter's views of *Erie* were shaped in significant part by those complex personal factors, it becomes easier to understand his egregious misinterpretation of Field and Holmes. If, in interpreting *Erie*, Frankfurter were aligning himself with Roosevelt and against Brandeis, who above all others would he wish to have on his side? Moreover, from the perspective of an old Progressive who had fought the bitter constitutional battles of the *Lochner* era, who would be most damning to link with Brandeis? How else could Frankfurter — acutely aware of the special relationship that had existed between Holmes and Brandeis — read Brandeis's emotion-tinged tribute in *Erie* and conclude that Brandeis had followed Field and rejected Holmes? [91]

Frankfurter's reaction to *Erie* seems both personal and idiosyncratic for another, more speculative, reason. At the core of his values and self-image lay a deep ambivalence about the fact that he was Jewish. He harbored an intense desire to assimilate, to embrace the culture of the Anglo-Saxon Protestant elite, and to become — and to be considered — a true and authentic "American." [92] Ironically, the dubious contrast he drew between the constitutional views of Holmes and Brandeis re-created on a jurisprudential level the political conflict he had witnessed the preceding year between Roosevelt and Brandeis. The constitutional contrast that he imagined between Holmes and Brandeis allowed him to reenact the choice he had made the previous year, once again rejecting Brandeis, this time in favor of the other object of his veneration. Both choices turned him away from Brandeis, a Jew closely linked with Zionism, and identified him with near perfect and "Progressive" embodiments of traditional, established, upper-class, old-family, Anglo-Saxon Protestant America.

Driven by these various motives, Frankfurter succeeded in ensuring that the new Court would ignore *Erie*'s constitutional language. Given the doubts and politics of the other new justices, it was likely an easy task.

The Roosevelt Court: Elaborating Serviceable Doctrine

The Roosevelt Court implemented *Erie* carefully but vigorously, enforcing a strict policy against forum shopping while ignoring Brandeis's constitutional language. The process required it to answer three major legal questions. The first was how federal judges should determine local law when there was no controlling decision by a state's highest court. The second was how, in suits involving parties from two or more states, they should decide *which* state's law to apply. The third was how they should identify the line between the "substantive" state rules that *Erie* required them to follow and mere "procedural" rules that fell outside the decision's mandate.

The Court answered the first question quickly and forcefully. Facing a lower judiciary that included a number of recalcitrant judges who resented *Erie*'s restriction on their independence,[93] the Roosevelt justices held that the lower courts had a "duty" to canvass and follow the decisions of all state courts.[94] In a series of cases in 1940 they held that the federal courts were bound by rulings of intermediate state courts[95] and, absent evidence that the state's highest court would hold differently, by rulings of state trial courts, even if the decisions of those courts were not binding on other state judges.[96] When state trial court decisions "stand as the only exposition of the law of the State," the Court declared in *Fidelity Union Trust Co. v. Field*, a federal court "was not at liberty to reject [them] merely because it did not agree with their reasoning."[97]

The Court addressed the second question almost as quickly and with equal clarity.[98] In 1941 it ruled in *Klaxon v. Stentor Electric Manufacturing Co.* that *Erie*'s "prohibition" against "independent determinations" of state law by federal courts "extends to the field of conflict of laws." In cases involving state law issues, *Klaxon* held, federal courts were bound to apply the choice-of-law rules of the state within which they sat. Although such rules were generally termed "procedural" in the legal vocabulary, the Court nevertheless treated them as "substantive" within the scope of *Erie*'s command. "Any other ruling would do violence to the principle of uniformity within a state, upon which the *Tompkins* decision is based," explained Justice Reed for a unanimous bench. "Whatever lack of uniformity this may produce between federal courts in different states is attributable to our federal system."[99] Choice-of-law rules embodied "local policies" which the federal courts could not "thwart."[100]

The Court answered the third question, how to distinguish substantive from procedural rules, in 1945 in *Guaranty Trust Co. v. York*, a decision that would stand for the next two decades as the Court's major statement on what became "the *Erie* doctrine."[101] There, the issue was whether a federal diversity court was required to apply a state statute of limitations—a provision that was generally considered a matter of "procedure." Trying to distinguish abstractly or logically between "substance" and "procedure" was useless, Frankfurter wrote for the Court, because each of the terms "implies different variables depending upon the particular problem for which it is used." [102] In the *Erie* context, he declared, courts should categorize as "procedural" any rule which, in practice, would be likely to "significantly affect the result of a litigation." That method was best because the "nub of the policy that underlies Erie" was that the "accident" of diverse citizenship should not lead to different results in federal and state courts. "[T]he intent of [*Erie*] was to insure that, in all cases where a federal court is exercising jurisdiction solely because of the diversity of citizenship of the parties," Frankfurter emphasized, "the outcome of the litigation in the federal court should be substantially the same, so far as legal rules determine the outcome of a litigation, as it would be if tried in a State court." [103] Diversity was intended only to protect nonresidents from local bias, and *Erie* was designed to eliminate forum shopping. "A policy so important to our federalism must be kept free from entanglements with analytical or terminological niceties." [104] Federal courts, therefore, were bound under *Erie* to apply all state laws—including those commonly considered "procedural"—if failure to do so would likely result in different outcomes in a federal court and a state court. Because a statute of limitations would terminate the case in a state court, it should be applied equally in a federal court.

Frankfurter's *York* opinion represented the crystallization of his thought on a number of problems related to *Erie*—not just how to define and enforce it but also how to limit it. First, Frankfurter designed *York* to lay to rest the idea that *Erie* had a genuine constitutional basis. He identified the case with a pragmatic social "policy," the effort to eliminate forum shopping. Burying his earlier-stated belief that *Erie* differed from Holmes's *Taxicab* dissent, Frankfurter equated the two opinions in *York*. He sought to negate *Erie*'s constitutional language by explaining Brandeis's opinion in terms of Holmes's general jurisprudential analysis. Quoting Holmes, Frankfurter wrote that *Swift* was the product of the nineteenth century's faith in a " 'brooding omnipresence' of Reason." Its doctrine was "congenial to the jurisprudential climate of the time." [105] *Erie,* in contrast, was the product of a twentieth-century Holmesian positivism. *Swift*'s fallacy was essentially jurisprudential, Frankfurter explained, and *Erie* simply "overruled a particular way of looking at law." [106] *Swift*'s overthrow, then, was best understood as a change in statutory construction resulting from a changed understanding about the philosophical meaning of the word *law.* Justifying the Court's awkward practice of ignoring Brandeis's constitutional language, Frankfurter used *York* to remake *Erie*'s doctrinal foundation. Brandeis's decision, he taught, was based solely on the "policy" of ending forum shopping and a changed "jurisprudential climate," not on the Constitution.

In private, Frankfurter acknowledged his purpose. It "never occurred to me that *York* involved any 'constitutional considerations,'" he wrote to Hart. "Of course Brandeis talked of constitutionality. But is it necessary for me to be bound by what he said?" *York,* Frankfurter explained, was based on the idea that *Erie* embodied a "policy of federal jurisdiction" and not a constitutional principle. "[T]he fact that Brandeis invoked constitutional considerations does not demonstrate their validity." His major concern, he made clear, was that a constitutional *Erie* created potential limits on the power of Congress.[107]

Second, *York* identified and limited *Erie*'s field of applicability. It extended only to those issues involving "state-created rights." Repeatedly Frankfurter emphasized that the crucial test of the doctrine's relevance was the source of the right being enforced.[108] *Erie,* in other words, did not apply when a federal court was adjudicating an issue of federal law. Frankfurter was attempting to formulate a general theory of Brandeis's decision, one that would clarify it and at the same time constrain it sharply.[109]

Third, *York* suggested that *Fidelity Union* and its companion cases from the 1940 term had served their purpose in overcoming lower court opposition to *Erie.* As long as the lower courts were making an honest effort to apply state law, Frankfurter believed, the Supreme Court should allow them more flexibility in meeting new problems. Reviewing cases based on state law drew the Court into areas where it had no expertise, and it deprived the Court of time to deal with cases that raised issues of federal law.[110] It was by design, then, that Frankfurter declared in *York* that the federal courts should follow state law "whether its voice be the legislature or its highest court." [111] Three years later a unanimous Court modified the *Fidelity Union* doctrine, although it reaffirmed the rule that decisions of state courts other than the "highest" one could bind a federal court if they were consistent and well settled.[112]

Frankfurter's decision in *York* was thus based on his determination to restrict *Erie* and prevent it from limiting congressional power or interfering with uniform federal law. It is ironic that Frankfurter—through his opposition to diversity, his association with Brandeis, and his opinion in *York*—became closely identified with a broad reading of *Erie.*[113] In fact, he was deeply suspicious of *Erie* and sought to constrain its reach. His most important and lasting contribution to the doctrine was his early and clear insistence that it simply did not apply when questions of federal law and federal rights were at issue.[114]

By substituting a monolithic "anti–forum-shopping" policy for the broader social concerns that had animated Brandeis, Frankfurter identified *Erie* with a practical purpose that was not only narrow but rigid and ultimately formalistic. *York*'s outcome test focused the "*Erie* doctrine" on one type of forum shopping and on one particular goal. It thereby ignored the broader concerns with unfair and abusive litigation tactics that had engaged Brandeis and helped inform his thinking about *Swift* and diversity jurisdiction. Brandeis chose for strategic reasons to drain his opinion of most of its equitable inspiration, and *York* helped ensure that whatever broader inspiration remained would be constricted, if not extinguished.

During the next decade the Court vigorously enforced *York*'s policy against forum shopping. Although its broad outcome test gave ruthless effect to that policy, *York* limited it to issues where the federal courts were enforcing state-created rights.[115] The *Erie* doctrine, Frankfurter noted in *York*, fostered "a sharper sense of what federal courts do when they enforce rights that have no federal origin."[116] *Erie*, especially as interpreted by *York*, made the question of which law was to be applied in the federal courts turn on the legislative source of the rights involved. That positivist emphasis coincided with the Roosevelt Court's deference to the legislature and its concern for the substantive social policies that legal rules embodied.

The Culture and Ideology of the Legal Academy: A Misbegotten Erie

For the courts and commentators addressing the technical problems that *Erie* raised, two broader concerns informed their views and helped shape their interpretation of Brandeis's decision. One was the continued commitment of the profession's elite to nationalism, professional craft values, and the superiority of the federal courts. The other was its desire to counter the dangers of legal realism and affirm the rational nature of the judicial process. Among many commentators, those concerns helped inspire a strikingly negative view of Brandeis's decision.

The elite of both the practicing bar and the teaching profession had embraced the national judiciary in the late nineteenth century, and their ardor remained unabated in the postwar decades. Many of *Erie*'s supporters and most of its critics disliked the severe restrictions that it, and especially its progeny, placed on the federal courts. "It has no doubt been difficult for many federal judges, traditionally among the ablest of our jurists," one commentator sympathized, "at times to subordinate their own ideas to the pronouncements of state courts."[117] Professor James W. Moore at Yale Law School criticized *Erie* and *Fidelity Union* for distorting the doctrine of precedent and thereby depriving the federal courts of necessary judicial flexibility. The latter case made state decisions "far more rigid and binding [in the federal courts] than in the [state] courts which establish them."[118] One writer bluntly demanded "protection of the federal courts from *Erie*," while another proclaimed that its doctrine placed "the mark of dependence and servility" on the national courts.[119]

Zechariah Chafee, Jr., a professor at Harvard and a renowned First Amendment scholar, represented the attitude of many elite lawyers. Shortly after *Erie* came down, he argued that in the area of unfair trade competition, one of his areas of expertise, *Erie* would prove "very damaging" because it decentralized the law where national uniformity was required. By 1947, he focused on the advantages *Swift* had offered and the evils that resulted from its overthrow. *Swift* had allowed "the Supreme Court and able circuit judges" to "operate independently of state idiosyncrasies during the formative period of our law," an arrangement that had brought "national uniformity." [120] To Chafee, the difference between state and federal courts was the difference between "idiosyncrasies" on the state side and "able" judges on the federal side.

Chafee saw *Erie* as a threat not only to national uniformity but also to the academic elite. *Swift* had led to "anomalies," he acknowledged, and those anomalies had proved "increasingly distasteful to men who thought seriously about law." To the extent that remedial action had been necessary, "there arose a growing hope that the ideal of national uniformity could be attained through other agencies than the federal courts." He announced those other agencies unabashedly. "Story himself made Harvard the first national law school where the desirability of rules of law was canvassed by teacher and students without regard to the particular state in which a student was going to practice," he explained. "In their classroom discussions the common law of the United States was taken as a reality." [121] The national law schools had helped to impose a practical uniformity on American law by teaching a single coherent common law and by supporting, where necessary, the passage of uniform state statutes. *Erie* only disrupted their growing success.

While the New Deal Court was suspicious of *Erie*'s constitutional language because it suggested limits on congressional power, many professional commentators criticized Brandeis's opinion because it limited the federal courts. They argued that the constitutional grant of "judicial power" conferred authority to render independent judgments on all common law issues within federal jurisdiction, and they pointed to the analogous power that the national courts asserted in admiralty and interstate controversies.[122] During the 1940s and early 1950s, these commentators generated a widespread belief that *Erie*'s constitutional language was only "dictum." [123] The *Cornell Law Quarterly* announced that "the constitutional argument has never been plausible," while *The Harvard Law Review* proclaimed it "thoroughly discredited." [124] Chafee scorned *Erie*'s constitutional language as a "comic element" that was "probably no longer accepted," while Brainerd Currie, another prominent scholar, dismissed it disdainfully as "a bit of judicial hyperbole" that "should not be permitted to mislead even the most literal-minded reader." [125]

Most commentators, moreover, including many who defended *Erie*, feared that it would disrupt or destroy the new Federal Rules of Civil Procedure, and they produced a massive literature calling for independence of the rules from *Erie* and especially from *York*.[126] Their often incisive analyses largely shared the assumption that strengthening federal procedural independence was desirable because the national courts were superior to the state courts. The legal elite identified with the federal courts, and its members looked suspiciously on whatever might restrict their authority.

To strengthen the position of the national judiciary and protect the Federal Rules, many writers began to revive the idea that there were general "principles" of the common law that the federal courts should apply "independently." To deny the federal courts the power to make "an independent judgment on matters of general law," declared one law review note, "is to emasculate the federal judicial power; to make automatons of federal judges who must perforce apply illogical, antiquated and locally characterized law, regardless of their own concepts and integrity." [127] *Klaxon* was "outrageous" and "absurd" in forcing federal courts in different states to produce contrary results on the same facts, another scholar maintained. "The rules of conflict of laws grow out of the law of nations and principles of comity," and hence the federal courts should not be bound by state decisions but only by those general principles.[128] Another article charged that *Erie* led to "chaos" and that Brandeis had been "influenced by a rational abhorrence of the possibility of contradictory rules within one geographical area." [129] The article's four authors assumed that the principles of the common law were clear and that the federal courts could elaborate them more effectively than could state courts. Their claim that Brandeis's motivations lay in a "rational" abhorrence of conflicting rules revealed the chasm that separated Brandeis's Progressivism from the concerns and assumptions of many postwar commentators.

The profession's social orientation and the interests of its legal elite were nowhere more clearly illustrated than in the views of the leaders of prewar legal realism. Critics of the old Court and in most cases supporters of the New Deal, the realists had rejected the idea that courts "found" law and had insisted that social results constituted the proper test of a rule's desirability. The political and intellectual crisis of the late 1930s and 1940s, however, generated a powerful need to reaffirm the ideal of legal objectivity and rationality. Juxtaposed to the behavior of the "totalitarian" legal systems of Nazi Germany and Stalinist Russia, the realists' most extreme claims — that there was no demonstrable rational or moral basis to the law and that law was whatever public officials would enforce — seemed dangerous and anti-democratic.[130] Political conservatives, moreover, exploited the new postwar mood by attempting to link the image of a cynical and debilitating realism with the jurisprudence of the Roosevelt Court, thereby discrediting both.[131] At the same time, with substantive due process interred and the commerce power expanded, the realists came to regard much of their prewar criticism as outmoded. They realized the need for "constructive" commentary, and they were attracted to social values that appeared nonpartisan and consensual, attributes they viewed as inconsistent with the twin evils they had fought: "liberty of contract," with its contrary-to-fact presumptions, and totalitarianism, with its ideological fanaticism. By the early 1940s, then, the old realists downplayed or ignored *Erie*'s social concerns and focused instead on a newly pivotal issue: the ways that *Erie* and its progeny compromised the full judicial process — rational in method and superior in quality — of the federal courts.

The decision, both hailed and condemned as the symbol of a newly triumphant Holmesian realism, provoked little reaction from leading realists other than disdain for its doctrinal results that constrained the power of the federal courts.[132] Most of the leading realists — including Arthur L. Corbin, Karl N. Llewellyn, Max Radin, Jerome Frank, Judge Joseph C. Hutcheson, Thomas Reed Powell, Charles E. Clark, and Walter Wheeler Cook — expressed their disapproval.[133] The social and political significance of Brandeis's decision was lost in part because the old Progressive wing of the legal elite, the most likely source of a vigorous defense of *Erie*'s social and political values, criticized it sharply. Indeed, the realist attack, like the assault of much of the legal academic elite, seemed to incorporate and echo the values that the ABA had proclaimed throughout the 1930s, the primacy of the federal courts and the need at all costs to protect their power and prestige.

Although the realists vaguely supported *Erie*'s immediate social result, they joined in the assault on its constitutional language and hammered incessantly on the claim that its doctrine forced the federal courts to follow state precedents "mechanically."[134] Its doctrine prevented federal judges from using their best judgment, drawing on the complete range of appropriate legal sources, and fulfilling their true judicial function. If *Erie* "is a direction to substitute an omnipresence brooding over Pennsylvania alone, in place of the roc-like bird whose wings have been believed to overspread forty-eight states," Corbin declared even before *Fidelity Union* came down, "something has indeed been lost."[135] He could see in *Erie* only a limitation on the federal judicial craft and harm to the common law's seamless web. Three years later, in a critique of *Erie* and especially of *Fidelity Union*, Corbin advanced his most extreme charge: The doctrine's rigidity deprived parties in diversity suits of a truly judicial forum and hence denied them due process of law.[136]

In spite of the familiar-sounding attack on a new "mechanical" jurisprudence, the realists' assault reflected their profound bias toward the federal courts far more than it did their prewar critique of legal reasoning. "Are the federal courts to take their state law from a justice of the peace?" Powell exclaimed with mocking incredulity.[137] "Why should we abdicate our judicial functions and even prostitute our intellectual capacities," Clark asked in 1945 after his appointment to the federal bench, "to discover not state law, but the particular views a state judge may have uttered many years ago under quite different circumstances?"[138] The judicial approach required by *Fidelity Union,* Cook agreed, was "so inadequate" that in choice-of-law issues it would cause "great harm."[139] Not surprisingly, Frank turned the most colorful, and subsequently most widely quoted, phrase. *Erie,* he announced, turned the federal judge into a "ventriloquist's dummy."[140]

Although the realists' critique had some merit after *Fidelity Union,* it was misguided and overblown.[141] In part, they objected to the policies that state laws enforced, but that objection went to *Erie*'s substantive merits, not to any "mechanical" method it forced on federal judges. In part, too, they objected to the absence, incompleteness, or relative antiquity of relevant state decisions, but that objection raised no insurmountable or unusual problems. Precedents often failed to provide clear or up-to-date answers to new questions, and where state decisions provided little or no guidance other legal sources were properly available to federal judges. Fairly considered, even *Fidelity Union* and its 1940 companions did not deny that.

More telling, the realists ignored two critical and highly "realist" considerations. First, in the immediate aftermath of *Erie* many lower court judges had used a variety of techniques to avoid following applicable state court decisions. It was their recalcitrance that forced the Court to adopt strong measures to limit their discretion and enforce *Erie*'s mandate.[142] The realists ignored the practical, administrative problems involved in ensuring institutional enforcement of the new doctrine. Second, they criticized *Erie* from a socially abstract point of view. They ignored their own earlier insistence that legal rules represented policy choices and that the judicial process was at least partly guided by the underlying values of the judges. In its place, they substituted the assumption that judicial decisions were relatively objective, that they were based only indirectly on policy choices, and that professional craft skills could guide judges in formulating "proper" decisions. Ultimately, what the realists objected to was not the imposition of some "mechanical" decision-making process but the hierarchical subordination of the federal courts — which they admired and with which they identified — to the state courts they so clearly disdained.

Consistent with their commitment to craft values and the prestige of the federal courts, the realists were also animated by a nationalist and reformist perspective that further discounted *Erie*'s value. They were professional legal reformers who wished to see their ideas accepted across the nation. Clark had

drafted the Federal Rules of Civil Procedure; Llewellyn was the principal architect of the Uniform Commercial Code; Corbin was the author of a massive and
masterly treatise on contract law and a major formulator of the American Law
Institute's *Restatement of the Law of Contracts;* Cook was a specialist in conflict
of laws who hoped to see the Supreme Court create a unified body of national
choice-of-law rules. Exhibiting the nationalist presuppositions that drove the
realists' critique of *Erie,* Cook charged that even on the "simplest" of issues
"the state decisions are hopelessly contradictory and chaotic." Assuming the superiority of the federal courts, he argued that they "may take a broader, a less
parochial, view of these matters than state courts." Assuming the possibility of
an objectively "rational" analysis of conflict-of-law issues and the desirability of
national uniformity, he criticized *Erie* and *Klaxon* for depriving federal judges
of their independence and for continuing the "present chaos." "Might it not be
better," he asked, "to let the federal courts — ultimately the Supreme Court —
work out a national system governing the 'choice of law' when these questions
arise?"[143] The realists disliked *Erie*'s decentralizing thrust, and they recognized
that the decision, by fragmenting the "general" common law taught in the
law schools, undermined their position as authoritative expounders of its basic
principles.[144]

While Brandeis and the realists shared many values, their different emphases were revealing. Brandeis was concerned with "realism" in the sense of
determining how a rule would operate in a given social context. He made his
decision in part on that basis, and it was that basis that the realists subordinated
to nationalism, professional craft values, and the independence of the federal
courts. From the variety of problems that *Erie* raised, the realists identified the
"mechanical" nature of the ensuing judicial process as the most important and
disruptive. Their selection was based on social criteria different from those Brandeis had used. Without analyzing or generally considering problems of social
context or differential litigation results, they criticized *Erie* for its alleged technical flaws, its distortion of judicial craft procedures, and its limitation on the
independence of the federal courts.

Given such a response from the socially oriented, New Deal wing of the
legal elite, it was natural that the parameters of debate over *Erie* would grow increasingly circumscribed and that questions about the impact of social inequality
on the legal process would be subordinated and largely ignored. The interpretation that Brandeis invited with his neutral conceptualistic language and that
Frankfurter developed with his narrow and formal approach in *York* was confirmed by the realists with their analytic focus on an abstract judicial process
and their commitment to the power and prestige of the national courts.

The Postwar Constitution and the Struggle for
Brandeis's Mantle: A Restrained Erie

Forced by novel issues to move beyond its shared New Deal values, the Roosevelt Court began to fragment in the 1940s. Black and Frankfurter emerged as polar figures advocating sharply different prescriptions for the Court. Both were rooted in the Progressive past, and both sought to develop judicial methods to avoid what they saw as the subjectivism of the old Court. Frankfurter emphasized the need for "judicial restraint," a high degree of deference to the decisions of other branches of government and a strict adherence to jurisdictional limitations. Black, in contrast, embraced a "literalist" theory, insisting that the Court was limited to enforcing only those rights explicitly granted by the Constitution. Black, however, read the Fourteenth Amendment broadly, claiming that it incorporated the first eight amendments of the Bill of Rights and hence made them enforceable against the states. His theory of "incorporation," together with his belief that the rights granted by the First Amendment were "absolute," enabled him to justify a vigorous judicial activism in favor of individual liberties. To Frankfurter, Black's approach represented both excessive judicial interventionism and a new reign of personal values; to Black, Frankfurter's views were not only amorphous and subjective but self-deluding.[145]

Responding to the postwar challenges of realism and totalitarianism in the context of the overarching constitutional debate between Black and Frankfurter, scholars attempted to integrate the insights of legal realism into broader frameworks that affirmed the authority of limiting and objective legal principles. The resulting jurisprudence of institutional process that marked the 1950s and 1960s acknowledged a subjective element in judicial decisions, assumed that logic by itself was an insufficient tool, and incorporated the idea that judicial decisions were rooted in social contexts and purposes. Its advocates maintained, however, that there were empirically demonstrable and rationally justifiable constraints that should and did guide judges in reaching valid and rationally justifiable decisions.[146]

The first constraint scholars identified was social. Judges were creatures of their time, cognizant of the general needs of their society and sharing its most fundamental goals and values. Upon reflection, judges could identify those social considerations with reasonable accuracy; they could also shape, within acceptable limits of disagreement, legal rules to serve those considerations.[147] If judges paid close heed to society's consensual values and remained free of "ideological" fanaticism, they would be both restrained and enlightened in their judgments.

The second constraint was institutional. Judges occupied a specific role that imposed a range of external and internal limits on their behavior. One was

the system of appellate courts and the advocacy of counsel who raised and explored salient issues.[148] Another was the "maturing of collective thought," the
idea that judges conferred with their colleagues and reached group judgments
that transcended narrow individual views.[149] A third was jurisdiction, which
prevented judges from deciding cases until a series of significant preliminary
requirements had been met.[150] The institutional role cabined judges, and close
attention to its demands provided reliable guidance.

The third constraint was intellectual and professional. Judges had a duty
to explain their decisions, to give clear and persuasive reasons for the choices
they made. To the extent that they fulfilled their duty, they seriously limited
themselves, channeled their decisions within accepted limits, and convinced the
public of their legitimacy. To the extent that they failed, the professional apparatus, especially the law reviews, would operate to undermine their decisions and
call the judges themselves before the bar of their intellectual peers.[151] Exacting
doctrinal analysis was crucial, not because "logic" dictated results, but because
well-reasoned opinions could persuade a craft-validated institutional audience
according to accepted canons of professional argument.

During the 1950s the jurisprudence of institutional process came to dominate academic legal thought. One variant, emphasizing what its proponents
called "reasoned elaboration" and "process jurisprudence," was inspired by
Frankfurter and associated with Harvard Law School.[152] The major constraints
on the judicial process, it stressed, were jurisdictional limitations, collective judicial reasoning, the demands of professional craftsmanship, and judicial passivity
absent a compelling cultural consensus to take action. A second variant, less influential at the time but more indicative of the shift that had taken place since
the 1930s, came from Karl Llewellyn, legal realism's most creative theorist.[153]
In his rich if eccentric magnum opus, *The Common Law Tradition*, he identified
fourteen institutional constraints and argued that a practical "situation-sense"
led judges toward the rational and optimal resolution of legal conflicts. Reason, Llewellyn insisted, could extract from human nature and prevailing social
conditions a rationally knowable and objective "immanent law" that ought to
control decisions.[154]

As the jurisprudence of institutional process spread during the 1950s, it
affected *Erie* in two ways. First, in emphasizing the need for restraints on judicial judgment and the importance of legal rules, it reflected and encouraged a
rationalist and anti-positivist attitude that helped restore faith in the existence
of legal and moral principles. Although the realists disliked *Erie*, many of its
critics, and even some of its supporters, identified it with a realist philosophy of
law. Its quotations from Holmes and its "philosophical" interpretation in *York*
gave plausibility to the charge and convinced some that it was built on "shaky

theoretical foundations." [155] The jurisprudence of institutional process tended to discredit *Erie*'s positivism and to support those who claimed that it fragmented the true common law and impaired the federal judicial process.

Llewellyn made the connection explicit. Acknowledging that the common law was the law of the states, he nevertheless described judicial lawmaking as a process of shaping and articulating a generalized and objective "immanent law" in the light of "sound reason." [156] Consequently, he saw *Erie* as dysfunctional because it subordinated the superior national courts to the state courts. He bristled when he reflected that *Erie* allowed "even 'any jackleg judge' of an inferior State court" to bind the judgment of a federal court. Brandeis's decision gave state judges the authority to "control the Federal court absolutely," he protested, "control without regard to the sense of the ruling or to its possible or probable reversal." [157]

Second, the jurisprudence of institutional process highlighted *Erie*'s technical flaws. *Erie* reversed a Supreme Court precedent that had stood for ninety-six years. So much for continuity. Even worse, as critics repeatedly pointed out, the parties had never called for a reconsideration of *Swift*. Both sides had, in fact, agreed that *Swift* controlled. So much for deciding only issues squarely presented. Still, there was more. The constitutional issue had never been briefed or argued, and in any case a constitutional holding was unnecessary and easily avoidable. So much for institutional restraint. *Erie*'s flaws, however, remained to be fully detailed. Brandeis's opinion had not clearly and persuasively explained its rationale; it had not elaborated precisely why *Swift* was unconstitutional. There was no agreement on *Erie*'s constitutional basis, and no agreement that the opinion meant—or even legitimately could mean—what it explicitly said. So much for reasoned elaboration.

Erie's flaws posed special difficulties for many of the proponents of process jurisprudence. Frankfurter was closely identified with Brandeis and, through *York* and his opposition to diversity, with *Erie* itself. He and many of his allies had been personally associated with Brandeis, and they shared many of his values. Moreover, Brandeis exerted a powerful intellectual attraction for them because he had emphasized the importance of careful opinion writing and the exercise of judicial restraint. *Erie* loomed as a flagrant and inexplicable anomaly.

With the advent of the Warren Court in 1954, amid a mounting national debate over constitutional law and the proper role of the Supreme Court, *Erie*'s "anomalous" quality became particularly embarrassing to the advocates of process jurisprudence. Urging a narrowly limited role for the Court, Frankfurter held himself out as the spokesman for reason and restraint as opposed to what he considered Black's result-oriented and politically motivated jurisprudence. He urged his former students and law clerks to criticize the Court for its activism and, implicitly, to defend his own views.[158] The major statements of reasoned elaboration, often appearing in the *Harvard Law Review* and written in most cases by Frankfurter's former students and clerks, generally defended his view of the Court and the Constitution. In contrast, those who rejected process jurisprudence or advocated a more active role for the Court in protecting civil rights and liberties often sympathized with Black and challenged Frankfurter's philosophy of restraint.[159]

The debate evolved, on one of its many levels, into a contest over the mantle of Brandeis's authority, which remained intact in the 1950s. Scholars sympathetic to Black and an activist federal judiciary heralded Brandeis as one of their own. They emphasized his innovative and reform-oriented jurisprudence, and they minimized his concern with restraint. Brandeis typically had not made "too ascetic a dissociation between his views of public policy and his opinions," wrote Max Lerner,[160] while Samuel Konefsky described the justice as "by nature a fighter for causes." [161] Political and social liberalism guided Brandeis's work on the Court, declared the political scientist C. Herman Pritchett, and he "could never quite believe that it was wrong for him as a judge to further the liberal goals of public policy in which he believed as a man." [162] Alpheus Mason's biography, published in 1946, focused on Brandeis's commitment to reform and enshrined his image as a liberal social activist.[163] Fred Rodell, a professor at Yale Law School and Frankfurter's most relentless critic, made the point most forcefully. "Brandeis was the crusader," he asserted. "No less than McReynolds, on the far side of the fence, did Brandeis seek to write his own economic ideas into law." [164]

Frankfurter bitterly resented the image of Brandeis as a judicial activist who could be seen as even remotely similar to Black. As he had suppressed his initial view of *Erie* to create a serviceable and nonconstitutional jurisprudential interpretation in *York,* so he moved beyond his private view in 1940 that Brandeis should have been "ashamed" of his result-oriented behavior. His new goal was to use Brandeis's career to construct a powerful anti-Black counterimage. When Louis Jaffe, another of Frankfurter's former students who had clerked for Brandeis, criticized those who stressed Brandeis's judicial reformism, Frankfurter congratulated him enthusiastically. "Your disassociation of Brandeis from the 'activists,' " he cheered, "is as true as it is good." It was essential to separate Brandeis from "those who really think that law is only the 'manipulation of symbols' for immediate, predetermined ends." [165] Ultimately, Frankfurter could not restrain himself, and in 1957 he entered the contest from the Supreme Court bench. Commentators often neglected "Mr. Justice Brandeis's" rigorous focus on "what business comes to the Court and how the Court deals with it," he wrote. To Brandeis, such jurisdictional rules "were not technicalities" but essentials. "He deemed wise decisions on substantive law within the indispensable area of the Court's jurisdiction dependent on a limited volume of business and on a truly deliberative process."[166]

Frankfurter controlled Brandeis's Court papers. After denying access to Mason, who had portrayed an activist Brandeis, he opened the papers to Alexander M. Bickel, one of his former clerks. He encouraged Bickel to produce a detailed study of Brandeis's judicial methods that would replace the image of a socially motivated dissenter with a portrait of a more self-restrained and institutionally oriented consensus builder.[167] Indeed, Frankfurter quashed the somewhat confrontational title that Bickel initially proposed — A Climate of Dissent — in favor of one that was as mundane as possible, The Unpublished Opinions of Mr. Justice Brandeis. The title minimized Brandeis's role as a partisan and focused on his commitment to the Court's internal process of cooperative and collective judicial deliberation.[168]

Bickel's book argued that Brandeis had been the effective advocate of reason and restraint within the Court and that the process of constitutional adjudication could be, and often was, a process of disinterested and open-minded rational analysis. Stressing Brandeis's commitment to procedural and jurisdictional limitations, Bickel used his first chapter to spotlight a striking lesson in judicial integrity. Examining an appeal involving the second federal child labor law, a centerpiece of Progressive reform, Bickel argued that Brandeis had come to believe that the underlying suit was jurisdictionally improper. As a result, he maintained, Brandeis concluded that the Court should not hear the appeal but should remand with a direction to dismiss. In blocking the case, Bickel suggested, Brandeis had prevented the formation of a majority that would likely have upheld the statute's constitutionality. The case was powerful evidence, therefore, "of the rigid integrity with which Brandeis adhered to his jurisdictional scruples, no matter if to do so was to oppose a substantive result he himself desired."[169] Bickel's interpretation of the child labor case was both highly speculative and dubious in the extreme. It did, however, perfectly serve his "Frankfurterian" goal.[170]

Developing his central theme in a series of brilliant essays, Bickel replaced the image of Brandeis the judicial activist with the image of Brandeis the paragon of reason and restraint. His book, as one reviewer noted, showed Brandeis's "scrupulous devotion to the judicial process."[171] The artful, sophisticated, and impassioned Progressive had been born again as the austere, ideal, and self-denying "Brandeis of Ashwander."[172]

Other Frankfurterian scholars joined the effort.[173] Ernest J. Brown of Harvard sought to sanctify Willing and Brandeis's opposition to the declaratory judgment. The case exemplified the idea of judicial restraint, Brown argued, because it showed that Brandeis "was consistently on the alert to oppose extensions of judicial authority." Further, Brown explained, Brandeis's eventual acceptance of the Declaratory Judgment Act showed that he readily acted against his own beliefs when they conflicted with the law.[174] Paul Freund, another Harvard professor who had studied under Frankfurter and clerked for Brandeis, pointed to the series of decisions that Brandeis had written in the 1930s under the Full Faith and Credit Clause. The doctrinally proper disposition, Freund declared with a triumphant rhetorical flourish, led Brandeis "to reject the claims of a widow, an orphan, and a workingman." Brandeis was not cruel, but neither was he directly result-oriented. He was, after all, "a constitutional judge, not a jury lawyer."[175] He was, in other words, Frankfurter, not Black. Indeed, by the end of the 1950s the new and carefully constructed image of "Brandeis of *Ashwander*" bore a much closer resemblance to Frankfurter than it did to its ostensible subject.[176]

Although far removed from the major constitutional controversies of the 1950s, *Erie* became relevant to the raging debate through the struggle for Brandeis's mantle. In the process of revising Brandeis' image, scholars sympathetic to Frankfurter and the ideal of reasoned elaboration began emphasizing *Erie*'s self-denying elements. Dean Erwin N. Griswold of Harvard, who had "qualms" two decades earlier over *Erie*'s flaws, now stressed that "the result reached by Justice Brandeis was one which cut down the scope of activity of the federal courts."[177] Freund struck the same note, emphasizing that "if [the justice] was guilty of violating his own principles he did so in the interest of enforcing a larger self-restraint on federal courts."[178] The ultimate synthesis came from Wallace Mendelson, a scholarly proponent of Frankfurter's judicial philosophy. *Erie* and *Ashwander,* Mendelson proclaimed, were not in fact contrary at all. "The two opinions are expressions in different contexts of a single principle — judicial self-restraint in deference to other agencies of government."[179] Thus, even if they acknowledged that *Erie* was something of a "sport" in Brandeisian jurisprudence, the proponents of process jurisprudence managed to justify it as part of the justice's broader practice of restraint. Thus, *Erie* evidenced Brandeis's all-encompassing commitment to judicial restraint and, by implication, showed that Brandeis rejected Black's deeply flawed constitutional activism.

Revealingly, the Frankfurterian scholars explained *Erie* with little or no reference to any political and social motives that Brandeis might have had for developing his ideas of restraint and seeking to restrict the federal courts. Indeed, for them *Erie*'s abstract and conceptual treatment of forum shopping and the fact that it reversed a judgment for an injured individual were perfect. Both confirmed the decision's strict social neutrality. Brandeis's sole motive in *Erie* was seemingly to honor an unyielding commitment to the abstract standards of judicial propriety.[180] That conclusion, of course, was quite the opposite of Frank-furter's view in 1938, when he described *Erie*'s "vital aspect" as the violation of those very standards of propriety.

By the end of the 1950s, some of the nation's most prominent and in-fluential scholars were portraying *Erie* as standing for a generalized principle of judicial restraint. That image, along with their reinterpretation of Brandeis's jurisprudence, invoked his authority on behalf of their position in the decade's constitutional and jurisprudential debates. Their portrayal of *Erie* was incom-plete and misleading, and their reinterpretation of Brandeis was overdrawn. Not only did the proponents of restraint and process jurisprudence minimize the ways in which Brandeis's social concerns influenced his judicial behavior, but they failed to explore adequately the ways in which the political context of the 1920s and 1930s gave to his judicial restraint a profoundly different social mean-ing than it had in the 1950s. Similarly, they highlighted the "neutral" nature of his forum-shopping analysis and banished the possibility that it could embody any broader or more challenging social inspiration. Finally, they distorted Bran-deis's principle of legislative primacy, transforming it from a limitation on the federal courts' nonconstitutional lawmaking power into a far more general re-quirement that the federal courts defer broadly to all agencies of government — even in areas that implicated constitutional values. *Erie*, in fact, gave no support to that sweeping and abstract mandate. Nevertheless, the advocates of process jurisprudence succeeded in remolding the image of Brandeis and, as a corollary, the image of *Erie* itself.

A new historical context gave scholars who admired both the absent Brandeis and the embattled Frankfurter new eyes with which to see. When they looked at *Erie*, they saw the judicial deference they favored and closed their eyes to the social purposiveness they disclaimed.

Henry M. Hart, Jr., and the Power of Transforming Vision

9

T he career of Henry M. Hart, Jr.—a student of Frankfurter's, a clerk to Brandeis, and by the 1950s one of the nation's most influential authorities on the federal judicial system—exemplified the ways in which American legal thinking changed between the Depression and the cold war. A New Dealer who became a critic of the Warren Court, Hart personified the shift from social reform to cultural reaffirmation. His brilliant and multilayered portrait of the federal judicial system illustrated the way that changing cultural preconceptions and personal politics molded both systematic legal theory and technical case analysis. Indeed, Hart produced a powerful vision of the national judiciary and a compelling new image of *Erie* that elided its Progressive political and social values and transformed it into an abstract symbol of federalism and the rule of law.

A Westerner at Harvard: From Progressivism to Anti-Communism

Born in Butte, Montana, in 1904, Henry Hart journeyed east for his higher education. Graduating from Harvard College in 1926, he remained on campus to receive an LL.B. in 1930 and a graduate law degree the following year. Mature, brilliant, and politically Progressive, he quickly became one of Frankfurter's most highly prized students. When he completed his graduate work, Hart received Frankfurter's nod to serve as Brandeis's law clerk. Already an admirer of the justice, the young man was profoundly impressed with Brandeis's intellect, integrity, and social commitment. Brandeis refused "to consider law in any other terms," Hart declared approvingly, "than those of its bearing upon the realities of social and economic life." The justice represented to his young clerk all that was best in the inspiring tradition of Progressivism. "As a critic of American life," he reflected, Brandeis "is in his own person a link between all the principal movements of protest and reform from the muckrakers of the nineties to the New Deal."[1] When Hart finished his clerkship, Frankfurter arranged to bring him back to Harvard as an assistant professor of law. "[Y]ou ought to know," he wrote his protégé in early 1932, "that no one has been more eagerly wanted all the years since I have been on the faculty."[2]

When Hart returned to Cambridge, Frankfurter quickly drew him into his projects. He invited his junior colleague to teach his course on federal jurisdiction while he was on leave,[3] and the following year the two collaborated on a new installment of "The Business of the Supreme Court."[4] Frankfurter also found an outlet for Hart's political interests by providing access to the pages of *The New Republic,* where in a series of unsigned editorials Hart defended the New Deal, urged economic redistributionism, and supported an expansive view of congressional power. Government, he insisted in 1935, must reduce the "fantastic inequalities in personal incomes and estates."[5] He joined the American Civil Liberties Union and the smaller and vigorously left-wing Cambridge Teacher's Union, an affiliate of the American Federation of Labor and a center for many of the university's radical activists. By 1937, his colleague Thomas Reed Powell was chiding him for living in "sociological heat" and exhibiting a "mood of intense knight-errantry."[6]

The Supreme Court infuriated the young Hart. An opinion by Justice Roberts was "in the tradition of unreality of too much of our constitutional law," and one of Justice McReynold's dissents was a "public misfortune."[7] The Court's decision invalidating the Railroad Retirement Act showed "reckless irresponsibility" and "evil implications,"[8] while *United States v. Butler,*[9] which declared the Agricultural Adjustment Act unconstitutional, was "incredibly stupid."[10] The Depression demanded substantial reforms, and one way or another the New Deal would bring them about. For a half century the Supreme Court had been "a prop to the dominant system of free corporate enterprise," Hart charged. "As that system decays, so the prop is failing."[11]

His loyalty to Roosevelt and the New Deal survived the acid test. In the spring of 1937, at Frankfurter's urging, Hart took up the administration's cause in the all-consuming debate over the Court bill. Addressing the League of Women Voters in Washington, D.C., he drew on the writings of James Bradley Thayer, a fountainhead of the Progressive doctrine of minimalist judicial review, to demonstrate the extent of the Court's abuses.[12] Unless a statute's unconstitutionality was "so manifest as to leave no room for reasonable doubt," the Court was obliged to respect the judgment of Congress. The judiciary was neither authorized nor qualified to make judgments of policy. American constitutional law, Hart insisted, "was founded on confidence in the legislature not distrust."[13] Affirming the constitutional standard of Progressivism, he insisted that Congress held primary lawmaking authority: "judgments of policy are the sole function of the legislature, and judgments of constitutionality its function in the first instance." But, he charged, pressure from the bar and "the comfortable classes" had generated an intense fear of social legislation and induced the Court to transgress the legitimate bounds of its authority.[14]

As the Court fight ended, foreign policy was fast becoming a predominant national concern. Widespread opposition existed to American involvement in any European war, and an emotional domestic debate intensified after the Nazi invasion of Poland in 1939. The American Communist Party, responding to the Nazi-Soviet nonaggression pact signed only days before the invasion, abruptly abandoned its strategy of forming a "common front" against fascism and, instead, condemned the war as a cynical struggle between imperialist rivals. The party supported pacifists, isolationists, and other groups determined to prevent American involvement. At the same time, public support for American aid to England and France grew steadily, and calls for immediate intervention began to appear with increasing frequency. By early 1940, the administration was directly, if covertly, providing military and economic support for the war against Germany.

Hart's sympathies were fervently interventionist. He was outraged by Nazi barbarities and believed that the United States had to join the opposition. His political commitment to Roosevelt induced him to follow the president's international leadership, and a year of service in the Office of the Solicitor General in 1937–38 pulled him even closer to the administration. He was also especially sensitive to Nazi anti-Semitism. His friendship with Brandeis and Frankfurter helped shape his views, and his frequently unsuccessful efforts to find positions for Jewish law graduates—even those at the top of their classes—convinced him directly of the evils of anti-Semitism.[15] Finally, Hart was bitterly disillusioned by the cynical opportunism of the Communist Party in abandoning the common front and following blindly the dictates of Soviet foreign policy. As the debate over America's course began to divide the Cambridge community, he grew angry and then contemptuous of party members and their allies who fought to keep the United States out of the war.

Opposition to war was strong at Harvard, as it was in many university communities. The "Cambridge Professional Branch" of the Communist Party of New England issued leaflets exhorting citizens to "KEEP AMERICA OUT OF THE IMPERIALIST WAR," and a new Communist-backed labor organization calling itself "The Yanks Are Not Coming" began agitating against American involvement.[16] Area students rallied against American involvement, and the Cambridge Teachers' Union, which counted among its members a number of avowed Marxists, was a hub of anti-interventionism.

In the spring of 1940 the Harvard Student Union asked the Teachers' Union to make a formal contribution to its newly established Anti-War Chest. Unalterably opposed to the anti-war effort, convinced that the request would fragment the union, and angered by what he regarded as the duplicity of many of the organization's left-wing members, Hart urged his colleagues to refuse. "On the great problems of America's destiny," he charged in a hastily called and tumultuous meeting, "we are thus asked to take counsel with those whose minds and spirit permit them to confront the collapse of European civilization with a jeer." [17] His motion to table the students' request was defeated by one vote, and again by a single vote the union agreed to make the contribution. Hart and ten others resigned. [18]

Although a variety of motives spurred his resignation, Hart explained it to friends who remained in the union as primarily a response to manipulative and dishonest tactics employed by Communists and fellow travelers. He suspected that several union members had joined the party while keeping their membership secret, [19] and he felt that others "consciously and likewise unavowedly follow its line." [20] The debate on the Student Union's request was marked by the "almost total absence of any condemnation of Nazism," he pointed out, and it lacked "any honest recognition of the bitterness of the alternatives involved." Only "unspoken assumptions" could explain the constrained and inadequate discussion. "Put shortly, I thought that the dominant note of the prevailing speakers coincided unpleasantly with the Communist party line," he declared. "I did not like it." [21] It was "intellectually contemptible" to mask a party position behind a facade, "a fraud which those who are exchanging views in good faith are entitled to resent." [22]

Hart's experience with the Teachers' Union brought him into working contact with Marxism and left-wing activism, and it made him deeply suspicious of both. As the crisis of the late 1930s moved him toward interventionism, Communist denunciations of the "imperialist" war seemed "vicious nonsense" that was "antagonistic to national well-being." [23] There were, he concluded, "basic weaknesses in the Marxist view of society" that "cripple effective thinking on contemporary events." [24] Communism and Nazism, he came to believe, were forces equally hostile to free debate and American national interests. After his resignation from the Teachers' Union, his anti-Communist position never wavered. [25]

Lessons of War and Government Service

While Hart was cutting his ties to much of the Left, he was drawn increasingly into government service, where he became absorbed with problems of administrative law and statutory construction. [26] After his year with the solicitor general he returned to Harvard but continued to carry government responsibilities. In 1939 he worked on a study for the Immigration and Naturalization Service and from 1939 to 1941 served on the attorney general's Committee on Administrative Procedure. During 1940–41 he left Cambridge for a year with the Office of the Attorney General, and American entry into the war brought him to Washington for the duration. He served in the Office of Price Administration from 1942 to 1945 and then for an additional year as general counsel in the Office of Economic Stabilization.

Hart's work for the INS convinced him of the equal legitimacy of two important goals: creating fair administrative procedures and identifying dangerous subversives. In 1939 he recommended broad and detailed changes in the procedures for admission, naturalization, and deportation of aliens, emphasizing the need to professionalize the INS and protect the rights of aliens.[27] By early 1941, however, considering the "possible future dangers" that "undesirable aliens" could present, he suggested "selective internment in the case of any emergency."[28] The world crisis accentuated the need "to make reasonable inquiry into the loyalty and political attitudes of applicants for citizenship."[29] During the war Hart urged the attorney general to provide additional resources to the INS so that procedural reforms designed to treat aliens with justice while safeguarding the national interest could be implemented effectively.[30]

From his years with the OPA and OES, Hart also learned a lesson in economic organization. The OPA operated during and briefly after the war to control inflation and ration scarce resources, and its efforts were generally successful. Between 1943 and 1945 consumer prices rose less than 2 percent.[31] Looking back on the experience, however, Hart was struck by the astonishing complexity of the OPA's task. By its very nature, he pointed out, such an effort was "certain to be carried out imperfectly" and could never reach "any close approximation of individual equity."[32] Success required "over-whelming" popular support, and the OPA had succeeded only because the war had provided "almost self-evident" goals. Without such war-induced unity, economic controls would prove inefficient, inequitable, and destructive. Then, the "job becomes one of anticipating market demand," a job that "cannot sensibly and efficiently be done by the government."[33] A decentralized market approach where "the opportunity to go ahead is widely diffused," he concluded, was "calculated to produce a better use of the human resources involved."[34]

From his experience, Hart came to believe that government was a subtle and complex process that required both the cooperation of different branches with diverse institutional expertise and a sensitive recognition that the entire process had limits to its effectiveness. The comprehensive interactions among those varied institutions was the ultimate reality of human government. Law, consequently, must be understood and designed to deal with that interconnected and imperfect reality. The legal system, therefore, should be seen primarily as a method of integrating diverse but potentially complementary institutional processes. Issues concerning individual rights should be properly managed by procedures designed to guarantee each person fair access to the most appropriate and competent decision-making institution.

Reconceiving Law in the Postwar World

In the fall of 1946, Hart returned to Harvard. The lessons of his wartime experiences were still largely inchoate, and he felt keenly the need to think them through. Newly appreciative of American virtues, he was optimistic about the nation's future and determined to do his part in learning to understand and protect American society. He was convinced that the central fact of modern society was the interdependence of individuals and institutions. Equally, he was aware that some of his political views from the 1930s were of dubious relevance in the new context of a "deferential" Supreme Court and a conservative Congress, an expanding bureaucratic state and a booming economy, and an international cold war and a threat of domestic subversion.

Hart began his reconsideration in light of three distinct but ultimately complementary assumptions. The first was the paramount necessity of defending American freedoms in a newly dangerous world. He shared the common abhorrence of "totalitarianism" that Nazism and Stalinism had generated, and he was moved, as were so many of his contemporaries, by the desire to understand and preserve the open and free society in the United States.[35] Vividly recalling his final days in the Teachers' Union, he accepted with alacrity "the long-run job of making Communism seem as unattractive and freedom as attractive as we believe them to be."[36] The need to reaffirm American values and institutions was compelling, and Hart looked at the nation's legal system with fond new eyes.

Second, Hart had come to believe that law must be grounded on rational and moral principles. When he returned to Harvard, he entered an intellectual environment conducive to that belief. Responding to the intellectual crises of the 1930s and 1940s, Harvard College had just published a fervent call for a return to "basic values" in American education. The law school, inspired by Professor Lon L. Fuller, a legal philosopher and an early critic of legal realism, began a "Faculty Discussion Group in Jurisprudence" to explore the foundations of legal theory. In 1950, the school completed a general revision of its curriculum that attempted to infuse legal philosophy into standard courses and encourage students to study jurisprudence.[37] "[T]he whole of legal philosophy," explained Fuller, who chaired the curriculum revision committee, "should be animated by the desire to seek out those principles by which men's relations in society may be rightly and justly ordered." [38]

Hart found the new emphasis appealing. Before the war he had become acquainted with Fuller when the latter moved to Harvard in 1939, and their meeting struck an intellectual spark. After Hart returned, the two became close friends and intellectual allies.[39] Quickly emerging as one of the leaders of the faculty discussion group, Hart began studying and teaching jurisprudence.[40] He agreed with Fuller and other critics of legal realism who charged that identifying law with government behavior and removing moral elements from legal analysis were philosophically inadequate and practically dangerous.[41] Declaring that he had been "puzzled for a long time" about Holmes's jurisprudence, he announced in 1951 that its flaw was an "uncompromising positivism" that led "to the deadly bog of behaviorism." [42] The political and social turmoil of the twentieth century demanded a commitment to the "moral claims of settled law in a constitutional democracy," and positivism and legal realism were destructive "now when the foundations of all things are being reexamined." [43]

Third, drawing on his wartime insights, Hart assumed that law could best be understood as a system of institutionalized decision making. Such an approach encouraged "the habit of mind which pictures the legal system as a going whole and seeks to understand the respective functions and interrelationships of all its component processes." [44] Although he did not fully elaborate his jurisprudence of process until the early 1950s, he began sketching its outlines shortly after he returned to Harvard.[45] He hoped to encompass both the dynamics of law and its practical limits and to synthesize the fact of legal change with the principles that should guide that change. He focused on law as a cohesive and rational system, and he framed its prescriptions in terms of the allocation of institutional competencies. "Problems arising in a court call for a perceptive awareness not only of what courts are for," he explained, "but of what a legislature is for and sometimes also of what an administrative agency is for and of what matter can best be left to private decision." [46]

The idea of law as process fit nicely with Hart's conviction that the law should be based on principles. It provided a method of transcending the split between "is" and "ought," between law as force and law as ethics, which Holmes and the realists had stressed. "Law as it is is a continuous process of becoming," Hart argued, echoing Fuller. "If morality has a place in the 'becoming,' it has a place in the 'is.' " [47] The idea of law as process avoided the static conceptualism the realists had mocked. It was a concept rooted in empirically observable behavior and hence seemed to preempt the realists on one of their strongest points. At the same time it allowed principles a central role. Principles of morality, determined by right reason, guided human action and were therefore by definition part of the law's process of "becoming." Principles of institutional efficiency, drawn from experience, determined relative competencies for various kinds of decision making.

The idea of law as institutional process equally served Hart's purpose of demonstrating the nation's virtues and preserving its stability. Minimizing social conflict and economic inequality, he rested his image of the legal process on the assumption that America was a cohesive society unified by commonly shared values. Confining institutional competencies to narrow scope, he implicitly denied the authority of any institution to initiate major social change. Avoiding questions of substantive law, which inevitably implicated conflicting social interests, he made procedure supreme. "[T]hose procedures and their accompanying doctrines and practices will come to be seen," he maintained, "as the most significant and enduring part of the whole legal system, because they are the matrix of everything else."[48] Established procedures, if fair, defined social justice. "It seems to me that whatever is in accord with established procedures of this kind is just, provided only that the procedures are fair."[49]

Hart conducted his intellectual reconsideration in a postwar context dominated by three changes that had occurred since the 1930s. First, the war had ended the Great Depression, and the anticipated postwar recession had not materialized. Haunted by their memory of a decade of acute economic hardship, Americans enthusiastically embraced the new prosperity and the economic system that produced it. Second, both the executive branch under President Harry S Truman and the Supreme Court under the rubric of "judicial restraint" had lost power in relation to Congress. Controlled since the Court fight by a coalition of Republicans and southern Democrats, Congress was intent on reasserting its powers and limiting or, if possible, dismantling parts of the New Deal. Third, the international cold war and domestic anti-Communism were the defining political issues. Domestic liberalism was on the defensive, and political initiative lay with anti-Communists and the bipartisan conservative majority in Congress.

The campaign against subversion and alien ideas grew fierce in the late 1940s. Truman announced his determination to oppose Communist expansion abroad and attempted to meet the threat of domestic subversion by instituting a government Loyalty Program.[50] His actions, however, seemed only to confirm the charges of anti-Communists that the Soviet Union presented a deadly threat and that the government was riddled with security risks. The trials of Alger Hiss and the Rosenbergs provided further evidence that Soviet agents were at work in the United States. Local and state investigations into subversive activities multiplied, and the press joined in a clamor for effective measures to expose covert Communist agents. When the Soviet Union exploded an atomic bomb in 1949 and Communist North Korea invaded non-Communist South Korea in the summer of 1950, the fear of a worldwide Communist conspiracy grew frenzied.

Congress became the national base of the anti-subversion campaign. In 1940 it had passed the Smith Act, which required the registration of aliens and made it a crime to conspire to overthrow or to advocate overthrowing the government of the United States.[51] In 1947 the first Republican-controlled Congress since 1930 amended the National Labor Relations Act with the anti-labor Taft-Hartley Act, mandating among its other requirements that union officials sign affidavits denying membership in the Communist Party and belief in Communist ideas.[52] Frightened by the Soviet threat and seeking to strike a fatal blow against the New Deal and the liberal and Democratic executive branch, Congressional Republicans and southern Democrats began to investigate domestic subversion in and out of government. By the end of the decade dozens of congressional committees were probing alleged subversive activities, and the House Committee on Un-American Activities and the Internal Security Subcommittee of the Senate Judiciary Committee exercised power unrivaled in twentieth-century congressional history.[53] Then, in early 1950, Republican Senator Joseph McCarthy of Wisconsin burst into the headlines with claims that he had evidence that hundreds of "traitors" were occupying government posts with the knowledge of their superiors.[54] McCarthy began his own investigations, dominating the headlines and spearheading the anti-Communist crusade for the next five years.

Congress responded with more anti-Communist legislation. The Internal Security Act of 1950, passed over Truman's veto, required Communist groups to register with the attorney general and to file membership lists and financial statements.[55] Further, it prohibited Communists from working in defense plants or receiving passports, and it established the Subversive Activities Control Board to enforce its provisions. Most strikingly, it authorized the government, upon the president's declaration of a national emergency, to arrest persons it considered likely to engage in espionage or sabotage and to hold them in special detention camps. Two years later Congress passed the Walter-McCarran Immigration and Nationality Act, again over a presidential veto.[56] Eliminating racial restrictions on immigration, the act authorized the exclusion or deportation of subversive aliens, the denaturalization of recent citizens, and serious restrictions on the procedural rights of those whom the government selected for scrutiny.

Although many lawyers and law professors thought it wise to remain silent, some protested the anti-subversive campaign. Zechariah Chafee, Jr., acknowledged the dangers of subversion and the threat of the Soviet Union, but he called for an end to abuses inspired by ignorance, politics, and hatred. "Never in our lifetimes," he exclaimed, "have American citizens spewed such virulence against American citizens." [57] Walter Gellhorn, another prominent civil libertarian, also recognized the Communist threat but deplored the excesses of the anti-subversion campaign. "If our freedoms are lost," he declared, "it will be because our own timidity, our own lack of confidence in the solidity of American institutions and traditions, led to their repudiation by us rather than to their destruction by others." [58]

Hart took a middle road. He defended the efforts to expose Communists and to bar them from government, but he disliked some of the extreme measures they inspired. He contributed to the defense fund for Alger Hiss [59] and made known his disdain for McCarthy.[60] At the same time, he criticized suggestions that declaratory judgments be available to protect individuals from possible future prosecutions under anti-subversion laws that arguably violated the First Amendment,[61] and he believed that those accused of being Communists should simply appear before their accusers and answer their questions.[62] He accepted loyalty oaths as both "a healthy and valuable instrument" of democratic government and a useful method of limiting "the whole fantastic program for prior investigation of every Government employee." [63]

After Congress passed the Walter-McCarran Act, Hart took his strongest critical stand. Interested from his prewar days in immigration problems, he was outraged that a xenophobic Congress would deny aliens even minimal procedural guarantees. In 1952 he joined his colleague Louis Jaffe in urging the President's Commission on Immigration and Naturalization to alter the law that "bristles with hostility to aliens" and constituted "a bacchanalia of meanness." [64] The act subjected permanent alien residents to the almost uncontrolled discretion of the attorney general, whose decisions (because Congress retained for itself the power of review) were "likely to be dictated by political rather than administrative standards." [65] Further, Hart and Jaffe attacked the unfair presumption the act created that enabled the government to prove more easily that an alien had procured his citizenship by fraud. Congress, Hart and Jaffe charged, had created "a new status of probationary, second-class citizenship." [66] Finally, they argued, the procedure established for deportation and exclusion hearings denied aliens the most significant innovation of the Administrative Procedure Act, the guarantee of an independent trial examiner. The act provided the victim little but "discreditable double-talk." [67]

Although both called for liberalized standards, narrower administrative discretion, and more elaborate review procedures, Hart advanced a more demanding position than Jaffe. Alone, he suggested that deportation of permanent resident aliens should be allowed only after adjudication through a full "judicial process." [68] The anti-Communist crusade, like the wartime hunt for fascist infiltrators, deepened Hart's faith in the truth-finding virtues of the courts and the social benefits of their exacting processes.

Reversing Branch Affinities: From Legislative to Judicial Primacy

Hart's concern with immigration convinced him that Congress had acted on the basis of ignorance and cruelty, and his changing social and economic ideas reinforced a deepening suspicion of government and the legislature.[69] "[N]o sensible person," he declared in 1951, "ought to think seriously in terms of a socialist economy."[70] The proper role of government was secondary and enabling. "We need to consider government, first, as a facility in establishing fruitful conditions under which people can work out as many as possible of their own problems for themselves without further intervention from the government," he explained in 1955, and "secondly, as a facility also in providing readily available and effective official procedures for the settlement of those problems which fail of satisfactory adjustment at the primary and basic level of private decision."[71]

Hart, who had insisted in 1937 that the Constitution "was founded on confidence in the legislature,"[72] grew intensely wary of the uses that Congress could make of its broad powers.[73] As he came to believe in the paramount virtues of private enterprise and the inability of government to efficiently regulate the economy, and as he watched the Senate and House committees with their anti-Communist extremists and ill-advised legislative proposals, Congress loomed increasingly as a menace. Not only did it have difficulty drafting legislation capable of effectively channeling private decision making, but it was also unable to oversee administration of the legislation it passed. "One of our serious problems now is the adequacy of Congress to be an effective check on error in government efficiency," he claimed. "Anyone who thinks seriously of that as a problem must shrink from the idea of loading onto Congress additional burdens of areas now carried privately."[74]

As Hart recognized the dangers of legislative power and the institutional weaknesses of Congress, he saw more clearly the contrasting "strengths of the judicial process." Common law adjudication "permits principles to be worked pure and the details of implementing rules and standards to be developed in the light of intensive examination of the interaction of the general with the particular."[75] He identified the courts with the rule of "principle" and—spurning the Progressive constitutional tradition and erasing his New Deal past—suggested that "[p]erhaps judges are less likely than other officials to develop unreasonable principles of action."[76] Judges operated on principle, and they had a finer capacity to select those that were reasonable. Moreover, judges applied their principles under the duty of explaining them rationally and publicly. "Adjudication involves choice between two alternatives, one of which is regarded as right," he explained. " 'Right' means rationally justifiable by reasoning from settled or properly assumed premises." [77]

The courts appeared superior not just because of their greater rationality, but because they confined themselves to the "intensive examination" of "the particular." Assuming that there were "settled or properly assumed premises" of the existing legal order, Hart preferred judicial to legislative action because its reach and impact was far more circumscribed. The courts dealt only with the individual case, not general issues. The common law, he argued, was "the most flexible and least constraining of all the techniques of coercive governmental action." [78]

In the 1930s the young Progressive had depicted the courts as incompetent to formulate policy and Congress as expert; by the 1950s he portrayed the courts as refined instruments of reason and the legislature as the voice of ignorance and partisanship. Congress made decisions "only under the pressure of immediate and strongly-felt political interests." Conversely, the "opportunity for long-range and systematic thinking lies with the courts and the legal profession, with such help as political science can muster." Serious scholarly and judicial thinking, he hoped, could "carry with Congress the weight which only disinterestedness and sound reasoning can command." [79]

By 1957, Hart was prepared to identify "a disease which infects the whole attitude of our generation toward the growth of the law." The disease was "denigration of the capacity and responsibility of the courts to develop the law creatively" and "a naive and uncritical faith in the capacity of legislatures to do the job which the courts ought to do." [80] The difference between the methods of courts and legislatures went not just to "competence" but to the intrinsic quality and desirability of the kinds of law each made. His course in "The Legal Process" stressed the contrast "between the characteristic generality and even-handedness of decisional law and the tendency toward arbitrary classification and unequal treatment in statutory law." [81]

Hart did not replace his earlier Progressive idea of legislative primacy with one of an overt judicial primacy. As a matter of formal theory, he accepted the proposition that the two branches had an "essentially collaborative relationship." [82] The nature of the collaboration that he thought proper, however, placed the courts in the dominant position. Their principled and rational method was superior to the legislature's ad hoc and partisan method, and their "even-handedness" contrasted favorably with the "arbitrary" nature of legislative enactments. Free choice and the market regulated most "private activity in the society," and the courts were best suited to handle whatever "general directive arrangements" they required. The legislature, conversely, properly played a role that was "secondary in the sense of second-line." It was "an intermittently intervening, trouble-shooting, back-stopping agency."[83] Finally, even when the legislature properly intervened, the courts' practical expertise and their method of "intensive examination" made them indispensable guides to successful legislation. "For the future will not be tolerable," he warned, "unless the courts' search for justice informs, first, the drafting of the statutes, and, then, their interpretation and application."[84] Thus, the courts were not merely the interpreters of the legislature; they were also its mentors.[85]

Indeed, Hart came to believe, the courts were mentors for the whole of American government. "The prime significance of judicial review," he explained in 1954, was "not to be found in what happens in the courts." Rather, it was found first "in what happens in Congress in the shaping of legislation." Then it was found "throughout the rest of the government in the shaping of executive and administrative decisions." Finally, it was found everywhere. "[T]he body of principle developed by this process of intensive analysis, which exists only because the courts have the responsibility of an independent judgment," he declared, "ramifies out and influences the whole course of government."[86]

Hart's de facto commitment to judicial primacy and his fear of the legislature, together with his desire to provide procedural protections for the individual, made him acutely wary of "judicial restraint." The New Deal had created numerous regulatory agencies, and the Roosevelt Court had narrowed the scope of judicial review accorded their decisions. Ominously, the Court had on several occasions during and after the war given evidence, especially in its treatment of aliens, that it might carry restraint to the point of ignoring the procedural due process rights of individuals faced with government prosecution.[87] Moreover, when the war induced a more drastic expansion of administrative powers, in order to minimize delay and obstruction Congress had experimented with restricting even further the right of individuals to obtain judicial review of agency actions.[88]

Most significantly, Hart was haunted by the threat to judicial independence that lay in congressional control over the jurisdiction of the federal courts. The Norris-LaGuardia Act, which he had approved as a young man, exemplified a method by which Congress could alter substantive rights by simply depriving the federal courts of jurisdiction to hear certain claims.[89] Voicing the typical Progressive view, for example, a legal writer in 1940 had urged Congress "to preserve its own authority over a judiciary of its own creation" by using its power over jurisdiction "aggressively." "The basic assumptions of representative government and majority rule demand it."[90] Indeed, dissenting in 1932, the year Congress passed the Norris-LaGuardia Act, Brandeis himself had vigorously affirmed the broad power of Congress over the jurisdiction of the federal courts. "The jurisdiction of those courts," Brandeis had declared, "is subject to the control of Congress."[91]

By the early 1950s, Hart harbored the gravest reservations about the Progressive view of legislative primacy and the power of Congress to control the jurisdiction of the national courts. How, he asked anxiously, could congressional power over the federal courts "be reconciled with the basic presuppositions of a regime of law and of constitutional government?"[92] Although the "actual plan of the Constitution" made "political processes" the arbiter of most intragovernmental conflicts, it "uses the courts primarily as last-ditch agencies of 'sober second thought' for the protection of individual rights." And the courts, especially the Supreme Court, "again and again contribut[ed] to the stability of the government" and contributed "continuously to the general sense of security against arbitrary governmental action."[93] The major political and constitutional need of the postwar period, he believed, was to protect freedom, democracy, and broad realms of private decision making. To Hart, that meant one thing: defending and strengthening the structural position of the national judiciary in the general scheme of American government. Judicial review, he insisted, was "essential as a safeguard against arbitrary action by the legislature."[94]

Hart's growing fear of government action led him to see Brandeis anew. Although he continued to admire and respect the justice, Hart came to ignore Brandeis as the great Progressive defender of the legislature and to conceive of him as the methodical opponent of arbitrary government. The Court's excessive "judicial restraint" in economic matters, he declared in 1954, rejected "the whole apparatus for curbing genuinely arbitrary exercise of governmental power which Brandeis through the years had so laboriously and imaginatively put together."[95] As Frankfurter had done, Hart paid Brandeis the ultimate tribute: When he changed, he changed Brandeis right along with him.[96]

A Vision of "The Federal System"

Those convictions and values, filtered through a powerful sense of professional craftsmanship, provided the inspiration for Hart's commanding portrait of the American legal system. In 1953, together with Herbert Wechsler of the Columbia Law School, he published the most brilliant casebook to come out of the American law schools, a book that one scholar fairly called "the definitive text on the subject of federal jurisdiction in spite of its casebook label."[97] The following year Hart addressed a special Conference on Federalism held at Columbia University where he summarized and elaborated many of the ideas his casebook suggested.[98] Together, the two events established him as one of the nation's foremost authorities on the American legal system.

As Frankfurter had attempted on a smaller and far less sophisticated scale twenty-five years earlier, Hart and Wechsler presented the problems of federal jurisdiction in broad terms of government structure.[99] The casebook form they chose and the ideological orientation they espoused, however, distinguished their effort from Frankfurter's. Hart and Wechsler imposed a coherent pattern on their materials, creating an image of *The Federal Courts and the Federal System* that was stunning in its complexity and compelling in its subtlety. They painted the national judicial system on the richly textured background of interrelated state and federal legislative, executive, judicial, and administrative powers. Two generations of law students absorbed their fundamental assumptions about the nature and role of the federal courts from "Hart and Wechsler." [100]

Hart had a vision of the whole, and he embodied that vision in a panoramic portrait of the American legal system. "It seemed to me, and came to seem increasingly," he declared three years after the casebook appeared, "that you could not think straight about the law unless you thought about its purposes and took sides on hard questions about which purposes should be furthered and which not." [101] He understood that the only way to impose coherent and compelling meaning on the complex, changing, ambiguous, and historically partisan materials of American constitutionalism—the only way successfully to impose his own meaning on ideas such as federalism and cases such as *Erie*—was to construct a system capable of encompassing the vague and unruly elements of jurisprudential debate and assigning to each a specific meaning consistent with that system's structure and purposes.

Federalism constituted the book's central image: its complexity was delineated in intricate detail; its desirability conveyed in every nuance. During the late 1940s and early 1950s numerous American intellectuals sought the "genius" of America, and it seemed reasonable that the nation's "special" nature might be found in its decentralized structure. Indeed, Hart announced, his goal was precisely to capture "the whole genius and dynamics of the federal system." [102] The casebook and his Columbia address were brilliant statements of the uniqueness and superiority of American government. They constituted the paramount contribution of the law schools to the federalism renaissance of the postwar decades.[103]

The book's image of the federal system served Hart's intellectual and political purposes well. Although the idea of federalism was critical to any understanding of the national courts, Hart made it a controlling ideological force that purportedly carried specific normative implications. Federalism was a counterbalance to the centralization of the New Deal and a counter-ideal to the nightmare of "totalitarianism." Americans could "rejoice" in the diversity and fluidity that federalism allowed and in the "multiplication of opportunities and resources for fruitful action" that it created.[104] Federalism recognized that the "manifold processes of private adjustment" were "the prime motive power of social life."[105] That truth, Hart announced proudly, was "a fact of social dynamics which not even the masters of Soviet Russia may escape."[106]

The concept of federalism also furnished Hart with a response to the cynicism of legal realism, for it was based on "principles" that were rationally knowable and—as he believed American experience demonstrated—empirically successful. The proven advantages of the federal system as well as its perennial institutional tensions were "impressive mainly as evidence of the sound architecture and good working order of the system as a whole."[107] Any problems that federalism created were minor and more than offset by the general social welfare that it underwrote. "The resulting disparities in the formal law of different states," he explained, "are notable chiefly as reflections of a necessary independence and even competition in the wise guidance of social affairs, entailing in most cases no sacrifice of any comparably important social value."[108]

Functionally, each institution of state and national government had its proper place. Federal law was essentially "interstitial," and even the most elaborate statutory scheme assumed and required the common law background of state law to fill out its meaning. The different bodies of state and federal law were so inextricably intertwined that the "rule of law" necessitated the most careful analysis of institutional interrelationships and the most subtle evaluation of competing interests before the proper laws could be identified and applied.[109] The implicit and explicit message of the Hart and Wechsler casebook was that the federal system operated according to a set of rigorous and knowable limitations: the boundaries of federal and state authority, the proper scope and institutional capacity of the various lawmaking agencies, the systemic coherence and intellectual delicacy of formal doctrine, and the existence of essentially "correct"— or at least manifestly "better"—answers to all jurisprudential and jurisdictional questions.

Although Hart emphasized the limits to both national power generally and national judicial power in particular, he regarded the national courts as the dominant institution in the federal system. Drawing on their broader national viewpoint, and, if necessary, the Constitution, the federal courts served the essential function as the day-to-day managers of governmental powers. In relation to diversity suits, he argued, "[t]he federal courts are in a peculiarly disinterested position to make a just determination as to which state's laws ought to apply where this is disputed."[110] In federal question cases "the need for uniformity may be so pressing that sole responsibility for establishing it, or for working out the content of the needed regulation, cannot feasibly be entrusted to a legislature."[111] Accordingly, he urged the federal courts to develop a "federal common law" based on substantive and jurisdictional statutes, and he criticized the Supreme Court for showing "diffidence in the creative exercise of federal judicial power after federal concern has been asserted" by Congress.[112] Such diffidence, he pointed out, "thrust upon Congress a burden of exclusive responsibility for the interstitial development of legal doctrine—a burden which it is wholly unequipped to bear." [113] In every area, the requirements of a working federalism necessitated a strong and creative system of national courts to provide guidance, restraint, and justice. Hart stressed the importance of limits on federal judicial power, then, not because he saw it as undesirable or because he wanted a passive national judiciary. Rather, he saw the national courts as central to the operation of the entire federal system, and he believed that they alone (in contrast to the other branches and agencies of government) had to be independently and ultimately self-regulating.

Hart's image of the federal system was both an answer to the threat implicit in congressional control over federal jurisdiction and a supplementary injunction to the federal courts to develop the law "creatively" in establishing an optimal "regime of law." [114] In his famous "Dialogue" about legislative and judicial power, originally published in the *Harvard Law Review* and substantially reprinted in his casebook, Hart argued at length that the congressional power to make "Exceptions" to the Supreme Court's appellate jurisdiction did not allow such changes "as will destroy the essential role of the Supreme Court in the constitutional plan." [115] The Constitution, "in whole not in part," limited the power of Congress and prohibited any use that "violates a necessary postulate of constitutional government—that a court must always be available to pass on claims of constitutional right to judicial process." [116] As long as Congress maintained any federal courts, it could not restrict their jurisdiction in order to preclude them from enforcing valid constitutional claims. "[J]urisdiction," he insisted, "always is jurisdiction only to decide constitutionally." [117] Further, he argued that Congress in practice simply could not do without the national courts. "Were the framers wholly mistaken in thinking that, as a matter of the hard facts of power, a government needs courts to vindicate its decisions?" he asked rhetorically. "Is there some new science of government that tells how to do it in some other way?" [118] Hart's image of the complexity and interrelatedness of the federal system was designed to show, in the most minute and convincing detail, exactly why the federal courts were essential to the nation's government and well-being.

The systemic argument of *The Federal Courts and the Federal System* was complex and often implicit, but nevertheless coherent and compelling. Its major premise was the principle that jurisdiction existed "only to decide constitutionally." [119] Its minor premise lay in its intricate exposition of the pivotal role the federal courts played in managing the subtle, complicated, and intertwining problems that challenged "the whole genius and dynamics of the federal system." The argument concluded that, if Congress were ever to try to manipulate jurisdiction to destroy constitutional rights, it would face an insoluble dilemma: if it left the federal courts with any jurisdiction at all, they would still be compelled to enforce the Constitution; if it abolished their jurisdiction, the nation's complex and delicate federal system would disintegrate into unmanageable chaos.

Erie *Reimagined*

In Hart's vision, diversity jurisdiction took on a new meaning. Although Wechsler was less favorably disposed toward it than was Hart and the casebook presented contentions for and against its utility, Hart wrote the section dealing with diversity and impressed his distinctive views on the topic.[120] The jurisdiction was rooted in the specific language of the Constitution, he argued, and it was a crucial symbol and instrument of national unity. More practically, it was the method by which the federal courts could, even though they applied state substantive law, provide a "juster justice than state courts."[121] Hart failed to explain the nature of his "juster justice," but he was confident that the national judiciary could provide it. The federal courts were especially "disinterested," they followed more efficient procedures, and they were, somehow, better able to discern and enforce the proper principles of justice.[122] Hart defended diversity, the jurisdiction that Brandeis and Frankfurter had attacked as disruptive and unnecessary, precisely because it offered an expanded arena for the federal courts to demonstrate their superiority and to develop more fully the basic principles of a sound national jurisprudence.[123]

From such a perspective, *Erie* emerged reborn and luminous. Hart's initial reaction to Brandeis's decision, published in 1940, had been ambivalent and typical of the reaction of many prewar legal Progressives. In general, he approved the decision, pointing out that *Swift* had brought not uniformity but a "deepening uncertainty" and an "[e]xploitation of the divergencies" between state and federal decisions which was an "offense to the ideal of law."[124] He emphasized that *Swift* had become "vulnerable to attack" because of its broad extension "and because of its discriminatory operation, in combination with doctrines of corporate citizenship, in favor of foreign corporations engaged in local business."[125] At the same time, however, Hart had serious reservations. He pointed out that the decision to overrule *Swift* had been made "without notice to the litigants or benefit of argument."[126] He noted, too, that Brandeis's opinion was "less clear" than the concurrence and that its constitutional argument was both "new" and "uncertain."[127] Finally, like a good New Dealer, he worried that the decision seemed to be based on "an outright prohibition upon hypothetical specific legislation." The constitutional problems the decision raised and the criticisms it provoked "may well be thought to vindicate afresh," he concluded disapprovingly, "the two canons invoked by Mr. Justice Butler in his dissent against deciding constitutional issues without clear necessity and against deciding any debatable issue without argument by the parties." [128]

By the early 1950s Hart saw a dramatically different *Erie*. Gone were references to the lack of restraint in deciding the case.[129] Gone, too, were doubts about the craftsmanship of the opinion. On the contrary, Hart asserted broadly and confidently that Brandeis had "marshalled" a "battery of considerations" to support his decision.[130] Gone, most obviously, were the Progressive concerns over the ability of foreign corporations to exploit jurisdictional rules and the danger that the decision might impose limitations on congressional power. Gone, finally, were doubts about the opinion's constitutional rationale. *Erie*, in fact, embodied fundamental constitutional principles. It was, Hart proclaimed grandly, "superbly right." [131]

According to Hart, Brandeis's opinion represented the most basic legal and constitutional principles. First, it rejected "the notion that the decisional rules of the state courts had a status inferior to state statutes." [132] Second, it ended the "dual and often inconsistent systems of substantive law" that *Swift* had engendered and thus removed an "offense to the most basic concepts of justice according to law." [133] *Erie* rested on two separate and independent constitutional grounds: a structural principle of federalism based on the overarching "constitutional plan" that required judicial and legislative powers to be coextensive,[134] and a fairness theory rooted in the Due Process Clause that condemned *Swift* for imposing on individuals "inconsistent systems of law." [135] Raising the stakes as high as they could be raised, Hart depicted *Erie* as standing triumphantly not only for a principle of American federalism but also for the ideal of the rule of law itself.

Erie's positivism Hart simply ignored.[136] In its place he saw only "principle." Eliding the idea of sovereign authority, he identified the decision with the idea of due process, injecting into *Erie*'s constitutional language an important but vague concept of "justice."

In the context of Hart's powerful and compelling image of the federal system, *Erie* indeed seemed seminal. For the generations of law students who learned federal jurisdiction from the Hart and Wechsler casebook, the meaning of *Erie* was powerfully, if somewhat imprecisely, etched. To those who believed in neutral principles, *Erie* seemed rational and proper. To those who reflected on history or the opinion's author, it seemed fitting that Brandeis had produced a monument to the "principle of federalism." [137]

Federalism was an important element of *Erie*, as were both the axiom of coextensive powers and a powerful concern for practical justice. But Hart's *Erie* was not Brandeis's *Erie*. Hart's version denied both the social and political purposes that had animated Brandeis's efforts. It was even more abstract than Brandeis's version, representing a tautological idea of federalism — that state law should apply where it should apply — and an unexceptionable idea of due process — that people should not be bound by inconsistent formal rules. Hart's idea of coextensive powers merely tidied up the "logic of federalism," and his idea of due process — like his cognate concept of a "juster justice" — had no determinate political or social resonance. For Hart, *Erie* represented a neutral allocative principle unrelated to either social issues or problems of economic inequality. Absent were both Brandeis's profound commitment to legislative primacy and his concern with the practical advantages that wealth and power bestowed on private litigants.[138] Hart elevated *Erie* to the rank of first principles by stripping it of political and social content and by denying the Progressive values that had inspired it.

Hart's method of abstraction was apparent in his synthesis of *Erie* with *Southern Pacific Co. v. Jensen* and its progeny.[139] The principle of federal supremacy in admiralty, he believed, embodied in consistent but obverse form the "logic of federalism" for which *Erie* stood: the principle that the federal and state courts should each be authoritative in their respective spheres. "The same logic of federalism which underlay *Erie*," he explained, "eventually prompted the Supreme Court to hold that the state courts in saving clause cases must respect the same principles of substantive obligation which the federal courts enforced in admiralty."[140] Thus, he maintained that the "logic of federalism" had caused *Jensen* and that the "same logic" guided the Court, twenty years later, in *Erie*.

The problem with his synthesis, of course, was that it contradicted history and misrepresented Brandeis. First, it ignored the social and political differences between *Jensen* and *Erie*. The former asserted and enlarged federal judicial power; the latter limited it. The former insisted on greater uniformity by expanding the reach of national law; the latter allowed greater diversity by expanding the scope of state law. Equally important, when decided, the former had defeated individuals asserting claims under state workmen's compensation statutes; while the latter had aided individuals asserting claims against corporations under state common law. Second, Hart's synthesis employed an overtly anti-historical and conceptualistic method to explain doctrinal change. Not only did it designate an abstract "logic of federalism" as the cause of historical evolution, but it conceived of that logic as a timeless force. Both *Erie* and *Jensen* were products of that "logic." Moreover, Hart's claim that the logic had "eventually" caused *Jensen* implied that the logic existed independently of the two decisions and antedated both of them. Legal change, therefore, appeared as an abstract process driven by a growing recognition of the true "logic of federalism." Finally, and most critical, Hart's synthesis ignored two historically dispositive facts: Brandeis, the architect of *Erie*'s "logic," had dissented in *Jensen* and subsequently called for its overruling;[141] and McReynolds, the author of *Jensen* and many of its progeny, had dissented in *Erie*. In treating *Jensen* and *Erie* as the embodiments (indeed, as the results) of the same "logic of federalism" Hart substituted an extraneous conceptual scheme for historical processes and imposed an ideology of rational progress on the pivotal — and invariably political — jurisprudential conflicts in the American past.

Hart's synthesis, in fact, reflected and helped shape a maturing twentieth-century theory of federal judicial power. Since the Civil War, the jurisdiction and authority of the national judiciary had expanded with the burgeoning power of the national government, and in the early twentieth century the Supreme Court had begun to reorient the lower courts away from common law issues and toward questions of federal law. Gradually, the Court and the profession reconceived their structural role in the national legal system. No longer considered inferior, as they had been in the early nineteenth century, or even equivalent to the state courts, the federal courts grew far more powerful and prestigious. They came to be seen as special authorities on an increasingly pervasive national law and as the "primary vindicators" of supreme federal statutory and constitutional rights. To postwar commentators, then, it made sense that *Jensen* and *Erie* were compatible. The former asserted the lawmaking authority of the federal courts over "national" concerns, while the latter consigned to the state courts lawmaking authority over less important "local" matters. It was, however, that increasingly dominant twentieth-century view of the federal judicial power, not a timeless "logic of federalism," that made Hart's synthesis seem reasonable and even "right" in a new age. Indeed, the triumph of that twentieth-century view made Hart appear to his contemporaries and successors as an advocate for a sophisticated legal "federalism" rather than as what he was — the prophet of a new, intricate, and exceptionally sophisticated version of judicial nationalism.[142]

Hart replaced Brandeis's idea of legislative primacy with the more neutral concept of institutional "collaboration." More important, although he formally acknowledged the power of the legislature, he subtly qualified it in theory and portrayed it as secondary in practice. Embracing the axiom of coextensive powers, Hart nevertheless designed his system to amplify the role of the federal courts, creating for them a practical independence from congressional power.[143] While Brandeis intended *Erie* to impose tight limits on the lawmaking power of the federal courts and subordinate that power to congressional initiative, Hart minimized those restrictions or dropped them entirely.

Hart's amplification of federal judicial power appeared in a variety of doctrinal arguments. He maintained that the federal courts should have an independent judgment in diversity cases on choice-of-law issues;[144] that they had inherent power even when enforcing state-created rights to grant "a fuller and fairer remedy" than state courts could grant;[145] that their "federal question" jurisdiction included not only cases presenting claims based on federal law but also cases in which a "proposition of federal law" was essential to plaintiff's cause of action;[146] that they could reinterpret state law when incorporating it to serve federal purposes;[147] that they could exercise an expansive "protective jurisdiction" and decide state law issues independently under their "federal question" jurisdiction in the absence of either diversity of citizenship or a substantive claim based on federal law;[148] that they were able to develop federal common law in advance of, or beyond, congressional action in areas where they viewed national uniformity as desirable;[149] that they properly created special federal equitable remedies to protect against unconstitutional actions by state officials;[150] that there were special areas in which they could make substantive law even though Congress itself could not;[151] and that they properly enforced the mandate of the Fourteenth Amendment broadly against all state officials who acted "under color of law."[152] Hart stretched the Court's decisions to insist on the right of federal courts to review the actions of administrative agencies, both the evidence in the record supporting their decisions and all questions of law that related to any legal duties and liabilities they imposed. Such review, he insisted, was essential for "the supremacy of law."[153] He advanced a broad view of federal habeas corpus, construed the Court's ambiguous precedents to stretch the reach of the federal writ, and urged the national judiciary to protect "fundamental constitutional rights" by giving "close scrutiny" to state court procedural rules that threatened to foreclose federal habeas relief.[154] He sought to establish the independence of the federal courts from congressional power in theory by his constitutional argument against the "political" manipulation of jurisdiction, and he sought to establish their independence in practice by his pervasive argument that the practical complexities of the federal system absolutely required a powerful national judiciary. Even in areas of express federal authority, he insisted, Congress was "wholly unequipped to bear" the burden of lawmaking alone.[155] The existence of complexity demanded specialists in complexity, and any serious restriction on federal jurisdiction would be a national disaster.

Hart repeatedly insisted that the federal courts were capable of providing—indeed, that they were specifically designed to provide—a "juster justice" than the state courts.[156] When he considered federal habeas corpus jurisdiction, he insisted on a "felt sense of justice" that demanded federal judicial relief for substantive state wrongs.[157] When he taught "protective jurisdiction," he urged the aggressive use of federal judicial power to protect federal rights and interests and to ensure the availability of a truly superior federal justice. In his class, a former student recalled, he was "passionate" when he advocated his expansive "protective jurisdiction."[158] He expounded his "juster justice" ideal, another noted, with "grandeur."[159]

Given his intense commitment to the ideal of a "juster justice," Hart's response to *Erie*'s social purposes was striking and disappointing. He essentially dismissed Brandeis's concern with the "practical discrimination" that had occurred under *Swift*. Forum shopping, Hart commented, was merely "a minor consideration which Brandeis mentioned in passing."[160] Insofar as jurisdictional statutes created an inequality between in-state and out-of-state parties, his proposed solution was simply — and not surprisingly — to expand federal jurisdiction. "[T]he federal government, confident of the justice of its own procedures" should make the "federal forum equally accessible to both litigants."[161] Beyond that, the policy of eliminating forum shopping was an unworthy "triviality."[162] Passing over the specific social problem that *Erie* had addressed, he failed to see in it any broader concern with the impact of social and economic inequality on the legal system's ability to deliver practical justice. His crabbed and sterile view of *Erie*'s social purposes contrasted with his richly imaginative and transforming portrayal of its political purposes.

Hart also heaped scorn on the Roosevelt Court's post-*Erie* cases that implemented the policy against forum shopping. The Court had become "obsessed" with a false problem.[163] "[T]he Supreme Court since 1938," he charged, "has persistently depreciated the foundations of principle of Justice Brandeis' opinion and moved steadily in the direction of degradation of federal justice."[164] Although he sharply criticized *Fidelity Union*, his major targets were *York* and *Klaxon*.[165]

Hart attacked *York* on several grounds, charging that its outcome test was incoherent and unprincipled.[166] His central objection, however, was that it offered "no stopping place" in making a federal diversity court "only another court of the state."[167] By seeking to make the outcome of federal and state litigations identical, *York* "leaves the diversity jurisdiction without intelligible rationale — or at least without a function of any consequence."[168] His assertion was at best contentious. If the purpose of diversity jurisdiction was to protect nonresidents from biased tribunals, as Frankfurter maintained, it would clearly have an "intelligible rationale" even with a strict *York* outcome test.[169] Hart, however, discarded that rationale and pressed for a much broader one — to provide a "juster justice." He rejected Frankfurter's rationale, and *York*, not because they were unintelligible but because they were restrictive.

If Hart disliked *York*, he despised *Klaxon*. "[T]he only sound solution," he announced, "is a complete overruling."[170] In 1958, adopting the vengeful stance of Cato the Elder, he addressed the Judicial Conference of the Third Circuit on the topic "*Klaxon Delendum Est.*"[171] *Klaxon* harmed the federal system because it increased legal uncertainty in diversity cases by destroying *Erie*'s "assurance of the uniform enforcement in any federal court of whatever state law was applicable" [172] and because it "paralyzed the capacities of the federal courts" to elaborate "the principles of the conflicts of law" and thereby promote uniformity.[173] "The federal courts," he insisted, "are in a peculiarly disinterested position to make a just determination as to which state's laws ought to apply where this is disputed." [174]

Hart believed that choice of law presented the most readily identifiable area where his "juster justice" was possible. "The principles of the conflict of laws have the function of preventing the plaintiff's choice of the state in which he brings his action from affecting the outcome of it, where justice forbids such an effect," he explained. "But state courts may reject or misapply these principles, and state legislatures may tell them to do so." [175] He simply assumed that the federal courts were more likely to administer "justice" than were state courts and that the inevitably resulting differences between federal and state choice-of-law rules would not cause significant harm. Moreover, he assumed that general "principles" were sufficiently authoritative to overcome the right of the states to enforce, within constitutional limits, their own substantive policies through their own choice-of-law rules.[176] Unspecified "principles" could of their own authority limit otherwise constitutionally valid state actions, perhaps Hart's most extreme anti-positivist contention. He made that assumption, too, despite the fact that the choice-of-law field was almost universally recognized as the most notoriously unsettled, confused, and probably arbitrary area of the common law.[177]

Hart's analysis of the increased "uncertainty" that *Klaxon* caused was revealing. He suggested that litigants could seldom predict in which state a future suit would be brought. "Why should forum-shopping between different courts in the same state have been regarded as the *summum malum* of diversity litigation," he asked, "while forum-shopping among courts in different geographical areas was dismissed as an inescapable weakness of a federal system?" [178] From Hart's viewpoint, of course, there was no reason for such a choice, for he assumed the existence of Brandeis's abstract universe of mobile litigant atoms. In practice, however, there was — as Brandeis well knew — a simple and compelling reason to prefer intrastate uniformity. Most individuals were not able to exploit the interstate litigation opportunities the federal system provided; typically they chose to file, for very real and pressing human reasons, in their state of residence. In that context the preference for intrastate uniformity in choice-of-law rules worked in the vast majority of cases to deprive nonresidents of precisely the kind of choice-of-law advantage that Brandeis had designed *Erie* to eliminate.[179]

In attacking *York* and *Klaxon*, Hart suggested a different test for delineating the area in which the federal courts should be bound by state decisions under *Erie*. Where the rule in question affected "primary activity"—where it determined the "plainly substantive" rights people relied on in their everyday "pre-litigation life"—the federal courts should follow the laws of the states; in other areas, they should be free to develop their own independent rules.[180] The fatal evil of *Swift*, he argued, was that it subjected citizens "at the crucial level of everyday activity to dual and often inconsistent systems of substantive law, without means of foretelling which system, in the unforeseeable contingency of litigation, was going to apply."[181] The flaw in *York* and *Klaxon* was that they perpetuated the uncertainty concerning which state's law would apply and forced the federal courts to mirror that condition of uncertainty.

Hart's concept of "primary activity" allowed him to conceive of the social problems relating to diversity jurisdiction from the viewpoint of "rational" individuals guided by their knowledge of relevant legal rules. "People repeatedly subjected, like Pavlov's dogs, to two or more inconsistent sets of directions, without means of resolving the inconsistencies, would not fail in the end to react as the dogs did," he argued. "The society, collectively, would suffer a nervous breakdown."[182] Hart's concept of "primary activity" shifted the analysis of the *Swift-Erie* problem from a social to a psychological level that emphasized the intellectual uncertainty of rational actors trying to discern which forum, and hence which rule, would judge their behavior. It implied, too, a single resolution. The problems of social life were to be solved by announcing and enforcing clear legal rules.

This concept of primary activity, however, obscured the critical varieties of prelitigation behavior. Most people, most of the time, acted with little conscious reference to the formal rules of law that might ultimately govern their behavior. Some people, sometimes, engaged in specifically planned legal activities. Finally, a relatively few people, in special and identifiable positions, sponsored elaborate behavior directed toward establishing complex legal positions and conducting anticipated litigations that were crucial or recurring. Hart's concept of primary activity was relevant primarily to the second type of behavior, though even there the concept was misleading. Typically, those who engaged in planned activities could specify the scope of their undertaking and choose the substantive law and the particular forum that would resolve their disputes. In contrast, Hart's concept of primary activity had little relevance to the first type of behavior and excluded the third type. People seldom felt psychological pressure from legal rules in their everyday activities; when they engaged in sophisticated and purposeful prelitigation behavior, they often did so under conditions of extreme inequality. Wealth, power, education, social position, access to skilled counsel, and ability to exploit institutional complexities and burdens were prerequisites for, and instruments of, such sophisticated and purposeful litigation planning. In obscuring those varieties of behavior, "primary activity" implied the irrelevance of those social attributes that were of greatest importance in actual litigations.

The social problem that *Erie* had sought to remedy was one not of psychological uncertainty but of inequitable social consequences. Hart's concept of primary activity incorporated the real world into his analysis through a comprehensive abstraction that denied, by implication, the existence of patterned and differential social results. It assumed coherence and unity in the underlying social order, and it focused on the need for consistent formal rules rather than on the way economic inequities influenced the tactical uses parties made of procedural and jurisdictional rules.[183]

Hart's vision of the federal system imposed a new image on *Erie* and reshaped ideas about federal jurisdiction and the proper role of the national judiciary. Hart strengthened the moral claims of the domestic status quo and made abstract reasoning the touchstone for jurisdictional analysis. He gave powerful force to the idea that *Erie* had a constitutional basis, but he replaced its Progressive premise of legislative primacy with a vision of the institutional centrality of the federal courts. He did so, moreover, within a framework that minimized the problem of forum shopping and conceived of litigants as fungible abstractions. He made an abstract concept of federalism an ostensibly meaningful normative criterion, one that seemed a neutral allocative principle but which, in fact, served primarily to magnify the role of the national judiciary as the manager of the nation's legal system.

Frankfurter, not surprisingly, recognized the direction of his former student's evolving jurisprudence. Hart's defense of diversity jurisdiction and attack on *Klaxon*, the justice wrote privately, "does not correspond with what I conceive to be actualities." Reiterating his claim that diversity was wasteful, Frankfurter echoed the traditional Progressive refrain that the jurisdiction worked to the advantage of "powerful moneyed interests."[184] More important, he pointed out that Hart's thinking had grown not only too abstract but too nationalistic. In dissent from the high bench he rejected Hart's argument for an expansive federal "protective" jurisdiction. On the basis of nothing but "a beguiling phrase," the justice declared, "the 'arising under' jurisdiction of the federal courts would be vastly expanded." Hart's theory "cannot be justified under any view of the allowable scope to be given to Article III."[185] Privately, Frankfurter expressed his concern directly. "Aren't you, in your very deep attachment to federalism," he queried, "a little neglectful of one-half of federalism—the importance of the state's share in the process?"[186]

Hart responded publicly two years later in the *Harvard Law Review*.

Frankfurter, he noted in passing, was a justice "who never seems to be wanting in deference to the states." [187]

Irony Again: The Perplexing Persistence of Historical Change

Hart's subsequent elaboration of his process jurisprudence represented an extension of the themes he had developed by the mid-1950s. Increasingly, he emphasized the primacy of procedural rules, the role of the judiciary in elaborating principle, and the technical apparatus of the legal process as opposed to the significance of substantive social results.[188] Continuing to stress the need for judicial development of the law, he explicitly rejected the restrictive argument — which Brandeis had repeatedly urged — that courts should for the most part refrain from acting in areas where the legislature had decided not to act. Such deference was merely "avoiding responsibility" and was "a manifestation in exaggerated form of the contemporary cult of the legislature." [189] Rather, as the courts improved in the performance of their role, he believed, legislatures would be required to do less.[190]

Hart's version of process jurisprudence began to take on a new emphasis in the late 1950s as the dominant issues and ruling branch affinities of American politics were completing their postwar realignment. The Warren Court initiated a new phase of judicial activism, invoking constitutional principle to abolish legalized racial segregation and statutory construction to restrict the campaign against subversion. The former represented the judicial creation of admittedly new or undeveloped constitutional principles that mandated sweeping social change, while the latter often involved the questionable treatment of statutory language and history. Often the Court failed to make a "reasoned elaboration" of the grounds for its decisions.[191] Although he strongly supported the Court's focal decision in *Brown v. Board of Education*, Hart was disturbed by what he regarded as the unreasoned uses the Court made of its authority.[192]

Responding to the mounting attacks on the Warren Court and to Frankfurter's continued pleas for support, Hart in 1959 launched a scathing attack on the Warren Court's methods and apparent biases. The Court was overworked largely because it repeatedly violated its own rules on granting *certiorari*, wrote confused opinions that provided inadequate guidance to the lower courts, failed to examine complicated issues "open-mindedly and thoroughly," and seemed to reject "the ideal of collective deliberation," which could lead it to wiser judgments.[193] The Court had failed in its primary task of "articulating and developing impersonal and durable principles" of law.[194]

In the 1960s Hart came to stand as a legal and political conservative. He deplored the Warren Court's growing activism and persistently shoddy reasoning.[195] Increasingly, he acknowledged the "conservatism" of his position, and he rested on his faith in the virtues of American institutions.[196] Criticizing the use of civil disobedience, he argued in 1965 that there was no justification for pursuing social objectives outside established institutions. In his final years, he sought to ground his views in some ultimate system of jurisprudence, but neither the time remaining nor the task chosen allowed him to fulfill his quest.[197]

When Hart died in 1969 his social and political views had changed drastically from the 1930s. Yet there were ironies in the masterful image of the federal system that he had created. Hart, a representative of the intellectual reaffirmation of America that dominated so much of the postwar period, was motivated to protect and magnify the federal courts in order to encourage them in the defense of basic and hotly contested procedural and constitutional rights. He was sensitive to anti-Communist excesses as well as to the dangers of big government, and he hoped to protect the individual—helpless alien as well as regulated businessperson—confronted with government coercion. He retained, therefore, a critical link with the evolving Progressive-liberal tradition as it tried to adjust to a dramatically changed postwar world.

A second, greater irony was that Hart's image of the federal system, an abstract conception rooted in the embrace of established values and institutions, implied a justification for the kind of Warren Court activism he came to deplore. Persistently minimizing the general desirability of legislation, Hart elevated—and almost sanctified—the methods and principles of the judiciary. Supporters of school desegregation and advocates of expanded civil rights and liberties could defend a more liberal judiciary on the basis of his compelling portrait of the federal courts in the federal system. Indeed, in 1959 Hart became one of the first writers to suggest a fundamental institutional and nationalist theory as a defense for the Warren Court's expansion of federal habeas corpus: "a state prisoner ought to have an opportunity for a hearing on a federal constitutional claim in a federal constitutional court."[198] His image of the national judiciary—its independence, its authority, its creative responsibilities, its inspiring role as the provider of a "juster justice," and its centrality to the ideal of constitutional government and "the supremacy of law"—could convey a drastically different but equally inspiring message in a new politico-constitutional age. After all, his casebook proclaimed, the federal courts were "the primary forum for the vindication of federal rights."[199] And, doubling the irony, to the opponents of the newly activist and liberal federal judiciary, Hart's image of the complex federal system continued to warn fiercely against the wisdom and practicality of retaliation through jurisdictional restrictions. The judicial activism that Hart came to criticize blossomed luxuriously in the 1960s and 1970s, and his dazzling image

of the nature and role of the federal courts may have nourished that activism indirectly, as much as his overt arguments developed the more restrictive message
of process jurisprudence.[200]

Some scholars have argued that Hart rejected Warren Court activism because it contradicted his constraining ideas concerning institutional competence
and the proper limits of adjudication.[201] They have suggested that his inability
to deal adequately with the Warren Court, and especially his failure to integrate
its desegregation decisions into his jurisprudence, helps explain his subsequent
inability to complete either his long-planned work on jurisprudence or his working manuscript on *The Legal Process*.[202] Their argument, however, is incomplete.
Warren Court liberal activism distressed Hart — indeed, perplexed him deeply —
not merely because he was unable to reconcile its decisions with his own professional standards. The Warren Court confounded him because it embodied, albeit
in a form he found unsatisfactory, many of his fundamental values and ideals:
judicial creativity, protection of individual liberty, institutional recognition of
moral principles, the lawmaking primacy of the federal courts, the inspiring
effort to establish a "juster justice," and a deep belief in the cause of racial justice itself. The Warren Court did not contradict his jurisprudence but drove a
wedge between its two distinct parts. Hart's intellectual problem with the Warren Court was that, after its birth, he was never able satisfactorily to bring those
two parts together again.

Perhaps, too, the most general conclusion to be drawn from Hart's vision
of *Erie* and the federal judicial system is that legal abstraction, while never
socially neutral, always remains socially volatile. Without constant reference to
changing social dynamics and consequences, students of procedure can scarcely
know what they are talking about. Whatever social purposes abstract analyses
might be designed to serve, historical changes continually refit them to new
and unexpected ends. The yawning historical chasm that separated Brandeis and
political Progressivism from the liberal judicial activists of the Warren Court, for
example, was nowhere more strikingly illustrated than by the fact that Brandeis,
a forceful advocate of social reform and broadened civil liberties, had dreamed
in the 1920s of the outright repeal of the Fourteenth Amendment, the foundation of nationalized constitutional liberties to a later reformist generation thrice
removed.

Cold War Politics and Neutral Principles

IO

THE FEDERAL JUDICIAL POWER IN A NEW AGE

Hart and Wechsler's casebook appeared in 1953, and the following year the Supreme Court decided *Brown v. Board of Education*, declaring racial segregation in public schools unconstitutional.[1] The public image and political role of the federal courts was quickly and profoundly transformed.

During the late 1940s and early 1950s liberals had grown increasingly suspicious of the legislative branch, and after 1954 they moved enthusiastically to embrace the national courts. They regarded state legislatures as dangerous and saw Congress as controlled by economic conservatives, anti-Communists, and segregationists. Then, suddenly, the Supreme Court transformed itself into "the Warren Court," first and foremost using the Constitution to prohibit legalized racial segregation, then beginning to protect civil liberties against the excesses of anti-Communism. Eventually the Warren Court extended the Bill of Rights to the states, broadened the mandate of the Equal Protection Clause, and noticeably (albeit selectively) addressed the claims of the poor and the outcast. Liberals came to hail the new Court as the guardian of individual freedoms and the nation's principal governmental agent of domestic social—and, indeed, moral—reform.

The Warren Court completed the reversal of political assumptions and branch affinities begun in 1937. Increasingly comfortable with the legislative branch, conservatives identified the judiciary with social activism and radicalism. Most Americans came to believe that the federal courts responded positively to causes identified with post–New Deal liberalism and that Congress was the force maintaining the status quo. Although the reality was more complex, the contrasting images found acceptance across the political spectrum and helped reshape the nation's basic politico-constitutional assumptions and all their de facto corollaries.

The Early Warren Court

In 1953 President Dwight D. Eisenhower, who had returned the Republicans triumphantly to national office only the year before, made what appeared to be a shrewd decision. He named Earl Warren of California as chief justice. A supporter of states' rights with extensive law enforcement experience as district attorney and state attorney general, Warren had been a popular three-term governor and the Republican vice presidential candidate in 1948. Although he was a known supporter of civil rights, his record as governor was mixed and his views moderate.[2]

In May 1954 the new Warren Court announced its decision in *Brown v. Board of Education,* unanimously holding that "separate but equal" facilities in the public schools violated the Constitution's guarantee of "Equal Protection of the Laws."[3] During its next four terms the Court relied on *Brown* to declare racial segregation unconstitutional in public beaches, golf courses, buses, and parks.[4] Then in 1958, faced with powerful resistance in the South, it met the challenge to its authority head on. In a highly unusual opinion separately signed by each of the nine justices, the Court proclaimed that "the federal judiciary is supreme in the exposition of the law of the Constitution," that *Brown* was "the supreme law of the land," and that "[e]very state legislator and executive and judicial officer is solemnly committed by oath . . . 'to support this Constitution.'"[5] By "this" Constitution the Court emphatically meant the Constitution that it, and it alone, expounded. *Brown* heralded not only new social values and constitutional doctrines but also a new institutional dynamism. It committed the federal judiciary to eliminate legalized racial segregation, and it led the Court to proclaim itself the ultimate voice of the Constitution.

Opposition to *Brown* quickly escalated as additional desegregation decisions came down and southerners began to realize their sweeping implications.[6] "The South," Senator James Eastland of Mississippi proclaimed, "will not abide by, or obey, this legislative decision by a political court."[7] White "Citizens' Councils" blossomed across the South and occasionally appeared in the North, while southern legislatures and governors announced their determination to prevent the destruction of racial segregation. In March 1956 ninety-six southern congressmen signed a "Southern Manifesto," accusing the Court of usurping the powers of Congress, the states, and the people. Echoing the attacks of old Progressives, the manifesto charged that the justices "undertook to exercise their naked judicial power and substituted their personal political and social ideas for the established law of the land."[8]

As southern opposition mounted, the Court edged into a second area that was, in one sense, more dangerous than segregation: the domestic anti-Communist campaign. Despite its powerful political base in the South, legalized racial segregation seemed morally unacceptable to a majority of Americans.[9] Further, in the context of the cold war and the growing importance of "non-aligned" African and Asian nations, *Brown* served as a useful tool for American propaganda, demonstrating that the nation repudiated racism.[10] When the Court took on the domestic anti-subversion campaign, however, it ran not with but against the cold war mentality and created an opposition that was national in scope, fervent in belief, and both distinct from and morally stronger than southern segregationism.

The Court was likely encouraged to act because by 1956 the worst of the second Red Scare apparently had passed.[11] The Republican victory in 1952 removed a driving political motivation behind the Republican charge of "twenty years of treason" that had fueled much of the anti-Communist campaign, and Eisenhower eased the nation's sense of immediate confrontation with communism when he brought the Korean War to an end in 1953. Moreover, his election helped force Senator Joseph McCarthy, the decade's inquisitor, to employ more extreme and isolating tactics that eventually led the Senate to censure him in December 1954. Criticism of the excesses of the anti-subversion campaign became increasingly forceful, especially in the self-consciously anti-Communist liberal press.[12]

The Court, too, was changing. The galvanizing appointment of William J. Brennan, Jr., to replace Sherman Minton, a Truman appointee with little enthusiasm for judicial activism or civil liberties, strengthened the activist wing, while Warren himself was moving closer to the libertarian position of Justices Hugo L. Black and William O. Douglas.[13] Moreover, since the beginning of the Roosevelt Court, several justices had been drawn to the idea that, having abandoned its earlier role as protector of private property, the Court should adopt a new role as guardian of individual liberties.[14] Widening government involvement in the everyday lives of its citizens, with the nightmare image of totalitarianism fresh in mind, made that role seem to many both reasonable and desirable.[15]

Four decisions in 1956 announced the change. The Court blocked the efforts of the Subversive Activities Control Board, restricted the operation of the Federal Loyalty Program, and prevented New York from firing a college teacher on the ground that he had invoked the Fifth Amendment before a Senate investigating committee.[16] Perhaps most striking was the fourth decision, which held that federal statutes preempted the field of anti-subversion and thereby invalidated anti-sedition provisions in the laws of forty-two states.[17] Sharp criticism erupted in Congress and the press. The decisions, McCarthy charged, "handed another solid victory to the Communist Party."[18]

The next year the Court acted even more broadly. It held that the Due Process Clause prohibited state bar associations from denying admission on the ground of past membership in the Communist Party,[19] and a month later it held that persons accused of violating loyalty laws had the right to inspect the records on which the government based its prosecution.[20] Then on June 17 the Court announced four separate decisions that broadly restricted anti-subversion investigations or prosecutions.[21] "[W]hat shall we say," asked Republican Senator William E. Jenner of Indiana, "of this parade of decisions that came down from our highest bench on Red Monday after Red Monday?"[22]

The Politics of Reversed Branch Affinities

Hostile reaction snowballed with each new decision. Eastland suggested that only "some secret, but very powerful Communist or pro-communist influence" could explain the Court's actions.[23] Its work stemmed from "a combination of charity and ideological sympathy," charged William H. Rehnquist, an Arizona lawyer and future chief justice. "Communists, former Communists, and others of like political philosophy scored significant victories."[24] The National Governors' Conference adopted a resolution criticizing two of the Court's decisions and calling on Congress to alter the statutes the Court had construed. By the end of 1956 over seventy bills to overrule specific decisions or curtail the Court's power had been introduced in the Eighty-Fourth Congress.[25]

While southern segregationists and extreme anti-Communists were in the forefront, other ostensibly conservative forces joined the attack. Following the Court's decision to open up government files, Eisenhower exclaimed that he had "never been so mad in my life."[26] The American Bar Association refused to adopt a resolution defending the Court, and bar associations across the nation reacted angrily at the Court's restrictions on their control over membership. Decisions broadening the rights of criminal defendants angered many, especially law enforcement groups.[27] In 1957 the International Association of Chiefs of Police and the American Legion accused the Court of undermining law and order across the nation.[28]

Business groups joined the attack, enraged in particular over *Railway Employees' Department v. Hanson*, a 1956 decision that restricted state right-to-work laws on the ground that a federal statute preempted the area.[29] The National Right-To-Work Committee, the United States Chamber of Commerce, the National Association of Manufacturers, and the American Farm Bureau Federation had argued before the Court on the losing side in *Hanson*, and their resentment stoked anti-Court hostility. The NAM mounted an intense lobbying effort for legislation to prevent the Court's continued use of the preemption doctrine.[30]

Finally, in 1958 the Conference of Chief Justices of the States entered the arena. The group heard a scathing report on the Warren Court's decisions and by a vote of thirty-six to eight adopted a series of resolutions that preached de-centralization and constitutional fundamentalism to the Supreme Court. "[T]his Conference hereby respectfully urges that the Supreme Court of the United States . . . exercise one of the greatest of all judicial powers—the power of judicial self-restraint." [31]

As *Time* magazine announced that the Court had taken a "deliberate course to the left," political liberals rose to its defense.[32] The report of the Conference of Chief Justices, declared Alexander Bickel, a Yale professor and an ardent proponent of *Brown*, was "inexplicable" and "inexcusable." [33] The Supreme Court was charged with the duty of forcing a sober second look in a time of turmoil, argued the political scientist C. Herman Pritchett, and the "Warren Court is performing this highest of judicial functions." [34]

The attacks on the Court swelled to a peak in 1958. Dozens of anti-Court bills were introduced in the Eighty-Fifth Congress, some aimed at individual decisions and others targeting the Court itself.[35] Seeking to unite the anti-Court forces behind a consensus proposal, Jenner sponsored a bill that struck directly at the Court. Relying on the congressional power to make "Exceptions" to its appellate jurisdiction,[36] his bill barred review of any case that called into question any action of a congressional committee, any dismissal of an executive branch employee on security grounds, any state anti-subversion program, any school board regulation relating to subversive activities, and any state bar regulation concerning admission to practice.[37] Quickly, Jenner's bill became the focus of the anti-Court drive.

Support for the bill came from segregationist Democrats, conservative Republicans, and a number of groups and individuals identified with the political right, including the Anti-Communist League of America, the Veterans of Foreign Wars, and the American Coalition of Patriotic Societies.[38] Many of its advocates raised issues that were perennial and troubling, accusing the Court of inadequate reasoning and subjective decision making. "[W]e witness today the spectacle of a Court constantly changing the law, and even changing the meaning of the Constitution," Jenner declared, "in an apparent determination to make the law of the land what the Court thinks it should be." [39] The Court, critics charged, had usurped the powers of the other branches of government. "Not only has the Court dealt deadly blows to the constitutional principle of States' rights and to the lawmaking power of the legislative branch of the Federal Government," declared Democratic Senator Strom Thurmond of South Carolina, "but the Court has also struck at the fundamental authority vested in the executive branch." [40]

Opposition came from northern and liberal congressmen, most Democrats and some Republicans, and a lineup of groups traditionally identified with mid-twentieth-century liberalism: the American Civil Liberties Union, the National Lawyers Guild, the American Jewish Congress, the National Association for the Advancement of Colored People, the American Federation of Labor-Congress of Industrial Organizations, and Americans for Democratic Action. They, too, raised serious issues. Joseph L. Rauh, speaking for the ADA, quoted Henry Hart's argument — "written," he assured the committee, "before this particular controversy arose" — that congressional power over jurisdiction was implicitly limited by an overarching constitutional structure and could not be used to "destroy the essential role of the Supreme Court in the constitutional plan." [41] Other opponents argued that removing the Court's jurisdiction would inevitably lead to drastic differences in the law throughout the country, while most emphasized the need to protect a free and independent judiciary. "[E]ven if we disagreed with the decisions," explained a representative of the National Lawyers Guild, echoing the American Bar Association in the 1930s, "we would oppose this bill as endangering the integrity of our judicial system." [42] Fighting an anti-Court majority on the Senate Judiciary Committee, four liberal members led by Senator Thomas Hennings of Missouri defended the Court's "so-called unpopular decisions" on the ground that they merely "insisted on giving the same individual legal rights of due process to all Americans." [43]

Supporters of the Jenner bill avoided the race issue, and some were undoubtedly motivated solely by considerations of national security or congressional responsibility. Race, nevertheless, largely drove the anti-Court effort. The issue marshalled southern votes against the Court and presented frightening prospects to blacks. "It is particularly dangerous to allow local school boards under the guise of curbing subversive activities to penalize teachers for belonging to such organizations as the NAACP," argued future Justice Thurgood Marshall, the association's counsel in *Brown*. "Such punitive action against teachers has already been tried in the States of Georgia and South Carolina." [44] Throughout the South, states had used a variety of "legal" methods to defeat the NAACP. Four states passed laws requiring teachers to divulge all their organizational affiliations, and two made membership in the NAACP grounds for dismissal.[45] "The truth," a Georgia legislator insisted in 1958, was that "this agitation over civil rights" was simply "the work of the Communist party." [46] Although the Jenner bill did not directly touch *Brown*, the emotions it generated were rooted in the passionate racial confrontation of the 1950s.

The reversal of branch affinities was obvious. The arguments of the bill's supporters tracked the Progressive critique of the "old Court," while liberals echoed the arguments made twenty years earlier by the opponents of Roosevelt's Court bill. "[I]n the 1930s when liberals thought the Federal judiciary was leaning too far to the right," declared the rabidly anti-Communist Clarence Manion, "they sponsored and won approval of legislation which took away the jurisdiction of the Federal courts in important fields." [47] He itemized the Norris-LaGuardia Act, the Johnson Act, and the Tax Injunction Act. Liberals recognized the incongruity. "I must say right at the outset that I find it somewhat strange for an organization of liberals to be the outspoken defenders of the Supreme Court while conservative groups lead the attack," Rauh pointed out. He readily conceded that liberals "have been wrong at times in the past when they went after the Court for decisions reached." Then, palinode delivered, he announced the true principle. Experience "may warrant the deduction that any time you go after the Court because of your personal views on decisions, a dangerous point has been reached." The Jenner bill was a challenge, Rauh declared, not to liberals but to conservatives. "One may well ask, where are the people who fought against Franklin Roosevelt's 'court packing' plan 20 years ago; where do they stand today on this grave new assault upon the Court?" [48]

As the showdown on the Jenner bill neared, the conservative establishment reluctantly and grudgingly answered Rauh's question. Attorney General William P. Rogers announced the administration's opposition, emphasizing the Court's necessary constitutional role and the need for national uniformity that it alone could provide. The Jenner bill "represents a retaliatory approach of the same general character as the Court packing plan proposed in 1937," he declared. "I disapproved of such an approach then and I do now." [49] For its part, the ABA was trapped. In 1937 it had mounted a frenzied campaign to defeat Roosevelt's proposal on the basis of constitutional principle, and in 1949 it had adopted a resolution calling for a constitutional amendment to deprive Congress of its power to restrict the Court's appellate jurisdiction in matters arising under the Constitution. At the same time, a large number of its members supported the Jenner bill passionately. After long debate in its House of Delegates, and haunted by its prior stands on principle, it finally announced its opposition. It did so quite minimally, however. The House of Delegates adopted a simple compromise resolution that relied exclusively on its 1949 action while pointedly "reserving our right to criticize decisions of any court in any case and without approving or disapproving any decisions of the Supreme Court of the United States." [50]

The opposition of the administration and the ABA, added to that of a number of prominent law firms and law schools that liberals had mobilized, swung the forces of institutional respectability into play and deprived the bill of essential support.[51] Jenner and the committee majority responded by adopting a softened compromise measure put together by Senator John Marshall Butler, a conservative Republican from Maryland.[52] The final Jenner-Butler bill deleted four of the five sections of the original proposal and added three new ones. It still deprived the Supreme Court of appellate jurisdiction in cases involving bar admissions, but its new provisions did not attempt to limit the Court directly.

The first new provision strengthened the position of congressional investigating committees; the second restricted the preemption doctrine and allowed for the operation of state anti-subversion legislation unless explicitly prohibited by Congress; and the third broadened the language of the anti-Communist Smith Act that the Court had construed restrictively.[53]

Throughout the summer of 1958, supporters of the Jenner-Butler bill sought to bring it to the floor, and liberals tried to kill it by delay. Senate Democratic Majority Leader Lyndon Johnson of Texas, desperately trying to prevent a split in his party and preserve his reputation as a harmonizer, agreed to stall.[54] By August, however, the pressure from the anti-Court faction grew insistent, and Johnson consented to bring the bill to the floor. A group of ten liberal senators, led by Hennings and Hubert Humphrey of Minnesota, then confronted Johnson and threatened to turn the debate into a broad attack on the segregationist motives behind the proposal.[55] They agreed not to force the race issue if Johnson would help defeat the bill. In the closing weeks of the Eighty-Fifth Congress the Jenner-Butler bill finally came to a vote. The Senate tabled it, by a vote of forty-nine to forty-one.[56]

With one relatively minor exception, a bill to modify the result of the Court's decision granting access to government files, the anti-Court bills failed. Although several passed the House, the Senate refused to act. The drive continued in the next Congress, but it lacked the intensity of the previous year. Jenner had retired, and six other anti-Court Republicans failed to win new terms.[57] The elections of 1958 were, in fact, a major liberal victory, and their results moderated the tone of the new Congress.

The Court itself helped deflate any renewed efforts, muting its assertiveness during the next three terms. Frankfurter and to a lesser extent Justice John M. Harlan, who had replaced Jackson in 1955, moved further from the Warren-Black-Douglas wing, and the Court's decisions were frequently narrower and often favored the government. Although the Court remained firm on desegregation, its decisions in other areas were mild and mixed.[58] The Warren Court would enter a second and far broader activist phase in 1962, but its later decisions would only confirm and strengthen the political realignments that had been forged in the late 1950s.[59]

Corollary: The Peripheral Politics of Diversity Jurisdiction

While the Eighty-Fifth Congress struggled with the Jenner-Butler bill, it also considered once again the question of diversity jurisdiction. Bills to restrict diversity had been intermittently introduced, and almost wholly ignored, in the years after the war. By the mid-1950s, however, support gathered behind two quite different bills.

The first was drafted and endorsed by the Judicial Conference of the United States under the prodding of Congressman Emmanuel Celler of New York, chairman of the House Judiciary Committee. Celler was dissatisfied with the continual need to create new judgeships to cope with mounting dockets.[60] The Judicial Conference had assigned the matter to a committee chaired by the venerable Judge John J. Parker of the Fourth Circuit, who had vigorously fought the Norris bill a quarter of a century earlier. Insisting that diversity was "essential to the proper administration of justice under the system of dual sovereignty,"[61] Parker produced a report that praised diversity for protecting "the commercial as well as the political fabric of the country."[62] Acknowledging the problem of congestion, his committee recommended that the jurisdictional amount be raised and that the "citizenship" of a corporation be expanded to include not only its state of incorporation but also the state where it maintained its "principal place of business."[63] The Judicial Conference accepted the report and forwarded its recommendations to Congress.[64]

The second bill was more radical and, to liberals at least, far more suspect. In March 1955, Congressman William M. Tuck, backed by his fellow Virginian Howard Smith, the powerful chairman of the House Rules Committee, introduced a bill that not only raised the jurisdictional amount but also excluded corporations from diversity jurisdiction.[65] Tuck and Smith were both economic conservatives, outspoken critics of desegregation, and determined advocates of states' rights. "This measure," Tuck declared, "is designed to relieve the Federal courts of litigation of a trifling or less substantial nature and to confer jurisdiction in such cases upon the State courts where it belongs." Although his arguments echoed those of Norris and other Progressives, the historical context and Tuck's hard states' rights rhetoric evidenced a profoundly different social meaning. The segregationist animus against *Brown* reverberated through his defense of the bill. "[A] greedy and Gargantuan Central Government in the last few years has usurped the powers of the States by expanding its activities into almost every phase of our existence," he protested bitterly, "and we can feel its tentacles in all walks of life."[66]

In 1957, the House Judiciary Committee held hearings at which Tuck and a representative of the Judicial Conference, Judge Albert B. Maris of the Third Circuit, appeared as witnesses. The following year the Committee reported favorably on a bill that adopted the proposals of the Judicial Conference. It raised the jurisdictional amount to $10,000 and adopted the "principal place of business" provision.[67] The House added an amendment that prohibited removal of any action based on a state workmen's compensation law. All the provisions were justified as methods of combating "congestion," and both Houses quickly passed them.[68]

The changes in diversity jurisdiction came easily and went unnoticed beyond the legal profession. Although the amendments were minor, what Congress did and what it failed to do were revealing. Like the politics of the Jenner bill, passage of the final diversity bill symbolized the difference between the 1930s and the 1950s. It rang down the curtain on diversity jurisdiction as a significant partisan political issue and confirmed that the age of Progressivism had long since passed.

The bill was based on a contradiction. Its supporters declared that alleviating the burden of "congested" dockets was essential, but experience suggested that the bill would provide little or no relief.[69] Given inflation, population growth, economic expansion, and ever increasing automobile traffic, there was no reason to assume that raising the jurisdictional amount would do the job, and the Parker committee acknowledged as much.[70] The "principal place of business" provision seemed equally ineffective. Docket statistics showed that the restriction would eliminate only 6 percent of corporate diversity cases and only 1.4 percent of the total civil caseload.[71] To be sure, diversity actions were sometimes complex and more commonly went to trial than did certain other kinds of actions, but the available figures suggested that the new restriction would have little discernible effect on the dockets.[72]

The triviality of the bill's likely impact was strikingly apparent when compared with the results that the alternative would have accomplished. Tuck's bill, Judge Maris acknowledged, "would unquestionably effect a much greater reduction in the caseload in the Federal courts."[73] Indeed, the Tuck bill would eliminate more than twelve thousand diversity cases per year and cut the total federal civil caseload by an impressive 25 percent.[74]

Therefore, although Congress discussed the amendments almost solely in terms of congestion, it acted on different grounds. The Tuck bill, clearly effective in terms of the ostensible goal, was quietly shelved in favor of a bill that never offered the possibility of doing more than slowing slightly the continued growth of the federal caseload. That contradiction was hardly surprising; for, however abstruse the debate, jurisdiction remained ultimately an issue of social policy and political power. The decision Congress made in revising the Judicial Code reflected two preferences that it regarded as far more significant than the problem of congestion.

The first preference was the same one that led it to reject the overtly anti-Court measures. Whatever its merits, the Tuck bill was a calculated strike at the federal courts, rooted in the same southern animus that had driven the Jenner-Butler bill to the brink of passage. In that atmosphere, liberals were in no mood to cut the jurisdiction of the federal courts by 25 percent, regardless of the subject matter involved. Southerners and anti-Communists, their attention focused on measures that would more nearly achieve their overriding political purposes, were unwilling to make the restriction of diversity jurisdiction a major goal.

The second preference was to accord national corporations the place they deserved in the legal system and to retain truly national affairs in the national courts. Few liberals in the 1950s rejected large corporations on principle or feared them with the intensity of their Progressive forebears. On the contrary, most accepted them as inevitable and desirable instruments of American progress, and they saw no need to alter jurisdictional rules to restrict their private litigation. Further, to the extent that liberals remained suspicious of the power and policies of large corporations, they were happy to keep them in the federal courts. After two decades of Democratic appointments, the national courts were at least as liberal as most state courts and frequently more so.

For their part, too, corporations still believed that they were better off in the federal courts. "[T]here is a great bulk of expert opinion from those who litigate in the courts," the Parker committee had declared, "that local prejudice continues to exist, and that the Federal courts are in truth a strong protection against it." [75] Questioned during the hearings, Judge Maris confirmed those views. "[M]y impression is that counsel for large corporate interests that operate through the country would be strongly opposed" to restrictions. Furthermore, he added, "I think that they would be very bitterly opposed to Governor Tuck's bill." [76]

The 1958 amendments did place one new restriction on general diversity jurisdiction, the "principal place of business" test. That provision confirmed the altered assumptions of the new age. The justification for the amendment rested on the image of the scheming "local" corporation that obtained an out-of-state charter for the sole purpose of gaining access to a federal court in suits involving essentially local matters. The image of the *Taxicab* case was summoned to exemplify the kinds of "frauds and abuses" the amendment would prohibit. Diversity and the doctrine of corporate citizenship, the Parker committee declared, "has given rise to the evil that a corporation which is in reality a local institution, engaged in a local business and locally owned, is enabled to drag its litigation into the Federal courts because it has obtained a charter from another State." [77] Thus, some local corporations enjoyed an unfair advantage over other local corporations, and the "principal place of business" amendment would eliminate their tactic.[78] The social goal that had animated Progressives — to aid uninformed and financially pressed individuals litigating against large national corporations — no longer shaped the debate. The justification Congress accepted for restricting diversity was to protect honest local businesses faced with unfair competition from conniving local businesses.

The distinction between "local" and "national" corporations implied a largely unspoken but pervasive premise: although still formally creatures of local law, corporations that conducted business across the nation properly deserved access to the federal courts. That premise was different from the traditional premise that corporations needed diversity to protect against local prejudice. Although many still assumed that such prejudice existed, that fear was no longer determinative. Rather, the proponents of the amendment recognized that large corporations were fundamental instruments of the nation's business, and they assumed that those corporations had a legitimate claim on the national courts. That newly dominant assumption symbolized the transformation that had occurred. Congress used the "principal place of business" amendment to discipline the scheming local corporation while blessing the judicially developed doctrine of corporate citizenship and guaranteeing to national business its right of access to the federal courts.

The amendment also suggested the drastic change that had occurred in the social significance of diversity. Individual claimants were no longer generally disadvantaged by the jurisdiction; to the contrary, they commonly regarded the federal courts as particularly desirable forums. The specific legal and social conditions that had inspired Progressives had passed away, and the jurisdiction's new critics focused on different problems, such as congestion and scheming local corporations. In that context the *Taxicab* decision, which involved a socially minor matter of strategic reincorporation that happened to provoke a famous dissent, misleadingly came to symbolize the social abuses that had marked the history of diversity jurisdiction.

If the struggle over the Jenner-Butler bill revealed the political fissures in American society, the easy passage of the diversity amendments manifested its underlying agreement. The national corporation was accepted and accorded protection, and the problem of the federal caseload was increasingly considered a technical matter to be entrusted to expert administrators. Broader and more awkward questions concerning the unfair impact of economic inequality on the administration of justice went unasked.[79]

The fates of the Jenner-Butler bill and the diversity amendments symbolized the gulf that separated the 1930s from the 1950s. Diversity's social significance had changed, and general concern with economic inequality and fear of corporate power had substantially diminished. In their place at center stage stood race and the cold war. The old Court that had raised the protection of property to a position of constitutional primacy was gone, replaced by a new Court in the process of raising individual freedom and equality to a similar position. The wings of the political spectrum marched past one another in reshaping their views about the nature and scope of the federal judicial power.

Stratagem: Reorienting the Debate

In the spring of 1959 Chief Justice Warren addressed the annual meeting of the prestigious American Law Institute. Founded in 1923 by some of the
most prominent leaders of the bench and bar, the ALI was organized to help
abolish "confusion" in the common law. Toward that end, over the years it produced a series of "Restatements" of traditional common law subjects. Elaborate,
detailed, and copiously footnoted, the "Restatements" imposed patterns on the
cases and symbolized a unified common law. Throughout the years, too, the institute stood as an ideological voice of the nation's legal elite. Its membership,
limited to a small number of individuals of prominence and position, included
many of the nation's most influential judges, scholars, and practitioners. Indeed,
traditionally the chief justice of the United States honored the institute's annual
meeting with an address.

In 1959 Warren welcomed the opportunity. Distressed over mounting
caseloads and disappointed with the 1958 amendments, he told the ALI that
"serious delay and congestion" were "daily risking the loss of public respect
and confidence" in the federal courts. Bills introduced in the new Congress to
restrict or abolish diversity jurisdiction evidenced the need for reform. "The
very breadth of these proposals," Warren suggested, "points up the need for a
full review of the diversity jurisdiction, conducted in the light of current judicial statistics and prevailing economic and social conditions." Warren urged the
institute to undertake a "special study" of the subject. "It is essential that we
achieve a proper jurisdictional balance between the Federal and State court systems, assigning to each system those cases most appropriate in the light of the
basic principles of federalism."[80] Adopting Warren's suggestion, the institute
agreed to undertake such an effort.

Although Warren was concerned with the federal caseload, far more substantial dangers helped inspire his proposal. Diversity and "congestion," after
all, had been persistent problems for seventy-five years. Indeed, had Warren
thought significant action imperative, he could have urged support for one or
more of the pending bills designed to curtail diversity jurisdiction. The year,
however, was 1959, and his paramount concern was the segregationist and anti-
Communist drive against the federal judiciary. In and out of Congress vitriol
against him and his Court was widespread. In both 1957 and 1958, for example,
when the chief justice attended the annual meeting of the American Bar Association, critics seized the opportunity to attack him and the federal courts to
his face, charging a variety of transgressions that included imposing subjective values and "advancing the cause of Communism." Angered and insulted,
Warren resigned.[81] "If the Court cannot rely upon the main national body of

the legal profession to treat it fairly in times of stress," he later warned, then it was "defenseless against the most powerful and reactionary interests in the nation." [82]

An astute politician, Warren recognized the utility of committing the question of jurisdictional reform to the blue-ribbon ALI. It would "profession-alize" the issue and put the weight of the institute behind a proposal whose gestation would take years. "Such a study," Warren noted casually, "is necessarily of a long-range nature." [83] The fact that the institute was conducting a study would constitute a powerful argument for congressional delay and undermine those who would use docket problems as an excuse to strike a quick political blow at the national courts. Further, Warren's emphasis on "the basic principles of federalism" cleverly placed his suggestion on a lofty plane, discrediting by implication partisan proposals aimed at reversing specific decisions. Indeed, what more effective political stance was there for the chief of the nationalizing Warren Court than as an advocate for "the basic principles of federalism"?

While some members of the ALI surely sympathized with Warren's tactic, all knew that diversity remained a controversial subject within the profession even absent the complications of national politics. One group, led by Justice Frankfurter, urged the drastic curtailment or abolition of the jurisdiction. They wished to protect the prerogatives of the states, rationalize the structure of the legal system, and enhance the elite status of the federal courts. [84] The jurisdiction's accepted rationale — protection against local prejudice — insulted the states; *Erie* denied the federal courts an authoritative voice on state law; the existence of two judicial systems only encouraged forum shopping; and petty cases squandered federal resources. [85] "[L]ittle, if any, reason exists today," declared Professor Philip Kurland of the University of Chicago, a former law clerk of Frankfurter's and a vigorous academic proponent of decentralization, "for the continuance of diversity jurisdiction." [86]

A rival group defended diversity and even advocated its expansion. [87] Congestion, they maintained, could be solved through more efficient administration and new judgeships. [88] The right of access to the federal courts, declared one ALI member, was "an attribute of national citizenship" that gave the federal courts "a vital role to play in strengthening the national fabric." [89] The defenders argued that diversity helped to create a fruitful interchange between local and national legal systems, advanced the cause of procedural reform, and prevented the federal courts from becoming narrowly specialized tribunals. Composed of political liberals solicitous of the federal courts, business lawyers who used diversity for their corporate clients, and members of the trial bar who cherished the general tactical advantage that a choice of forums offered, the defenders of diversity jurisdiction exhibited a strongly nationalistic orientation and — like the jurisdiction's opponents — a fervent belief in the superiority of the federal courts.[90]

As the debate fragmented the profession along preexisting fault lines, the institute hastened to adopt a neutralist stance. The members of its advisory committee and the study's drafters — called "reporters" — insisted that they would examine all elements of federal jurisdiction, not just diversity. "The objective of this Study is that cases be divided between the state and federal courts in a manner grounded on rational principle," they asserted.[91] "What I am hoping to do and what I regard as our mandate from the American Law Institute," explained Professor Richard H. Field of Harvard Law School, the project's chief reporter, "is to try to put these matters on a basis of what is, objectively speaking, the proper function of federal courts vis-à-vis state courts in the diversity area."[92] With alacrity the institute seized on Warren's phrase "the basic principles of federalism" — as resonant as it was indeterminate — because its members knew that their effort involved not only perennially troubling legal issues but divisive political and professional conflicts as well.

The lure of the phrase "basic principles of federalism" was powerfully appealing to the members of the ALI. Not only did it imply a rationale that would sharply distinguish their efforts from partisan politics and the self-interest of the trial lawyers, but it also harmonized with their broader commitment to the ideas of process jurisprudence. By the late 1950s many lawyers, especially law school teachers, were committed to the search for "neutral principles" and the practice of "reasoned elaboration." How could an activist judiciary be reconciled with the ideal of popular government? How could the Court be protected from retaliation by the legislature? The answer, many concluded, was that judicial independence could be justified and the courts defended from legislative attack only if judges acted within narrow limits, reached decisions on the basis of "neutral" principles, and produced "well crafted" opinions that related those principles to the specific results reached.[93]

Process jurisprudence was the product of complex historical and cultural forces. The crises of the 1930s and 1940s generated an absorbing need in the postwar decades for social consensus, institutional stability, and political caution. The powerful movement for black civil rights and the chaotic campaign against internal subversion fragmented Americans along social and moral, as well as political and ethnic, lines. Commitment to social consensus made the existence of "basic principles" a matter of compelling faith, while the eruption of bitter new domestic conflicts necessitated an appeal to their authority. In that context the ideals of process jurisprudence fostered the belief that legal analysts could extract from American experience truly "basic principles of federalism" that could be used to reorder the jurisdiction of the national courts rationally and properly.

The ALI Study: Neutral Principles and the Federal Judicial Power

The 1958 revision of the Judicial Code "certainly rests on no general structure of thought," Henry Hart told the ALI. It "was the work of plumbers." [94] The institute was determined that its product would be different.

It was. The effort took ten laborious years, and not until the ALI's annual meeting in 1969 did Herbert Wechsler, the institute's director, announce completion of its *Study of the Division of Jurisdiction Between State and Federal Courts*. "[T]he Reporters and the Advisors and the Institute have believed that there are principles of federalism," he proclaimed, "and they are given effect in the recommendations made." [95] Just as Wechsler believed neutral principles should distinguish judicial opinions from legislative choices, so he thought that they distinguished the institute's proposals from those of politicians and agitators. [96]

In spite of inevitable disagreements and compromises, the institute largely succeeded in carrying its principled approach to fruition. The drafters had the advantages of those empowered to put ideas into written form, and they also had the time and expertise necessary to build a broad technical foundation for their proposals. They had the further advantage of an overriding faith in a set of ideas that explained what they were doing and why. Taking the high ground, the reporters and the advisory committee effectively disarmed much of their internal opposition with their steady commitment to principle. [97]

THE TRIUMPH OF FORMAL STRUCTURE

The *Study* was carefully and self-consciously organized around a commitment to the "basic principles of federalism." The ALI "accepted the thesis of the Chief Justice that there are basic principles of federalism and that it is essential to allocate judicial business between state and federal courts in the light of those principles," Field explained. "This thesis has dominated the thinking of my associates as Reporters and myself." [98]

The most fundamental of those principles, the *Study* declared, was the "political axiom" that Alexander Hamilton enunciated in the Eightieth *Federalist* that the reach of the judicial and legislative powers should be coextensive. From that premise the *Study* drew two conclusions. The first was that whenever the federal courts exercised diversity jurisdiction "the state's judicial power is less extensive than its legislative power." Diversity, therefore, was "an undesirable interference with state autonomy" that should be retained "only upon a showing of strong reasons therefor." The second conclusion was the complement of the first. The federal courts should be "concentrated upon the adjudication of rights created by federal substantive law." [99] In addition to recommending that diversity jurisdiction be narrowed, the *Study* proposed that federal question jurisdiction be extended. Absent substantial countervailing considerations, explained Professor Charles Alan Wright of the University of Texas, an associate reporter, "questions of federal law are best left to the federal courts."[100]

The ALI confirmed and expanded *Erie*'s central role in the jurisdictional jurisprudence Hart and Wechsler had inspired. Its various drafts consistently emphasized that Brandeis's decision was foundational.[101] *Erie*, they proclaimed, was a twentieth-century restatement of Hamilton's "political axiom." "If *Erie* had a constitutional base," the *Study* declared, "it was the absence of federal legislative power as to the run of factual situations presented in diversity cases."[102] Like Hamilton's Eightieth *Federalist,* Brandeis's decision embodied a fundamental principle of federalism, the theory of coextensive powers. So viewed, *Erie* provided a principled basis for limiting diversity jurisdiction by undergirding "the basic proposition that federal courts should not be called upon for the administration of state law."[103] Equally, it provided a principled basis for extending the jurisdiction of the national courts to all cases involving federal law issues. "In such adjudication the federal courts speak with the authority which they lack in diversity cases since *Erie R.R. v. Tompkins,*" and there they can "exercise the creative function which is essential to their dignity and prestige."[104]

Although the ALI *Study* did not specifically identify additional "basic principles of federalism," it assumed two others. One was an "original purpose" principle. The Constitution had included diversity jurisdiction, the *Study* argued, in order to protect out-of-state litigants against local prejudice and, secondarily, to foster a sense of national unity. "If general diversity jurisdiction is to be retained, it must be because these basic reasons for it continue to have validity."[105] The other principle related to "participation": those who became "participants in the general life" of a state, regardless of their formal citizenship, were not "genuine out-of-staters." Such persons "had reason and opportunity" to exert political influence in the states where they were involved, and consequently they should not be regarded as "strangers" there. As participants in local activities, "they are properly held to have accepted the hazards of that state's system as it exists."[106]

In addition, the institute relied on judgments about relevant "modern conditions."[107] The "nationalizing function" that diversity performed had "no present relevance" to twentieth-century America, nor was the danger of local prejudice against out-of-staters a serious matter. "[T]he social and economic incentives to interstate movement and business today are so great as to override any risk of injustice in state courts," the *Study* declared. Moreover, "none of the significant prejudices which beset our society today begins or ends when a state line is traversed."[108] Diversity, then, could be safely restricted.

Conversely, the "principles" and "modern conditions" relevant to federal question jurisdiction suggested the opposite conclusion: the need for expansion. Federal law had grown in scope and complexity, and the federal courts had developed "considerable expertness" in its interpretation and application.[109] Additionally, the structure and organization of the federal judicial system promised a "greater uniformity" in the development of national law than state courts could achieve.[110] Finally, the *Study* maintained, "lack of sympathy — or even hostility" toward federal law on the part of state courts could frustrate the actual "vindication" of federal rights beyond the institutional capacity of the Supreme Court to review and rectify.

The institute adopted the central proposition that the federal district courts were not only forums for interpreting federal law but also, and more important, the practical "vindicators" of federal rights. Owing to the critical task of fact finding, their jurisdiction should extend beyond technical federal questions to include all claims based on federal law, even when the only disputed issues were factual.[111] Moreover, if federal courts sat to vindicate federal rights, they should also have jurisdiction over cases where defendants raised federal counterclaims or defenses.[112] Their jurisdiction, the *Study* announced, "should extend to all cases in which the meaning or application of the Constitution, laws, or treaties of the United States, is a principal element in the position of either party."[113] Consequently, the *Study* called for the severe restriction of the "well-pleaded complaint rule" and a far-reaching expansion of federal question jurisdiction. Its vibrant "vindication" theory was "not now the law," it acknowledged. "It is [nevertheless] the rationale on which the present proposals are based."[114]

The ALI *Study* set forth a series of interrelated recommendations. First, it adopted several restrictions that would likely reduce diversity actions by at least 50 percent.[115] It proposed that parties be prevented from "manufacturing" diversity through the appointment of out-of-state executors and administrators and that plaintiffs be precluded from suing citizens of other states in the federal courts of the plaintiffs' home states.[116] Additionally, it proposed that out-of-state commuters and foreign corporations maintaining permanent local business establishments not be considered "genuine out-of-staters" and that they should, therefore, be denied the right to invoke diversity jurisdiction in the state where they worked or conducted business.

Second, the institute urged that diversity be broadened to address special problems. Partnerships and unincorporated associations that enjoyed legal capacity were to be regarded as "citizens" of the state of their principal place of business,[117] and defendants otherwise able to remove were to be allowed to do so even when plaintiffs joined a citizen of the forum state as a codefendant.[118] Further, the *Study* proposed that diversity be broadened to allow federal courts

to hear multistate, multiparty suits where state rules of venue or personal jurisdiction prevented a plaintiff from bringing suit in any single state forum.[119]

Third, the *Study* proposed a substantial expansion of federal question
jurisdiction. It recommended the almost complete elimination of the jurisdictional amount and the broadening of "pendent" jurisdiction, which allowed
federal courts in the absence of diversity jurisdiction to hear state law claims
related to federal questions.[120] Further, it suggested expanding the reach of the
national courts over distant defendants by establishing nationwide service of
federal process. "No federal question case," it announced, "should be denied a
federal forum because of restrictive rules of venue or process."[121] Most significant, it recommended that removal from state court be allowed on the basis of
federal law issues that appeared in defenses or counterclaims.[122]

The *Study* was an impressive document that offered a systematic and
comprehensive set of proposals for jurisdictional reform. Exemplifying the ideal
of a rational legal system, it was a sophisticated and detailed effort to apply
coherent principles of political and legal theory to the structure of federal jurisdiction.

SOCIAL VALUES: THE INDETERMINACY OF ABSTRACTION

The ALI *Study*, however, had its flaws. It proclaimed allegiance to two
basic goals. The first was to alleviate "congestion"; the second was to implement the "basic principles of federalism." Both supported the *Study*'s claim to
social and political neutrality. In execution, however, both proved inadequate
and misleading.

The first of the *Study*'s formal goals, ending "congestion," was relegated
to a minor role. The institute repeatedly emphasized that the burdens of heavy
dockets, which could "paralyze" the federal judiciary, gave a "special urgency"
to its work. At the same time, it also accepted the proposition that its primary
purpose was to "allocate judicial business between state and federal courts in
the light of those [basic] principles" of federalism.[123] Its proposals expanded federal question jurisdiction massively, while enlarging diversity in some ways and
constricting it in others. "It may well be that the end result of our work will be a
net increase in the workload of the federal courts," the chief reporter acknowledged. "Be that as it may, our concern is not with judicial statistics but rather
that cases be divided between state and federal courts in a manner grounded on
rational principle."[124] The institute's first neutral goal thus collapsed in the face
of its second goal.[125]

The basic principles of federalism, however, provided little more direction. The *Study*'s use of Hamilton's "political axiom" showed their malleability.
As the institute acknowledged, Hamilton had offered his axiom as part of a

political argument "in justification of the federal judicial power."[126] An extreme centralizer in a decentralized era, and a would-be aristocrat disdainful of popular sovereignty, Hamilton saw a national court system as a force fostering commerce, centralization, and a dominant propertied class. He advanced his axiom to link the unpopular federal judicial power, not yet embodied in a lower court system and facing determined political opposition, to the legitimacy and authority of the popular, constitutionally more powerful, and authentically "republican" legislative branch. Although his contention may have been an "axiom," its inspiration was not geometrical symmetry but political leverage.

Similarly, Brandeis designed *Erie* for his own political purposes. Believing in democracy and the legislature as much as Hamilton feared them, and seeking to limit the federal courts as much as Hamilton sought to strengthen them, Brandeis applied the axiom for a political purpose that was precisely the opposite of Hamilton's. *Erie* not only deprived the federal courts of the power to make law in areas "confessedly" beyond the reach of Congress but also implied that the courts could make law within the legislative power only after Congress had chosen to act in those areas. Thus, while Brandeis embraced the principle of coextensive powers, he used it to support a second principle—legislative primacy—that subordinated the lawmaking power of the federal courts to that of Congress. Although in one sense they assumed the "same" axiom, *Erie* and the eightieth *Federalist* were historical and political opposites.

The ALI *Study*, however, embraced both statements of the axiom. As Hart had done in embracing both *Erie* and *Jensen*, it did so by merging them into a new, higher, and transforming abstraction. The *Study*'s use of the axiom was inconsistent with both Hamilton's purpose and Brandeis's. Unlike Hamilton, the institute used the axiom to limit the judicial power in diversity; unlike Brandeis, it used the axiom to expand the judicial power over federal questions. Moreover, in trying to make the judicial power of the states coextensive with their legislative power, the *Study* obscured the foundation of Brandeis's constitutional jurisprudence—the democratic accountability and lawmaking primacy of the legislature.[127]

The ALI homogenized the conflicting purposes of Hamilton and Brandeis and thereby created, in the guise of a neutral principle, its own new and transforming jurisdictional axiom: the federal courts should have jurisdiction over all cases involving any significant federal issue. The recommendations concerning federal question jurisdiction, Wechsler explained, "are enormously important extensions of federal jurisdiction, premised on the proposition that the application and interpretation of federal law is *uniquely* the function of the federal courts, under what the Chief Justice in his speech to us called the principles of federalism."[128] The increase in federal judicial power in the recommendations was quite apparent, but when and how had the proposition that the "interpretation of federal law is *uniquely* the function of the federal courts" been incorporated into the nation's basic principles of federalism? How, indeed, was it consistent with the institute's subsidiary principle of "originalism"? The proposition was not in the Constitution, and the Founders who passed the First Judiciary Act rejected it. Indeed, as a general proposition, it had no support in the history of the American dual-court system. In adopting the axiom of coextensive powers as a "basic principle of federalism," the institute imagined its own new premise for its own new ends.[129]

Although it justified drastic changes, the institute's newly fashioned axiom did not logically determine the nature of the *Study*'s recommendations concerning diversity jurisdiction.[130] The axiom of "coextensive powers" could not, after all, determine *which* diverse citizens should be allowed to invoke the jurisdiction and which not. To close that logical gap, the *Study* referred to its "participation" and "original purpose" principles.

The principle of "participation" declared that those who became "participants in the general life of the state" should no longer be regarded as " 'true' out-of-staters," and hence no longer able to invoke diversity.[131] The "principle" was freshly minted and dubious, and its obvious purpose was acknowledged. The principle simply embodied an adroit reversal of traditional relationships: instead of diversity existing to encourage out-of-staters to transact local business, the transaction of local business transformed "out-of-staters" into local "participants" in order to deny them use of diversity. The new principle substituted the concept of " 'true' out-of-stater" for the constitutional one of legal citizenship and served as an expedient rationalizing device to prevent some citizens from using diversity.

The "original purpose" principle held that diversity jurisdiction was proper only when it served its "originally designed" purpose of protecting out-of-staters against local prejudice.[132] The institute gave no reason for limiting diversity to such a rigid purpose. It did not, after all, try to limit federal question jurisdiction to any such original purpose. Congressional power in general, including the power to create lower federal courts and to establish their jurisdiction, was held to no original purpose. The *Study* never explained why, as long as the jurisdiction extended to citizens of different states, Congress could not use it to implement any constitutionally proper purpose it chose.

More revealing, the institute was willing to jettison its "original purpose" principle when its view of social policy suggested the wisdom of a broader diversity jurisdiction. Owing to the "complexity and rapid communication which characterize our modern society," the *Study* explained, litigation was increasingly national in scope. "[E]fficient disposition of lawsuits involving such complex transactions often calls for bringing in multiple parties, perhaps from several different places."[133] The institute consequently recommended that diversity be expanded to give federal courts jurisdiction over multistate disputes which, because of the requirements of personal jurisdiction or venue, could not be brought in any single state court. "This is not the first time," the *Study* declared, "that diversity jurisdiction has been expanded to meet new national needs of this kind."[134]

The institute reconciled its expansive proposal to meet "new national needs" by redefining the "original purpose" of diversity. The jurisdiction had been designed to protect against "the prejudice or reasonable fear of prejudice against outsiders from other states or, in broader terms, the lack of confidence in the adequacy of state court justice."[135] Lawyers certainly knew the utility of shifting to "broader terms" when their argument stumbled. Regarding the issue of multistate jurisdiction, the *Study* pointed out, "neither state courts nor federal courts now adequately deal" with such problems.[136] Hence, the syllogism concluded, multistate jurisdiction fit the "original purpose" of remedying "inadequate" state judicial systems.

The proposed multistate jurisdiction illustrated the selective policy judgments that lay behind the institute's proposals. First, although the new jurisdiction would expand the federal caseload, the "urgent" anti-congestion policy inexplicably gave way to the different policy of fostering national commercial transactions. Second, in its explanation of why "participation" would deprive persons of " 'true' out-of-stater" status, the *Study* bluntly stated that, owing to their activities within the state, "they are properly held to have accepted the hazards of that state's system as it exists."[137] When the institute addressed the multistate jurisdiction, however, it did not apply the same reasoning. It refused to find that persons who chose to engage in multiparty, multistate transactions assumed the same risk.

The ALI *Study*, then, was not the neutral document that its proponents claimed. The anti-congestion policy was readily and frequently subordinated to other interests. Principles, basic and otherwise, were molded anew. Logical rigor, though successful in giving the *Study* a consistent formal structure, was a mere tool of the substantive policies that the institute chose to adopt.

SANITIZING THE HISTORICAL AND SOCIAL

The *Study of the Division of Jurisdiction Between State and Federal Courts* treated the judicial power as a problem of abstract logic and thereby passed over the true social significance of jurisdictional rules. It praised diversity jurisdiction, for example, for its "spectacularly achieved" commercial and nationalizing results.[138] It did so, apparently, for the sole purpose of proclaiming that there was no longer any general reason to use the jurisdiction to protect commerce or foster nationalism.[139] "Although the weight of history is not to be ignored nor its lessons overlooked," the *Study* explained, "the problem is one to be solved in the light of the conditions existing today."[140] Fair enough. The institute's failure, however, was that it ignored the truly critical lesson of the history of diversity jurisdiction: formally "neutral" jurisdictional rules implicate complex questions about the relationship of social and economic inequality to the principle of equal justice under the law. The institute created an abstract history that had no place for such a lesson.

The *Study*'s treatment of the origin of federal question jurisdiction was even more revealing. Congress granted the jurisdiction, it claimed, to avoid a problem of doctrinal uncertainty. "In 1875, when this jurisdiction was finally granted, it was by no means clear that the state courts could be required to entertain claims arising under federal law," it explained. "There may have seemed no alternative but to grant such jurisdiction to the lower federal courts."[141] As Hart had designated "the logic of federalism" as the historical cause of both *Erie* and *Jensen,* so the *Study* portrayed doctrinal uncertainty as the cause of jurisdictional expansion. Its explanation in effect denied the entire history of late Reconstruction. Despite any doctrinal uncertainty, Congress conferred federal question jurisdiction on the national courts in 1875 not because it doubted its formal authority over state courts but because it sought specifically to bypass those courts for compelling reasons of national policy.[142]

As the *Study* sanitized the past, it treated the present abstractly. The institute did little to discover what its proposed changes would in fact accomplish, and it was content to work with available statistical compilations and to rely on the collective experience of its members. "In truth," acknowledged one reporter, "no one knows what the exact effect will be."[143] That collective experience hardly represented the experience of most lawyers, especially those who represented Americans in lower- and middle-income groups. To the extent that the interests of the nonelite bar—and, through them (possibly), the interests of poorer Americans—were represented by associations of trial lawyers, there was strong opposition to the institute's proposals. The National Association of Claimants Counsel of America and the National Board of the American Trial Lawyers Association both opposed what they termed the "emasculation" of diversity jurisdiction.[144] Although their protests were undoubtedly self-serving, as supporters of the ALI proposals charged, it was also possible that they spoke indirectly for the legal interests of otherwise voiceless and poorer citizens.[145] That possibility deserved consideration. When the representative of the Claimants Counsel spoke at the institute's annual meeting in 1963, however, none of the reporters bothered to respond.[146]

The *Study* also reflected the legal elite's national orientation and special commitment to the federal judiciary. It assumed the paramount importance of federal law and the qualitative superiority of the national courts. "Without disparagement of the quality of justice in many state courts throughout the country," it declared, "it may be granted that often the federal courts do have better judges, better juries, and better procedures." [147] In fact, the institute recommended restricting diversity in part because state law actions typically were neither critical in terms of national policy nor interesting in terms of professional concerns. Nearly two-thirds of diversity cases, declared Judge Henry J. Friendly, a member of the advisory committee, involved run-of-the-mill claims involving "insurance and personal injuries." [148] The elite bar handled few such claims, and diversity actions seldom presented professionally exciting or innovative legal issues. The jurisdiction, Friendly believed, gave rise to "the dullest cases." [149] The state courts, far more numerous and carrying vastly larger caseloads, were readily available to handle such routine matters.

The same biases inspired the institute to recommend the creation of a special multistate diversity jurisdiction. Such a jurisdiction would bring a burgeoning, economically important, and professionally exciting class of problems into the federal courts. Yet the institute's proposal was complicated, required the litigation of difficult threshold questions, and had not been shown empirically to be necessary.[150] Further, the *Study* acknowledged that the expanding ability of state courts to assert personal jurisdiction over distant defendants rendered most multistate problems potentially resolvable in those courts.[151] Finally, and most striking, the *Study* acknowledged that its proposed multistate jurisdiction "represents a transfer of power from the state courts" that "will involve a greater incursion on state power than is true of general diversity." [152] That multistate "incursion" would be greater because the institute also recommended the abrogation of much established law, including Hart's bête noire, *Klaxon v. Stentor.*[153] "Since state choice-of-law may embody policy," the *Study* explained, "the [multistate] jurisdiction created for present purposes must necessarily contain the power and the actual likelihood of undercutting local policies in cases within its scope." [154] When the institute adopted its multistate recommendations, then, it was increasing "congestion," redefining diversity's "original purpose," creating a complicated new procedure, and consciously violating the axiom of coextensive powers, the *Study*'s self-proclaimed core principle of federalism. Nevertheless, the institute persisted. The recommendation was based on a policy of facilitating national commerce, but it was inspired by the commitment of the institute's members to the special status of the federal courts and their own professional fascination with an exciting new legal arena.

The *Study*'s recommendations for broadening federal question jurisdiction revealed a similar concern with the special role of the national judiciary. In the context of the late twentieth century the institute's proposed expansions meant a considerable shift of power to the federal courts. The fact that national law was growing rapidly in scope and importance, together with the *Study*'s theory that the district courts should function as the "vindicators" of federal rights, meant that control of federal question jurisdiction would confer control of the nation's judicial future. Through a vibrantly expanding Fourteenth Amendment and broadened civil rights remedies, many instances of "prejudice" against which diversity might have afforded protection now presented federal questions over which the national courts had general jurisdiction. "[I]f people are raising claims under the Constitution of the United States," Wright asked, "why should they not have access to a federal forum?" [155] Although members of the institute spoke conscientiously of federalism, they reformulated its theory to ensure the increasing centrality of the federal courts in the nation's legal system.

Equally revealing were the limits the institute accepted on that expansion. The struggle for black civil rights in the 1950s and 1960s had generated strong support for the idea that the district courts should function as the "vindicators" of federal rights. "In the civil rights movement," wrote one liberal lawyer unconnected with the institute, it was clear that "the state's legal institutions were and are the principal enemy." [156] Segregationist legal tactics and the hostility of southern state courts were widely recognized and documented, but the institute avoided the challenge.[157] "Recent litigation involving civil rights has dramatized the necessity for an independent system of federal courts to vindicate federal law," it declared, "but it would be unfortunate if this particular class of cases, which forms a statistically small part of federal question litigation, were to dominate thinking as to the whole area of how the federal question should be handled." [158]

The explanation rang hollow. The institute had readily ignored the significance of statistical representativeness when it recommended its new multiparty, multistate jurisdiction. Moreover, its expressed concern was without foundation. It was not necessary for civil rights cases to "dominate thinking" about federal question jurisdiction in order to allow the federal courts to vindicate national law in the area. Indeed, both the Federal Judicial Code and the *Study*'s own recommendations included special sections covering civil rights cases.[159] The institute did not, then, refrain from treating such cases separately. Rather, it refrained from treating them favorably.[160]

If federal defenses were to be heard in federal courts because state courts might be "unsympathetic," however, and if the proper role of the district courts was to "vindicate" federal rights, then there was no area of the law more powerfully in need of federal intervention than the methodical political prosecutions of blacks and civil rights workers in the South.[161] The institute, however, refused to recommend any such change. It chose, instead, to urge the expansion of federal diversity jurisdiction over multiparty, multistate litigation.[162]

The Question of Relevance

In 1969 the ALI submitted its completed *Study* to the Judicial Conference of the United States. Not surprisingly, the conference reacted gingerly. Encouraging members of the federal judiciary to submit written comments,[163] it warily passed the buck to Congress in the fall of 1970.[164] When the Senate Judiciary Committee specifically asked for its judgment, the conference declared the *Study* "well conceived" but expressed its preference for other, narrower proposals.[165]

In the early 1970s, when a Senate subcommittee held extensive hearings on the ALI proposals, familiar arguments and interests were heard.[166] The legislative process, however, worked in its own way. Divided by many of the substantive problems that the institute had ignored, Congress refused to act. The proposals were far too broad and revolutionary to attract widespread support, and beyond their theoretical coherence there was simply no significant reason to adopt them. Moreover, the institute's stance of social neutrality — a claim usually critical for the success of procedural reform efforts — was belied by the drastic and, ultimately, partisan nature of its proposals.[167] The meticulously crafted *Study* soon sank from public view.

The *Study* failed not only as a set of practical proposals but also as a theoretical effort. First, it did not explain why an increase in internal coherence that failed to achieve its purported policy goal of alleviating "congestion" could justify an alteration in existing jurisdictional rules that would cause unknown but significant changes in the operation of the legal system. Second, it failed to demonstrate that its heralded "principles" were either "basic" or "of federalism" (at least, in the form that the institute chose to cast them). Indeed, it reshaped its central principle, the "political axiom" of Hamilton and Brandeis, and applied it to radical new purposes. Third, the *Study* made basic policy choices without justifying — or even clearly acknowledging — what it was doing. Worse, it made policy choices while pretending it was doing something else. Finally, and in some ways most disappointing, it refrained from making a logical policy choice in the one crucial area where its own "principles" called for forthright action: the protection of federal civil rights. Rigorously conceived and elegantly reasoned, the institute's product was neither logically compelling nor socially useful.

The *Study* was the signature product of the American legal academic elite at a historical moment.[168] It reflected both the awesome intellectual strengths of that elite as well as its constrained social orientation. The *Study* did not consistently serve any external interests, and its underlying viewpoint did not mask economic drives or serve the purposes of class or party. Instead, it reflected the view of elite professionals in thrall to a misguided and inappropriate jurisprudence and committed to expanding the prestige and power of the federal courts.

Despite its neutral stance, intellectual flaws, and doomed legislative fate, the *Study* did provide substantial help to the Warren Court. In immediate and practical terms, it wheeled the idea of neutral principles forward to relieve the anti-Court siege. The institute's decade-long project helped to defuse segregationist and anti-Communist attacks on the Court. More generally, it served to delegitimize overtly political efforts to use the power of Congress over federal jurisdiction to discipline the national judiciary. In broader political and ideological terms, the *Study* embraced and articulated the nationalist vision of the federal courts as the authoritative interpreters of federal law and the primary vindicators of federal rights. On the highly rarefied level of generalized jurisdictional theory, it elaborated, justified, and certified an ideology of federal judicial nationalism that paralleled the highly controversial institutional jurisprudence that the Warren Court was so vigorously developing in practice. In the august voice of the profession's elite and under the authoritative banner of the principles of federalism, the *Study* shaped Brandeis's opinion in *Erie* to help advance the most sweeping plan to implement the twentieth-century view of the national courts that had ever been put forward for serious public consideration.

To Century's End

II

MEANING, POLITICS, AND THE

CONSTITUTIONAL ENTERPRISE

Duric the last quarter of the twentieth century, while massive social transformations continued to reshape the nation and its political culture, the fundamental branch affinities that had evolved during the postwar decades (spurred and symbolized by *Brown* and *Roe v. Wade*) weakened and showed signs of fracturing.[1] Changes in political orientations and shifts in power relations among the three branches of government began to jar the expectations of both liberals and conservatives.[2] A pervasive sense of social and ideological fragmentation spurred a burgeoning effort to rethink basic assumptions and inspired a proliferation of what came to be called "constitutional theory."[3]

Political liberals still tended to identify with the national government, especially its judiciary, and to look with skepticism on both state courts and legislatures. They upheld the authority of the national courts, urged their primacy in hearing federal law claims, and defended their efforts to protect and expand individual noneconomic rights. Consistently, they opposed the periodic efforts of conservatives to use the power of Congress to restrict their jurisdiction over such focal issues as busing, abortion, and school prayer.[4] Their faith in the federal courts began to waver, however, after Presidents Richard M. Nixon, Ronald Reagan, and George Bush succeeded in filling the lower judiciary with large numbers of conservative judges and appointing to the Supreme Court a series of justices unsympathetic to the Warren Court.[5] By 1992, in fact, approximately 70 percent of all federal judges were Reagan or Bush appointees.[6] Under Chief Justice Warren E. Burger, appointed by Nixon in 1969, and especially Chief Justice William H. Rehnquist, another Nixon appointee who was elevated to the center chair by Reagan in 1986, the Court narrowed the range of claims that the national courts could hear and came to favor business over government and both over aggrieved individuals. The Rehnquist Court sought to force federal law claims into the state courts "in the expectation that relief will be denied," charged an ardent defender of the Warren Court. As a result, "the fundamental framework of American government is now very much at risk." [7]

While many liberals clung to their faith in the national courts, others accepted, however reluctantly, the need to rethink their premises. "The passion of the 1960s and the image of the heroic federal judge," a commentator acknowledged in 1995, "have by now escaped our collective grasp." [8] Perhaps most surprising, some — led by none other than Justice William J. Brennan, the leading figure in the establishment of liberal federal judicial nationalism — began turning hopefully to the state courts. They argued that those courts could and should take up the role of guaranteeing and expanding those individual noneconomic rights the United States Supreme Court seemed ready to abandon. [9]

On the other side of the political spectrum, conservatives continued to castigate the national judiciary. The federal courts regularly "invaded legislative prerogatives," charged a former Reagan administration official, and the "incoherent" and "unpredictable Constitutional rulings" of the liberal Court turned on "the ideosyncracies [*sic*] of the individual justices." [10] For "the last four decades," a conservative scholar charged in 1993, the Court "has operated almost without exception to move public policy choices in a left-liberal direction." [11] A more extreme reaction came from Robert H. Bork, a law professor and former Nixon administration official who became a cause celebre when a Democratic Senate rejected his nomination to the Court. The federal courts were controlled by a liberal intellectual class, he claimed, and their radical egalitarianism was destroying American society. The only solution, Bork suggested, reaching back to borrow a plank from La Follette and his Progressive Party, was to amend the Constitution to allow Congress to override Supreme Court decisions. [12]

As liberals had begun to rethink their premises, however, conservatives were similarly reconsidering their positions and beginning to modify their own branch affinities. Increasingly they were drawn to the Rehnquist Court's more congenial political orientation. They approved its efforts to tighten restrictions on access to federal forums, defer more broadly to state courts, discourage tort and civil rights suits against business and government, and move toward a more decentralized brand of federalism. [13] Even more striking, conservative politicians and legal thinkers helped revive the deep suspicion of government and legislatures that had dominated the legal profession in the late nineteenth and early twentieth centuries. [14] The administrative state and the representative branch, after all, held the power to regulate the economy broadly and adopt systematically redistributive policies. Some even began to embrace once more the idea of a new conservative judicial activism that would vigorously protect private property against government regulation and methodically enforce the values they associated with market economics. "The clear lesson" of the *Lochner* era, University of Chicago law professor Richard A. Epstein declared in 1996, was that the Supreme Court failed "to take its jurisprudence of individual rights and limited government far enough." In the future, he urged, the Court should "guard against legislative abuse" by applying "a beefed-up *Lochner* across the board." [15]

A Different Legal Process: Reshaping Erie, from Warren to Rehnquist

Not surprisingly, those sweeping changes helped alter professional thinking about the nature of federal judicial power. *Erie*'s promise as both a politico-constitutional instrument and an ideological Rorschach test remained vibrant. In the 1940s the Roosevelt Court produced a New Deal version designed to protect both resident plaintiffs and the power of Congress. Simultaneously, professional commentators committed to national law, uniform procedure, and the elite status of the federal judiciary constructed a negative *Erie* — one that purportedly advanced spurious constitutional claims, disrupted the uniformity of American law, and corrupted the integrity of the federal judicial process itself. During the following decade the jurisprudence of institutional process rescued Brandeis's decision from such disrepute by establishing the image of a constitutionally sound and institutionally sophisticated *Erie*. The allocative *Erie*s of the 1950s — both the Frankfurterian icon of judicial restraint and the Hartian exemplar of the rule of law — minimized de facto problems of litigation inequality and highlighted concerns for federalism and neutral principles. Given that evolution, it was hardly surprising that the massive changes of the late twentieth century produced more new versions of Brandeis's decision.

In 1965, in *Hanna v. Plumer* the Warren Court reinterpreted *Erie*, using Brandeis's decision to expand national powers, focus concern on inequitable litigation effects, and strengthen the authority and independence of the federal courts.[16] *Hanna* presented a conflict between a state procedural rule and a Federal Rule of Civil Procedure. In a diversity action for tort damages, the plaintiff had followed the federal requirement for service of process and failed to comply with the state rule. After the statute of limitations had run, the district court granted summary judgment, dismissing the suit on the ground that under *York* the state rule controlled and hence that service under the federal rule was invalid. The suit, consequently, had not been properly "commenced" within the prescribed limitations period.[17] Granting *certiorari* "[b]ecause of the threat to the goal of uniformity of federal procedure," the Supreme Court reversed, holding that the federal rule, not the state rule, controlled. For two reasons, it explained, *Erie* and *York* did not require the federal court to follow state law. First, application of the federal rule did not conflict with the practical social policies the two cases embodied.[18] Second, and "more fundamental," neither case properly applied when the contested federal rule was one of the Federal Rules of Civil Procedure. Those rules were promulgated pursuant to the Rules Enabling Act, and Congress had constitutional authority to prescribe procedural rules for the national courts.[19]

The *Hanna* decision was typical of the Warren Court. Ensuring the uniformity of federal procedure and guaranteeing its independence from the states, the decision asserted federal authority broadly and exemplified the Court's nationalizing tendencies. The chief justice wrote the opinion, which reflected many of the deepest values that he and his Court shared.

First, *Hanna* emphasized that problems of forum choice should be examined in light of practical issues of litigation fairness. *Erie* was "rooted" in "the realization that it would be unfair" for litigation results to differ merely because suits were brought in different courts, and it was designed to end a systematic de facto abuse, "the practice of 'forum shopping' which had grown up in response to the rule of *Swift v. Tyson*." [20] Insisting that *Erie*'s goal was to negate rules that "unfairly discriminate" against forum residents, the chief justice enthusiastically supported Brandeis's assertion—often questioned, and even derided, as lacking coherent doctrinal meaning—that *Swift* denied resident litigants the "equal protection of the law." [21] To Warren, this statement was compelling not because of its basis in doctrinal logic or constitutional theory but because of its grounding in social practices and moral ideals. *Erie*'s purpose was, indeed, to recognize and resolve "equal protection problems," the chief justice twice insisted.[22] It was to ensure that the application of the rules of law respecting forum choice did not result in the unfair treatment of any class of litigants. Amplifying *Erie*, Warren stressed its pragmatic social mandate. Brandeis's decision had "twin aims," he declared: not only the "discouragement of forum-shopping" but also "the avoidance of inequitable administration of the laws." [23]

Warren's elaboration was critical. There was, after all, nothing inherently unfair about offering parties a choice of forums. Such a choice was intrinsic to the nation's dual federal-state court system and to the practice of concurrent jurisdiction. Indeed, in addition to allowing federal-state forum choice, the law often allowed parties to choose between judicial and nonjudicial forums, between different state courts in the same state, and between different courts in different states. *Hanna* recognized and made explicit the fact that *Erie* had condemned "forum shopping" not across the board or in the abstract but only where a specific practice operated in a de facto unfair way.

The Federal Rule of Civil Procedure properly applied, Warren explained, because on the facts of *Hanna* it did not foster or allow practical unfairness. He based that conclusion on the critical role of timing in litigation. At the point when plaintiff initiated suit, the federal rule conferred no particular advantage that gave the choice of forum an unfair significance. *Swift*, of course, had done just the opposite, announcing prior to suit that forum choice would determine which of two different substantive laws applied to a claim. Conversely, once a party had selected a forum, Warren reasoned, the matter assumed a different status. Then, variations in the procedures to be subsequently followed in state and federal courts might lead to different results, but such differences would not be unfair, assuming that the applicable rules were reasonable and the parties had notice of them. If parties failed to comply with reasonable, relevant, and known procedural rules after they had chosen the forum, they could not claim unfairness, and certainly not any structural or systemic unfairness.[24]

Similarly, *Hanna* reflected the Warren Court's nationalism. It construed *Erie* as representing a broad theory of national power, and it implicitly dismissed the constitutional relevance of any theory of independently limiting "reserved" powers. "We are reminded by the *Erie* opinion that neither Congress nor the federal courts can, under the guise of formulating rules of decision for federal courts, fashion rules which are not supported by a grant of federal authority contained in Article I or some other section of the Constitution; in such areas state law must govern because there can be no other law."[25] According to *Hanna*, then, *Erie* did not offer any new constitutional doctrine concerning reserved powers or the Tenth Amendment. It merely "reminded" the courts of what was ostensibly a fundamental and long-established principle. The Constitution's positive "grant of federal authority" was the sole determinant of the scope of national power, and the Tenth Amendment imposed no independent or substantive limit on that authority.

Indeed, *Hanna* announced a broad and important constitutional principle of national authority and federal independence from state procedural rules. "For the constitutional provision for a federal court system (augmented by the Necessary and Proper Clause)," it explained, "carries with it congressional power to make rules governing the practice and pleading in those courts." That power, moreover, was exceptionally broad. Congress could authorize independent federal rules to control any issue, no matter how important, as long as the rules met the most flaccid of standards: they were required to be "rationally capable of classification" as procedural.[26]

Finally, *Hanna* typified the Warren Court by using *Erie* to affirm the breadth and independence of federal judicial power. Although its interpretation of *Erie*'s fairness concern and its constitutional principle reflected Brandeis's views, its treatment of *Erie*'s theory of federal judicial power did not. "[N]either Congress nor the federal courts," *Hanna* declared, could "fashion rules" that were not supported by some "grant of federal authority." That statement implied a proposition that was both fundamental and inconsistent with Brandeis's decision. The federal courts, *Hanna* suggested, could "fashion rules" in any area where a constitutional grant gave authority to the federal government. The judicial power was coextensive not only with the legislative power but also with the constitutional power of the federal government. Moreover, the lawmaking power of the federal judiciary was not dependent upon prior legislative action. It could, apparently, initiate federal lawmaking in any area where national power existed. Accepting *Erie*'s basic constitutional premise concerning coextensive powers, *Hanna* ignored its limiting corollary that the federal courts should not make law in areas that Congress had left to the states.

As the Warren Court shaped *Erie* in light of its commitment to activist judicial lawmaking and the values of an egalitarian nationalism, the new conservative, Republican-appointed justices who began to reorient the Court after the mid-1970s attempted to mold it to their own purposes.[27] During the preceding fifteen years, charged Justice Rehnquist in 1974, "there has been a dramatic shift of power from the legislative to the judicial branch."[28] The new justices sought to restrict the access of disfavored plaintiffs' groups to the national courts and to expand procedural and jurisdictional doctrines that would prevent the lower courts from hearing their cases. As part of their effort, they used *Erie* to challenge liberal judicial lawmaking, and by the 1980s the profession was debating the merits of their purportedly "new" *Erie*.[29]

The conservatives' immediate target was the expanding range of private remedies the federal courts were creating for those injured by actions that violated the Constitution and federal statutes. The substantial restraining influence that *Erie* had exercised over the Court's lawmaking in the 1940s and 1950s — a result of the justices' Progressive and New Deal heritage — had weakened by the early 1960s, and the liberal activists on the Warren and early Burger Courts made new law with increasing boldness.[30] During those years they drastically expanded the relief available against state officials under the federal civil rights laws, and they created a range of new "private rights of action" that allowed aggrieved individuals to sue federal officials as well as private individuals and institutions.[31] Although they continued to develop areas of "specialized federal common law" involving the operations of the national government, their judicial creation and expansion of private remedies for constitutional and statutory violations provoked the conservatives' strongest opposition.

In 1970 the conservative scholar Philip B. Kurland of the University of Chicago sounded the warning. *Erie* had been "the last great judicial upheaval on behalf of the states," he announced, and liberal justices were subverting it. "[T]he Warren Court's decisions" were working "an erosion of the constitutional authorization and a destruction of the statutory basis for the *Erie* doctrine." The Court had "amended" the Rules of Decision Act illegitimately "to provide that the federal courts may—even in the absence of constitutional, treaty, or statutory command—create their own rules." According to Kurland, the Court had repudiated Brandeis's assertion that there was no "general" federal common law. "[W]e are now told that there is a federal common law which is to be as 'general' as the Court wishes to make it." [32]

A decade of attacks by Kurland and others eventually found effective voice on the Court. At the end of the 1970s Rehnquist and Justice Lewis F. Powell, Jr., another Nixon appointee, took the lead in reviving *Erie* as a constitutional restraint on federal judicial lawmaking. In 1979 in *Cannon v. University of Chicago* they protested the Court's decision to imply a private right of action for gender discrimination under a federal education statute.[33] Powell launched a fundamental assault, indicting the majority on constitutional grounds.[34] Identifying the liberals' approach with "the regime of *Swift v. Tyson*," he leveled against it *Erie*'s indictment that "the unconstitutionality of the course pursued has now been made clear." [35] In creating private rights of action which Congress had not authorized, Powell argued, the Court had "assume[d] the legislative role." He seized on Brandeis's prudential corollary, advanced it as a substantial restraint on federal judicial lawmaking, and identified it expressly with fundamental constitutional principles. Creating private causes of action without congressional approval was "not faithful to constitutional principles" and "cannot be squared with the doctrine of separation of powers." [36] *Erie*, he insisted, was designed to limit the federal courts and to preserve the lawmaking primacy of Congress.

In succeeding cases Rehnquist developed Powell's argument and applied it to delegitimize federal judicial lawmaking in other areas. In 1980 he rejected the Court's "legislative role" in creating private causes of action to remedy constitutional violations. "The determination by federal courts of the scope of such a remedy," he charged, "involved the creation of a body of common law analogous to that repudiated in *Erie*." Rehnquist repeatedly emphasized that the jurisdiction of the federal courts was limited and that they "do not have the authority to act as general courts of common law absent authorization by Congress." *Erie*, he maintained, "expressly rejected" the majority's contrary position.[37] In 1981 he finally invoked Brandeis's decision on behalf of a restrictive conservative majority, using it in *Milwaukee v. Illinois* to abolish the Court's recently developed federal common law nuisance action for interstate water pollution. The decision to make federal law and displace state law, he insisted, was constitutionally the responsibility of Congress, not the courts. "*Erie*," Rehnquist declared, "recognized as much." [38]

Reacting to the growing political resentment against liberal judicial activism, the Nixon and Reagan justices altered the Court's course and reoriented its values. Drawing on the Powell-Rehnquist *Erie*, they curtailed the creation of new private rights of action and limited the availability of those already in existence. The Court registered the impact of Powell's opinion in *Cannon* almost immediately, narrowing the grounds on which it would imply rights of action from federal statutes and making a clearly expressed congressional intent its only criterion.[39] Similarly, the Court gradually, if less explicitly, adopted new and more restrictive standards that made the creation of implied constitutional rights of action extremely difficult.[40]

Although the Powell-Rehnquist "new" *Erie* recognized Brandeis's decision as a limit on federal judicial lawmaking, it ignored important aspects of his opinion. First, it did not address two elements of *Erie*'s constitutional theory that were problematic for its sweeping rhetoric: the principle of coextensive powers, and the declaration that state law applied "[e]xcept in matters governed by the Federal Constitution or by Acts of Congress."[41] The former qualified, and gave a special constitutional meaning to, the claim that the federal courts lacked "general" lawmaking powers. The latter meant that *Erie* had, at most, an uncertain relevance to causes of action directly based on, and intended to implement, federal statutory and constitutional provisions. Both Powell and Rehnquist seemed to be aware of the analytic gap. They failed to delineate the decision's exact doctrinal relevance, cited it only for broad propositions relating to the federal judiciary's lack of general common law powers, and essentially identified it with a broad principle of separation of powers.[42]

Second, and more obvious, the Powell-Rehnquist version failed to acknowledge *Erie*'s broader social inspiration. The two justices were concerned only with the issue of judicial lawmaking; *Erie*'s progressive social purpose was irrelevant to them. Indeed, the Court that gave birth to the "new" *Erie* showed a marked insensitivity to the substantive social inequities that had helped inspire Brandeis's decision. While the Court continued to apply *Hanna*'s "twin aims of *Erie*" test in cases of federal-state conflicts,[43] it seemed far more concerned with restricting access to the federal courts than remedying—or even recognizing—any socially "inequitable administration" of the law.[44] To a large extent, the Rehnquist Court ignored the ways in which social and economic inequality imposed de facto limitations on the ability of aggrieved persons to seek judicial relief. It construed *Erie* and *Hanna* rigidly to approve truly inequitable forum shopping tactics, and it strengthened the right of economically powerful and legally sophisticated parties to control forum choice and thereby impose heavy practical burdens and legal disadvantages on their unsuspecting adversaries.[45] The same Court that avidly embraced *Erie*'s Progressive constitutional purpose was blind to its underlying Progressive social purpose.

While the Powell-Rehnquist *Erie* provoked vigorous debate, a number of legal scholars (most of whom were political liberals sympathetic to Warren Court values) countered its implications by developing elaborate theories to support the institutional centrality of the federal courts and their power to make law.[46] The boldest and most original formulation came from Louise Weinberg, a professor at University of Texas Law School, who argued for an expansive federal judicial power that authorized the national courts to make law actively, broadly, and independently of Congress. Weinberg rejected the claim that *Erie* limited the federal courts, and she countered the constraining *Erie* of Powell and Rehnquist with her own vision of a vibrantly empowering *Erie*. As both Hart and the ALI had done before her, Weinberg made Brandeis's decision the centerpiece of a provocative effort to reconceive the scope and nature of the federal judicial power.[47]

Citing *Marbury v. Madison* for the proposition that the duty of courts is "to say what the law is," Weinberg argued in 1994 that *Marbury*'s judicial duty existed "even in the absence of any constitutional, legislative, or pre-existing decisional text." [48] She followed this with a pivotal question: "What is the source of law when a court that must decide a clearly 'federal' question finds that it has only inchoate national policy to work with?" Her answer was straightforward. "In such cases courts must face the antecedent problems of identifying national policy and its bounds, and striking a policy balance." [49] Thus, she maintained, "judicial power to fashion federal law flows from an identified national interest." Further, the Constitution commanded the federal courts to make new law to serve evolving national interests. "[A] judicial duty to fashion federal law when the national interest so requires," she declared, "is imposed by the Supremacy Clause." [50]

Weinberg's theory was sweeping and innovative. It assumed that courts could properly identify issues that were "clearly 'federal' " and that a new and supreme federal law should govern them. It assumed that the courts, independent of other institutions of government, were empowered to decide when those issues were "federal." It assumed, finally, that "inchoate national policy" or "inchoate federal policy" existed, that the federal courts had a duty to implement it, and that such inchoate policy justified the courts in making new federal law.[51] Her theory therefore authorized — indeed, required — the federal courts to make law even in the absence of constitutional and statutory provisions whenever they, in their independent opinion, thought an issue should be nationalized.

Reconceiving *Erie*, Weinberg transformed Brandeis's decision into the foundation for an expansive theory of federal judicial power.[52] She began with two propositions. One, clearly valid, was that the federal common law under *Swift* had in theory been "state" law. From that fact, she drew a fundamental conclusion. Although *Erie* overturned *Swift*, it "could not have declared [truly] federal rules of decision unconstitutional." [53] *Erie*, therefore, did not impose any limits on authentically "federal" law. The other proposition, more controversial but nevertheless consistent with Brandeis's theory, held that *Erie* was a constitutional decision based on the proper scope of national lawmaking power. Weinberg denied that *Erie* rested on "equal protection," the Tenth Amendment, or theories of separation of powers. Instead, she declared, *Swift*'s flaw — and the constitutional basis of *Erie* — lay in "the sheer lack of national lawmaking power over state law issues." [54]

On that foundation, Weinberg shaped *Erie* to make three transforming points. First, because "*Erie*'s explicit holding is that case law *is* entitled to the same deference as statute law," *Erie* analogously supported the proposition that federal law should not distinguish between legislative and judge-made rules. Rather, *Erie* suggested that both were equally legitimate.[55] Second, because *Erie* declared that Congress "has no power to declare substantive rules of common law," it constituted "a specific holding about the power of Congress as well as the federal courts." Consequently, she argued, "it is hard to make the argument that *Erie* saves for Congress powers that federal courts do not have." [56] By upholding the principle of coextensive powers, in other words, *Erie* supported the idea that the lawmaking powers of the federal courts were equal to those of Congress and could be exercised as fully and independently. Third, because *Erie* embraced a positivist conception of law, it made sovereignty the ultimate test of lawmaking power.[57] It held "that American law must be either federal or state law; there can be no hybrid third option." [58] Accordingly, *Erie* established that "[t]here is no general *state* common law either" and, hence, that federal judicial lawmaking power was no more limited in national areas of authority than state judicial power was in state areas.[59] In making law, then, the federal courts did not exercise any specially "limited lawmaking powers" inferior to those of the state courts. In all areas committed to national authority they held the full lawmaking power of the national government.[60]

Weinberg used those three elements of *Erie* — the equation of legislative and judge-made law, the principle of coextensive powers, and the embrace of constitutional positivism — to support one paramount conclusion. When "the national interest so requires, Congress has power to federalize a matter previously governed by state law." Therefore, it "would seem that that basic power must also inhere in courts." [61]

From Weinberg's perspective, the judicial power was exceptionally broad, limited not so much by express constitutional provisions as by an amorphous concept of "inchoate" national interests and policies. "[T]oday it is understood," she claimed, "that the power of Congress to federalize any issue is adequate to the national interest in doing so." [62] Indeed, the Supremacy Clause not only guaranteed the supremacy of federal law but also created a presumption against the application of state law. "It would seem," she explained, "that it is only in the absence of an overriding national interest that the nation may not trench on historic state power." Accordingly, the federal courts could make law on their own whenever they considered it appropriate to effectuate a national interest, and they could do so over the broadest area, wherever there was a "national interest in doing so." Weinberg added a single caveat. "Of course, as Justice Brandeis suggests in *Erie*, the power of courts to make federal law is no greater than the power of Congress to make federal law."[63]

The caveat, of course, was ironic. Weinberg's *Erie* was no more the *Erie* of Brandeis than the *Erie* of Hart or Rehnquist had been. As those predecessors had done, she ignored *Erie*'s social dimension. In Weinberg's case, the neglect was not for lack of sympathy but because she saw the issue of judicial lawmaking as the defining issue of her day.[64] More significantly, although she rightly discerned Brandeis's theory of coextensive powers, she ignored — indeed, buried — his prudential corollary as a serious limitation on federal judicial lawmaking. Wholly out of contact with the political values of Progressivism, she reflected not Brandeis's *Erie* but the views of Warren Court liberal nationalists who sought to repudiate the premises of a restrictive Rehnquist Court judicial conservatism.[65] In reacting to the new politics of the late twentieth century and the doctrinal potential of the Powell-Rehnquist *Erie*, she inverted the values of Brandeis's opinion to serve the cause that he and his Progressives colleagues had fought so resolutely and, by the 1990s, so long ago.

Law and Some Considerations of History

Brandeis's decision was rooted in the politico-constitutional culture of early twentieth-century Progressivism and the values and judgments of an unusual individual. That truth, of course, did not stop subsequent commentators from shaping the case, consciously or not, to their own times and purposes. Indeed, historical change and the processes of interpretation made such new versions inevitable.

Considered as a historical phenomenon, then, *Erie* suggests several general observations. One is that the decision's de facto social significance changed substantially over the course of its first half century. Originally, by requiring the national courts to apply state common law, it eliminated the divergent and often pro-corporate federal common law and thereby deprived national corporations of a significant litigation advantage. As Democratic judicial appointments transformed the political orientation of the national courts in the 1940s, however, *Erie* limited their ability to shape the common law in more liberal directions. That limitation proved relatively unimportant for liberals in the 1950s and 1960s when state courts were expanding common law remedies against corporate abuses. By the 1980s, however, as state courts became more conservative and as business-sponsored "tort reforms" succeeded in many jurisdictions, *Erie* tended increasingly to require the national courts to apply a more pro-defendant body of state common law.[66]

A second observation is that commentators have seen in Brandeis's opinion an unusually wide range of legal propositions and values. This wealth of interpretation is the result of a combination of factors. The opinion's relatively terse and misleading language compounded the normal problems of interpretation and guaranteed a wide range of diverse readings. So, too, did both the massive contextual shift that pulled the case from its original cultural moorings and the politico-constitutional realignments that subsequently inspired new uses for it. Finally, *Erie*'s kaleidoscopic quality resides in the fact that it addressed or implicated a stunning range of fundamental legal issues: federalism, *stare decisis*, separation of powers, forum shopping, judicial lawmaking, the scope of congressional power, the nature and basis of judicial authority, problems of jurisdictional manipulation and exploitative litigation tactics, the New Deal constitutional revolution, philosophical positivism and the "declarative" theory of law, and the proper constitutional role of the national judiciary. Given these factors, it is not surprising that *Erie* produced a panorama of divergent interpretations.

A third general observation is that the variety of interpretations highlighted not only a rich diversity but also a revealing consensus. Brandeis's decision, most commentators implied, concerned legal doctrines, constitutional principles, and jurisprudential theories. Although they readily acknowledged *Erie*'s facial concern with forum shopping, after the 1940s they tended to minimize and sterilize that concern. Commentators construed the opinion's language concerning forum shopping in a variety of ways: abstractly, as presenting a timeless problem of the nation's dual court system; narrowly, limiting its meaning to a historically specific set of conditions that had withered or disappeared; and formally, constricting its significance to differences that existed between the procedural rules applied in state and federal courts. Some even dismissed *Erie*'s concern with forum shopping altogether. No less an authority than Henry Hart, after all, labeled it "a minor consideration" and a "triviality."[67]

The loss of *Erie*'s social inspiration stemmed from a variety of factors. To a large extent, Brandeis himself was responsible. His tactical decision to cast his opinion in abstract terms served his immediate purposes, but it also resulted in a desiccated socio-legal inspiration that was unable to survive the next generation.[68] The loss was also due to growing preference of plaintiffs for a federal forum and the consequent transformation that occurred in the social uses of diversity jurisdiction. Together, those developments minimized *Erie*'s Progressive resonance and deprived it of much of its social relevance. Conditions in the legal academy facilitated the process of loss. The difficulty of studying de facto claim-disputing patterns, the irresistibly formalist and normative compulsions of law school scholarship, and the professional rewards and attractions of relatively traditional doctrinal work combined to direct the attention of most scholars elsewhere. Those who continued to examine questions involving social inequality focused on other more specific and immediately compelling areas such as civil rights litigation and poverty law. Finally the loss of *Erie*'s social inspiration was also due to something more—a broad professional reluctance to confront fully the awkward and embarrassing extent to which de facto social inequalities distorted the workings of the legal system and frustrated many of its proclaimed ideals.

While Brandeis's opinion encouraged a variety of interpretations, one formulation failed to capture and sustain the profession's imagination. In 1938 *Erie* stood—indeed, it still stands—as a potential cornerstone for a fundamental proposition that goes far beyond the narrow and historically specific issue of federal-state forum shopping under *Swift v. Tyson*. The proposition is as follows: legal analysis should systematically examine the dynamics of litigation practice, consider more thoroughly the role of social inequalities in determining the results of procedural and jurisdictional rules applied in the various de facto litigation processes that mark different fields of practice, and seek continually to recraft those rules in order to maximize the ability of litigants—particularly the weak, unsophisticated, and practically disadvantaged—to secure practical justice. That rich and challenging potential, however, was seldom alluded to, let alone explored in detail. Indeed, citing *Erie* in support of any such proposition, at least since the end of World War II, would have provoked little but rejection, puzzlement, amusement, or scorn. The astonishing persistence and vitality that marked debate over *Erie*'s constitutional significance and philosophical underpinnings stands in illuminating contrast to the narrowness and formality that characterized discussions of its social significance.

A fourth general observation is that *Erie* has served, somewhat ironically, as a major force in the development of the twentieth-century concept of the federal courts. In the eighteenth and early nineteenth centuries the federal judiciary was small and relatively weak, and into the twentieth century state law claims brought under diversity jurisdiction constituted a major part of its business.[69] In contrast, state courts were more prominent and numerous, and they handled the overwhelming bulk of the nation's judicial business. More important, they heard many of the nation's important and controversial cases, and they were considered appropriate and desirable forums for litigating issues of federal law. By the early twentieth century, however, the situation had changed. The national courts had increased, in number and in power. They were regarded as the specialized and authoritative voices of a supreme federal law and as the protectors of fundamental new federal rights. Although they continued to hear large numbers of relatively small private law cases, they were more frequently the forums that heard and decided the most important and controversial cases — usually involving "federal" and "public" law issues. Conversely, the state courts declined in both prestige and relative power. They continued to do the overwhelming bulk of the nation's judicial business, but their work became more heavily concentrated in the mass processing of routine and typically uncontested private law disputes. The state courts were, in the view of many, no longer desirable or even appropriate forums to hear many federal law claims, particularly the truly "important" ones.

The twentieth-century view of the federal courts evolved from a long and overlapping series of historical changes. The Civil War and Reconstruction led to centralizing constitutional amendments and dramatic expansions of federal jurisdiction, while an integrating national market and a narrow judicial selection process in the late nineteenth century induced the national courts to foster a vibrant interstate commerce and protect its various instruments. The rise of a preeminent and powerful corporate legal elite and the emergence of a specialized national law-teaching profession created articulate and compelling advocates for the congenial view that the federal courts were superior to state courts and the chosen instruments for the development of a modern national judicial system and an integrated and expansive national law. In the decades surrounding the turn of the century the Supreme Court expanded federal judicial protection for private property rights against government action and, as part of its effort, began reorienting the lower courts away from ordinary issues of state law and toward the enforcement of federal regulatory schemes and the vindication of federal constitutional rights. The spread of jurisprudential positivism, focusing attention sharply on the sovereign source of legal authority, linked the federal courts ever more tightly to federal question jurisdiction and issues of national law while identifying diversity jurisdiction as anomalous and inappropriate. Subsequent events — World War I and the Red Scare, the New Deal and the rise of a centralized bureaucratic state, World War II and the haunting image of totalitarianism, the cold war and McCarthyism, the civil rights movement and a subsequent series of civil rights and civil liberties revolutions — solidified and strengthened that evolving twentieth-century view. During the same decades a massive socio-cultural evolution was under way, leaving the nation without recognized political, cultural, and moral authorities capable of articulating and establishing consensual norms. Federal law grew in sweep and importance; the national courts became its essential agents of enforcement; and the Supreme

Court tended to serve as a voice of moral and cultural, as well as legal, authority.[70] The convergence of the Warren Court and the ALI study in the 1960s symbolized and confirmed the triumph of that twentieth-century view in the judiciary and among the professional elite.

Placed in the context of that long-term evolution, *Erie*'s major significance to the American legal system emerges as twofold. Considered narrowly and technically, it provided a constitution-based working definition of "state" law and thereby established an essential foundation for the continued operation of legal federalism in a new age of centralization, nationalization, and globalization. *Erie* joined the Court's 1875 decision in *Murdock v. City of Memphis* to identify in institutional terms the ways in which "state" law existed as an independent and authoritative body of rules.[71] *Murdock* held that the Supreme Court lacked jurisdiction to review state court judgments that were properly based on state law grounds, thereby making the state courts the final authorities on certain legal issues. *Erie* paralleled *Murdock*'s result, holding that on essentially the same legal issues the state courts were final authorities and, consequently, that the federal courts were required to follow their decisions on those issues. More important, *Erie* strengthened the *Murdock* rule by lending it constitutional authority. *Murdock* had avoided the Constitution and rested on statutory grounds, though its construction of the relevant legislation seemed questionable if not erroneous. By adopting a parallel rule and basing it on the Constitution, *Erie* provided authority for the proposition that the decision in *Murdock*—regardless of doubts about its statutory reasoning—had been correct because its holding was required by the Constitution.[72]

Considered broadly and in terms of constitutional authority, *Erie* took shape as a pillar of the twentieth-century view of the federal courts and the national legal system. Brandeis's decision was not, as Kurland claimed, a "great judicial upheaval on behalf of the states."[73] To the contrary, its greatest significance lay in precisely the opposite direction. Judge Henry J. Friendly was closer to the mark when he identified it as the case that "caused the principle of a specialized federal common law to "develop."[74] Even Friendly, however, understated its significance, for *Erie* did far more than stimulate a "new" federal common law. Rather, *Erie* was a specializing and nationalizing decision that could readily be adapted to the twentieth-century restructuring of the role and image of the federal judiciary. It helped bring diversity jurisdiction into ever growing disfavor, passed responsibility for routine and workaday common law questions to the state courts, and defined both the federal judicial power and the special province of the federal courts as the development and vindication of a supreme national law. *Erie* expanded the social and cultural power of the federal judiciary, confirming and accelerating its ascension to the position of indisputable authority on national law and the final voice on the most pressing and fundamental national controversies.[75]

The fifth observation is that although Brandeis enjoyed many successes (not least of which was *Erie*), the pressures of historical change and the dynamics of institutional power seem to have doomed much of his constitutional enterprise. Among his principal goals, Brandeis sought to restrain federal judicial lawmaking and to protect the authority of the states. Those goals helped turn him against *Swift* and diversity jurisdiction. In retrospect, what he failed to realize was that *Swift* and diversity not only expanded federal judicial power but imposed limitations as well. Of primary importance, both combined to entrench the national courts in a position of ambiguous equality with the state courts. Diversity jurisdiction focused the federal courts on ordinary common law disputes, crowded their dockets with cases presenting state law issues, and diverted their attention from the need to make truly national rules of law. Similarly, *Swift* kept the realm of "general" law—that is, "state" law—broad and undefined, freed the state courts from federal supervision and review in developing general common law doctrines, and obscured the extent to which the federal courts could develop rules of federal judge-made law that would carry the mandate of the Supremacy Clause. Although *Erie* constrained the federal courts in some ways, it also channeled them in new directions where they could enjoy freedom and, eventually, even greater power. In the late twentieth century, the United States—with its centralized national government, integrated national economy, and global environment that intensified pressures for national and international consistency, uniformity, and efficiency—those new directions offered the federal courts opportunities to assert a far more influential and sweeping lawmaking authority than they could have wielded under *Swift*.

Similarly, some of the related ideas that Brandeis advanced also contributed to frustrating his broader enterprise. He repeatedly insisted, for example, that the paramount role of the federal courts, and certainly the Supreme Court, was to deal with issues of national importance and national law. "[T]he special province of this Court," he declared, "is the Federal Law." [76] Again, he urged that the Supreme Court be given almost complete discretion to select the cases it would hear and that its docket be substantially lightened. A sharply reduced docket and tight control over its content, he explained, would enable the Court "to give adequate consideration to the adjudication of great issues of government." [77] In retrospect, the irony is clear. By focusing the national courts on distinctively federal law matters, by encouraging the Supreme Court to specialize in the "great issues of government," and by urging that the justices be given discretion to pick and choose among the cases they would decide, he helped to point the federal courts toward their richest area of action, spur a dynamic expansion of national law and federal judicial power, and encourage future Supreme Courts to set their own agendas in shaping the "great issues of government" of their day.

Brandeis, both intentionally and unintentionally, helped inspire the twentieth-century view of the federal courts that emerged during his life and became dominant in the century's second half. Although his purpose was to limit federal judicial power in opposition to the efforts of anti-Progressives like Brewer, many of the ideas he advanced most ardently led through the tangles of history in the opposite direction. Those ideas included his beliefs that diversity jurisdiction should be abolished, that federal courts should concentrate on federal law, that the Supreme Court should have discretion to focus on great issues of government, that the national judicial system should be rationalized, that the concept of "liberty" in the Fourteenth Amendment should be broadened, and that the Supreme Court should serve as a wise teacher to the nation.

That irony suggests another: however widely accepted *Erie*'s constitutional theory might be, its prudential corollary seems likely, in practice, to prove more aspirational than directive. For example, despite the Rehnquist Court's rhetorical attacks on "judicial activism" and its embrace of an ostensibly restrictive "new" *Erie*, it hardly abjured the creation of federal common law. In its most significant decision in this area, *Boyle v. United Technologies Corp.*, the Court minted a supervening federal common law defense to state tort claims that allowed government contractors to avoid suits brought by individuals injured by defective products.[78] Revealingly, *Boyle* ignored the fact that Congress had long considered and repeatedly refused to enact a bill designed to provide special protections for government contractors. More important, to erect some cover of authority for its lawmaking, the Court was compelled to rely on badly strained analogies and dubiously elastic language. The result was a decision that provided methodological license for expansive judicial lawmaking that could range far beyond the command of any constitutional or statutory provision.[79]

Boyle revealed not merely the substantive social values of the Rehnquist Court but the uncertain practical import of *Erie*'s prudential corollary. Although Powell was no longer on the Court, Rehnquist readily joined the five-justice *Boyle* majority. So, too, did Justice Antonin Scalia, a recent Reagan appointee who, like the chief justice, had repeatedly insisted on the limited nature of federal judicial power.[80] Scalia maintained that the Court could not properly imply private rights of action under federal statutes, for example, and several months after *Boyle* he urged the Court to adopt "the categorical position that federal private rights of action will not be implied."[81] Scalia wrote the majority opinion in *Boyle* notwithstanding his oft-stated general views and the obvious contrary promptings of the Powell-Rehnquist *Erie*. Indeed, and not surprisingly, in *Boyle* it was the Court's liberals who saw the virtues of limiting federal judicial law-making. Writing for four dissenters, Brennan invoked *Erie* to condemn the majority's efforts.[82] "We are judges," he chastised his colleagues, "not legislators." [83]

The importance of *Erie*'s prudential corollary (including the refurbished version that Powell and Rehnquist offered) was of uncertain import, however, not merely because substantive social values shaped the justices' conclusions concerning the desirability of judicial lawmaking. It was also of doubtful significance because the social and institutional trajectory of the twentieth century challenged the corollary's wisdom and utility, and hence its power to command judicial allegiance. In an age when organized and sophisticated interest groups methodically pressed the judicial system for advantage, the courts constantly heard cases that allowed or required them to choose between identifiable and conflicting social policies.[84] In an age when judges—certainly those on the United States Supreme Court—recognized the interpretative problems that inhered in the authoritative sources they construed, they understood the potential range of the discretion they enjoyed. And in an age of accelerating interstate and international integration they could not deny the compelling need for effective national ordering in those areas they valued most highly and thought most essential to the nation's well-being.[85] Combined with the widespread acceptance of the twentieth-century view of the federal courts, those complex forces boded ill for any consistent and highly restrictive interpretation of *Erie*'s prudential corollary.

History and Some Considerations of Law

By the century's last decade there was relatively widespread consensus that *Erie* was a decision of fundamental importance and considerable agreement that it reached constitutional stature. Hart, Warren, Powell, Rehnquist, and Weinberg all agreed with that. Most commentators continued to see federalism as *Erie*'s basic value, though an increasing number emphasized its roots in ideas concerning separation of powers. A majority recognized, correctly, that in varying ways the case served both those principles.[86] Doubters nevertheless persisted, and the Powell-Rehnquist version inspired some liberals to question or reject *Erie*'s constitutional status. Unlike the skeptics who commented on *Erie* during its first two decades, however, few scorned the decision, rejected its legitimacy, or dismissed its constitutional stature out of hand.

There was also some general agreement on two other distinct but counter-poised propositions. One was that *Erie* limited, albeit somewhat vaguely and imprecisely, the lawmaking powers of the national judiciary. The other was that it inspired, and even justified, a "special" federal common law based on constitutionally granted national lawmaking powers. Whether and to what extent those two propositions were consistent, and where the line between them should be drawn, remained subjects of profound professional controversy across a wide range of doctrines and areas. Much of the debate over *Erie* focused on this controversy as century's end approached.

Despite its status as a landmark, *Erie* declined somewhat in relative importance during the century's final quarter. Many of the complex technical problems that it created had been worked out as practical matters, and the nation's dominant constitutional controversies centered on areas that seemed remote from *Erie*'s reach.[87] Diversity jurisdiction fell into ever deeper judicial and scholarly disfavor, and commentators increasingly concentrated on "federal questions" and national law issues to which *Erie* was peripheral at best.

By the 1970s, moreover, the authority that had resided in wearing Brandeis's mantle had largely dissipated, and *Erie* was left with little of its author's social, political, and moral resonance. That result was not surprising because case law does, indeed, work itself pure. Whether or not it evolves toward "righter" rules, as that expression has been used to suggest, judge-made law does come to represent more abstract propositions by its refined process of sloughing off— and, where necessary, dismissing, altering, uncovering, or simply inventing— the historical specifics that gave rise to prior judicial decisions and then shaped their practical meanings. So, too, with *Erie*.

Brandeis was concerned with limiting federal judicial lawmaking, but neither *Erie*'s language nor any simple set of rules could fully and finally delineate the "proper" scope of such lawmaking. In different historical periods the nature of specific issues, the dynamics of driving social conflicts, and the contours of the dominant politico-constitutional culture combined to shape varying understandings of the "proper" scope of judicial lawmaking.

Indeed, Brandeis was not averse to making law himself. He pushed the Court to make law under both the Commerce Clause and the Full Faith and Credit Clause in order to restrict interstate forum shopping and rationalize the national legal system. Similarly, he was willing to expand the noneconomic constitutional rights of individuals. When the Court was prepared to announce and enforce such rights, he joined its opinions.[88] When the Court refused to take such actions, he sometimes dissented forcefully, urging the Court to protect freedom of speech,[89] expand noneconomic due process liberty and privacy rights,[90] and impose general "decency" limits on the actions the federal government could take against individuals.[91]

To some extent his judicial lawmaking can be minimized. His doctrine of Commerce Clause venue, his restrictive rulings based on the Full Faith and Credit Clause, and the decency limits he urged on the federal government, for example, were limited and easily distinguishable from the kind of judicial lawmaking the Court practiced under *Swift*. They were comparatively narrow ventures, and they were directed for the most part to the internal operations of the courts themselves.[92] Most important, they were subject to the power of Congress to alter or reject.[93]

When Brandeis sought to expand fundamental "liberty" rights, of course, he accepted the need for judicial lawmaking that was both more substantial in scope and more independent of congressional revision. Here, again, his efforts can be minimized, for they were in part a forced response to the constitutional principles of the Court's anti-Progressive majority. Contrary to his urgings, the Court repeatedly held that the Constitution protected "fundamental" liberty rights. "Despite arguments to the contrary which had seemed to me persuasive, it is settled that the due process clause of the Fourteenth Amendment applies to matters of substantive law as well as to matters of procedure," he explained in 1927. "Thus all fundamental rights comprised within the term liberty are protected by the Federal Constitution from invasion by the States." Given the majority's premise, Brandeis had little trouble beginning to suggest other rights that should be considered fundamental. "The right of free speech, the right to teach and the right of assembly are, of course, fundamental rights."[94] To some extent, then, Brandeis urged judicial lawmaking to enforce noneconomic liberty rights because the Court had embraced an overarching principle that in his view demanded such extensions in logic and justice.

Although his constitutional lawmaking can thus be minimized, it cannot and should not be explained away. Brandeis also made law because he prized certain personal liberties and social values most dearly. He believed that they were essential for full human development, and he recognized that they often needed judicial protection to ensure their free exercise.[95] He viewed his efforts as limited in scope, justified by compelling reasons, subject in some part to congressional modification, and based directly on express provisions of the Constitution. Still, he did make law, and in viewing his actions as limited and justified he undoubtedly reflected the conviction of most judges who decide in good faith that they must go beyond the letter of constitutional and statutory provisions.

Although Brandeis was committed to the principle of legislative primacy, he did not view it as an absolute value. Primacy, after all, was not supremacy. Indeed, *Erie* was not inconsistent with his constitutional lawmaking. It posed no problem for the kind of law that Brandeis made. State law simply did not apply, he wrote in *Erie*, "in matters governed by the Federal Constitution."[96]

In light of both *Erie*'s meaning and Brandeis's jurisprudence, then, the most that can fairly be drawn from the opinion as a constitutional guide is four general and elastic propositions. First, where Congress cannot legislate, the federal courts cannot make nonconstitutional rules of law. Second, where Congress has enacted legislation within its authority and the issue before the court directly implicates statutory provisions, the federal courts may make rules to supplement and effectuate those provisions. Third, where Congress can legislate but has not, the federal courts should be extremely hesitant to make new legal rules. When compelling reasons support such action, however, they may make law in certain special contexts, especially those where the issue directly involves federal judicial processes or the internal operations of the federal courts. Fourth, regardless of the authority of Congress, the Court may make rules that are necessary to enforce and protect constitutional rights, privileges, and limitations.

Concluding with propositions so general and elastic, this study seems to have little utility as a matter of "law" or normative "legal history." Such narrowly "historical" analyses, however, have their own virtues. They illuminate the inevitably evolving practice of American constitutional government and highlight its massive complexities and enduring tensions. They also help us understand the true nature of our operational "rule of law," that special historico-cultural practice that is as substantial and essential as it is manipulable and constructed. Ultimately, such histories suggest that we may understand far more about the nation's constitutional enterprise by recognizing its social and cultural foundations and its human and institutional dynamics than by straining to structure sets of formally consistent propositions or fabricating historical pedigrees for temporarily useful normative propositions.

Those observations suggest that the future vitality of *Erie*'s constitutional theory, and especially its prudential corollary, rests where Brandeis would likely have agreed that it inevitably must: in society's most deeply informed judgments about pursuing individual freedom and the common good through the instruments of popular government. *Erie*'s teachings are fundamental, but they are largely directional and aspirational, not specifically determinative. The twenty-first century, moreover, will pose its own distinct and now unfathomable challenges. Because *Erie*'s constitutional theory addresses a central tension in the American legal system, its scope cannot be "resolved" as long as Americans pursue their creaking but worthy project of constitutional government.

In that ongoing enterprise, Brandeis and *Erie* emerge as imperfect but admirable. *Erie*'s "technical" flaws are, at most, minor. More important, its incompletely expressed constitutional theory is, in its basic import, sufficiently clear. Indeed, its theory is both well-grounded and fundamentally sound. It implemented constitutional principles that protect the values of federalism, separation of powers, and popular government while preserving the full constitutional authority of the Court. Further, the fact that its constitutional theory was not fully articulated is understandable even if regrettable. The Supreme Court is, after all, a majoritarian institution, and Brandeis could write only what four other justices would accept.

Although the imperfections that have drawn the most criticism are either minor or understandable, a little-noticed flaw is more troublesome. Brandeis designed *Erie*'s social analysis to disguise what he was doing and why he was doing it. He used "facts" that misled and reasons that obscured. To some extent the fault can be mitigated. He did not ultimately rest *Erie* on its social analysis, nor did the social analysis misrepresent his own genuine dislike of manipulative forum shopping. Indeed, Brandeis had sought to constrain such tactics in other contexts, specifically to limit the ability of individual plaintiffs to use unreasonable forums against corporate defendants. Finally, he used his misleading analysis for a variety of pragmatic reasons that made his tactic seem prudent and desirable for the Court itself. Practical considerations and the demands of a majoritarian institution committed to publishing reasoned opinions make such obfuscating strategies inevitable. They should not, however, allow such judicial craft to pass unnoticed and unexamined.[97]

Brandeis's opinion likely contains yet another flaw. It may have misconstrued the "original intent" of the framers who enacted Section 34. Recent research examining the provision has seriously challenged the historical work that Brandeis cited and, further, has made a strong case that the framers could not have intended the section to carry the meaning Brandeis attributed to it.[98] Moreover, other historical studies have shown that the jurisprudential ideas Story articulated in *Swift* were common and widely accepted by American lawyers in the late eighteenth and early nineteenth centuries. *Swift*'s jurisprudence may be closer to the intent of those who drafted and ratified Section 34 than was *Erie*'s limited positivism.[99]

Assuming that Brandeis was mistaken in his historical claim concerning Section 34, several conclusions are warranted. The most obvious is that the episode constitutes another telling lesson about the pitfalls of relying on "original intent" where the historical record is less than ample and the showing less than highly probable. Another conclusion is that whatever the First Congress intended with Section 34, it surely did not intend the large-scale social practice that had evolved under *Swift* by the end of the nineteenth century. A third conclusion is that the evidence casts little light on *Erie* itself because Brandeis decided the case not on historical grounds but on grounds of *Swift*'s "defects, political and social." A final conclusion is that *Erie* is far more wisely and properly judged in light of more than two hundred years of American history and the problems and needs of the present than it is by any "intent" of those who drafted and adopted the First Judiciary Act.

One final issue remains. Was it proper for Brandeis to allow his own social and political values to influence his judicial decision? The answer, in the context of the American constitutional enterprise, if not according to everyone's normative jurisprudential theory, must be that both his decision and his behavior were proper. Supreme Court justices constantly face complex and deeply problematic issues, and they are often influenced—indeed, in many cases they must be influenced—by their personal values, beliefs, assumptions, and expectations.[100] The relevant questions (neither of which is answerable with precision or complete objectivity) are whether the justices are influenced by "improper" considerations and, ultimately but unavoidably, how Americans judge the quality of their values, the force of their reasons, the breadth of their fairness, and the nature of the consequences they bring about.

In the case of Brandeis and *Erie* the answer to the first question seems relatively straightforward, if not incontestable. The relevant personal considerations were hardly improper. Brandeis's actions were obviously not "corrupt" in any way. He did not act out of self-advantage, personal favoritism, or narrow political partisanship. His decision was based on his best, good-faith, and well-informed judgments about constitutional principles and public policy. His views, often disputed, were within the parameters of the nation's constitutional tradition and its ongoing interpretative project. Although his forum-shopping analysis was misleading, he used it to bring about greater fairness and equality in the operation of the legal system. Further, he sought to extend this fairness and equality to all parties, corporate defendants as well as individual plaintiffs.

The answer to the second question is, of course, more subjective and conducive to dispute. This book takes the position that in deciding *Erie*, Brandeis acted admirably and well as a constitutional judge. It views Brandeis not as an icon of "judicial restraint" or as a prophet of "neutral principles," but as an exemplar of deep commitment to democratic ideals, substantively just principles, wise and evenhanded administration of law, and the institutional requirements of balanced constitutional government. He was imperfect, but he did better than most.[101]

Brandeis's opinion in *Erie* illustrates his greatness as a judge sitting on that most unusual bench, the United States Supreme Court. Beyond his obvious characteristics—intelligence, dedication, discipline, honesty, and hard work—Brandeis combined three more complex and value-laden qualities that shaped both *Erie* and his general jurisprudence. First, he retained an unyielding faith in two paramount and, in his mind, profoundly linked values: human reason and popular government. He believed that careful analysis, methodical education, and determined action can enable human beings to create social and political structures that fit their ordinary capacities and empower them to control and improve their common life. Second, he understood that arbitrary and contingent social factors limit human potential, and he empathized with the relatively weak and disadvantaged. He had the intellectual honesty to recognize the ways that social inequalities allow some individuals to exploit others, and he had the decency and courage to attempt to alleviate some of those inequalities and reduce some of that exploitation. Third, he maintained an inclusive social and constitutional vision. Brandeis accepted the legitimacy of a wide range of interests and concerns, and he sought to harmonize them in a higher common good. He recognized the need for corporate business as much as he understood the need for labor unions. He understood the importance of private property and the values of the entrepreneur as much as he recognized the need for government regulation and protective social legislation. He valued the noneconomic individual freedoms and personal privacy rights that all individuals could enjoy. He embraced the idea of federalism, regarding it not as a rigid norm or a cynical excuse but as an evolving ideal to be tested by its social results. Those complex qualities—faith in reason and democracy, determination to alleviate contingent social injustice, and a balanced, inclusive, tolerant, and pragmatic vision—informed *Erie* and gave Brandeis's overarching constitutional jurisprudence its integrity, its power, and its virtue.

Notes

INTRODUCTION

1 304 U.S. 64 (1938); *Erie* has been hailed for more than half a century as a "great case" and a jurisprudential "landmark," but it has also provoked an unusual amount and range of discord. One prominent theorist, for example, explains that *Erie* "is by no means simply a case" but rather "the very essence of our federalism"; another cites it as illustrating an exemplary mode of constitutional interpretation; a third sees it as embodying a revolution in twentieth-century legal thinking; a fourth conceives it as the inspiration for a fundamental reorientation in American jurisprudence following World War II. John Hart Ely, "The Irrepressible Myth of *Erie*," 87 *Harvard Law Review* 693, 695 (1974); Philip Bobbitt, *Constitutional Interpretation* (Cambridge, Mass., 1991), 158–59; Cass R. Sunstein, *The Partial Constitution* (Cambridge, Mass., 1993), 54–55; Bruce A. Ackerman, *Private Property and the Constitution* (New Haven, Conn., 1977), 272 n. 4.

The use of *Erie* as symbolic, exemplary, or representative is widespread. *See, e.g.,* Abram Chayes, "How Does the Constitution Establish Justice?" 101 *Harvard Law Review* 1026 (1988) (*Erie* is an example of the confused understanding of the nature of federal judicial power and the design of the Constitution in establishing justice, at 1029–31); Steven Stark, "The Real Meaning of *Erie*," 17 *Connecticut Law Review* 723 (1985) (*Erie* "has no meaning at all" but gained "notoriety" because it is "a case that explains how the [law] game is played," at 728); John W. Johnson, *American Legal Culture, 1908–1940* (Westport, Conn., 1981) (*Erie* is an example of the growing influence of law reviews because it "wrote the thesis of [a specific] law review article into law," at 64); William R. Casto, "The *Erie* Doctrine and the Structure of Constitutional Revolutions," 62 *Tulane Law Review* 907 (1988) (*Erie* is the result of generational change and the triumph of legal positivism: "an anticlimactic consequence of an ideological revolution," at 950); Lawrence Lessig, "Understanding Changed Readings: Fidelity and Theory," 47 *Stanford Law Review* 395 (1995) (*Erie* is the result of "a transformation in legal discourse" and part of a "pattern" of twentieth-century legal change that can be termed the "*Erie* effect," at 432, 433); Richard A. Posner, *Law and Legal Theory in England and America* (New York, 1996) ("The jurisprudential debate in *Swift* and *Erie* illustrates the difference between contextual and acontextual definitions of 'law,' " at 1); Kelly D. Hine, "The Rule of Law Is Dead, Long Live the Rule: An Essay on Legal Rules, Equitable Standards, and the Debate Over Judicial Discretion," 50 *Southern Methodist University Law Review* 1769, 1773 (1997) (*Erie* is the culmination of a historical move toward legal determinacy and the rule of law).

2 For recent discussions of some of the differences between "forensic" or "law office history" and the historian's analysis of people, events, ideas, and institutions related to "law,"
see Martin S. Flaherty, "History 'Lite' in Modern American Constitutionalism," 95 *Columbia Law Review* 523 (1995); John Phillip Reid, "Law and History," 27 *Loyola of Los Angeles
Law Review* 193 (1993); and Carol Greenhouse, "Just in Time: Temporality and the Cultural
Legitimation of Law," 98 *Yale Law Journal* 1631 (1989).

3 The cites are, respectively, Frank I. Michelman, "Property, Federalism, and Jurisprudence:
A Comment on *Lucas* and Judicial Conservatism," 35 *William and Mary Law Review* 301,
319 (1993); and Akhil Reed Amar, "Law Story," 102 *Harvard Law Review* 688, 693 (1989).

4 326 U.S. 99 (1945); 380 U.S. 460 (1965); 441 U.S. 677 (1979).

5 The legal literature on "original intent" (including its variations such as "original meaning" and "original understanding") has grown immense. *See, e.g.,* Jack N. Rakove, *Original
Meanings: Politics and Ideas in the Making of the Constitution* (New York, 1996), and the
excellent review by Christopher L. Eisgruber, "Early Interpretations & Original Sin," 95
Michigan Law Review 2005 (1997). For a provocative recent critique *see* Christine A. Desan,
"The Constitutional Commitment to Legislative Adjudication in the Early American Tradition," 111 *Harvard Law Review* 1381 (1998), and for a more general discussion in terms of the
historical writing *see* David Harlan, *The Degradation of American History* (Chicago, 1997).

6 Many legal commentators, of course, adopt various analytic limitations to formalize the idea
of original intent in order to render it more malleable and useful. As a means to construct
normative legal arguments, such a strategy is understandable and probably unavoidable. As
a method of exploring and understanding past events, it is distorting and ultimately arbitrary. To the extent that one makes the quest for an original intent a truly historical inquiry,
the concept becomes diffuse, subjective, highly complex, partly unspecifiable, and to some
extent ultimately unknowable. Its normative implications are few and general at best, and its
legal significance tends to become vague, uncertain, and nondirective. To the extent that one
limits the quest by eliding historical complexities and adopting simplifying and restrictive
assumptions, the concept becomes increasingly predetermined, formalistic, expedient, and
arbitrary. Its normative implications tend to flow ever more directly from the number and
nature of the limiting assumptions. *See, e.g.,* Ronald Dworkin, *A Matter of Principle* (Cambridge, Mass., 1985), 34–57; Richard A. Epstein, *Takings: Private Property and the Power of
Eminent Domain* (Cambridge, Mass., 1985), 26–29; Antonin Scalia, *A Matter of Interpretation: Federal Courts and the Law* (Princeton, N.J., 1997), 37–41.

7 Thus, although the book assumes much of the "postmodern" critique of human inquiry, it
regards the insights of that critique as ultimately preliminary. For a recent example of a sensible discussion of both the strengths and limits of historical analysis applied to legal issues,
see Martin S. Flaherty, "The Most Dangerous Branch," 105 *Yale Law Journal* 1725 (1996).
More generally, *see* Joyce Appleby, Lynn Hunt, and Margaret Jacob, *Telling the Truth about
History* (New York, 1994).

CHAPTER 1. THE PREMISE OF AN AGE

1 Similar conflicts marked earlier periods. *See, e.g.,* Richard Ellis, *The Jeffersonian Crisis:
Courts and Politics in the Young Republic* (New York, 1971); Charles M. Cook, *The American
Codification Movement: A Study of Antebellum Legal Reform* (Westport, Conn., 1981).

2 *E.g.,* Nathan Miller, *Theodore Roosevelt: A Life* (New York, 1992), 522.

3 Roscoe Pound, "Common Law and Legislation," 21 *Harvard Law Review* 383, 384 (1908).

4 Felix Frankfurter, *Law and Politics: Occasional Papers of Felix Frankfurter, 1913–1938;* Archibald MacLeish and E. F. Pritchard, Jr., eds. (New York, 1962 [1939]), 4.

5 Learned Hand, *The Spirit of Liberty: Papers and Addresses of Learned Hand,* Irving Dilliard, ed. (New York, 1959), 15.

6 Felix Frankfurter to Benjamin Flexner, Feb. 16, 1921, Frankfurter Papers, Box 55, folder 1038.

7 Herbert Croly, *Progressive Democracy* (New York, 1914), 366, 368.

8 Pound, "Common Law and Legislation," 384. *See, e.g.,* Croly, *Progressive Democracy,* 362–71; Walter Lippmann, *Drift and Mastery* (New York, 1914), 157; Edward A. Purcell, Jr., "Learned Hand: The Jurisprudential Trajectory of an Old Progressive," 43 *Buffalo Law Review* 873, 890–94 (1995); Clarence E. Wunderlin, Jr., *Visions of a New Industrial Order: Social Science and Labor Theory in America's Progressive Era* (New York, 1992), 26.

9 Charles F. Amidon to Oliver Wendell Holmes, Jr., Jan. 19, 1911, Holmes Papers, Box 37, folder 20.

10 Quoted in David Brody, *Steelworkers in America: The Nonunion Era* (New York, 1960), 264.

11 United States Industrial Commission, *Report of the Industrial Commission on the Relations and Conditions of Capital and Labor Employed in Manufactures and General Business* (Washington, D.C., 1901), Vol. 7, at 657.

12 Learned Hand to Gilbert Roe, Nov. 7, 1913, Hand Papers, Box 37, folder 13.

13 Hand, *Spirit of Liberty,* 19.

14 Charles A. Beard, *The Supreme Court and the Constitution* (New York, 1912); Beard, *An Economic Interpretation of the Constitution* (New York, 1913).

15 Lawrence M. Friedman, *A History of American Law,* 2d ed. (New York, 1985), 355–63.

16 Loren P. Beth, *The Development of the American Constitution, 1877–1917* (New York, 1971), 83.

17 *E.g.,* John R. Schmidhauser, *Judges and Justices: The Federal Appellate Judiciary* (Boston, 1979), ch. 3; Gerald G. Eggert, *Railroad Labor Disputes: The Beginnings of Federal Strike Policy* (Ann Arbor, Mich., 1967), 234–35.

18 John R. Schmidhauser, "The Justices of the Supreme Court: A Collective Portrait," 3 *Midwest Journal of Political Science* 1 (1959).

19 *See, e.g.,* Charles W. McCurdy, "American Law and the Marketing Structure of the Large Corporations, 1875–1890," 38 *Journal of Economic History* 631 (1978); *Welton v. Missouri,* 91 U.S. 275 (1875).

20 Edward A. Purcell, Jr., *Litigation and Inequality: Federal Diversity Jurisdiction in Industrial America, 1870–1958* (New York, 1992), 61–86.

21 *Compare Loewe v. Lawlor,* 208 U.S. 274 (1908) with *United States v. E.C. Knight Co.,* 156 U.S. 1 (1895). *See* Beth, *Development of the American Constitution,* ch. 5.

22 *Pollock v. Farmers' Loan & Trust Co.,* 157 U.S. 429 (1895).

23 State courts had begun to develop the doctrine in the middle of the nineteenth century. Howard Gillman, *The Constitution Besieged: The Rise and Demise of Lochner Era Police Power Jurisprudence* (Durham, N.C., 1993), 45–60.

24 *Santa Clara County v. Southern Pacific Railroad Co.,* 118 U.S. 394 (1886).

25 *Chicago, Milwaukee & St. Paul Railway. Co. v. Minnesota,* 134 U.S. 418, 458 (1890).

26 *Allgeyer v. Louisiana,* 165 U.S. 578 (1897); *Chicago, Burlington & Quincy Railroad v. Chicago,* 166 U.S. 226 (1897); *Lochner v. New York,* 198 U.S. 45 (1905).

27 Donald Richberg, "The Menace of Government by Injunction," *The Locomotive Engineers Journal* (January 1923), 11, 13, Richberg Papers, Box 5, folder 1922–23.

28 William D. Guthrie, *Lectures on the Fourteenth Article of Amendment* (Boston, 1898), 45.

29 The idea that the courts were "formalist" in the period from 1877 to 1937 derives from this premise and from the respective strategies of the two opposing sides. The fact that judicial "formalism" remained a major issue among historians for more than half a century testifies to the scope and intensity of the long struggle as well as to the triumph after 1937 of the Progressive view. As a category for either legal or historical analysis, "formalism" is partial, misleading, and largely off the point.

30 Arnold M. Paul, *Conservative Crisis and the Rule of Law: Attitudes of Bar and Bench, 1887–1895* (New York, 1960), ch. 10; Samuel Haber, *The Quest for Authority and Honor in the American Professions, 1750–1900* (Chicago, 1991), esp. ch. 6.

31 Christopher G. Tiedeman, *A Treatise on the Limitations of Police Power in the United States* (St. Louis, 1886), vii. *See* William P. LaPiana, "Jurisprudence of History and Truth," 23 *Rutgers Law Journal* 519 (1992).

32 Robert Stevens, *Law School: Legal Education in America from the 1850s to the 1980s* (Chapel Hill, N.C., 1983); William P. LaPiana, *Logic & Experience: The Origin of Modern American Legal Education* (New York, 1994).

33 Robert H. Wiebe, *The Search for Order, 1877–1920* (New York, 1967), 117.

34 Gerald Carson, *A Good Day at Saratoga* (Chicago, 1978), 12.

35 *See, e.g.,* Jerold S. Auerbach, *Unequal Justice: Lawyers and Social Change in Modern America* (New York, 1976), ch. 1; Friedman, *History of American Law,* 606–29, 633–54; Wayne K. Hobson, "Symbol of the New Profession: Emergence of the Large Law Firm, 1870–1915," in Gerard W. Gawalt, ed., *The New High Priests: Lawyers in Post-Civil War America* (Westport, Conn., 1984), 3–27; Robert W. Gordon, "Legal Thought and Legal Practice in the Age of American Enterprise, 1870–1920," in Gerald L. Geison, ed., *Professions and Professional Ideologies in America* (Chapel Hill, N.C., 1983), 70–110.

36 William C. Miller, *Men in Business* (Cambridge, Mass., 1952), 276–88.

37 Albert Martin Kales, "The Next Step in the Evolution of the Case-book," 21 *Harvard Law Review,* 92, 114 (1907). *See* Alexander M. Bickel and Benno C. Schmidt, Jr., *The Judiciary and Responsible Government, 1910–1921* (New York, 1984), 15, 16; Michael Kammen, *A Machine that Would Go of Itself: The Constitution in American Culture* (New York, 1986), chs. 7–8.

38 Guthrie, *Lectures on the Fourteenth Article of Amendment,* 31.

39 *Id.* at 31–32. *See* Purcell, *Litigation and Inequality,* 287–91.

40 *See, e.g.,* Joseph W. Bailey, "The American Judiciary," 1 *American Bar Association Journal* 496 (1915); Henry Schofield, "Swift v. Tyson: Uniformity of Judge-Made State Law in State and Federal Courts," 4 *Illinois Law Review* 533 (1910); Edward C. Eliot, "The Common Law of the Federal Courts," 36 *American Law Review* 498 (1902); Frederick Green, "The Law as Precedent, Prophecy, and Principle: State Decisions in the Federal Courts," 19 *Illinois Law Review* 217, 223 (1924).

41 Simeon E. Baldwin, *The American Judiciary* (New York, 1914 [1905]), 75, 77, 171.

42 *Id.* at 375.

43 *Id.* at 383.

44 *Id.* at 374.

45 *Id.* at 382.

46 *Id.* at 385–86.

47 *Id.* at 386.

48 Alan F. Westin, "The Supreme Court, the Populist Movement and the Campaign of 1896," 15 *Journal of Politics* 3, 38 (1953).

49 John W. Akin, "Aggressions of the Federal Courts," 32 *American Law Review* 669, 679 (September–October 1898).

50 L. B. Boudin, "Government by Judiciary," 26 *Political Science Quarterly* 238 (1911).

51 198 U.S. 45 (1905).

52 Learned Hand, "Due Process of Law and the Eight-Hour Day," 21 *Harvard Law Review* 495, 508 (1908). *See* Paul Kens, *Judicial Power and Reform Politics: The Anatomy of Lochner v. New York* (Lawrence, Kans., 1990).

53 *See* William G. Ross, *A Muted Fury: Populists, Progressives, and Labor Unions Confront the Courts, 1890–1937* (Princeton, N.J., 1994).

54 *E.g.,* William Jennings Bryan, "The People's Law," address at Columbus, Ohio, Mar. 12, 1912, Bryan Papers, Box 49; Donald Richberg, "Constitutional Growth Through Recall of Decisions," *Annals of the American Academy of Political and Social Science* (March 1914), 25. *See* Stephen Stagner, "The Recall of Judicial Decisions and the Due Process Debate," 24 *American Journal of Legal History* 257 (1980).

55 Act of Feb. 11, 1903, 30 Stat. 823; Act of June 29, 1906, 34 Stat. 584, 592; Act of June 18, 1910, 36 Stat. 539, 557; Act of Mar. 4, 1913, 37 Stat. 1013, 1014. *See generally* John E. Lockwood, Carlyle E. Maw, and Samuel L. Rosenberry, "The Use of the Federal Injunction in Constitutional Litigation," 43 *Harvard Law Review* 426 (1930).

56 Act of Apr. 5, 1910, 36 Stat. 291; Act of Jan. 28, 1915, 38 Stat. 804; Act of June 5, 1920, 41 Stat. 988. *See, e.g.,* Sen. Rep. No. 432, 61 Cong., 2 sess. (1910); and H.R. Rep. No. 513, 61 Cong., 2 sess. (1910).

57 *See generally* Kenneth M. Murchison, *Federal Criminal Law Doctrines: The Forgotten Influence of National Prohibition* (Durham, N.C., 1995); Richard F. Hamm, *Shaping the Eighteenth Amendment: Temperance Reform, Legal Culture, and the Polity, 1880–1920* (Chapel Hill, N.C., 1995).

58 John D. Hicks, *Republican Ascendency, 1921–1933* (New York, 1960), 260; American Law Institute, *A Study of the Business of the Federal Courts: Part I, Criminal Cases* (Philadelphia, 1934), 32–38, Detailed Table 1 at 107; *id. Part II, Civil Cases* (Philadelphia, 1934), Detailed Table 1 at 111; 72 *Cong. Rec.*, 71 Cong., 2 sess. (1930), 4962–63, 7462–63.

59 "Greater Judicial Efficiency," 7 *American Bar Association Journal* 533 (1921).

60 72 *Cong. Rec.*, 71 Cong., 2 sess. (1930), 4966. *See, e.g.,* 62 *Cong. Rec.*, 67 Cong., 2 sess. (1921), 146–69; 67 *Cong. Rec.*, 69 Cong., 1 sess. (1926), 12540–42.

61 John E. Semonche, *Charting the Future: The Supreme Court Responds to a Changing Society, 1890–1920* (Westport, Conn. 1978), 424–25.

62 Paul L. Murphy, *The Constitution in Crisis Times, 1918–1969* (New York, 1972), ch. 2. *E.g., Adkins v. Childrens Hospital*, 261 U.S. 525 (1923).

63 *Hammer v. Dagenhart*, 247 U.S. 251 (1918); *Bailey v. Drexel Furniture Co.*, 259 U.S. 20 (1922). *See generally* Stephen B. Wood, *Constitutional Politics in the Progressive Era: Child Labor and the Law* (Chicago, 1968).

64 Donald R. Richberg, *Tents of the Mighty* (New York, 1930), 160, 166.

65 LeRoy Ashby, *The Spearless Leader: Senator Borah and the Progressive Movement in the 1920s* (Urbana, Ill., 1972), 31–32; Steven F. Lawson, "Progressives and the Supreme Court: A Case for Judicial Reform in the 1920s," 42 *Historian* 419 (1980); Erik Olssen, "The Progressive Group in Congress, 1922–1929," 42 *Historian* 244 (1980); Ross, *Muted Fury*, ch. 8.

66 *E.g.,* Sen. Rep. No. 842, 69 Cong., 1 sess. (1926) (a bill limiting the power of judges to express

to the jury their "personal opinion" about credibility of witnesses or weight of evidence). See Ross, *Muted Fury*, chs. 8–13.

67 Robert M. La Follette, "Supreme Court Rules the Nation" (Madison, Wisc.) *Capitol Times* June 29, 1922, La Follette Family Papers, Series B, Robert M. La Follette, Box 226.

68 Kenneth Campbell MacKay, *Progressive Movement* (New York, 1947), 11, 144.

69 Charles Evans Hughes, speech at St. Paul, Minn., Oct. 25, 1924, Hughes Papers, Box 181, file no. 18.

70 "The Endless Battle for Constitutional Principle," 12 *American Bar Association Journal*, 464, 465 (1926).

71 Quoted in newspaper report, *The Virginia Pilot and the Norfolk Standard*, Feb. 9, 1928, McReynolds Papers, Box 4, folder F-2.

72 *See generally* Thomas K. McCraw, *TVA and the Power Fight* (Philadelphia, 1971); Lockwood, Maw, and Rosenberry, "The Use of the Federal Injunction in Constitutional Litigation."

73 *Chicago, Milwaukee & St. Paul Railroad Co. v. Minnesota*, 134 U.S. 418 (1890); *Smyth v. Ames*, 169 U.S. 466 (1898); *Ex parte Young*, 209 U.S. 123 (1908).

74 *Prentis v. Atlantic Coast Line Co.*, 211 U.S. 210 (1908); *Bacon v. Rutland Railroad Co.*, 232 U.S. 134 (1914).

75 *Pacific Telephone & Telegraph Co. v. Kuykendall*, 265 U.S. 196 (1924); *Porter v. Investors Syndicate*, 286 U.S. 461 (1932).

76 Sen. Rep. No. 125, Pt. 2, 73 Cong., 1 sess. (1933), p. 5.

77 David E. Lilienthal, "The Federal Courts and State Regulation of Public Utilities," 43 *Harvard Law Review* 379, 381 n. 6 (1930).

78 *Interborough Rapid Transit Co. v. Gilchrist*, 25 F.2d 164, 26 F.2d 912 (S.D.N.Y. 1928), *reversed*, 279 U.S. 159 (1929).

79 S. 4491 and H.R. 95, 70 Cong., 1 sess. (1928); H.R. 135, 71 Cong., 1 sess.; S. 3085, 71 Cong., 2 sess (1930).

80 Press release of Sen. Robert F. Wagner (undated), Frankfurter Papers, Box 179, folder 3456.

81 69 *Cong. Rec.*, 70 Cong., 1 sess., 3472, 3473 (1928). *See* Sen. Rep. No. 701, 72 Cong., 1 sess. (1932).

82 Lilienthal, "Federal Courts and State Regulation of Public Utilities," at 416, 419, 421, 422.

83 John E. Benton to George W. Norris, Apr. 12, 1932, Norris Papers, Tray 42, Box 8. *See, e.g.*, Russell B. Harrison, to Norris, Feb. 24, 1934, and J. F. Shaughnessy to Sen. Tasker L. Oddie, Mar. 24, 1932, Norris Papers, Tray 78, Box 6.

84 Clyde L. Seavey, Address before National Association of Railroad and Utilities Commissioners, *circa* 1931, Norris Papers, Tray 42, Box 8.

85 Hiram W. Johnson to Chas. K. McClatchy, Feb. 23, 1934, Johnson Papers, Part III, Box 16. *See generally* Richard Coke Lower, *A Bloc of One: The Political Career of Hiram W. Johnson* (Stanford, Calif., 1993).

86 Spencer Olin, *California's Prodigal Son: Hiram Johnson and the Progressives, 1911–1917* (Berkeley, Calif., 1968), 35–39.

87 Hiram W. Johnson to J. Earl Langdon, Dec. 8, 1933, Johnson Papers, Part III, Box 15.

88 S. 3243, 72 Cong., 1 sess. (1932).

89 *See, e.g.*, letters collected in Norris Papers, Tray 78, Box 6.

90 Edward W. Everett to Members of Committee on Jurisprudence and Law Reform, Mar. 8, 1934, Baker Papers, Box 21, "ABA—1934"; Clarence E. Martin to J. Harvey Covington,

May 20, 1933, Baker Letters, Box 20, "ABA — 1934"; Edward W. Everett to Newton D. Baker, Dec. 12, 1933, Baker Papers, Box 20, "ABA — 1933."

91 Hiram W. Johnson to Hiram W. Johnson, Jr., Feb. 11, 1934, Johnson Papers, Part VI, Box 6.
92 Hiram W. Johnson to Hiram W. Johnson, Jr., May 13, 1934, Johnson Papers, Part VI, Box 6.
93 78 *Cong. Rec.*, 73 Cong., 2 Sess. (1934), 8322 (Congressman O'Connor of New York).
94 78 *Cong. Rec.*, 73 Cong., 2 Sess. (1934), 8337 (Congressman McGugin of Kansas).
95 78 *Cong. Rec.*, 73 Cong., 2 Sess. (1934), 8332.
96 78 *Cong. Rec.*, 73 Cong., 2 Sess. (1934), 8331.
97 Edward W. Everett to Members of Committee on Jurisprudence and Law Reform, Mar. 8, 1934, Baker Papers, Box 21, "ABA — 1934."
98 Throughout the debate, advocates of the Johnson bill repeatedly invoked the magic of Roosevelt's name and emphasized his support. 78 *Cong. Rec.*, 73 Cong., 2 sess. (1934), 8339, 8340, 8342, 8350, 8415, 8435. *Accord* Edward W. Everett to Earl W. Evans, Mar. 6, 1934, Baker Papers, Box 21, "ABA — 1934."
99 Quoted in Judson King, "The Stake of the Consumer and Investor" (from Franklin D. Roosevelt, Special Message to the Legislature, Jan. 27, 1930), at 22, pamphlet enclosed with letter from George W. Norris to Hiram Johnson, Sept. 17, 1932, Johnson Papers, Part III, Box 62.
100 Homer S. Cummings to Franklin D. Roosevelt, Apr. 20, 1934, Roosevelt Papers, OF 41, Box 114; and Cummings to Roosevelt, May 14, 1934, Roosevelt Papers, OF 5708, Box 3; Max Freedman, ed., *Roosevelt & Frankfurter: Their Correspondence, 1928–1945* (Boston, 1967), 198–99.
101 Hiram W. Johnson to Chas. K. McClatchy, Feb. 23, 1934, Johnson Papers, Part III, Box 16.
102 Hiram W. Johnson to Chas. K. McClatchy, May 11, 1934, Johnson Papers, Part III, Box 16. *See* Note, "Limitation of Lower Federal Court Jurisdiction Over Public Utility Rate Cases," 44 *Yale Law Journal* 119 (1934).
103 *See, e.g.,* 46 American Bar Association *Reports,* 325–40 (1928). There were, of course, many varieties of professional law reform and reformers. *See, e.g.,* William P. LaPiana, " 'A Task of No Common Magnitude': The Founding of the American Law Institute," 11 *Nova Law Review* 1085 (1987); N. E. H. Hull, "Restatement and Reform: A New Perspective on the Origins of the American Law Institute," 8 *Law and History Review* 55 (1990); Michael Ariens, "Progress Is Our Only Product: Legal Reform and the Codification of Evidence," 17 *Law & Social Inquiry* 213 (1992); Lawrence M. Friedman, "Law Reform in Historical Perspective," 13 *St. Louis University Law Journal* 351 (1969); John Henry Schlegel, *American Legal Realism and Empirical Social Science* (Chapel Hill, N.C., 1995), ch. 1.
104 David Wigdor, *Roscoe Pound: Philosopher of Law* (Westport, Conn., 1974), 126–27.
105 Alpheus Thomas Mason, *William Howard Taft: Chief Justice* (New York, 1964), chs. 2, 4; Peter Graham Fish, *The Politics of Federal Judicial Administration* (Princeton, N.J., 1973), chs. 1–2; Fish, "William Howard Taft and Charles Evans Hughes: Conservative Politicians as Chief Judicial Reformers," 1975 *Supreme Court Review* 123, 129–30.
106 *See* Fish, *Politics of Federal Judicial Administration,* chs. 1–3.
107 The American Judicature Society, founded in 1913, quickly lent its support to the effort. *See, e.g.,* "A Fundamental Principle Violated," 1 *Journal of the American Judicature Society* 13 (1917).
108 17 Stat. 197 (1872), then codified as 28 USCA 724.
109 46 *Cong. Rec.*, 61 Cong., 3 sess. (1910), 25; quoted in Mason, *William Howard Taft,* 52.

110 37 American Bar Association *Reports*, 35–36, 142, 434–35 (1912).

111 Thomas W. Shelton to Frederick L. Wadhams, Mar. 4, 1920, Walsh Papers, Box 281, "Judi-ciary." *Accord* Shelton to Thomas J. Walsh, May 12, 1926, Walsh Papers, Box 302. For discus-sions of the history of the ABA bill and the Rules Enabling Act, *see* Peter Charles Hoffer, "Text, Translation, Context, Conversation: Preliminary Notes for Decoding the Delibera-tions of the Advisory Committee that Wrote the Federal Rules of Civil Procedure," 37 *American Journal of Legal History* 409 (1993); Janice Toran, " 'Tis a Gift To Be Simple: Aes-thetics and Procedural Reform," 89 *Michigan Law Review* 352 (1990); Stephen N. Subrin, "How Equity Conquered the Common Law: The Federal Rules of Civil Procedure in His-torical Perspective," 135 *University of Pennsylvania Law Review* 909 (1987); Stephen B. Bur-bank, "The Rules Enabling Act of 1934," 130 *University of Pennsylvania Law Review* 1015 (1982); Subrin, "Federal Rules, Local Rules, and State Rules: Uniformity, Divergence, and Emerging Procedural Patterns," 137 *University of Pennsylvania Law Review* 1999 (1989).

112 *E.g.*, Edmund M. Morgan, "Judicial Regulation of Court Procedure," 2 *Minnesota Law Re-view* 81, 86 (1918); Henry W. Taft, "Uniformity of Procedure in the Federal Courts," 12 *American Bar Association Journal* 20 (1926).

113 Roscoe Pound, "The Rule-Making Power of the Courts," 12 *American Bar Association Jour-nal* 599, 603 (1926).

114 Purcell, *Litigation and Inequality*, 150–54.

115 Carl Wheaton, "Procedural Improvements and the Rule-Making Power of Our Courts," 22 *American Bar Association Journal*, 642, 644 (1936).

116 *See, e.g.*, the opposition to the ABA bill reflected in George W. McClintic to Thomas J. Walsh, May 20, 1926, Walsh Papers, Box 302, "Procedural bill"; Fish, "William Howard Taft and Charles Evans Hughes," 137.

117 John H. Wigmore, "All Legislative Rules for Judiciary Procedure Are Void Constitution-ally," 23 *Illinois Law Review*, 276, 278 (1928).

118 "Uniform Judicial Procedure," 7 *American Bar Association Journal* 121 (1921).

119 "Improved Methods of Judicial Procedure," 12 *American Bar Association Journal* 546, 547 (1926).

120 Mason, *William Howard Taft*, 91.

121 Thomas W. Shelton to Roscoe Pound, Apr. 5, 1926, Pound Papers, Series II, Box 32, folder 25. *See* Shelton to Pound, Jan. 31, 1923, *id.*

122 Freedman, ed., *Roosevelt & Frankfurter*, 319.

123 Thomas J. Walsh to R. W. Oglesby, Mar. 22, 1927, Walsh Papers, Box 302, "Procedural bill"; George W. Norris to Charles B. Letton, June 8, 1926, Norris Papers, Tray 6, Box 8, "Judi-ciary (reform of) (1913–1931)"; Thomas W. Shelton to Roscoe Pound, Dec. 4, 1926, Pound Papers, Series II, Box 32, folder 25.

124 Hiram W. Johnson to Hiram W. Johnson, Jr., Apr. 7, 1934, Johnson Papers, Part VI, Box 6.

125 *See, e.g.*, Edson R. Sunderland, "The Grant of Rule-Making Power to the Supreme Court of the United States," 32 *Michigan Law Review* 1116, 1128 (1934).

126 One proponent of the bill acknowledged, "[t]he amount of litigation carried on in the federal courts is insignificant compared with that transacted in the courts of the States." Sunder-land, "Grant of Rule-Making Power," 1126.

127 Learned Hand to Thomas J. Walsh, May 25, 1926, Walsh Papers, Box 302; Learned Hand to Albert Cummins, Feb. 1, 1924, Hand Papers, Box 18, folder 10; Charles E. Clark, "The Pro-posed Federal Rules of Civil Procedure," 22 *American Bar Association Journal*, 447 (1936).

128 Charles E. Clark and James Wm. Moore, "A New Federal Civil Procedure," 44 *Yale Law Journal* 387, 390 (1935).

129 Charles Evans Hughes to Harlan F. Stone, Mar. 7, 1935, Stone Papers, Box 81. *See* George W. McClintic to Thomas J. Walsh, May 20, 1926, Walsh Papers, Box 302, "Procedure bill"; 57 American Bar Association *Reports* 118–19, 575 (1932); Harlan F. Stone to C. C. Burlingham, Mar. 13, 1935, Stone Papers, Box 81.

130 Sen. Rep. No. 1174, 69 Cong., 1 Sess. (1926), 22 (minority views of Sen. Walsh). *See* Thomas J. Walsh to Robert Jackson, Apr. 19, 1927, Walsh Papers, Box 302; Walsh to Gilbert P. Bullis, Nov. 2, 1926, Walsh Papers, Box 302.

131 Thomas J. Walsh, "Rule-Making Power on the Law Side of Federal Practice," 13 *American Bar Association Journal,* 87, 90 (1927).

132 Sen. Rep. No. 1174, 69 Cong., 1 sess. (1926), 33–34.

133 Walsh, "Rule-Making Power on the Law Side," 91. *See* Sen. Rep. No. 1174, 69 Cong., 1 sess. (1926), 26–27.

134 Sen. Rep. No. 1174, 69 Cong., 1 sess. (1926), 13; Thomas W. Shelton to Roscoe Pound, Aug. 21, 1922, Pound Papers, Series II, Box 32, folder 25; Thomas W. Shelton, "Report No. 3 to Committee on Uniform Judicial Procedure," Nov. 28, 1922, Pound Papers, Series II, Box 32, folder 25.

135 Thomas W. Shelton to Roscoe Pound, Feb. 8, 1924, Pound Papers, Series II, Box 32, folder 25. *Accord* Shelton to Pound, Aug. 4, 1925, and Dec. 4, 1926, *id.*

136 *E.g.,* Thomas J. Walsh to Albert E. Cummins, Dec. 3, 1924, Walsh Papers, Box 281, "Legislation File"; Thomas W. Shelton to Walsh, May 12, 1926, Walsh Papers, Box 302, "Procedural Bill."

137 Quoted in Mason, *William Howard Taft,* 94. *See* Roscoe Pound, "Senator Walsh on Rule Making Power on the Law Side of Federal Practice," 13 *American Bar Association Journal* 84 (1927).

138 Sen. Rep. No. 440, 70 Cong., 1 sess. (1928).

139 Quoted in Mason, *William Howard Taft,* 94.

140 57 American Bar Association *Reports,* 118–19, 575 (1932); 58 *id.,* 110 (1933).

141 *See* Homer S. Cummings, "Immediate Problems for the Bar," 20 *American Bar Association Journal* 212 (1934).

142 Authur M. Schlesinger, Jr., *The Age of Roosevelt: The Coming of the New Deal* (Boston, 1965), 549.

143 Cummings, "Immediate Problems for the Bar," 212, 213; Sen. Rep. No. 1049, 73 Cong., 2 sess. (1934), 1; H.R. Rep. No. 1829, 73 Cong., 2 sess. (1934), 2.

144 48 Stat. 1064 (1934), then codified as 28 USCA 723b, 723c. *See* H.R. Rep. No. 1829, 73 Cong., 2 sess. (1934); Homer S. Cummings to Franklin D. Roosevelt, June 12, 1934, Roosevelt Papers, OF 5708, Box 5.

145 *See generally* Peter H. Irons, *The New Deal Lawyers* (Princeton, N.J., 1982); William E. Leuchtenburg, *The Supreme Court Reborn: The Constitutional Revolution in the Age of Roosevelt* (New York, 1995); and Barry Cushman, *Rethinking the New Deal Court: The Structure of a Constitutional Revolution* (New York, 1998).

146 Leonard Baker, *Back to Back: The Duel Between FDR and the Supreme Court* (New York, 1967), 108; "Statement of Mr. Wm. Nelson Cromwell," Committee of the Bar for Hoover in the State of New York, Hoover Papers, Pres. Subj. File — Judiciary, Sup. Ct. of United States, Correspondence, Box 192. On the attitude of elite lawyers toward the New Deal *see* Ronen

Shamir, *Managing Legal Uncertainty: Elite Lawyers in the New Deal* (Durham, N.C., 1995).

147 *See* materials collected in Roosevelt Papers, OF 41 A, Box 116. *See also, e.g.,* Hiram W. Johnson to Hiram W. Johnson, Jr., Dec. 27, 1935, Johnson Papers, Part VI, Box 7; Franklin D. Roosevelt to Homer S. Cummings, Jan. 14, 1936, Roosevelt Papers, OF 10, Box 6.

148 Homer S. Cummings to Franklin D. Roosevelt, June 2, 1936, Roosevelt Papers, OF 10, Box 5. *See also* Homer S. Cummings to Franklin D. Roosevelt, July 19, 1935, Roosevelt Papers, OF 10, Box 4; Robert H. Jackson, *The Struggle for Judicial Supremacy: A Study of a Crisis in American Power Politics* (New York, 1941), 118–19; Cummings to Roosevelt, Jan. 21, 1936, Roosevelt Papers, OF 10, Box 5; Sen. Doc. Nos. 25–33, 37–44, 75 Cong., 1 sess. (1937); Frederic C. Howe to George W. Norris, June 4, 1937, Norris Papers, Tray 79, Box 6, File: Judicial Anti-Injunction, 1933–"; Sen. Res. No. 82, 75 Cong., 1 sess. (1937); William H. Harbaugh, *Lawyer's Lawyer: The Life of John W. Davis* (New York, 1973), 365–72.

149 *Morehead v. New York ex rel. Tipaldo,* 298 U.S. 587 (1936); *United States v. Butler,* 297 US 1 (1936).

150 297 U.S. at 78, 87 (Stone, J., dissenting).

151 Jackson, *Struggle for Judicial Supremacy,* x, xi.

152 William E. Leuchtenburg, "The Origins of Franklin D. Roosevelt's 'Court-Packing' Plan," 1966 *Supreme Court Review* 347, 373.

153 Franklin D. Roosevelt, "A Recommendation to Reorganize the Judicial Branch of the Federal Government," H.R. Doc. No. 142, 75 Cong., 1 sess. (1937).

154 *Id.* at 4.

155 *Id.* at 6–7.

156 Herbert Hoover, *Addresses Upon the American Road, 1933–1938* (New York, 1938), 230.

157 Samuel I. Rosenman, ed., *The Public Papers and Addresses of Franklin D. Roosevelt,* Vol. 5 (1937) (New York, 1941), 75–77.

158 *Id.* at 126, 128. *See* Freedman, ed., *Roosevelt & Frankfurter,* 381.

159 James MacGregor Burns, *Roosevelt: The Lion and the Fox* (New York, 1956), 300.

160 Burns, *Roosevelt,* 298–99; Baker, *Back to Back,* 72–78.

161 Statement of Hon. Burton K. Wheeler, Hearings before the Senate Judiciary Committee, Mar. 22, 1937, 75 Cong., 1 sess. (1937), 487–92.

162 *West Coast Hotel v. Parrish,* 300 U.S. 379 (1937).

163 *National Labor Relations Board v. Jones & Laughlin Steel Co.,* 301 U.S. 1 (1937).

164 *Steward Machine Co. v. Davis,* 301 U.S. 548 (1937); *Helvering v. Davis,* 301 U.S. 619 (1937).

165 *E.g.,* Thurman Arnold, *Voltaire and the Cowboy,* Gene M. Gressley, ed. (Boulder, Colo., 1977), 250, 252–53; Hiram W. Johnson to Matt. I Sullivan, Apr. 13, 1937, Johnson Papers, Part VI, Box 7; Diary of J. F. T. O'Connor, Vol. 5, Mar. 29, 1937, O'Connor Papers; Leuchtenburg, *Franklin D. Roosevelt and the New Deal,* 237.

166 Baker, *Back to Back,* 225–31; Burns, *Roosevelt,* 306; George F. Sparks, ed., *A Many-Colored Toga: The Diary of Henry Fountain Ashurst* (Tucson, Ariz., 1962), 374.

167 Rosenman, ed., *Papers and Addresses of Franklin D. Roosevelt,* Vol. 5 (1937), 338–42; Sen. Rep. No. 963, 75 Cong., 1 sess. (1937); 50 Stat. 751 (1937); Homer S. Cummings to Franklin D. Roosevelt, Aug. 17, 1937, Roosevelt Papers, OF 41 A, Box 117.

168 50 Stat. 738 (1937).

169 *E.g., United States v. Butler,* 297 U.S. 1, 78–79 (Stone, J., dissenting); Jackson, *Struggle for Judicial Supremacy,* vi–vii.

170 Leuchtenburg, *Franklin D. Roosevelt and the New Deal,* 251.

171 Alan Brinkley, *The End of Reform: New Deal Liberalism in Recession and War* (New York, 1995); James T. Patterson, *Congressional Conservatism and the New Deal: The Growth of the Conservative Coalition in Congress, 1933–1939* (Lexington, Ky., 1967); Richard Polenberg, *Reorganizing Roosevelt's Government: The Controversy Over Executive Reorganization, 1936–1939* (Cambridge, Mass., 1966); Barry D. Karl, *Executive Reorganization and Reform in the New Deal: The Genesis of Administrative Management, 1900–1939* (Cambridge, Mass., 1963); Barry D. Karl, *The Uneasy State* (Chicago, 1983).

172 *See* Brinkley, *The End of Reform;* Sidney M. Milkis, *The President and the Parties: The Transformation of the American Party System Since the New Deal* (New York, 1993); John W. Jeffries, "The 'New' New Deal: FDR and American Liberalism, 1937–1945," 105 *Political Science Quarterly* 397 (1990).

CHAPTER 2. EXPANDING THE FEDERAL JUDICIAL POWER

1 On the Court's acceptance of reform legislation *see* Melvin I. Urofsky, "Myth and Reality: The Supreme Court and Protective Legislation in the Progressive Era," 1983 *Yearbook of the Supreme Court Historical Society* 53; for the complex roots of its jurisprudence *see* Howard Gillman, *The Constitution Besieged: The Rise and Demise of Lochner Era Police Power Jurisprudence* (Durham, N.C., 1993). On the Court's failure to protect noneconomic rights, *see, e.g., Patterson v. Colorado*, 205 U.S. 454 (1907) (First Amendment); *Giles v. Harris*, 189 U.S. 475 (1903) (black voting rights); *United States v. Ju Toy*, 198 U.S. 253 (1905) (due process for alleged aliens claiming citizenship); Michael J. Klarman, "Race and the Court in the Progressive Era," 51 *Vanderbilt Law Review* 881 (1998).

2 *Hale v. Henkel*, 201 U.S. 43, 76 (1906).

3 Questions about the Court's motivations have long been debated. As we Americans have moved further from the experiences of those who felt the harsh consequences of industrialization, their cries have grown fainter. As we have grown more accustomed to, and satisfied with, the benefits of large-scale corporate capitalism, their fears and protests have seemed increasingly dubious. And as our faith in the ability and integrity of government has declined, their proposals for "regulation and reform" have steadily lost favor. Recent decades, therefore, have cast new and more favorable light on the turn-of-the-century Court. Indeed, its accomplishments are admired by both contemporary conservatives who preach the virtues of the market and contemporary liberals who honor the federal courts as instruments of social reform.

The justices on the turn-of-the-century Court were not in any simple sense "pro-corporate," and all of them—even the most staunchly "conservative"—acceded to a broad range of regulatory efforts. All the justices wished to check government favoritism and the creation of legal privilege, and they all believed in such time-honored American ideals as popular government, individual liberty, and (as an essential element of the latter) the right to private property. To some extent, too, they were influenced by the Jacksonian commitment to equality, the free-labor ideas of the anti-slavery movement, and ideas associated with classical and neoclassical economics.

Although those ideas and values helped shape the attitudes of the justices, by themselves they determined neither the nature of the Court's jurisprudence nor the content of its decisions. In fact, most Americans agreed with most of those general ideas and values. The question the Court faced in each case was what they meant on the particular facts presented and in the radically new social context of the late nineteenth and early twentieth century.

What exactly was "liberty"? Whose liberty would be protected, against whom, under what conditions, and to what extent? Indeed, the votes of the individual justices were often influenced by a wide range of case-specific concerns that included race, federalism, the particular governmental agency or state involved, and the specific activity or commodity that was being regulated.

A number of intangible and complex factors also influenced their work. One was the fact that the justices constituted a remarkably similar, if not insular, social group. Trained and experienced at the bar, steeped in the revered common law, and coming largely from the ranks of the corporate elite, they were highly successful Anglo-Saxon males, predominantly Protestant, college-educated, and middle class in upbringing. They shared high social status, a cult of masculinity, and connections with powerful political and economic actors. Consequently, to varying degrees they began to share concerns about the dangerous potential of labor unions, "populistic" democracy, rapacious legislatures, the industrial working class, and "hordes" of non–Anglo-Saxon Protestant immigrants.

A second critical factor was that the justices lived in a period marked profoundly by a sense of class conflict, social fragmentation, and loss of moral and cultural order. Urbanization and suburbanization, Darwinism and a broader secular naturalism, the influx of Jews and Catholics from southern and eastern Europe, and the appearance of a new kind of commercial culture based on advertising and mass marketing combined to challenge the dominance of Protestantism, the verities of Victorian morality, and the traditional assumptions of American politics. Together, those forces generated a variety of internal doubts and a strongly felt need for order and authority. Increasing the ability of the federal courts to supervise national affairs and ensure the rule of law seemed a natural and desirable way to deal with those problems.

A third critical factor was the ambivalence the justices shared with most Americans concerning industrialization and its far-reaching consequences. On the one hand they were concerned with the harsh human consequences of industrialism, the unprecedented power of the new national corporations, and, as Justice Rufus Peckham rued, the closing of economic opportunities for "small dealers and worthy men" (*United States v. Trans-Missouri Freight Association*, 166 U.S. 290, 323 (1897)). On the other hand, they were awed and fascinated with the wonders of industrial progress. "It cannot be to the real interest of anyone to injure or cripple the resources of the railroad companies of the country," Peckham also believed, "because the prosperity of both the railroads and the country is most intimately connected" (*Ex parte Young*, 209 U.S. 123, 166 (1908)). For such a social group as the justices, it would have been difficult to prevent the latter from outweighing the former and, in critical cases, trumping laws designed to assist disfavored social groups and purposes.

4 *Chicago, Milwaukee and St. Paul Railway Co. v. Minnesota*, 134 U.S. 418, 458 (1890).

5 134 U.S. at 461 (Bradley, J., dissenting with Gray and Lamar, JJ.).

6 *Lochner v. New York*, 198 U.S. 45, 57 (1905).

7 *Mobile and Ohio Railroad Co. v. Tennessee*, 153 U.S. 486 (1894); *Muhlker v. New York and Harlem Railroad Co.*, 197 U.S. 544 (1905). *See* James W. Ely, Jr., *The Chief Justiceship of Melville W. Fuller, 1888–1910* (Columbia, S.C., 1995), 103–17.

8 *Chicago, Burlington and Quincy Railroad Co. v. Chicago*, 166 U.S. 226 (1897) (Takings Clause); *Hale v. Henkel*, 201 U.S. 43 (1906) (Fourth Amendment).

9 *E.g., Cleveland, Cincinnati, Chicago and St. Louis Railway Co. v. Illinois*, 177 U.S. 514 (1900).

See David P. Currie, *The Constitution in the Supreme Court, the Second Century: 1888–1986* (Chicago, 1990), 31–40; Ely, *The Chief Justiceship of Melville W. Fuller*, 140–48; Alexander M. Bickel and Benno C. Schmidt, *The Judiciary and Responsible Government, 1910–1921* (New York, 1984), 265–70; Charles W. McCurdy, "American Law and the Marketing Structure of the Large Corporation, 1875–1890," 38 *Journal of Economic History* 631 (1978).

10 The Court ruled several congressional statutes unconstitutional. *E.g., Employers' Liability Cases*, 207 U.S. 463 (1908); *Adair v. United States*, 208 U.S. 161 (1908). Usually, however, it treated congressional power more broadly. *E.g., Swift v. United States*, 196 U.S. 375 (1905); *Houston, East and West Texas Railway Co. v. United States*, 234 U.S. 342 (1914). *See generally* Owen M. Fiss, *Troubled Beginnings of the Modern State, 1888–1910* (New York, 1993).

11 *E.g., Interstate Commerce Commission v. Cincinnati, New Orleans & Texas Pacific Railway*, 167 U.S. 479 (1897) (denying the commission power to set rates); *Johnson v. Southern Pacific Co.*, 196 U.S. 1 (1904) (broadly construing the railroad Safety Appliance Act). *See* Ely, *Fuller Court*, 91–94; Edward A. Purcell, Jr., *Litigation and Inequality: Federal Diversity Jurisdiction in Industrial America, 1870–1958* (New York, 1992), 164.

12 *See, e.g.,* Rudolph J. R. Peritz, *Competition Policy in America, 1888–1992: History, Rhetoric, Law* (New York, 1996), 26–58.

13 *Texas & Pacific Railway Co. v. Abilene Cotton Oil Co.*, 204 U.S. 426 (1907); Bickel and Schmidt, *Judiciary and Responsible Government*, 270–75; Stephen A. Gardbaum, "The Nature of Preemption," 79 *Cornell Law Review* 767 (1994).

14 The Court's landmark decision establishing the right to a "fair return" on investment for regulated companies required elaborate fact-finding to determine whether challenged rates were "reasonable." *Smyth v. Ames*, 169 U.S. 466, 546–47 (1898).

15 *Reagan v. Farmers' Loan and Trust Co.*, 154 U.S. 362 (1894); *Smyth v. Ames*, 169 U.S. 466 (1898); *Prout v. Starr*, 188 U.S. 537 (1903); *Gunter v. Atlantic Coast Line Railroad Co.*, 200 U.S. 273 (1906).

16 *Siler v. Louisville & Nashville Railroad Co.*, 213 U.S. 174 (1909).

17 The lower federal court began to appoint receivers in the 1870s, and in the 1890s the Supreme Court approved their general efforts in a series of decisions. *See* Charles Warren, "Federal and State Court Interference," 43 *Harvard Law Review* 345, 364–66; Robert W. Gordon, "Legal Thought and Legal Practice in the Age of American Enterprise," in Gerald L. Geison, *Professions and Professional Ideologies in America* (Chapel Hill, N.C., 1983), 70, 101–7. After the turn of the century the Court approved more extended postdischarge supervision by federal courts. *E.g., Wabash Railroad Co. v. Adelbert College*, 208 U.S. 38 (1908); *Palmer v. Texas*, 212 U.S. 118 (1909).

18 *Corbus v. Alaska Treadwell Gold Mining Co.*, 187 U.S. 455 (1903); *Venner v. Great Northern Railway Co.*, 209 U.S. 24 (1908). *See* Herbert Hovenkamp, *Enterprise and American Law, 1836–1937* (Cambridge, Mass., 1991), 44–45.

19 *E.g., Dietzsche v. Huidekoper*, 103 U.S. 494 (1881); *Julian v. Central Trust Co.*, 193 U.S. 93 (1904); *Gunter v. Atlantic Coast Line Railroad Co.*, 200 U.S. 273 (1906). *See generally* Warren, "Federal and State Court Interference."

20 *E.g., Davis & Farnum Manufacturing Co. v. Los Angeles*, 189 U.S. 207 (1903); *Dobbins v. Los Angeles*, 195 U.S. 223 (1904).

21 209 U.S. 123 (1908). For background on the case *see* Richard C. Cortner, *The Iron Horse and the Constitution: The Railroads and the Transformation of the Fourteenth Amendment* (West-

port, Conn., 1993), chs. 6–8. For a thoughtful view that minimizes the importance of *Young*, *see* Ann Woolhandler, "The Common Law Origins of Constitutionally Compelled Remedies," 107 *Yale Law Journal* 77, 81 (1997).

22 *See, e.g.,* Burton D. Wechsler, "Federal Courts, State Criminal Law and the First Amendment," 49 *New York University Law Review* 741 (1974).

23 The Court had long been able to avoid the Eleventh Amendment when necessary. During Reconstruction, however, it gave the amendment a greater breadth which required, in turn, a further narrowing after 1890. *See* John V. Orth, *The Judicial Power of the United States: The Eleventh Amendment in American History* (New York, 1987).

24 The requirement of an independent legal wrong was stated, *e.g.,* in *Pennoyer v. McConnaughy*, 140 U.S. 1, 10 (1891). *See* Currie, *The Constitution in the Supreme Court, The Second Century,* 50–54.

25 *E.g., Tennessee v. Union and Planters' Bank,* 152 U.S. 454 (1894). The Court developed the "well-pleaded complaint" rule after Congress conferred federal question jurisdiction on the national courts in 1875. It used the rule as a device to narrow that jurisdiction and control the growing federal caseload. It also expanded the rule's reach in the 1890s prior to its general reorientation of the lower courts away from diversity issues and toward federal law issues after 1900. Purcell, *Litigation and Inequality,* 268–72. Even after 1900, however, it continued to enforce the rule. *E.g., Louisville & Nashville Railroad Co. v. Mottley,* 211 U.S. 149 (1908). It was for that reason, among others, that *Young's* implied federal cause of action was of such importance. *See generally* Michael G. Collins, "The Unhappy History of Federal Question Removal," 71 *Iowa Law Review* 717 (1986).

26 *E.g., Fitts v. McGhee,* 172 U.S. 516, 530 (1899).

27 *E.g.,* Benno C. Schmidt, Jr., "Juries, Jurisdiction, and Race Discrimination: The Lost Promise of *Strauder v. West Virginia*," 61 *Texas Law Review* 1401, 1441 and n. 187 (1983).

28 209 U.S. at 176.

29 *Willcox v. Consolidated Gas Co.,* 212 U.S. 19, 39–40 (1909).

30 *Home Telephone and Telegraph Co. v. Los Angeles,* 227 U.S. 278, 284, 285 (1913).

31 At various times and in various areas during the nineteenth century, of course, the Court had sought to bring certain cases involving federal questions within the jurisdiction of the lower federal courts. *See, e.g.,* Orth, *Judicial Power of the United States,* ch. 3; Woolhandler, "Common Law Origins," 89–99. Until the early twentieth century, however, the Court treated diversity jurisdiction relatively favorably and, in some ways, more favorably than federal question jurisdiction. Purcell, *Litigation and Inequality,* 266–91; Woolhandler, "Common Law Origins," 130.

32 *Prentis v. Atlantic Coast Line Co.,* 211 U.S. 210 (1908); *Bacon v. Rutland Railroad Co.,* 232 U.S. 134 (1914).

33 *E.g., Western Union Telegraph Co. v. Kansas,* 216 U.S. 1 (1910); *Pullman Co. v. Kansas,* 216 U.S. 56 (1910). States could not directly limit federal jurisdiction. Because they had the power to exclude foreign corporations from conducting intrastate business, however, many of them compelled those corporations to accept limits on their ability to use the federal courts in exchange for the right to do local business. Under the doctrine of "unconstitutional conditions" the Court began systematically striking down those state-imposed limits. *See* Gerard C. Henderson, *The Position of Foreign Corporations in American Constitutional Law: A Contribution to the History and Theory of Juristic Persons in Anglo-American Law* (Cambridge, Mass., 1918), esp. ch. 8.

34 The requirement was a basic principle of equity which Congress put into statutory form in Section 16 of the Judiciary Act of 1789. Although the Court had touched on the issue as early as 1819, the nature and basis of the controlling rule remained unsettled into the early twentieth century. The Court held state court remedies "adequate" to defeat federal equity jurisdiction, *e.g.,* in *Insurance Co. v. Bailey,* 80 U.S. (13 Wall.) 616 (1871) and *Cable v. United States Life Insurance Co.,* 191 U.S. 288 (1903). See John Norton Pomeroy, Jr., *Pomeroy's Equity Jurisprudence and Equitable Remedies* (San Francisco, Calif., 1905), Vol. 2, 1154 n. 46. Major milestones toward establishing the ultimate rule included *McConihay v. Wright,* 121 U.S. 201, 205–6 (1887); *Smyth v. Ames,* 169 U.S. 466, 516 (1898); and *Singer Sewing Machine Corp. v. Benedict,* 229 U.S. 481 (1913). By the 1920s the Court stated the rule flatly. *E.g., Chicago, Burlington & Quincy Railroad Co. v. Osborne,* 265 U.S. 14, 16 (1924); *Risty v. Chicago, Rock Island & Pacific Railway Co.,* 270 U.S. 378, 388 (1926). *See generally* Note, "Effect of the Existence of an Adequate Remedy at Law in the State Courts on Federal Equity Jurisdiction," 49 *Harvard Law Review* 950 (1936); Benjamin F. Keller, "Jurisdiction of the Federal Equity Courts as Affected by State Statutes," 47 *American Law Review* 190 (1913).

35 209 U.S. at 166.

36 Purcell, *Litigation and Inequality,* 262–91. Similarly, the Court rigorously enforced the anti-removal provision of the Federal Employers' Liability Act, a measure that was compatible with the Court's effort after 1900 to reorient the workload of the lower courts away from private law tort claims and toward issues of broader national importance. *E.g., Kansas City Southern Railway Co. v. Leslie,* 238 U.S. 599 (1915); *Southern Railway Co. v. Lloyd,* 239 U.S. 496 (1916).

37 *Doctor v. Harrington,* 196 U.S. 579 (1906) (shareholder derivative suits); *Re Metropolitan Railway Receivership,* 208 U.S. 90 (1908) (railroad receivership).

38 *Madisonville Traction Co. v. Saint Bernard Mining Co.,* 196 U.S. 239 (1905). The decision was arguably inconsistent with *Upshur County v. Rich,* 135 U.S. 467 (1890). The Court had often used diversity jurisdiction to bring important national issues into the federal courts. *See* Purcell, *Litigation and Inequality,* 255–56; Woolhandler, "Common Law Origins," 89–99.

39 *Deposit Bank v. Frankfort,* 191 U.S. 499, 517 (1903). *Accord Gunter v. Atlantic Coast Line Railroad Co.,* 200 U.S. 273, 290–91 (1906). *See* Stephen B. Burbank, "Interjurisdictional Preclusion, Full Faith and Credit and Federal Common Law: A General Approach," 71 *Cornell Law Review* 733, 751–52 (1986).

40 *General Oil Co. v. Crain,* 209 U.S. 211 (1908).

41 *Second Employers' Liability Cases,* 223 U.S. 1 (1912); *Seaboard Air Line Railway v. Horton,* 233 U.S. 492 (1914). *Accord Southern Railway Co. v. Gray,* 241 U.S. 333 (1916).

42 The old rule was stated, *e.g.,* in *Egan v. Hart,* 165 U.S. 188, 191 (1897); and *E. Bement & Sons v. National Harrow Co.,* 186 U.S. 70, 83 (1902). The new rule was suggested in *Kansas City Southern Railway Co. v. C. H. Albers Commission Co.,* 223 U.S. 573, 591–94 (1912); *Cedar Rapids Gas Light Company v. City of Cedar Rapids,* 223 U.S. 655, 668–69 (1912); and *Washington v. Fairchild,* 224 U.S. 510, 526–28 (1912). *See* Richard F. Wolfson and Philip B. Kurland, *Robertson and Kirkham's Jurisdiction of the Supreme Court of the United States* (New York, 1951), 191–207.

43 *Creswill v. Grand Lodge Knights of Pythias of Georgia,* 225 U.S. 246, 261 (1912).

44 *Cedar Rapids Gas Co. v. Cedar Rapids,* 223 U.S. 655, 668–69 (1912). Although the Court sometimes suspected state court decisions, it seldom acknowledged the fact. For a rare example, *see Terre Haute and Indianapolis Railroad Co. v. Indiana,* 194 U.S. 579, 589 (1904).

45 *Deposit Bank v. Frankfort,* 191 U.S. 499, 518 (1903). The Court's concern with maintaining

federal jurisdiction was so intense that in 1908 it suggested in *dictum* that there were constitutional limits on the power of Congress to place "exceptions and regulations" on its
appellate jurisdiction. *United States v. Bitty,* 208 U.S. 393, 399–400 (1908). Similarly, following the lynching of an imprisoned black defendant in 1906, the Court in an extraordinary
move initiated its own contempt proceeding against local officials in Tennessee for willful
disregard of its order staying execution pending appeal. *United States v. Shipp,* 214 U.S. 386,
414, 425 (1909). Although singular, the action symbolized the Court's determination to see
its mandate enforced. *See* Willard L. King, *Melville Weston Fuller: Chief Justice of the United
States, 1888–1910* (Chicago, 1950), 323–27.

46 If, as Owen Fiss has recently written, Brewer and Justice Rufus Peckham were the "intellectual leaders" of the Court, Brewer probably had both the greater influence and the broader
and more activist jurisprudence. Fiss, *Troubled Beginnings of the Modern State,* 28, 33–37.

47 The most complete account of Brewer's life is Michael J. Brodhead, *David J. Brewer: The Life
of a Supreme Court Justice, 1837–1910* (Carbondale, Ill., 1994). J. Gordon Hylton has written
three insightful articles: "David Josiah Brewer and the Christian Constitution," 81 *Marquette
Law Review* 417 (1998); "David Josiah Brewer: A Conservative Justice Reconsidered," 1994
Supreme Court History 45; and "The Judge Who Abstained in *Plessy v. Ferguson:* Justice David
Brewer and the Problem of Race," 61 *Mississippi Law Journal* 315 (1991). For a critical account
see Arnold M. Paul, "David J. Brewer," in Leon Friedman and Fred L. Israel, eds., *The Justices
of the United States Supreme Court, 1789–1969, Their Lives and Major Opinions,* 4 Vols. (New
York, 1969), 1515; for a sympathetic account *see* Ralph E. Gamer, "Justice Brewer and Substantive Due Process: A Conservative Court Revisited," 18 *Vanderbilt Law Review* 61 (1965).

48 Cyrus W. Field was a successful manufacturer, merchant, and newspaper owner, best known
for promoting the first trans-Atlantic telegraph cable. David Dudley Field was a leader of
the New York bar and one of the nation's most prominent legal reformers. He drafted the
Field Code of civil procedure to modernize the common law and influenced the subsequent
development of civil procedure in both the federal courts and in the courts of England.
Stephen J. Field served as chief justice of the California Supreme Court, where he also helped
promote the reform of civil procedure. In 1863 he was named to the United States Supreme
Court by Abraham Lincoln and served there for thirty-four years. Henry M. Field, the least
well known of the brothers, was a prominent clergyman as well as a writer and editor. *See*
Brian J. Moline, "David J. Brewer," in Clare Cushman, ed., *The Supreme Court Justices: Illustrated Biographies, 1789–1995,* 2d ed. (Washington, D.C., 1995), 251, 252.

49 Hylton, "David Josiah Brewer and the Christian Constitution," 419–22.

50 The most recent biography of Field is Paul Kens, *Justice Stephen Field: Shaping Liberty from
the Gold Rush to the Gilded Age* (Lawrence, Kans., 1997).

51 David J. Brewer, "The Supreme Court of the United States," 33 *Scribner's Magazine* 273, 279
(1903).

52 David J. Brewer, "The Nation's Safeguard," *Proceedings of the New York State Bar Association,* 16th Annual Meeting (New York, 1893), 39.

53 Brewer, "Nation's Safeguard," 40.

54 David J. Brewer, "The Nation's Anchor," 57 *Albany Law Journal* 166, 170 (1898).

55 *Id.,* 169.

56 *South Carolina v. United States,* 199 U.S. 437, 448 (1905) (Brewer, J.).

57 David J. Brewer, "The Federal Judiciary," *Twelfth Annual Meeting of the Bar Association of
the State of Kansas,* 81, 83 (1895).

58 *Church of the Holy Trinity v. United States,* 143 U.S. 457 (1892) (Brewer, J.).

59 David J. Brewer, "Protection to Private Property from Public Attack," 55 *New Englander and Yale Review* (August, 1891), 97, 98. *Accord Budd v. New York,* 143 U.S. 517, 548, 550 (1892) (Brewer, J., dissenting).

60 Brewer, "Protection to Private Property," 108.

61 Brewer, "Nation's Safeguard," 39.

62 Brewer, "Supreme Court," 273, 276, 277.

63 Brewer, "Nation's Anchor," 167.

64 Brewer, "Federal Judiciary," 83.

65 Brewer, "Nation's Safeguard," 46.

66 David J. Brewer, "Growth of the Judicial Function," *Report of the Organization and First Annual Meeting of the Colorado Bar Association,* 82, 90 (1898).

67 Brewer, "Nation's Safeguard," 44.

68 David J. Brewer, address to the Colorado Bar Association, *Report of the Sixth Annual Meeting,* 46, 47 (1903).

69 *United States v. Detroit Timber and Lumber Co.,* 200 U.S. 321, 339 (1906) (Brewer, J.).

70 *Mississippi Mills v. Cohn,* 150 U.S. 202 (1893).

71 *E.g., Leadville Coal Co. v. McCreery,* 141 U.S. 475 (1891); *Louisville Trust Co. v. Louisville, New Albany and Chicago Railway Co.,* 174 U.S. 674 (1899).

72 Brewer, "Nation's Anchor," 167. Brewer defended federal equity jurisdiction broadly, *e.g.,* in *Reagan v. Farmers' Loan and Trust Co.,* 154 U.S. 362 (1894).

73 Brewer, "Growth of the Judicial Function," 90.

74 Brewer, "Federal Judiciary," 83.

75 Brewer, "Nation's Safeguard," 41.

76 Brewer, "Supreme Court," 284.

77 Brewer joined the Court in invalidating government action, *e.g.,* in *Lake Shore and Michigan Southern Railway Co. v. Smith,* 173 U.S. 684 (1899); he dissented from denial of a challenge to state action, *e.g.,* in *Magoun v. Illinois Trust and Savings Bank,* 170 U.S. 283, 301 (Brewer, J., dissenting); *Freeport Water Co. v. Freeport City,* 180 U.S. 587, 601 (White, J., dissenting, joined by Brewer, Brown, and Peckham, JJ.); and *Atkin v. Kansas,* 191 U.S. 207, 224 (Fuller, C.J., and Brewer and Peckham, JJ., dissenting).

78 Concerning workers: *e.g., Holden v. Hardy,* 169 U.S. 366, 398 (1898) (Brewer, J., dissenting); *McLean v. Arkansas,* 211 U.S. 539, 552 (1909) (Brewer, J., dissenting). Concerning labor unions: *e.g., In re Debs,* 158 U.S. 564 (1895) (Brewer, J.); *Adair v. United States,* 208 U.S. 161 (1907); *Loewe v. Lawlor,* 208 U.S. 247 (1908). Concerning tort claimants: *e.g., Union Pacific Railway Co. v. Botsford,* 141 U.S. 250, 258 (1891) (Brewer, J., dissenting); *Northern Pacific Railway Co. v. Dixon,* 194 U.S. 338 (1904) (Brewer, J.); *Schlemmer v. Buffalo, Rochester and Pittsburg Railway Co.,* 205 U.S. 1, 14 (1907) (Brewer, J., dissenting); *The Employers' Liability Cases,* 207 U.S. 463, 504 (1908) (Peckham, J., concurring, joined by Brewer, J.).

79 Brewer dissented from decisions upholding police power regulations, *e.g.,* in *Knoxville Iron Co. v. Harbison,* 183 U.S. 13, 22 (1901); and *North American Cold Storage Co. v. Chicago,* 211 U.S. 306 (1908). He dissented more frequently than any justice except Harlan. King, *Melville Weston Fuller,* 340–41.

80 Brewer, "Protection to Private Property," 109.

81 *Chicago & Northwestern Railway Co. v. Dey,* 35 F. 866 (Cir. Ct. S.D. Iowa 1888) (Brewer, C.J.); *Budd v. New York,* 143 U.S. 517, 548 (1892) (Brewer, J., dissenting); *Brass v. North Dakota,* 153

U.S. 391, 405 (1894) (Brewer, J., dissenting); *Reagan v. Farmers' Loan and Trust Co.*, 154 U.S. 362 (1894) (Brewer, J.).

82 Brewer, "Protection to Private Property," 102.

83 *Monongahela Navigation Co. v. United States*, 148 U.S. 312, 326, 327 (1893) (Brewer, J.); *Chicago, Burlington and Quincy Railroad Co. v. Chicago*, 166 U.S. 226, 258, 259 (1897) (Brewer, J., dissenting).

84 There were also, of course, apparent inconsistencies. *Compare, e.g.:* on statutory construction, *Church of the Holy Trinity v. United States*, 143 U.S. 457 (1892) *with Clyatt v. United States*, 197 U.S. 207 (1905); on statutory provisions providing for attorneys' fees, *Gulf, Colorado and Santa Fe Railway Co. v. Ellis*, 165 U.S. 150 (1897) *with Atchison, Topeka and Santa Fe Railroad Co. v. Matthews*, 174 U.S. 96 (1899). *See* Hylton, "The Judge Who Abstained in *Plessy v. Ferguson*," 353–58.

85 *E.g., Atchison, Topeka and Sante Fe Railroad Co. v. Matthews*, 174 U.S. 96 (1899) (Brewer, J.); *Smiley v. Kansas* 196 U.S. 447 (1905) (Brewer, J.). *See* Ely, *The Chief Justiceship of Melville W. Fuller*, 75; Hylton, "David Josiah Brewer and the Christian Constitution," 423.

86 Brodhead, *David J. Brewer*, 105–8, 116–38, 168–87; Hylton, "The Judge Who Abstained in *Plessy v. Ferguson*," 353–58.

87 Illustrating the complexities of Supreme Court judging, Brewer did not invariably join the Court's efforts to expand federal judicial power. *See Madisonville Traction Co. v. Saint Bernard Mining Co.*, 196 U.S. 239, 257 (1905) (Brewer, J., dissenting); *Deposit Bank v. Frankfurt*, 191 U.S. 499, 521 (1903) (Brewer, J., dissenting); Brodhead, *David J. Brewer*, 172.

88 *Budd v. New York*, 143 U.S. 517, 548, 551 (Brewer, J., dissenting). On the centrality of Brewer's religious convictions to his whole life *see* Brodhead, *David J. Brewer*, 179–80; Hylton, "David J. Brewer and the Christian Constitution," esp. 422–25.

89 Brewer, "Protection to Private Property," 107–8.

90 Further illustrating the complexities that inevitably mark any significant judicial career, Brewer wrote for the Court in upholding the right of the states to establish a "red light" district over the objections of nearby property owners. *L'Hote v. New Orleans*, 177 U.S. 587 (1900).

91 *See* Purcell, *Litigation and Inequality*, 78–81, 287–89; Hylton, "David Josiah Brewer and the Christian Constitution," 422–25.

92 42 U.S. (16 Pet.) 1 (1842).

93 On Story *see* R. Kent Newmyer, *Supreme Court Justice Joseph Story: Statesman of the Old Republic* (Chapel Hill, N.C., 1985), esp. 97–114, 332–43; Gerald T. Dunne, *Justice Joseph Story and the Rise of the Supreme Court* (New York, 1970), esp. 403–20.

94 The Rules of Decision Act, Section 34 of the Judiciary Act of 1789, provided: That the laws of the several states, except where the constitution, treaties, or statutes of the United States shall otherwise require or provide, shall be regarded as rules of decision in trials at common law in the courts of the United States in cases where they apply." 1 Stat. 92 (1789). The provision had remained essentially unchanged since 1789.

95 Although the *Swift* doctrine allowed the federal courts to avoid state judicial decisions, it was also used in some contexts to narrow or avoid state statutes. *E.g.*, William A. Fletcher, "The General Common Law and Section 34 of the Judiciary Act of 1789: The Example of Marine Insurance," 97 *Harvard Law Review* 1513, 1554 (1984); Herbert Hovenkamp, *Enterprise and American Law, 1836–1937* (Cambridge, Mass., 1991), 81–92.

96 In spite of the language in *Swift*, it is doubtful that Story accepted a simple "declaratory"

theory of law. His view, based largely on the customs and practice of the commercial world as well as on the common law, was more sophisticated, complex, and practical. Newmyer, *Supreme Court Justice Joseph Story*, 342; Dunne, *Justice Joseph Story*, 412–14; Tony Freyer, *Harmony & Dissonance: The Swift and Erie Cases in American Federalism* (New York, 1981), 37; Morton J. Horwitz, *The Transformation of American Law, 1780–1860* (Cambridge, Mass., 1977), 245–52. See generally G. Edward White, *The Marshall Court and Cultural Change, 1815–1835* (New York, 1988), 836–83.

97 *Kuhn v. Fairmont Coal Co.*, 215 U.S. 349 (1910).

98 For general discussions of *Swift*, *see* Tony A. Freyer, *Forums of Order: The Federal Courts and Business in American History* (Greenwich, Conn., 1979); Freyer, *Harmony & Dissonance;* William P. LaPiana, "*Swift v. Tyson* and the Brooding Omnipresence in the Sky: An Investigation of the Idea of Law in Antebellum America," 20 *Suffolk University Law Review* 771 (1986); Randolph Bridwell and Ralph U. Whitten, *The Constitution and the Common Law: The Decline of the Doctrines of Separation of Powers and Federalism* (Lexington, Mass., 1977).

99 Brewer joined the Court in striking down the first Federal Employers' Liability Act, which had limited the federal common law of torts, *The Employers' Liability Cases*, 207 U.S. 463 (1908), and in voiding the federal Erdman Act, which restricted the ability of interstate railroads to terminate workers for joining labor unions, *Adair v. United States*, 208 U.S. 161 (1908). The result of both cases was that the relevant federal common law was left in place.

100 *South Carolina v. United States*, 199 U.S. 437, 449 (1905) (Brewer, J.).

101 149 U.S. 368 (1893).

102 The Court had previously applied the *Swift* doctrine to industrial torts, but it had sometimes reached decisions favoring injured plaintiffs while failing to establish clearly that the controlling law was "general." Purcell, *Litigation and Inequality*, 72–82.

103 *Id.*, 78–82.

104 Brewer, "Nation's Safeguard," 39.

105 149 U.S. at 411, 401.

106 *Martin v. Atchison, Topeka and Sante Fe Railroad Co.*, 166 U.S. 399 (1897); *Texas & Pacific Railway Co. v. Bourman*, 212 U.S. 536 (1909). In the most divisive fellow-servant case that the Court heard following *Baugh*, Brewer wrote for a five-justice majority denying recovery in *Northern Pacific Railway Co. v. Dixon*, 194 U.S. 338 (1904).

107 Brodhead, *David J. Brewer*, 109.

108 181 U.S. 92 (1901).

109 *Id.* at 100.

110 *Id.* at 94–95.

111 *Id.* at 95–99.

112 *Smith v. Alabama*, 124 U.S. 465, 478 (1888). The most widely cited authority was *Wheaton v. Peters*, 33 U.S. (8 Pet.) 591, 658 (1834). Brewer was not the only justice to muddy the waters, however. See *Bucher v. Cheshire Railway Co.*, 125 U.S. 555, 583 (1888).

113 181 U.S. at 103. He used similarly unhelpful and conclusory language at another point, citing Chancellor Kent, Blackstone, and *Black's Law Dictionary*. *Id.* at 101–2.

114 *Id.* at 102.

115 Brewer's stress on basic justice was also evident in his equity receivership decisions, where he developed another brand of independent federal judge-made law to deal with complex, multistate reorganizations. See *Kneeland v. American Loan and Trust Co.*, 136 U.S. 89 (1890);

Leadville Coal Co. v. McCreery, 141 U.S. 475 (1891); *Louisville Trust Co. v. Louisville, New Albany and Chicago Railway Co.*, 174 U.S. 674 (1899). Because Section 34 applied only to actions at common law, the independent federal judge-made rules applied in equity proceedings did not technically fall within the *Swift* doctrine.

116 *Carpenter v. Providence Washington Insurance Co.*, 41 U.S. (16 Pet.) 495, 511 (1842).

117 *E.g., Paul v. Virginia*, 75 U.S. (8 Wall.) 168 (1868); *Ducat v. Chicago*, 77 U.S. (10 Wall.) 410 (1870).

118 *E.g., Nutting v. Massachusetts*, 183 U.S. 553 (1902).

119 *E.g., Iowa Life Insurance Co. v. Lewis*, 187 U.S. 335 (1902); *Northern Assurance Co. v. Grand View Building Association*, 183 U.S. 308 (1902). *See* Purcell, *Litigation and Inequality*, 64–72.

120 *See, e.g., Mutual Life Insurance Co. of New York v. Hill*, 193 U.S. 551 (1904); *Mutual Life Insurance Co. of New York v. Cohen*, 179 U.S. 262 (1900).

121 Brewer frequently extolled the virtues of localism. *E.g.*, David J. Brewer, "Address to the Law School," *1900 Commencement Annual, University of Wisconsin* (Madison, Wisc., 1900), i, x.

122 Brewer, "Address to the Law School," xvii.

123 Morton Keller, *The Life Insurance Enterprise, 1885–1910: A Study in the Limits of Corporate Power* (Cambridge, Mass., 1963), esp. ch. 14.

124 Brewer's equity receivership decisions similarly exemplified the Court's practical instrumentalist approach. *See, e.g., Louisville Trust Co. v. Louisville, New Albany and Chicago Railway Co.*, 174 U.S. 674, 682–83, 688–89 (1899).

125 In an earlier decision, 185 U.S. 125 (1902), the Court tentatively accepted jurisdiction and overruled without prejudice Colorado's demurrer.

126 *Kansas v. Colorado*, 206 U.S. 46, 57–64 (1907).

127 *Id.* at 65.

128 *Id.* at 68.

129 *Id.* at 66.

130 *Id.* at 69.

131 *Id.* at 72.

132 *Id.* at 66.

133 *Id.* at 69.

134 One justice did not participate, and two concurred without opinion in the result only.

135 206 U.S. at 81.

136 *Id.* at 82.

137 *Id.* at 83–84.

138 *Id.* at 82.

139 *Id.* at 89.

140 *Id.* at 90.

141 *Id.* at 94.

142 *Id.* at 95.

143 *Id.* at 96. Brewer quoted the latter phrase, as well as a much longer excerpt, from his opinion in *Western Union*.

144 *Id.* at 97.

145 *Id.* at 98.

146 *Id.* at 118.

147 In combination with the jurisdictional grant in Article III, either clause could have justified national law-making authority and provided a role for Congress.

148 *In re Debs*, 158 U.S. 564 (1895).

149 *Id.* at 599.

150 Felix Frankfurter and Nathan Greene, *The Labor Injunction* (New York, 1930), 17; Edwin
Walker to Richard Olney, Sept. 14, 1894, Olney Papers. *See* Gerald G. Eggert, *Richard Olney:
Evolution of a Statesman* (University Park, Pa., 1974); Ray Ginger, *The Bending Cross: A
Biography of Eugene Victor Debs* (New Brunswick, N.J., 1949).

151 Brewer, "Nation's Anchor," 168.

152 *United States v. Kane*, 23 F. 748 (C.C.D. Colo. 1885).

153 Brewer, "Nation's Safeguard," 43.

154 *E.g.*, James L. High, *A Treatise on the Law of Injunctions*, 4th ed. rev. (Chicago, 1905), Vol. 2,
1409–10. *See generally* Arnold M. Paul, *Conservative Crisis and the Rule of Law: Attitudes of
Bar and Bench, 1887–1895* (Ithaca, N.Y., 1960); William E. Forbath, *Law and the Shaping of
the American Labor Movement* (Cambridge, Mass., 1991), 59–97; Daniel R. Ernst, *Lawyers
Against Labor: From Individual Rights to Corporate Liberalism* (Urbana, Ill., 1995), 76–89.

155 158 U.S. at 600.

156 Brewer drew heavily on the argument of Attorney General Richard Olney, who stressed the
nuisance theory in his brief and oral argument. *See* Eggert, *Richard Olney*, 153–55, 166–68.

157 158 U.S. at 578–82.

158 *Id.* at 581.

159 *Id.* at 582.

160 There was no evidence in the record suggesting that criminal enforcement efforts by local,
state, or national officials had been hindered by hostile juries. Indeed, there was scarcely any
relevant record at all. *Id.* at 565–73. Even more striking, Brewer's own opinion evidences
the contrary-to-fact nature of his fear of a jury-induced breakdown of law enforcement:
"Whatever any single individual may have thought or planned, the great body of those who
were engaged in these transactions contemplated neither rebellion nor revolution, and when
in the due order of legal proceedings the question of right and wrong was submitted to the
courts, and by them decided, they unhesitatingly yielded to their decisions." *Id.* at 598.

161 *Id.* at 582.

162 *Id.* at 581.

163 Intriguingly, Brewer did not cite the one federal statute that might have authorized the president to act against the strike. Fiss, *Troubled Beginnings of the Modern State*, 72.

164 *Missouri Pacific Railway Co. v. United States*, 189 U.S. 274, 284, 288–89 (1903) (Brewer, J.,
dissenting). The sentence quoted in the text omits the Court's citation to *Debs*.

165 158 U.S. at 587.

166 *Id.* at 593.

167 *Id.* at 592.

168 *Id.* at 592.

169 206 U.S. at 90.

CHAPTER 3. PROGRESSIVE JUDICIAL REFORM AFTER WORLD WAR I

1 Mark DeWolfe Howe, ed., *Holmes-Laski Letters: The Correspondence of Mr. Justice Holmes
and Harold J. Laski, 1916–1935* (Cambridge, Mass., 1953), Vol. 1, 428 (Laski).

2 Edward A. Purcell, Jr., *Litigation and Inequality: Federal Diversity Jurisdiction in Industrial
America, 1870–1958* (New York, 1992), ch. 1.

3 Purcell, *Litigation and Inequality*, chs. 2 and 4.

4 *See, e.g.*, Mitchell Wendell, *Relations Between the Federal and State Courts* (New York, 1949), 170–74, 185–86; George C. Holt, *The Concurrent Jurisdiction of the Federal and State Courts* (New York, 1888), 159–88.

5 Purcell, *Litigation and Inequality*, 64–86.

6 Simon Newcomb, "Employer's Liability," 82 *The Nation* 440, 441 (1906). *See* "The Flexibility of Law," 96 *The Outlook* 850 (Dec. 17, 1910).

7 William Jennings Bryan, "Popular versus State's Rights," 9 *The Reader* 461, 463 (1907).

8 *E.g.*, William H. Rand, Jr., "Swift v. Tyson versus Gelpcke v. Dubuque," 8 *Harvard Law Review* 328 (1894); William M. Meigs, "Shall the State Courts Adopt the Federal Doctrine of 'General Principles of Jurisprudence'?" 29 *Central Law Journal* 465 (1889); J. B. Heiskell, "Conflict Between Federal and State Decisions," 16 *American Law Review* 743 (1882); William B. Hornblower, "Conflict Between Federal and State Decisions," 14 *American Law Review* 211 (1880); George Wharton Pepper, *The Border Land of Federal and State Decisions* (Philadelphia, 1889).

9 Pepper, *Border Land*, 78.

10 *See* Tony A. Freyer, *Forums of Order: The Federal Courts and Business in American History* (Greenwich, Conn., 1979), 99–136; Freyer, *Harmony and Dissonance: The Swift & Erie Cases in American Federalism* (New York, 1981); William R. Casto, "The *Erie* Doctrine and the Structure of Constitutional Revolutions," 62 *Tulane Law Review* 907, 921–30 (1988).

11 Oliver Wendell Holmes, Jr., *Collected Legal Papers* (New York, 1952 [1920]), 167.

12 Oliver Wendell Holmes, Jr., *The Common Law*, Mark DeWolfe Howe, ed. (Boston, 1963 [1881]), 5.

13 Mark DeWolfe Howe, ed., *Holmes-Pollock Letters: The Correspondence of Mr. Justice Holmes and Sir Frederick Pollock, 1874–1932* (Cambridge, Mass., 1961 [1941]), Vol. 1, 157.

14 *Id.*, Vol. 1, 157.

15 215 U.S. 349 (1910).

16 *Id.* at 371, 372 (Holmes, J., dissenting).

17 *Lochner v. New York*, 198 U.S. 45, 74 (1905) (Holmes, J., dissenting).

18 Howe, ed., *Holmes-Pollock Letters*, Vol. 1, 160.

19 *Swift*'s defenders often accepted positivist ideas and did not think that Story's decision assumed or required any "declaratory" theory of law. *See* Tony Freyer, *Harmony & Dissonance: The Swift and Erie Cases in American Federalism* (New York, 1981), 97.

20 Wilbur Larremore, "Stare Decisis and Contractual Rights," 22 *Harvard Law Review* 182, 189 (1909).

21 Herbert Pope, "The English Common Law in the United States," 24 *Harvard Law Review* 6, 30 (1911).

22 American Bar Association, *Reports*, Vol. 6 (1920), at 494.

23 *Id.* at 494.

24 Felix Frankfurter and Nathan Greene, *The Labor Injunction* (New York, 1930), 89–105. The great power of the injunction as an anti-union instrument was due not just to the unfavorable nature of the substantive law involved. It was also the result of the speed and ease with which preliminary orders could be obtained, the scope of their prohibitions, the difficulty of defending against a contempt proceeding brought to punish violations, and the fact that an *ex parte* or "preliminary" order—"temporary," in theory—was usually adequate in practice to destroy the force behind the unionization effort. *See* Felix Frankfurter and Nathan Greene, "Labor Injunction," 8 *Encyclopaedia of the Social Sciences* (New York, 1932), 653; William E.

Forbath, *Law and the Shaping of the American Labor Movement* (Cambridge, Mass., 1991), 59–97; Daniel R. Ernst, *Lawyers Against Labor: From Individual Rights to Corporate Liberalism* (Urbana, Ill., 1995), 76–89.

25 *Loewe v. Lawlor*, 208 U.S. 274 (1908); *Gompers v. Buck's Stove & Range Co.*, 221 U.S. 418 (1911). Employers could circulate among themselves "blacklists" that identified "troublemakers" who were not to be hired. Francis Bowes Sayre, "Labor and the Courts," 39 *Yale Law Journal* 682, 703–4 (1930).

26 Irving Bernstein, *The Lean Years: A History of the American Worker, 1920–1933* (Baltimore, 1966), 200.

27 Samuel Gompers, "Taft, the Injunction Standard Bearer," 14 *American Federationist* 791 (1907). *See* Christopher L. Tomlins, *The State and the Unions: Labor Relations, Law, and the Organized Labor Movement in America, 1880–1960* (New York, 1985), 61–67.

28 D. M. Means, "Contempt of Court," 70 *The Nation* 412 (1900).

29 *Truax v. Corrigan*, 257 U.S. 312, 369, nn. 38 and 39 (1921) (Brandeis, J., dissenting).

30 Edwin E. Witte, "The Federal Anti-Injunction Act," 16 *Minnesota Law Review* 638 (1932).

31 Arthur S. Link, *Woodrow Wilson and the Progressive Era, 1910–1917* (New York, 1954), 69–73.

32 26 Stat. 209 (1914).

33 *Duplex Printing Press Co. v. Deering*, 254 U.S. 443 (1921).

34 *Id.* at 478.

35 Learned Hand to Felix Frankfurter, Feb. 11, 1921, Frankfurter Papers, Box 63, folder 1220.

36 257 U.S. 312 (1921).

37 Frankfurter and Greene, *The Labor Injunction*, 210; Charles Warren to George W. Norris, Mar. 24, 1932, and Warren to Hatton W. Sumners, Apr. 30, 1932, Norris Papers, Tray 42, Box 8, file: "Limiting Jurisdiction of Federal Courts."

38 30 Stat. 424 (1898).

39 *Coppage v. Kansas*, 236 U.S. 1, 27, n. 1 (1915).

40 208 U.S. 161, 175 (1908).

41 236 U.S. 1, 9, 13, 14 (1915).

42 245 U.S. 229 (1917). *See* Winthrop D. Lane, *Civil War in West Virginia: A Story of the Industrial Conflict in the Coal Mines* (New York, 1921), esp. 68–73.

43 245 U.S. at 232–34. *See* Bernstein, *Lean Years*, 196–200.

44 245 U.S. at 251, 253.

45 *Id.* at 251.

46 *Id.* at 252.

47 *Id.*

48 *Id.* at 260. *See also id.* at 248.

49 *Id.* at 255–56.

50 *Id.* at 251.

51 *Id.* at 254.

52 *Id.* at 246 (emphasis added).

53 For a probing analysis of the anti-union bias in the federal labor decisions *see* Dianne Avery, "Images of Violence in Labor Jurisprudence: The Regulation of Picketing and Boycotts, 1894–1921," 37 *Buffalo Law Review* 1, 13 (1989).

54 Clever pleading and alignment of parties could often succeed in creating diversity jurisdiction. *See, e.g., Detroit Tile & Mosaic Co. v. Mason Contractors' Association*, 48 F. 2d. 729 (C.C.A. 6th 1931); *Vonnegut Machinery Co. v. Toledo Machine & Tool Co.*, 263 F. 192 (N.D.

Ohio W.D. 1920); *Dial-Overland Co. v. Willys-Overland, Inc.*, 263 F. 171 (N.D., Ohio, W.D., 1919). Such tactics did not always work. *E.g., Niles-Bemont-Pond Co. v. Iron Moulders' Union*, 254 U.S. 77 (1920); *Davis v. Henry*, 266 F. 261 (C.C.A. 6th 1920).

55 245 U.S. at 251.

56 *Id.* at 251. *See* Thomas Reed Powell, "The Supreme Court's Control Over the Issue of Injunctions in Labor Disputes," 13 *Proceedings of the Academy of Political Science* 37, 46 (1928).

57 245 U.S. at 252.

58 *Id.* at 257.

59 Francis Bowes Sayre, "Labor and the Courts," 39 *Yale Law Journal* 682, 691 n. 38 (1930).

60 Sayre, "Labor and the Courts"; Charles E. Carpenter, "Interference with Contract Relations," 41 *Harvard Law Review* 728 (1928); Francis Bowes Sayre, "Inducing Breach of Contract," 36 *Harvard Law Review* 663 (1923); Note "Tortious Interference with Contractual Relations in the Nineteenth Century: The Transformation of Property, Contract, and Tort," 93 *Harvard Law Review* 1510 (1980).

61 *Neves v. Scott*, 54 U.S. (13 How.) 268 (1851); *Guffey v. Smith*, 237 U.S. 101 (1915); Armistead M. Dobie, *Handbook of Federal Jurisdiction and Procedure* (St. Paul, Minn., 1928), 659–60; Note, "The Equitable Remedial Rights Doctrine: Past and Present," 67 *Harvard Law Review* 836 (1954).

62 *Mason v. United States*, 260 U.S. 545, 559 (1923).

63 *See, e.g., Northwestern Mutual Life Insurance Co. v. McCue*, 223 U.S. 234 (1912).

64 Robert K. Murray, *Red Scare: A Study in National Hysteria, 1919–1920* (New York, 1955).

65 *Vonnegut Machinery Co. v. Toledo Machine & Tool Co.*, 263 F. 192, 202 (N.D. Ohio, W.D. 1920).

66 Walter Wheeler Cook, "The Injunction in the Railway Strike," 32 *Yale Law Journal* 166 (1922); Donald Richberg, "The Menace of Government by Injunction," *The Locomotive Engineers Journal* 11 (January 1923), Richberg Papers, Box 5, folder 1922–23. *See* Colin J. Davis, *Power at Odds: The 1922 National Railroad Shopmen's Strike* (Urbana, Ill., 1997).

67 Quoted in Henry P. Pringle, *The Life and Times of William Howard Taft* (New York, 1939), Vol. 2, at 967.

68 In *Montgomery v. Pacific Electric Railway Co.*, 293 F. 680 (C.C.A. 9th 1923), for example, the court invalidated a California anti–yellow dog statute on the basis of *Coppage* and then affirmed an injunction protecting the employer's contractual relationship with its workers. *See also, e.g., Kinloch Telephone Co. v. Local Union No. 2 of International Brotherhood of Electrical Workers*, 275 F. 241 (C.C.A. 8th 1921); *Armstrong v. United States*, 18 F. 2d 371 (C.C.A. 7th 1927); *Alco-Zander Co. v. Amalgamated Clothing Workers of America*, 35 F. 2d 203 (E.D.Pa. 1929).

69 Bernstein, *Lean Years*, 200.

70 Bernstein, *Lean Years*, 200–1; Sen. Rep. No. 1060, 71 Cong., 2 Sess., part 2 (1930), "Minority Views" at 7; Edwin E. Witte, *The Government in Labor Disputes* (New York, 1932), Appendix B.

71 Bernstein, *Lean Years*, 84.

72 35 Stat. 65 (1908) and 36 Stat. 291 (1910); 41 Stat. 988 (1920).

73 *See* Richard Lowitt, *George W. Norris*, 3 Vols. (Urbana, Ill., 1963–78).

74 Lowitt, *Norris*, Vol. 2, at 277–86, 435–41. *See id.* at 161–63, 414–19.

75 George W. Norris to Virginia Laurenson, Apr. 22, 1922, Norris Papers, Tray 6, Box 8, file: "Judiciary (reform of) (1913–1931)."

76 *New York Times*, Apr. 23, 1922, sec. 6, at 5.

77 Thomas J. Walsh, "The Overburdened Supreme Court," 1922 *Virginia Bar Association Reports* 216, 234.

78 276 U.S. 518 (1928).

79 The *Taxicab* case did not present the kind of case that spurred the attacks of Populists and Progressives. It became a symbol because it was a Supreme Court decision, because it prompted a great dissent, and because it constituted a useful tool for Progressive polemics. Subsequently, it remained a symbol because the legal profession lost contact with the social history of diversity jurisdiction and the federal common law, mistaking the symbol for the reality, and because casebook editors found the case a convenient and formalistic way to introduce law students to what became "the *Erie* doctrine." *See* Purcell, *Litigation and Inequality*, 239–40.

80 276 U.S. at 533, 534 (Holmes, J., dissenting).

81 *See, e.g.,* Augustus N. Hand to Felix Frankfurter, July 17, 1928, Frankfurter Papers, Box 63, folder 1213.

82 Thomas J. Walsh to Felix Frankfurter, Apr. 27, 1928, Frankfurter Papers, Box 110, folder 2299; Louis D. Brandeis to Felix Frankfurter, May 8, 1928, Frankfurter Papers, Box 27, folder 436.

83 *See generally* John Henry Schlegel, *American Legal Realism and Empirical Social Science* (Chapel Hill, N.C., 1995); Neil Duxbury, *Patterns of American Jurisprudence* (New York, 1995), chs. 1–3.

84 For criticisms, *see* Armistead M. Dobie, "Frictional Points of Conflict Between State and Federal Courts," 19 *Virginia Law Review* 485 (1933); Thomas W. Shelton, "Concurrent Jurisdiction—Its Necessity and Its Dangers," 15 *Virginia Law Review* 137, 153 (1928); Charles I. Dawson, "Conflict of Decisions Between State and Federal Courts in Kentucky, and the Remedy," 20 *Kentucky Law Journal* 1 (1931); W. Barton Leach, "State Law of Evidence in Federal Courts," 43 *Harvard Law Review* 554 (1930). For support *see* Robert C. Brown, "Jurisdiction of the Federal Courts Based on Diversity of Citizenship," 78 *University of Pennsylvania Law Review* 179 (1929).

85 *E.g.,* Dobie, "Frictional Points of Conflict," 487; Dawson, "Conflict of Decisions Between State and Federal Courts in Kentucky," 9; Shelton, "Concurrent Jurisdiction," 153.

86 The Institute of Law at Johns Hopkins University, established in 1929 by several leading realists, attempted to study the practical differences between federal and state courts through questionnaires to practicing lawyers. Although they concluded that the critics had not established their case against *Swift* and diversity, they did recommend some changes to prevent "undue discrimination against the poor litigant." *See* Hessel E. Yntema, "The Jurisdiction of the Federal Courts in Controversies Between Citizens of Different States—II," 19 *American Bar Association Journal* 149, 153 (1933).

87 Charles E. Clark, "Diversity of Citizenship Jurisdiction of the Federal Courts," 19 *American Bar Association Journal* 499 (1933).

88 *Id.* at 503.

89 Felix Frankfurter, "The Place of the Supreme Court in Our Government," radio speech on May 13, 1930, over the National Broadcasting Corp, Frankfurter Papers, Box 196.

90 Concerning the anti-Semitism of the bar and the ABA, *see* Robert Stevens, *Law School: Legal Education in America from the 1850s to the 1980s* (Chapel Hill, N.C., 1983), 100–101, 126 n. 18, 180 n. 3, 184 n. 41, 109 n. 67; Jerold S. Auerbach, *Unequal Justice: Lawyers and Social Change in Modern America* (New York, 1976), esp. chs. 2 and 4.

91 Felix Frankfurter and James M. Landis, *The Business of the Supreme Court: A Study in the*

Federal Judicial System (New York, 1928). See Edward A. Purcell, Jr., "Reconsidering the Frankfurterian Paradigm: Reflecting on Histories of Lower Federal Courts," 24 *Law and Social Inquiry* (1999).

92 Felix Frankfurter, "Distribution of Judicial Power Between United States and State Courts," 13 *Cornell Law Quarterly* 499, 526 (1928).

93 *Id.* at 529.

94 *Id.* at 524–25.

95 Felix Frankfurter, "The Federal Courts," 58 *The New Republic* 273, 276 (1929).

96 Frankfurter, "Distribution of Judicial Power," 524–25.

97 Frankfurter, "Federal Courts," 276.

98 Frankfurter, "Distribution of Judicial Power," 523.

99 William Starr Myers, ed., *The State Papers and Other Public Writings of Herbert Hoover*, Vol. 1 (New York, 1934), 6.

100 Willis Van Devanter to Dennis T. Flynn, Oct. 31, 1930, Van Devanter Papers, Box 15, Letterbook 43.

101 *E.g.*, Felix Frankfurter to George W. Norris, Jan. 5, 1932, Mar. 10, 1932, and Apr. 13, 1932; Norris to Frankfurter, Mar. 11, 1932, and Apr. 11, 1932, Norris Papers, Tray 42, Box 8, file: "Limiting Jurisdiction of Federal Courts"; Frankfurter to Norris, May 15, 1929, Norris Papers, Tray 78, Box 8, file: "Limiting Jurisdiction of Federal Courts."

102 Among other things, his proferred bills raised the jurisdictional amount to $10,000, treated corporations as citizens of every state in which they did business, amended the Rules of Decision Act to reverse *Swift*, and restricted the jurisdiction of the federal courts to enjoin the enforcement of state laws regulating intrastate public utilities. Felix Frankfurter to George W. Norris, May 15, 1929, Norris Papers, Tray 78, Box 8, file: "Limiting Jurisdiction of Federal Courts, 1929–30"; Frankfurter to Norris, Apr. 13, 1932, Tray 42, Box 8, file: "Limiting Jurisdiction of Federal Courts."

103 *See, e.g.*, George W. Norris to Sen. William King, July 9, 1928, Norris Papers, Tray 42, Box 2; Norris to Sam G. Bratton, Aug. 11, 1928, Norris Papers, Tray 42, Box 2, file: "S. 3151 (70th)"; Norris to William D. Mitchell, May 28, 1930, Norris Papers, Tray 78, Box 8, file: "Limiting Jurisdiction of Federal Courts, 1929–30"; Norris to Felix Frankfurter, Mar. 11, 1932, Norris Papers, Tray 42, Box 8, file: "Limiting Jurisdiction of Federal Courts."

104 Gurney E. Newlin, "Proposed Limitations Upon Our Federal Courts," 15 *American Bar Association Journal* 401, 404 (1929).

105 John J. Parker, "The Federal Jurisdiction and Recent Attacks Upon It," 18 *American Bar Association Journal* 433, 439 (1932).

106 John J. Parker to Edward W. Everett, Apr. 4, 1932, Parker Papers, Box 8, folder 145.

107 Edward W. Everett to John J. Parker, Apr. 2, 1932, Parker Papers, Box 8, folder 145.

108 Paul Howland, "Shall Federal Jurisdiction of Controversies Between Citizens of Different States Be Preserved?" 18 *American Bar Association Journal*, 499, 500 (1932).

109 *Id.* at 502.

110 The Supreme Court's opinion repeatedly and explicitly stated that the relevant Kentucky "law" was a matter of common or general law. *Black & White Taxicab and Transfer Co. v. Brown & Yellow Taxicab and Transfer Co.*, 276 U.S. 518, 525, 526–27, 528, 529, 530 (1928).

111 Herbert Hoover, "Strengthening of Procedure in the Judicial System," Sen. Doc. No. 65, 72 Cong., 1 sess. (1932), x; William D. Mitchell to George W. Norris, May 26, 1930, Norris Papers, Tray 78, Box 8, file: "Limiting Jurisdiction of Federal Courts."

112 William D. Mitchell to George W. Norris, Dec. 2, 1931, Norris Papers, Tray 78, Box 8, file: "Limiting Jurisdiction of Federal Courts, 1929–30"; William D. Mitchell to George W. Norris, May 26, 1930, Norris Papers, Tray 78, Box 8, file: "Limiting Jurisdiction of Federal Courts"; Myers, ed., *State Papers and Other Public Writings of Herbert Hoover*, Vol. 2, 129, 133–34.

113 Diary of James Henry MacLafferty, Sept. 8, 1930, MacLafferty Papers, Box 1.

114 *Id.*, Dec. 24, 1930, MacLafferty Papers, Box 1. *See also id.* Jan. 4, 1931.

115 William D. Mitchell to Charles A. Boston, Feb. 9, 1931, Norris Papers, Tray 78, Box 8, file: "Limiting Jurisdiction of Federal Courts, 1929–30."

116 "Limiting Jurisdiction of the Federal Courts," Hearings before the Committee on the Judiciary of the House of Representatives, 72 Cong., 1 sess. (1932) at 10.

117 Silas H. Strawn, "The Federal Courts: Jurisdiction Based on Diverse Citizenship," Statement of the President of the American Bar Association "submitted for the information of members with the view that they may desire to express individual viewpoints, in the premises, to their members of Congress" (Washington, D.C., 1932); Clayton H. Kinney to Warren R. Austin, Mar. 16, 1932, Norris Papers, Tray 42, Box 8, file: "Limiting Jurisdiction of Federal Courts"; David Kay, Jr. to George W. Norris, Apr. 15, 1932, Norris Papers, Tray 78, Box 6, file: "Johnson Bill."

118 *See* the collection of documents in Norris Papers, Tray 79, Box 8, file: "Protesting Passage Limiting Jurisdiction of Federal Courts"; W. Calvin Chesnut to John J. Parker, July 13, 1932, Parker Papers, Box 22, folder 557; Parker to Chesnut, July 18, 1932, Parker Papers, Box 22, folder 558.

119 A copy of the ABA brief may be found in the Norris Papers, Tray 79, Box 8, file: "Protesting Passage Limiting Jurisdiction of Federal Courts." For the *Journal*'s campaign, *see, e.g.*, "Diversity of Citizenship and the Presidential Message," 18 *American Bar Association Journal* 215 (1932).

120 James F. Ailshie to Edward W. Everett, Dec. 1, 1933, Baker Papers, Box 20, "ABA-1933."

121 Herman Oliphant to Felix Frankfurter, May 6, 1929, Frankfurter Papers, Box 150, folder 3049.

122 Newton Baker to Edward W. Everett, Oct. 10, 1933, and Oct. 31, 1933, Baker Papers, Box 20, file: "ABA-1933"; Charles E. Clark to Paul Howland, Mar. 12, 1932, Parker Papers, Box 8, folder 144; Clark to Paul Howland, Apr. 15, 1932, and Clark to George W. Norris, Apr. 22, 1932, Norris Papers, Tray 42, Box 8, file: "Limiting Jurisdiction of Federal Courts."

123 Charles E. Clark to Paul Howland, Mar. 12, 1932, Parker Papers, Box 8, folder 144; Charles E. Clark to George W. Norris, Apr. 22, 1932, Norris Papers, Tray 42, Box 8, file: "Limiting Jurisdiction of Federal Courts." *See, e.g.*, "Limiting Jurisdiction of Federal Courts—Pending Bills—Comment by Members of the Chicago University Law Faculty," 31 *Michigan Law Review* 59 (1932).

124 *See, e.g.*, 74 *Cong. Rec.* 71 Cong., 3 sess. (1931), 3126–27.

125 Fiorello LaGuardia to George W. Norris, Apr. 23, 1932, Norris Papers, Tray 42, Box 8, file: "Limiting Jurisdiction of Federal Courts."

126 "Limiting Jurisdiction of Federal Courts," Hearings before the Committee on the Judiciary of the House of Representatives, 72 Cong., 1 sess. (1932), at 65 (statement of Washington Bowie).

127 *See* Wayne K. Hobson, "Symbol of the New Profession: Emergence of the Large Law Firm, 1870–1915," in *The New High Priests: Lawyers in Post-Civil War America* (Westport, Conn., 1984), 3–27.

128 57 *Reports of the American Bar Association* 102 (1932). The association's enthusiasm for the cause of diversity contrasted sharply with its refusal to take any action to defend the most basic due process rights of the period's "controversial" criminal defendants: Sacco and Vanzetti, Tom Mooney, and the "Scottsboro boys"—the last so badly outraged by the legal system that the Supreme Court twice reversed their convictions. *See, e.g.*, Auerbach, *Unequal Justice*, 145–46; exchange of letters—dated Apr. 13, 14, 19, 24, and 26, and May 11 and 12, 1933—between Newton Baker and Clarence E. Martin (president of the ABA), Baker Papers, Box 20, "ABA-1933"; Gurney E. Newlin (president of the ABA) to Felix Frankfurter, June 24 [*sic*, probably a mistaken date that should read June 14], 1929, and Frankfurter to Newlin, June 24, 1929, Landis Papers (L.C.), Box 5, "FF"; *Powell v. Alabama*, 287 U.S. 45 (1932). *See* Dan T. Carter, *Scottsboro: A Tragedy of the American South* (Baton Rouge, La., 1969); James Goodman, *Stories of Scottsboro* (New York, 1994).

129 Sen. Rep. No. 530, 72 Cong., 1 sess. (1932), 16.

130 *Id.* at 3.

131 *Id.* at 23. On this point, there seems little question that Norris was correct.

132 John H. Walker to Felix Frankfurter, May 28, 1921, Frankfurter Papers, Box 110, folder 2293; Donald R. Richberg, "The Menace of Government by Injunction," *The Locomotive Engineers Journal* 11 (January 1923), Richberg Papers, Box 5, folder 1922–23; Mollie Ray Carroll, *Labor and Politics* (New York, 1923), 158–62.

133 "What to Do," 32 *The New Republic* 136 (Oct. 4, 1922).

134 "Labor's Position in the 1924 Campaign," Farmer Labor Association Papers, Box 1; *The Facts: La Follette-Wheeler Campaign Textbook* (Chicago, 1924), La Follette Family Papers, Series B, Robert M. La Follette, Box 206.

135 Bernstein, *Lean Years*, 394–95.

136 *Taliaferro v. United States.*, 290 F. 906 (C.C.A. 4th 1923).

137 George Wharton Pepper, "Injunctions in Labor Disputes," *Report of the Forty-Seventh Annual Meeting of the American Bar Association*, Vol. 49 (1924), 174–80.

138 Donald Richberg Papers, Box 33.

139 *E.g.*, John P. Frey, *The Labor Injunction: An Exposition of Government by Judicial Conscience and Its Menace* (Cincinatti, Ohio, 1923); Walter Nelles, "A Strike and Its Legal Consequences—An Examination of the Receivership Precedent for the Labor Injunction," 40 *Yale Law Journal* 507 (1931); Frankfurter and Greene, *Labor Injunction;* Sayre, "Labor and the Courts"; Thomas Reed Powell, "Supreme Court's Control Over the Issue of Injunctions in Labor Disputes," 13 *Proceedings of the Academy of Political Science* 37 (1928); Witte, *Government in Labor Disputes.*

140 Felix Frankfurter to Oliver Wendell Holmes, Jr., Jan. 14, 1921, Holmes Papers, Box 30, folder 16. *See* Frankfurter, *Law and Politics*, 41–47, 218–21.

141 Felix Frankfurter to Thomas J. Walsh, Dec. 18, 1926, Frankfurter Papers, Box 110, folder 2299. Frankfurter identified closely with the federal courts. "The federal judiciary is my earliest legal love," he boasted. Felix Frankfurter to Charles E. Clark, Feb. 2, 1933, Frankfurter Papers, Box 134, folder 2764.

142 Frankfurter and Greene, *Labor Injunction*, 13–14.

143 *Id.* at 17.

144 Frankfurter and Greene, *Labor Injunction*, 96. *See also id.* at 87.

145 Felix Frankfurter to Charles Amidon, Mar. 15, 1932, Frankfurter Papers, Box 20, folder 260. *See* Frankfurter to Charles E. Clark, Mar. 25, 1932, Frankfurter Papers, Box 44, folder 775.

146 *See* responses in Frankfurter Papers, Box 150, folders 3051 and 3052.

147 Lowett, *Norris*, Vol. 1, 125. *See* Lowett, *Norris*, Vol. 2, 518–27; Norris, *Fighting Liberal*, 308–17; George W. Norris to A. B. Critchfield, Apr. 26, 1922, Norris Papers, Tray 6, Box 8, file "Judiciary (reform of) (1913–1931)."

148 *Bedford Cut Stone Co. v. Journeymen Stone Cutters' Association*, 274 U.S. 37 (1927).

149 *United Mine Workers v. Red Jacket Consolidated Coal & Coke Co.*, 18 F. 2d 839 (C.C.A. 4th 1927), *cert. denied*, 275 U.S. 536 (1927). *See* Bernstein, *Lean Years*, 211–15; Mason, *William Howard Taft*, 228–30.

150 Edwin E. Witte, "The Federal Anti-Injunction Act," 16 *Minnesota Law Review* 638, 647–48 (1932); Edwin E. Witte to Roger Baldwin, Dec. 24, 1931, Norris Papers, Tray 79, Box 7, file: "Judicial Anti-Injunction, 1929–33"; Bernstein, *Lean Years*, 395–96; Sen. Doc. No. 327, 71 Cong., 3 sess. (1931).

151 Gilbert Roe to Andrew Furuseth, Jan. 17, 1928, La Follette Family Papers, Series H, Papers of Gilbert Roe, Box 8; Edwin E. Witte to Roger Baldwin, Dec. 24, 1931, Norris Papers, Tray 79, Box 7, file: "Judicial Anti-Injunction, 1929–33"; Roscoe Pound to William Green, July 9, 1928, Frankfurter Papers, Box 59, folder 1144; Felix Frankfurter to George W. Norris, June 21, 1928, Frankfurter Papers, Box 87, folder 1788; Sen. Doc. No. 327, 71 Cong., 3 sess. (1931).

152 *See, e.g.,* "Outline of Explanation of Bill Drafted to Limit and Define the Jurisdiction of the Federal Courts in Labor Cases," Frankfurter Papers, Box 161, folder 3208.

153 Roscoe Pound to William Green, July 9, 1928, Frankfurter Papers, Box 59, folder 1144; Gilbert Roe to Andrew Furuseth, Jan. 17, 1928, La Follette Family Papers, Series H, Roe Papers, Box 8; Edwin E. Witte to Roger N. Baldwin, Dec. 24, 1931, and Felix Frankfurter to Furuseth, Mar. 23, 1931, Norris Papers, Tray 79, Box 7, file: "Judicial Anti-Injunction, 1929–33"; Donald Richberg to George W. Norris, June 19, 1928, Frankfurter Papers, Box 87, folder 1788; Frankfurter to Richberg, June 20, 1928, Frankfurter Papers, Box 96, folder 1971; Frankfurter to Herman Oliphant, June 15, 1928, Frankfurter Papers, Box 87, folder 1798; Oliphant to Frankfurter, June 16, 1928, Frankfurter Papers, Box 87, folder 1798; Richberg, "Memorandum Concerning Amendments to Anti-Injunction Bill Suggested by the American Federation of Labor," Norris Papers, Tray 42, Box 8, file: "Anti-Injunction 1929–32"; Bernstein, *Lean Years*, 396.

154 George W. Norris to Felix Frankfurter, Apr. 21, 1928, Frankfurter Papers, Box 87, folder 1788; Norris, *Fighting Liberal*, 312.

155 The original draft is reprinted in Frankfurter and Greene, *Labor Injunction*, 279–88.

156 Charles F. Amidon to Felix Frankfurter, Feb. 2, 1930, Frankfurter Papers, Box 20, folder 260. *See* Felix Frankfurter, Edwin E. Witte, and Herman Oliphant, "Observations on Injunction Bill Endorsed by AF of L," Frankfurter Papers, Box 161, folder 3207.

157 *See* Matthew Woll to George W. Norris, June 13, 1929, Norris Papers, Tray 42, Box 8, file: "Anti-Injunction 1929–32"; Bernstein, *Lean Years*, 400–403.

158 *International Organization, United Mine Workers of America v. Red Jacket Consolidated Coal & Coke Co.*, 18 F.2d 839 (C.C.A. 4th 1927). Felix Frankfurter to George W. Norris, May 9, 1930, Norris Papers, Tray 79, Box 7, file: "Judicial Anti-Injunction, 1929–33." *See* Peter Graham Fish, "*Red Jacket* Revisited: The Case that Unraveled John J. Parker's Supreme Court Appointment," 5 *Law and History Review* 51 (1987).

159 *See, e.g.,* "Smothering a Strike by Injunction," 74 *The Literary Digest* 7 (Sept. 16, 1922); Donald Richberg to George W. Norris, Feb. 29, 1932, Norris Papers, Tray 42, Box 7, file: "Wilkerson Nomination."

160 72 *Cong. Rec.*, 71 Cong., 2 sess. (1930), 8487; Bernstein, *Lean Years*, 411–12.

161 *Texas & New Orleans Railroad Co. v. Brotherhood of Railway & Steamship Clerks*, 281 U.S. 548, 570–71, 565, 568 (1930).

162 Bernstein, *Lean Years*, 410–11.

163 Witte, "Federal Anti-Injunction Act," 639.

164 *Id.* at 640.

165 Arthur M. Schlesinger, Jr., *The Crisis of the Old Order, 1919–1933* (Boston, 1957), 238–39.

166 *See, e.g.* 75 *Cong. Rec.*, 72 Cong., 1 sess. (1932), 4502 *et seq.*, 4618 *et seq.*, 4680 *et seq.*, 4689 *et seq.*, 4768 *et seq.*, 4915 *et seq.;* Sen. Rep. No. 163, 72 Cong., 1 sess. (1932); H.R. Rep. 669, 72 Cong., 1 sess. (1932).

167 75 *Cong. Rec.*, 72 Cong., 1 sess. (1932), 5019, 5511; Witte, "Federal Anti-Injunction Act," 641–42.

168 Diary of James Henry MacLafferty, Mar. 8, 1932, at 2, MacLafferty Papers, Box 1.

169 Henry W. Taft to Herbert Hoover, Mar. 23, 1932, Hoover Papers, Pres. Subj. File-Anti- Trust Laws, Box 64.

170 Diary of James Henry MacLafferty, Mar. 10, 1932, at 3, MacLafferty Papers, Box 1.

171 *Id.*, Mar. 8, 1932, at 2 and Mar. 10, 1932, at 3, MacLafferty Papers, Box 1.

172 75 *Cong. Rec.*, 72 Cong., 1 sess. (1932), 5474.

173 *See* Andrew Furuseth to George W. Norris, Jan. 7, 1932, Norris Papers, Tray 42, Box 8, file: "Anti-Injunction, 1929–32."

174 *E.g., Sheldon v. Sill*, 49 U.S. (8 How.) 441 (1850); *Kline v. Burke Construction Co.*, 260 U.S. 226 (1922).

175 *International Organization, United Mine Workers of America v. Red Jacket Consolidated Coal & Coke Co.*, 18 F.2d 839, 840 (C.C.A. 4th 1927).

176 Purcell, *Litigation and Inequality*, ch. 7.

177 *See* Hiram Johnson to George W. Norris, Feb. 26, 1934, Norris Papers, Tray 78, Box 6, file: "Johnson Bill."

CHAPTER 4. LITIGANT STRATEGIES AND JUDICIAL DYNAMICS

1 Aaron L. Danzig, "Erie v. Tompkins at 50: Due a Respectful Burial?" *New York Law Journal*, Feb. 26, 1988, at 6. Another account, based on an unpublished manuscript by Danzig, contains additional — and slightly different — information. *See* Bob Rizzi, "Erie Memoirs Reveal Drama, Tragedy," 63 *Harvard Law Record* 2 (Sept. 24, 1976). *See generally* Tony Freyer, *Harmony & Dissonance: The Swift & Erie Cases in American Federalism* (New York, 1981), 122–42.

2 Tompkins so described his injury in his trial testimony. Quoted in Irving Younger, "What Happened in *Erie*," 56 *Texas Law Review* 1011, 1014 (1978). Subsequently, one of his attorneys described the "dark object" as "a black wing of destruction soaring toward him." Danzig, "Erie v. Tompkins at 50," 6.

3 Younger, "What Happened in *Erie*," at 1012–13.

4 *Id.* at 1012–13; Danzig, "Erie v. Tompkins at 50," 6.

5 Venue was, of course, proper in both states, and Tompkins's claim was above the jurisdictional minimum of $3,000. Given the extent of the Erie's operations, it is possible that Tompkins could also have brought his suit in a state court in one or more other states. Any such state court, however, following common choice-of-law rules, would most likely have applied the substantive tort law of Pennsylvania, the place of injury.

6 *Falchetti v. Pennsylvania Railroad Co.*, 307 Pa. 203 (1932).

7 A second, and powerful, practical motive also spurred Tompkins's attorneys to the same decision. They were New York practitioners who were not licensed to practice in Pennsylvania. Younger, "What Happened in *Erie*," 1016.

8 *Id.*, 1016.

9 The Erie offered Tompkins $7,500 to settle the case prior to the appeal, but his attorneys—confident that the judgment would stand—persuaded him not to accept it. Younger, "What Happened in *Erie*," 1021–22.

10 *Tompkins v. Erie Railroad Co.*, 90 F.2d 603 (2d Cir. 1937). The Second Circuit did not cite *Swift* but relied, instead, on *Baugh*.

11 Danzig, "Erie v. Tompkins at 50," 6.

12 302 U.S. 671 (1937). For the Erie's procedural maneuvering to obtain a stay of the Second Circuit's judgment, see Younger, "What Happened in *Erie*," 1023–24.

13 Nemeroff, Danzig, and Hunt did not appear in the Supreme Court but arranged special counsel for the appeal. *See Erie Railroad Co. v. Tompkins*, 304 U.S. 64, 68 (1938). The briefs of both parties on the petition for *certiorari* and on the merits are reprinted in Philip B. Kurland and Gerhard Casper, eds., *Landmark Briefs and Arguments of the Supreme Court of the United States: Constitutional Law*, Vol. 35 (Arlington, Va., 1975), 601.

14 Danzig, "Erie v. Tompkins at 50," 6.

15 Kurland and Caspar, eds., *Landmark Briefs*, Vol 35, 708 (br. for pet. at 27). Kiendl's brief on the merits is also reprinted in Frederick C. Hicks, *Materials and Methods of Legal Research*, 3d rev. ed. (Rochester, N.Y., 1942), 391 (quote at 412).

16 Kurland and Caspar, eds., *Landmark Briefs*, Vol. 35, at 716 (br. for Pet. at 35).

17 *Id.* at 709 (br. for Pet. at 28).

18 *Id.* at 699–703 (Br. for Pet. at 18–22). The Erie's brief relied principally on *Falchetti v. Pennsylvania Railroad Co.*, 307 Pa. 203 (1932).

19 Kurland and Caspar, eds., *Landmark Briefs*, Vol. 35, 705, 708–19 (br. for Pet. at 24, 27–38).

20 Kiendl's explanation is set forth in Hicks, *Materials and Methods of Legal Research*, 376–77 and discussed in Freyer, *Harmony & Dissonance*, 130.

21 Hicks, *Materials and Methods of Legal Research*, 376.

22 The Court granted *certiorari* on Oct. 11, 1937. *Erie Railroad Co. v. Tompkins*, 302 U.S. 671 (1937). The railroad's main brief was submitted on Jan. 3, 1938, and its reply brief on Jan. 24. Hicks, *Materials and Methods of Legal Research*, 389.

23 *Black and White Taxicab and Transfer Co. v. Brown and Yellow Taxicab and Transfer Co.*, 276 U.S. 518, 532 (1928) (Holmes, J., dissenting).

24 Freyer, *Harmony & Dissonance*, 101–22.

25 *Hawks v. Hamill*, 288 U.S. 52 (1933); *Trainor Co. v. Aetna Casualty & Surety Co.*, 290 U.S. 47 (1933); *Mutual Life Insurance Co. of New York v. Johnson*, 293 U.S. 335 (1934); *Boseman v. Connecticut General Life Insurance Co.*, 301 U.S. 196 (1937).

26 There is no transcript of the oral argument. Kiendl's recollections are contained in a document he sent to Frederick C. Hicks. Hicks, *Materials and Methods of Legal Research*, 376–77.

27 Quoted in Elliott Cheatham, "Comments by Elliott Cheatham on the True National Common Law," 18 *American University Law Review* 372, 374 (1969).

28 Hicks, *Materials and Methods of Legal Research*, 376–77.

29 *Burnet v. Coronado Oil & Gas Co.*, 285 U.S. 393, 405, 405–6 (Brandeis, J., dissenting).

30 *Id.* at 406 n. 1, 407 n. 2, and 48 n. 3.

31 *Id.* at 407–8.

32 Only eighteen months earlier, another member of the Court, Justice Harlan F. Stone, had spoken at a conference on "The Future of the Common Law" held as part of the highly publicized Harvard tercentenary celebration. There, Stone had also advanced a flexible idea of *stare decisis* and cited Brandeis's discussion in *Burnet* for the proposition that appellate courts "on occasion" showed "a readiness frankly to overrule" precedents that were "undesirable." Harlan F. Stone, "The Common Law of the United States," 50 *Harvard Law Review* 4, 9 and n. 12.

33 Edward A. Purcell, Jr., *Litigation and Inequality: Federal Diversity Jurisdiction in Industrial America, 1870–1958* (New York, 1992), 28–86, 256–62.

34 Kurland and Casper, eds., *Landmark Briefs*, at 706 (Br. for Pet. at 25). See also *id*. at 627 and n. 1.

35 *Id*. at 627 n.1 (br. in support of Pet. at 20).

36 Younger, "What Happened in Erie," 1025, 1026.

37 It is surprising, and may be revealing, that sometime after 1938 Kiendl destroyed his files on *Erie*. Freyer, *Harmony & Dissonance*, 12.

38 *E.g., Erie,* 304 U.S. at 80, 82 (Butler, J., dissenting). This charge and some of the considerations involved are summarized in Henry J. Friendly, "In Praise of Erie—and of the New Federal Common Law," reprinted in Friendly, *Benchmarks: Selected Papers by an Eminent Federal Judge* (Chicago, 1967), 155, 171 n. 71.

39 On the basic issue of *Swift*'s validity, the lack of briefing was relatively insignificant. *Swift*'s legitimacy and social significance had been broadly and thoroughly explored in the legal literature for decades.

40 244 U.S. 205, 218, 255 (1917). Although Holmes and Brandeis occasionally applied *Swift* when writing for the Court, they avoided its doctrine where possible. *Salem Trust Co. v. Manufacturers' Finance Co.,* 264 U.S. 182 (1924); Melvin I. Urofsky and David W. Levy, *Letters of Louis D. Brandeis* (Albany, N.Y., 1978), Vol. 5, 174. *See also Paine Lumber Co. v. Neal,* 244 U.S. 459 (1917).

41 276 U.S. 518, 532 (1928).

42 *Brinkerhoff-Faris Trust & Savings Co. v. Hill,* 281 U.S. 673, 681 n. 8 (1930).

43 Harlan F. Stone to Pierce Butler, Feb. 8, 1927, Stone Papers, Box 73. *See also, Waggoner Estate v. Wichita County,* 273 U.S. 113 (1927) (Stone, J.); *Edward Hines Yellow Pine Trustees v. Martin,* 268 U.S. 458 (1925) (Stone, J.).

44 Harlan F. Stone to Felix Frankfurter, Sept. 23, 1931, Frankfurter Papers, Box 105, folder 2182.

45 Harlan F. Stone, "The Common Law in the United States," 50 *Harvard Law Review* 4, 8 (1936). *See also id*. at 10, 20; Alpheus Thomas Mason, *Harlan F. Stone: Pillar of the Law* (New York, 1956), 327–35.

46 Cardozo did not return to the Court after December 1937 and died on July 9, 1938. Although no direct evidence exists, there is some reason to think that he approved the majority's decision. First, he issued the stay that kept the appeal alive and enabled the railroad to bring the case to the Supreme Court. *See* Danzig, "Erie v. Tompkins at 50," 6. Second, in late August, a month after Cardozo's death, Judge Irving Lehman reported a conversation he had had with Cardozo shortly before his death. "Cardozo," Lehman told Brandeis, "was deeply interested in the Tompkins decision, and happy that he had had something to do with the case earlier." Melvin I. Urofsky and David W. Levy, *"Half Brother, Half Son": The Letters of Louis D. Brandeis to Felix Frankfurter* (Norman, Okla., 1991), 617.

47 Merlo J. Pusey, *Charles Evans Hughes* (New York, 1951), Vol. 2, 710.

48 *Id*., Vol. 2, 710. Although Hughes raised the possibility of overruling *Swift* when he intro-

duced *Erie* in conference, Pusey himself remarks, presumably reflecting what Hughes told him, that "[m]ost of the credit for this overturn goes to Justice Brandeis." *Id.* at 711.

49 *See generally* Purcell, *Litigation and Inequality,* ch. 9.

50 *See, e.g.,* Barry Cushman, "A Stream of Legal Consciousness: The Current of Commerce Doctrine from *Swift* to *Jones & Laughlin,*" 61 *Fordham Law Review* 105, 146–54, 157–58; Stephen Gardbaum, "New Deal Constitutionalism and the Unshackling of the States," 64 *University of Chicago Law Review* 483 (1997).

51 *See* Alpheus T. Mason, "Owen Josephus Roberts," in John A. Garraty, ed., *Dictionary of American Biography,* Supp. Vol. 5 (New York, 1977), 571, 573–76; Charles A. Leonard, *A Search for a Judicial Philosophy: Mr. Justice Roberts and the Constitutional Revolution of 1937* (Port Washington, N.Y., 1971), 180.

52 Quoted in David Burner, "Owen J. Roberts," *The Justices of the Supreme Court, Their Lives and Major Opinions,* ed. Leon Friedman and Fred L. Israel, 4 Vols. (New York, 1969), Vol. 3, 2263.

53 After leaving the Court, Roberts destroyed his papers. Mason, "Owen Josephus Roberts," 576. His willingness to act in spite of the fact that the appellant did not call for *Swift*'s overthrow may have been influenced by criticism he received for his alleged "switch" in the spring of 1937. *See* Edward A. Purcell, Jr., "Rethinking Constitutional Change," 80 *Virginia Law Review* 277, 288–90 (1994).

54 Charles Evans Hughes, *The Autobiographical Notes of Charles Evans Hughes,* ed. David J. Danelski and Joseph S. Tulchin (Cambridge, Mass., 1973), 298.

55 Danelski and Tulchin, "Editors' Introduction," in Hughes, *Autobiographical Notes,* xx.

56 *See, e.g., United States v. Butler,* 297 U.S. 1 (1936) (Roberts, J.).

57 Labor and administrative law cases were clear exceptions. *See* C. Herman Pritchett, *The Roosevelt Court: A Study in Judicial Politics and Values, 1937–1947* (Chicago, 1948), 191, 208.

58 Virginia Van Der Veer Hamilton, *Hugo Black: The Alabama Years* (Birmingham, Ala., 1972), 76–77; Gerald T. Dunne, *Hugo Black and the Judicial Revolution* (New York, 1977), 92–97, 183-84; Tony Freyer, "Introduction," in Freyer, ed., *Justice Hugo Black and Modern America* (Tuscaloosa, Ala., 1990), 21–25; Howard Ball, "Justice Hugo L. Black: A Magnificent Product of the South," in Freyer, ed., *Justice Hugo Black,* 31–35; Roger K. Newman, *Hugo Black: A Biography* (New York, 1994), 150–51.

59 Quoted in John P. Frank, "Hugo L. Black," *Justices of the Supreme Court,* ed. Friedman and Israel, Vol. 3, 2326.

60 Jerome L. Clark, "Interview with Associate Justice Hugo Black, Supreme Court Building, Washington, D.C., July 2, 1958," Black Papers, Box 43, file: "Noe-Nor," at 2.

61 Hugo Black, Jr., *My Father: A Remembrance* (New York, 1975), 78. See also *id.* at 81; Dunne, *Hugo Black,* 131; *Cong. Rec.* 75 Cong., 1 sess. (1937), 9220.

62 Harold L. Ickes, *The Secret Diary of Harold L. Ickes,* Vol. 2, *The Inside Struggle, 1936-1939* (New York, 1954), 183, 190–91, 196; James MacGregor Burns, *Roosevelt: The Lion and the Fox* (New York, 1956), 312; Hamilton, *Hugo Black,* 273; Newman, *Hugo Black,* 233–46.

63 John P. Frank, "The New Court and the New Deal," in Stephen Strickland, ed., *Hugo Black and the Supreme Court: A Symposium* (New York, 1967), 41–50; Randolph E. Paul, "Federal Taxation: Questions of Power and Propriety," in *id.,* 166–73.

64 Letter from George W. Norris to Henry F. Ashurst, Aug. 17, 1937, "Extracts from the Congressional Record Relative to the Nomination of the Honorable Hugo L. Black to be an Associate Justice of the Supreme Court," Sen. Doc. No. 118, 75 Cong., 1 sess. (1937), 9.

65 302 U.S. 419, 423 (1938) (Black, J., dissenting).

66 Carl Brent Swisher, "History's Panorama and Justice Black's Career," in Strickland, ed., *Hugo Black and the Supreme Court*, 282 n. 35.

67 303 U.S. 77, 83 (1938) (Black, J., dissenting).

68 H. L. Mencken, by 1937 a persistent critic of the New Deal, termed the solitary dissent in *Connecticut General* "completely cuckoo" and proclaimed that he could "see little in Black except a Cracker demagogue." Quoted in Dunne, *Hugo Black and the Judicial Revolution*, 179. Many Progressives and New Dealers, however, expressed delight with his performance. Norris, William O. Douglas, and Harold Ickes wrote to tell him, in Norris's words, "how much pleasure and comfort" his dissents gave them. Norris to Black, undated (Black's response to Norris was dated Jan. 28, 1938), Black Papers, Box 253, file: "McCart v. Indianapolis Water Co." *See* Ickes to Black, Feb. 16, 1938, Black Papers, Box 254, file: "General Life Insurance v. Johnson"; Douglas to Black, Feb. 4, 1938, Black Papers, Box 59, file: "W. O. Douglas."

69 *See* John D. Fassett, *New Deal Justice: The Life of Stanley Reed of Kentucky* (New York, 1994).

70 Stanley Reed, "The Constitution of the United States," 22 *American Bar Association Journal* 601 (1936); C. Herman Pritchett, "Stanley Reed" in *Justices of the Supreme Court*, ed. Friedman and Israel, Vol. 3, 2373.

71 Stanley Reed to Louis D. Brandeis, Mar. 21, 1938, Brandeis Court Papers, Box 107, folder 7, "*Erie*."

72 Freyer, *Harmony & Dissonance*, 131–35, 147–53.

73 Draft opinion, undated but apparently written between Mar. 4 and Mar. 7, 1938, Brandeis Court Papers, Box 107, folder 5, "*Erie*." For general background on the case's history, see Freyer, *Harmony & Dissonance*, 122–42. For a different view of Brandeis's role and *Erie*'s origins, *see* William R. Casto, "The *Erie* Doctrine and the Structure of Constitutional Revolutions," 62 *Tulane Law Review* 907 (1988).

74 Draft opinion, dated Mar. 7, at 3, Brandeis Court Papers, Box 107, folder 5, "*Erie*." This draft also cited Charles Warren's reseach on the Judiciary Act of 1789, Warren, "New Light on the History of the Federal Judiciary Act of 1789," 37 *Harvard Law Review* 49 (1926).

75 Draft opinion, dated Mar. 7, at 3, Brandeis Court Papers, Box 107, folder 5, "*Erie*."

76 Draft opinion, dated Mar. 9, at 4, Brandeis Court Papers, Box 107, folder 5, "*Erie*."

77 Draft opinion, dated Mar. 10, at 4, Brandeis Court Papers, Box 107, folder 6, "*Erie*."

78 Based on his discovery and analysis of drafts of the First Judiciary Act, Warren had published an article arguing that the framers of Section 34 had intended to include both statutes and judicial decisions in the word *laws* and, hence, that *Swift* was wrongly decided. Warren, "New Light on the History of the Federal Judiciary Act of 1789." Brandeis cited, but did not substantively rely on, Warren's research. Subsequent research has undermined Warren's position. Wilfred J. Ritz, *Rewriting the History of the Judiciary Act of 1789: Exposing Myths, Challenging Premises, and Using New Evidence*, ed. Wythe Holt and L. H. LaRue (Norman, Okla., 1990).

79 Draft opinion, dated Mar. 21, at 8, Brandeis Court Papers, Box 107, folder 7, "*Erie*."

80 Hugo L. Black to Louis D. Brandeis, March 22, 1938, Brandeis Court Papers, Box 107, folder 7, "*Erie*."

81 Single-page memo titled "Supreme Court of the United States," appended to draft opinion, "as circulated March 21 with corrections," Brandeis Court Papers, Box 107, folder 7, "*Erie*." The change appeared in 304 U.S. 64 (1938), at 80, n. 24.

82 W. Graham Claytor, undated memo entitled "Pennsylvania Law," Brandeis Court Papers, Box 107, folder 5, "*Erie*."

83 This seems particularly likely given two added considerations. One is that the choice-of-law rules of all the states apparently called for the application of Pennsylvania law (the place of injury) in such a case. The other is that, contemporaneously with his opinion in *Erie*, Brandeis wrote an opinion recognizing the choice-of-law issue that *Erie* created (choosing *which* state's law applied) and choosing to leave the question open. *Ruhlin v. New York Life Insurance Co.*, 304 U.S. 202 (1938). *See* George Dargo, *A History of the United States Court of Appeals for the First Circuit*, Vol. I (Washington, D.C., 1993), 134–35 and n. 7.

84 Stanley Reed to Louis D. Brandeis, Mar. 21, 1938, Brandeis Court Papers, Box 107, folder 7, "*Erie*."

85 Draft concurrence of Justice Reed, Brandeis Court Papers, Box 107, folder 9, "*Erie*."

86 Mason, *Harlan Fiske Stone*, 478.

87 Harlan F. Stone to Louis D. Brandeis, Mar. 23, 1938, Brandeis Court Papers, Box 107, folder 7, "*Erie*."

88 Pusey, *Charles Evans Hughes*, Vol. 2, 711.

89 Hugo L. Black to Louis D. Brandeis, Mar. 22, 1938, Brandeis Court Papers, Box 107, folder 7, "*Erie*."

90 Notation in Brandeis's handwriting on letter, Harlan F. Stone to Louis D. Brandeis, March 23, 1938, Brandeis Court Papers, Box 107, folder 7, "*Erie*."

91 Harlan F. Stone to Louis D. Brandeis, Mar. 25, 1938, Brandeis Court Papers, Box 107, folder 7, "*Erie*."

92 Draft opinion, dated Mar. 21, "as circulated," Brandeis Court Papers, Box 107, folder 7, "*Erie*" (emphasis added on language deleted).

93 Harlan F. Stone to Louis D. Brandeis, Mar. 25, 1938, and draft opinion, dated Mar. 21 "as circulated with corrections," Brandeis Court Papers, Box 107, folder 7, "*Erie*." The changes were incorporated in the final opinion, 304 U.S. at 77–78 (emphasis added on new language).

94 Harlan F. Stone to Louis D. Brandeis, Mar. 25, 1938, Brandeis Court Papers, Box 107, folder 7, "*Erie*."

95 This is suggested by a brief note, Pierce Butler to Louis D. Brandeis, Mar. 28, 1938, Brandeis Court Papers, Box 114, folder 18.

96 Hughes's "return" is in Brandeis Court Papers, Box 107, folder 9, "*Erie*."

97 Pusey, *Charles Evans Hughes*, Vol. 1, vii.

98 *Id.*, Vol. 2, at 711.

99 Mason, *Harlan Fiske Stone*, 479, 480.

100 A fuller account of the drafting process in *Erie*, based on a review of Brandeis's Court papers, is given in Freyer, *Harmony & Dissonance*, 131–42.

101 Harlan F. Stone to Louis D. Brandeis, Mar. 23, 1938, Brandeis Court Papers, Box 107, folder 7, "*Erie*."

102 *E.g.*, Pusey unquestioningly accepted Charles Warren's inconclusive argument that the history of Section 34 proved that the construction of the statute given in *Swift* was erroneous, misstated the *Swift* doctrine (ignoring the fact that it carved out certain "local" law areas in which the federal courts had a duty to follow state law), and asserted that the federal courts applied different rules from the state courts "in every state" (ignoring the fact that some federal courts tended to follow local law in many areas and that some states had adopted some of the rules of the federal common law).

103 In fairness to Mason, it must be noted that he repeatedly sought, and was denied, access to Brandeis's papers. Alexander Bickel, who was apparently the first scholar to notice the

significance of Brandeis's notation on Stone's letter, concluded that Mason's account was "badly garbled." Alexander Bickel to Felix Frankfurter, May 7, 1959, Frankfurter Papers, Box 24, folder 358.

104 304 U.S. at 77–78, 80.

105 *Id*. at 78.

106 *Id*. at 72, 78.

107 303 U.S. 161 (1938).

108 303 U.S. 161, 172, 175 (1938) (Black, J., dissenting). *See* Hugo L. Black to Arthur B. Foster, Feb. 21, 1938, Black Papers, Box 254, *"Connecticut General Life Insurance v. Johnson."*

109 *E.g.*, Williams, *Hugo L. Black*, 79–81; Wesley McCune, *The Nine Young Men* (New York, 1947), 31–32; Swisher, "History's Panorama and Justice Black's Career," in Strickland, ed., *Hugo Black and the Supreme Court*, 83. Black is given a more moderate influence in Dunne, *Hugo Black and the Judicial Revolution*, 183–84.

110 Mason, *Harlan Fiske Stone*, 478, note.

111 Handwitten notation on Black's "return" of draft dated Apr. 19, 1938, Brandeis Court Papers, Box 107, folder 9, *"Erie."*

112 303 U.S. at 175.

113 Mason, *Harlan Fiske Stone*, 467–76; Harlan F. Stone to Marshall and Lauson Stone, Jan. 7, 1938, Stone Papers, Box 3; Stone to Felix Frankfurter, Feb. 1938, Stone Papers, Box 13; Newman, *Hugo Black*, 272–79; Dunne, *Hugo Black and the Judicial Revolution*, 187–90.

114 *See* Urofsky and Levy, eds., *Letters of Louis D. Brandeis*, Vol. 5, 552, 608; Felix Frankfurter to Louis D. Brandeis, May 20, 1938, Frankfurter Papers, Box 29, folder 481. Brandeis's ready praise for Reed contrasted sharply with his warnings about Black. *See* Urofsky and Levy, eds., *"Half Brother, Half Son,"* 607, 608, 610.

115 *See* Dunne, *Hugo Black*, 187.

116 *See, e.g.*, Ball, "Justice Hugo L. Black," in Freyer, ed., *Justice Hugo Black*, 41–42; Dunne, *Hugo Black*, 163, 187, 228–31, 252; Norman Redlich, "Hugo Black Enters His Hundredth Year: Some Heavenly Reflections on the Constitution," in Freyer, ed., *Justice Hugo Black*, 307; Mason, *Harlan Fiske Stone*, 765–69; Lash, ed., *From the Diaries of Felix Frankfurter*, 182; Freedman, ed., *Roosevelt & Frankfurter*, 457; Baker, *Brandeis and Frankfurter*, 424; John T. Noonan, review of *Hugo Black and the Judicial Revolution* by Gerald T. Dunne, 9 *Southwestern Law Review* 1127, 1130- 32. *But see* Newman, *Hugo Black*, 273, 285, 323; Ickes, *Secret Diary*, Vol. 2, 483.

117 *See* 304 U.S. 72, 79–80. Both points, too, were added particularly in response to Justice Butler's dissent. In the Mar. 21 draft, the sentence on pp. 79–80 of the final published opinion did not appear. The reference to Section 34 as "declarative" of the law was originally confined to a footnote. In the final opinion the footnote was moved to the text, and Brandeis added a second, similar quote plus three supporting citations to the new footnote 2.

118 Single-page memo titled "Supreme Court of the United States," appended to draft opinion, "as circulated March 21 with corrections," Brandeis Court Papers, Box 107, folder 7, *"Erie."* *Compare* draft opinion, dated Mar. 10, at 4–5 (quoting Holmes but not Field) *with* draft opinion dated Mar. 17, at 7 (quoting Holmes and adding two sentences from Field's dissent in *Baugh*) and *with* draft opinion "as circulated March 21 with corrections," at 7 (still quoting only two sentences from Field's dissent in *Baugh*), Brandeis Court Papers, Box 107, folders 6 and 7, *"Erie."*

119 Pusey, *Charles Evans Hughes*, Vol. 2, 711.

after the event, and it could have been colored by the dominant professional opinion in the late 1940s that *Erie*'s constitutional language was unsound.

121 Harlan F. Stone to Felix Frankfurter, Apr. 29, 1938, Frankfurter Papers (H.L.S.), Box 171, folder 17.

122 It was also a group product that required compromise. *Compare* Alan Barth, *Prophets with Honor: Great Dissents and Great Dissenters in the Supreme Court* (New York, 1974), ch. 1.

CHAPTER 5. THE JUDGE AS HUMAN

1 There is an extensive and excellent biographical literature on Brandeis. *See, e.g.,* Alfred Lief, *Brandeis: The Personal History of an American Ideal* (New York, 1936); Alpheus T. Mason, *Brandeis: A Free Man's Life* (New York, 1946); Melvin I. Urofsky, *A Mind of One Piece: Brandeis and American Reform* (New York, 1971); Allon Gal, *Brandeis of Boston* (Cambridge, Mass., 1980); Melvin I. Urofsky, *Louis D. Brandeis and the Progressive Tradition* (Boston, 1981); Bruce Allen Murphy, *The Brandeis/Frankfurter Connection: The Secret Political Activities of Two Supreme Court Justices* (New York, 1982); Lewis J. Paper, *Brandeis* (Englewood Cliffs, N.J., 1983); Philippa Strum, *Louis D. Brandeis: Justice for the People* (Cambridge, Mass., 1984); Thomas K. McCraw, *Prophets of Regulation: Charles Francis Adams, Louis D. Brandeis, James M. Landis, and Alfred E. Kahn* (Cambridge, Mass., 1984); Leonard Baker, *Brandeis and Frankfurter: A Dual Biography* (New York, 1984); Robert A. Burt, *Two Jewish Justices: Outcasts in the Promised Land* (Berkeley, Calif., 1988); Nelson L. Dawson, ed., *Brandeis and America* (Lexington, Ky., 1989); Philippa Strum, *Brandeis: Beyond Progressivism* (Lawrence, Kans., 1993); Clyde Spillenger, "Elusive Advocate: Reconsidering Brandeis as People's Lawyer," 105 *Yale Law Journal* 1445 (1996). *See generally* Gene Teitelbaum, *Justice Louis D. Brandeis: A Bibliography of Writings and Other Materials on the Justice* (Littleton, Colo., 1988).

2 Urofsky, *A Mind of One Piece*, ch. 2.

3 The colloquy was recalled in a letter to Brandeis written by William E. Smythe and dated June 2, 1916, quoted in Mason, *Brandeis*, note at 504–5.

4 Mason, *Brandeis*, 323–33. *See, e.g.,* Louis D. Brandeis, *Business — A Profession* (Boston, 1914), 51–64, 198–217, 255–312; Robert Kanigal, *The One Best Way: Frederick Winslow Taylor and the Enigma of Efficiency* (New York, 1997), 429–43. For the importance of "efficiency" ideas to early-twentieth-century Progressivism, *see* Samuel Haber, *Efficiency and Uplift: Scientific Management in the Progressive Era, 1890–1920* (Chicago, 1964); Samuel P. Hays, *Conservation and the Gospel of Efficiency: The Progressive Conservation Movement, 1890–1920* (Cambridge, Mass., 1959).

5 *Muller v. Oregon*, 208 U.S. 412 (1908).

6 Brandeis also became a major figure in American Zionism in the years after 1912, and his ideas about Jews and a Jewish homeland were shaped to a large extent by his ideas about Progressivism, democracy, and the United States. *See, e.g.,* Urofsky, *Louis D. Brandeis and the Progressive Tradition*, ch. 5; Strum, *Brandeis*, chs. 13–14.

7 Quoted in John E. Semonche, *Charting the Future: The Supreme Court Responds to a Changing Society, 1890–1920* (Westport, Conn., 1978), 313.

8 *Id.* at 315.

9 Alexander M. Bickel, *The Unpublished Opinions of Mr. Justice Brandeis* (Chicago, 1957).

10 The discussion that follows summarizes key aspects of Brandeis's judicial career and synthesizes his judicial philosophy. As such, it minimizes the changes that occurred while he was

jurisprudence, and it reflects the fact that Brandeis remained remarkably consistent over the years in his basic values and attitudes.

From another perspective, however, one could trace different phases and emphases in Brandeis's judicial career. In simplified and schematic terms, there were at least four such phases: First, from 1916 to approximately 1921 Brandeis seemed most determined to support and defend Progressive programs and policies, and he did so relatively forcefully and overtly. Second, from approximately 1922 to 1933 Brandeis altered his tactics, serving his goals somewhat less directly and seeking to moderate the Court's actions and deflect the majority's values. His altered approach was the result of his failure to prevail in a number of early cases, his clear recognition (especially following the appointments of Taft, Sutherland, and Butler in 1921–22) of his minority position, his increased willingness to compromise and save his energies for particularly critical issues, his recognition of the limited impact he could have, and his growing respect for and identification with the Court as an institution. It was during this period that he began developing in detail his ideas about judicial restraint, giving greater weight to structural matters and the claims of institutional efficiency, and pressing to expand the reach of the Fourteenth Amendment to include noneconomic rights. Third, from 1933 through 1937 Brandeis was caught between conflicting pressures: his fervent Progressivism, his enthusiasm for much of the New Deal, and his stalwart opposition to the views of the Court's conservative majority increasingly struggled with his growing sense of unease and, on occasion, outright dislike for some of the New Deal's centralizing measures and rhetoric. For the first time since World War I he enjoyed considerable influence within the administration, and he sought to influence the New Deal's course while retaining his judicial distance. Finally, from the spring of 1937 until he resigned in 1939, Brandeis was in a strikingly new position on the Court. For the first time he was in the constitutional majority, and he worked with considerable freedom and success to reshape doctrine along his chosen lines.

11 On Brandeis's attitude toward "reasonableness" *see* Burt, *Two Jewish Justices*, 20–34.

12 244 U.S. 147 (1917).

13 *Id.* at 149, 153. *Compare Southern Pacific Co. v. Jensen*, 244 U.S. 205 (1917).

14 *See* Kurt Wetzel, "Railroad Management's Response to Operating Employees' Accidents, 1890–1913," 21 *Labor History* 351–368 (Summer, 1980).

15 244 U.S. at 164–65.

16 *Id.* at 165.

17 *Id.* at 166.

18 "Conversations Between L[ouis]. D. B[randeis]. and F[elix]. F[rankfurter]," Frankfurter Papers, Box 224, at 24 [hereafter, "Brandeis-Frankfurter Conversations"].

19 Brandeis-Frankfurter Conversations, 19 (emphasis in original).

20 252 U.S. 189 (1920).

21 252 U.S. 220, 237 (Brandeis, J., dissenting).

22 Brandeis-Frankfurter Conversations, 3.

23 *Id.* at 17, 10.

24 *Id.* at 21.

25 *Duplex Printing Press Co. v. Deering*, 254 U.S. 443, 479, 485 (1921) (Brandeis, J., dissenting).

26 *New State Ice Co. v. Liebmann*, 285 U.S. 262, 280, 311 (1932) (Brandeis, J., dissenting).

27 264 U.S. 504 (1924).

28 Brandeis-Frankfurter Conversations, 8.

29 Melvin I. Urofsky and David W. Levy, eds., *Letters of Louis D. Brandeis* (Albany, N.Y., 1978), Vol. 5, 126.

30 264 U.S. at 520.

31 *Id.* at 530. *Cf. St. Louis & O'Fallon Railway Co. v. United States,* 279 U.S. 461, 488 (1929) (Brandeis, J., dissenting).

32 264 U.S. at 534.

33 Brandeis-Frankfurter Conversations, 15.

34 Urofsky and Levy, eds., *Letters of Louis D. Brandeis,* Vol. 5, 75.

35 *Compare* Stephen L. Winter, "The Metaphor of Standing and the Problem of Self-Governance," 40 *Stanford Law Review* 1371 (1988).

36 *E.g., Lipke v. Lederer,* 259 U.S. 557, 563 (1922) (Brandeis, J., dissenting); *King Manufacturing Co v. City Council of Augusta,* 277 U.S. 100, 115 (1928) (Brandeis, J. dissenting); *Hill v. Wallace,* 259 U.S. 44, 72 (1922) (Brandeis, J., concurring); *Fidelity and Deposit Co. of Maryland v. Tafoya,* 270 U.S. 426, 437 (1926) (Brandeis, J., concurring in the dissent of McReynolds, J.). *See* Harlan F. Stone to Alfred Lief, Feb. 4, 1936, Stone Papers, Box 19; Bickel, *Unpublished Opinions.*

37 297 U.S. 288, 341.

38 *Id.* at 346.

39 *Id.* at 347.

40 *Id.* at 348.

41 Urofsky and Levy, eds., *Letters of Louis D. Brandeis,* Vol. 5, 324.

42 *Id.,* Vol. 5, 368. *See id.,* Vol. 5, 83, 160, 324, 326; Brandeis-Frankfurter Conversations, 1, 8, 14, 28–29.

43 Strum, *Brandeis: Beyond Progressivism,* 131.

44 *See* Frederick Schauer, "Ashwander Revisited," 1995 *Supreme Court Review* 71.

45 *See* Burt, *Two Jewish Justices,* ch. 2.

46 Urofsky and Levy, eds., *Letters of Louis D. Brandeis,* Vol. 5, 64.

47 *Id.,* Vol. 5, 75. *See also id.,* Vol. 5, 63, 128.

48 Bickel, *Unpublished Opinions,* ch. 4.

49 *United Mine Workers of America v. Coronado Coal Co.,* 259 U.S. 344 (1922). *See* Bickel, *Unpublished Opinions,* ch. 5.

50 *New State Ice Co. v. Liebmann,* 285 U.S. 262, 280, 311 (1932) (Brandeis, J., dissenting). *Accord Adams v. Tanner,* 244 U.S. 590, 597 (1917) (Brandeis, J., dissenting); *Quaker City Cab Co. v. Pennsylvania,* 277 U.S. 389, 403 (1928) (Brandeis, J., dissenting); *Liggett v. Lee,* 288 U.S. at 517, 541 (1933) (Brandeis, J., dissenting).

51 262 U.S. 553 (1923).

52 Brandeis-Frankfurter Conversations, 8. *See* Urofsky and Levy, eds., *Letters of Louis D. Brandeis,* Vol. 5, 105.

53 298 U.S. 238 (1936). *See* Paul L Murphy, *The Constitution in Crisis Times, 1918–1969* (New York, 1972), 149–50.

54 257 U.S. 282 (1921).

55 39 Stat. 726 (1916).

56 256 U.S. at 303.

57 *Id.* at 298.

58 *Id.* at 298–99.

59 *E.g., Eureka Pipe Line Co. v. Hallanan,* 257 U.S. 265, 277 (1921) (Brandeis, J., dissenting). *See*

Edward A. Purcell, Jr., *Litigation and Inequality: Federal Diversity Jurisdiction in Industrial America, 1870–1958* (New York, 1992), 55–58.

60 *St. Joseph Stock Yards Co. v. United States,* 298 U.S. 38, 73, 93 (1936) (Brandeis, J., concurring, arguing against expanded judicial review of certain questions of fact in appeals from administrative orders).

61 *See, e.g.,* Paper, *Brandeis,* 372–77.

62 Urofsky and Levy, eds., *Letters of Louis D. Brandeis,* Vol. 5, 129. *See* Felix Frankfurter to Edwin E. Borchard, Apr. 2, 1928, Frankfurter Papers, Box 25, folder 388.

63 Brandeis-Frankfurter Conversations, 18.

64 *See, e.g., Piedmont & Northern Railway Co. v. United States,* 280 U.S. 469 (1930).

65 Edwin Borchard, *Declaratory Judgments* (Cleveland, Ohio, 1934), 237–43. The declaratory judgment had roots in English equity practice prior to its formal adoption by statute. Stephen C. Yeazell, *From Medieval Group Litigation to the Modern Class Action* (New Haven, Conn., 1987).

66 *Id.* at 244–45.

67 *E.g.,* Edwin M. Borchard, "The Declaratory Judgment — A Needed Procedural Reform," 28 *Yale Law Journal* 3 (1918); Borchard, "Judicial Relief for Peril and Insecurity," 45 *Harvard Law Review* 793 (1931); Borchard to George Sutherland, Apr. 15, 1927, Sutherland Papers, Box 5; Borchard to Harlan F. Stone, Mar. 1, 1928, Stone Papers, Box 6.

68 45 *Reports of the American Bar Association,* 59, 260 (1920).

69 Edwin M. Borchard, "The Uniform Act on Declaratory Judgments," 34 *Harvard Law Review,* 697, 698–700 (1921); Borchard, *Declaratory Judgments,* 245; Borchard, "The Supreme Court and the Declaratory Judgment," 14 *American Bar Association Journal* 633 (1928).

70 Edson R. Sunderland, "A Modern Evolution in Remedial Rights — the Declaratory Judgment," 16 *Michigan Law Review* 69, 69–70 (1917).

71 Borchard, "The Supreme Court and the Declaratory Judgment," 635.

72 179 N.W. 350, 351 (1920).

73 Borchard, *Declaratory Judgments,* 249, n. 4.

74 179 N.W. at 365.

75 *Id.* at 351.

76 Borchard, *Declaratory Judgments,* 252. *Compare* Borchard, "Uniform Act on Declaratory Judgments," 34 *Harvard Law Review* at 702.

77 Victor A. Olander to William Green, Jan. 7, 1929, enclosed with Andrew Furuseth to George W. Norris, Jan. 10, 1929, Norris Papers, Tray 42, Box 1, file: "Judiciary Committee, 1929."

78 Felix Frankfurter, "A Note on Advisory Opinions," 37 *Harvard Law Review* 1002, 1003 (1924).

79 *Id.* at 1003, 1004.

80 *Id.* at 1005, 1007.

81 *Id.* at 1007.

82 *Id.* at 1005.

83 *Id.* at 1008. In Massachusetts, the Supreme Judicial Court had constitutional authority to issue advisory opinions, and it had ruled that statutes prohibiting yellow dog contracts were unconstitutional. When the state legislature tried to pass such a bill in 1932, its opponents charged the supporters with willfully defying the court. Frankfurter defended the bill, arguing that the earlier advisory opinion was not binding. Felix Frankfurter, "Court's Advisory Opinion Not Necessarily Final," *Boston Herald,* Feb. 27, 1932, Frankfurter Papers, Box 197, folder 7.

84 Everett P. Wheeler to Thomas J. Walsh, Feb. 24, 1923, Walsh Papers, Box 281, "Legislation." *See* Wheeler to Walsh, Mar. 18, 1922, Apr. 4, 1922, and Nov. 17, 1923, Walsh Papers, Box 281, "Legislation."

85 Arthur H. Vanderberg to William D. Mitchell, Jan. 30, 1934, Mitchell Papers, Box 1 (emphasis in original).

86 *E.g.*, Thomas J. Walsh to Everett P. Wheeler, Mar. 1, 1923, and Walsh to Richard P. Ernst, Feb. 20, 1923, Walsh Papers, Box 281, file: "Legislation."

87 The Court had avoided addressing the constitutionality of declaratory judgments for more than a decade. In two decisions it ruled that the judicial power did not preclude judgments rendered without accompanying orders of execution: *Fidelity National Bank v. Swope*, 274 U.S. 123, 132 (1927); *Old Colony Trust Co. v. Commissioner of Internal Revenue*, 279 U.S. 716, 725 (1929). Further, in three cases under the Due Process Clause, one involving a zoning ordinance and two relating to civil liberties issues, it held that judgment could be granted in advance of actual injury. *Euclid v. Ambler Realty Co.*, 272 U.S. 365 (1926); *Terrace v. Thompson*, 263 U.S. 197 (1923); *Pierce v. Society of Sisters*, 268 U.S. 510 (1925).

At the same time, however, in other contexts the Court implied or stated that the federal judiciary could not render declaratory relief. In some cases the statements were clearly dicta, and in others it was not clear whether the holding was based simply on the absence of a congressional enabling act or on the ultimate mandate of Article III. *New Jersey v. Sargent*, 269 U.S. 328, 334–35 (1925); *Liberty Warehouse Co. v. Grannis*, 273 U.S. 70, 76 (1927); *Liberty Warehouse Co. v. Burley*, 276 U.S. 71, 89 (1928); *Arizona v. California*, 283 U.S. 423, 462–63 (1931); *Piedmont v. Northern Railway Co.*, 280 U.S. 469, 477 (1930).

88 277 U.S. 274 (1928). *See* H.R. Rep. Nos. 288 and 366, 70 Cong., 1 sess (1928); 69 *Cong. Rec.*, 70 Cong., 1 sess., 2032 (1928); Subcommittee of Senate Committee on Judiciary, Hearings on H.R. 5632, 70 Cong., 1 sess. (1928); William H. King to Edwin M. Borchard, Feb. 22, 1928, Stone Papers, Box 6.

89 277 U.S. at 289.

90 *Id.* at 284.

91 *Id.* at 289.

92 *Id.*

93 The procedural situation that resulted was uncertain, but it was possible that plaintiffs could still have obtained their remedy under Illinois law in a state court. 277 U.S. at 290.

94 *Id.* at 291. *See* Paul A. Freund, *On Law and Justice* (Cambridge, Mass., 1968), 141.

95 277 U.S. at 291.

96 Andrew Furuseth to George W. Norris, Jan. 10, 1929, Norris Papers, Tray 42, Box 1, file: "Judiciary Committee, 1929."

97 H.R. Rep. No. 94, 71 Cong., 2 sess. (1929); H.R. Rep. No. 627, 72 Cong., 1 sess. (1932); 71 *Cong. Rec.* 10564–65, 71 Cong., 2d sess. (1930).

98 69 *Cong. Rec.* 2028, 70 Cong., 1 sess. (1928).

99 *See, e.g.*, Note, "The Constitutionality of the Proposed Federal Declaratory Judgment Act," 38 *Yale Law Journal* 104, 107 (1928).

100 Borchard, "Supreme Court and the Declaratory Judgment," 639.

101 Felix Frankfurter and James M. Landis, *The Business of the Supreme Court: A Study in the Federal Judicial System* (New York, 1928), v.

102 Note, "Declaratory Relief in the Supreme Court," 45 *Harvard Law Review* 1089, 1090–91 (1932).

103 *Id.* at 1095.

104 *Id.* at 1096.

105 Charles E. Clark to Felix Frankfurter, June 1, 1932, Frankfurter Papers, Box 44, folder 775. Another leading realist, Walter Wheeler Cook, agreed with Clark. Cook to Harlan F. Stone, Apr. 29, 1927, Stone Papers, Box 10.

106 Edwin M. Borchard, "Declaratory Judgments in Federal Courts," 41 *Yale Law Journal* 1195, 1197 (1932). *See id.* at 1198.

107 Felix Frankfurter to Charles E. Clark, June 2, 1932, Frankfurter Papers, Box 44, folder 775.

108 Thurman Arnold and Harry Shulman were two of the relatively small number of legal Progressives who seemed to agree with Brandeis and Frankfurter. *See* Arnold to Frankfurter, May 12, 1932, and undated (circa June 1932) Frankfurter Papers, Box 21, folder 286; Shulman to Frankfurter, Oct. 12, 1932, Frankfurter Papers, Box 102, folder 2115.

109 Charles E. Clark to Felix Frankfurter, June 3, 1932, Frankfurter Papers (H.L.S.), Box 183, folder 20.

110 *See* the series of letters from Borchard to Stone in 1927, 1928, and 1933 in Stone Papers, Box 6. *See also* Walter Wheeler Cook to Stone, Apr. 29, 1927, Stone Papers, Box 10; Stone to William Howard Taft, Apr. 18, 1927, Stone Papers, Box 53, "Fidelity National Bank v. Swope." In 1927 Stone had joined the Court's opinion in *Liberty Warehouse Co. v. Grannis,* 273 U.S. 70 (1927), which contained language similar to Brandeis's language in *Willing.*

111 *See* Holmes's "return" on Stone's concurrence in *Willing,* Stone Papers, Box 55, "*Willing v. Chicago.*" Cardozo had written the Senate Judiciary Committee in 1928 supporting adoption of the proposed federal declaratory judgment act. Sen. Rep. No. 1005, 73 Cong., 2 sess. (1934), 1.

112 Borchard, "Declaratory Judgments in Federal Courts," 1196 n. 5.

113 288 U.S. 249, 264 (1933).

114 *See id.* at 262; *Alabama v. Arizona,* 291 U.S. 286, 291 (1934).

115 Borchard, *Declaratory Judgments,* 296.

116 Felix Frankfurter and Henry M. Hart, Jr., "The Business of the Supreme Court at October Term, 1932," 47 *Harvard Law Review* 245, 285, 286 (1933). *See Skelly Oil Co. v. Phillips Petroleum Co.,* 339 U.S. 667 (1950) (Frankfurter, J.).

117 Homer S. Cummings to Franklin D. Roosevelt, June 13, 1934, Roosevelt Papers, OF 5708, Box 4.

118 Sen. Rep. No. 1005, 73 Cong., 2 sess. (1934), 5. *See* H.R. Rep. No. 1264, 73 Cong., 2 sess. (1934). *See also* Edwin M. Borchard to William H. King, Feb. 4, 1928, and Mar. 8, 1928, and King to Borchard, Feb. 22, 1928, Stone Papers, Box 6.

119 297 U.S. at 347, 348.

120 Although Brandeis has attracted an unusually large number of fine biographers, they have generally paid little attention to *Erie,* Brandeis's motives in writing the decision, or its place in his jurisprudence. The reasons are understandable. A biographer has too much other ground to cover, and the case seems too technical for general interest. The most extensive treatment of *Erie* in a biography is in Paper, *Brandeis,* 378–85. Brief references are the common approach. *E.g.,* Strum, *Louis D. Brandeis,* 364, and Dawson, *Brandeis and America,* 144. *Erie* does not even appear in the index of some works on Brandeis. *E.g.,* Mason, *Brandeis;* Baker, *Brandeis and Frankfurter.* Failure to make connections between Brandeis the man, the Progressive, and the judge on the one side and *Erie* on the other may help explain why legal scholars have been able to treat the case relatively abstractly and ahistorically and why *Erie*

has so commonly been understood as simply another example of Brandeis's commitment to federalism and the authority of the states.

121 *See* Charles E. Clark, "State Law in the Federal Courts: The Brooding Omnipresence of Erie v. Tompkins," 55 *Yale Law Journal* 267, 295 (1946).

122 *Hawks v. Hamill*, 288 U.S. 52, 58 (1933); *Mutual Life Insurance Co. v. Johnson*, 293 U.S. 335 (1934).

123 Kiendl's argument for distinguishing *Swift* might have appealed to Cardozo. *See* Alfred S. Konefsky, "How to Read, or at Least Not Misread, Cardozo in the *Allegheny College* Case," 36 *Buffalo Law Review* 645 (1988).

124 *See* Henry J. Friendly, *Benchmarks* (Chicago, 1967), 157–64.

125 For the breakup of Roosevelt's congressional coalition, *see* James Patterson, *Congressional Conservatism and the New Deal* (Lexington, Ky., 1967); Richard Polenberg, *Reorganizing Roosevelt's Government: The Controversy Over Executive Reorganization, 1936–39* (Cambridge, Mass., 1966).

126 *See, e.g.,* C. Herman Pitchett, *The Roosevelt Court: A Study in Judicial Politics and Values* (Chicago, 1969 [1948]), 300–301.

127 For attacks on the Supreme Court during the 1920s and 1930s *see* Paul L. Murphy, *The Constitution in Crisis Times, 1918–1969* (New York, 1972), chs. 2–5; Edward S. Corwin, *Twilight of the Supreme Court* (New Haven, Conn., 1934); William G. Ross, *Muted Fury: Populists, Progressives, and Labor Unions Confront the Courts, 1890–1937* (Princeton, 1994), chs. 8–13.

128 Willard Hurst to Felix Frankfurter, May 24, 1938, Frankfurter Papers, Box 127, folder 2648. *See* Harold L. Ickes, *The Secret Diary of Harold L. Ickes: The Inside Struggle, 1936–1939* (New York, 1954), 365.

129 *E.g.*, Urofsky and Levy, eds., *Letters of Louis D. Brandeis*, Vol. 4, 520, 528; *Liggett v. Lee*, 288 U.S. 517, 541 (1933) (Brandeis, J., dissenting in part); Paul A. Freund, "Mr. Justice Brandeis," in *Mr. Justice*, ed. Allison Dunham and Philip B. Kurland (Chicago, 1956); Urofsky, *A Mind of One Piece;* Bickel, *Unpublished Opinions,* ch. 7.

130 Brandeis was not, of course, a stereotyped "states'-rights" advocate, nor was he opposed to bigness under any and all circumstances. He strongly believed in the exercise of the constitutionally granted powers of the federal government, consistently defending, for example, an expansive interpretation of the commerce power. When large-scale organization was necessary, and especially when it served the values of efficiency or competition, he was ready to accept it. Bigness, however, not smallness was what required special justification. See, *e.g.*, *American Column and Lumber Co. v. United States*, 257 U.S. 377 (1921) (Brandeis, J., dissenting); *Chicago Board of Trade v. United States*, 246 U.S. 231 (1918); Urofsky and Levy, eds., *Letters of Louis D. Brandeis*, Vol. 5, 41.

131 Urofsky and Levy, eds., *Letters of Louis D. Brandeis*, Vol. 4, 497–99, Vol. 5, 17, 45–46; Freund, "Mr. Justice."

132 Urofsky and Levy, eds., *Letters of Louis D. Brandeis*, Vol. 5, 46.

133 Brandeis-Frankfurter Conversations, at 24. *See, e.g.*, *Arkansas Railroad Commission v. Chicago, Rock Island & Pacific Railroad Co.*, 274 U.S. 597 (1927) (Brandeis, J.); *Public Utilities Commission of Rhode Island v. Attleboro Steam & Electric Co.*, 273 U.S. 83, 91 (1927) (Brandeis, J., dissenting).

134 *New State Ice Co. v. Liebmann*, 285 U.S. 262, 311 (1932) (Brandeis, J., dissenting).

135 Quoted in Freund, "Mr. Justice," at 112. *See* Bickel, *Unpublished Opinions*, ch. 10, esp. 225, 234.

136 His attitude in this regard may have been influenced further by his Kentucky upbringing and

the anti–federal court bias of his beloved uncle Lewis N. Dembitz. *See* William M. Wiecek, "Clio as Hostage: The United States Supreme Court and the Uses of History," 24 *California Western Law Review* 227, 243 (1988).

137 Urofsky and Levy, eds., *Letters of Louis D. Brandeis*, Vol. 5, 556. *See* Arthur M. Schlesinger, Jr., *The Age of Roosevelt: The Politics of Upheaval, 1935–36* (Cambridge, Mass., 1966 [1960]), 312–16.

138 *Schechter Poultry Co. v. United States*, 295 U.S. 495 (1935).

139 Quoted in Schlesinger, *The Age of Roosevelt*, 280. *See* Urofsky and Levy, eds., *Letters of Louis D. Brandeis*, Vol 5, 537.

140 Otis L. Graham, *An Encore for Reform: The Old Progressives and the New Deal* (New York, 1967), 124–25. On the same day the Court announced its unanimous decision that the NIRA was unconstitutional, *A.L.A. Schechter Poultry v. United States*, 295 U.S. 495 (1935), Brandeis wrote for the Court in another unanimous decision declaring the New Deal's Frazier-Lemke Act of 1933 unconstitutional. *Louisville v. Radford*, 295 U.S. 555 (1935). For Brandeis's attitude toward the New Deal, *see* Mason, *Brandeis*, 613–27; Strum, *Brandeis*, 348–53.

141 302 U.S. 783 (1937); Urofsky and Levy, *"Half Brother, Half Son,"* 606. *Erie* helped spur a brief protest in the Senate against the new Rules. 83 *Cong. Rec.* 75 Cong., 1 sess (1938), 8473–83.

142 Brandeis's views are reported in Paul A. Freund, *On Understanding the Supreme Court* (Boston, 1949), 58; Freund, "Mr. Justice Brandeis," 111.

143 Quoted in Robert E. Sherwood, *Roosevelt and Hopkins: An Intimate History* (New York, 1948), 90. *See* Murphy, *Constitution in Crisis Times*, 179–85; Urofsky and Levy, eds., *Letters of Louis D. Brandeis*, Vol. 5, 588 n. 1; Mason, *Brandeis*, 624–26.

144 Mason, *Brandeis*, 626–27; Baker, *Brandeis and Frankfurter*, 329–30.

145 Urofsky and Levy, eds., *Letters of Louis D. Brandeis*, Vol. 5, 584.

146 Pusey, *Charles Evans Hughes*, Vol. 2, 753. *See* Robert H. Jackson, *The Struggle for Judicial Supremacy: A Study of a Crisis in American Power Politics* (New York, 1941), 190. In private, Brandeis responded by arguing that age had nothing to do with a "conservative mentality." Urofsky and Levy, eds., *Letters of Louis D. Brandeis*, Vol. 5, 588 n. 1; Mason, *Brandeis*, 624–25. Ironically, however, a decade earlier Brandeis had come to believe that Holmes — of all people — had grown more conservative with respect to property issues as he had aged. Strum, *Louis D. Brandeis*, 313.

147 Mason, *Brandeis*, 633.

148 Paper, *Brandeis*, 365–66.

149 Baker, *Brandeis and Frankfurter*, 333–36. Brandeis's cooperation with Hughes and Van Devanter in undermining the Court-packing plan angered a number of New Dealers, including Dean Acheson, Harold Ickes, and Tommy Corcoran, all of whom remained loyal to the president. *See, e.g.*, Ickes, *Secret Diary: The Inside Struggle, 1936–1939*, 424, 471, 505, 539–40, 559; Charles A. Fecher, ed., *The Diary of H. L. Mencken* (New York, 1989), 112–13; Michael E. Parrish, *Felix Frankfurter and His Times* (New York, 1982), 274; Murphy, *Brandeis/Frankfurter Connection* (New York, 1982), 179–84.

150 In two other contemporaneous cases, Brandeis wrote for the Court and disposed of issues which, judged by his philosophy of restraint, arguably should have been remanded. *Thompson v. Consolidated Gas Utilities Corp.*, 300 U.S. 55, 74–76 (1937); *Kellogg Co v. National Biscuit Co.*, 305 U.S. 111, 113 n. 1 (1938).

151 Quoted in Mason, *Brandeis*, 495.

152 Mark DeWolfe Howe, ed., *Holmes-Laski Letters: The Correspondence of Mr. Justice Holmes*

and Harold J. Laski, 1916–1935 (Cambridge, Mass., 1953), Vol. 2, 1055. On the relationship between Holmes and Brandeis *see* Samuel J. Konefsky, *The Legacy of Holmes and Brandeis: A Study in the Influence of Ideas* (New York, 1956).

153 *See, e.g.,* Robert M. Mennel and Christine L. Compston, eds., *Holmes & Frankfurter: Their Correspondence, 1912–1934* (Hanover, N.H., 1996), 68, 137, 169–70, 198. In his effort Brandeis was not alone. *See, e.g.,* G. Edward White, *Justice Oliver Wendell Holmes: Law and the Inner Self* (New York, 1993), 355–56, 369, 427–30, 484.

154 Quoted in Alpheus Thomas Mason, *William Howard Taft: Chief Justice* (New York, 1965), 220. *See id.,* 227–28; Paper, *Brandeis,* 281–82, 309–14. Although the two justices shared many views, they also differed in significant ways. *See, e.g.,* Strum, *Louis D. Brandeis,* 309–38; Paper, *Brandeis,* 307–9; Bickel, *Unpublished Opinions,* ch. 10.

155 Oliver Wendell Holmes, Jr., to Felix Frankfurter, Nov. 21, 1927, Holmes Papers, Box 29, folder 11; Mennel and Compston, eds., *Holmes & Frankfurter,* 162, 218, 223, 266.

156 Oliver Wendell Holmes, Jr., to Felix Frankfurter, Jan. 26, 1924, Holmes Papers, Box 29, folder 8.

157 Howe, ed., *Holmes-Laski Letters,* Vol. 1, 304, 297.

158 Howe, ed., *Holmes-Laski Letters,* Vol. 1, 485. *See* Urofsky and Levy, eds., *Letters of Louis D. Brandeis,* Vol. 4, 450, and Vol. 5, 364.

159 Howe, ed., *Holmes-Laski Letters,* Vol. 1, 485. Brandeis "never fails to offer a strong hand," Holmes wrote in 1931. "I am fortunate in my friend." Mennel and Compston, eds., *Holmes & Frankfurter,* 267.

160 Felix Frankfurter to Charles E. Clark, Jan. 17, 1930, Frankfurter Papers, Box 42, folder 774. Holmes put his remark in print in his introduction to Frankfurter's collection of essays honoring Brandeis. Oliver Wendell Holmes, Jr., "Introduction," in Felix Frankfurter, ed., *Mr. Justice Brandeis* (New York, 1972 [1932]), unpaginated. *See* Mennel and Compston, eds., *Holmes & Frankfurter,* 175, 176, 184, 236, 271.

161 Brandeis-Frankfurter Conversations, at 27.

162 Strum, *Louis D. Brandeis,* 370.

163 Paper, *Brandeis,* 326–27.

164 Felix Frankfurter to Charles Amidon, Mar. 15, 1932, Frankfurter Papers, Box 20, folder 260.

165 Paper, *Brandeis,* 327; White, *Oliver Wendell Holmes,* 470.

166 White, *Oliver Wendell Holmes,* 472.

167 Willard Hurst to Felix Frankfurter, May 24, 1938, Frankfurter Papers, Box 127, folder 2648.

168 *Kuhn v. Fairmont Coal Co.,* 215 U.S. 349, 370 (1910).

169 244 U.S. 205, 218 (1917).

170 *Black & White Taxicab and Transfer Co. v. Brown & Yellow Taxicab and Transfer Co.,* 276 U.S. 518, 532, 533 (Holmes, Brandeis, and Stone, JJ., dissenting). *See* the special concurrence that Holmes and Brandeis filed in *Salem Trust Co. v. Manufacturers' Finance Co.,* 264 U.S. 182 (1924); Urofsky and Levy, eds., *Letters of Louis D. Brandeis,* Vol. 5, 174.

171 Oliver Wendell Holmes, Jr., to Baroness Moncheur, Apr. 6, 1928, Holmes Papers, Box 36, folder 23.

172 Oliver Wendell Holmes, Jr., to Felix Frankfurter, Apr. 21, 1928, Holmes Papers, Box 36, folder 23.

173 Howe, ed., *Holmes-Laski Letters,* Vol. 2, 1007. *See also id.,* Vol. 2, 214.

174 *See* Oliver Wendell Holmes, Jr., to Barroness Moncheur, Jan. 27, 1928, Holmes Papers, Box 36, folder 22; Mark DeWolfe Howe, ed., *Holmes-Pollock Letters: The Correspondence of*

Mr. Justice Holmes and Sir Frederick Pollock, 1874–1932 (Cambridge, Mass., 1961 [1941]), Vol. 2, 136.

175 Urofsky and Levy, eds., *Letters of Louis D. Brandeis*, Vol. 5, 335.

176 Holmes's statement appears on his "return" of Stone's draft concurrence. Stone Papers, Box 55, "Willing v. Chicago."

177 304 U.S. 64, 79.

178 Urofsky and Levy, eds., *Letters of Louis D. Brandeis*, Vol. 5, 518.

CHAPTER 6. "DEFECTS, SOCIAL"

1 *Erie Railroad Co. v. Tompkins*, 304 U.S. 64, 74 (1938).

2 *Black and White Taxicab and Transfer Co. v. Brown and Yellow Taxicab and Transfer Co.*, 276 U.S. 518, 532, 533 (1928) (Holmes, J., dissenting).

3 *See, e.g.*, Melvin I. Urofsky and David W. Levy, *Letters of Louis D. Brandeis* (New York, 1978), Vol. 5, 66–67; Louis D. Brandies, *Business—A Profession* (Boston, 1914); Louis D. Brandeis, *Other People's Money and How Bankers Use It* (New York, 1914); Louis D. Brandeis, *The Curse of Bigness* (New York, 1935).

4 277 U.S. 389 (1928).

5 *Id.* at 403 (Brandeis, J., dissenting). *See* Alexander M. Bickel, *The Unpublished Opinions of Mr. Justice Brandeis* (Chicago, 1957), ch. 7, esp. at 157.

6 277 U.S. at 410. *Accord Kentucky, Finance Corp. v. Paramount Auto Exchange Corp.*, 262 U.S. 544, 551 (1923) (Brandeis and Holmes, JJ., dissenting).

7 Harry Shulman, "Memorandum of Talk with L[ouis]. D[embitz]. B[randeis].—December 8, 1933," Frankfurter Papers (H.L.S.), Box 188, folder 8; Urofsky and Levy, eds., *Letters of Louis D. Brandeis*, Vol. 5, 482.

8 Urofsky and Levy, eds., *Letters of Louis D. Brandeis*, Vol 5, 84. *See id.*, Vol. 4, 130.

9 *Id.*, Vol. 5, 360; Melvin I. Urofsky and David W. Levy, eds., *"Half Brother, Half Son": The Letters of Louis D. Brandeis to Felix Frankfurter* (Norman, Okla., 1991), 351.

10 Urofsky and Levy, eds., *Letters of Louis D. Brandeis*, Vol. 5, 193. *See id.* at 45–46; *Whitney v. California*, 274 U.S. 357, 372, 375 (1927) (Brandeis, J., concurring).

11 288 U.S. 517, 565, 566, 567 (1933) (Brandeis, J., dissenting).

12 Bickel, *Unpublished Opinions*, 157. *See* Urofsky and Levy, eds., *Letters of Louis D. Brandeis*, Vol. 5, 482.

13 *See, e.g.*, Brandeis, *Business—A Profession*, 333–41.

14 Urofsky and Levy, eds., *Letters of Louis D. Brandeis*, Vol. 5, 75.

15 *Mortensen v. Security Insurance Co.*, 289 U.S. 702 (1933) (Brandeis, J., dissenting).

16 Urofsky and Levy, eds., *Letters of Louis D. Brandeis*, Vol. 5, 170, 337.

17 Alpheus T. Mason, *Brandeis—A Free Man's Life* (New York, 1946), 257–58.

18 Richard Lowitt, *George W. Norris: The Making of a Progressive, 1861–1912* (Syracuse, N.Y., 1963), 239.

19 Richard Lowitt, *George W. Norris: The Persistence of a Progressive, 1913–1933* (Urbana, Ill., 1971), 16, 18.

20 Mason, *Brandeis*, 600; Urofsky and Levy, eds., *"Half Brother, Half Son,"* 590.

21 Mason, *Brandeis*, 493.

22 Louis D. Brandeis to Thomas J. Walsh, May 14, 1926, Walsh Papers, Box 302, "Procedural Bill." *See* Walsh to John C. Shea, Oct. 1, 1929, Walsh Papers, Box 302, "Procedural bill."

23 Mason, *Brandeis*, 603–6; James M. Landis, "Mr. Justice Brandeis: A Law Clerk's View," 5–6, Landis Papers, Box 169; Bruce Allen Murphy, *The Brandeis/Frankfurter Connection: The Secret Political Activities of Two Supreme Court Justices* (New York, 1982), 121–23.

24 Thomas J. Walsh to Felix Frankfurter, Feb. 23, 1926, Frankfurter Papers, Box 134, folder 2774; Urofsky and Levy, eds., *Letters of Louis D. Brandeis*, Vol. 5, 322. *See also id.*, Vol. 5, 330, 368, 377.

25 Urofsky and Levy, eds., *Letters of Louis D. Brandeis*, Vol. 5, 322, 327, 330, 368; Urofsky and Levy, eds., *"Half Brother, Half Son,"* 325–26; James M. Landis to Felix Frankfurter, Mar. 9, 1926, Frankfurter Papers, Box 134, folder 2774.

26 Urofsky and Levy, eds., *Letters of Louis D. Brandeis*, Vol. 5, 322.

27 *See, e.g., id.*, Vol. 4, 559.

28 *Id.*, Vol. 5, 221, 224, 235, 247, 306, 315; Murphy, *Brandeis/Frankfurter Connection*, 75–92.

29 *Id.*, Vol. 5, 60, 90, 174, 298, 308, 309.

30 *E.g.*, Felix Frankfurter, "Distribution of Judicial Power Between United States and State Courts," 13 *Cornell Law Quarterly* 499 (1928). *See* Louis D. Brandeis to Felix Frankfurter, Feb. 16, 1928, Frankfurter papers, Box 27, folder 435; Urofsky and Levy, eds., *Letters of Louis D. Brandeis*, Vol. 5, 373; Frankfurter to George W. Norris, Dec. 21, 1928, Norris Papers, Tray 42, Box 2, file: "Judiciary Committee, 1928"; Frankfurter to William D. Mitchell, Mar. 15, 1929, Frankfurter Papers, Box 84, folder 1725.

31 Murphy, *Brandeis/Frankfurter Connection*, 40–42. *See, e.g.*, Urofsky and Levy, eds., *Letters of Louis D. Brandeis*, Vol. 5, 187, 372; Michael E. Parrish, *Felix Frankfurter and His Times: The Reform Years* (New York, 1982), 162; Donald A. Ritchie, *Landis* (Cambridge, Mass., 1980), 28.

32 Urofsky and Levy, eds., *Letters of Louis D. Brandeis*, Vol. 5, 364.

33 R. Walton Moore to Felix Frankfurter, Mar. 12, 1928, Frankfurter Papers, Box 134, folder 2763.

34 Henry J. Friendly, "The Historic Basis of Diversity Jurisdiction," 41 *Harvard Law Review* 483 (1928).

35 Urofsky and Levy, eds., *Letters of Louis D. Brandeis*, Vol. 5, 327.

36 See Felix Frankfurter to R. Walton Moore, Apr. 18, 1928, Frankfurter Papers, Box 80, folder 1620; R. Walton Moore to Felix Frankfurter, Apr. 21, 1928, Frankfurter Papers, Box 134, folder 2763.

37 Urofsky and Levy, eds., *Letters of Louis D. Brandeis*, Vol. 5, 337.

38 Felix Frankfurter to Thomas J. Walsh, Apr. 23, 1928, Frankfurter Papers, Box 110, folder 2299.

39 Thomas J. Walsh to Felix Frankfurter, Apr. 27, 1928, Frankfurter Papers, Box 110, folder 2299.

40 Louis D. Brandeis to Felix Frankfurter, May 8, 1928, Frankfurter Papers, Box 27, folder 436.

41 *Gay v. Ruff*, 292 U.S. 25, 35, 37 (1934) (Brandeis, J.).

42 Quoted in Nelson L. Dawson, *Louis D. Brandeis, Felix Frankfurter, and the New Deal* (Hamden, Conn., 1980), 20.

43 Felix Frankfurter to George W. Norris, Feb. 18, 1936, Norris Papers, Tray 27, Box 5, file: "Supreme Court and AAA Decision."

44 Felix Frankfurter to George W. Norris, Feb. 18, 1936, Norris Papers, Tray 27, Box 5, file: "Supreme Court and AAA Decision"; Frankfurter to Norris, Mar. 4, 1936, Norris Papers, Tray 27, Box 2, file: "Supreme Court, 1935–36"; Norris to Frankfurter, Mar. 24, 1936, Norris Papers, Tray 27, Box 2, file: "Supreme Court, 1935–36."

45 Urofsky and Levy, eds., *Letters of Louis D. Brandeis*, Vol. 2, 210–11. *Compare* his earlier view, *id.*, Vol. 1, 283–84.

46 For Brandeis's early views see Mason, *Brandeis*, 141–52, 289–315, 357–62; Allon Gal, *Brandeis of Boston* (Cambridge, Mass., 1980), 55–65; Urofsky and Levy, eds., *Letters of Louis D. Brandeis*, Vol. 1, 232–33; Brandeis, *Business—A Profession*, 88–89.

47 Two were based exclusively on diversity: *Hitchman Coal & Coke Co. v. Mitchell*, 245 U.S. 229 (1917); and *American Steel Foundries v. Tri-City Central Trades Council*, 257 U.S. 184 (1921). Two were based on federal question jurisdiction under the Sherman Act but brought additionally as diversity suits: *Duplex Printing Press Co. v. Deering*, 254 U.S. 443 (1921); and *United Mine Workers v. Coronado Coal Co.*, 259 U.S. 344 (1922).

48 245 U.S. at 271.

49 274 U.S. 37, 56 (1927) (Brandeis, J., dissenting).

50 *Id.* at 59.

51 *Id.* at 58.

52 *Id.* at 65.

53 Quoted in Mason, *Brandeis*, 259.

54 Urofsky and Levy, eds., *Letters of Louis D. Brandeis*, Vol. 5, 279.

55 "Conversations between L[ouis]. D[embitz]. B[randeis]. and F[elix]. F[rankfurter].," Frankfurter Papers, Box 257, at 20 (copy also in Box 224) (hereafter, "Brandeis-Frankfurter Conversations").

56 *Id.*, Vol. 5, 60. *See id.* at 68.

57 Urofsky and Levy, eds., *Letters of Louis D. Brandeis*, Vol. 5, 281. *See* Felix Frankfurter, " 'Reminds of Involuntary Servitude,' " 50 *The New Republic* 262 (1927).

58 Urofsky and Levy, eds., *Letters of Louis D. Brandeis*, Vol. 5, 322.

59 *Id.*, Vol. 5, 317, 322, 386–87, 414.

60 See, *e.g.*, *Bendix Products Corp. v. Beman*, 14 F. Supp. 58 (N.D., Ill., 1936).

61 303 U.S. 41 (1938).

62 *See also Santa Cruz Fruit Packing Co. v. National Labor Relations Board*, 303 U.S. 453 (1938).

63 *Levering & Garrigues Co. v. Morrin*, 71 F. 2d 284 (C.C.A. 2d 1934), *cert. denied*, 297 U.S. 595 (1935).

64 *United States Coal Companies v. Rice*, 80 F. 2d 1 (C.C.A. 7th 1935), *cert. denied*, 297 U.S. 714 (1936).

65 257 U.S. 312 (1921).

66 254 U.S. 443 (1921).

67 *Levering & Garrigues Co. v. Morrin*, 71 F. 2d 284 (C.C.A. 2d 1934), *cert. denied*, 293 U.S. 595 (1935).

68 *Russell v. United States*, 86 F. 2d 389 (C.C.A. 8th 1936); *New Negro Alliance v. Sanitary Grocery Co.*, 92 F. 2d 510 (C.C.A. D.C. 1937).

69 Note, 50 *Harvard Law Review*, 1295, 1298 (1937).

70 47 Stat. 70, Sec. 13 (a)–(c).

71 *Donnelly Garment Co. v. International Ladies' Garment Workers' Union*, 21 F. Supp. 807, 815 (W.D. Mo. 1937).

72 Note, "Constitutionality of State Statute Limiting Injunctions in Labor Disputes," 46 *Yale Law Journal* 1064, 1066 (1937).

73 *Senn v. Tile Layers Protective Union*, 301 U.S. 468 (1937) (Brandeis, J.).

74 *Lauf v. E. G. Shinner & Co.*, 303 U.S. 323 (1938); *New Negro Alliance v. Sanitary Grocery Co.*, 303 U.S. 552 (1938).

75 *Lauf v. E.G. Shinner & Co.*, 303 U.S. at 327.

76 Brandeis could not have missed the dissent in *Donnelly*. Behind the Norris-LaGuardia Act, it stated, "is the figure, sinister or saintly (the reader may take his choice)," of "Professor Frankfurter of the Harvard Law School. From High Olympus, more than once, he has moved the pawns upon the nation's chess board and, it is whispered, on occasion has even sought to check the king." The dissent identified Frankfurter as one of the authors of the Norris-LaGuardia Act and described *The Labor Injunction* as a book "written to promote this law." Then, it quoted a long passage from the book which contained, in turn, a long quote from Brandeis's own condemnation of the labor injunction in his dissent in *Duplex v. Deering*. 21 F. Supp. at 821–22.

77 21 F. Supp. 817, 821–22, 31 (Otis, D.J., dissenting).

78 *International Ladies' Garment Workers' Union v. Donnelly Garment Co.*, 304 U.S. 243 (1938).

79 Personal jurisdiction was an insufficient limit for several reasons. First, states commonly required foreign corporations to agree to subject themselves to personal jurisdiction on a wide range of claims, occurring both in and out of state, as a condition for permission to do local business. Second, the elaborate interstate activities of foreign corporations increasingly gave them such a sufficiently substantial presence in many states that they became subject to jurisdiction there on out-of-state claims. Third, from the late nineteenth century the Supreme Court itself, reacting to the growth of interstate business and travel, continuously expanded the authority of the states to assert personal jurisdiction over nonresidents who performed actions or conducted regular business within their borders. *See, e.g.*, Austin W. Scott, "Jurisdiction over Nonresidents Doing Business Within a State," 32 *Harvard Law Review* 871 (1919).

80 Purcell, *Litigation and Inequality*, ch. 8. Brandeis helped move the Court toward accepting the discretionary doctrine of *forum non conveniens*, which allowed judges to dismiss suits brought in "inconvenient" forums. *See, e.g.*, *Canada Malting Co., Ltd. v. Paterson Steamships, Ltd.*, 285 U.S. 413 (1932) (Brandeis, J.); *Broderick v. Rosner*, 294 U.S. 629 (1935) (Brandeis, J.).

81 Purcell, *Litigation and Inequality*, ch. 8.

82 262 U.S. 312 (1923).

83 *Id.* at 316. Brandeis used the same phrase again in *Hoffman v. Foraker*, 274 U.S. 21, 23 (1927).

84 *Michigan Central Railroad Co. v. Mix*, 278 U.S. 492 (1929).

85 *Allgeyer v. Louisiana*, 165 U.S. 578 (1897); *New York Life Insurance Co. v. Head*, 234 U.S. 149 (1914); *Aetna Life Insurance Co. v. Dunken*, 266 U.S. 389 (1924).

86 *Home Insurance Co. v. Dick*, 281 U.S. 397 (1930) (Brandeis, J.). Brandeis also sought to limit the Court's use of the Due Process Clause to protect the authority of the states to regulate instate business activities. *See, e.g.*, *Mutual Life Insurance Co. of New York v. Liebing*, 259 U.S. 209 (1922) (Holmes, J.); *Bothwell v. Buckbee, Mears Co.*, 275 U.S. 274 (1927) (Brandeis, J.).

87 Since the late nineteenth century, increasing multistate activities had forced the Court to begin addressing new claims made under the Full Faith and Credit Clause. Prior to World War I its use of the clause was generally limited to enforcing judgments. With respect to choice-of-law questions, the Court's decisions were few and tentative, and the scope given to the clause was quite narrow. *See, e.g.*, Stephen I. Langmaid, "The Full Faith and Credit Required for Public Acts," 24 *Illinois Law Review* 383 (1929); G. W. C. Ross, "Has the Conflict of Laws Become a Branch of Constitutional Law?" 15 *Minnesota Law Review* 161 (1931); Edward S. Corwin, "The 'Full Faith and Credit' Clause," 81 *University of Pennsylvania Law Review* 371 (1933).

88 *Broderick v. Rosner*, 294 U.S. 629, 643 (1935).

89 *John Hancock Mutual Life Insurance Co. v. Yates*, 299 U.S. 178 (1936).

90 *Broderick v. Rosner*, 294 U.S. at 642.

91 *Ohio v. Chattanooga Boiler & Tank Co.*, 289 U.S. 439, 442 (1933).

92 286 U.S. 145 (1932).

93 *Id.* at 159.

94 *Id.* at 158. In a different context Brandeis easily followed the traditional tort rule. *Young v. Masci*, 289 U.S. 253, 258 (1933) (Brandeis, J.).

95 *Kryger v. Wilson*, 242 U.S. 171, 176 (1916). Brandeis followed such cases as *Finney v. Guy*, 189 U.S. 335 (1903), and *Allen v. Alleghany Co.*, 196 U.S. 458 (1905).

96 *Kryger v. Wilson*, 242 U.S. at 176. Brandeis insisted that the *Swift* doctrine had no role in the state courts or in the Supreme Court's review of their decisions. *Brinkerhoff-Faris Trust & Savings Co. v. Hill*, 281 U.S. 673, 681 n. 8 (1930). Indeed, in *Brinkerhoff* Brandeis cited *Kryger* for the still valid proposition that the Court's power to review state decisions was limited "to their decisions on federal questions." *Id.*, 281 U.S. at 680 n. 6.

97 *Bradford Electric Light Co., Inc. v. Clapper*, 286 U.S. at 163-64 (Stone, J., concurring).

98 *Id.* at 163.

99 Brandeis limited his acceptance of due process limits on choice-of-law issues by stressing the right of states to apply their own law whenever the relevant activities occurred within their borders. *E.g., Bothwell v. Buckbee, Mears Co.*, 275 U.S. 274 (1927) (Brandeis, J.).

100 *Bradford*, 286 U.S. at 164.

101 The following year their disagreement widened. *See Yarborough v. Yarborough*, 290 U.S. 202, 213 (1933) (Brandeis, J., for the Court with Stone, J., dissenting).

102 H. Parker Sharp and Joseph B. Brennan, "The Application of the Doctrine of Swift v. Tyson Since 1900," 4 *Indiana Law Journal* 367, 370 (1929).

103 Mitchell Wendell, *Relations Between the Federal and State Courts* (New York, 1949), 170-74.

104 Edward Thompson Company, *Federal Law of Contracts* (St. Paul, Minn., 1934), Vol. 2, 476.

105 Between approximately 1900 and 1920 a series of statutes and judicial decisions had narrowed the realm of the federal common law and moderated its harshness in the contentious area of employee torts. Purcell, *Litigation and Inequality*, 160-72, 175-76, 245-46.

106 300 U.S. 203 (1937).

107 *Id.* at 215.

108 300 U.S. 227 (1937).

109 When *Erie* was under consideration, cases before the Court suggested that Brandeis's earlier concern about the declaratory judgment had some basis. *See Anniston Manufacturing Co. v. Davis*, 301 U.S. 337, 354-55 (1937); *Electric Bond & Share Co. v. Securities and Exchange Commission*, 303 U.S. 419, 443 (1938).

110 300 U.S. at 234.

111 For the company's argument, *see id.* at 232-33; for the Court's ruling, *see id.* at 239.

112 *Id.* at 240, 244.

113 304 U.S. at 74.

114 *Id.* at 75.

115 *Id.* at 74.

116 *Id.* at 75.

117 *Id.* at 76.

118 *Id.* at 76-77.

119 *Id.* at 73-74.

120 *Id.* at 76.

121 *Id.* at 76–77.

122 Purcell, *Litigation and Inequality,* 198, 209.

123 *Id.* at 177–87, 209. *See, e.g., Alabama & Vicksburg Railway Co. v. Journey,* 257 U.S. 111 (1921); *Michigan Central Railroad Co. v. Mix,* 278 U.S. 492 (1929); *Denver & Rio Grande Western Railroad Co. v. Terte,* 284 U.S. 284 (1932).

124 *See* Purcell, *Litigation and Inequality,* 179–80. The federal common law was not, of course, invariably favorable to defendants. *Id.* at 63, 175–76.

125 A plaintiff would not be "forum shopping" interstate if she brought suit in the defendant's home state because she could not obtain personal jurisdiction over the defendant in any other state. Such a plaintiff might, of course, be able to forum shop if there were one or more other states where the defendant was subject to personal jurisdiction.

126 Brandeis attempted to limit the "changing residence" option for FELA plaintiffs in *Michigan Central Railroad Co. v. Mix,* 278 U.S. 492, 495 (1929).

127 288 U.S. 517, 572 (Brandeis, J., dissenting). *Accord Kentucky Finance Corp. v. Paramount Auto Exchange Corp.,* 262 U.S. 544, 551 (1923) (Brandeis and Holmes, JJ., dissenting); *Power Manufacturing Co. v. Saunders,* 274 U.S. 490, 497 (1927) (Holmes and Brandeis, JJ., dissenting); *Compania General De Tabacos De Filipinas v. Collector of Internal Revenue,* 275 U.S. 87, 99 (1927) (Holmes and Brandeis, JJ., dissenting).

128 Urofsky and Levy, eds., *Letters of Louis D. Brandeis,* Vol. 5, 67.

129 288 U.S. at 568.

130 *Federal Trade Commission v. Gratz,* 253 U.S. 421, 429, 438 (1920) (Brandeis, J., dissenting). *Cf. American Column & Lumber Co. v. United States,* 257 U.S. 377, 413, 416 (1921) (Brandeis, J., dissenting).

131 Dean Acheson, *Morning and Noon* (Boston, 1965), 83–84.

132 Robert M. Mennel and Christine L. Compston, eds., *Holmes & Frankfurter: Their Correspondence, 1912–1934* (Hanover, N.H., 1996), 194.

133 American Law Institute, *A Study of the Business of the Federal Courts, Part II, Civil Cases* (Philadelphia, 1934).

134 When dealing with diversity suits, Brandeis sometimes showed little concern with some of the tactics individual claimants used to avoid the federal courts. *See Mecom v. Fitzsimmons Drilling Co., Inc.,* 284 U.S. 183 (1931). Moreover, although he had joined the Court's decision blocking another plaintiff's anti-removal device, *Lee v. Chesapeake & Ohio Railway Co.,* 260 U.S. 653 (1923), within a short time he changed his mind. Urofsky and Levy, eds., *"Half Brother, Half Son,"* 229. *See* Purcell, *Litigation and Inequality,* 181–83.

135 Bickel, *Unpublished Opinions,* ch. 1, 5, esp. 97.

136 *Id.* at 118.

137 American Law Institute, *A Study of the Business of the Federal Courts;* Charles E. Clark, "Diversity of Citizenship Jurisdiction of the Federal Courts," 19 *American Bar Association Journal* 499 (1933).

138 304 U.S. at 77. *See* Harlan Fiske Stone to Louis D. Brandeis, Mar. 25, 1938, Brandeis Court Papers, Box 107, folder 7, "Erie."

139 *Erie* Draft, Mar. 21, [1938], Brandeis Court Papers, Box 107, folder 7, *"Erie."*

140 Undated fragment, Brandeis Court papers, Box 107, folder 5, *"Erie."*

141 304 U.S. at 75.

142 They were codified in 1938 as 28 U.S.C. Secs. 41 (1) and 71. The former was the general diversity jurisdiction statute; the latter was the diversity removal statute.

143 Choice of forum would be limited, of course, by such restrictions as venue and personal jurisdiction. *See, e.g., Lee v. Chesapeake & Ohio Railway Co.,* 260 U.S. 653 (1923).

144 Brandeis's decision not to include his contemplated discussion of *Baugh* (a case in which a railroad had taken advantage of more favorable federal common law by removing) but to focus instead on the *Taxicab* case (a case in which a corporation had taken advantage of more favorable federal common law by reincorporating and then initiating suit as plaintiff) accomplished the same purpose.

145 It is possible that Brandeis formulated his dichotomy as an ironic — and perhaps even somewhat vengeful — response to the Court's equal protection decisions. During his tenure the Court had repeatedly applied the equality clause to protect foreign corporations against allegedly discriminatory state laws, denying that there was any relevant "real and substantial difference" (*Power Manufacturing Co. v. Saunders,* 274 U.S. 490, 493 (1927)) between foreign and domestic corporations or individuals and partnerships. Brandeis — sometimes vehemently — and Holmes consistently dissented from those decisions. *See, e.g., Power Manufacturing,* 274 U.S. at 497 (Holmes and Brandeis, JJ., dissenting); *Kentucky Finance Corp v. Paramount Auto Exchange Corp.,* 262 U.S. 544, 551 (1923) (Brandeis and Holmes, JJ., dissenting); *Quaker City Cab Co. v. Pennsylvania,* 277 U.S. 389, 403 (1928) (Brandeis and Holmes, JJ., dissenting); *Liggett v. Lee,* 288 U.S. 517, 541 (1933) (Brandeis, J., dissenting). Similarly, Brandeis often dissented from the Court's use of the Equal Protection Clause to protect corporations from allegedly discriminatory taxation. *See, e.g., Concordia Insurance Co. v. Illinois,* 292 U.S. 535, 550 (1934) (Cardozo, J., dissenting, joined by Brandeis and Stone, JJ.).

In *Erie* Brandeis could not formally rely on the equality clause because the Court held that it applied only to the states, not to the federal government. Given his statement that *Swift* "rendered impossible equal protection of the law," however (*Erie,* 304 U.S. at 75), it seems likely that he intended the "citizen/noncitizen" dichotomy to evoke the classification issue in the equal protection cases and to suggest that those decisions, juxtaposed to the *Swift* doctrine, illustrated the Court's underlying bias in favor of corporations. The dichotomy, after all, stressed the fact that the "noncitizen" — which, as the justices knew full well, typically was a foreign corporation — was given a systematic and unfair advantage over the "citizen" — typically, also in the justices's common knowledge, an individual plaintiff.

146 *E.g., Board of Trade of the City of Chicago v. United States,* 246 U.S. 231, 238 (1918) (Brandeis, J.). *Accord Burns Baking Co. v. Bryan,* 264 U.S. 504, 517 (1924) (Brandeis, J., dissenting); *O'Gorman & Young v. Hartford Fire Insurance Co.,* 282 U.S. 251 (1931) (Brandeis, J.); *New State Ice Co. v. Liebman,* 285 U.S. 262, 280 (1932) (Brandeis, J., dissenting); *St. Joseph Stock Yards Co. v. United States,* 298 U.S. 38, 73 (1936) (Brandeis, J., concurring). *See* Strum, *Brandeis,* 351 and 469 n. 22.

CHAPTER 7. "DEFECTS, POLITICAL"

1 Brandeis's efforts varied greatly. At the most extreme, he expressed the desire to have the Fourteenth Amendment repealed in order to curb judicial excesses. Narrowly and technically, he developed doctrines to limit the Court's opportunities to intervene in local and regulatory matters. *E.g., King Manufacturing Co. v. City Council of Augusta,* 277 U.S. 100, 115 (1928) (Brandeis, J., dissenting); *Railroad Commission of California v. Los Angeles Railway Commission,* 280 U.S. 145, 158 (1929) (Brandeis, J., dissenting); *Ashwander v. Tennessee Valley Authority,* 297 U.S. 288, 341 (1936) (Brandeis, J., concurring).

2 Louis D. Brandeis, *The Curse of Bigness* (New York, 1935), 73.

3 *Id.* at 73.

4 *Myers v. United States,* 272 U.S. 52, 240, 294–95 (1926) (Brandeis, J., dissenting).

5 *Id.* at 318.

6 *Id.* at 319. See Melvin I. Urofsky and David W. Levy, eds., *Letters of Louis D. Brandeis* (New York, 1972), Vol. 2, 603–10.

7 Urofsky and Levy, eds., *Letters of Louis D. Brandeis,* Vol. 1, 335.

8 *Id.,* Vol. 2, 297.

9 *Muller v. Oregon,* 208 U.S. 412 (1908).

10 Brandeis, *Curse of Bigness,* 52–69.

11 *Id.,* 65. *See* Philippa Strum, *Louis D. Brandeis: Justice for the People* (Cambridge, Mass., 1984), 335.

12 248 U.S. 215, 248 (1918) (Brandeis, J., dissenting).

13 *Id.* at 262.

14 *Id.* at 267.

15 *Id.* at 264, 263. He offered a similar analysis in *Duplex Printing Co. v. Deering,* 254 U.S. 443, 479, 485, 488 (1921) (Brandeis, J., dissenting).

16 Brandeis developed, for example, a range of doctrines to limit the opportunities of the federal courts to intervene in the work of regulatory agencies. *E.g., Ohio Valley Water Co. v. Ben Avon Borough,* 253 U.S. 287, 292 (1920) (Brandeis, J., dissenting); *Federal Trade Commission v. Gratz,* 253 U.S. 421, 429 (1920) (Brandeis, J., dissenting); *Great Northern Railway Co. v. Merchants Elevator Co.,* 259 U.S. 285 (1922) (Brandeis, J.); *St. Joseph Stock Yards Co. v. United States,* 298 U.S. 38, 73 (1936) (Brandeis, J., dissenting).

17 Urofsky and Levy, eds., *Letters of Louis D. Brandeis,* Vol. 2, 640.

18 *New State Ice Co. v. Liebmann,* 285 U.S. 262, 311 (Brandeis, J., dissenting).

19 Urofsky and Levy, eds., *Letters of Louis D. Brandeis,* Vol. 1, 407.

20 *Id.,* Vol. 5, 45.

21 *Erie Railroad Co. v. Tompkins,* 304 U.S. 64, 75, 76 (1938).

22 "Proposed New Footnote 24, p. 8," Brandeis Court Papers, Box 107, folder 8, "Erie." Because *Swift* required the federal courts to follow state statutes, his statement could refer only to congressional legislation.

23 Alpheus T. Mason, *Brandeis: A Free Man's Life* (New York, 1946), 153.

24 Mason, *Brandeis,* 164–71.

25 *Id.* at 177. *See* Alpheus Thomas Mason, *The Brandeis Way: A Case Study in the Workings of Democracy* (Princeton, 1938), 300; Louis D. Brandeis, *Business—a Profession* (New York, 1971 [1914]), 182–97.

26 Brandeis, *Business—A Profession,* 109–22.

27 *Id.* at 118.

28 *E.g., id.* at 130.

29 *Id.* at 123–24, 130–31.

30 *Id.* at 126–27, 157–63, 181–85 (quote at 183).

31 Urofsky and Levy, eds., *Letters of Louis D. Brandeis,* Vol. 5, 601.

32 *Id.,* Vol. 5, 595.

33 Morton Keller, *The Life Insurance Enterprise, 1885–1910: A Study in the Limits of Corporate Power* (Cambridge, Mass., 1963), 257, 258.

34 Brandeis, *Business: A Profession,* 135–37.

35 *Id.* at 134–35.

36 In 1913 the Court reaffirmed its long-established rule in *New York Life Insurance Co. v. Deer Lodge County,* 231 U.S. 495, 510 (1913).

37 Louis D. Brandeis, *Other People's Money and How the Bankers Use It* (New York, 1914), 60.

38 Edward A. Purcell, Jr., *Litigation and Inequality: Federal Diversity Jurisdiction in Industrial America, 1870–1958* (New York, 1992), 64–72, 205–16.

39 *O'Gorman & Young v. Hartford Fire Insurance Co.,* 282 U.S. 251 (1931); *Bothwell v. Buckbee, Mears Company,* 275 U.S. 274 (1927).

40 246 U.S. 357 (1918).

41 *Id.* at 366.

42 *Id.* at 373, 375, 377.

43 *Id.* at 382.

44 *Id.*

45 *Id.* at 383.

46 He believed that *Mason v. United States,* 260 U.S. 545 (1923), had in effect acknowledged that *Swift* embodied a constitutional principle when it declared — as Brandeis quoted in *Erie* — that the "statute, however, is merely declarative of the rule which would exist in the absence of the statute," 304 U.S. at 72. In a footnote *(Erie,* 304 U.S. at 72 n. 2), Brandeis quoted almost identical language from an earlier Court decision, *Hawkins v. Barney's Lessee,* 30 U.S. (5 Pet.) 457, 464 (1831).

47 Brandeis, of course, on occasion made law in advance of congressional action. *See* Chapter 11 of this volume.

48 *See, e.g., Marin v. Augedahl,* 247 U.S. 142, 154–55 (1918) (Clarke, J., dissenting, joined by Brandeis and Pitney). Brandeis drew on a long tradition of criticism directed against *Swift* that had maintained that its doctrine was unconstitutional. *See* Tony Freyer, *Harmony & Dissonance: The Swift & Erie Cases in American Federalism* (New York, 1981), 101–22, 142–53.

49 304 U.S. at 72.

50 The quotation spoke of "general" law issues "where the state tribunals are called upon to perform *the like functions as ourselves,* that is, to ascertain upon general reasoning and legal analogies, what is the true exposition of the contract or instrument, or what is the just rule furnished by the principles of commercial law to govern the case." *Id.* at 71–72 (emphasis added).

51 304 U.S. at 76. *See also id.* at 75.

52 Louis D. Brandeis to Stanley Reed, Mar. 24, 1938, Brandeis Court Papers, Box 107, folder 7, "Erie."

53 304 U.S. at 78.

54 Urofsky and Levy, eds., *Letters of Louis D. Brandeis,* Vol. 5, 98. *See, e.g., Arkansas Railroad Commission v. Chicago, Rock Island & Pacific Railroad Co.,* 274 U.S. 597 (1927) (Brandeis, J.).

55 Urofsky and Levy, eds., *Letters of Louis D. Brandeis,* Vol. 5, 247. *See id.,* Vol. 5, 199.

56 *International News Service v. Associated Press,* 248 U.S. 215, 248, 267 (1918) (Brandeis, J., dissenting); Urofsky and Levy, eds., *Letters of Louis D. Brandeis,* Vol. 5, 344.

57 Urofsky and Levy, eds., *Letters of Louis D. Brandeis,* Vol. 5, 129. *See Ashwander v. Tennessee Valley Authority,* 297 U.S. 288, 341 (1936) (Brandeis, J., concurring); Alexander M. Bickel, *The Unpublished Opinions of Mr. Justice Brandeis* (Chicago, 1957), ch. 1.

58 *Southern Pacific Co. v. Jensen,* 244 U.S. 205 (1917) ("general maritime law," at 216); *Chelentis v. Luckenbach Steam Ship Co.,* 247 U.S. 372 (1918); *Knickerbocker Ice Co. v. Stewart,* 253 U.S. 149 (1920); *Washington v. Dawson,* 264 U.S. 219 (1924). *See* Note, "From Judicial Grant

to Legislative Power: The Admiralty Clause in the Nineteenth Century," 67 *Harvard Law Review* 1214 (1954).

59 244 U.S. 205 (1917). On the admiralty jurisdiction and its relation to *Erie*, *see* William A. Fletcher, "The General Common Law and Section 34 of the Judiciary Act of 1789: The Example of Marine Insurance," 97 *Harvard Law Review* 1513 (1984).

60 244 U.S. 205, 222 (1917) (Holmes, J., dissenting).

61 *Id.* at 225–27 (Pitney, J., dissenting).

62 *Chelentis v. Luckenbach Steam Ship Co.*, 247 U.S. 372, 385 (1918) (Brandeis, Pitney, and Clarke, JJ., dissenting without opinion).

63 *Knickerbocker Ice Co. v. Stewart*, 253 U.S. 149, 166 (1920) (Holmes, J., dissenting, joined by Pitney, Brandeis, and Clarke, JJ.); *Washington v. Dawson*, 264 U.S. 219, 228 (1924) (Brandeis, J., dissenting).

64 "Conversations between L[ouis]. D[embitz]. B[randeis]. and F[elix]. F[rankfurter].," Frankfurter Papers, Box 257, at 18 (hereafter, "Brandeis-Frankfurter Conversations").

65 *See* the series: *Western Fuel Co. v. Garcia*, 257 U.S. 233 (1921); *Grant Smith-Porter Ship Co. v. Rohde*, 257 U.S. 469 (1922); *State Industrial Commission of the State of New York v. Nordenholt Corp.*, 259 U.S. 263 (1922); *Panama Railroad Co. v. Johnson*, 264 U.S. 375 (1924); *Messel v. Foundation Co.*, 274 U.S. 427 (1927); *Smith & Son v. Taylor*, 276 U.S. 179 (1928); *John Baizley Iron Works v. Span*, 281 U.S. 222, 232 (1930) (separate opinion by Stone, J., joined by Holmes and Brandeis, JJ.); *Kellogg & Sons, Inc. v. Hicks*, 285 U.S. 502 (1932). An interesting twist occurred in *Minnie v. Port Huron Terminal Co.*, 295 U.S. 647 (1935), where Brandeis had apparently trapped himself doctrinally.

66 In *Red Cross Line v. Atlantic Fruit Co.*, 264 U.S. 109 (1924), Brandeis won a rare victory over McReynolds in the maritime area, limiting the *Jensen* decision and helping to uphold a New York statute which made contracts to arbitrate future disputes specifically enforceable as applied to a maritime contract.

67 *Washington v. Dawson*, 264 U.S. 219, 231 (1924) (Brandeis, J., dissenting). *See id.* at 228- 29; Urofsky and Levy, eds., *Letters of Louis D. Brandeis*, Vol. 5, 116.

68 264 U.S. at 229. *See id.* at 230, 233 n. 9, 234–37.

69 *Id.* at 234.

70 U.S. Constitution, Art I, sec. 8, cl. 4. *See* 264 U.S. at 235.

71 264 U.S. at 237.

72 David W. Robertson, *Admiralty and Federalism* (Mineola, N.Y., 1970), 142–46; Grant Gilmore and Charles L. Black, Jr., *The Law of Admiralty* (Brooklyn, 1957), 42.

73 *See, e.g., Panama Railroad Co. v. Johnson*, 264 U.S. 375, 385–87 (1924).

74 304 U.S. at 72.

75 *E.g., Kentucky Whip & Collar Co. v. Illinois Central Railroad Co.*, 299 U.S. 334 (1937); *Santa Cruz Fruit Packing Co. v. National Labor Relations Board*, 303 U.S. 453 (1938). *See* Barry Cushman, *Rethinking the New Deal Court: The Structure of a Constitutional Revolution* (New York, 1998), chs. 10–12.

76 *State of Missouri v. Holland*, 252 U.S. 416 (1920). Although the issue was not "settled," Progressive legal thinkers generally denied the theory of a substantive Tenth Amendment, *e.g.*, Thomas Reed Powell, "The Child Labor Law, the Tenth Amendment, and the Commerce Clause," 3 *Southern Law Quarterly* 175, 189 (1918). *See* Aviam Soifer, "Truisms that Never Will Be True: The Tenth Amendment and the Spending Power," 57 *University of Colorado Law Review* 793, 801–11 (1986).

77 *See United States v. Beatty,* 297 U.S. 1, 78 (1936) (Stone, J., dissenting); Alpheus T. Mason, *Harlan Fiske Stone: Pillar of the Law* (New York, 1956), 406–11, 553–54; *United States v. Darby,* 312 U.S. 100 (1941) (Stone, J.). Like Brandeis, Stone also concurred in Hughes's opinion in *Schechter.*

78 Brandeis-Frankfurter Conversations, p. 24. *See, e.g., Kane v. New Jersey,* 242 U.S. 160, 168 (1916).

79 304 U.S. at 78–79.

80 The Tenth Amendment provides: "The powers not delegated to the United States by the Constitution, nor prohibited by it to the States, are reserved to the States respectively, or to the people."

81 *Baugh,* 149 U.S. 368, at 401; *Erie,* 304 U.S. at 78–79.

82 *Baugh,* 149 U.S. at 401; *Erie,* 304 U.S. at 79 (emphasis added). Contrast with the language in Brandeis's draft dated Mar. 21 at 7, Brandeis Court Papers, Box 107, folder 7, "*Erie.*"

83 Item 1 on undated memo, "The Supreme Court of the United States," Brandeis Court Papers, Box 107, folder 7, "*Erie.*"

84 *E.g., United States v. Butler,* 297 U.S. 1, 63–64, 68 (1936) (Roberts, J.); *United States v. Constantine,* 296 U.S. 287, 295–96 (1935) (Roberts, J.).

85 *Schechter Poultry Corp. v. United States,* 295 U.S. 495, 545–50 (1935) (Hughes, C.J.); *Carter v. Carter Coal Co.,* 298 U.S. 238, 317–18 (1936) (Hughes, C.J., separate opinion). *See* Charles Evans Hughes, *The Supreme Court of the United States: Its Foundation, Methods and Achievements: An Interpretation* (New York, 1928), 95–96.

86 The exception was *Schechter Poultry Co. v. United States,* 295 U.S. 495 (1935), where a unanimous Court invalidated the poorly drafted and chaotically administered National Industrial Recovery Act—the one piece of New Deal legislation that Brandeis truly hated as centralization run rampant. In the Court's other opinions that suggested a substantive Tenth Amendment during the critical years from 1935 to 1937 Brandeis dissented: *United States v. Constantine,* 296 U.S. 287, 297 (Cardozo, Brandeis, and Stone, JJ., dissenting); *United States v. Butler,* 297 U.S. 1, 78 (Stone, Brandeis, and Cardozo, JJ., dissenting); *Carter v. Carter Coal Co.,* 298 U.S. 238, 324 (Cardozo, Brandeis, and Stone, JJ., dissenting); *Ashton v. Cameron County Water Improvement District No. One,* 298 U.S. 513, 532 (1936) (Cardozo, Brandeis, and Stone, JJ., and Hughes, C.J., dissenting).

87 *Compare Baugh,* 149 U.S. at 401, with *Erie,* 304 U.S. at 79.

88 Draft opinion marked "As circulated March 21 with corrections," at 8, Brandeis Court Papers, Box 107, folder 7, "*Erie.*"

89 304 U.S. 87.

90 Item 4, undated memo (circa mid-April 1938), Brandeis Court Papers, Box 107, folder 7, "*Erie*"; 304 U.S. at 79–80.

91 Harlan F. Stone to Louis D. Brandeis, Mar. 23, 1938, Brandeis Court Papers, Box 107, folder 7, "*Erie.*"

92 304 U.S. at 78.

93 If Brandeis's principle of legislative primacy provided the constitutional underpinning of *Erie,* two additional conclusions, not discussed elsewhere, follow. First, Brandeis did not view his opinion as challenging congressional authority to establish rules of procedure for the federal courts. Although he dissented from the Court's adoption of the Federal Rules of Civil Procedure, 302 U.S. 783 (1937), he did not do so because he regarded the Rules Enabling Act as unconstitutional. *See* Paul A. Freund, *On Understanding the Supreme Court*

(Boston, 1949), 58; Freund, "Mr. Justice Brandeis," in Allison Dunham and Philip B. Kurland, eds., *Mr. Justice* (Chicago, 1956), 111. Second, Charles Warren's research into the origins of the Judiciary Act of 1789 (Charles Warren, "New Light on the History of the Federal Judiciary Act of 1789," 37 *Harvard Law Review* 49 (1923)), cited in 304 U.S. at 73 n. 5, had no significant impact on Brandeis's decision. Although Brandeis cited Warren's article, he did not follow its logical conclusion—that Reed's concurrence was correct and that the Court should simply alter its construction of the statute. Rather, Brandeis made it explicit that it was the "unconstitutionality of the course pursued" that required *Swift*'s overthrow. For Brandeis, whatever practical significance Warren's research may have had most likely lay in supporting the proposition that the Founders who sat in the First Congress had not assumed that they could, consistent with the Constitution they had just written and adopted, pass legislation allowing the federal courts to ignore state decisions when hearing diversity suits. Warren's conclusions have been severely undermined by Wilfred J. Ritz, *Rewriting the History of the Judiciary Act of 1789: Exposing Myths, Challenging Premises, and Using New Evidence*, ed. Wythe Holt and L. H. LaRue (Norman, Okla., 1990).

94 *E.g.*, "Address by Mr. Justice Black," 13 *Missouri Bar Journal* 173, 175 (1942). *See* John J. Parker, "Erie v. Tompkins in Retrospect: An Analysis of Its Proper Area and Limits," 35 *American Bar Association Journal*, 19, 21 (1949); Gerald T. Dunne, *Hugo Black and the Judicial Revolution* (New York, 1977), 182–84.

95 Holmes's view was also likely driven by his resentment—perhaps stemming in some part from his own days as a state court judge—against the "arrogant assumption" of federal judges in rendering an "independent" opinion on what was a matter solely within the authority of the states. Mark DeWolfe Howe, ed., *Holmes-Pollock Letters: The Correspondence of Mr. Justice Holmes and Sir Frederick Pollock, 1874–1932* (Cambridge, Mass., 1961), Vol. 2, 214–15; Arthur E. Sutherland, "Recollections of Justice Holmes," Felix Frankfurter Papers, Box 146, folder 2967.

96 *See, e.g.*, Oliver Wendell Holmes, Jr., *Collected Legal Papers* (New York, 1952 [1920]), 167–202, 310–16.

97 Mark DeWolfe Howe, ed., *Holmes-Laski Letters: The Correspondence of Mr. Justice Holmes and Harold J. Laski, 1916–1935* (Cambridge, Mass., 1953), Vol. 2, 1089 (emphasis in original).

98 Howe, ed., *Holmes-Pollock Letters*, Vol. 2, 215.

99 Howe, ed., *Holmes-Laski Letters*, Vol. 2, 823.

100 *Id.*, Vol. 2, 822.

101 *Id.*, Vol. 2, 823.

102 304 U.S. at 79 (quoting from 276 U.S. at 533 [three places], 533–34 [one place], and 535 [one place]).

103 ". . . outside of any particular state but obligatory within it." *Id.* at 79.

104 ". . . unless and until changed by [state] statute." *Id.*

105 The same, of course, may be said of a good many "positivist" and "realist" thinkers who were nevertheless charged with taking such positions. *See, e.g.*, Wilfrid E. Rumble, "The Legal Positivism of John Austin and the Realist Movement in American Jurisprudence," 66 *Cornell Law Review* 986 (1981).

106 Holmes would have agreed with this approach to the role of the judge. *See* Thomas C. Grey, "Molecular Motions: The Holmesian Judge in Theory and Practice," 37 *William and Mary Law Review* 19 (1995).

107 In accepting the narrowly positivist contention that courts made law, Brandeis embraced

nothing beyond what most judges and legal scholars — including many supporters of *Swift* — themselves accepted. *Northwestern Life Insurance Co. v. McCue*, 223 U.S. 234, 246 (1912) (McKenna, J.); *Bond v. Hume*, 243 U.S. 15, 21–22 (1917) (White, C.J.); *Gordon v. Ware National Bank*, 132 F. 444, 449 (C.C.A. 8 1904); *Galbraith v. Illinois Steel Co.*, 133 F. 485 (C.C.A. 7 1904), *cert. denied*, 201 U.S. 643 (1906); Alexander Lincoln, "The Relation of Judicial Decisions to the Law," 21 *Harvard Law Review* 120 (1907); Edward C. Eliot, "The Common Law of the Federal Courts," 36 *American Law Review* 498, 502 (1902); Henry Schofield, "Swift v. Tyson: Uniformity of Judge-Made State Law in State and Federal Courts," 4 *Illinois Law Review* 533, 536–37 (1910); G. Edward White, *Justice Oliver Wendell Holmes: Law and the Inner Self* (New York, 1993), 184; Freyer, *Harmony & Dissonance*, 97, 152.

By the 1930s, in fact, there were relatively few legal thinkers who refused to accept the proposition that, on at least some level, courts did not merely "find" law but "made" it. *See, e.g., Clark v. Willard*, 292 U.S. 112, 123–24, 128–29 (1934) (Cardozo, J.). In 1935 the Fourth Circuit applied federal common law and refused to follow a contrary state rule. The federal rule "is not avoided by the declaration of a state court that its decision is grounded in public policy," it declared, "for it is equally well settled that in matters of general law the federal courts determine such matters of public policy for themselves." *Citizens National Bank v. Waugh*, 78 F. 2d 325, 328 (4th Cir. 1935). Thus, the Fourth Circuit, a strong proponent of the federal common law, saw no need for a "found" law theory and openly acknowledged that in applying *Swift* the federal courts made choices of social policy.

For a similar view of the jurisprudential background to *Erie, see* Jack Goldsmith and Steven Walt, "*Erie* and the Irrelevance of Legal Positivism," 1997 Working Papers Series, University of Virginia School of Law, Paper No. 97, at 15.

108 The Commerce Clause functioned similarly with respect to relations between the federal and state governments. *E.g., Western Union Telegraph Co. v. Brown*, 234 U.S. 542 (1914).

109 The problem first arose with respect to "wrongful death" statutes, which states began to adopt in the 1870s and which had become common by the 1890s. *See, e.g., Dennick v. Railroad Company*, 146 U.S. 657 (1880); *Stewart v. Baltimore & Ohio Railroad Co.*, 168 U.S. 445 (1897). Because the new action was statutory, and because the statutes explicitly changed the common law, the federal courts could not avoid the choice-of-law issue by relying solely on federal common law.

110 *Pennoyer v. Neff*, 95 U.S. 714 (1877), was the foundation, even though technically the Court did not there apply the Due Process Clause. *Pennoyer* was followed, however, by innumerable decisions that did apply the clause. *E.g., Riverside and Dan River Cotton Mills v. Menefee*, 237 U.S. 189 (1915). Brandeis wrote for the Court in applying the due process limit to personal jurisdiction: *Philadelphia & Reading Railway Co. v. McKibben*, 243 U.S. 264 (1917); *Rosenberg Bros. & Co., Inc. v. Curtis Brown Co.*, 260 U.S. 516 (1923).

111 *E.g., Allgeyer v. Louisiana*, 165 U.S. 578 (1897); *Chicago, Burlington & Quincy Railroad Co. v. Chicago*, 166 U.S. 226 (1897); *Blackstone v. Miller*, 188 U.S. 189 (1903); *Union Refrigerator Transit Co. v. Kentucky*, 199 U.S. 194 (1905). *See* Joseph H. Beale, "Jurisdiction to Tax," 32 *Harvard Law Review* 587, 592, 603 (1919).

112 *Bonaparte v. Tax Court*, 104 U.S. 592 (1881).

113 The Court regularly relied on common law choice-of-law principles, *e.g., Dennick v. Railroad Co.*, 103 U.S. 11 (1880), and *Northern Pacific Railroad Co. v. Babcock*, 154 U.S. 190 (1894), sometimes vaguely mixed with constitutional references, *e.g., Western Union Telegraph Co. v. Brown*, 234 U.S. 542 (1914).

114 *Converse v. Hamilton,* 224 U.S. 243, 260 (1912).

115 The Full Faith and Credit Clause, U.S. Constitution, Art. IV, sec. 1, provides in relevant part: "Full faith and credit shall be given in each state to the public acts, records, and judicial proceedings of every other state."

116 *Supreme Council of the Royal Arcanum v. Green,* 237 U.S. 531, 542 (1915). *Accord Modern Woodmen of America v. Mixer,* 267 U.S. 544 (1925).

117 *New York Life Insurance Co. v. Head,* 234 U.S. 149, 162 (1914). *Accord National Mutual Building and Loan Association v. Brahan,* 193 U.S. 635, 647 (1904) *(dictum); Olmsted v. Olmsted,* 216 U.S. 386, 395 (1910) *(dictum); Hartford Accident & Indemnity Co. v. Delta & Pine Land Co.,* 292 U.S. 143 (1934). The early cases were often unclear as to their constitutional basis. *See, e.g.,* G. W. C. Ross, "Has the Conflict of Laws Become a Branch of Constitutional Law?" 15 *Minnesota Law Review* 161, 177–78 (1931).

118 266 U.S. 389, 399 (1924).

119 *Bond v. Hume,* 243 U.S. 15, 25 (1917). *See* E. Merrick Dodd, Jr., "The Power of the Supreme Court to Review State Decisions in the Field of Conflict of Laws," 39 *Harvard Law Review* 533 (1926).

120 *Kryger v. Wilson,* 242 U.S. 171, 176 (1916).

121 *Bradford Electric Light Co., Inc. v. Clapper,* 286 U.S. 145, 156 (1932).

122 *Broderick v. Rosner,* 294 U.S. 629, 642 (1935).

123 281 U.S. 397, 408 (1930).

124 *Id.* at 408 n. 5. *See New York Life Insurance Co. v. Dodge,* 246 U.S. 357, 377 (1918) (Brandeis, J., dissenting); *Compania General De Tabacos De Filipinas v. Collector of Internal Revenue,* 275 U.S. 87, 99 (1927) (Holmes and Brandeis, JJ., dissenting); *Bothwell v. Buckbee, Mears Co.,* 275 U.S. 274 (1927) (Brandeis, J.).

125 American Law Institute, *Restatement of the Law of Conflict of Laws* (St. Paul, Minn., 1934), Secs. 42–43, 59–70, at 72–74, 92–104; *Alaska Packers Association v. Industrial Accident Commission of California,* 294 U.S. 532, 540, 547 (1935) (Stone, J.). *Accord* Ross, "Has the Conflict of Laws Become a Branch of Constitutional Law?" 161, 171, 172, 178 n. 79; Stephen I. Langmaid, "The Full Faith and Credit Required for Public Acts," 24 *Illinois Law Review* 383, 402 (1929); George Wilfred Stumberg, *Principles of Conflict of Laws* (Chicago, 1937), 52–65; Robert H. Jackson, "Full Faith and Credit—The Lawyer's Clause of the Constitution," 45 *Columbia Law Review* 1, 11 (1945).

126 *Alaska Packers,* 294 U.S. at 547. *See* Paul A. Freund, *On Law and Justice* (Cambridge, Mass., 1968), 183.

127 Similarly, Brandeis sought to ensure that the state courts would recognize and enforce federal law where it controlled. *See McKnett v. St. Louis & San Francisco Railway Co.,* 292 U.S. 230 (1934) (Brandeis, J.).

128 While the Due Process Clause could disable a forum state from applying its own law, whether statutory or judge-made, the Full Faith and Credit Clause distinguished between the two types of "law." It was generally agreed that statutes came within the category of a state's "public acts" that the clause made binding on other states. It was well settled that judicial *judgments* were within the clause's category of "judicial proceedings" that were also binding on other states. The enforcement of such judgments was the most common and unexceptional use to which courts put the clause. In contrast, there was almost no authority for the proposition that judicial decisions *as common law precedents* qualified as either "public acts" or "judicial proceedings" within the clause. Thus, unlike the Due Process Clause, the Full

Faith and Credit Clause clearly distinguished statutory law from common law. That fact, however, does not detract from the point in the text that both clauses focused judicial attention on the concept of legislative jurisdiction and provided limits to a state's use of its own law, whether statutory or judge-made. Indeed, in *Clapper* Brandeis seemed to suggest that state common law might come within the "public acts" provision of the Full Faith and Credit Clause. *Bradford Electric Light Co. v. Clapper*, 286 U.S. 145, 154 (1932). *See* Walter Wheeler Cook, *The Logical and Legal Bases of the Conflict of Laws* (Cambridge, Mass., 1942), 80–81.

129 American Law Institute, *Restatement of the Law of Conflict of Laws*, Sec. 59, at 92. *Accord* Stumberg, *Principles of Conflict of Laws*, 63 n. 32.

130 Robert A. Burt makes a similar point in *Two Jewish Justices: Outcasts in the Promised Land* (Berkeley, Calif., 1988), 23.

131 *Erie*, 304 U.S. at 74.

132 *Id.* at 75.

133 *Pennsylvania Railroad Co. v. Hughes*, 191 U.S. 477, 486 (1903).

134 *United States v. Thompson*, 93 U.S. 586, 588–89 (1876); *Bethell v. Demaret*, 77 U.S. (10 Wall.) 537 (1870); *Marrow v. Brinkley*, 129 U.S. 178 (1889).

135 *Delmas v. Insurance Co.*, 81 U.S. (14 Wall.) 661, 666 (1871).

136 *Pennsylvania Railroad Co. v. Hughes*, 191 U.S. at 486.

137 *See, e.g., Cole v. Pennsylvania Railroad Co.*, 43 F. 2d 953 (C.C.A. 2d 1930).

138 The issue had been partially raised and apparently settled de facto in *Murdock v. Memphis*, 20 Wall. (87 U.S.) 590 (1874). The Court did not, however, actually rule on the constitutionality of federal appellate review over state common law issues. *See* William M. Wiecek, "*Murdock v. Memphis:* Section 25 of the 1789 Judiciary Act and Judicial Federalism," in Maeva Marcus, ed., *Origins of the Federal Judiciary: Essays on the Judiciary Act of 1789* (New York, 1992), 223–47.

139 *Kryger v. Wilson*, 242 U.S. 171, 176 (1916) (Brandeis, J.). *Accord Tidal Oil Co. v. Flanagan*, 263 U.S. 444 (1924); *Fleming v. Fleming*, 264 U.S. 29 (1924).

140 281 U.S. 673 (1930).

141 *Id.* at 682 n. 8, citing *Fleming v. Fleming*, 264 U.S. 29, 31 (1924); *Tidal Oil Co. v. Flanagan*, 263 U.S. 444, 451 (1924); *Moore-Mansfield Construction Co. v. Electrical Installation Co.*, 234 U.S. 619 (1914); *Bacon v. Texas*, 163 U.S. 207, 220–24 (1896); *Central Land Co. v. Laidley*, 159 U.S. 103 (1895).

142 304 U.S. 92 (1938).

143 Quoted in *Hinderlider*, 304 U.S. at 99.

144 *Id.* at 109–10 and n. 12.

145 *Id.* at 110.

146 206 U.S. 46 (1907).

147 Prior to *Hinderlider*, Brandeis had been reminded pointedly of the power of Brewer's opinion in *Kansas v. Colorado* when the majority quoted from it at length in *Carter v. Carter Coal Co.*, 298 U.S. 238, 293–94 (1936), one of the "old" Court's last major pronouncements on the Tenth Amendment.

148 304 U.S. at 110.

149 304 U.S. at 78.

150 206 U.S. at 97.

151 304 U.S. at 104 (emphasis added).

152 U.S. Constitution, Art. I, sec. 10.

153 304 U.S. at 105. *See* Frankfurter and Landis, "The Compact Clause of the Constitution—A Study in Interstate Adjustments," 34 *Yale Law Journal* 685 (1925). Holmes had adopted a similar, but less explicit, approach to limiting judicial power and recognizing legislative options in *Missouri v. Illinois and the Sanitary District of Chicago,* 200 U.S. 496, 518–21 (1906) (Holmes, J.).

154 The expansive ideas about the reach of federal judicial power and the Court's practices in asserting that power broadly occurred not only in relatively well-known and high-profile cases but also in a variety of other more "ordinary," less politically controversial cases. *E.g., Coombes v. Getz,* 285 U.S. 434, 448 (1932) (Cardozo, J., dissenting, joined by Brandeis and Stone, JJ.); *Sanders v. Armour Fertilizer Works,* 292 U.S. 190, 206 (1934) (Cardozo, J., dissenting, joined by Hughes, C.J., and Brandeis and Stone, JJ.); *Georgia Railway & Electric Co. v. Decatur,* 295 U.S. 165, 171 (1935) (Stone, J., dissenting, joined by Brandeis and Cardozo).

155 *Myers v. United States,* 272 U.S. 52, 240, 292–93 (1926) (Brandeis, J., dissenting). *Accord* Brandeis, *Other People's Money,* 4–5.

CHAPTER 8. EROSION AND CREATION OF MEANING IN AN AGE OF TRANSITION

1 Alpheus Thomas Mason, *Harlan F. Stone: Pillar of the Law* (New York, 1956), 477, note.

2 Felix Frankfurter to Harlan F. Stone, Apr. 27, 1938, Stone Papers, Box 13.

3 Harlan F. Stone to Felix Frankfurter, Apr. 29, 1938, Stone Papers, Box 13.

4 Note, "Congress, the Tompkins Case, and the Conflict of Laws," 52 *Harvard Law Review* 1002 (1939).

5 T. A. Cowan, "Constitutional Aspects of the Abolition of Federal 'Common Law'," 1 *Louisiana Law Review* 161, 173 (1938).

6 Augustus N. Hand to Felix Frankfurter, May 10, 1938, Frankfurter Papers (H.L.S.), Box 171, folder 17; Thomas Reed Powell, "A Constitution for an Indefinite and Expanding Future," 14 *Washington Law Review* 99, 116 (1939).

7 Harry Shulman, "The Demise of Swift v. Tyson," 47 *Yale Law Journal* 1336, 1343 (1938).

8 *See, e.g.,* editorial, "Erie Railroad Case," 24 *American Bar Association Journal* 372 (1938).

9 Charles T. McCormick and Elvin Hale Hewins, "The Collapse of 'General' Law in the Federal Courts," 33 *Illinois Law Review* 126, 133 (1938).

10 John J. Parker, "Erie v. Tompkins in Retrospect: An Analysis of Its Proper Area and Limits," 35 *American Bar Association Journal* 19 (1949).

11 McCormick and Hewins, "Collapse of 'General' Law in the Federal Courts," at 144; Irving Long, "A Warning Signal for Municipal Bond Holders: Some Implications of Erie Railroad v. Tompkins," 37 *Michigan Law Review* 589 (1939).

12 Albert J. Schweppe, "What Has Happened to Federal Jurisprudence?" 24 *American Bar Association Journal* 421, 423 (1938). *See also* Arthur G. Powell, "The Constitutional Convention and Swift v. Tyson," 24 *American Bar Association Journal* 862 (1938) (letter).

13 Testimony of Robert H. Jackson before the Senate Judiciary Committee, "Reorganization of the Federal Judiciary," Hearing on the President's Bill to Reorganize the Federal Judiciary, S. 1392, 75 Cong., 1 sess. (1937), 38.

14 G. Edward White, *The American Judicial Tradition: Profiles of Leading American Judges* (New York, 1976), 230–39.

15 Robert H. Jackson, "The Rise and Fall of Swift v. Tyson," 24 *American Bar Association Journal* 609 (1938).

16 *Id.* at 614.

17 *Id.* at 644.

18 *See, e.g.,* James T. Patterson, *Grand Expectations: The United States, 1945–1974* (New York, 1996); Alonzo L. Hamby, *Liberalism and Its Challengers: From F.D.R. to Bush,* 2d ed. (New York, 1992); William L. O'Neill, *American High: The Years of Confidence, 1945–1960* (New York, 1986); John Patrick Diggins, *The Proud Decades: America in War and Peace, 1941–1960* (New York, 1988); Lary May, ed., *Recasting America: Culture and Politics in the Age of the Cold War* (Chicago, 1989); William H. Chafe, *The Unfinished Journey: America Since World War II* (New York, 1986).

19 Quoted in Robert Lekachman, *The Age of Keynes* (New York, 1966), 171, 170.

20 *See* Lekachman, *Age of Keynes,* ch. 6; Alan Brinkley, *The End of Reform: New Deal Liberalism in Recession and War* (New York, 1995). The problem of corporate power remained a muted and relatively professionalized political concern. *See* Rudolph J. R. Peritz, *Competition Policy in America, 1888–1992: History, Rhetoric, Law* (New York, 1996), ch. 4.

21 For a discussion of the intellectual left, *see* William L. O'Neill, *The Great Schism: Stalinism and the American Intellectuals* (New York, 1982); John P. Diggins, *Up from Communism: Conservative Odysseys in American Intellectual History* (New York, 1975); Mary Sperling McAuliffe, *Crisis on the Left: Cold War Politics and American Liberals, 1947–1954* (Amherst, Mass., 1978); Richard H. Pells, *The Liberal Mind in a Conservative Age: American Intellectuals in the 1940s & 1950s* (New York, 1985); Alan M. Wald, *The New York Intellectuals: The Rise and Decline of the Anti-Stalin Left from the 1930s to the 1980s* (Chapel Hill, N.C., 1987); Robert Griffith, "Old Progressives and the Cold War," 66 *Journal of American History* 334 (1979).

22 For the anti-Communist campaign, *see* Stanley I. Kutler, *The American Inquisition: Justice and Injustice in the Cold War* (New York, 1982); Michael Paul Rogin, *The Intellectuals and McCarthy: The Radical Spectre* (Cambridge, Mass., 1967); Ellen W. Schrecker, *No Ivory Tower: McCarthyism & the Universities* (New York, 1986); Robert Griffith, *The Politics of Fear: Joseph R. McCarthy and the Senate* (New York, 1970); Richard Gid Powers, *Not Without Honor: The History of American Anticommunism* (New York, 1995).

23 *See, e.g.,* Herbert Wechsler, "Stone and the Constitution," 46 *Columbia Law Review* 764 (1946); Paul L. Murphy, *The Constitution in Crisis Times, 1918–1969* (New York, 1972), ch. 6; David Yassky, "Eras of the First Amendment," 91 *Columbia Law Review* 1699 (1991).

24 For changes in law *see* Murphy, *Constitution in Crisis Times,* esp. chs. 7–10; Morton J. Horwitz, *The Transformation of American Law, 1870–1960* (New York, 1992), esp. chs. 7–9.

25 *See* Edward A. Purcell, Jr., *Litigation and Inequality: Federal Diversity Jurisdiction in Industrial America, 1870–1958* (New York, 1992), 45–58, 154–60, 219–24, 230–31.

26 *E.g., Wickard v. Filburn,* 317 U.S. 111 (1941). *Compare* William E. Leuchtenburg, *The Supreme Court Reborn: The Constitutional Revolution in the Age of Roosevelt* (New York, 1995), ch. 8, *with* Barry Cushman, *Rethinking the New Deal Court: The Structure of a Constitutional Revolution* (New York, 1998), chs. 10–12.

27 *Compare United States v. Butler,* 297 U.S. 1 (1936), *with Helvering v. Davis,* 301 U.S. 619 (1937), and *Wickard v. Filburn,* 317 U.S. 111 (1942).

28 *United States v. South-Eastern Underwriters Association,* 322 U.S. 533 (1944); *Polish National Alliance of the United States of North America v. National Labor Relations Board,* 322 U.S. 643 (1944). Not only did the Court expand the commerce power, but it subsequently decided — contrary to earlier cases — that Congress had the power to authorize continued state regulation over interstate commerce in insurance and that it was not required to enact a nationally uniform law. *See* 59 Stat. 33 (1945); *Prudential Insurance Co. v. Benjamin,* 328 U.S. 408 (1946).

29 *D'oench, Duhme & Co., Inc. v. Federal Deposit Insurance Corporation*, 315 U.S. 447 (1942); *Clearfield Trust Co. v. United States*, 318 U.S. 363 (1943).

30 For more than two decades after *Erie* the Court remained highly restrained and cautious in expanding the new federal common law. *E.g., United States v. Standard Oil of California*, 332 U.S. 301 (1947); *Bank of America v. Parnell*, 352 U.S. 29 (1956).

31 *See* C. Herman Pritchett, *The Roosevelt Court: A Study in Judicial Politics and Values, 1937–1947* (Chicago, 1969 [1948]); Melvin I. Urofsky, *Division and Discord: The Supreme Court Under Stone and Vinson, 1941–1953* (Columbia, S.C., 1997); Frances Howell Rudko, *Truman's Court: A Study in Judicial Restraint* (Westport, Conn., 1988); Mary Frances Berry, *Stability, Security and Continuity: Mr. Justice Burton and Decision-making in the Supreme Court, 1945–1958* (Westport, Conn., 1978); Stephen Gardbaum, "New Deal Constitutionalism and the Unshackling of the States," 64 *University of Chicago Law Review* 483 (1997).

32 The Court, for example, elaborated a series of "abstention" doctrines designed to prevent federal judicial action in cases within their jurisdiction. *See, e.g., Railroad Commission of Texas v. Pullman Co.*, 312 U.S. 496 (1941); *Burford v. Sun Oil Co.*, 319 U.S. 315 (1943); *Douglas v. City of Jeannette*, 319 U.S. 157 (1943).

33 Harlan F. Stone to Owen J. Roberts, Jan. 3, 1941, quoted in Mason, *Stone*, 480, note.

34 The Court did not refer to the constitutional issue again for eighteen years. *See Bernhardt v. Polygraphic Co. of America*, 350 U.S. 198, 202, 208 (1956).

35 *United States v. Darby*, 312 U.S. 100, 124 (1941); *Case v. Bowles*, 327 U.S. 92, 101–2 (1946). *See* Mason, *Stone*, 406–11, 550–56.

36 On the bench Frankfurter continued to advise Roosevelt and other New Dealers. *See* Bruce Allen Murphy, "Elements of Extrajudicial Strategy: A Look at the Political Roles of Justices Brandeis and Frankfurter," 69 *Georgetown Law Journal* 101, 115–18 (1980).

37 Felix Frankfurter to Harlan F. Stone, May 9, 1938, Frankfurter Papers, Box 105, folder 2195.

38 Felix Frankfurter to Harlan F. Stone, Apr. 27, 1938, Stone Papers, Box 13; Frankfurter to Stone, May 9, 1938, Frankfurter Papers, Box 105, folder 2195.

39 Felix Frankfurter to Stanley Reed, May 14, 1942, Frankfurter Papers, Box 92, folder 1922.

40 *See* Felix Frankfurter to Harlan F. Stone, May 9, 1938, Stone Papers, Box 13; Frankfurter to Stone, Feb. 3, 1945, Stone Papers, Box 75.

41 Felix Frankfurter to Harlan F. Stone, Feb. 3, 1945, Stone Papers, Box 75.

42 Felix Frankfurter to Harlan F. Stone, Feb. 3, 1945, Stone Papers, Box 75. Frankfurter maintained that his interpretation of *Erie* was also supported by both Reed's concurrence and Butler's dissent. *Id.*

43 "I am not now prepared to hold," he wrote in early 1945, "that Congress would not have power to formulate a code of law in diversity cases." Felix Frankfurter to Harlan F. Stone, Feb. 3, 1945, Stone Papers, Box 75. *See* Frankfurter to Henry M. Hart, Jr., May 3, 1954, Frankfurter Papers (H.L.S.), Box 185, folder 15.

44 *See, e.g.,* Robert M. Mennel and Christine L. Compston, eds., *Holmes & Frankfurter: Their Correspondence, 1912–1934* (Hanover, N.H., 1996), xxxvi.

45 For the quote, *see Erie*, 304 U.S. at 78–79; for the reference to "reserved" powers, *see Erie*, 304 U.S. at 80, and *Baugh*, 149 U.S. at 399, 401.

46 304 U.S. at 79–80.

47 Felix Frankfurter to Harlan F. Stone, Feb. 3, 1945, Stone Papers, Box 75.

48 Neither in *Kuhn* nor in the *Taxicab* case did Holmes discuss congressional power. Rather,

in both he emphasized *Swift*'s transgressions against state authority. *Kuhn v. Fairmont Coal Co.*, 215 U.S. 349, 370, 372 (1910); *Black & White Taxicab*, 276 U.S. at 533-34.

In neither did Holmes cite or refer to Field's dissent. His refusal was undoubtedly quite purposeful. In *Taxicab* he cited *Baugh*, but only the majority opinion and only for the proposition that a state statute could change the common law. Holmes undoubtedly wished to avoid Field's reliance on the Tenth Amendment, and he almost certainly did not want to share his cherished jurisprudential position with Field. For his vanity, ambition, and desire to appear intellectually independent and original, *see, e.g.,* G. Edward White, *Justice Oliver Wendell Holmes: Law and the Inner Self* (New York, 1993), 125-27, 152, 193, 215, 296-97, 322, 354, 452, 476-77. For an interesting parallel, *see Burrill v. Locomobile Co.*, 258 U.S. 34 (1922) (Holmes, J.); Ann Woolhandler, "The Common Law Origins of Constitutionally Compelled Remedies," 107 *Yale Law Journal* 77, 138-41 (1997).

49 *Compare Black & White Taxicab*, 276 U.S. at 533 *with Baugh*, 149 U.S. at 394; Holmes scorned the idea of a "transcendental body of law outside of any particular State but obligatory within it," *Black & White Taxicab*, 276 U.S. at 533; Field (quoting an earlier treatise) dismissed the idea that "there is an atmosphere of general law floating about all the states, not belonging to any of them." *Baugh*, 149 U.S. at 399.

50 *Compare Black & White Taxicab*, 276 U.S. at 535 *with Baugh*, 149 U.S. at 397, 398;

51 *Compare Black & White Taxicab*, 276 U.S. at 534 *with Baugh*, 149 U.S. at 397.

52 *Baugh*, 149 U.S. at 399, 401.

53 *Compare Black & White Taxicab*, 276 U.S. at 533, 535, *with Baugh*, 149 U.S. at 394, 398, 401, 402-3.

54 Felix Frankfurter to Harlan F. Stone, Feb. 3, 1945, Stone Papers, Box 75.

55 *See, e.g.,* Charles W. McCurdy, "Justice Field and the Jurisprudence of Government-Business Relations: Some Parameters of Laissez-Faire Constitutionalism, 1863-1897," 61 *Journal of American History* 970 (1975).

56 Felix Frankfurter to Harlan F. Stone, Apr. 27, 1938, Stone Papers, Box 13. *Accord* Max Freedman, ed., *Roosevelt & Frankfurter: Their Correspondence, 1928-1945* (Boston, 1967), 456.

57 Quoted in Michael E. Parrish, *Felix Frankfurter and His Times: The Reform Years* (New York, 1982), 267.

58 Parrish, *Felix Frankfurter and His Times,* 262. Two scholars have suggested that the change in their relationship was already under way by 1933. David W. Levy and Bruce Allen Murphy, "Preserving the Progressive Spirit in a Conservative Time: The Joint Reform Efforts of Justice Brandeis and Professor Frankfurter, 1916-1933," 78 *Michigan Law Review* 1252, 1300-1301 (1980).

59 Robert E. Sherwood, *Roosevelt and Hopkins: An Intimate History* (New York, 1948), 90.

60 Melvin I. Urofsky and David W. Levy, eds., *"Half Brother, Half Son": The Letters of Louis D. Brandeis to Felix Frankfurter* (Norman, Okla., 1991), 593.

61 Freedman, ed., *Roosevelt & Frankfurter,* 377.

62 *Id.* at 372.

63 *Id.* at 381-87, 392, 399.

64 *See, e.g.,* Felix Frankfurter to Monte Lemann, Apr. 1, 1937, Frankfurter Papers, Box 765, folder 1530; Frankfurter to Charles C. Burlingham, Apr. 29, 1937, Apr. 29, 1937, Frankfurter Papers, Box 34, folder 580.

65 Freedman, ed., *Roosevelt & Frankfurter,* 380-81. *See generally* Nelson L. Dawson, *Louis D. Brandeis, Felix Frankfurter, and the New Deal* (Hamden, Conn., 1980), ch. 9.

66 *See* Harold L. Ickes, *The Secret Diary of Harold L. Ickes: The Inside Struggle, 1936–1939,* (New York, 1954), Vol. 2, 424 (July 16, 1938).

67 Freedman, ed., *Roosevelt & Frankfurter,* 392.

68 Felix Frankfurter to Charles C. Burlingham, June 9, 1937, Frankfurter Papers, Box 34, folder 580. Frankfurter reacted similarly when New York's liberal Democratic governor Herbert Lehman came out against the Court bill. Dawson, *Louis D. Brandeis, Felix Frankfurter, and the New Deal,* 150.

69 Felix Frankfurter to Charles E. Wyzanski, Jr., Apr. 13, 1937, Frankfurter Papers, Box 149, folder 3033.

70 300 U.S. 379 (1937).

71 Felix Frankfurter to Monte Lemann, Apr. 1, 1937, Frankfurter Papers, Box 76, folder 1530.

72 Urofsky and Levy, eds., *"Half Brother, Half Son,"* at 594 and n. 1 (letter no. 618). *See* Felix Frankfurter to Monte Lemann, July 2, 1937, Frankfurter Papers, Box 76, folder 1530.

73 Felix Frankfurter, *The Commerce Clause Under Marshall, Taney, and Waite* (Chicago, 1964 [1937]). *See* Freedman, ed., *Roosevelt & Frankfurter,* 366.

74 Felix Frankfurter to C. C. Burlingham, Apr. 29, 1937, Frankfurter Papers, Box 34, folder 580. *Accord* Freedman, ed., *Roosevelt and Frankfurter,* 392.

75 Felix Frankfurter and James M. Landis, *The Business of the Supreme Court: A Study in the Federal Judicial System* (New York, 1928), 310.

76 *Id.* at 310. *See* Frankfurter, *The Commerce Clause,* 65.

77 Mennel and Compston, eds., *Holmes & Frankfurter,* 86.

78 Felix Frankfurter, "The Red Terror of Judicial Reform," reprinted in Frankfurter, *Law and Politics: Occasional Papers of Felix Frankfurter, 1913–1938,* ed. Archibald MacLeish and E. F. Prichard, Jr. (New York, 1962 [1939]), 15. *See also id.* at 6–7, 12–13, 30, 41–47, 54.

79 Felix Frankfurter to C. C. Burlingham, Apr. 29, 1937, Frankfurter Papers, Box 34, folder 580.

80 Felix Frankfurter to Charles E. Wyzanski, Jr., Apr. 13, 1937, Frankfurter Papers, Box 149, folder 3033.

81 Felix Frankfurter to C. C. Burlingham, Apr. 29, 1937, Frankfurter Papers, Box 34, folder 580.

82 Felix Frankfurter to Harry Shulman, May 23, 1938, Frankfurter Papers (H.L.S.), Box 171, folder 17.

83 Felix Frankfurter to Harry Shulman, May 23, 1938, Frankfurter Papers (H.L.S.), Box 171, folder 17.

84 Quoted in Parrish, *Felix Frankfurter and His Times,* 275.

85 Ickes, *Secret Diary,* Vol. 2, 471. *See, e.g.,* George W. Norris to Herbert Agar, Aug. 23, 1938, and Norris to Jacob Billikopf, Aug. 12, 1938, Norris Papers, Tray 78, Box 5, file: "Judiciary Committee, 1939–40."

86 The widely shared assumption was that ethnicity and geography would prevent Roosevelt from appointing Frankfurter, a Jew from Massachusetts, to the Court while Brandeis, another Jew from Massachusetts, remained a member.

87 Parrish, *Felix Frankfurter and His Times,* 274.

88 Felix Frankfurter to Louis D. Brandeis, May 20, 1938, Frankfurter Papers, Box 29, folder 481. On the alteration in their friendship, *compare* Parrish, *Felix Frankfurter and His Times,* 259–63, 267–71; Bruce Allen Murphy, *The Brandeis/Frankfurter Connection: The Secret Political Activities of Two Supreme Court Justices* (New York, 1982), 155–58, 172–84, 418 n. 112; Harry N. Hirsch, *The Enigma of Felix Frankfurter* (New York, 1981), 114–24; Dawson, *Louis D. Brandeis, Felix Frankfurter, and the New Deal,* ch. 9.

89 Felix Frankfurter to Henry M. Hart, Jr., Mar. 17, 1940, Hart Papers, Box 5, folder 19.

90 Quoted in Parrish, *Felix Frankfurter and His Times*, 260.

91 Frankfurter's keen desire to separate Holmes from Brandeis was apparent in his response to a letter from J. Willard Hurst written shortly after *Erie* came down. Hurst, who had been Brandeis's law clerk the preceding term, wrote Frankfurter speculating that Brandeis had used *Erie* to pay tribute to Holmes and that there was "feeling there so deep as to be avoided" (Hurst to Frankfurter, May 24, 1938, Frankfurter Papers, Box 127, folder 2648). Responding quickly, Frankfurter took keen exception to Hurst's speculation concerning Brandeis's "deep" feelings for Holmes and his motives for writing *Erie* (Frankfurter to Hurst, June 10, 1938, Frankfurter Papers, microfilm, Reel 39). Even if Frankfurter had been correct in identifying a constitutional difference between Holmes and Brandeis, that difference would hardly have disproved Hurst's speculation as to Brandeis's personal feelings and motivations in writing his opinion. Surely, Holmes and Brandeis had been particularly close, and surely *Erie* did place "considerable stress" on the name and words of a single deceased justice who had, after all, written only dissents on the point. Further, Frankfurter stretched in the letter to magnify differences between the two justices. Unlike Brandeis, he told Hurst, Holmes "did not suggest disturbing the original *Swift v. Tyson* doctrine." That claim was technically correct, but it was also an incomplete and misleading statement of Holmes's attitude toward *Swift* and his view of what the law should be. Holmes undoubtedly would have been delighted with *Erie*'s references to him and his jurisprudential theory as well as with its legal result in overturning *Swift*.

   I am indebted to Professor Daniel R. Ernst for calling my attention to Frankfurter's response to Hurst's letter.

92 "Felix Frankfurter was the assimilationist's dream come true," Alfred S. Konefsky has written. He "constantly worked to remind everyone that he was both an American and that he was socially desirable. He was consumed with his need to know, or at least be acquainted with, the 'right' people." Alfred S. Konefsky, "Men of Great and Little Faith: Generations of Constitutional Scholars," 30 *Buffalo Law Review* 365, 375 (1981). *Accord*, Robert A. Burt, *Two Jewish Justices: Outcasts in the Promised Land* (Berkeley, Calif., 1988), esp. 37–48, 123–29.

93 For an example of the continued effort to maintain as much slack as possible in *Erie*'s application, *see* the opinion of Judge John Parker in *New England Mutual Life Insurance Co. v. Mitchell*, 118 F.2d 414 (1941).

94 *West v. American Telephone & Telegraph*, 311 U.S. 223, 237 (1940). The recalcitrance of the lower courts and the tactical uses of the declaratory judgment were both on view in one of the decisions the Supreme Court reversed. See *Stoner v. New York Life Insurance, Co.*, 311 U.S. 464 (1941).

95 *See, e.g., Six Companies of California v. Joint Highway District No. 13 of California*, 311 U.S. 180 (1940); *Stoner v. New York Life Insurance Co.*, 311 U.S. 464 (1940); *West v. American Telephone and Telegraph Co.*, 311 U.S. 223 (1940).

96 *Fidelity Union Trust Co. v. Field*, 311 U.S. 169 (1940).

97 311 U.S. 169, 179.

98 The Court left the choice-of-law issue open in a case decided only weeks after *Erie*. See *Ruhlin v. New York Life Insurance Co.*, 304 U.S. 202 (1938).

99 *Klaxon Co. v. Stentor Electric Manufacturing Co., Inc.*, 313 U.S. 487, 496 (1941).

100 *Klaxon*, 313 U.S. at 496.

101 326 U.S. 99 (1945). *See* Felix Frankfurter to Harlan F. Stone, Jan. 27, 1945, Frankfurter Papers, Box 106, folder 2205. The case also decided that the *Erie* doctrine applied in federal equity.

102 *Id.* at 108. Frankfurter had suggested this analysis in his dissent in *Sibbach v. Wilson*, 312 U.S. 1, 16 (1941) (Frankfurter, J., dissenting).

103 326 U.S. at 109.

104 *Id.* at 110.

105 *Id.* at 102, 103.

106 *Id.* at 101.

107 Felix Frankfurter to Henry M. Hart, Jr., May 3, 1954, Frankfurter Papers (H.L.S.), Box 185, folder 15.

108 326 U.S. at 101, 102, 105–9, 112.

109 Convinced that the Court's role was the exposition of federal law, Frankfurter had grown distressed with suggestions that *Erie* and state law could be determinative in cases involving federal law. *See* Felix Frankfurter to Harlan F. Stone, Apr. 23, 1942, Frankfurter Papers, Box 106, folder 2199; Frankfurter to Stone, Nov. 27, 1942, Stone Papers, Box 74; *Holmberg v. Armbrecht*, 327 U.S. 392, 395 (1946) (Frankfurter, J.).

110 Felix Frankfurter to Stanley Reed, May 14, 1942, Frankfurter Papers, Box 92, folder 1922.

111 326 U.S. at 112.

112 *King v. Order of United Commercial Travellers*, 333 U.S. 153, 158 (1948). *See* Robert H. Jackson, *Full Faith and Credit — The Lawyer's Clause of the Constitution* (New York, 1945), 1 n. 1.

113 *E.g.*, Arthur John Keefe, John J. Gilhooley, George H. Bailey, and Donald S. Day, "Weary Erie," 34 *Cornell Law Quarterly* 494, 504 and n. 55 (1949). *See* Mary Brigid McManamon, "Felix Frankfurter: The Architect of 'Our Federalism,' " 27 *Georgia Law Review* 697, 708–9, 749–51, 754–55, 777–80 (1993).

114 *See, e.g., Pope & Talbot, Inc. v. Hawn*, 346 U.S. 406, 414, 416 (1953) (Frankfurter, J., concurring).

115 *Angel v. Bullington*, 330 U.S. 183 (1947); *Ragan v. Merchants Transfer Co.*, 337 U.S. 530 (1949); *Cohen v. Beneficial Loan Corp.*, 337 U.S. 541 (1949); *Woods v. Interstate Realty Co.*, 337 U.S. 535 (1949).

116 *Guaranty Trust Co. v. York*, 326 U.S. at 112.

117 Frank W. Snepp, "The Law Applied in the Federal Courts," 13 *Law and Contemporary Problems* 165, 180 (1948).

118 James Wm. Moore and Robert Stephen Oglebay, "The Supreme Court, Stare Decisis and Law of the Case," 21 *Texas Law Review* 514, 525 (1943).

119 Richard L. Braun, "The Erie Case and the Federal Rules — A Prediction," 39 *Georgetown Law Journal* 600, 607 (1951); Lawrence Earl Broh-Kahn, "Uniformity Run Riot — Extensions of the Erie Case," 31 *Kentucky Law Journal* 99, 111 (1941).

120 Zechariah Chafee, Jr., "Do Judges Make or Discover Law?" 91 *Proceedings of the American Philosophical Society* 405, 415 (1947). *See* Donald L. Smith, *Zechariah Chafee, Jr.: Defender of Liberty and Law* (Cambridge, Mass., 1986).

121 Chafee, "Do Judges Make or Discover Law," at 416.

122 Maxwell H. Herriott, "Has Congress the Power to Modify the Effect of Erie Railroad Co. v. Tompkins?" 26 *Marquette Law Review* 1, 10 (1941). *See* Schweppe, "What Has Happened to Federal Jurisprudence?"; Thomas Reed Powell, "Some Aspects of American Constitutional Law," 53 *Harvard Law Review* 529 (1940); Wolfson, "Uniform Law and the Federal Courts Under the Erie Doctrine," 23 *Temple Law Quarterly* 404 (1950).

123 *See, e.g.*, McCormick and Hewins, "The Collapse of 'General' Law in the Federal Courts,"
     at 134; Keefe, Gilhooley, Bailey, and Day, "Weary Erie," at 497 (1949); "Developments in the
     Law: Declaratory Judgments—1941–1949," 62 *Harvard Law Review* 787 n. 128, 1031 (1949);
     Moore and Oglebay, "The Supreme Court, Stare Decisis and Law of the Case," at 526. *See
     also* Wolfson, "Uniform Law and the Federal Courts Under the Erie Doctrine"; Note, "Erie
     R.R. v. Tompkins and the Federal Rules," 62 *Harvard Law Review* 1030 (1949); Broh-Kahn,
     "Uniformity Run Riot"; Edward S. Stimson, "Swift v. Tyson—What Remains? What Is
     (State) Law?" 24 *Cornell Law Quarterly* 54 (1938); Shulman, "The Demise of Swift v. Tyson."

124 Elizabeth Storey Landis and William B. Landis, Jr., "Federal Interpleader," 34 *Cornell Law
     Quarterly*, 403, 414 (1949); Note, "Developments in the Law: Declaratory Judgments, 1941–
     1949," 62 *Harvard Law Review* 787, 805 n. 128 (1949).

125 Chaffee, "Do Judges Make or Discover Law?" 414; Brainerd Currie, "Change of Venue and
     the Conflict of Laws," 22 *University of Chicago Law Review* 405, 468 (1955).

126 The early literature on *Erie* and the Federal Rules was extensive. *See, e.g.,* Lehan Kent
     Tunks, "Categorization and Federalism: 'Substance' and 'Procedure' after Erie Railroad v.
     Tompkins," 34 *Illinois Law Review of Northwestern University* 271 (1939); Alexander Holtzoff,
     "The Federal Rules of Civil Procedure and Erie Railroad Co. v. Tompkins," 24 *Journal of the
     American Judicature Society* 57 (1940); Bernard C. Gavit, "States' Rights and Federal Proce-
     dure," 25 *Indiana Law Review* 1 (1949).

127 Wolfson, "Uniform Law and the Federal Courts Under the Erie Doctrine," at 404.

128 *Id.* 117. *See* Broh-Kahn, "Uniformity Run Riot."

129 Keefe, Gilhooley, Bailey, and Day, "Weary Erie," at 494, 526.

130 Edward A. Purcell, Jr., *The Crisis of Democratic Theory: Scientific Naturalism and the Problem
     of Value* (Lexington, Ky., 1973), esp. chs. 5 and 9.

131 Felix Morley, "Affirmation of Materialism," *Barron's*, June 18, 1951, at 3. *See* Purcell, *Crisis of
     Democratic Theory*, 159–78; G. Edward White, *Patterns of American Legal Thought* (India-
     napolis, 1978), 194–226.

132 *See, e.g.*, Parker, "Erie v. Tompkins in Retrospect," 20–21; Gerald T. Dunne, *Hugo Black and
     the Judicial Revolution* (New York, 1977), 182–83.

133 *E.g.*, Thomas Reed Powell, "Some Aspects of American Constitutional Law," 53 *Harvard
     Law Review* 529, 542, 551–52 (1940); Arthur L. Corbin, "The Laws of the Several States," 50
     Yale Law Journal 762 (1941); Karl N. Llewellyn, *The Common Law Tradition: Deciding Ap-
     peals* (Boston, 1960), 417–18 and n. 34; Max Radin to Felix Frankfurter, Dec. 2, 1943, Frank-
     furter Papers, Box 92, folder 1906; *Richardson v. Commissioner of Internal Revenue*, 126 F. 2d
     562, 567 (C.C.A. 2d 1942) (Frank, J.); Charles E. Clark, "State Law in the Federal Courts:
     The Brooding Omnipresence of Erie v. Tompkins," 55 *Yale Law Journal* 267, 291 (1946).

134 *See* Joseph C. Hutcheson, Jr., address at symposium, "The Erie-Tompkins Case and the
     Doctrine of Precedent, Advance or Retreat?" 14 *University of Cincinnati Law Review* 259,
     271–74 (1940); Clark, "State Law in the Federal Courts," 279, 285; Powell, "Some Aspects
     of American Constitutional Law," 542; Corbin, "Laws of the Several States," 763 n. 6; Cook,
     Logical and Legal Bases of the Conflict of Laws, 136–47.

135 Arthur L. Corbin, "The Common Law of the United States," 47 *Yale Law Journal* 1351, 1353
     (1938).

136 Corbin, "Laws of the Several States," 768, 774.

137 Quoted in Kenneth C. Cole, "Erie v. Tompkins and the Relationship Between Federal and
     State Courts," 36 *American Political Science Review* 885, 889 n. 9 (1942).

138 Clark, "State Law in the Federal Courts," 291. *Accord 165 Broadway Building, Inc. v. City Investing Co.,* 120 F. 2d 813, 818 (2d Cir. 1941) (Clark, J.). *See* Stephen N. Subrin, "Charles E. Clark and His Procedural Outlook: The Disciplined Champion of Undisciplined Rules," in Peninah Petruck, ed., *Judge Charles Edward Clark* (New York, 1991), 115.

139 Cook, *Logical and Legal Bases of the Conflict of Laws,* 151.

140 *Richardson v. Commissioner of Internal Revenue Service,* 126 F. 2d 562, 567 (C.C.A. 2d 1942) (Frank, J.). Quoted, *e.g.,* in Wechsler, "Federal Jurisdiction and the Revision of the Judicial Code," 13 *Law and Contemporary Problems* 216, 239 (1948); *Gaunt v. John Hancock Mutual Life Insurance Co.,* 160 F. 2d 599, 603, 604 (Clark, J., concurring). *Accord* Jackson, *Full Faith and Credit,* 1 n. 2.

141 For somewhat different views from judges, *see, e.g.,* Calvert Magruder, "Trials and Tribulations of an Intermediate Appellate Court," 44 *Cornell Law Quarterly* 1, 6 (1958); Charles E. Wyzanski, *A Trial Judge's Freedom and Responsibility* (New York, 1952), 22; *Ruhlin v. New York Life Insurance Co.,* 304 U.S. 202, 208 (Reed, J.).

  For different views from scholars, *see* Bertram Harnett and John V. Thornton, "Precedent in the Eerie-Tompkins Manner: A Decade in Retrospect," 24 *New York University Law Quarterly Review* 770 (1949); James A. Gorrell and Ithamar D. Weed, "Erie Railroad: Ten Years After," 9 *Ohio State Law Journal* 276, 288–90 (1948); Marquis L. Smith, "Erie Railroad *versus* Tompkins: Two Years After," 12 *Rocky Mountain Law Review* 184 (1940); Michael C. Dorf, "Prediction and the Rule of Law," 52 *U.C.L.A. Law Review* 651, 696–709 (1995). *See generally* Kurland, "Mr. Justice Frankfurter, the Supreme Court and the Erie Doctrine in Diversity Cases," 205–14.

142 *Cf.* Maxwell L. Stearns, "Standing and Social Choice: Historical Evidence," 144 *University of Pennsylvania Law Review* 309, 393–99 (1995).

143 Cook, *Logical and Legal Bases of the Conflict of Laws,* 136. *See also* Cook, "Powers of Congress," 433–34.

144 The realists would seem to fit Robert Wiebe's description of the new "national class" that developed in the early twentieth century. Robert H. Wiebe, *Self-Rule: A Cultural History of American Democracy* (Chicago, 1995), 140–50, 199–201.

145 *See* James F. Simon, *The Antogonists: Hugo Black, Felix Frankfurter and Civil Liberties in Modern America* (New York, 1989).

146 *E.g.,* Lon L. Fuller, "Reason and Fiat in Case Law," 59 *Harvard Law Review* 376 (1946). *See* Neil Duxbury, *Patterns of American Jurisprudence* (New York, 1995), ch. 4; William W. Fisher III, "The Development of Modern American Legal Theory and the Judicial Interpretation of the Bill of Rights," in Michael J. Lacey and Knud Haakonssen, *A Culture of Rights: The Bill of Rights in Philosophy, Politics, and Law, 1789–1991* (Cambridge, England, 1991); Horwitz, *Transformation of American Law,* esp. ch. 9; Gary Peller, "Neutral Principles in the 1950s," 21 *University of Michigan Journal of Law Reform* 561 (1988); Mark Tushnet, "Truth, Justice, and the American Way: An Intepretation of Public Law Scholarship in the Seventies," 57 *Texas Law Review* 1307 (1979).

147 Fuller, "Reason and Fiat," 34.

148 *Id.* at 35.

149 *Id.* at 36.

150 *Id.* at 37.

151 *Id.* at 38.

152 Many of the later themes identified with the jurisprudence of institutional process were sug-

gested in Frankfurter's early writings. *See, e.g.,* Felix Frankfurter and Henry M. Hart, Jr., The Business of the Supreme Court at October Term, 1932," 47 *Harvard Law Review* 245 (1933).

153 Karl N. Llewellyn, *Jurisprudence: Realism in Theory and Practice* (Chicago, 1962), chs. 12 and 15. *See* Duxbury, *Patterns of American Jurisprudence*, ch. 3.

154 Karl N. Llewellyn, *The Common Law Tradition: Deciding Appeals* (Boston, 1960), 122. *See id.* at 127, 157, 241, 270.

155 Kenneth C. Cole, "Erie v. Tompkins and the Relationship Between Federal and State Courts," 36 *American Political Science Review* 885, 895 (1942). For criticisms of *Erie, see* Lawrence Earl Broh-Kahn, "Amendment by Decision — More on the *Erie* Case," 30 *Kentucky Law Journal* 3 (1941); Bernard C. Gavit, "States' Rights and Federal Procedure," 25 *Indiana Law Journal* 1 (1949); Parker, "*Erie v. Tompkins* in Retrospect,"; Edward S. Stimson, "Swift v. Tyson — What Remains?" 24 *Cornell Law Quarterly* 54 (1938); Note, "Swift v. Tyson Overruled," 24 *Virginia Law Review* 895 (1938).

156 Llewellyn, *Common Law Tradition*, 417–18.

157 *Id.* at 417.

158 *E.g.,* Felix Frankfurter to Alexander M. Bickel, Mar. 18, 1963, and Oct. 8, 1964, Frankfurter Papers, Box 24, folder 359; Felix Frankfurter to Henry M. Hart, Jr., June 29, 1956, and July 18, 1957, Hart Papers, Box 3, folder 3.

159 *E.g.,* Braden, "Search for Objectivity in Constitutional Law," 57 *Yale Law Journal* at 588; Fred Rodell, *Nine Men: A Political History of the Supreme Court from 1790 to 1955* (New York, 1955), 269–73.

160 Max Lerner, *Ideas Are Weapons* (New York, 1943), 83.

161 Samuel J. Konefsky, *The Legacy of Holmes and Brandeis: A Study in the Influence of Ideas* (New York, 1961 [1956]), 106.

162 C. Herman Pritchett, *The Roosevelt Court: A Study in Judicial Politics and Values, 1937–1947* (Chicago, 1969 [1948]), 266. *See* Mark DeWolfe Howe, ed., *Holmes-Laski Letters: The Correspondence of Mr. Justice Holmes and Harold J. Laski, 1916–1935* (Cambridge, Mass., 1953), Vol. 1, at 556.

163 Mason, *Brandeis. See* Henry J. Friendly, book review, 56 *Yale Law Journal* 423, 424 (1947).

164 Rodell, *Nine Men*, 227.

165 Felix Frankfurter to Louis Jaffe, Mar. 18, 1947, Frankfurter Papers, Box 70, folder 1384. *Cf.,* Michael Ariens, "A Thrice-Told Tale, or Felix the Cat," 107 *Harvard Law Review* 620, 667–75 (1994).

166 *Ferguson v. Moore-McCormack Lines, Inc.,* 352 U.S. 521, 524, 525 (1957) (Frankfurter, J., dissenting).

167 *See* Felix Frankfurter to Alexander M. Bickel, Aug. 29, 1956, Frankfurter Papers, Box 24, folder 356.

168 Edward A. Purcell, Jr., "Alexander M. Bickel and the Post-Realist Constitution," 11 *Harvard Civil Rights/Civil Liberties Law Review* 521, 529 (1976). *See id.* at 529–32; Bickel, *Unpublished Opinions*, ch. 9; Philip B. Kurland, "Mr. Justice Frankfurter, the Supreme Court and the Erie Doctrine in Diversity Cases," 67 *Yale Law Journal* 187 (1957).

169 Bickel, *Unpublished Opinions*, 17. *Accord* Paul A. Freund, *On Law and Justice* (Cambridge, Mass., 1968), 140–41; Alexander M. Bickel and Harry H. Wellington, "Legislative Purpose and the Judicial Process: The Lincoln Mills Case," 71 *Harvard Law Review* 1, 28–29 (1957). *See* Purcell, "Alexander M. Bickel and the Post-Realist Constitution," 528–32.

170 A subsequent scholar, evaluating Bickel's contention in the context of a general study of the

Court and the problem of child labor, concluded that Bickel's interpretation was "not simply improbable but unlikely in the highest degree." Stephen B. Wood, *Constitutional Politics in the Progressive Era* (Chicago, 1968), 249.

171 Adrian S. Fisher, review of *The Unpublished Opinions of Mr. Justice Brandeis* by Alexander M. Bickel, 67 *Yale Law Journal* 1148, 1149 (1958).

172 Bickel, *Unpublished Opinions*, 20.

173 Louis Jaffe, review of Mason, *Brandeis: A Free Man's Life*, 14 *University of Chicago Law Review* 526 (1947); Paul A. Freund, "Mr. Justice Brandeis: A Centennial Memoir," 70 *Harvard Law Review* 769 (1957); Erwin N. Griswold, "Foreword: Of Time and Attitudes — Professor Hart and Judge Arnold," 74 *Harvard Law Review* 81 (1960); Bickel and Wellington, "Legislative Purpose and the Judicial Process," 28–29; Felix Frankfurter to Henry Hart, May 3, 1954, Hart Papers, Box 3, folder 2.

174 Ernest J. Brown to Max Lerner, Feb. 26, 1964, Hart Papers, Box 4, folder 19. *Accord* Paul A. Freund, "Mr. Justice Brandeis," at 788.

175 Freund, *On Law and Justice*, 139, 140. Freund apparently considered the line so effective that he repeated it in another essay. *See id.* at 210.

176 *See* Clyde Spillenger, "Reading the Judicial Canon: Alexander Bickel and the Book of Brandeis," 79 *Journal of American History* 125 (1992).

177 Erwin N. Griswold to Harlan F. Stone, May 4, 1938, Stone Papers, Box 15; Griswold, "Foreword: Of Time and Attitudes," 91 and n. 42.

178 Freund, *On Law and Justice*, 141.

179 Wallace Mendelson, *The Constitution and the Court* (New York, 1959), 211.

180 Brandeis "gave primacy to the canon of self-limitation," Freund wrote. "That was still the first mark of the master." Freund, *On Law and Justice*, 143.

CHAPTER 9. HENRY M. HART, JR., AND THE POWER OF TRANSFORMING VISION

1 Henry M. Hart, Jr., review of *Brandeis: Lawyer and Judge in the Modern State* by Alpheus Thomas Mason, 82 *University of Pennsylvania Law Review* 668 (1934).

2 Felix Frankfurter to Henry M. Hart, Jr., Feb. 2, 1932, Hart Papers Box 2, folder 29.

3 Henry M. Hart, Jr., to Roscoe Pound, Oct. 2, 1933, Hart Papers, Box 5, folder 17.

4 Felix Frankfurter and Henry M. Hart, Jr., "The Business of the Supreme Court at October Term, 1934," 49 *Harvard Law Review* 68 (1935).

5 [Henry M. Hart, Jr.], unsigned editorial, "Unshackling the Tax Power," 81 *The New Republic* 319 (1935), Hart Papers, Box 29, folder 3.

6 Thomas Reed Powell to Henry M. Hart, Jr., Oct. 18, 1937, Hart Papers, Box 5, folder 18. For Hart's membership in the ACLU *see* Lucille Banner to Henry M. Hart, Jr., Nov. 20, 1935, Hart Papers, Box 1, folder 5.

7 [Henry M. Hart, Jr.], unsigned editorial, "The Supreme Court Eats Crow," 78 *The New Republic* 146 (1934), Hart Papers, Box 29, folder 1; [Henry M. Hart, Jr.], unsigned editorial, "The Florida Chain Store Case," 74 *The New Republic* 230 (1933), Hart Papers, Box 29, folder 1.

8 [Henry M. Hart, Jr.], unsigned editorial, "A Dred Scott Decision," 83 *The New Republic* 34 (1935).

9 297 U.S. 1 (1936).

10 Henry M. Hart, Jr., to Bruce Bliven, Jan. 6, 1936, Hart Papers, Box 5, folder 13. *See* Hart, "Processing Taxes and Protective Tariffs," 49 *Harvard Law Review* 610 (1936); Hart, "The Constitution Is What the Judges Say It Is" (draft, circa 1936), Hart Papers, Box 24, folder 3.

11 [Henry M. Hart, Jr.], unsigned editorial, "Unshackling the Tax Power," 81 *The New Republic* 319 (1935), Hart Papers, Box 29, folder 3.

12 The Progressives interpreted Thayer through their own political purposes and attributed to him a narrower doctrine of judicial review than he had actually advanced. *See* Edward A. Purcell, Jr., "Learned Hand: The Jurisprudential Trajectory of an Old Progressive," 43 *Buffalo Law Review* 873, 884–96 (1995).

13 Henry M. Hart, Jr., "The American System of Constitutional Law," speech given at dinner sponsored by the League of Women Voters, Washington, D.C., May 4, 1937, Hart Papers, Box 22, folder 3, at 19.

14 *Id.* at 16–17. *See* Henry M. Hart, Jr., "The United States Supreme Court: An Argument on the President's Side," *Harvard Alumni Bulletin* 767, 769 (1937); and drafts, Henry M. Hart, Jr., to *New York Times* and Charles Merz to Hart, Mar. 22, 1937, Hart Papers, Box 5, folder 10; Hart, "A Correction," letter to the *Boston Herald,* Apr. 3, 1937, Red Set, Henry M. Hart, Harvard Law School Library.

15 Henry M. Hart, Jr., to Felix Frankfurter, Feb. 19, 1937, Hart Papers, Box 2, folder 30. *See* Frederick Bernays Wiener to Henry M. Hart, Jr., Aug. 3, 1929, Hart Papers, Box 6, folder 23; Ganson Purcell to Henry M. Hart, Jr., Nov. 9, 1932, Hart Papers, Box 5, folder 20.

16 *See* leaflet and materials in Hart Papers, Box 31, folder 9; Lawrence S. Wittner, *Rebels Against War: The American Peace Movement, 1933–83* (Philadelphia, 1984), 23. *See* Robert Cohen, *When the Old Left Was Young: Student Radicals and America's First Mass Student Movement, 1929–1941* (New York, 1993), ch. 9.

17 Henry M. Hart, Jr., speech delivered at meeting of Cambridge Teachers Union, May 22, 1940, Hart Papers, Box 31, folder 9, at 3.

18 *The Harvard Crimson,* May 27, 1940, at 1. *See* letter "To the Editor of the Harvard *Crimson,*" May 29, 1940, Hart Papers, Box 31, folder 9.

19 Harry Levin to Henry M. Hart, Jr., June 14, 1940, Hart Papers, Box 31, folder 9.

20 Henry M. Hart, Jr., to "Mattie" [F. O. Matthiessen] May 25, 1940, Hart Papers, Box 31, folder 9. Hart was apparently correct in his estimate. *See* Ellen W. Schrecker, *No Ivory Tower: McCarthyism & the Universities* (New York, 1986), ch. 2.

21 Henry M. Hart, Jr., to "Matty" [F.O. Matthiessen], May 25, 1940, Hart Papers, Box 31, folder 9, at 4.

22 *Id.* at 5.

23 *Id.* at 6.

24 *Id.*

25 Hart's experience was typical of many intellectuals who shared left-wing sympathies in the 1930s. *See, e.g.,* William L. O'Neill, *The Great Schism: Stalinism and the American Intellectuals* (New York, 1982); John P. Diggins, *Up from Communism: Conservative Odysseys in American Intellectual History* (New York, 1975); Alan M. Wald, *The New York Intellectuals: The Rise and Decline of the Anti-Stalinist Left from the 1930s to the 1980s* (Chapel Hill, N.C., 1987), Part III.

26 *See* William N. Eskridge, Jr., and Philip P. Frickey, "An Historical and Critical Introduction to *The Legal Process,*" in Henry M. Hart, Jr., and Albert M. Sacks, *The Legal Process: Basic Problems in the Making and Application of Law,* ed. Eskridge and Frickey (Westbury, N.Y., 1994), lxxiv–vii (hereafter, "Eskridge and Frickey, *Legal Process*").

27 Henry M. Hart, Jr., "Report on Immigration Procedures" (1939), Hart Papers, Box 23.

28 Immigration and Naturalization Service, "Committee on Legislation," minutes of meeting on Jan. 7, 1941, Hart Papers, Box 43, folder 3, at 5.

29 Henry M. Hart, Jr., "Memorandum," June 12, 1942, Hart Papers, Box 43, folder 1.

30 Henry M. Hart, Jr., to Francis Biddle, Feb. 2, 1942, Hart Papers, Box 1, folder 8.

31 Richard Polenberg, *War and Society: The United States, 1941–1945* (Philadelphia, 1972), 32. *See* Henry M. Hart, Jr., to Edwin C. Pearce, Oct. 13, 1945, Hart Papers, Box 5, folder 21.

32 Henry M. Hart, Jr., typescript of speech at Harvard Law School forum on "Legal Problems of Mobilization," Apr. 6, 1951, at 5, Hart Papers, Box 22, folder 11.

33 Henry M. Hart, Jr., unedited transcript of speech at symposium on "Freedom and Planning," Chicago, 1951, at 43. Hart Papers, Box 22, folder 12. *Accord*, Hart, speech on "Legal Problems of Mobilization," at 22.

   It is necessary to note that Hart rejected the transcript, terming it "a complete hash" of his remarks. Hart to Archer O'Reilly, Jr., July 10, 1951, Hart Papers, Box 22, folder 12. I quote from the transcript in spite of his disavowal for two reasons. First, his objections seemed to go principally to the lack of "unity, emphasis and coherence" in the transcript as a whole. Second, the transcript seems consistent with his general views on the basic subjects addressed: the importance of private decision making and decentralization and the dangers of government regulation and legislative activism.

34 Hart, speech at "Freedom and Planning" symposium, at 47. *See* Henry M. Hart, Jr., "An Imaginary Memorandum," typescript dated Nov. 30, 1950, Hart Papers, Box 24, folder 12.

35 Robert Allen Skotheim, *American Intellectual Histories and Historians* (Princeton, 1966); Edward A. Purcell, Jr., *The Crisis of Democratic Theory: Scientific Naturalism and the Problem of Value* (Lexington, Ky., 1973).

36 Henry M. Hart, Jr., to Warren A. Seavey, Dec. 11, 1950, Hart Papers, Box 6, folder 15. *See* "Comment of Professor Hart," in Arthur E. Sutherland, ed., *Government Under Law* (Cambridge, Mass., 1956), 143.

37 Henry M. Hart, Jr., "The New Third-Year Program," *Harvard Law School Bulletin*, April 1950, 1. Hart and Fuller attempted to develop a jurisprudence that could encompass realism and then subordinate it to orderly rational and moral principles. For discussions of Harvard after the war *see* Laura Kalman, *Legal Realism at Yale, 1927–1960* (Chapel Hill, N.C., 1986), 207–28; Arthur E. Sutherland, *The Law at Harvard: A History of Ideas and Men, 1817–1967* (Cambridge, Mass., 1967), chs. 9–10.

38 Lon L. Fuller, "The Course in Jurisprudence," *Harvard Law School Bulletin* (April 1950), 4. For Fuller, *see* Robert S. Summers, *Lon L. Fuller* (Stanford, Calif., 1984); Fuller, *The Law in Quest of Itself* (Boston, 1940); Fuller, *The Morality of Law* (New Haven, Conn., 1964).

39 Summers, *Lon L. Fuller*, 6, 14; Eskridge and Frickey, *Legal Process*, lxxxiii.

40 His course on "legislation," Hart wrote, should "more accurately have been called Process of Lawmaking, with a Heavy Infusion of Jurisprudence." Henry M. Hart, Jr., to Stanley Surrey, Feb. 18, 1950, Hart Papers, Box 6, folder 15.

41 Henry M. Hart, Jr., "Holmes' Positivism — An Addendum," 64 *Harvard Law Review* 929 (1951). *Compare* Lon L. Fuller, "Reason and Fiat in Case Law," 59 *Harvard Law Review* 376 (1946).

42 *Id.* at 930, 932.

43 *Id.* at 937.

44 Henry M. Hart, Jr., to Carl A. Auerbach, Mar. 4, 1959, Hart Papers, Box 1, folder 3.

45 For a detailed discussion of the evolution of Hart's thinking that led to *The Legal Process*, *see* Eskridge and Frickey, *Legal Process*, lxxvii–xcvi. For Hart's evolving ideas, *see, e.g.*, Henry M. Hart, Jr., "Some After-Thoughts on Justice," manuscript dated Feb. 6, 1949, Hart

Papers, Box 35, folder 7; Henry M. Hart, Jr., "Introductory Lecture" in undergraduate law course, 1955, Hart Papers, Box 22, folder 15.

46 Henry M. Hart, Jr., and Albert M. Sacks, *The Legal Process: Basic Problems in the Making and Application of Law* (Cambridge, Mass., Tentative Edition, 1958), iii (hereafter, "Hart and Sacks, *Legal Process*"). Although Hart and Sacks never published their working legal process materials, the 1958 "Tentative Edition" became the standard version for more than three decades. In 1994, the 1958 edition was finally and rightfully published with a superb historical introduction. *See* Eskridge and Frickey, *Legal Process*.

47 Hart, "Holmes' Positivism," at 930.

48 Hart and Sacks, *Legal Process*, 6; Eskridge and Frickey, *Legal Process*, 6. *Compare* Fuller, *Morality of Law*, 96–97; Lon L. Fuller, "Positivism and Fidelity to Law — A Reply to Professor [H.L.A.] Hart," 71 *Harvard Law Review* 630, 643 (1958).

49 Henry M. Hart, Jr., "Some After-Thoughts on Justice," Hart Papers, Box 35, folder 7, at 3. *Accord* Hart, "Holmes' Positivism," at 936–37.

50 Paul L. Murphy, *The Constitution in Crisis Times, 1918–1969* (New York, 1972), 257.

51 54 Stat. 670 (1940).

52 61 Stat. 136 (1947); *see* Michal R. Belknap, *Cold War Political Justice: The Smith Act, the Communist Party, and American Civil Liberties* (Westport, Conn., 1977); Peter L. Steinberg, *The Great "Red Menace": United States Prosecution of American Communists, 1947–1952* (Westport, Conn., 1984).

53 Walter Goodman, *The Committee: The Extraordinary Career of the House Committee on Un-American Activities* (New York, 1968); Michael Wrezin, "The Dies Committee," in Arthur M. Schlesinger, Jr., and Roger Bruns, eds., *Congress Investigates, 1792–1974* (New York, 1975); Kenneth O'Reilly, *Hoover and the Un-Americans: The F.B.I., H.U.A.C., and the Red Menace* (Philadelphia, 1983).

54 For the impact of McCarthy and his hearings on a young liberal lawyer, *see* Arthur L. Liman, *Lawyer: A Life of Counsel and Controversy* (New York, 1998), ch. 1. *See generally, e.g.,* Schrecker, *No Ivory Tower;* Stanley I. Kutler, *The American Inquisition: Justice and Injustice in the Cold War* (New York, 1982); Robert Griffith, *The Politics of Fear: Joseph R. McCarthy and the Senate* (New York, 1970).

55 64 Stat. 987 (1950).

56 66 Stat. 143 (1952).

57 Zechariah Chafee, Jr., "Investigations of Radicalism and Laws Against Subversion," in *Civil Liberties Under Attack*, ed. Henry Steele Commager (Philadelphia, 1951), 46.

58 Walter Gellhorn, "A General View," in Gellhorn, ed., *The States and Subversion* (Ithaca, N.Y., 1952), 391.

59 Alger Hiss to Henry M. Hart, Jr., Mar. 25, 1949, Hart Papers, Box 3, folder 23.

60 Henry M. Hart, Jr., "Professor Crosskey and Judicial Review," 67 *Harvard Law Review* 1456, 1475 (1954).

61 Henry M. Hart, Jr., to Kenneth Culp Davis, Nov. 15, 1952, Hart Papers, Box 2, folder 1.

62 *See* Leo Sheiner to Henry Hart, Apr. 10, 1954, with attachment, and Richard H. Field to Leo Sheiner, Apr. 20, 1954, Hart Papers, Box 6, folder 15.

63 "Memorandum: First gropings for an approach to the loyalty problem," Henry M. Hart, Jr., to David F. Cavers, undated (circa 1952), Hart Papers, Box 36, folder 2, at 1.

64 "Statement of Henry M. Hart, Jr., and Louis L. Jaffe to the President's Commission on Immigration and Naturalization," presented in Washington, D.C., by Louis L. Jaffe, Oct. 28, 1952,

at 2, Henry M. Hart, Jr., Red Set, Harvard Law School Library (hereafter, "Statement of Hart and Jaffe"). Jaffe's intellectual journey is recounted in Morton J. Horwitz, *The Transformation of American Law: The Crisis of Legal Orthodoxy, 1870–1960* (New York, 1992), 237–40.

65 "Statement of Hart and Jaffe," at 6.

66 *Id.* at 8.

67 *Id.* at 16.

68 *Id.* at 19.

69 *Id.* at 5.

70 Henry M. Hart, Jr., speech at symposium on "Freedom and Planning," Chicago, 1951, Hart Papers, Box 22, folder 12, at 47. *See* Hart to Archer O'Reilly, Jr., July 10, 1951, Hart Papers, Box 22, folder 12.

71 Henry M. Hart, Jr., "Comment for the Conference on Government Under Law," Sept. 22, 1955, Hart Papers, Box 22, folder 4, at 10. *See* "Comment of Profesor Hart," in Sutherland, ed., *Government Under Law,* 141–45.

72 Henry M. Hart, "The American System of Constitutional Law," speech given at dinner sponsored by the League of Women Voters, Washington, D.C., May 4, 1937, Hart Papers, Box 22, folder 3, at 19.

73 Henry M. Hart, Jr., "The Relations Between State and Federal Law," 54 *Columbia Law Review* 489, 539 (1954). *See* Eskridge and Frickey, *Legal Process,* lxxx.

74 Hart, speech at symposium on "Freedom and Planning," 48–49.

75 Henry M. Hart, Jr., "The Aims of the Criminal Law," 23 *Law and Contemporary Problems* 401, 429–30 (1958). *Accord* Henry M. Hart, Jr., "What Part Should Courts Play in Lawmaking?" summary of speech to the Columbus Bar Association, Nov. 16, 1954.

76 Hart, "Relations Between State and Federal Law," 519.

77 Henry M. Hart, Jr., to Lon L. Fuller, Nov. 5, 1957, Hart Papers, Box 3, folder 6.

78 Hart, "Relations Between State and Federal Law," 494. *See* Anthony J. Sebok, "Reading *The Legal Process,*" 94 *Michigan Law Review* 1571 (1996).

79 *Id.* at 541.

80 Henry M. Hart, Jr., "Talk for the Harvard Law School Association of New Jersey," May 23, 1957, Hart Papers, Box 22, folder 17, at 7–8. *Accord* Hart and Sacks, *The Legal Process,* 496–521.

81 Henry M. Hart, Jr., to Allen M. Singer, Feb. 5, 1959, at 3, Hart Papers, Box 6, folder 14. *Accord* Henry M. Hart, Jr., "Comment on Courts and Lawmaking," in Monrad G. Paulsen, ed., *Legal Institutions Today and Tomorrow* (New York, 1959), 40–49.

   The Hart and Sacks text, *The Legal Process,* is built on an analysis of the comparative "institutional competencies" of various lawmaking agencies (courts, legislatures, administrative agencies, private contractual agreements) to determine which agencies are best adapted for what jobs, and it is built further on the principle of "institutional settlement," the idea that people should accept the decisions of lawmaking agencies when the institutionally proper agency has made the decision and when it did so according to its prescribed procedures. Despite that "comparative" and "procedural" foundation, however, *The Legal Process* is focused on judicial lawmaking and conveys the message that courts (and private individuals) are generally far better and more desirable lawmakers than are legislatures and, to a lesser extent, administrative agencies. Thus, as a general matter, Hart's broader social orientation meant that the principle of institutional competency identified the courts as the most desirable and competent of lawmaking institutions. "Within the limits fixed by established remedies, in other words, the common law provides a comprehensive, underlying body of law adequate for the resolution of all the disputes that may arise within the social order," Hart and Sacks, *The Legal Process,* 647. *See* Vincent A. Wellman, "Dworkin and the Legal Process Tradition: The Legacy of Hart & Sacks," 29 *Arizona Law Review* 413 (1987); Neil Duxbury, "Faith in Reason: The Process Tradition in American Jurisprudence," 15 *Cardozo Law Review* 601 (1993).

82 Henry M. Hart, Jr., to Allen M. Singer, Feb. 5, 1959, at 3, Hart Papers, Box 6, folder 14.

83 Eskridge and Frickey, *Legal Process,* 164.

84 Hart, "Talk for the Harvard Law School Association of New Jersey," at 26.

85 *See also* Hart, "Aims of the Criminal Law," at 59. *See* Hart and Sacks, *Legal Process,* 647, 783; Fuller, "Reason and Fiat in Case Law," 393–94.

86 Hart, "Professor Crosskey and Judicial Review," 1485, 1486.

87 Henry M. Hart, Jr., "The Power of Congress to Limit the Jurisdiction of Federal Courts: An Exercise in Dialectic," 66 *Harvard Law Review* 1362, 1380–83, 1391–96 (1953). *See Estep v. United States,* 327 U.S. 114 (1946); *United States ex rel. Knauff v. Shaughnessy,* 338 U.S. 537 (1950); *Shaughnessy v. United States ex rel. Mezei,* 345 U.S. 206 (1953); *Falbo v. United States,* 320 U.S. 549 (1944).

88 *Id.* at 1367 n. 20, 1372–75. *See Lockerty v. Phillips,* 319 U.S. 182 (1943), and *Yakus v. United States,* 321 U.S. 414 (1944).

89 *Id.* at 1363–64.

90 Robert Jennings Harris, *The Judicial Power of the United States* (Binghamton, N.Y., 1940), 144.

91 *Crowell v. Benson,* 285 U.S. 22, 65, 86 (1932) (Brandeis, J., dissenting).

92 Hart, "The Power of Congress to Limit the Jurisdiction of Federal Courts," 1363.

93 Hart, "Professor Crosskey and Judicial Review," 1461.

94 "Comment of Professor Hart," in Sutherland, ed., *Government Under Law,* 139.

95 Henry M. Hart, Jr., to Charles E. Wyzanski, Jr., Mar. 22, 1954, at 4, Hart Papers, Box 7, folder 2.

Brandeis did, of course, oppose "arbitrary" government action, especially when certain noneconomic, individual freedoms were at stake. As Hart's general social and political views changed, he came to stress those aspects of Brandeis's legacy and to ignore other aspects. Most revealing, the quote in the text is taken from Hart's remarks concerning the Court's decision in *Olsen v. Nebraska,* 313 U.S. 236 (1941), which set forth an extremely deferential standard for the review of state economic regulation. Hart's comment ignored two significant considerations. First, Brandeis's view of "arbitrary" government action in such cases was far more limited than it was in, for example, First Amendment cases. Therefore, even if Brandeis had disagreed with some of the language in *Olsen,* he would likely have agreed with its result. Second, *Olsen* presented Hart with a particularly problematic case, for *Olsen* overruled *Ribnik v. McBride,* 277 U.S. 350 (1928), where the "old" Court had invalidated a state effort to regulate employment agencies. Hart ignored the fact that in *Ribnik,* Brandeis and Holmes had joined Stone's powerful dissent that broadly defended the state's right to regulate the activity. Moroever, the majority in *Ribnik* relied on the Court's decision the previous year in *Tyson & Brother v. Banton,* 273 U.S. 418 (1927), which overturned a similar state effort to regulate the resale price of theater tickets. As in *Ribnik,* Brandeis dissented in *Tyson,* joining separate opinions by both Holmes and Stone which upheld highly deferential theories of state regulatory power. Regardless of "reasonable differences of opinion as to the wisdom" of the state's effort, Stone wrote in his *Ribnik* dissent, the choice "should be left where, it seems to me, it was left by the Constitution—to the states and to Congress," 277 U.S. at 375. On his "return" on Stone's draft dissent, Brandeis wrote simply but emphatically, "Yes, indeed!" Quoted in Alpheus Thomas Mason, *Harlan Fiske Stone: Pillar of the Law* (New York, 1956), 239.

96 In 1954 Judge Charles E. Wyzanski gave a lecture on Brandeis at the university named in Brandeis's honor, emphasizing his practical reform orientation and his support of broad congressional power. Asked for his comments, Hart took exception to several of Wyzanski's assertions. Brandeis, Hart wrote, was not merely practical and empirical but also "had an intensely philosophical bent." The justice had "very consciously used basic premises arrived at by abstract thinking as a framework within which to search, by the empirical method, for concretely workable solutions." Brandeis had been concerned primarily with decentralization, with opposition to arbitrary power, and with fostering private initiative. He was, in short, very similar to the Henry Hart of the early 1950s. After his detailed criticism of Wyzanski's lecture, Hart closed with a word of commendation. "Among many things which stirred my enthusiasm," he wrote the author, "was your treatment at the end of the significance of Brandeis' seeming change of outlook as he grew older." Henry M. Hart, Jr., to Charles E. Wyzanski, Jr., Mar. 22, 1954, Hart Papers, Box 7, folder 2.

97 The casebook is Henry M. Hart, Jr., and Herbert Wechsler, *The Federal Courts and the Federal System* (Brooklyn, 1953). The quote is from Philip B. Kurland, review of *The Federal Courts and the Federal System,* by Henry M. Hart, Jr., and Herbert Wechsler, 67 *Harvard Law Review* 906, 907 (1954).

98 Hart, "Relations Between State and Federal Law."

99 Felix Frankfurter and James Landis, *The Business of the Supreme Court* (New York, 1928); Felix Frankfurter and Wilbur G. Katz, *Cases and Other Authorities on Federal Jurisdiction and Procedure* (Chicago, 1931).

100 For general discussions of Hart & Wechsler, *see* Akhil Reed Amar, "Law Story," 102 *Harvard Law Review* 688 (1989); Michael Wells, "Behind the Parity Debate: The Decline of the Legal Process Tradition in the Law of Federal Courts," 71 *Boston University Law Review* 609 (1991); Gary Peller, "Neutral Principles in the 1950s," 21 *University of Michigan Journal of Law Reform* 561 (1988); "Symposium: Reflections on the Hart and Wechsler Paradigm," 47 *Vanderbilt Law Review* 953 (1994); Michael Wells, "Busting the Hart & Wechsler Paradigm," 11 *Constitutional Commentary* 557 (1994); Richard H. Fallon, Jr., "Comparing Federal Courts 'Paradigms,'" 12 *Constitutional Commentary* 3 (1995); Michael Wells, "Positivism and Antipositivism in Federal Courts Law," 29 *Georgia Law Review* 655 (1995); Michael Wells, "Who's Afraid of Henry Hart?" 14 *Constitutional Commentary* 175 (1997).

101 Henry M. Hart, Jr., "Thomas Reed Powell," 69 *Harvard Law Review* 804 (1956).

102 Henry M. Hart, Jr., "The Place of the Federal Courts in the Constitutional Plan," (undated draft, circa 1955), Hart Papers, Box 24, folder 4, at 21.

103 *See* Purcell, *The Crisis of Democratic Theory,* ch. 11.

104 Hart, "Relations Between State and Federal Law," 490.

105 *Id.* at 490, 489.

106 *Id.* at 490.

107 *Id.* at 542.

108 *Id.* at 491.

109 *E.g.,* Hart and Wechsler, *Federal Courts and the Federal System,* 435–36, 481–83, 607–10, 694–700, 794–97, 884–85.

110 Hart, "Relations Between State and Federal Law," 515.

111 *Id.* at 530.

112 *Id.* at 530.

113 *Id.* at 534.

114 Hart and Wechsler, *Federal Courts and the Federal System,* xiii.

115 Hart, "Power of Congress to Limit the Jurisdiction of Federal Courts," at, 1365. *See* Hart and Wechsler, *Federal Courts and the Federal System,* 312–40.

In his "Dialogue" Hart acknowledged that Congress could, if determined, destroy the jurisdiction of the federal courts and that the state courts were thus, in some ultimate and desperate sense, the "primary guarantors of constitutional rights" (Hart, "Power of Congress to Limit the Jurisdiction of Federal Courts," at 1401). He insisted, however, that as long as the federal courts — or any court — had jurisdiction, they had jurisdiction only to decide cases according to the Constitution, regardless of whatever jurisdictional restraints Congress might impose (*id.* at 1402). Some scholars have regarded Hart's argument as too weak a defense of the federal courts, and others have assumed that his final reliance on the state courts meant that the state courts were his principal or preferred reliance. Both views seem mistaken, and both seem to miss the reason he employed the highly unusual dialogue form. Hart's "Dialogue" was — and remains — a brilliant, powerful, and tenacious lawyerly brief on behalf of the federal courts and the ideal of the rule of law in the midst of an unwieldy and ragged body of constitutional case law that posed a variety of difficult and complex challenges. Although he finally acknowledged the state courts as the "ultimate" defenders of constitutional rights, he did so as the lawyer's fallback position, not because he regarded the state courts as his preferred defenders. His position, and the position that he defended so indefatigibly in the "Dialogue" and elsewhere, was that the "national courts" were properly "the primary forum for the vindication of federal rights." Hart and Wechsler, *Federal Courts and the Federal System,* 727.

116 Hart, "Power of Congress to Limit the Jurisdiction of Federal Courts," 1372.

117 *Id.* at 1402. When Supreme Court justices wrote opinions that ignored "the painful forward steps" toward constitutional government and the rule of law, Hart maintained, "they write without authority for the future." And "so long as courts of the United States sit" to hear cases, "[t]he appeal to principle is still open." *Id.* at 1396.

118 *Id.* at 1397.

119 *Id.* at 1372.

120 Henry M. Hart, Jr., to Philip B. Kurland, Apr. 22, 1954, Frankfurter Papers (H.L.S.), Box 185, folder 15.

121 Hart and Wechsler, *Federal Courts and the Federal System,* 652, 659; Hart, "Relations Between State and Federal Law," 513.

122 *See, e.g.,* Hart, "Relations Between State and Federal Law," 531.

123 Privately, Hart criticized Frankfurter for allowing his personal hostility to diversity to influence his decisions on the Court. Henry M. Hart, Jr., to Felix Frankfurter, Apr. 22, 1954, enclosing copy of Hart to Kurland, Apr. 22, 1954 (the quotation is taken from the latter), Frankfurter Papers (H.L.S.), Box 185, folder 15.

124 Henry M. Hart, Jr., "The Business of the Supreme Court at the October Terms, 1937 and 1938," 53 *Harvard Law Review* 579, 608 (1940).

125 *Id.* at 608.

126 *Id.* at 610.

127 *Id.* at 610 n. 64, 609.

128 *Id.* at 611.

129 One of the most significant elements of the casebook was the coherent, suggestive, and sometimes (as Hart admitted privately, Hart to Kurland, Apr. 22, 1954, Hart Papers, Box 185, folder 15) "tendentious" questions that the authors used to explore the issues and illuminate the materials. The questions following *Erie* ignored the issue of the decision's procedural propriety and raised no questions about the opinion. They focused on problems involved in implementing the *Erie* principle, especially those related to *York* and *Klaxon*. *See* Hart and Wechsler, *Federal Courts and the Federal System*, 892–97.

130 Hart, "Relations Between State and Federal Law," 512.

131 Hart, "Place of the Federal Courts in the Constitutional Plan," 40.

132 Hart, "Relations Between State and Federal Law," 506.

133 *Id.* at 505, 506.

134 Hart and Weshsler, *Federal Courts and the Federal System*, 634. *See* Hart, "Relations Between State and Federal Law," at 512; Hart and Wechsler, *Federal Courts and the Federal System*, 31; Wechsler, "Federal Jurisdiction and the Revision of the Judicial Code," 13 *Law and Contemporary Problems* 216, 239, nn. 119 and 121 (1948); Hart, "Place of the Federal Courts in the Constitutional Plan," Hart Papers, Box 24, folder 4.

135 Hart, "Place of the Federal Courts in the Constitutional Plan," 37–38; Hart, "Relations Between State and Federal Law," 505–6, 512–13; Hart and Wechsler, *Federal Courts and the Federal System*, 616.

136 Hart and Wechsler, *Federal Courts and the Federal System*, 620.

137 *Id.* at 633.

138 *See* Hart, "Relations Between State and Federal Law," 497.

139 244 U.S. 205 (1917).

140 Hart, "Relations Between State and Federal Law," 532.

141 *Washington v. Dawson*, 264 U.S. 219, 228 (1924) (Brandeis, J., dissenting).

142 Alfred S. Konefsky has called my attention to the similarities between Hart and Joseph Story. They, of course, had differences, but both believed: the law should be based on and drawn from general principles rooted in reason, practice, and social needs; society needed clear and specific rules of law, and the courts were the branch of government best able to state and develop such rules; the legislative branch should be regarded with skepticism; the federal courts were essential instruments of American government and should be used to advance and institutionalize what they regarded as a broader national viewpoint; and a rigorously trained national legal elite was essential to staff the legal system and make it operate most effectively. Ironically, in fact, Hart attempted to do with *Erie* much of what Story had attempted to do with *Swift*.

143 Hart, "Relations Between State and Federal Law," 512.

144 Hart and Wechsler, *Federal Courts and the Federal System*, 635–36; Hart, "Relations Between State and Federal Law," 514–15.

145 Hart and Wechsler, *Federal Courts and the Federal System*, 652.

146 *Id.* at 769, 774–75.

147 *Id.* at 456–57, 696. *Cf., id.* at 483–84.

148 *Id.* at 744–47.

149 Hart, "Relations Between State and Federal Law," 530, 534; Hart and Wechsler, *Federal Courts and the Federal System,* 483–84, 681–91. Hart did not think the federal courts should make federal common law broadly or in most areas of "primary behavior" where the states had traditionally controlled. He thought they should act only in critical areas where national interests and authority were apparent. *Cf.,* Note, "The Competence of Federal Courts to Formulate Rules of Decision," 77 *Harvard Law Review* 1084 (1964).

150 Hart and Wechsler, *Federal Courts and the Federal System,* 818. *Compare* Hart, "Relations Between State and Federal Law," at 522–24 and n. 124.

151 Hart and Wechsler, *Federal Courts and the Federal System,* 371–72.

152 *Id.* at 829, 833.

153 *Id.* at 321–22 (quotation at 321). *Accord* Hart, "Power of Congress to Limit the Jurisdiction of the Federal Courts," 1372.

154 Henry M. Hart, Jr., "Foreword: The Time Chart of the Justices," 73 *Harvard Law Review* 84, 116, 117 (1959).

155 Hart to Kurland, Apr. 22, 1954, Frankfurter Papers (H.L.S.), Box 185, folder 15.

156 Hart and Wechsler, *Federal Courts and the Federal System, e.g.,* 636, 652, 659, 672.

157 Hart, "Foreword: The Time Chart of the Justices," 118.

158 Interview with Harry H. Wellington, Jan. 22, 1997, New York, N.Y.

159 Henry P. Monaghan, review of Paul M. Bator, Paul J. Mishkin, David L. Shapiro, and Herbert Wechsler, *Hart and Wechsler's The Federal Courts and the Federal System,* 87 *Harvard Law Review* 889, 893 (1974).

160 Hart, "Relations Between State and Federal Law," 513.

161 *Id.* at 508. *See id.* at 513 and n. 80.

162 Hart, "Relations Beween State and Federal Law," 512, 513. Charles E. Clark echoed Hart's claim that *Erie*'s concern with forum shopping was a "triviality." *Jaftex Corp. v. Randolph Mills, Inc.,* 282 F. 2d 508, 514 (2d Cir. 1960) (Clark, J.).

163 Hart, "Relations Between State and Federal Law," 513.

164 *Id.* at 510.

165 *Fidelity Union Trust Co. v. Field,* 311 U.S. 169 (1940).

166 *See* Hart and Wechsler, *Federal Courts and the Federal System,* 659–60; Hart, "Relations Between State and Federal Law," 508; Hart to Kurland, Apr. 22, 1954, Frankfurter Papers (H.L.S.), Box 185, folder 15.

167 Hart and Wechsler, *Federal Courts and the Federal System,* 678.

168 Hart to Kurland, Apr. 22, 1954, Frankfurter Papers (H.L.S.), Box 185, folder 15. *See also* Hart, "Relations Between State and Federal Law," 512.

169 *See, e.g., Lumbermen's Mutual Casualty Co. v. Elbert,* 348 U.S. 48, 53 (Frankfurter, J., concurring).

170 Henry M. Hart, Jr. to Ivan C. Rutledge, June 5, 1958, Hart Papers, Box 6, Folder 8. *See also* Hart and Wechsler, *Federal Courts and the Federal System,* 634.

171 Henry M. Hart, Jr., to Harry E. Kalodner, May 1, 1958, Hart Papers, Box 4, folder 7. The title means "*Klaxon* must be destroyed."

172 Hart and Wechsler, *Federal Courts and the Federal System,* 635.

173 Hart, "Relations Between State and Federal Law," 513, 514; Hart and Wechsler, *Federal Courts and the Federal System*, 897.

174 Hart, "Relations Between State and Federal Law," 515. *See also* Hart and Wechsler, *Federal Courts and the Federal System*, 636.

175 Henry M. Hart, Jr., "Notes for the Discussion with Mr. Denham," undated memorandum, circa 1953, at 6, Hart Papers, Box 22, folder 13.

176 *See, e.g.,* Hart and Wechsler, *Federal Courts and the Federal System*, 635.

177 The field of "choice of law" was quite unsettled in the postwar decades. "Not only is precedent relatively sparse in this area; that which exists is frequently misleading. Guidance therefore cannot be sought, as in many other branches of the law, from an accepted body of settled rules. Rather, the judge frequently finds himself forced to pursue the inquiry into basic questions of policy and value." Elliott E. Cheatham and Willis L. M. Reese, "Choice of the Applicable Law," 52 *Columbia Law Review* 959 (1952).

178 Hart and Wechsler, *Federal Courts and the Federal System*, 635.

179 For Frankfurter's criticism of Hart's attack on *Klaxon, see* Felix Frankfurter to Henry M. Hart, Jr., Feb. 11, 1959, Hart Papers, Box 3, folder 3. *Cf.,* John Hart Ely, "The Irrepressible Myth of *Erie*," 87 *Harvard Law Review* 693, 714 n. 125 (1974). At the end of the twentieth century, despite the vast improvements in transportation, the overwhelming majority of plaintiffs still brought suit near their homes. *See* Michael E. Solimine, "The Quiet Revolution in Personal Jurisdiction," 73 *Tulane Law Review* 1, 56 (1998).

180 Hart, "Relations Between State and Federal Law," 508; Hart and Wechsler, *Federal Courts and the Federal System*, 616–17, 634–35; Hart to Kurland, Apr. 22, 1954, Frankfurter Papers (H.L.S.), Box 185, folder 15.

181 Hart, "Relations Between State and Federal Law," 505. *See also id.* at 489, 508; Hart and Wechsler, *Federal Courts and the Federal System*, 634.

182 *Id.* 489. *See* Hart and Wechsler, *Federal Courts and the Federal System*, 634.

183 *See, e.g.,* Hart, "Relations Between State and Federal Law," 489–91, 539–42; Hart, "Comment on Courts and Lawmaking," 40–48.

184 Felix Frankfurter to Henry M. Hart, Jr., Feb. 11, 1959, Hart Papers, Box 3, folder 3. Frankfurter wrote to a mutual friend that Hart "seems to me to become more and more Thomistic or geometric in his thinking." Quoted in Laura Kalman, *The Strange Career of Legal Liberalism* (New Haven, Conn., 1996), 256 n. 30, at 257.

185 *Textile Workers Union of America v. Lincoln Mills of Alabama*, 353 U.S. 448, 460, 474 (Frankfurter, J., dissenting). *See id.* at 473–77 and *Association of Westinghouse Salaried Employees v. Westinghouse Electric Corp.*, 348 U.S. 437, 452 n. 25 (Frankfurter, J.).

186 Felix Frankfurter to Henry M. Hart, Jr., July 18, 1957, Hart Papers, Box 3, folder 3. For Frankfurter's criticism of some of Hart's other arguments, *see, e.g.,* Frankfurter to Hart, June 19, 1956, June 25, 1956, and Feb. 11, 1959, Hart Papers, Box 3, folder 3; Frankfurter to Hart, May 3, 1954, Frankfurter Papers (H.L.S.), Box 185, folder 15.

187 Hart, "Time Chart of the Justices," 107 n. 68. *See* Hart and Wechsler, *Federal Courts and the Federal System*, 832.

188 Hart and Sachs, *Legal Process;* Hart, "Comment on Courts and Lawmaking," 40, 42.

189 Hart, "Comment on Courts and Lawmaking," 47.

190 *Id.* at 43.

191 For a discussion of the ways that reasoned elaboration restricted discretion, *see* Hart and Sachs, *Legal Process*, 168–78; Eskridge and Frickey, *Legal Process*, 150–57.

192 347 U.S. 483 (1954).

193 Hart, "Foreword: The Time Chart of the Justices," 96–98, 100, 111, 123, 124–25 (1959). Frankfurter had urged Hart to write such an article. Felix Frankfurter to Henry M. Hart, Jr., June 29, 1956, Hart Papers, Box 3, folder 3.

194 *Id.* at 99.

195 Hart wrote very little for publication during his last few years due to declining health. From the letters his students wrote it was possible to get a reasonably clear idea of the arguments he made to his classes. *See, e.g.,* Donald R. Spuehler to Henry M. Hart, Jr., Oct. 9, 1964, Hart Papers, Box 6, folder 15; Bernard Harvith to Henry M. Hart, Jr., Oct 30, 1962, Hart Papers, Box 3, folder 27; Richard E. Rubenstein to Henry M. Hart, Jr., Oct. 28, 1962, Hart Papers, Box 6, folder 8.

196 Memoranda from Henry M. Hart, Jr., to Jerome Skolnick, Oct 14, 1965, at 4, Hart Papers, Box 30, folder 2. *See* Hart to Skolnick, Oct. 25, 1965, *id.*

197 *See* Michael J. Henry, "Hart Converses on Law and Justice," *Harvard Law Record* (Feb. 28, 1963), 7–8; Derek C. Bok, "Professor Henry Melvin Hart, Jr.," 82 *Harvard Law Review* 1591, 1592 (1969). For his unfinished efforts, *see, e.g.,* "The Morality of Function," undated draft of speech given at Harvard Law School, circa 1963, Hart Papers, Box 23, folder 3; Henry, "Hart Converses on Law and Justice," at 7.

198 Hart, "Time Chart of the Justices," 106. Much of the argument Hart advanced concerning federal habeas corpus was incorporated by the Warren Court in one of its most aggressive expansions of federal jurisdiction. *See Fay v. Noia,* 372 U.S. 391, 411, 420, 421, 423, 427 (1963) (Brennan, J.). Hart's position was, in turn, rejected by the opponents of the Warren Court's habeas jurisprudence. *See Fay v. Noia,* 372 U.S. 448, 457–58 (Harlan, J., dissenting); Paul M. Bator, "Finality in Criminal Law and Federal Habeas Corpus for State Prisoners," 76 *Harvard Law Review* 441, 488–93 (1963).

199 Hart and Wechsler, *Federal Courts and the Federal System,* 727.

200 One of the earliest and most insightful theorists who elaborated and defended the relatively independent lawmaking role of the federal courts was a student of Hart's in the mid-1950s. Early in his career, Alfred Hill wrote extensively on *Erie. E.g.,* Hill, "The Erie Doctrine in Bankruptcy," 66 *Harvard Law Review* 1013 (1953). By the late 1960s Hill was exploring and justifying the Court's "creative" development of federal common law and judge-made remedies for constitutional violations. *See e.g.,* Hill, "The Law-Making Power of the Federal Courts: Constitutional Preemption," 67 *Columbia Law Review* 1024 (1967); Hill, "The Bill of Rights and the Supervisory Power," 69 *Columbia Law Review* 181 (1969). After Hart's death in 1969, Hill dedicated his next article—defending the Court's use of implied judicial remedies for constitutional violations—to Hart. Hill, "Constitutional Remedies," 69 *Columbia Law Review* 1109, 1112–13 (1969).

201 Hart did not oppose the Warren Court because he disliked its desgregation decisions. Kalman, *Strange Career of Legal Liberalism,* 34–35; Eskridge and Frickey, *Legal Process,* cxiii.

202 A variety of factors contributed to the failure of Hart and Sacks to publish *The Legal Process. See* Eskridge and Frickey, *Legal Process,* xcvii–c.

CHAPTER 10. COLD WAR POLITICS AND NEUTRAL PRINCIPLES

1 347 U.S. 483 (1954).

2 *See* Earl Warren, *The Memoirs of Earl Warren* (New York, 1977); Bernard Schwartz, *Super*

Chief: Earl Warren and His Supreme Court—A Judicial Biography (New York, 1983); G. Edward White, *Earl Warren: A Public Life* (New York, 1982).

3 *See* Gerald T. Dunne, *Hugo Black and the Judicial Revolution* (New York, 1977), ch. 14; Richard Kluger, *Simple Justice: The History of Brown v. Board of Education and Black America's Struggle for Equality* (New York, 1975); Michael D. Davis and Hunter R. Clark, *Thurgood Marshall: Warrior at the Bar, Rebel on the Bench* (New York, 1994), chs. 12–13; Philip Elman, "The Solicitor General's Office, Justice Frankfurter and Civil Rights Litigation, 1946–1960: An Oral History," 100 *Harvard Law Review* 817 (1987); Mark V. Tushnet, *The NAACP Legal Strategy Against Segregated Education, 1925–1950* (Chapel Hill, N.C., 1987). Michael J. Klarman has recently challenged many ideas about *Brown*'s social significance. *See, e.g.,* Klarman, "*Brown,* Racial Change, and the Civil Rights Movement," 80 *Virginia Law Review* 7 (1994); Klarman, "Rethinking the Civil Rights and Civil Liberties Revolutions," 82 *Virginia Law Review* 1 (1996).

4 *E.g., Mayor of Baltimore v. Dawson,* 350 U.S. 877 (1955); *Holmes v. City of Atlanta,* 350 U.S. 879 (1955); *Gayle v. Browder,* 352 U.S. 903 (1956); *New Orleans City Park Improvement Association v. Detiege,* 358 U.S. 54 (1958).

5 *Cooper v. Aaron,* 358 U.S. 1, 17–19 (1958).

6 *See,* Stephen L. Wasby, *The Impact of the United States Supreme Court: Some Perspectives* (Homewood, Ill., 1970), 169–85; Reed Sarratt, *The Ordeal of Desegregation: The First Decade* (New York, 1966).

7 Quoted in Neil R. McMillan, *The Citizens' Council: Organized Resistance to the Second Reconstruction, 1954–1964* (Urbana, Ill., 1971), 9.

8 102 *Cong. Rec.* 4515–16 (1956).

9 Kenneth M. Dolbeare, "The Public Views the Supreme Court," in Herbert Jacob, ed., *Law, Politics, and the Federal Courts* (Boston, 1967), 206.

10 Walter F. Murphy, *Congress and the Court: A Case Study in the American Political Process* (Chicago, 1962), 313. *See* Mary L. Dudziak, "Desegregation as a Cold War Imperative," 41 *Stanford Law Review* 61 (1988).

11 *See* Richard M. Fried, *Nightmare in Red: The McCarthy Era in Perspective* (New York, 1990); David M. Oshinsky, *A Conspiracy So Immense: The World of Joe McCarthy* (New York, 1983); Thomas C. Reeves, *The Life and Times of Joe McCarthy* (New York, 1982); David Caute, *The Great Fear: The Anti-Communist Purge Under Truman and Eisenhower* (New York, 1978).

12 *E.g.,* Telford Taylor, *Grand Inquest: The Story of Congressional Investigations* (New York, 1955), xvii.

13 G. Edward White, *The American Judicial Tradition: Profiles of Leading American Judges* (New York, 1976), 339. *See* Archibald Cox, *The Warren Court: Constitutional Decision as an Instrument of Reform* (Cambridge, Mass., 1968), 6.

14 *E.g., Palko v. Connecticut,* 302 U.S. 319 (1937); *United States v. Carolene Products Co.,* 304 U.S. 144 (1938); *West Virginia State Board of Education v. Barnette,* 319 U.S. 624 (1943).

15 Robert G. McCloskey, *The Modern Supreme Court* (Cambridge, Mass., 1972), 129–56.

16 *Communist Party v. Subversive Activities Control Board,* 351 U.S. 115 (1956); *Cole v. Young,* 351 U.S. 536 (1956); *Slochower v. Board,* 350 U.S. 513 (1956).

17 *Pennsylvania v. Nelson,* 350 U.S. 497 (1956). *See* Murphy, *Congress and the Court,* 322.

18 Quoted in Murphy, *Congress and the Court,* 324.

19 *Schware v. Board of Bar Examiners,* 353 U.S. 232 (1957); *Konigsberg v. State Bar of California,* 353 U.S. 252 (1957).

20 353 U.S. 657 (1957).

21 *Watkins v. United States,* 354 U.S. 178 (1957); *Sweezy v. New Hampshire,* 354 U.S. 234 (1957); *Yates v. United States,* 354 U.S. 298 (1957); *Service v. Dulles,* 354 U.S. 363 (1957).

22 "Limitation of Appellate Jurisdiction of the United States Supreme Court," Hearing before the Subcommittee to Investigate the Administration of the Internal Security Act and Other Internal Security Laws of the Committee of the Judiciary of the United States Senate, 85 Cong., 1 sess. (1957), 13 (hereafter, "Hearing on Limitation of Appellate Jurisdiction").

23 Quoted in Murphy, *Congress and the Court,* 89.

24 William H. Rehnquist, "The Bar Admission Cases: A Strange Judicial Aberration," 44 *American Bar Association Journal* 229, 232 (1958).

25 Murphy, *Congress and the Court,* 95–97.

26 Quoted in Dunne, *Hugo Black,* 329–30.

27 *Griffin v. Illinois,* 351 U.S. 12 (1956); *Mallory v. United States,* 354 U.S. 449 (1957).

28 Murphy, *Congress and the Court,* 119–20.

29 351 U.S. 225 (1956).

30 Murphy, *Congress and the Court,* 89–91, 92–93, 113, 202–5, 211; C. Herman Pritchett, *Congress Versus the Supreme Court* (New York, 1973), ch. 6.

31 The Council of State Governments, *Proceedings, Tenth Annual Meeting of the Conference of Chief Justices* (Chicago, 1958), 23.

32 Quoted in Dunne, *Hugo Black,* 333.

33 Alexander M. Bickel, "An Inexplicable Document," 139 *The New Republic* 9, 11 (1958).

34 C. Herman Pritchett, *The Political Offender and the Warren Court* (Boston, 1958), 74.

35 Murphy, *Congress and the Court,* 91–95.

36 U.S. Constitution, Art. III, Sec. 2, Cl. 2.

37 Hearing on Limitation of Appellate Jurisdiction, 1–2.

38 Pritchett, *Congress Versus the Supreme Court,* 127; Murphy, *Congress and the Court,* 157–62, 266–67.

39 Hearing on Limitation of Appellate Jurisdiction, 2.

40 *Id.* at 207.

41 *Id.* at 40, 49.

42 *Id.* at 477.

43 "Minority Views," Sen. Rep. No. 1586, 85 Cong., 2 sess. (1958), 13.

44 Hearing on Limitation of Appellate Jurisdiction, 487.

45 Jack W. Peltason, *Fifty-Eight Lonely Men: Southern Federal Judges and School Desegregation* (New York, 1961), 73.

46 Quoted in *id.* at 36.

47 Hearing on Limitation of Appellate Jurisdiction, 588.

48 *Id.* at 41, 47.

49 *Id.* at 573.

50 Murphy, *Congress and the Court,* 164–65; "Minority Appendix C," "Resolution Adopted by the House of Delegates, American Bar Association, Feb. 25, 1958," Sen. Rep. No. 1586, 85 Cong., 2 sess. (1958), 38.

51 "Appendix E," Sen. Rep. No. 1856, 85 Cong., 2 sess. (1958), 43–70; Donald J. Kemper, *Decade of Fear: Senator Hennings and Civil Liberties* (Columbia, Mo., 1965), 165–66.

52 Kemper, *Decade of Fear,* 166–68, 167–70.

53 Sen. Rep. No. 1586, 85 Cong., 2 sess. (1958), 2–3.

54 Murphy, *Congress and the Court*, 199–201.

55 Kemper, *Decade of Fear*, 173.

56 104 *Cong. Rec.*, 85 Cong., 2d sess. (1958), 18687.

57 Kemper, *Decade of Fear*, 183.

58 Paul Murphy, *The Constitution in Crisis Times, 1918–1969* (New York, 1972), 334–37; Dunne, *Hugo Black*, 351–52; Murphy, *Congress and the Court*, 229–35.

59 William J. Brennan, "An Invitation to State Courts," 13 *Litigation* 5 (1987); David P. Currie, *The Constitution in the Supreme Court: The Second Century, 1888–1986* (Chicago, 1990), chs. 12–13.

60 *See* Peter Graham Fish, *The Politics of Federal Judicial Administration* (Princeton, 1973); "Jurisdiction of Federal Courts Concerning Diversity of Citizenship," Hearing Before Subcommittee No. 3 of the Committee on the Judiciary, House of Representatives, 85 Cong., 1 sess. (1958), 10 (statement of Hon. Albert M. Maris) (hereafter, "Hearing Concerning Diversity of Citizenship").

61 John J. Parker, "Dual Sovereignty and the Federal Courts," 51 *Northwestern Law Review* 407, 408 (1956).

62 Hearing Concerning Diversity of Citizenship, 13.

63 *Id.* at 17–18; 24–25.

64 *Id.* at 26–27.

65 *Id.* at 2 (statement of Hon. William M. Tuck).

66 "Extension of Remarks of Hon. William M. Tuck," 101 *Cong. Rec.*, 84 Cong., 1st sess. (1955), at A 1815.

67 H.R. Rep. No. 1706, 85 Cong., 2 sess. (1958), 1–2.

68 104 *Cong. Rec.* 12683, 12689, 85 Cong., 2 sess. (1958); 72 Stat. 415 (1958).

69 104 *Cong. Rec.* 12683–90, 85 Cong., 2 sess. (1958); H.R. Rep. No. 1706, 85 Cong., 2 sess. (1958); Sen. Rep. No. 1830, 85 Cong., 2 sess. (1958).

70 Hearing Concerning Diversity of Citizenship, 15, 17.

71 *Id.* at 42–43; Sen. Rep. No. 1830, 85 Cong., 2 sess. (1958), 13.

72 Hearing Concerning Diversity of Citizenship, 43.

73 *Id.* at 34.

74 *Id.* at 42.

75 *Id.* at 12, 13.

76 *Id.* at 35.

77 *Id.* at 14.

78 *Id.* at 39. *See* 104 *Cong. Rec.*, 85 Cong., 2 sess. (1958), 12685 (statement of Congressman Celler); *id.* at 12688 (statement of Senator Keating).

79 The provision relating to workmen's compensation claims suggested the issue of social and economic inequality, but Congress did not pursue it. *See* 72 Stat. 415 (1958); 104 *Cong. Rec.*, 85 Cong., 2 sess. (1958), 12683; Sen. Rep. No. 1865, 85 Cong., 2 sess. (1958), 8–9.

80 "Speech of Earl Warren," American Law Institute, *Proceedings, 36th Annual Meeting, 1959* (Philadelphia, 1960), 29, 33, 34.

81 Warren, *Memoirs of Earl Warren*, 321–35.

82 *Id.* at 330. *See, e.g.*, Schwartz, *Super Chief*, 289, 299–300, 336–38.

83 "Speech of Earl Warren," 34.

84 *Lumbermen's Mutual Casualty Co. v. Elbert*, 348 U.S. 48, 60, 61 (1954) (Frankfurter, J. concurring).

85 *See Gibson v. Phillips Petroleum Co.*, 352 U.S. 874 (1956) (Frankfurter, J., dissenting). *See, e.g.*, Felix Frankfurter to Learned Hand, Mar. 28, 1957, Frankfurter Papers, Box 65, folder 1253; Frankfurter to Earl Warren, Jan. 28, 1960, Frankfurter Papers (H.L.S.), Box 188, folder 5; Frankfurter to Richard H. Field, June 13, 1960, Frankfurter Papers (H.L.S.), Box 188, folder 5.

86 Philip B. Kurland, "The Distribution of Judicial Power Between National and State Courts," 42 *Journal of the American Judicature Society* 159, 162 (1959).

87 James William Moore and Donald T. Weckstein, "Diversity Jurisdiction: Past, Present, and Future," 43 *Texas Law Review* 1 (1964).

88 *See, e.g.*, J. Skelley Wright, "The Federal Courts and the Nature and Quality of State Law," 13 *Wayne Law Review* 317 (1967); William L. Marbury, "Why Should We Limit Federal Diversity Jurisdiction?" 46 *American Bar Association Journal* 379 (1960); John P. Frank, "For Maintaining Diversity Jurisdiction," 73 *Yale Law Journal* 7 (1963).

89 Marbury, "Why Should We Limit Federal Diversity Jurisdiction," 382.

90 *See, e.g.*, Note, "ALI Proposals to Expand Federal Diversity Jurisdiction: Solution to Multi-party, Multistate Controversies?" 48 *Minnesota Law Review* 1109 (1964); Leslie L. Anderson, "The Problems of the Federal Courts—and How the State Courts Might Help," 54 *American Bar Association Journal* 352 (1968); Daniel J. Meador, "A New Approach to Limiting Diversity Jurisdiction," 46 *American Bar Association Journal* 383 (1960); David P. Currie, "The Federal Courts and the American Law Institute, Part I," 36 *University of Chicago Law Review* 1 (1968).

91 American Law Institute, *Study of the Division of Jurisdiction Between State and Federal Courts* (Philadelphia, 1969), 6 (hereafter, "ALI, *Study*").

92 Richard H. Field, "Proposals on Federal Diversity Jurisdiction," 17 *South Carolina Law Review* 669, 670 (1965).

93 *E.g.*, Alexander M. Bickel and Harry H. Wellington, "Legislative Purpose and the Judicial Process: The Lincoln Mills Case," 71 *Harvard Law Review* 1 (1957); Henry M. Hart, Jr., "Foreword: The Time Chart of the Justices," 73 *Harvard Law Review* 84 (1959); Herbert Wechsler, "Toward Neutral Principles of Constitutional Law," 73 *Harvard Law Review* 1 (1959).

94 Henry M. Hart, Jr., to Charles Bunn, circa Aug. 10, 1959, Hart Papers, Box 1, folder 19. The institute had appointed Bunn to begin preliminary work on the *Study*, and he asked Hart for suggestions.

95 American Law Institute, *Proceedings, 46th Annual Meeting, 1969* (Philadelphia, 1970), 18.

96 Wechsler, "Toward Neutral Principles."

97 *E.g.*, Charles Alan Wright, "Restructuring Federal Jurisdiction: The American Law Institute Proposals," 26 *Washington and Lee Law Review* 185, 207 (1969).

98 Richard H. Field, "Diversity of Citizenship: A Response to Judge Wright," 13 *Wayne Law Review* 489, 490 (1967).

99 ALI, *Study*, 99.

100 ALI, *Proceedings, 42nd Annual Meeting, 1965* (Philadelphia, 1966), 102.

101 *See, e.g.*, Richard H. Field, "Federal Diversity Jurisdiction—A Rebuttal," 17 *South Carolina Law Review* 685 (1965); Field, "Diversity of Citizenship: A Response to Judge Wright," 494.

102 ALI, *Study*, 443.

103 American Law Institute, *Study of the Division of Jurisdiction Between State and Federal Courts*, Part I, Official Draft (Philadelphia, 1965,), ix.

104 ALI, *Study*, 99.

105 *Id.* at 105.

106 *Id.* at 109. *See* Field, "Diversity of Citizenship: A Response to Judge Wright," 495.

107 *See* "Speech of Earl Warren," 34.

108 ALI, *Study*, 105, 106.

109 *Id.* at 164.

110 *Id.* at 165.

111 Paul J. Mishkin, "The Federal 'Question' in the District Courts," 53 *Columbia Law Review* 157, 170–71 (1953). Mishkin, a professor at the University of Pennsylvania who served as one of the reporters, was a significant voice in shaping the study. *See* ALI, *Study*, 163; Mishkin to Henry M. Hart, Jr., May 21, 1958, and Mishkin to *New York Times*, May 13, 1958, Hart Papers, Box 4, folder 28. Mishkin's emphasis on the federal courts as "vindicators" of federal rights reflected Hart and Wechsler's concept of "protective jurisdiction" and, more generally, typical twentieth-century attitudes about the proper role of the federal courts. *See* Henry M. Hart, Jr., and Herbert Wechsler, *The Federal Courts and the Federal System* (Brooklyn, 1953), 727, 744–47.

112 Federal question jurisdiction existed only when the requisite federal law issue appeared on the face of plaintiff's "well-pleaded complaint."

113 ALI, *Study*, 168.

114 *Id.* at 168. *See id.* at 164–72, 187–94, 478–79; American Law Institute, *Proceedings, 42nd Annual Meeting, 1965* (Philadelphia, 1966), 99–102, 118; Wright, "Restructuring Federal Jurisdiction: The American Law Institute Proposals," 198–200.

115 ALI, *Study*, App. B, 466–69.

116 *Id.* at 117–19, 123–25.

117 *Id.* at 114–17. *See, e.g., United Steelworkers of America v. R. H. Bouligny, Inc.*, 382 U.S. 145 (1965).

118 ALI, *Study*, 140–49.

119 *Id.* at 386–410. Hart, who served as a member of the advisory committee, had suggested this in his casebook. Hart and Wechsler, *Federal Courts and the Federal System*, 897.

120 ALI, *Study*, 176–82; 196–200, 207–16.

121 *Id.* at 217.

122 *Id.* at 196–200.

123 *Id.* at 1.

124 Field, "Diversity of Citizenship: A Response to Judge Wright," 490. *See also* Field, "Proposals on Federal Diversity Jurisdiction," 670–71; ALI, *Study*, App. B, 472.

125 The *Study* claimed weakly that its proposals would significantly cut the federal dockets. ALI, *Study*, 6; appendix B, *id.* at 465–76. The claim seemed implausible. *E.g.*, Orison S. Marden, "Reshaping Diversity Jurisdiction: A Plea for Study by the Bar," 54 *American Bar Association Journal* 453, 455 (1968).

126 ALI, *Study*, 99. *See generally* Gordon S. Wood, *The Radicalism of the American Revolution* (New York, 1991), 322–25, 261–65; Martin S. Flaherty, "History 'Lite' in Modern American Constitutionalism," 95 *Columbia Law Review* 523, 564–67 (1995).

127 The chief reporter exemplified the way in which the institute's approach implicitly ignored questions of legislative power and the right of Congress to make fundamental policy choices. The division of judicial power between the states and the nation "should rest on a principled basis," he argued, and basing jurisdiction on "the accident of citizenship" was "unprincipled." Field, "Diversity of Citizenship: A Response to Judge Wright," 492. Therefore, he set aside the fact that the Constitution itself had authorized jurisdiction based precisely on "citizenship" and—despite the fact that the Constitution also committed both the exis-

tence and jurisdiction of the federal courts to the judgment of Congress — maintained that jurisdiction was to be determined by recourse not to congressional policy choice or constitutional provision, but to vague principles.

128 ALI, *Proceedings, 46th Annual Meeting, 1969* (Philadelphia, 1970), 18.

129 The proposition was inconsistent, for example, with Hart's views. Henry M. Hart, Jr., "The Power of Congress to Limit the Jurisdiction of Federal Courts: An Exercise in Dialectic," 66 *Harvard Law Review* 1362, 1401–1402 (1953). The idea of coextensive powers has led to a range of diverse "theories." *Compare, e.g.,* Louise Weinberg, "Federal Common Law," 83 *Northwestern University Law Review* 805 (1989) and ch. 11, *infra;* G. Edward White, "Recovering Coterminous Power Theory: The Lost Dimension of Marshall Court Sovereignty Cases," in Maeva Marcus, ed., *Origins of the Federal Judiciary: Essays on the Judiciary Act of 1789* (New York, 1992), 66–105.

130 The *Study* acknowledged that its axiom served primarily to alter the burden of proof to require a particular justification for any use of diversity. A few pages later, however, it asserted a contrary burden of proof rule. *Compare* ALI, *Study,* 99 *with* 106.

131 ALI, *Study,* 110. *See id.* at 2.

132 *Id.* at 107. *See id.,* 105, 106.

133 *Id.* at 375.

134 *See also* Field, "Diversity of Citizenship: A Response to Judge Wright," 499; ALI, *Study,* 110.

135 ALI, *Study,* 105.

136 *Id.* at 110.

137 *Id.* at 109.

138 *Id.* at 105.

139 *Id.* at 105 and n. 10.

140 *Id.* at 102.

141 *Id.* at 162–63.

142 Donald H. Zeigler, "A Reassessment of the Younger Doctrine in Light of the Legislative History of Reconstruction," 1983 *Duke Law Journal* 987, 992–1020; William M. Wiecek, "The Reconstruction of Federal Judicial Power, 1863–1875," 13 *American Journal of Legal History* 333 (1969); Stanley I. Kutler, *Judicial Power and Reconstruction Politics* (Chicago, 1968).

143 Wright, "Restructuring Federal Jurisdiction: The American Law Institute Proposals," 194. *See* David L. Shapiro, "Federal Diversity Jurisdiction: A Survey and a Proposal," 91 *Harvard Law Review* 317, 331 (1977).

144 American Law Institute, *Proceedings, 40th Annual Meeting, 1963* (Philadelphia, 1964), 79–81; Donald J. Farage, "Proposed Code Will Emasculate Diversity Jurisdiction; Affect 55% of These Cases in Federal Court," 2 *Trial* 30 (1966); "Conflict Over Cut in Federal Civil Cases," 4 *Trial* 3 (1968).

145 *See, e.g.,* ALI, *Proceedings, 40th Annual Meeting, 1963* (Philadelphia, 1964), 108–09; Henry J. Friendly, *Federal Jurisdiction: A General View* (New York, 1973), 150; Field, "Proposals on Federal Diversity Jurisdiction," 670; Wright, "Restructuring Federal Jurisdiction: The American Law Institute Proposals," 207–08.

146 ALI, *Proceedings, 40th Annual Meeting, 1963* (Philadelphia, 1964), 81.

147 ALI, *Study,* 100. *See also* Shapiro, "Federal Diversity Jurisdiction," 330. The *Study* rejected Hart's ideal of a "juster justice" largely because it would endanger the federal courts by leading to overcrowding. ALI, *Study,* 100, 103, 104.

148 Friendly, *Federal Jurisdiction*, 145. *See also* Shapiro, "Federal Diversity Jurisdiction," 322 n. 28 and 319–20.

149 Friendly, *Federal Jurisdiction*, 144.

150 Currie, "Federal Courts and the American Law Institute, Part I," 29–32.

151 ALI, *Study*, 375–77.

152 *Id.* at 378.

153 *Klaxon Electric Manufacturing Co. v. Stentor*, 313 U.S. 487 (1941). Hart repeatedly pressed his argument for abolishing *Klaxon* on the institute and, in this instance, succeeded. Henry M. Hart, Jr., to the advisory committee, Feb. 19, 1964, Hart Papers, Box 1, folder 5. Support for his position was strong among legal scholars. *See, e.g.*, Harold W. Horowitz, "Toward a Federal Common Law of Choice of Law," 14 *U.C.L.A. Law Review* 1191 (1967); Elliott Cheatham, "Comments by Elliott Cheatham on the True National Common Law," 18 *American University Law Review* 372 (1969).

154 ALI, *Study*, 379. *See id.* at 402–4.

155 ALI, *Proceedings, 42nd Annual Meeting, 1965* (Philadelphia, 1966), 106–7.

156 Leon Friedman, ed., *Southern Justice* (New York, 1965), 7.

157 Friedman, ed., *Southern Justice;* Anthony G. Amsterdam, "Criminal Prosecutions Affecting Federally Guaranteed Civil Rights: Federal Removal and Habeas Corpus Jurisdiction to Abort State Court Trial," 113 *University of Pennsylvania Law Review* 793 (1965).

158 ALI, *Study*, 163.

159 In fairness to the ALI, it should be noted that the Warren Court also fell short on the issue. In 1966, over a dissent by Justice Douglas in which Warren, Brennan, and Fortas joined, five justices reversed the Fifth Circuit — the crucial "vindicator" of black civil rights in the 1950s and 1960s — and interpreted the federal civil rights removal statute, 28 U.S.C. Sec. 1343 (1) and (2), in a restrictive manner. The decision prevented a group of twenty-nine civil rights workers from removing a Mississippi criminal prosecution to federal court. *City of Greenwood v. Peacock*, 384 U.S. 808 (1966). The majority pointed out that "Congress, if it chose, could provide" broader removal jurisdiction in civil rights cases. *Id.* at 833. The *Study* offered an analogous justification for its position: "The Institute decided that if fundamental changes are to be made in that relationship [between federal and state courts] in the area of civil rights, such changes would more appropriately come in a civil rights bill than in a jurisdictional study." *Id.* at 205. In *Peacock*, of course, the justices were limited by their good-faith reading of the controlling statute. The ALI operated under no such limitation. Moreover, to the extent that an expansive interpretation of the existing civil rights removal statute might have seemed potentially too broad, the ALI could have drafted a narrower proposal that would still have met the immediate needs of protecting federal rights in the South.

160 *Id.* at 203–5. The existing language appeared in *id.* at 27 (Section 1312 [c]).

161 *See, e.g.*, Amsterdam, "Criminal Prosecutions Affecting Federally Guaranteed Civil Rights."

162 The institute did express sympathy for the plight of civil rights workers, and the reporters and some members urged the adoption of stronger protections. *See* ALI, *Study*, 205–6, and ALI, *Proceedings, 42nd Annual Meeting, 1965* (Philadelphia, 1966), 231–32. The final version liberalized somewhat the conditions under which civil rights workers might obtain federal injunctions against state prosecutions (ALI, *Study*, 308), but the relevant proposal remained too narrow and would have been far more cumbersome and ineffective than a removal statute.

In justifying its decision, the institute formally relied on the esthetics of professional craft. "An injunction is a far more delicate remedy that removal," the study explained, "since an injunction will issue only after a judicial determination of irreparable harm, while removal automatically brings the state proceeding to a halt." ALI, *Study,* 206. *See* David P. Currie, "The Federal Courts and the American Law Institute, Part II," 36 *University of Chicago Law Review* 268, 329–33 (1969). Although "delicate" remedies are usually highly desirable, to rely on such an analysis when addressing the problems of blacks and civil rights workers in the South during the 1960s seems both an egregious social misjudgment and an abuse of craft values. In light of the study's drastic recommendations in other areas, moreover, ALI members could hardly have believed that it was unwise or inappropriate to offer broader civil rights recommendations merely because such "radical" proposals might be "controversial" or unlikely to win congressional approval.

163 Annual Report of the Dirctor of the Administrative Office of the United States Courts, March 1970, *Reports of the Proceedings of the Judicial Conference of the United States* (Washington, D.C., 1971), 14.

164 *Id.,* October 1970, at 79; Annual Report of the Director of the Administrative Office of the United States Courts, March 1971, *Reports of the Proceedings of the Judicial Conference of the United States* (Washington, D.C., 1972), at 25.

165 *Id.,* October 1971, at 79.

166 Shapiro, "Federal Diversity Jurisdiction," 322–28.

167 *Compare, e.g.,* Deborah J. Barrow and Thomas G. Walker, *A Court Divided: The Fifth Circuit Court of Appeals and the Politics of Judicial Reform* (New Haven, Conn., 1988), 31.

168 Later commentators adopted considerably more flexible and pragmatic approaches to jurisdictional reform: *e.g.,* Henry J. Friendly, *Federal Jurisdiction: A General View* (New York, 1973); Richard A. Posner, *The Federal Courts: Crisis and Reform* (Cambridge, Mass., 1985); Erwin Chemerinsky and Larry Kramer, "Defining the Role of the Federal Courts," 1990 *Brigham Young University Law Review* 67. For the widespread acceptance of the twentieth-century view of the federal courts at century's end, *see* The Federal Courts Study Committee, *Report* (Washington, D.C., 1990); Judicial Conference of the United States, Committee on Long Range Planning, *Proposed Long-Range Plan for the Federal Courts* (Washington, D.C., 1995).

CHAPTER 11. TO CENTURY'S END

1 *See, e.g.,* Steve Fraser and Gary Gerstle, *The Rise and Fall of the New Deal Order, 1930–1980* (Princeton, N.J., 1989); James Patterson, *Grand Expectations: The United States, 1945–1974* (New York, 1996); 410 U.S. 113 (1973) (upholding a constitutional right to have an abortion).

2 On the changing politics of separation of powers ideas and branch affinities in the 1980s, *see, e.g.,* Geoffrey P. Miller, "From Compromise to Confrontation: Separation of Powers in the Reagan Era," 57 *George Washington Law Review* 401 (1989); William N. Eskridge, Jr., "Reneging on History? Playing the Court/Congress/President Civil Rights Game," 79 *California Law Review* 613 (1991).

3 *See, e.g.,* "Symposium: Fidelity in Constitutional Theory," 65 *Fordham Law Review* 1247 (1997); Stephen M. Griffin, *American Constitutionalism* (New York, 1996). Some liberals began deemphasizing the role of the courts generally. *See, e.g.,* Cass Sunstein, *The Partial Constitution* (Cambridge, Mass., 1993); Bruce Ackerman, *We the People: Foundations* (Cambridge, Mass., 1991). Other scholars have challenged the idea that the courts can and have had significant impact on the course of social change. *See, e.g.,* Michael J. Klarman, "Rethinking the

Civil Rights and Civil Liberties Revolutions," 82 *Virginia Law Review* 1 (1996); Gerald N. Rosenberg, *The Hollow Hope: Can Courts Bring About Social Change?* (Chicago, 1991). The fragmentation was equally apparent on the level of legal philosophy. *See, e.g.,* Gary Minda, *Postmodern Legal Movements: Law and Jurisprudence at Century's End* (New York, 1995).

4 For representative "liberal" positions *see* J. Skelly Wright, "Professor Bickel, The Scholarly Tradition, and the Supreme Court," 84 *Harvard Law Review* 769 (1971); Theodore Eisenberg, "Congressional Authority to Restrict Lower Federal Court Jurisdiction," 83 *Yale Law Journal* 499 (1974); Burt Neuborne, "The Myth of Parity," 90 *Harvard Law Review* 1105 (1977); Donald Zeigler, "Federal Court Reform of State Criminal Justice Systems: A Reassessment of the Younger Doctrine from a Modern Perspective," 19 *University of California at Davis Law Review* 31 (1985); Akhil Reed Amar, "A Neo-Federalist View of Article III: Separating the Two Tiers of Federal Jurisdiction," 65 *Boston University Law Review* 205 (1985).

5 *See, e.g.,* David M. O'Brien, "The Supreme Court and Intergovernmental Relations: What Happened to 'Our Federalism'?" 9 *Journal of Law and Politics* 609 (1993); Robin West, "Foreword: Taking Freedom Seriously," 104 *Harvard Law Review* 43 (1990); James F. Simon, *The Center Holds: The Power Struggle Inside the Rehnquist Court* (New York, 1995); Carl Tobias, "Keeping the Covenant on the Federal Courts," 47 *S.M.U. Law Review* 1861 (1994).

6 Mary L. Dudziak, "The Courts," in Stanley I. Kutler *et al.*, eds. *Encyclopedia of the United States in the Twentieth Century*, Vol. 1 (New York, 1996), 392.

7 Larry Yackle, *Reclaiming the Federal Courts* (Cambridge, Mass., 1994), 41, 2. *Accord e.g.,* Hugh C. MacGill, "The Role of the District Courts in a Changing Political Climate," 56 *Connecticut Bar Journal* 222 (1982); Erwin Chemerinsky, "The Values of Federalism," 47 *Florida Law Review* 499, 513 (1995).

8 Ann Althouse, "Federal Jurisdiction and the Enforcement of Federal Rights: Can Congress Bring Back the Warren Era?" 20 *Law and Social Inquiry* 1067, 1087 (1995). *See* the statement of Robert M. Cover in Robert M. Cover, Owen Fiss, and Judith Resnik, *Procedure* (Westbury, Conn., 1988), 730; Barry Friedman, review of *Reclaiming the Federal Courts* by Larry W. Yackle, 12 *Constitutional Commentary* 441 (1995).

9 *See, e.g.,* William J. Brennan, "State Constitutions and the Protection of Individual Rights," 90 *Harvard Law Review* 489 (1977); Brennan, "An Invitation to State Courts," 13 *Litigation* 5 (1987). *See* Ann Althouse, "Federalism, Untamed," 47 *Vanderbilt Law Review* 1207 (1994); Akhil Reed Amar, "Of Sovereignty and Federalism," 96 *Yale Law Journal* 1425 (1987); Burt Neuborne, "Foreword: State Constitutions and the Evolution of Positive Rights," 20 *Rutgers Law Journal* 881 (1989); Stephen A. Holmes, "Right to Abortion Quietly Advances in State Courts," *The New York Times*, Dec. 6, 1998, Sec. 1, p. 1.

10 Comments of Bruce Fein in "The Federal Courts: Have They Functioned as the Framers Intended?" 42 *The Record of the Association of the Bar of the City of New York* 980, 993, 999, 1000 (1987).

11 Lino A. Graglia, "Constitutional Interpretation," 44 *Syracuse Law Review* 631, 637 (1993).

12 Robert H. Bork, *Slouching Toward Gomorrah: Modern Liberalism and American Decline* (New York, 1996), 97, 117.

13 *E.g., Gregory v. Ashcroft*, 501 U.S. 452 (1991); *New York v. United States*, 505 U.S. 144 (1992); and *United States v. Lopez*, 514 U.S. 549 (1995). For general scholarly commentary *see, e.g.,* Gene R. Nichol, "Is There a Law of Federal Courts?" 96 *West Virginia Law Review* 147 (1993); H. Jefferson Powell, "The Oldest Question of Constitutional Law," 79 *Virginia Law Review* 633 (1993); John C. Yoo, "The Judicial Safeguards of Federalism," 70 *Southern Cali-*

fornia Law Review 1311 (1997); Bill Swinford and Eric N. Waltenburg, "The Supreme Court and the States: Do *Lopez* and *Printz* represent a broader pro-state movement? 14 *Journal of Law & Politics* 319 (1998).

14 *E.g.,* David Schoenbrod, *Power Without Responsibility: How Congress Abuses the People Through Delegation* (New Haven, Conn., 1993); "Symposium on the Theory of Public Choice," 74 *Virginia Law Review* 167 (1988).

15 Richard A. Epstein, review of *The Chief Justiceship of Melville W. Fuller, 1888–1910,* 40 *American Journal of Legal History* 109, 110 (1996). *Accord* Bernard H. Siegan, *Economic Liberties and the Constitution* (Chicago, 1980); David P. Bryden, "A Conservative Case for Judicial Activism," *The Public Interest,* No. 111, 72 (1993).

16 380 U.S. 460 (1965).

17 *Id.* at 461–62 and n. 1. The court of appeals affirmed the decision of the trial court.

18 *Id.* at 466–69.

19 *Id.* at 469–73 (quote at 469).

20 *Id.* at 467.

21 *Id.* at 468 n. 9; *Erie Railroad Co. v. Tompkins,* 304 U.S. 64, 75 (1938).

22 *Hanna v. Plumer,* 380 U.S. at 468, 469.

23 *Id.* at 468.

24 *Id.* at 469.

25 *Id.* at 471–72.

26 *Id.* at 472.

27 Legal commentators, naturally, participated in the effort. In 1974, for example, John Hart Ely, who had been the chief justice's law clerk during the term when *Hanna* was decided, defended the Warren Court's version of *Erie.* He trivialized *Erie*'s constitutional significance as a limitation on federal power (though acknowledging that *Erie* was a constitutional decision), dismissed out of hand the idea of a substantive Tenth Amendment, emphasized the lawmaking power of Congress and the Court, and stressed that litigation "fairness" was the proper test for judging forum shopping. *See* Ely, "The Irrepressible Myth of Erie," 87 *Harvard Law Review* 693 (1974). Moreover, as one commentator pointed out, Ely also reflected the Warren Court's heightened sensitivity to individual privacy rights. *See* Abram Chayes, "Some Further Last Words on Erie," 87 *Harvard Law Review* 741 (1974). Perhaps most revealing, Ely did not explore and seemed to reject *Erie* as a limit on the lawmaking powers of the federal courts. *See* Paul J. Mishkin, "Some Further Last Words on Erie—The Thread," 87 *Harvard Law Review* 1682 (1974). Ely's article earned widespread praise and acceptance during the decade that followed.

Along with its legal virtues, however, Ely's article exemplified the ahistorical method of traditional doctrinal scholarship. It explained the "myth" of *Erie*—the belief that the decision's constitutional stature made it relevant to a variety of disparate legal issues—as resulting from two factors. One—presumably offered with tongue in cheek—was the "accepting" nature of commentators who wrote on civil procedure matters. The other—which deserved "most of the blame"—was that the Supreme Court had, by faulty construction of the Rules Enabling Act, "created a need for limits" on the Federal Rules of Civil Procedure, which, in turn, a broad, amorphous, and "undefended" application of *Erie* came to fill. *Id.* at 698–99. Similarly, it explained the fact that the Court did not refer to *Erie*'s constitutional basis between 1938 and 1956 as a result of doctrinal logic: *Erie* made the Rules of Decision Act more broadly protective of state law than the Constitution, and hence the direct significance of its constitutional holding "was ended." Ely, "The Irrepressible Myth of Erie," at 704. In both instances, then, the article explained complex historical events involving the evolution of doctrine and the actions of the justices as the results of doctrinal logic. Its analysis exemplified the approach that had allowed Hart to synthesize *Erie* and *Jensen* and the ALI to equate Brandeis's use of coextensive powers with Hamilton's. That approach reflects accepted and standard methods of legal argument. It is not, however, historical analysis. Indeed, all three examples illustrate one of the reasons history and law are such profoundly different intellectual enterprises.

28 William H. Rehnquist, "Whither the Courts," 60 *American Bar Association Journal* 787 (1974).

29 *E.g.,* George D. Brown, "Of Activism and *Erie* — The Implication Doctrine's Implications for the Nature and Role of the Federal Courts," 69 *Iowa Law Review* 617 (1984); Donald L. Doernberg, "Juridical Chameleons in the 'New Erie' Canal," 1990 *Utah Law Review* 759.

30 *Compare, e.g., Wheeldin v. Wheeler,* 373 U.S. 647, 651 (1963) with *Bivens v. Six Unknown Named Agents of the Federal Bureau of Narcotics,* 403 U.S. 388 (1971). *See* H. Miles Foy, III, "Some Reflections on Legislation, Adjudication, and Implied Private Actions in the State and Federal Courts," 71 *Cornell Law Review* 501 (1986).

31 Classic cases include the following: (a) expanding plaintiffs' ability to sue state officials and local governments under the federal civil rights laws — *Monroe v. Pape,* 365 U.S. 167 (1961); *McNeese v. Board of Education,* 373 U.S. 668 (1963); *Monell v. New York City Department of Social Services,* 436 U.S. 658 (1978); (b) implying private rights of action against federal officials for violating constitutional rights — *Bivens v. Six Unknown Named Agents of the Federal Bureau of Narcotics,* 403 U.S. 388 (1971); *Davis v. Passman,* 442 U.S. 228 (1979); (c) implying private rights of actions against private parties for violations of federal statutes — *J.I. Case Co. v. Borak,* 377 U.S. 426 (1964); *Allen v. State Board of Elections,* 393 U.S. 544 (1969); *Superintendent of Insurance v. Bankers Life & Casualty Co.,* 404 U.S. 6 (1971).

32 Philip B. Kurland, *Politics, the Constitution, and the Warren Court* (Chicago, 1970), 61–63. *Accord* Henry P. Monaghan, book review, 87 *Harvard Law Review* 889, 892 (1974).

33 441 U.S. 677 (1979).

34 Rehnquist concurred on narrow grounds, emphasizing that the issue was one of congressional intent and warning Congress that in the future the Court would "be extremely reluctant to imply a cause of action." 441 U.S. at 718.

35 *Id.* at 732, 742 (quoting *Erie,* 304 U.S. at 77–78).

36 *Id.* at 730, 731.

37 *Carlson v. Green,* 446 U.S. 14, 31, 35, 37–38, 39, 44 (1980) (Rehnquist, J., dissenting).

38 *City of Milwaukee v. Illinois,* 451 U.S. 304, 312, 313 (1981). The Court had first recognized the cause of action in 1972 in *Illinois v. City of Milwaukee,* 406 U.S. 91 (1972).

39 *E.g., Touche Ross & Co. v. Redington,* 442 U.S. 560 (1979); *Transamerica Mortgage Advisors, Inc. v. Lewis,* 444 U.S. 11 (1979). The Court did not stop creating implied statutory rights of action completely, *e.g., Merrill Lynch, Pierce, Fenner & Smith v. Curran,* 456 U.S. 353 (1982), nor did it abrogate some well-established implied rights of action, *e.g., Herman & MacLean v. Huddleston,* 459 U.S. 375 (1983) (upholding an action long recognized by the lower courts under Sec. 10b of the Securities and Exchange Act of 1934).

40 *E.g., United States v. Stanley,* 483 U.S. 669 (1987); *Schweiker v. Chilicky,* 487 U.S. 412 (1988).

41 *Erie Railroad Co. v. Tompkins,* 304 U.S. 64, 78 (1938).

42 The Rehnquist Court used the idea of separation of powers frequently. The idea's mallea-

bility, however, led to diverse doctrinal results. *Compare, e.g., Allen v. Wright,* 468 U.S. 737 (1984) (using separation of powers to restrict standing in action challenging policy of federal agency) *with Lujan v. Defenders of Wildlife,* 504 U.S. 555 (1992) (using separation of powers to restrict congressional power to create federal law claims). Separation of powers ideas were easily made to support contrary arguments in *Lujan* and in *Franklin v. Gwinnett County Public Schools,* 503 U.S. 60 (1992).

43 *Walker v. Armco Steel Corp.,* 446 U.S. 740 (1980); *Burlington Northern Railroad Co. v. Woods,* 480 U.S. 1 (1987).

44 *See, e.g.,* Nancy Levit, "The Caseload Conundrum, Constitutional Restraints and the Manipulation of Jurisdiction," 64 *Notre Dame Law Review* 321 (1989).

45 *Ferens v. John Deere Co.,* 494 U.S. 516 (1990). Justice Scalia wrote an incisive dissent in which the Court's three remaining liberals joined. *Id.* at 518; *see* Edward A. Purcell, Jr., "Geography as a Litigation Weapon: Consumers, Forum-Selection Clauses, and the Rehnquist Court," 40 *U.C.L.A. Law Review* 423 (1992); Paul D. Carrington and Paul H. Haagan, "Contract and Jurisdiction," 1996 *Supreme Court Review* 331. The Rehnquist Court approved the imposition of practical burdens and costs relatively regularly as an indirect method of accomplishing its social goals. *See, e.g., Wards Cove Packing Co. v. Atonio,* 490 U.S. 642 (1989); *Webster v. Reproductive Health Services,* 492 U.S. 490 (1989).

46 Akhil Reed Amar, "A New-Federalist View of Article III: Separating the Two Tiers of Federal Jurisdiction," 65 *Boston University Law Review* 205 (1985); Martha A. Field, "Sources of Law: The Scope of Federal Common Law," 99 *Harvard Law Review* 881 (1986); Erwin Chemerinsky, "The Supreme Court, 1988 Term—Foreword: The Vanishing Constitution," 103 *Harvard Law Review* 43 (1989); Linda S. Mullenix, "Unconstitutional Rulemaking: The Civil Justice Reform Act and Separation of Powers," 77 *Minnesota Law Review* 1283 (1993).

47 Weinberg's views did not seem to persuade most legal scholars. *E.g.,* Martin H. Redish, "Federal Common Law and American Political Theory: A Response to Professor Weinberg," 83 *Northwestern University Law Review* 853 (1989).

48 5 U.S. (1 Cranch) 137 (1803).

49 Louise Weinberg, *Federal Courts: Cases and Comments on Judicial Federalism and Judicial Power* (St. Paul, Minn., 1994), 4.

50 Weinberg, *Federal Courts,* 16. *Accord id.* at 14; Weinberg, "Federal Common Law," 83 *Northwestern University Law Review* 805 (1989).

51 Weinberg, "Federal Common Law," 836.

52 Louise Weinberg, "The Curious Notion that the Rules of Decision Act Blocks Supreme Federal Common Law," 83 *Northwestern University Law Review* 860, 874 (1989).

53 Weinberg, *Federal Courts,* 10.

54 *Id.* at 13.

55 *Id.* at 12 (emphasis in original).

56 *Id.* at 13.

57 *Id.* at 16, 18, 19.

58 *Id.* at 15.

59 *Id.* at 14, quoting Weinberg, "Federal Common Law," at 819. *See id.* at 15, 17–19.

60 Weinberg, *Federal Courts,* 15.

61 *Id.* at 20. Weinberg continued, adding a qualification: "granting that prudential constraints may be placed upon its exercise." Throughout her writings she acknowledged differences between judicial and legislative lawmaking and pointed out that the federal courts would

likely defer to other government institutions in some cases or "borrow" existing state common law for federal purposes. Those qualifications, however, do not constitute limits on the nature of federal judicial power, and her overall argument suggests that the federal courts should overlook them relatively easily and make federal common law relatively readily.

62 *Id.* at 19, citing *Garcia v. San Antonio Metropolitan Transit Authority,* 469 U.S. 528 (1985).

63 Weinberg, *Federal Courts,* 20.

64 *E.g.,* Louise Weinberg, "Against Comity," 80 *Georgetown Law Journal* 53 (1991); Weinberg, "Holmes' Failure," 96 *Michigan Law Review* 691 (1997).

65 Much of this story is told in Laura Kalman, *The Strange Career of Legal Liberalism* (New Haven, Conn. 1996).

66 *E.g., Gasperini v. Center for Humanities, Inc.,* 116 S.Ct. 2211 (1996).

67 Henry M. Hart, Jr., "The Relations Between State and Federal Law," 54 *Columbia Law Review* 489, 513, 512 (1954). According to one scholar writing in 1989, the profession has neglected the whole area of forum shopping. Friedrich K. Juenger, "Forum Shopping, Domestic and International," 63 *Tulane Law Review* 553 (1989).

68 One example, chosen because it is an otherwise excellent discussion written by a particularly perceptive commentator, illustrates some of the unfortunate consequences of Brandeis's abstract language. *See* George D. Brown, "The Ideologies of Forum Shopping — Why Doesn't a Conservative Court Protect Defendants?" 71 *North Carolina Law Review* 649 (1993). In discussing *Erie* and the problems of forum shopping, the author construes *Erie* abstractly and misses the critical fact that it was most immediately concerned not with all federal diversity actions but with removed actions. That oversight, induced by the opinion's language, leads the author to misconceive the "pro-defendant results" (*id.* at 708) that have occurred in many of the Court's subsequent *Erie* decisions and to overlook two fundamental considerations: first, the *social* differences (*i.e.,* the nature of the parties involved and the frequency and types of the claims at issue) between state/state and state/federal forum shopping cases; second, the *historical* differences between those social differences as they existed prior to 1938 and in the late twentieth century. Those oversights, in turn, lead to two further mistakes in his analysis: first he concludes that *Erie*'s relevance to forum shopping is rooted in its federalism principle (*id.* at 711, 713, 720) rather than in its concern with the equitable administration of the law in social and practical terms; second, he assumes that the relevant decisions of the Burger and Rehnquist Courts were based substantively on *Erie* and *its* (federalism) values, as opposed to the distinct values and ideologies of a set of primarily "conservative" justices who shaped their own version of *Erie* for their own purposes.

69 Diversity jurisdiction did, of course, also allow parties to bring federal law issues to the national courts both prior to and after 1875. *See, e.g.,* Ann Woolhandler, "The Common Law Origins of Constitutionally Compelled Remedies," 107 *Yale Law Journal* 77 (1997).

70 For statements by the Supreme Court of the self-conscious twentieth-century view, occurring in the context of a dominant mid-century "liberalism," *see, e.g.,* the following opinions written by Justice Brennan: *Fay v. Noia,* 372 U.S. 391 (1963); *England v. Louisiana State Board of Medical Examiners,* 375 U.S. 411 (1964); *Dombrowski v. Pfister,* 380 U.S. 479 (1965); *Steffel v. Thompson,* 415 U.S. 452 (1974).

The Burger and Rehnquist Courts disagreed with many of the decisions and values of the Warren Court, employed a different constitutional rhetoric, and served a different set of values. Although they reoriented federal procedural and jurisdictional law significantly, they did not reject the twentieth-century paradigm itself so much as attempt to limit its scope, alter its institutional significance, and change the substantive values it served. *E.g., Michigan v. Long*, 463 U.S. 1032 (1983); *Yellow Freight System, Inc. v. Donnelly*, 494 U.S. 820 (1990). Of course, some of the Rehnquist Court justices launched direct attacks on the twentieth-century view. *E.g., Idaho v. Coeur d'Alene Tribe*, 117 S. Ct. 2028 (1997) (Parts II-B, II-C, and II-D of the opinion of Kennedy, J., joined by Rehnquist, C.J.). Their broadest success came in the special field of federal habeas corpus, where they succeeded in wiping out much of the habeas jurisprudence of the Warren Court, narrowing drastically the availability of the federal remedy for state prisoners. *E.g., Wainwright v. Sykes*, 433 U.S. 72 (1977); *Teague v. Lane*, 489 U.S. 288 (1989). In 1996 Congress adopted legislation that confirmed and apparently further tightened the Court's limitations on federal habeas corpus. *See Antiterrorism and Effective Death Penalty Act of 1996*, 110 Stat. 1214.

The continued general dominance of the twentieth-century view is evident in two distinct areas of political and professional consensus. The first involves the numerous amendments Congress has made to the Federal Judicial Code over the past half century. They have repeatedly expanded federal question jurisdiction while consistently limiting diversity jurisdiction. The second involves consensus committee reports prepared by elite groups of lawyers and judges addressing the future role of the federal judiciary. *E.g., Report of the Federal Courts Study Committee* (Washington, D.C., 1990).

For a brilliant critique of the dominant and, at the time, politically "liberal" view by a major conservative theorist, *see* Paul M. Bator, "The State Courts and Federal Constitutional Litigation," 22 *William and Mary Law Review* 605 (1981). Bator's views have been taken up by some of the Nixon and Reagan justices. *E.g., Webster v. Doe*, 486 U.S. 592, 606 (1988) (Scalia, J., dissenting); *Stone v. Powell*, 428 U.S. 465 (1976) (Powell, J.).

71 87 U.S. (20 Wall.) 590 (1875).

72 *See* William M. Wiecek, *"Murdock v. Memphis:* Section 25 of the 1789 Judiciary Act and Judicial Federalism," in Maeva Marcus, ed., *Origins of the Federal Judiciary: Essays on the Judiciary Act of 1789* (New York, 1992), 223–47; Field, "Sources of Law," 919–23.

73 Kurland, *Politics, the Constitution, and the Warren Court*, 61.

74 Friendly, "In Praise of *Erie*," at 407.

75 *Compare* Robert H. Wiebe, *Self-Rule: A Cultural History of American Democracy* (Chicago, 1995), 199–200, *with* William J. Novak, *The People's Welfare: Law and Regulation in Nineteenth-Century America* (Chapel Hill, N.C., 1996), 235–48.

76 *Railroad Commission of California v. Los Angeles Railway Corp.*, 280 U.S. 145, 158, 166 (Brandeis, J., dissenting); Melvin I. Urofsky and David W. Levy, eds., *Letters of Louis D. Brandeis*, Vol. 5 (Albany, N.Y., 1978), 160; Felix Frankfurter and James M. Landis, *The Business of the Supreme Court: A Study in the Federal Judicial System* (New York, 1928), 257.

77 *Id.* at 166.

78 *Boyle v. United Technologies Corp.*, 487 U.S. 500 (1988). *Cf. County of Oneida v. Oneida Indian Nation*, 470 U.S. 226 (1985).

79 *Boyle*, for example, authorized the federal courts to identify "uniquely federal interests" and to make law whenever it seemed necessary, in the judgment of the federal courts, to protect those interests (487 U.S. at 505). Instead of requiring the application of state law "[e]xcept in matters governed by the federal Constitution or by acts of Congress" (*Erie*, 304 U.S. at 78), *Boyle* allows the creation of federal common law in areas "committed by the Constitution and laws of the United States to federal control" (*Boyle* at 504). The sentence is critical because it refers not to the "statutes" of the United States but to its "laws." *Erie*, of course, states

that the term *laws* is meant to include judicial decisions as well as statutes, and in support of the sentence, *Boyle* cites *Clearfield Trust Co. v. United States,* 318 U.S. 363 (1943), an early post-*Erie* decision that authorized the creation of federal judge-made law to control issues involving the commercial paper of the federal government. Thus, *Boyle* seems to mean that the Court itself has the authority to identify "uniquely federal interests" whenever it sees fit and, absent any congressional action, make whatever federal law it wishes to cover the area. The decision was particularly egregious because Congress had repeatedly considered bills to establish such a federal law defense and had repeatedly refused to adopt them. *Boyle* thus provides strong support for Professor Weinberg's activist and nationalist interpretation of *Erie.*

Boyle's reasoning, however, is exceptionally dubious. The Court, for example, misconstrues a major precedent on which it relies. Compare *Boyle* 487 U.S. at 504 ("We have held that obligations to and rights of the United States under its contracts are governed exclusively by federal law") with the case cited in support, *United States v. Little Lake Misere Land Co.,* 412 U.S. 580 (1973) ("The government urges us to decide, virtually without qualification, that land acquisition agreements of the United States should be governed by federally created federal law. We find it unnecessary to resolve this case on such broad terms"), *id.* at 595. More important, *Boyle* identifies the "uniquely" federal interest at issue by reasoning *analogically* from two areas of federal common law and one federal statute that *extended* government liability. Basing federal judicial lawmaking on reasoning by analogy suggests, by itself, a likely conflict with *Erie.* Basing it on reasoning by analogy to other areas of law which are, themselves, judge-made, seems clearly inconsistent with *Erie.* Basing federal judicial lawmaking on distant and inapt analogies prepares the way for a wholesale — though, in terms of substantive policies, undoubtedly quite selective — rejection of *Erie*'s limits on federal common law.

Indeed, although *Boyle* misconstrued *Little Lake Misere,* an early Burger Court decision, it did draw some support from the latter's strikingly amorphous reasoning and strongly nationalizing thrust. *Little Lake Misere,* in fact, suggested a relatively clean doctrinal way to neutralize *Erie* as a restriction on federal judicial lawmaking. "The federal jurisdictional grant over suits brought by the United States is not in itelf a mandate for applying federal law in all circumstances," the Court wrote. "This principle follows from *Erie* itself, where, although the federal courts had jurisdiction over diversity cases, we held that the federal courts did not possess the power to develop a concomitant body of general federal law" (412 U.S. at 591). Thus, *Erie* could be negated as a doctrinal bar to federal judicial lawmaking by construing it to mean only that a relevant jurisdictional grant is not, by itself, enough to warrant federal judicial lawmaking. With *Erie* so limited, then, the presence of some "uniquely federal interest" — even if it is one identified only by the courts — would allow the creation of federal common law free from the limits of this narrowly "jurisdictional" *Erie.* This withered *Erie* is quite different from the vibrant version that Powell and Rehnquist advanced in the service of other substantive social goals.

80 *See, e.g., Agency Holding Corp. v. Malley-Duff & Associates,* 484 U.S. 143 (1987) (Scalia, J., dissenting).

81 *Thompson v. Thompson,* 484 U.S. 174, 188, 191 (Scalia, J., concurring).

82 487 U.S. at 516, 517–18.

83 *Id.* at 531.

84 *E.g.,* Gregory A. Caldeira and John R. Wright, "Organized Interests and Agenda Setting in the U.S. Supreme Court," 82 *American Political Science Review* 1009 (1997).

85 The Rehnquist Court, for example, while disclaiming "judicial activism" and employing the rhetoric of deference to the legislature, actively made law implementing its values, sometimes ignoring or setting aside congressional actions in the process. *See, e.g.*, Donald H. Zeigler, "The New Activist Court," 45 *American University Law Review* 1367 (1996); Frank I. Michelman, "Property, Federalism, and Jurisprudence: A Comment on *Lucas* and Judicial Conservatism," 35 *William and Mary Law Review* 301 (1993); Owen M. Fiss, *The Irony of Free Speech* (Cambridge, Mass., 1996). *Compare* Diana Gribbon Motz, "A Federal Judge's View of Richard A. Posner's *The Federal Courts: Challenge and Reform*," 73 *Notre Dame Law Review* 1029, 1039–42 (1998). Jonathan R. Macy, "Federal Deference to Local Regulators and the Economic Theory of Regulation: Toward a Public-Choice Explanation of Federalism," 76 *Virginia Law Review* 265 (1990).

86 *E.g.*, Richard B. Stewart and Cass R. Sunstein, "Public Programs and Private Rights," 95 *Harvard Law Review* 1195, 1224 (1982). To the extent that Brandeis's decision was taken to limit federal judicial lawmaking on separation of powers grounds, the limitation shifted the burden of asserting national control to Congress. Because congressional action is slower, more complicated, and subject to far more numerous and direct political checks than is judicial action, it is less likely to occur absent substantial popular support and sustained political pressure. Consequently, an *Erie* based on separation of powers principles serves to limit assertions of federal authority in new areas and, hence, to protect "federalism" interests, at least insofar as those interests are identified with national inaction. *See, e.g.*, Brown, "The Ideologies of Forum Shopping," 663; Redish, *Federal Courts in the Political Order*, 30–31.

87 Numerous problems, of course, remained. One was the range of choice-of-law problems that arose in mass toxic tort and other multistate, multiparty types of litigation. *See, e.g.*, Larry Kramer, "Choice of Law in Complex Litigation," 71 *New York University Law Review* 547 (1996); Linda Mullenix, "Class Resolution of the Mass Tort Case: A Proposed Federal Procedure Act," 64 *Texas Law Review* 1039 (1986).

88 *Silverthorne Lumber Co., Inc. v. United States*, 251 U.S. 385 (1920); *Gouled v. United States*, 255 U.S. 298 (1921); *Moore v. Dempsey*, 261 U.S. 86 (1923); *Meyer v. Nebraska*, 262 U.S. 390 (1923); *Pierce v. Society of Sisters*, 268 U S 510 (1925).

89 *E.g.*, *Gilbert v. Minnesota*, 254 U.S. 325, 334 (1920) (Brandeis, J., dissenting); *Schaefer v. United States*, 251 U.S. 466, 482 (1920) (Brandeis, J., dissenting); *Whitney v. California*, 274 U.S. 357, 372 (1927) (Brandeis, J., concurring).

90 *E.g.*, *United States v. Gault*, 271 U.S. 142, 152 (1926) (Brandeis, J., dissenting); *St. Joseph Stock Yards Co. v. United States*, 298 U.S. 38, 73, 77 (1936) (Brandeis, J., concurring). *See* Samuel D. Warren and Louis D. Brandeis, "The Right to Privacy," 4 *Harvard Law Review* 193 (1890).

91 *E.g.*, *Burdeau v. McDowell*, 256 U.S. 465, 476 (1921) (Brandeis, J., dissenting); *Olmstead v. United States*, 77 U.S. 438, 471 (1927) (Brandeis, J. dissenting); *Casey v. United States*, 276 U.S. 413, 421 (1928) (Brandeis, J., dissenting).

92 *See* Chapter 6 of this volume. *Cf.*, *Olmstead v. United States*, 277 U.S. 438, 471, 484–85 (1928) (Brandeis, J., dissenting).

93 Brandeis, of course, also "made law" in interpreting and developing federal statutes, *e.g.*, *Board of Trade of Chicago v. United States*, 246 U.S. 231 (1918).

94 *Whitney v. California*, 274 U.S. 357, 372, 373 (Brandeis, J., concurring). *Accord Gilbert v. Minnesota*, 254 U.S. 325, 334, 325 (Brandeis, J., dissenting).

95 *See generally* Vincent Blasi, "The First Amendment and the Ideal of Civic Courage: The Brandeis Opinion in *Whitney v. California*," 29 *William and Mary Law Review* 653 (1988);

David M. Rabban, "Free Speech in Progressive Social Thought," 74 *Texas Law Review* 951 (1996); Philippa Strum, *Brandeis: Beyond Progressivism* (Lawrence, Kans., 1993), ch. 6; Strum, *Louis D. Brandeis: Justice for the People* (Cambridge, Mass., 1989), 309–38.

96 304 U.S. at 78.

97 For examples of Brandeis's lack of judicial candor, *see* Bickel, *Unpublished Opinions of Mr. Justice Brandeis,* 94–97, 118–24, 157–58; Alexander M. Bickel and Benno C. Schmidt, Jr., *The Judiciary and Responsible Government, 1910–1921* (New York, 1984), 627–30; Strum, *Louis D. Brandeis,* 360–61; Walter Gellhorn and Clark Byse, *Administrative Law: Cases and Comments* (Mineola, N.Y., 1974), 417–19. *Willing v. Chicago Auditorium Association,* 277 U.S. 274 (1928), is probably the most extreme example.

98 *See* Wilfred J. Ritz, *Rewriting the History of the Judiciary Act of 1789: Exposing Myths, Challenging Premises, and Using New Evidence,* ed. Wythe Holt and L. H. LaRue (Norman, Okla., 1990). Ritz argues that Section 34 was most likely intended to do nothing more than direct the federal courts to use "American" rather than "British" law and, possibly, to serve as an "American" common law of crimes "stopgap" until Congress enacted a federal criminal code (*id.* at 11). Concerning *Erie,* the book concludes bluntly: "In short, on its historical basis, *Erie* is dead wrong" (*id.* at 148).

99 *See, e.g.,* G. Edward White, *The Marshall Court and Cultural Change, 1815–35* (New York, 1988); William P. LaPiana, "*Swift v. Tyson* and the Brooding Omnipresence in the Sky: An Investigation of the Idea of Law in Antebellum America," 20 *Suffolk University Law Review* 771 (1986); Randolph Bridwell and Ralph U. Whitten, *The Constitution and the Common Law: The Decline of the Doctrines of Separation of Powers and Federalism* (Lexington, Mass., 1977).

100 *See* Bickel, *Unpublished Opinions of Mr. Justice Brandeis.*

101 Brandeis, of course, had his flaws. He used people, sometimes ruthlessly, to serve his purposes; and he used legal doctrines and techniques to accomplish results he thought desirable. He could be self-righteous, uncompromising, and excessively demanding. Sometimes his views seemed rigid and ideological. *See, e.g.,* Paper, *Brandeis,* 335. While on the bench he engaged in political efforts that were dubious and, by later standards at least, unethical. *See, e.g.,* Murphy, *Brandeis/Frankfurter Connection, passim.* Perhaps most striking to later generations, his concern with the weak and disadvantaged did not extend noticeably to the plight of African Americans. *See, e.g.,* Strum, *Brandeis: Beyond Progressivism,* 141–42. *See also* n. 97 above.

Index